Approx. Scale
1:17 500 000

THE 5TH EDITION

The Canadian Oxford School Atlas

Edited by Walter G. Kemball

Oxford University Press (Canada)

The Canadian Oxford School Atlas

Oxford University Press (Canada)
70 Wynford Drive
Don Mills, Ontario M3C 1J9

Toronto Oxford New York Delhi Bombay
Calcutta Madras Karachi Petaling Jaya
Singapore Hong Kong Tokyo Dar es Salaam
Cape Town Melbourne Auckland

and associated companies in
Berlin Ibadan

Oxford is a trademark of Oxford University Press

First edition 1957
Second edition 1963
Third edition 1972
Fourth edition 1977
Fifth edition 1985

ISBN 0-19-5404580

Graphic design, atlas pages
John Marsh, MCSD
Graphic design, preliminary pages
Leslie Smart & Associates
Endpaper map:
compiled by Artplus Limited
Printed in Canada by
Bryant Press Limited

6789-2109

Contents

Canada: Tables and Graphs
Population 4A
Census Metropolitan Areas 6A
Travel 8A
Agriculture 9A
Forestry 12A
Mining 15A
Manufacturing 18A
The Labour Force 20A
The Canadian Economy: An Overview 21A
Electricity 22A

World: Tables and Graphs
Countries of the World: Selected Statistics 24A
Population Growth by Continent 27A
Economic Profiles 28A
Urbanization 30A
International Tourism, 1980 31A
Developed and Developing Countries 31A

The Arctic 1:25M 1

Canada Political 1:19M 2–3
Graphs: area of Canada and of provinces

Canada Physical 1:19M 4–5
Insets: retreat of ice sheet; vertical profile

Canada Climate 6–7
temperature; precipitation; growing season
Insets: air masses; ocean currents; snowfall
Graphs: climagraphs

Canada: Climate Regions; Physiographic Regions
1:35M 8

Canada: Soils; Vegetation 1:35M 9

Canada Population 1:35M 10
Graphs: CMA populations; population growth;
ethnic composition

Canada: Roads, Ports, Airports; Rail 1:35M 11
Inset: transcontinental travel
Graphs: movements of people and goods

Canada Agriculture 1:35M 12
Graphs: farm land-use; agricultural production;
size of farms

Canada Forestry 1:35M 13
Inset: fire risk
Graphs: forest products

Canada Fishing: Atlantic Coast; Pacific Coast
1:15M 14
Insets: freshwater fishing and salmon-spawning
Graphs: fish catch and products; exports and impor

Canada Mining: Metals; Industrial Minerals
1:35M 15
Graphs: mineral production; iron ore

Canada Energy: Coal and Electricity; Oil and Gas
1:35M 16–17
Inset: sunshine
Graphs: production and consumption; end use

Canada Manufacturing: Metals; Other Industries
1:35M 18–19
Insets: manufacturing: Kingston-Québec,
Windsor-Trenton 1:4M; acid rain
Graphs: production and labour; top industries;
iron and steel

he Territories Topographic 1:12M 20–21
Graphs: provincial statistics

estern Canada Topographic 1:8M 22–23
Graphs: provincial statistics

ntario and Québec Topographic 1:8M 24–25
Graphs: provincial statistics

astern Canada Topographic 1:8M 26
Graphs: provincial statistics

rban Land Use 27
Edmonton; Montréal; Toronto; Vancouver

ritish Columbia Topographic 1:5M 28–29
Insets: Vancouver Island and Vancouver; the economy
Graphs: production and employment; forestry statistics

lberta Topographic 1:5M 30
Inset: the economy
Graphs: GDP; production; employment

askatchewan Topographic 1:5M 31
Inset: the economy
Graphs: wheat production, production and employment

anitoba Topographic 1:5M 32–33
Insets: Winnipeg urban plan; Winnipeg transportation 1:400 000; wheat exports; the economy
Graphs: wheat production and exports; production and employment

ntario Topographic 1:6.5M 34–35
Insets: the economy; southern Ontario economy 1:3M
Graphs: production and employment

ébec Topographic 1:6.5M 36–37
nsets: the economy; James Bay Project 1:7.5M
Graphs: production and employment

ke Ontario and Upper St. Lawrence Topographic
.5M 38–39
nset: the St. Lawrence Seaway
Graphs: St. Lawrence Seaway traffic

antic Provinces Topographic 1:5M 40–41
nset: the economy
Graphs: production and employment; fishery catches and products

rth and South America Physical 1:44M 42–43
nsets: annual rainfall; build and minerals

rth and South America Agriculture
4M 44–45
nset: vegetation
Graphs: climagraphs

and S. America Population and Communications
4M 46–47
nset: political

. Political 1:12.5M 48–49
nsets: Hawaii; Alaska

stern U.S. Topographic 1:8M 50–51

stern U.S. Topographic 1:8M 52–53

rtheastern U.S. Topographic 1:2M 54–55

an Land Use: New York; Chicago; shington 56–57

xico, Central America and the ibbean 1:16M 58–59
sets: Bermuda 1:500 000; Panama Canal 1:1.5 M

South America Topographic 1:22M 60

Central America Topographic 1:7.875M 61

Europe Physical 1:19M 62
Graphs: climagraphs

Europe Climate 1:19M 63
Graphs: climagraphs

Europe Political 1:19M 64
Inset: European Economic Community

Europe Population and Communications
1:19M 65

Europe Agriculture 1:19M 66
Inset: vegetation

British Isles Topographic 1:4.750M 67
Insets: population; power

Western Europe Topographic 1:6.250M 68–69
Inset: the Ruhr 1:3M

Eastern Europe Topographic 1:6.250M 70–71
Inset: Scandinavia 1:19M

Urban Land Use: Paris, Moscow 72

Asia Political 1:44M 73

Asia Physical 1:44M 74

Asia Rainfall, Vegetation, Minerals 1:110M 75
Graphs: climagraphs

Asia Population and Communications 1:44M 76

Asia Agriculture 1:44M 77
Inset: monsoons

U.S.S.R. Topographic 1:25M 78–79

Western U.S.S.R. Topographic 1:12.5M 80–81

Middle East Topographic 1:12.5M 82–83
Inset: Israel

Southern Asia 1:12.5M 84

Southeast Asia Mainland Topographic 1:12.5M 85

China Topographic 1:19M 86–87

Eastern China Topographic 1:6.250M 88–89

Japan Topographic 1:6.250M 90
Inset: urban land use in Tokyo 1:400 000

Southeast Asia Topographic 1:19M 91

Australasia: Physical; Climate 1:44M 92
Insets: minerals and build

Australasia: Agriculture; Population and Communications 1:44M 93
Inset: vegetation
Graphs: climagraphs

Australasia Topographic 1:22M 94

New Zealand Topographic 1:7.5M 95

Australasia Political 1:44M 95

Africa Physical 1:44M 96

Africa Political 1:44M 97
Inset: annual rainfall, build and minerals

Africa Population and Communications 1:44M 98
Inset: vegetation
Graphs: climagraphs

Africa Agriculture 1:44M 99
Insets: tsetse fly
Graphs: climagraphs

North Africa Topographic 1:19M 100–101
Inset: Suez Canal 1:1.5M

Southern Africa Topographic 1:19M 102
Inset: Madagascar 1:19M

Atlantic Ocean 1:63M 103

Pacific Ocean 1:63M 104–105

World Political 1:88M 106–107
Insets: time zones
Graphs: land areas and populations

World Physical 1:88M 108–109
Insets: paleogeography; plate tectonics; volcanoes; natural hazards
Graph: geological time

World Climate 110–111
Precipitation; temperature; ocean currents
Insets: air masses; tropical revolving storms

World Climate Regions 1:180M 112
Inset: soils
Graphs: climatic regions; distribution of water

World Vegetation 1:180M 113
Inset: forest resources
Graph: land use

World Population 1:88M 114–115
Graphs: growth; birth/death; age/sex

World: Life Expectancy; Demography; Medical Care 1:180M 116
Graphs: infant mortality; doctors; etc.

World: Demography; Religions; Education
1:100M 117
Graph: expenditure on education

World Agriculture and Nutrition 1:88M 118–119
Insets: nutrition; food consumption
Graphs: food consumption; nutrition levels

World Energy: Oil; Gas; Coal; Electricity
1:180M 120–121
Graphs: consumption and reserves

World Energy Statistics 122
Inset: geothermal energy
Graphs: consumption and reserves

World: Iron and Steel; Mineral Production
1:180M 123

World GDP and Industry 1:88M 124–125
Inset: industrialization 1:180M
Graph: industrial contribution to GDP

World Manufacturing 126
Graphs: income per capita; vehicles per person; iron and steel production; manufacturing indices

World Transportation 1:100M 127
Inset: satellite receiving stations
Graphs: air travel; seaborne freight

Antarctica 1:25M 128

Gazetteer 1B

Canadian Statistics 1C

Canada
Population

The graph on page 10 shows the growth of Canada's population from 1851–1981. What this graph cannot show are the factors that contributed to this population growth.

There are two components to population growth. The first is net natural increase: the excess of births over deaths in any one period. The second is net migration: the excess (or otherwise) of immigration over emigration in any one period. Fig. 1 shows the role of each factor in the population of Canada for the period 1921–1981. Figs. 2 and 3 plot the components of population growth year-by-year for a short period. Fig. 3 particularly demonstrates the wide variations that can occur within a decade. (Net migration figures should always be treated with some caution, as accurate figures of emigration from Canada are not available, and must be estimated.)

So far we have looked only at the growth of population in Canada as a whole. When we come to examine population growth province by province, some startling variations appear, particularly in the net migration component of population change. The net migration figures for each province include Canadians who have moved into or out of another province, as well as immigrants moving into Canada and emigrants leaving it. Fig. 4 makes clear the shifts from province to province, which are of course not included in the net migration figures for the population growth of Canada as a whole.

Fig. 1: Growth of Canada's Population, 1921–1981

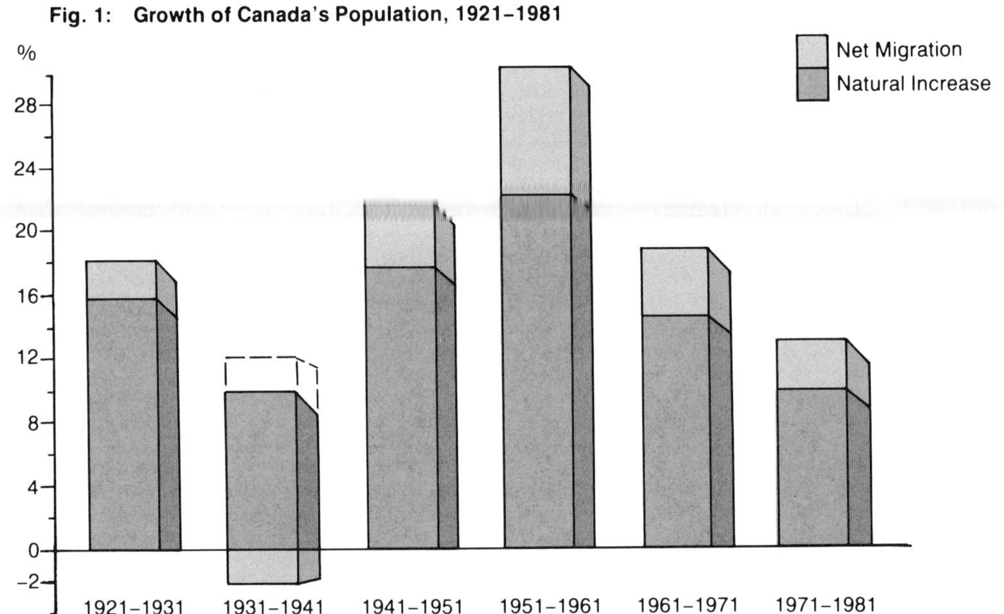
%
28
24
20
16
12
8
4
0
−2
Net Migration
Natural Increase
1921–1931
1931–1941
1941–1951
1951–1961
1961–1971
1971–1981

Based on data from Urquhart, M.C. (ed.), *The Historical Statistics of Canada* (Toronto: Macmillan, 1965) and *Statistics Canada, 1971 and 1981 Census*

Fig. 2: Vital Statistics, 1977–1981 **Fig. 3: Immigration and Emigration, 1977–1981**

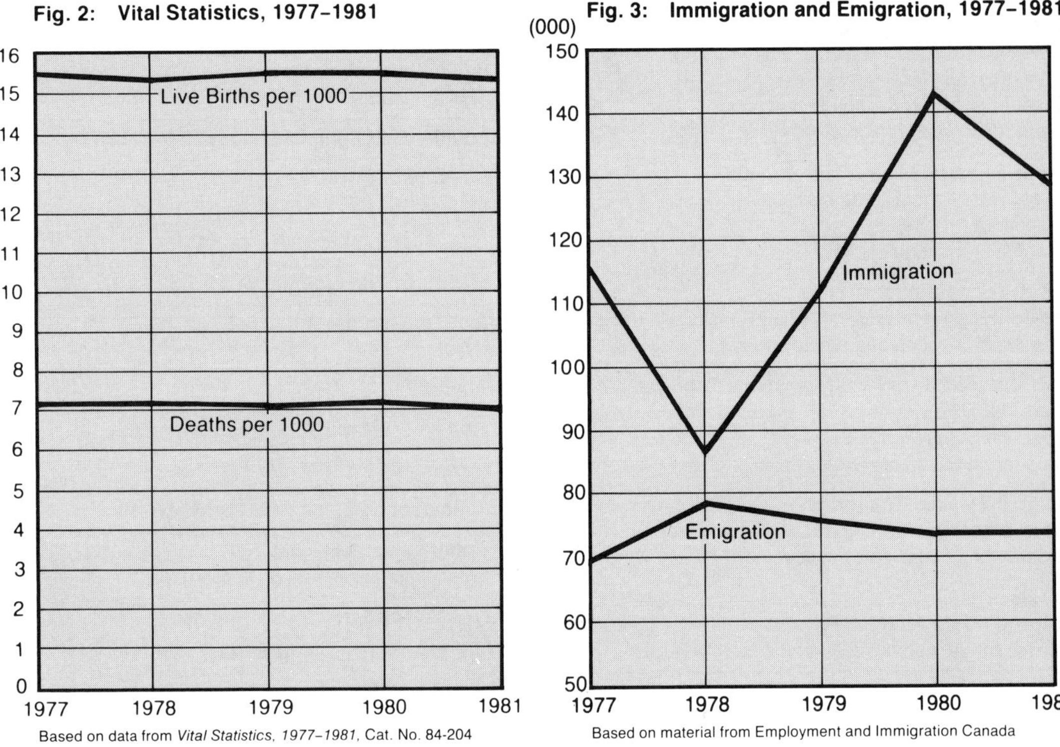
16
15
14
13
12
11
10
9
8
7
6
5
4
3
2
1
0
Live Births per 1000
Deaths per 1000
1977
1978
1979
1980
1981
(000)
150
140
130
120
110
100
90
80
70
60
50
Immigration
Emigration
1977
1978
1979
1980
198

Based on data from *Vital Statistics, 1977–1981*, Cat. No. 84-204

Based on material from Employment and Immigration Canada

Fig. 4: Interprovincial Migration, 1976–1981

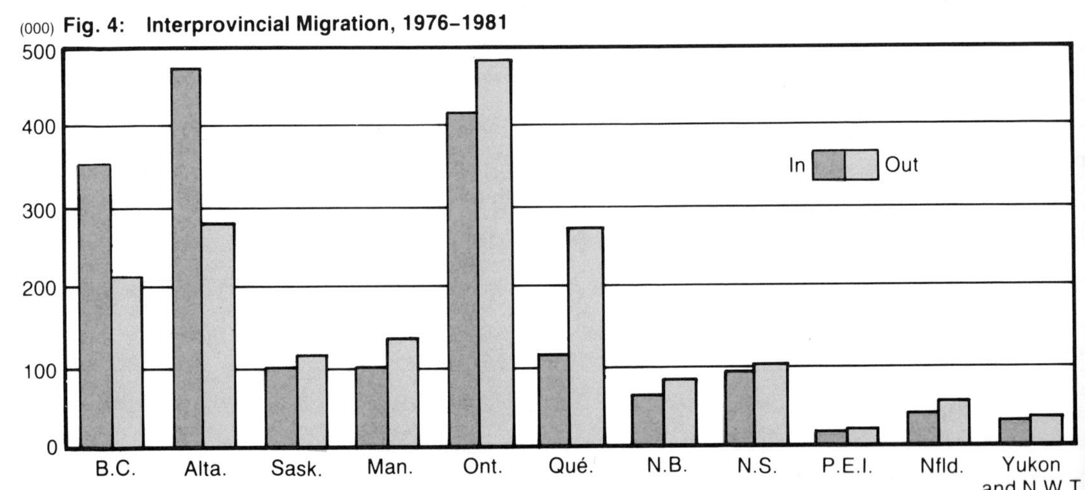
(000)
500
400
300
200
100
0
In
Out
B.C.
Alta.
Sask.
Man.
Ont.
Qué.
N.B.
N.S.
P.E.I.
Nfld.
Yukon and N.W.T

Based on data from Statistics Canada, *International and Interprovincial Migration in Canada*, Cat. No. 91–208

Fig. 5: Components of Population Change by Province, 1961–1981

Province or Territory	Total Population Change 1961–66	Natural Increase 1961–66	Net Migration 1961–66	Total Population Change 1966–71	Natural Increase 1966–71	Net Migration 1966–71	Total Population Change 1971–76	Natural Increase 1971–76	Net Migration 1971–76	Total Population Change 1976–81	Natural Increase 1976–81	Net Migration 1976–81
Newfoundland	36 000	60 000	–24 000	29 000	49 000	–20 000	36 000	45 000	–9 000	10 000	36 000	–26 000
Prince Edward Island	4 000	9 000	–5 000	3 000	5 000	–2 000	7 000	5 000	2 000	5 000	5 000	—
Nova Scotia	19 000	60 000	–41 000	33 000	37 000	–4 000	40 000	32 000	8 000	19 000	27 000	–8 000
New Brunswick	19 000	53 000	–34 000	18 000	35 000	–17 000	43 000	33 000	10 000	19 000	28 000	–9 000
Québec	522 000	458 000	64 000	247 000	289 000	–42 000	207 000	223 000	–16 000	204 000	265 000	–61 000
Ontario	725 000	488 000	237 000	742 000	373 000	369 000	561 000	328 000	233 000	361 000	301 000	60 000
Manitoba	41 000	70 000	–29 000	25 000	49 000	–24 000	33 000	45 000	–12 000	5 000	40 000	–35 000
Saskatchewan	30 000	76 000	–46 000	–29 000	51 000	–80 000	–5 000	38 000	–43 000	47 000	46 000	1 000
Alberta	131 000	135 000	–4 000	165 000	105 000	60 000	210 000	96 000	114 000	400 000	128 000	272 000
British Columbia	245 000	104 000	141 000	311 000	88 000	223 000	282 000	83 000	199 000	278 000	98 000	180 000
Yukon Territory and Northwest Territories	5 000	7 000	–2 000	10 000	7 000	3 000	11 000	6 000	5 000	4 000	7 000	–3 000
Canada	**1 777 000**	**1 520 000**	**257 000**	**1 554 000**	**1 088 000**	**466 000**	**1 425 000**	**934 000**	**491 000**	**1 352 000**	**981 000**	**371 000**

Based on Statistics Canada, *Historical Statistics and Census*, Cat. Nos. 91-208, 92-901, 84-204

Changes in the birth rate and life expectancy can greatly alter the age structure of the population. The age/sex pyramids provide a graphic illustration of changes in birth rates and of increased life expectancy among other things. It is more difficult to determine what effect migration has on the age structure, as migrants can be of all ages.

Fig. 6 Immigration to Canada by Country or Region of Last Permanent Residence, 1957–1981

	1957–61	1962–66	1967–71	1972–76	1977–81
Great Britain	183 443	172 633	174 234	140 152	82 050
France	16 023	23 882	31 231	17 702	10 400
Italy	115 280	105 388	74 535	24 910	12 166
West Germany	69 746	36 474	33 093	14 349	8 879
Other European	194 898	123 975	183 591	137 563	77 649
TOTAL EUROPEAN	**579 390**	**462 352**	**496 684**	**334 676**	**191 144**
Africa	7 089	15 333	18 813	44 684	23 808
Asia	19 543	37 317	109 086	208 794	226 347
Australasia	10 290	12 147	22 681	11 468	7 045
North and Central America	56 795	69 567	113 771	118 134	57 757
Other	16 636	25 128	76 959	144 225	78 957
TOTAL	**689 743**	**621 844**	**837 994**	**861 981**	**585 058**

Based on data from Urquhart, M.C. (ed), *The Historical Statistics of Canada* (Toronto: Macmillan, 1965) and on material from Employment and Immigration Canada

Fig. 7: The Changing Shape of Canada's Population, 1901–1981

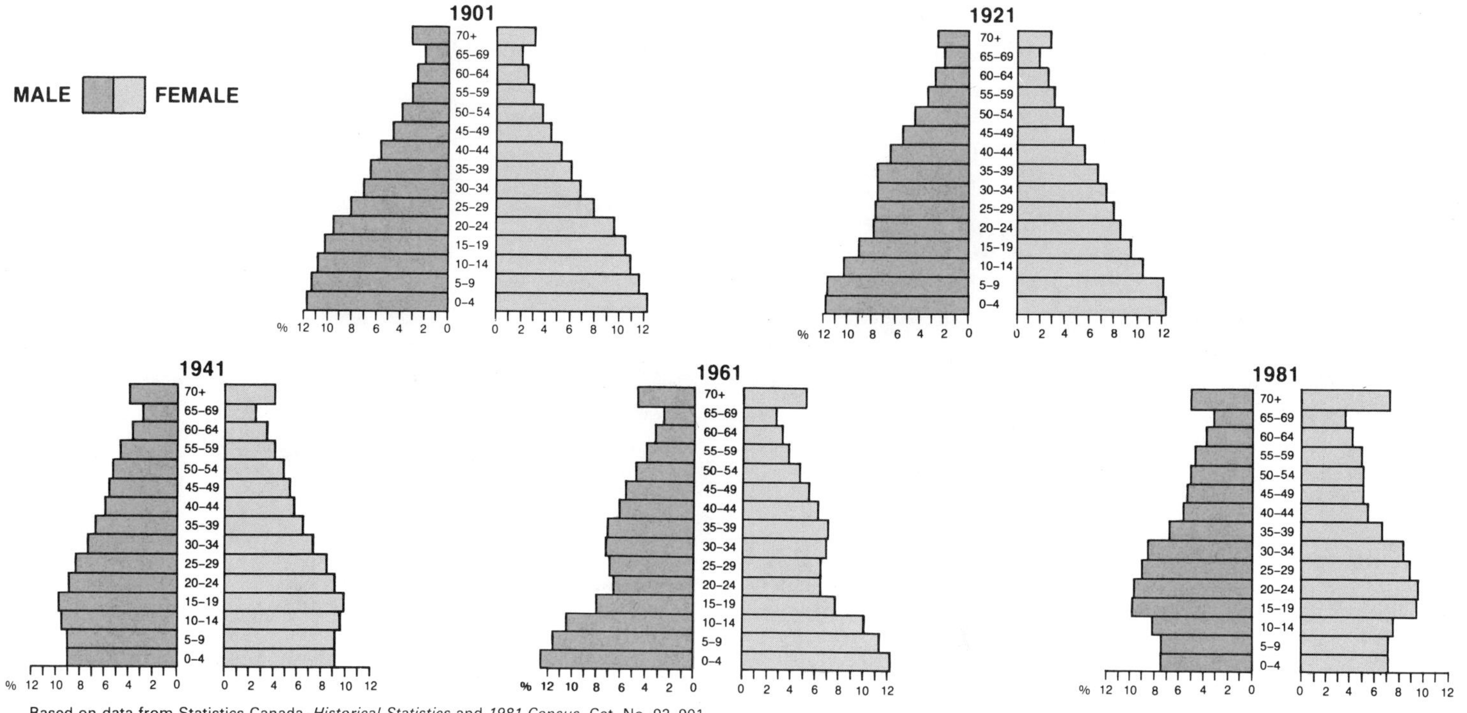
MALE
FEMALE
1901
1921
1941
1961
1981
70+
65–69
60–64
55–59
50–54
45–49
40–44
35–39
30–34
25–29
20–24
15–19
10–14
5–9
0–4
% 12 10 8 6 4 2 0
0 2 4 6 8 10 12

Based on data from Statistics Canada, *Historical Statistics* and *1981 Census*, Cat. No. 92–901

Fig. 8: Census Metropolitan Areas, 1971–1981

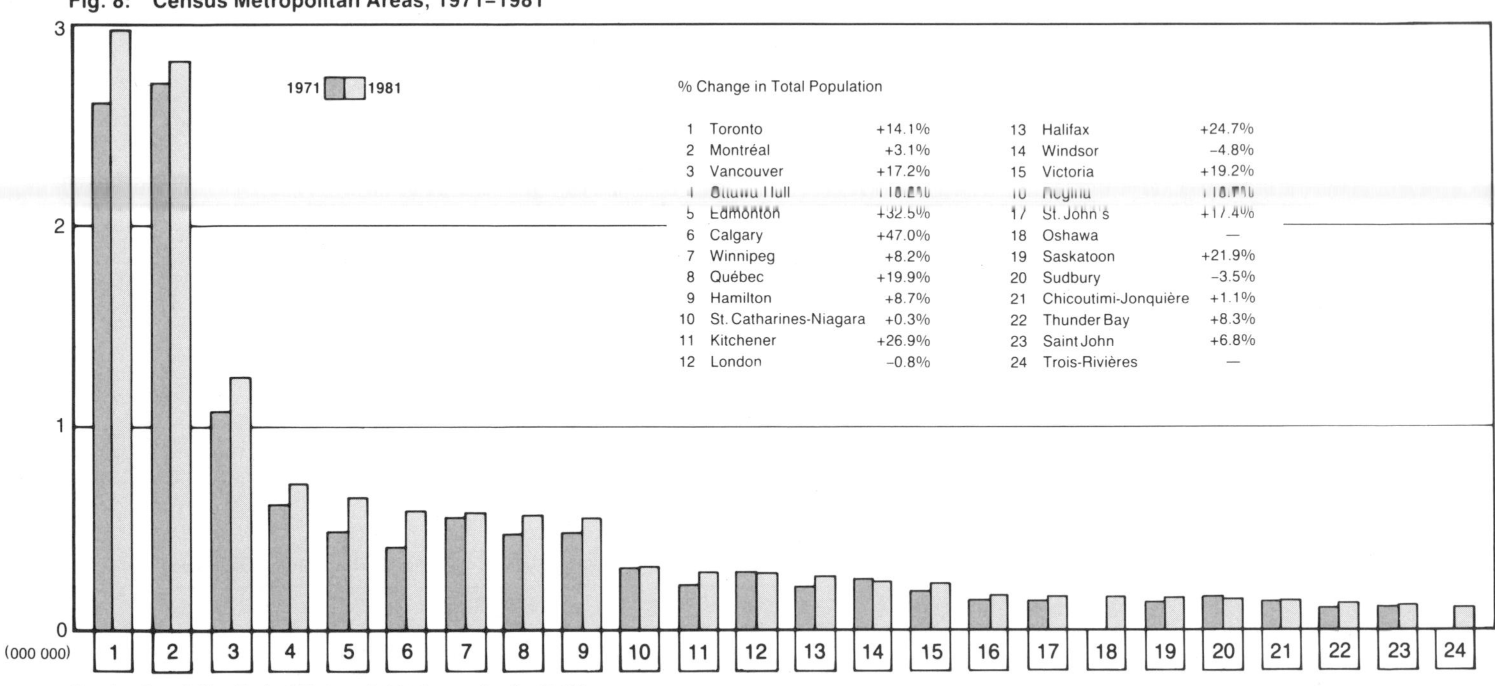

3
2
1
0
(000 000)
1971
1981
% Change in Total Population
1 Toronto +14.1%
2 Montréal +3.1%
3 Vancouver +17.2%
4 Ottawa-Hull
5 Edmonton +32.5%
6 Calgary +47.0%
7 Winnipeg +8.2%
8 Québec +19.9%
9 Hamilton +8.7%
10 St. Catharines-Niagara +0.3%
11 Kitchener +26.9%
12 London –0.8%
13 Halifax +24.7%
14 Windsor –4.8%
15 Victoria +19.2%
16 Regina
17 St. John's +17.4%
18 Oshawa —
19 Saskatoon +21.9%
20 Sudbury –3.5%
21 Chicoutimi-Jonquière +1.1%
22 Thunder Bay +8.3%
23 Saint John +6.8%
24 Trois-Rivières —
1 2 3 4 5 6 7 8 9 10 11 12 13 14 15 16 17 18 19 20 21 22 23 24

Based on *Canada Year Book, 1980–81*, and 1981 Census, Cat. No. 95-903

Rural/Urban Profiles

Census Metropolitan Areas

A census metropolitan area is a large urban centre and the surrounding area—roughly the daily commuting area—with a population of 100 000 or more.

In 1971 there were 22 CMAs in Canada; by the time of the 1981 census the number had grown to 24.

Canada's history has shown a steady trend towards increasing urbanization, as Fig. 9 shows.

The 1981 census showed that in most parts of Canada urban dwellers greatly outnumbered the rural population.

However, the 1981 census also showed that for the first time in Canada's history, the trend towards urbanization halted in the last decade. The total population grew by 12.9% between 1971 and 1981; the total rural population grew by 14.7% compared with a 12.3% growth in the urban population.

Fig. 9: Percentage of Population in Urban Areas, 1851–1971

Province	1851	1871	1891	1911	1931	1951	1961	1971
British Columbia	—	9.0	42.6	50.9	62.3	68.6	72.6	75.7
Alberta	—	—	—	29.4	31.8	47.6	63.3	73.5
Saskatchewan	—	—	—	16.1	20.3	30.4	43.0	53.0
Manitoba	—	—	23.3	39.3	45.2	56.0	63.9	69.5
Ontario	14.0	20.6	35.0	49.5	63.1	72.5	77.3	82.4
Québec	14.9	19.9	28.6	44.5	59.5	66.8	74.3	80.6
New Brunswick	14.0	17.6	19.9	26.7	35.4	42.8	46.5	56.9
Nova Scotia	7.5	8.3	19.4	36.7	46.6	54.5	54.3	56.7
Prince Edward Island	—	9.4	13.1	16.0	19.5	25.1	32.4	38.3
Newfoundland	—	—	—	—	—	43.3	50.7	57.2

Based on data from Stone, Leroy O., Urban Development in Canada; 1961 Census Monograph; 1971 Census of Canada

Fig. 10: Urban and Rural Population of Canada and the Provinces, 1981

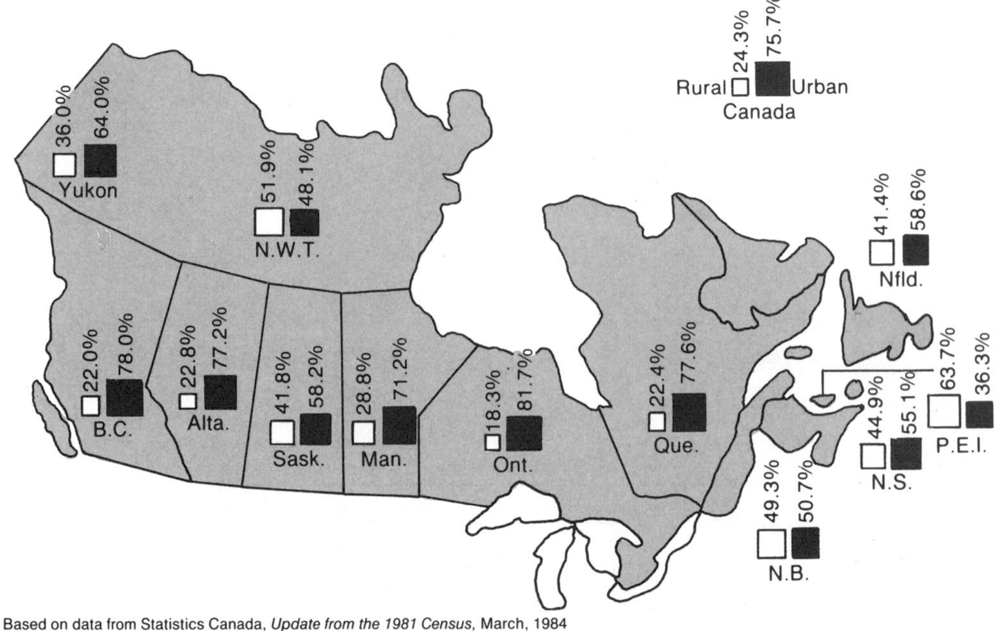

24.3%
75.7%
Rural
Urban
Canada
36.0%
64.0%
Yukon
51.9%
48.1%
N.W.T.
41.4%
58.6%
Nfld.
22.0%
78.0%
B.C.
22.8%
77.2%
Alta.
41.8%
58.2%
Sask.
28.8%
71.2%
Man.
18.3%
81.7%
Ont.
22.4%
77.6%
Que.
44.9%
55.1%
N.S.
63.7%
36.3%
P.E.I.
49.3%
50.7%
N.B.

Based on data from Statistics Canada, *Update from the 1981 Census*, March, 1984

The increase in the rural population does not mean, however, that Canadians are returning to life on the farm. For some decades, the farm population has been declining dramatically, in actual numbers as well as a percentage of the total population.

The emerging trends seem to be that nearly all census metropolitan areas grew in population over the last decade, with the greatest rates of growth being recorded in some western centres; and that in some of the largest centres, particularly in eastern Canada, the city core is declining in population as Canadians move out to the rural fringe areas of these centres to become part of the rural population. Between 1971 and 1976, population growth in these areas accounted for 25% of total rural growth; between 1976 and 1981 these areas accounted for nearly 50% of all rural growth.

In Québec 176 400 people lived in rural areas in 1981, and of these, one-half were in fringe areas neighbouring on large cities. Of the 84 900 people living in rural areas in Ontario, fully two-thirds lived in areas close to large urban centres. British Columbia, with the third largest rural population of all the provinces, had 40 percent of its 89 600 rural residents living in fringe areas in 1981.

Fig. 11 Farm Population in Canada, 1951–1981 (Census Farms Only)

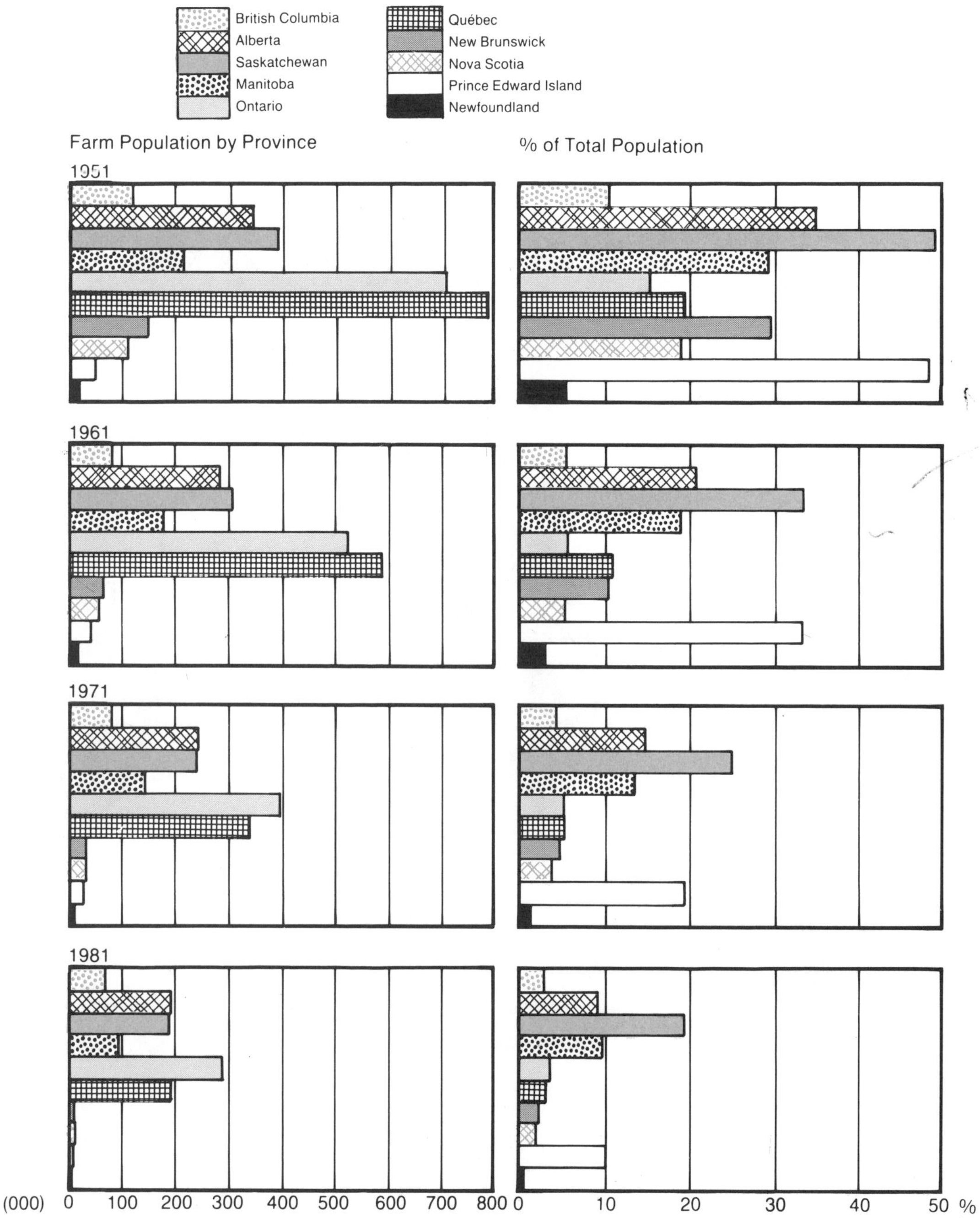

British Columbia
Alberta
Saskatchewan
Manitoba
Ontario
Québec
New Brunswick
Nova Scotia
Prince Edward Island
Newfoundland

Farm Population by Province

% of Total Population

1951

1961

1971

1981

(000) 0 100 200 300 400 500 600 700 800

0 10 20 30 40 50 %

Based on material from Statistics Canada, *Census of Canada, Agriculture*

Fig. 12 Population of the City Core, 1971–1981

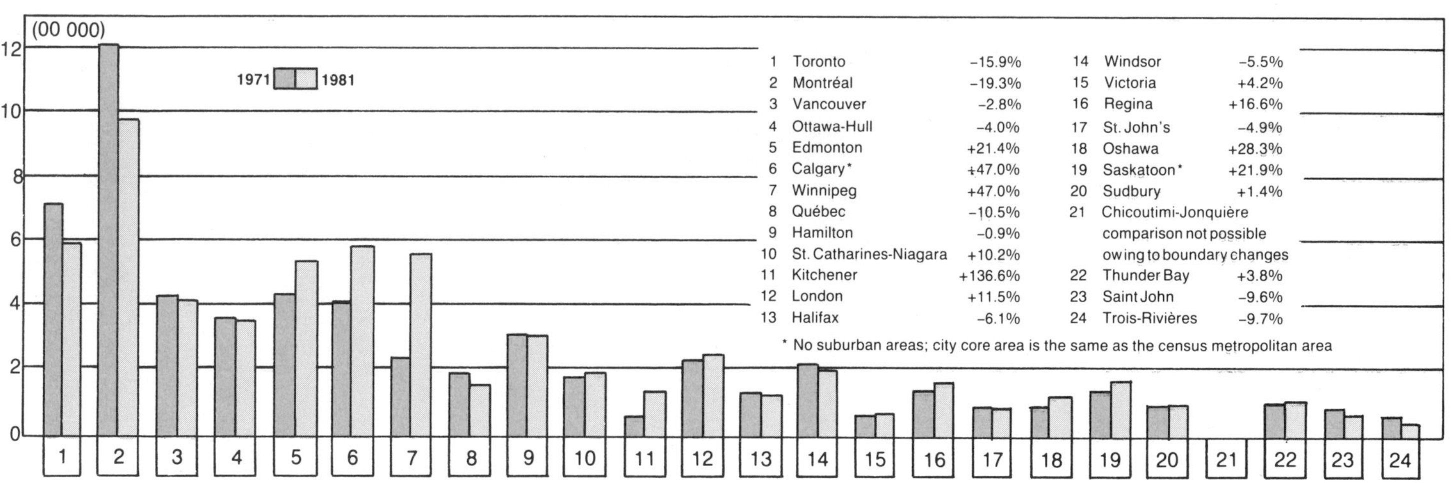
(00 000)
12
10
8
6
4
2
0
1971
1981
1 Toronto -15.9%
2 Montréal -19.3%
3 Vancouver -2.8%
4 Ottawa-Hull -4.0%
5 Edmonton +21.4%
6 Calgary* +47.0%
7 Winnipeg +47.0%
8 Québec -10.5%
9 Hamilton -0.9%
10 St. Catharines-Niagara +10.2%
11 Kitchener +136.6%
12 London +11.5%
13 Halifax -6.1%
14 Windsor -5.5%
15 Victoria +4.2%
16 Regina +16.6%
17 St. John's -4.9%
18 Oshawa +28.3%
19 Saskatoon* +21.9%
20 Sudbury +1.4%
21 Chicoutimi-Jonquière comparison not possible owing to boundary changes
22 Thunder Bay +3.8%
23 Saint John -9.6%
24 Trois-Rivières -9.7%
* No suburban areas; city core area is the same as the census metropolitan area
1
2
3
4
5
6
7
8
9
10
11
12
13
14
15
16
17
18
19
20
21
22
23
24

Based on data from *Canada Year Book, 1980–81*, and *1981 Census, Cat. No. 95–903*

Travel

Canadians are a nation of car-drivers. For commuting to work and short trips, and even for longer distances to some degree, the car is the preferred method of travel.

Approximately 73% of Canadian workers travel to work by car, 15% by public transport, and 10% walk. The increase in gasoline prices in recent years has had very little effect on how Canadians travel to work. For short-to-medium journeys within Canada, the car has been overwhelmingly the preferred method of transportation.

Plane travel in 1980 accounted for less than 6% of journeys within Canada, but represented 21% of expenditure on travel, while travel by car accounted for 72% of total expenditures.

The length of the trip plays a major part in the choice of means of transportation used. On longer trips of over 800 km one way, plane travel is used nearly as frequently as travel by automobile.

Fig. 13: Method of Transportation of Commuters, 1982

	(000)	(%)
Driving alone	4 624	52%
Driving with passenger(s)	656	7%
Riding as a passenger	1 034	12%
Sharing the driving	179	2%
Total cars	6 494	73%
Public transportation	1 340	15%
Walking	877	10%
Other	146	2%

Based on *Statistics Canada Cat. Nos. 87-503, 87-003*

Fig. 14: Medium and Long-distance Travel to Destinations within Canada, 1980

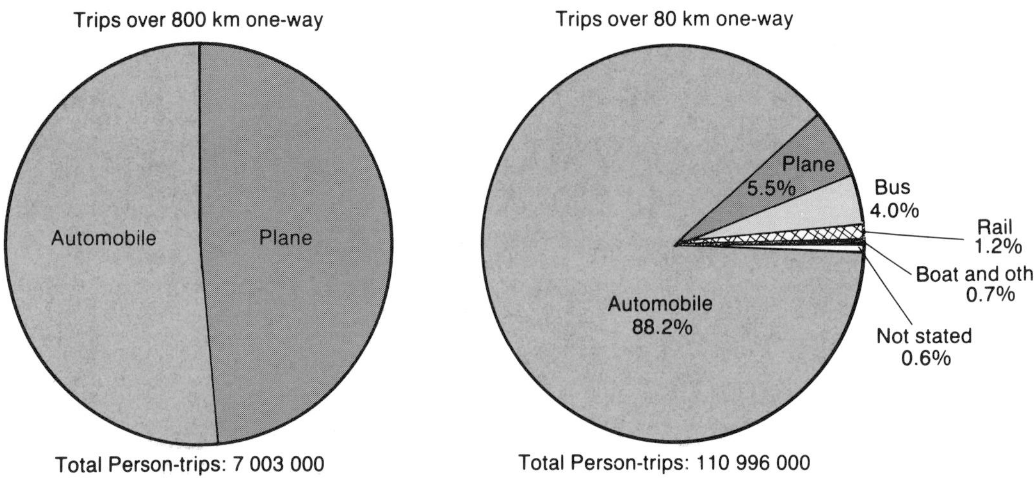
Trips over 800 km one-way
Automobile
Plane
Total Person-trips: 7 003 000
Trips over 80 km one-way
Plane
5.5%
Bus
4.0%
Rail
1.2%
Boat and other
0.7%
Not stated
0.6%
Automobile
88.2%
Total Person-trips: 110 996 000

Based on data from *Statistics Canada Cat. No. 87-504*

Fig. 15: Tourism Expenditure Estimates, 1983

	Expenditures ($000 000)
Newfoundland	310
Prince Edward Island	150
Nova Scotia	625
New Brunswick	380
Québec	3 225
Ontario	6 095
Manitoba	705
Saskatchewan	805
Alberta	2 430
British Columbia	2 860
Yukon/Northwest Territories	60
Canada	**18 550***

*Includes crew spending and fares to Canadian carriers

Based on data supplied by Tourism Canada

Natural Resources

Agriculture

Canada is the second largest country in the world in areal extent. It is not, however, the second largest agricultural country. Only a small percentage of the total area has the right combination of climate and soils to sustain profitable agriculture.

Fig. 16: Agricultural Land in Canada

Total area of Canada 100%
Total improved land 5.0%
Area suitable for agriculture 8.9%
Total land on farms 7.2%

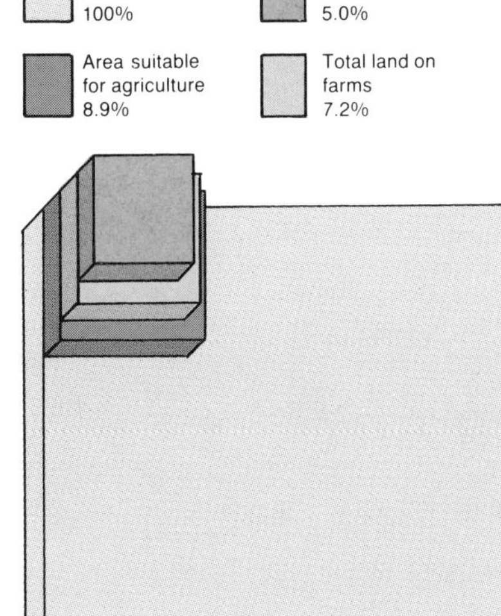

Based on Statistics Canada data quoted in Agriculture Canada. *Market Commentary: Farm Inputs and Finance*, Dec. 1983

The graph on page 12 of the atlas shows certain trends in agriculture over the past three decades. Fig. 17 shows these trends broken down by province. Although the total area in farms has decreased during this period, losses of farmland are offset to some extent by improvements to the land still in use for agricultural purposes, as Fig. 19 shows.

Fig. 17: Number of Farms and Average Size of Farms, 1951–1981

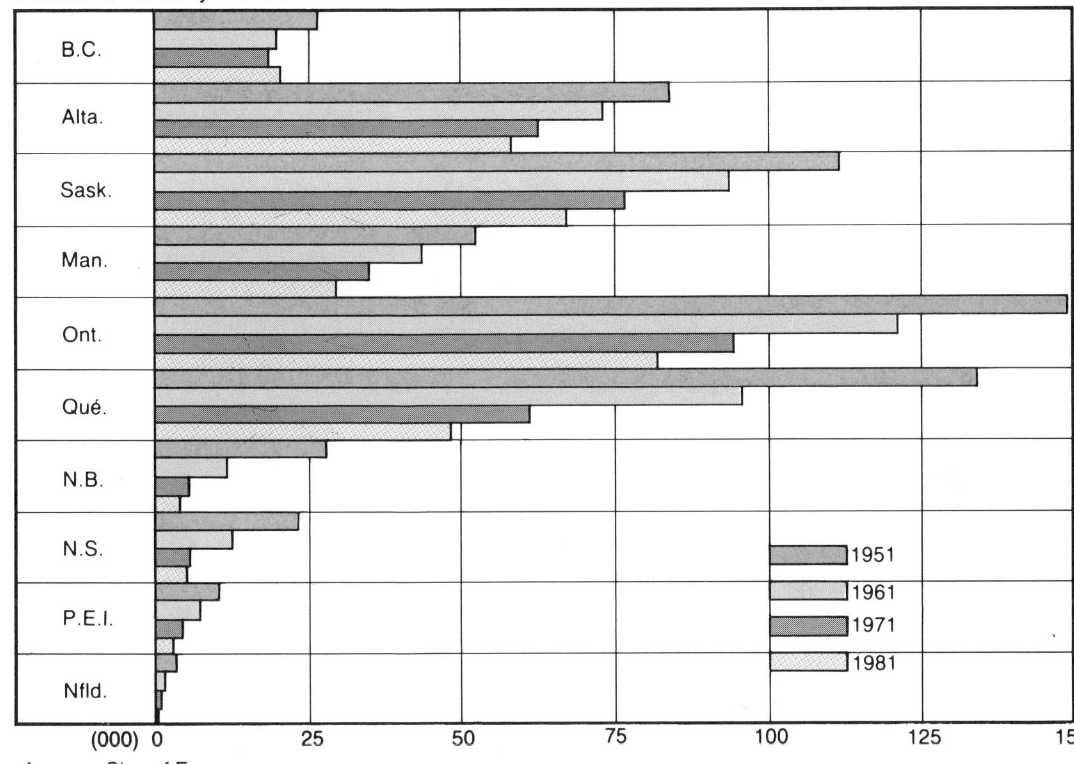
Number of Farms by Province
B.C.
Alta.
Sask.
Man.
Ont.
Qué.
N.B.
N.S.
P.E.I.
Nfld.
1951
1961
1971
1981
(000) 0
25
50
75
100
125
150

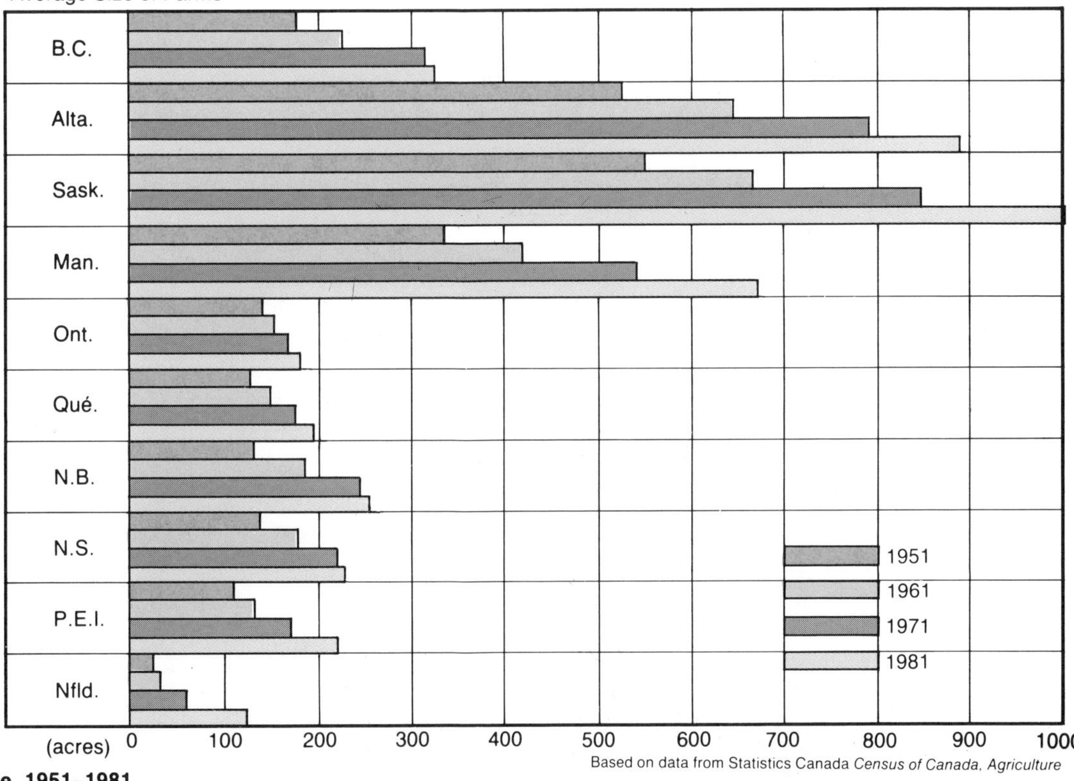
Average Size of Farms
B.C.
Alta.
Sask.
Man.
Ont.
Qué.
N.B.
N.S.
P.E.I.
Nfld.
1951
1961
1971
1981
(acres) 0
100
200
300
400
500
600
700
800
900
1000

Based on data from Statistics Canada *Census of Canada, Agriculture*

Fig. 18: Total Area of Farms, by Province, 1951–1981

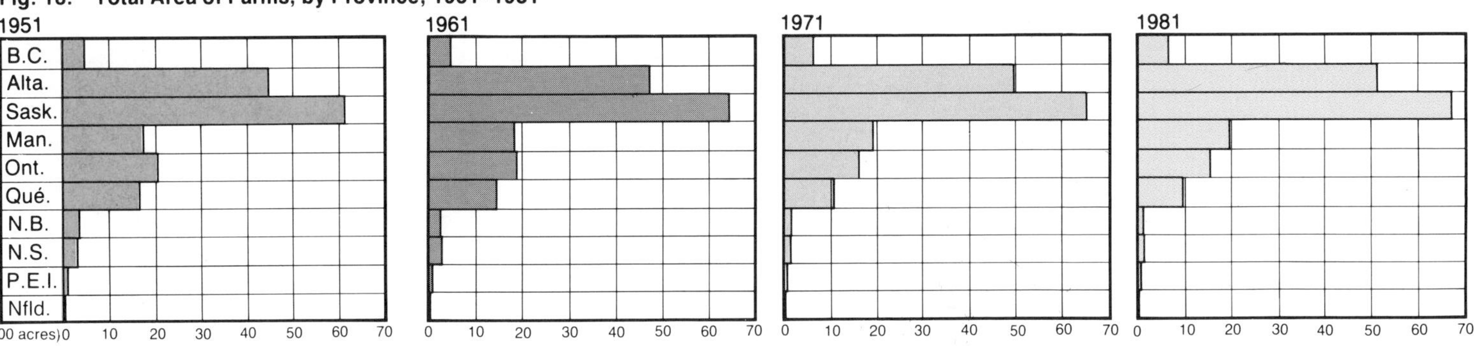
1951
1961
1971
1981
B.C.
Alta.
Sask.
Man.
Ont.
Qué.
N.B.
N.S.
P.E.I.
Nfld.
(00 000 acres) 0
10
20
30
40
50
60
70

Based on data from Statistics Canada, *Census of Canada, Agriculture*.

What implications do these trends have for farmers? Clearly the decline in the number of farms has meant financial hardship for some farmers, as Fig. 20 shows.

In Canada a distinction is made between census farms—farms with sales beyond a certain level operated for profit—and other farms. In 1971 a census farm was defined as a farm with annual sales exceeding $1200; in 1981 a census farm was defined as a farm with annual sales exceeding $2500.

Not all the decrease in farms was a decrease in commercial farms; many people who had run a small farm as a sideline to other employment also gave up, and so affected the total picture.

Fig. 19: Land Use of Occupied Farms

Improved Land
Unimproved Land

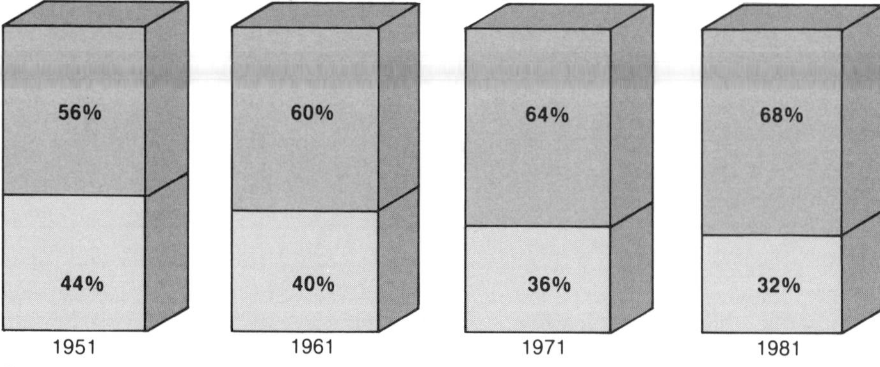
56%
44%
1951
60%
40%
1961
64%
36%
1971
68%
32%
1981

Based on data from *Agriculture Facts*, November 1983, Pub. 5032B, Minister of Supply and Services, Canada

Fig. 20: Number of Bankruptcies in Agriculture by Province

Province	1979	1980	1981	1982
British Columbia	8	8	7	3
Alberta	12	4	11	19
Saskatchewan	11	11	15	15
Manitoba	1	12	5	24
Ontario	39	94	112	132
Québec	7	31	35	115
New Brunswick	1	1	3	2
Nova Scotia	2	3	3	3
Prince Edward Island	1	0	0	2
Newfoundland	0	0	0	1
N.W.T. and Yukon	0	0	0	0
Canada	**82**	**164**	**191**	**316**
% Change		+100.0	+16.5	+65.4

Source: Market Commentary, December 1983, Agriculture Canada

Fig. 21: Census and Non-census Farms, 1971 and 1981

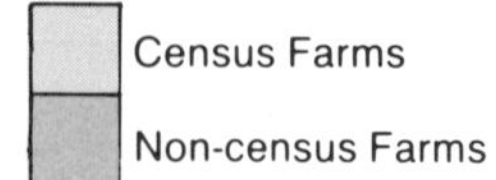
Census Farms
Non-census Farms

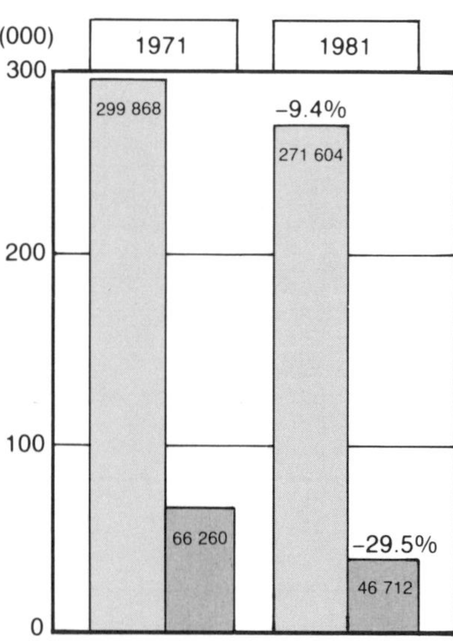
(000)
300
200
100
0
1971
1981
299 868
66 260
-9.4%
271 604
-29.5%
46 712

Based on data from *Agriculture Facts*, Pub. 5032B, November 1983, Minister of Supply and Services, Canada

What of the farmers who stayed in business? Direct comparisons are difficult, and allowances must be made for inflation when comparing dollar values, but even taking the changing value of the Canadian dollar into account, it is clear that some farmers became more prosperous, as Fig. 22 shows.

Fig. 22: Farms Classfied by Annual Sales

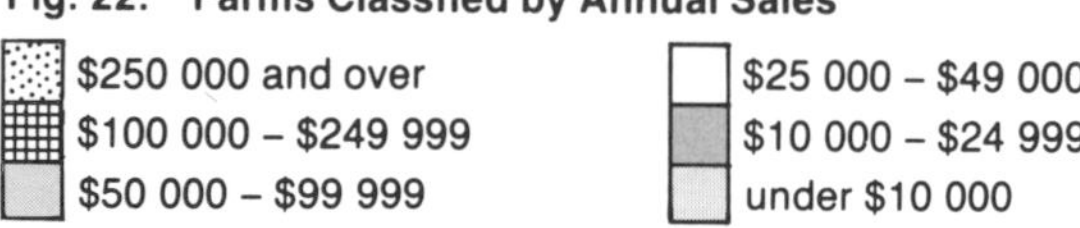
$250 000 and over
$100 000 – $249 999
$50 000 – $99 999
$25 000 – $49 000
$10 000 – $24 999
under $10 000

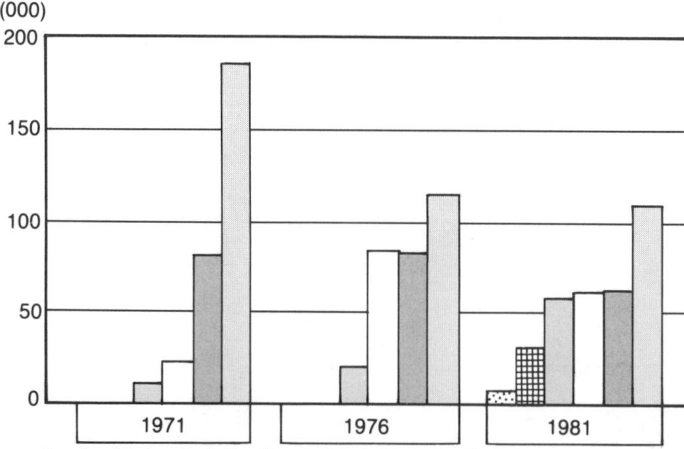
(000)
200
150
100
50
0
1971
1976
1981

Based on data from Agriculture Canada, *Selected Agricultural Statistics, Canada and the Provinces*

Agriculture plays an important part in Canada's economy, not only within the country but as a large item in our export trade.

The graph on page 33 shows Canada's world role as an exporter of wheat. Fig. 24 demonstrates the importance of grain exports relative to other types of agricultural exports; in the 1981–82 crop year 27.3 million tonnes of grains were exported: of these grains, 18 million tonnes were wheat.

Fig. 23: Agricultural Exports: ($000 000)

	1978	1979	1980	1981	1982
Western Europe	1 020	1 488	1 429	1 539	1 450
Eastern Europe	566	679	1 623	2 107	2 303
Japan	833	1 115	1 025	1 345	1 248
China	350	414	531	713	743
Other Asian	382	333	304	263	367
Central America	314	381	540	050	471
North America	793	1 027	1 116	1 264	1 610
Others*	572	671	1 144	891	1 112
Developed countries	3 294	4 433	3 627	4 226	4 390
Developing countries	1 536	1 667	1 604	1 386	1 629
Centrally planned countries	—	—	2 487	3 165	3 287

*Includes Middle East, Africa, Oceania, South America.
Based on data from *Agricultural Facts, 1983,* Minister of Supply and Services

Fig. 24: Canadian Agricultural Exports by Major Commodity Groups

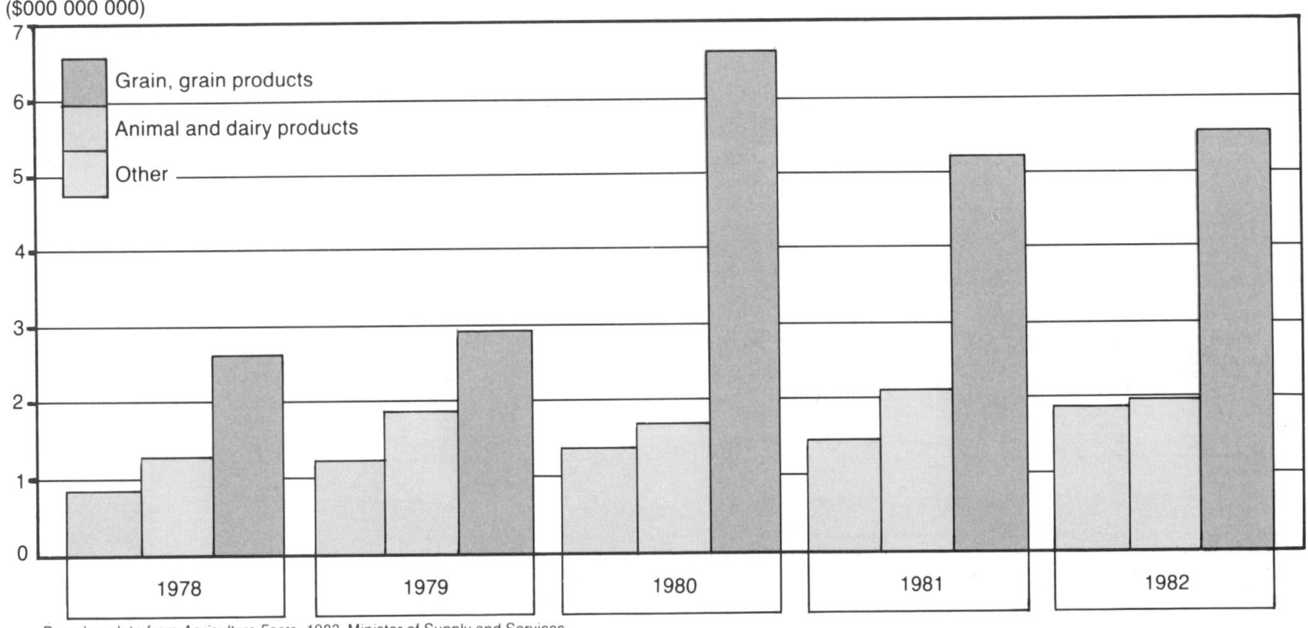
($000 000 000)
7
6
5
4
3
2
1
0
Grain, grain products
Animal and dairy products
Other
1978
1979
1980
1981
1982

Based on data from *Agriculture Facts, 1983,* Minister of Supply and Services

Fig. 25: Major Importers of Canadian Wheat

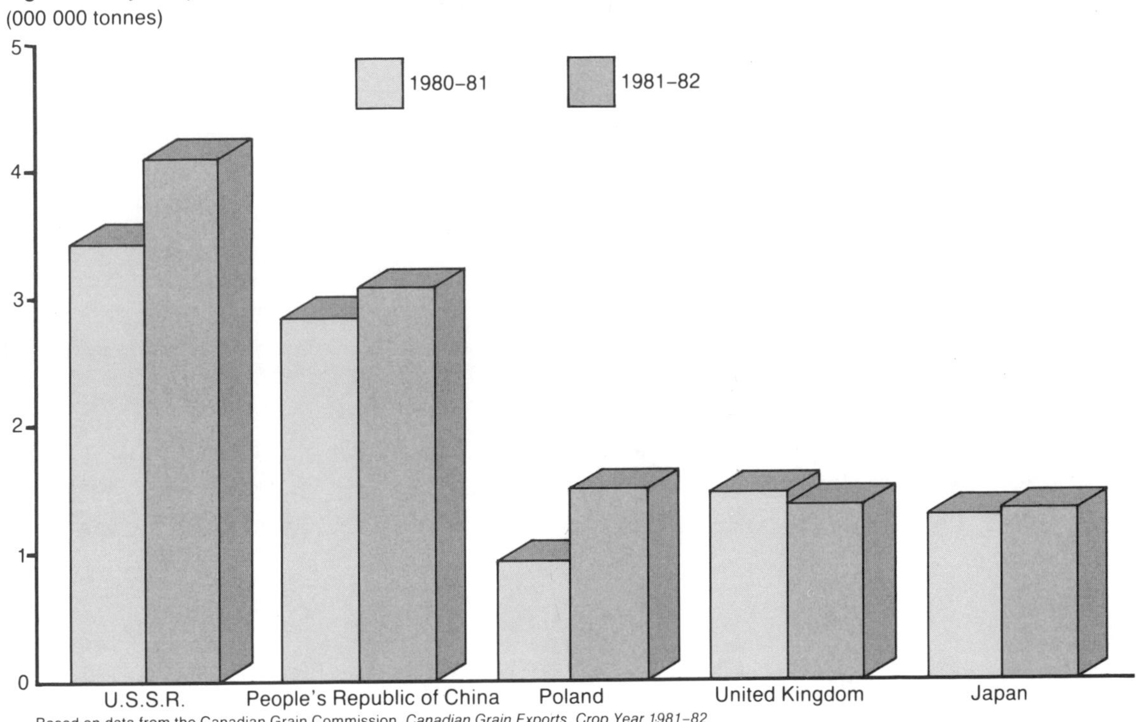
(000 000 tonnes)
5
4
3
2
1
0
1980–81
1981–82
U.S.S.R.
People's Republic of China
Poland
United Kingdom
Japan

Based on data from the Canadian Grain Commission, *Canadian Grain Exports, Crop Year 1981–82*

Forestry

About 47% of Canada's land area is forested land. Of this large area, 2 202 000 km²—24%—is in productive use by the forestry industry.

Figs. 26, 27, and 28, together with the information on pages 13 and 28–29, provide some information on the forestry industry in Canada, and on its dependence on a renewable resource.

Fig. 26: Annual Allowable Cut by Species Group, 1982

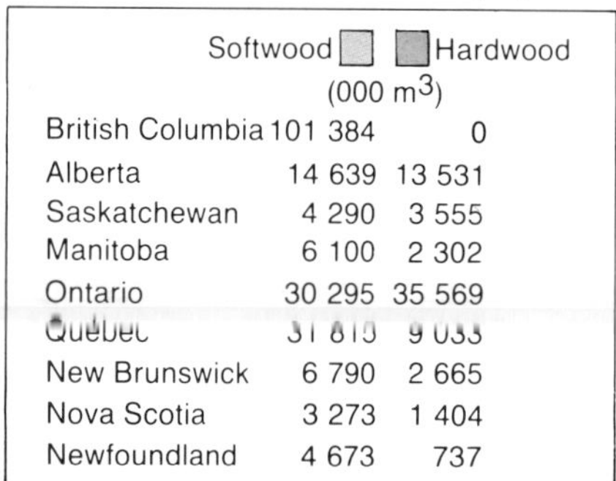

(000 m³)	Softwood	Hardwood
British Columbia	101 384	0
Alberta	14 639	13 531
Saskatchewan	4 290	3 555
Manitoba	6 100	2 302
Ontario	30 295	35 569
Québec	31 815	9 033
New Brunswick	6 790	2 665
Nova Scotia	3 273	1 404
Newfoundland	4 673	737

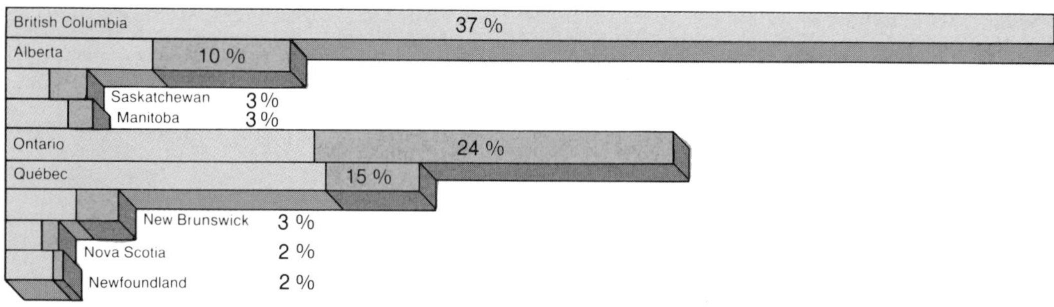
British Columbia 37 %
Alberta 10 %
Saskatchewan 3 %
Manitoba 3 %
Ontario 24 %
Québec 15 %
New Brunswick 3 %
Nova Scotia 2 %
Newfoundland 2 %

Based on data from Bowen, M.G., *Canada's Forest Inventory, 1976*, Canadian Forestry Service, Environment Canada, and direct communications with the provinces, 1982

Fig. 27: Silviculture Data, 5-Year Average (1975/76–1979/80)

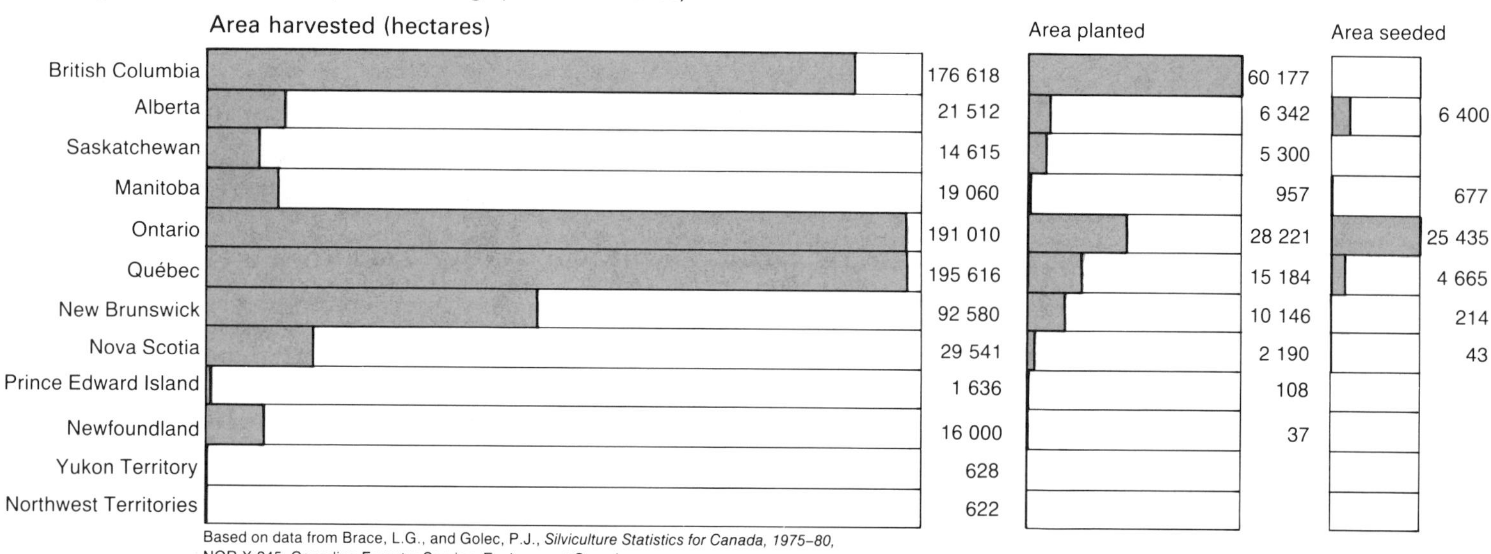
Area harvested (hectares)
Area planted
Area seeded
British Columbia 176 618 60 177
Alberta 21 512 6 342 6 400
Saskatchewan 14 615 5 300
Manitoba 19 060 957 677
Ontario 191 010 28 221 25 435
Québec 195 616 15 184 4 665
New Brunswick 92 580 10 146 214
Nova Scotia 29 541 2 190 43
Prince Edward Island 1 636 108
Newfoundland 16 000 37
Yukon Territory 628
Northwest Territories 622

Based on data from Brace, L.G., and Golec, P.J., *Silviculture Statistics for Canada, 1975–80*, NOR-X-245, Canadian Forestry Service, Environment Canada

Fig. 28: Gross Merchantable Volume of Wood on Productive Land, 1981

Area Class	B.C.	Alta.	Sask.	Man.	Ont.	Qué.	N.B.	N.S.	P.E.I.	Nfld.	Y.T.	N.W.T.	**Canada**
	Volume (000 000 m³)												
By age class													
Regeneration	1	1	—	—	17	160	—	1	—	—	—	—	**180**
Immature	1 569	979	—	371	2 151	1 149	154	12	—	—	209	144	**6 738**
Mature	6 272	326	—	239	467	2 824	353	139	—	69	40	301	**11 030**
Overmature	—	110	—	25	563	—	8	28	—	42	—	1	**777**
Uneven-aged	—	—	—	—	—	—	1	22	—	—	—	—	**23**
Undetermined	—	22	484	—	—	—	—	—	33	352	5	—	**896**
Total	7 842	1 438	484	635	3 198	4 133	516	202	33	463	254	446	**19 644**
By species:													
Softwoods: Spruce, Pine, Fir, Hemlock, Cedar, Douglas-fir	7 438	781	293	439	2 075	3 089	338	137	22	429	214	315	**15 570**
Hardwoods: Aspen/Poplar, Birch, Maple	404	657	191	196	1 123	1 044	178	65	11	34	40	131	**4 074**

Based on data from G.M. Bonnor, *Canada's Forest Inventory 1981*, Forestry Statistics and Systems Branch, Canadian Forestry Service, Environment Canada

The figures on this page show the amount of lumber cut over a thirty-year period, and the amount processed by the forestry industry into wood pulp, some of which is further processed into paper and related products, as Figs. 30 and 31 (page 14A) show.

Fig. 29: Lumber Production by Region, 1950–1982

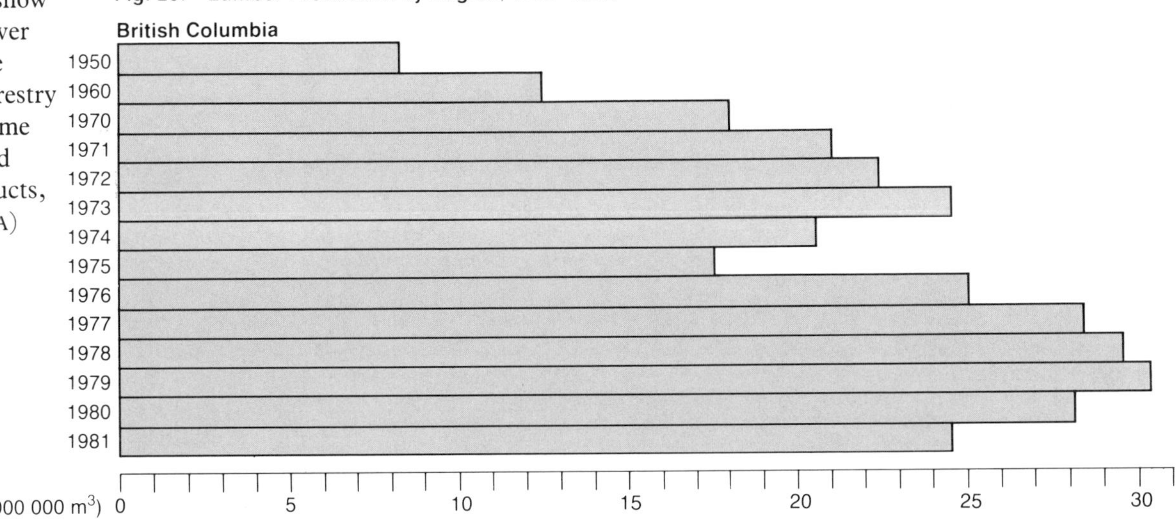
British Columbia
1950
1960
1970
1971
1972
1973
1974
1975
1976
1977
1978
1979
1980
1981
(000 000 m³) 0
5
10
15
20
25
30

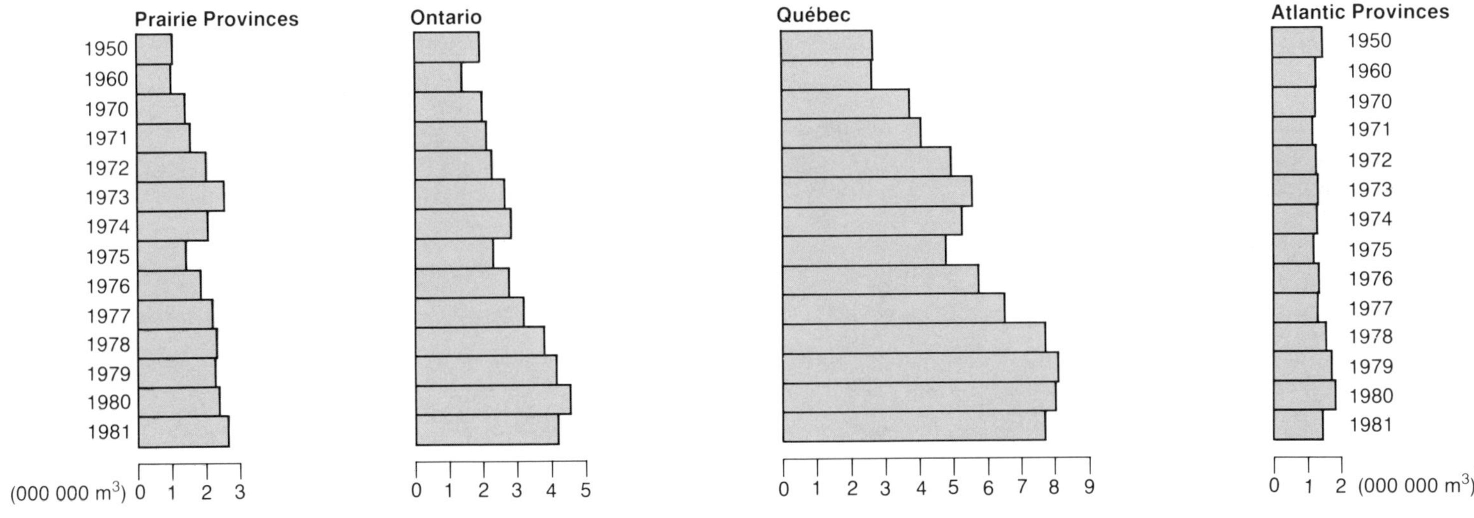
Prairie Provinces
Ontario
Québec
Atlantic Provinces
1950
1960
1970
1971
1972
1973
1974
1975
1976
1977
1978
1979
1980
1981
(000 000 m³) 0 1 2 3
0 1 2 3 4 5
0 1 2 3 4 5 6 7 8 9
0 1 2 (000 000 m³)

Based on data from *Statistics Canada, Cat. No. 25-202*

Fig. 30: Basic Paper and Paperboard Products by Category and Region, 1950–1981: (000 t)

	Québec			Ontario			British Columbia	Other provinces	Canada		
Year	Newsprint	Other paper and paperboard	Total	Newsprint	Other paper and paperboard	Total	Total paper and paperboard	Total paper and paperboard	Newsprint	Other paper and paperboard	Total
1950	2 510	499	3 009	1 125	602	1 727	452	993	4 826	1 355	6 180
1960	2 863	680	3 543	1 459	855	2 313	1 043	1 195	6 068	2 027	8 095
1970	3 766	1 298	5 064	1 686	1 198	2 883	1 675	1 631	7 996	3 256	11 252
1971	3 609	1 348	4 957	1 609	1 220	2 830	1 826	1 545	7 733	3 428	11 161
1972	3 793	1 529	5 322	1 625	1 310	2 935	1 834	1 791	8 079	3 803	11 882
1973	3 671	1 559	5 230	1 769	1 464	3 233	2 029	2 093	8 357	4 226	12 583
1974	4 079	1 657	5 736	1 778	1 626	3 404	1 952	2 128	8 710	4 508	13 219
1975	3 529	1 236	4 765	1 140	959	2 099	1 477	1 725	7 010	3 056	10 066
1976	3 931	1 447	5 378	1 411	1 181	2 592	1 977	1 844	8 063	3 728	11 791
1977	3 726	1 560	5 286	1 610	1 476	3 086	1 952	1 813	8 066	4 070	12 136
1978	4 124	1 830	5 954	1 663	1 654	3 317	2 137	1 967	8 739	4 637	13 376
1979	4 075	1 996	6 071	1 743	1 810	3 553	2 154	1 863	8 642	4 999	13 641
1980	3 800	1 853	5 653	1 734	1 788	3 522	2 147	2 063	8 368	5 017	13 385
1981	4 452	1 880	6 332	1 742	1 820	3 562	1 926	2 136	8 933	5 023	13 956

Based on data from *Statistics Canada, Cat. No. 36-204*

Fig. 31: Basic Paper and Paperboard Production by Kind, 1950–1981

Year	Newsprint	Book and writing	Wrapping	Paperboard	All other	Total
1950	4 825	194	202	796	163	**6 180**
1960	6 068	366	292	1 159	210	**8 095**
1970	7 996	821	438	1 678	319	**11 252**
1971	7 733	844	490	1 698	396	**11 161**
1972	8 079	881	542	1 941	439	**11 882**
1973	8 357	892	610	2 282	442	**12 583**
1974	8 710	1 056	643	2 338	470	**13 218**
1975	7 010	679	431	1 542	403	**10 066**
1976	8 063	842	526	1 908	453	**11 791**
1977	8 066	1 116	556	1 944	454	**12 136**
1978	8 739	1 377	628	2 171	460	**13 376**
1979	8 642	1 606	617	2 290	487	**13 641**
1980	8 368	1 636	544	2 319	517	**13 385**
1981	8 933	1 599	523	2 388	512	**13 956**
			(000 t)			

Based on data from *Statistics Canada Cat. No. 36-204*

Fig. 32 Estimated Value of Shipments of Forest Products, 1982

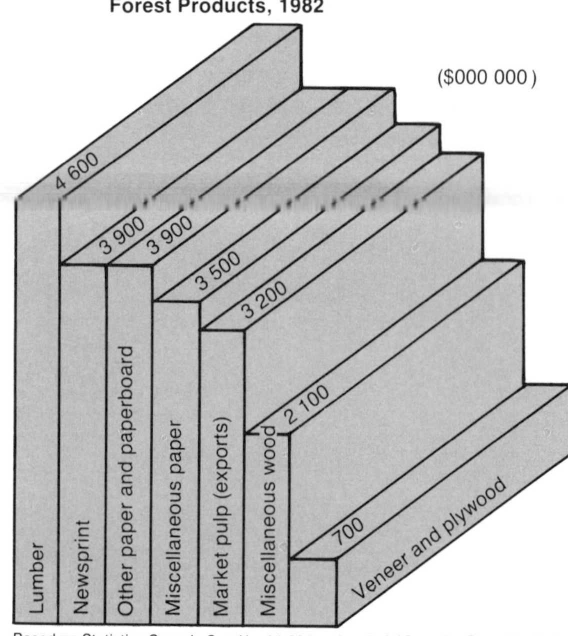
($000 000)
4 600
3 900
3 900
3 500
3 200
2 100
700
Lumber
Newsprint
Other paper and paperboard
Miscellaneous paper
Market pulp (exports)
Miscellaneous wood
Veneer and plywood

Based on *Statistics Canada Cat. No. 31-001* and material from the Canadian Pulp and Paper Association

Canada produces 9% of the total world output of lumber; 14% of all wood pulp; and 4% of paper and related products. Even though Canada is only a small producer, it nevertheless plays an important part in world exports, as Fig. 33 shows. The bulk of these exports (67%) goes to the U.S.

Fig. 33: World Exports of Forest Products, 1981

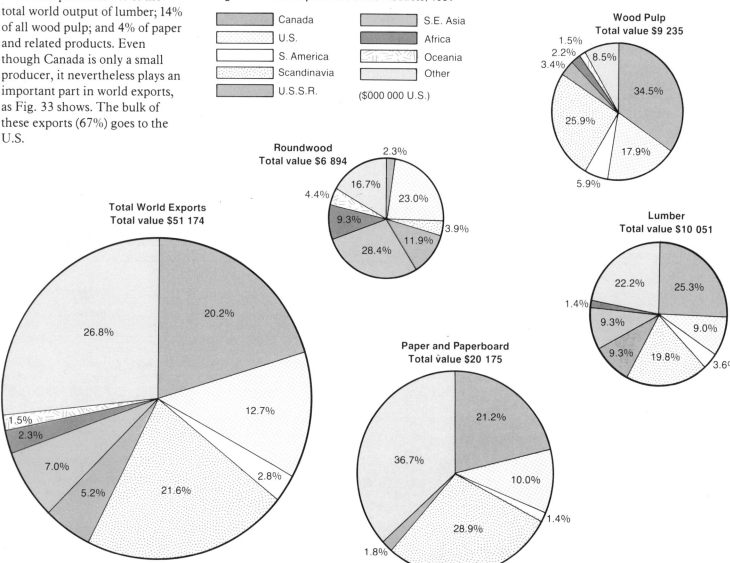

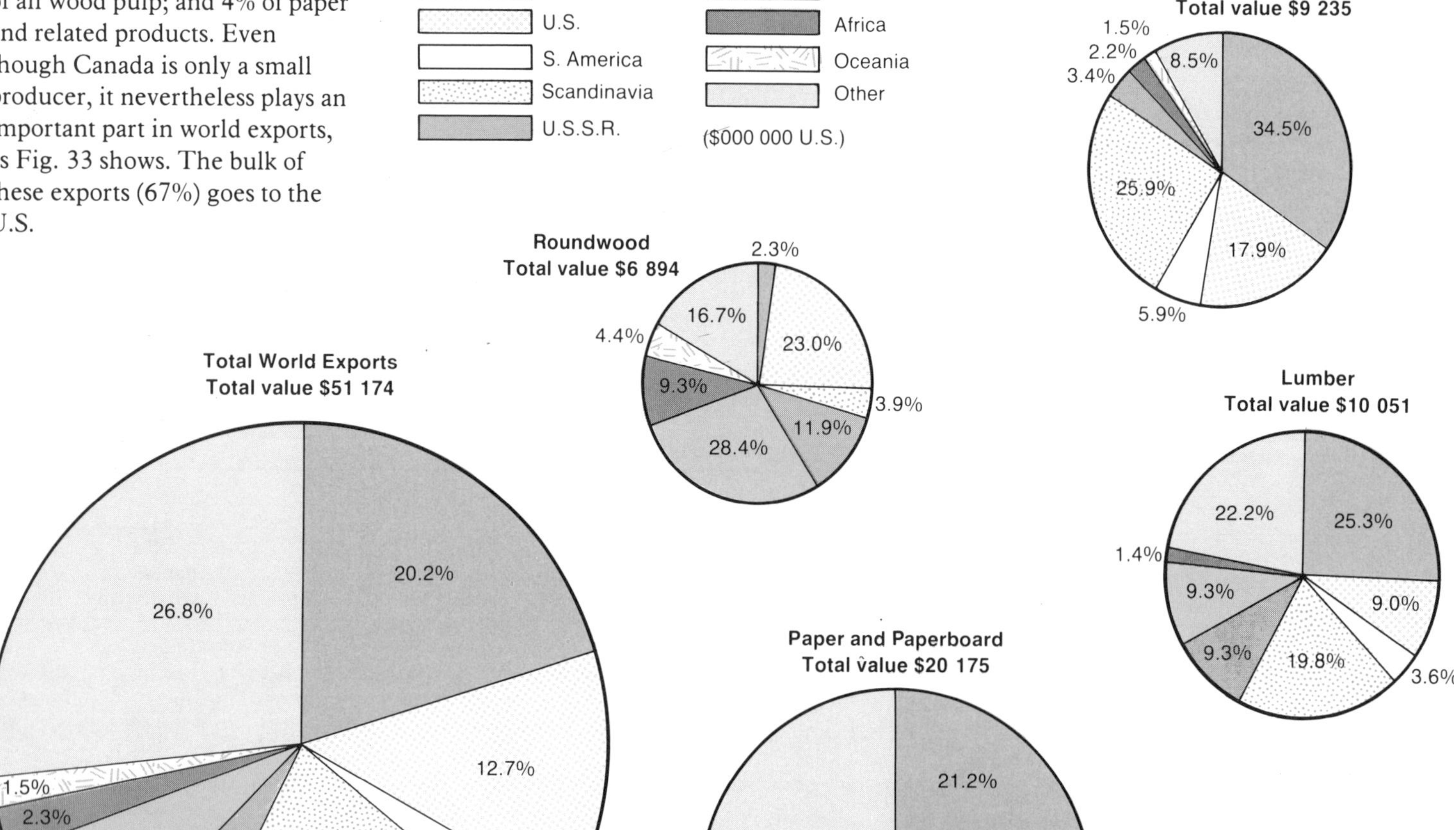
Canada
U.S.
S. America
Scandinavia
U.S.S.R.
S.E. Asia
Africa
Oceania
Other
($000 000 U.S.)
Wood Pulp
Total value $9 235
1.5%
2.2%
3.4%
8.5%
34.5%
25.9%
17.9%
5.9%
Roundwood
Total value $6 894
2.3%
16.7%
23.0%
4.4%
9.3%
3.9%
11.9%
28.4%
Total World Exports
Total value $51 174
20.2%
26.8%
12.7%
1.5%
2.3%
7.0%
2.8%
5.2%
21.6%
Lumber
Total value $10 051
22.2%
25.3%
1.4%
9.3%
9.0%
9.3%
19.8%
3.6%
Paper and Paperboard
Total value $20 175
21.2%
36.7%
10.0%
1.4%
28.9%
1.8%

Based on data from the *1981 Yearbook of Forest Products*, Food and Agriculture Organization of the United Nations

Mining

Canada's geological structure provides a rich variety of mineral resources, and these have been exploited for a long period. Fig. 36 on page 16A shows the value of minerals mined since 1886, and the dramatic increase in value in the last thirty years; Fig. 37 on page 17A gives a breakdown for this latter period by categories of minerals. For this same period Fig. 34 provides yet a further breakdown of six of the leading Canadian minerals.

Fig. 34: Percentage of Total Mineral Value Contributed by Selected Minerals 1951–1981

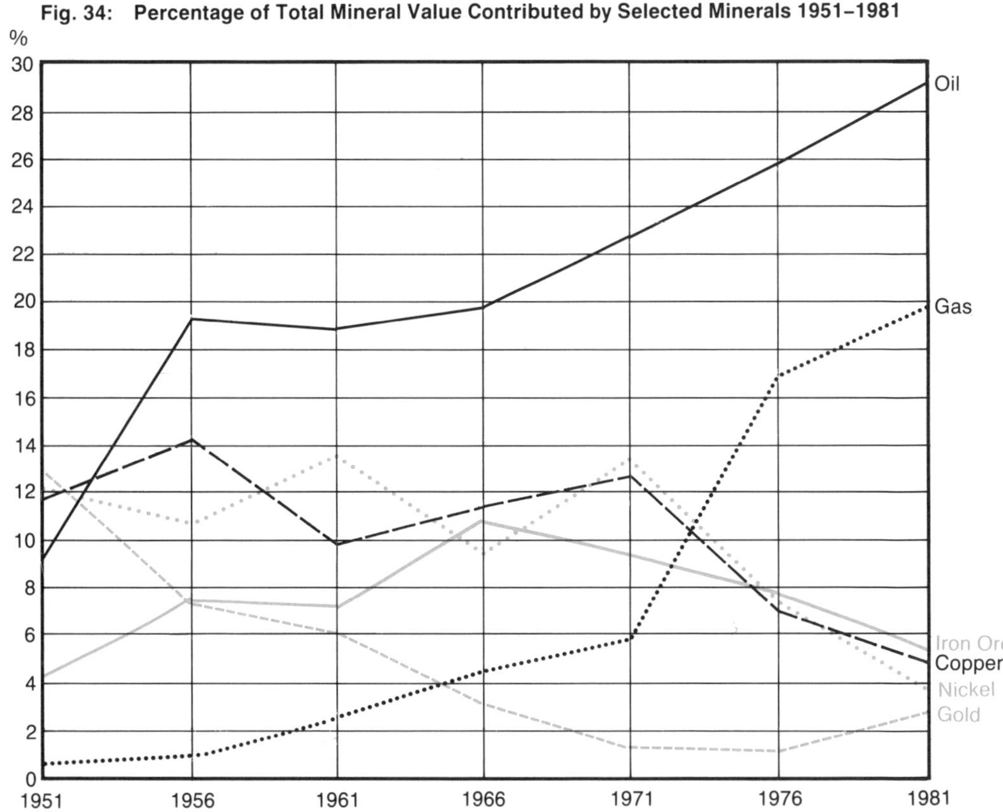
%
30
28
26
24
22
20
18
16
14
12
10
8
6
4
2
0
1951
1956
1961
1966
1971
1976
1981
Oil
Gas
Iron Ore
Copper
Nickel
Gold

Based on data from the *Canada Year Book, 1956, 1975, 1981*

Canada is a leading producer in the world of certain minerals, as demonstrated by Fig. 35; the contribution of those minerals to the value of all minerals mined in Canada (excluding fuels) can be determined by examining the graph on atlas page 15.

The fuel shortages of the 1970s have had a great impact on the quantity and value of oil and gas production in Canada. To include these fuels with statistics of other minerals could downplay the importance and diversity of other minerals. Atlas pages 16–17 contain some statistical data on fuels alone; atlas page 15 provides data on the relative values of other minerals when fuels are excluded. Figs. 34, 36, and 37 show what happens to the total picture when fuels and other minerals are combined.

Fig. 35: Canada's World Role as a Producer of Certain Important Minerals, 1980

	Rank of Six Leading Countries – % of World Total					
	1	2	3	4	5	6
Potash (K_2O equivalent) (000 t)	**Canada 26.4**	U.S.S.R. 24.4	East Germany 12.7	West Germany 9.7	U.S.A. 8.1	France 7.0
Nickel (mine production) (t)	**Canada 25.7**	U.S.S.R. 18.9	New Caledonia 11.4	Australia 9.8	Indonesia 5.4	Philippine Republic 5.1
Zinc (mine production) (000 t)	**Canada 18.4**	U.S.S.R. 17.4	Peru 8.5	Australia 8.1	U.S.A. 6.4	Mexico 4.1
Asbestos (000 t)	U.S.S.R. 44.6	**Canada 27.5**	South Africa 5.6	Zimbabwe 5.2	China 5.2	Italy 3.0
Titanium concentrates (Ilmenite) (000 t)	Australia 27.5	**Canada 18.0**	Norway 17.0	U.S.A. 10.2	U.S.S.R. 8.2	South Africa 7.1
Uranium (U concentrates) (t)	U.S.A. 38.2	**Canada 15.3**	South Africa 14.0	Niger 9.3	Namibia 9.2	France 6.0
Silver (kg)	U.S.S.R. 14.8	Mexico 14.3	**Canada 11.7**	Peru 11.7	U.S.A. 9.3	Australia 7.3
Molybdenum (Mo content) (t)	U.S.A. 63.5	Chile 12.4	**Canada 11.0**	U.S.S.R. 9.7	China 1.9	Peru 0.9
Platinum group metals (mine production) (kg)	U.S.S.R. 47.5	South Africa 45.3	**Canada 6.0**	Columbia 0.2	Australia 0.1	U.S.A. —
Gold (mine production) (kg)	South Africa 53.6	U.S.S.R. 20.5	**Canada 4.0**	China 3.7	Brazil 3.2	U.S.A. 2.4
Copper (mine production) (t)	U.S.A. 15.1	U.S.S.R. 14.7	Chile 13.6	**Canada 9.1**	Zambia 7.6	Zaire 5.9
Aluminum (primary metal) (t)	U.S.A. 29.0	U.S.S.R. 11.1	Japan 6.8	**Canada 6.7**	West Germany 4.6	Norway 4.1
Iron Ore (000 t)	U.S.S.R. 27.9	Brazil 11.1	Australia 10.9	China 8.6	U.S.A. 8.1	**Canada 5.6**

Based on data from *Statistical Summary of the Mineral Industry in Canada, 1981*, Department of Energy, Mines and Resources

Fig. 36: Value of Mineral Production, 1886–1981

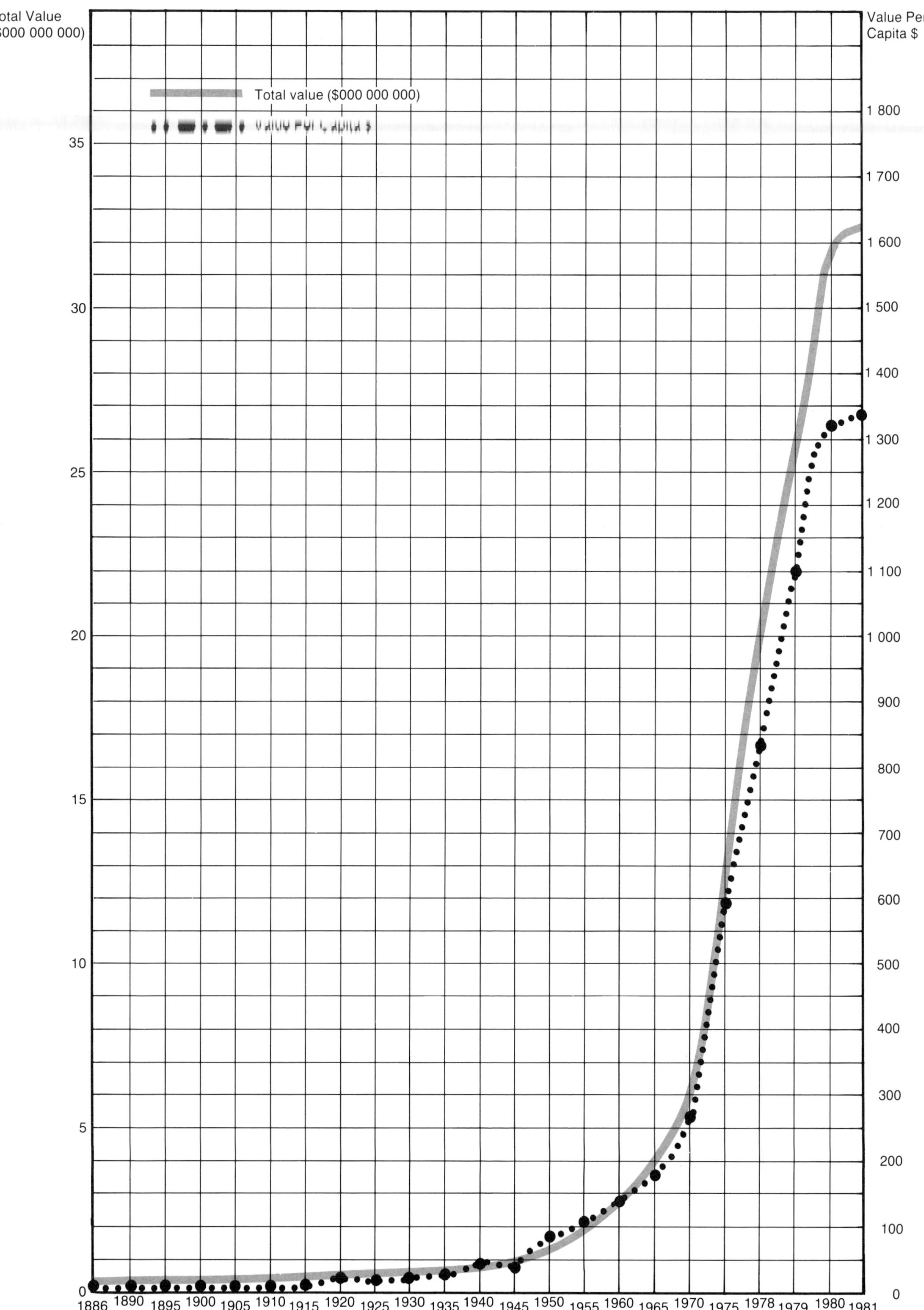
Total Value
($000 000 000)
Value Per
Capita $
Total value ($000 000 000)
35
30
25
20
15
10
5
0
1 800
1 700
1 600
1 500
1 400
1 300
1 200
1 100
1 000
900
800
700
600
500
400
300
200
100
0
1886
1890
1895
1900
1905
1910
1915
1920
1925
1930
1935
1940
1945
1950
1955
1960
1965
1970
1975
1978
1979
1980
1981

Based on data from Mineral Policy Sector, Energy, Mines and Resources Canada

Fig. 37: Value of Mineral Production; Per Capita Value of Mineral Production, 1952–81

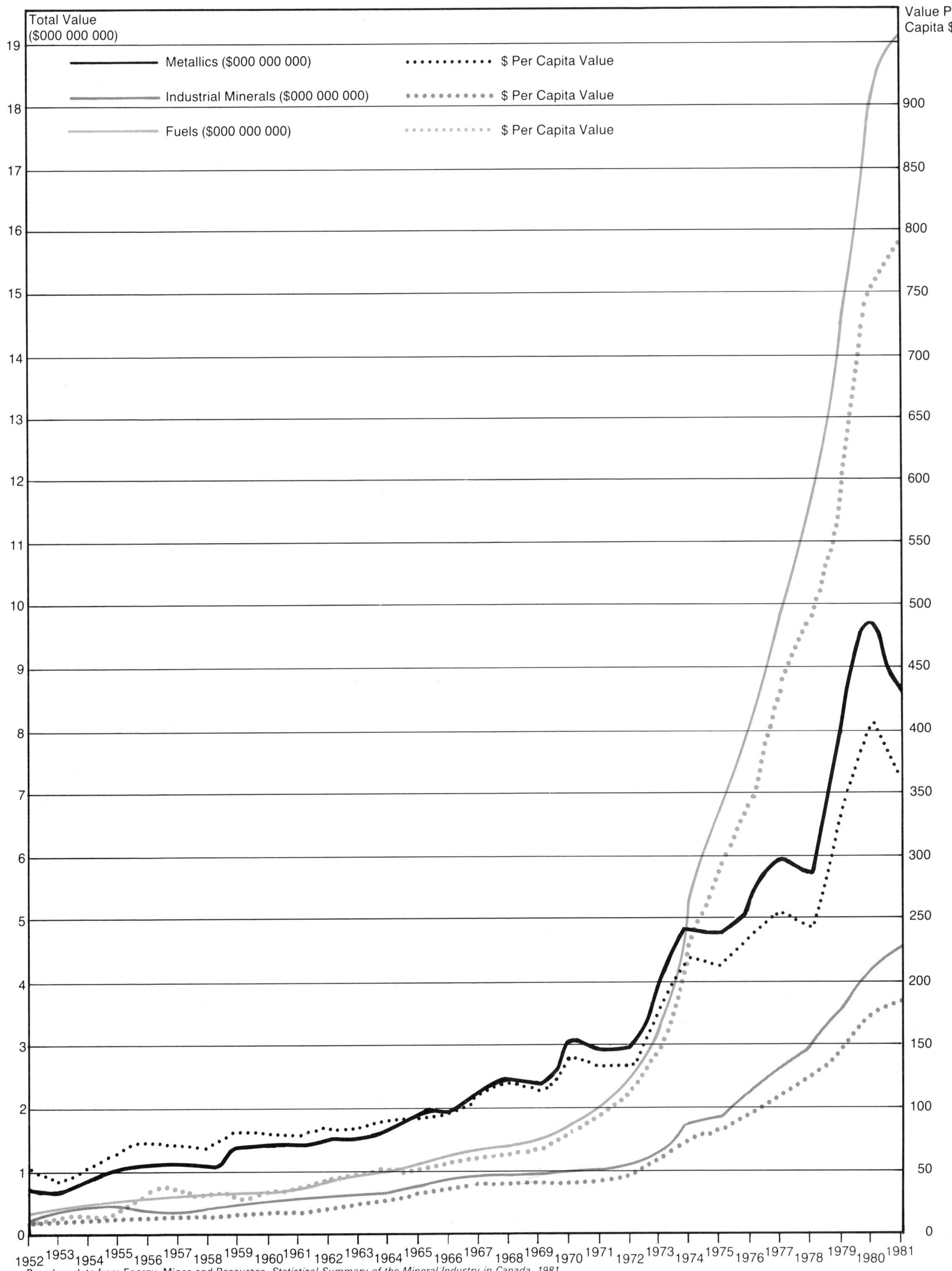
Total Value
($000 000 000)
Value Per
Capita $
Metallics ($000 000 000)
$ Per Capita Value
Industrial Minerals ($000 000 000)
$ Per Capita Value
Fuels ($000 000 000)
$ Per Capita Value
0
1
2
3
4
5
6
7
8
9
10
11
12
13
14
15
16
17
18
19
0
50
100
150
200
250
300
350
400
450
500
550
600
650
700
750
800
850
900
1952
1953
1954
1955
1956
1957
1958
1959
1960
1961
1962
1963
1964
1965
1966
1967
1968
1969
1970
1971
1972
1973
1974
1975
1976
1977
1978
1979
1980
1981

Based on data from Energy, Mines and Resources, *Statistical Summary of the Mineral Industry in Canada, 1981*

Manufacturing

The emphasis on Canada's natural resources should not obscure the fact that Canada is a highly developed manufacturing country with a wide diversity of industries, only some of which are resource-based. Fig. 38 shows the development of the manufacturing sector from 1920. Although inflation magnifies the apparent increase in dollar value over a period of time, the graph gives a good indication of the increasing importance of manufacturing industries to the Canadian economy.

The variety of kinds of manufacturing in a number of centres across the country is reflected in the following manufacturing profiles of selected cities; while the large centres in each province reflect general manufacturing to some degree, others stand out for their dependence on one industry.

Fig. 38: Manufacturing Industries, Selected Years, 1920–1981

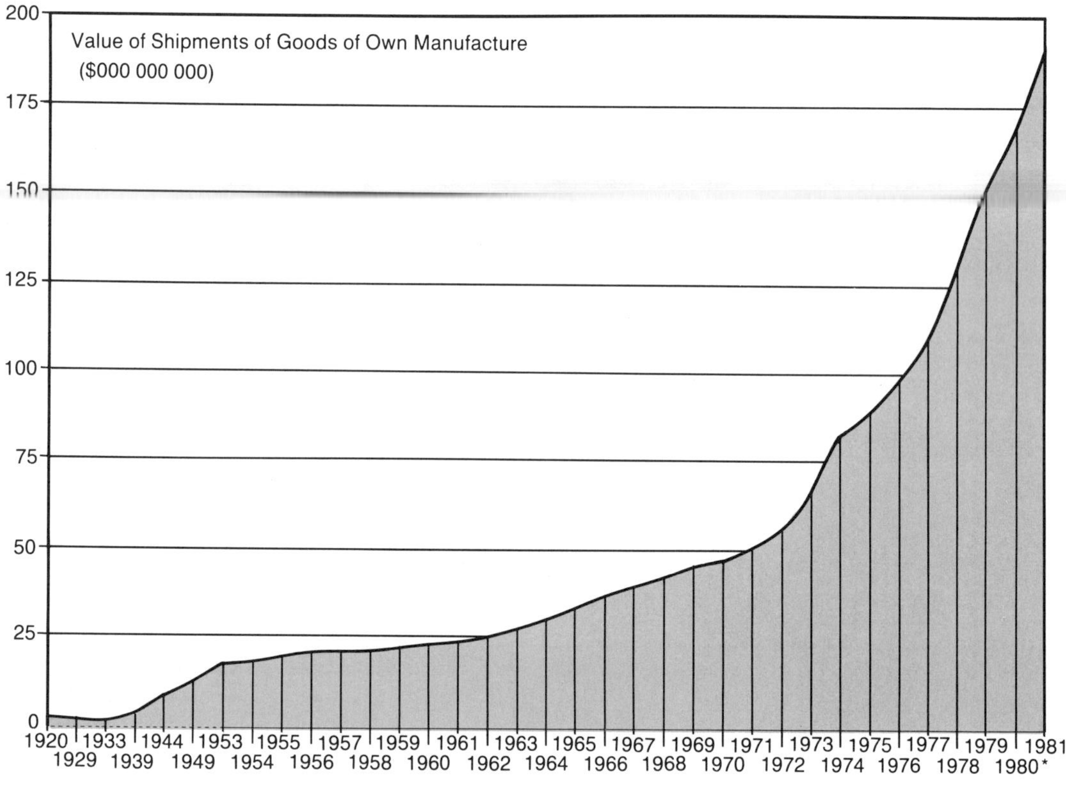
Value of Shipments of Goods of Own Manufacture
($000 000 000)
200
175
150
125
100
75
50
25
0
1920 1933 1944 1953 1955 1957 1959 1961 1963 1965 1967 1969 1971 1973 1975 1977 1979 1981
1929 1939 1949 1954 1956 1958 1960 1962 1964 1966 1968 1970 1972 1974 1976 1978 1980*

*Preliminary figures

Note: Before 1952, data represent gross value of production. Based on data from Statistics Canada, *Canada Handbook, 1984*

Fig. 39: Distribution of Industrial Activity by Industry Grouping within Selected Census Metropolitan Areas, 1980

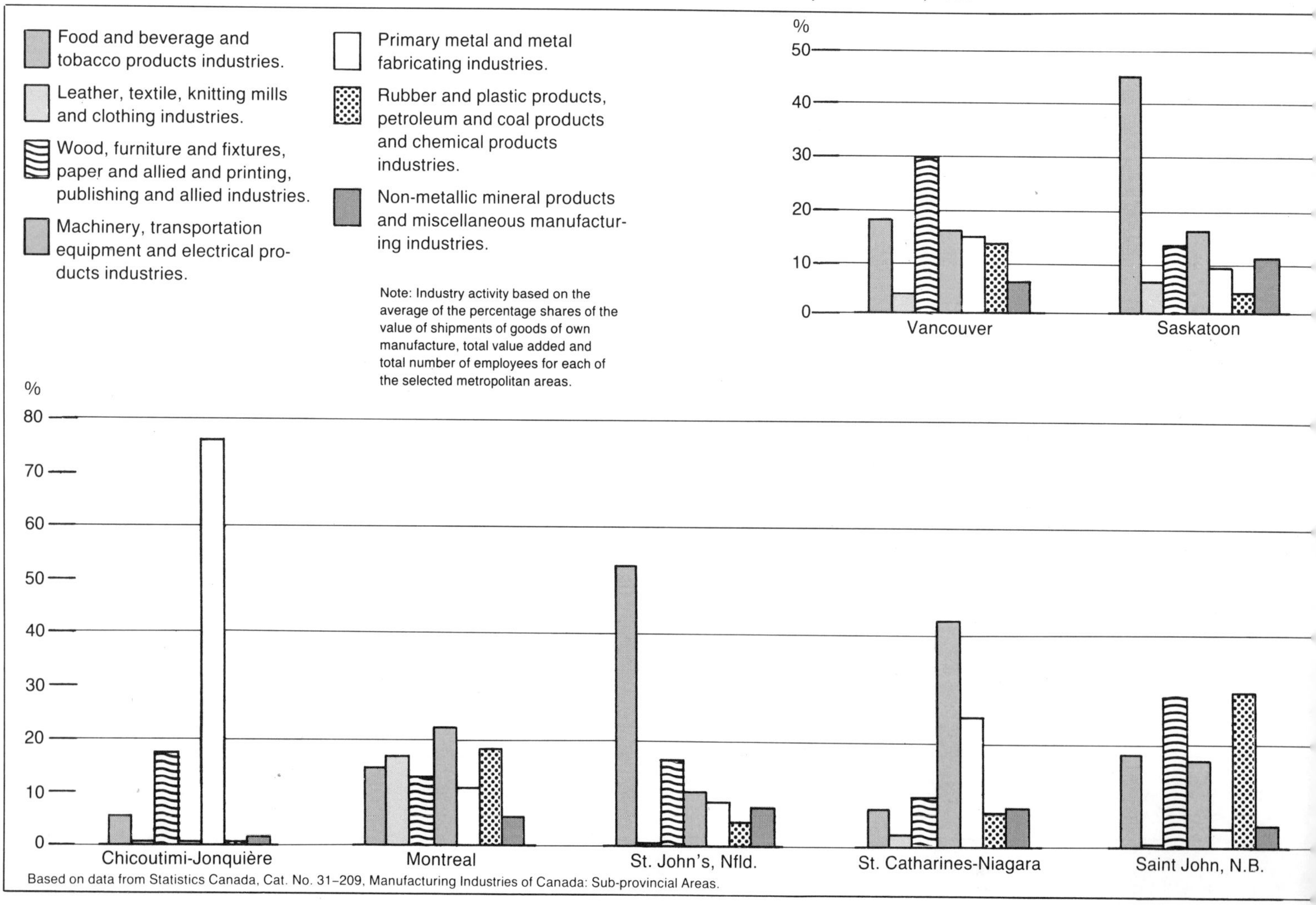

- Food and beverage and tobacco products industries.
- Leather, textile, knitting mills and clothing industries.
- Wood, furniture and fixtures, paper and allied and printing, publishing and allied industries.
- Machinery, transportation equipment and electrical products industries.
- Primary metal and metal fabricating industries.
- Rubber and plastic products, petroleum and coal products and chemical products industries.
- Non-metallic mineral products and miscellaneous manufacturing industries.

Note: Industry activity based on the average of the percentage shares of the value of shipments of goods of own manufacture, total value added and total number of employees for each of the selected metropolitan areas.

%
50
40
30
20
10
0
Vancouver
Saskatoon

%
80
70
60
50
40
30
20
10
0
Chicoutimi-Jonquière
Montreal
St. John's, Nfld.
St. Catharines-Niagara
Saint John, N.B.

Based on data from Statistics Canada, Cat. No. 31–209, Manufacturing Industries of Canada: Sub-provincial Areas.

Fig. 41 sets out the relative value of the major primary industries compared to manufacturing. Wood and paper industries have been shown separately from other manufacturing, to avoid distortion when comparisons with other forestry statistics are made.

Exports are another yardstick for measuring the importance of the various factors in the economy, and Fig. 40 shows the increasing role played by manufacturing in Canada's export trade.

Fig. 40: Canadian Exports by Commodity Group, 1950–1982

Year	Forest Products	Farm & Fish Products	Metals & Minerals	Chemicals & Fertilizers	Other Manufactures	Re-exports	Total
		($000 000)					
1950	1 102	935	605	93	368	39	**3 143**
1960	1 587	1 018	1 814	238	601	134	**5 390**
1970	2 929	1 864	4 815	533	6 260	419	**16 820**
1971	3 084	2 225	4 614	555	6 917	423	**17 818**
1972	3 601	2 331	4 928	588	8 215	477	**20 141**
1973	4 507	3 338	6 621	718	9 673	564	**25 421**
1974	5 586	4 110	10 050	997	10 935	766	**32 443**
1975	5 094	4 248	10 004	1 053	12 150	779	**33 328**
1976	6 534	4 429	10 860	1 415	14 413	825	**38 476**
1977	7 878	4 837	11 737	1 776	17 459	870	**44 554**
1978	9 566	5 656	12 808	2 375	21 854	923	**53 183**
1979	11 787	7 025	16 713	3 323	25 469	1 324	**65 641**
1980	12 698	8 682	21 864	4 077	27 126	1 713	**76 158**
1981	12 855	9 830	21 831	4 626	32 196	2 475	**83 811**
1982	11 961	10 482	20 490	4 102	34 794	2 706	**84 534**

Based on data from the *Bank of Canada Review*, June 1983

Fig. 41: Value of Production, 1981

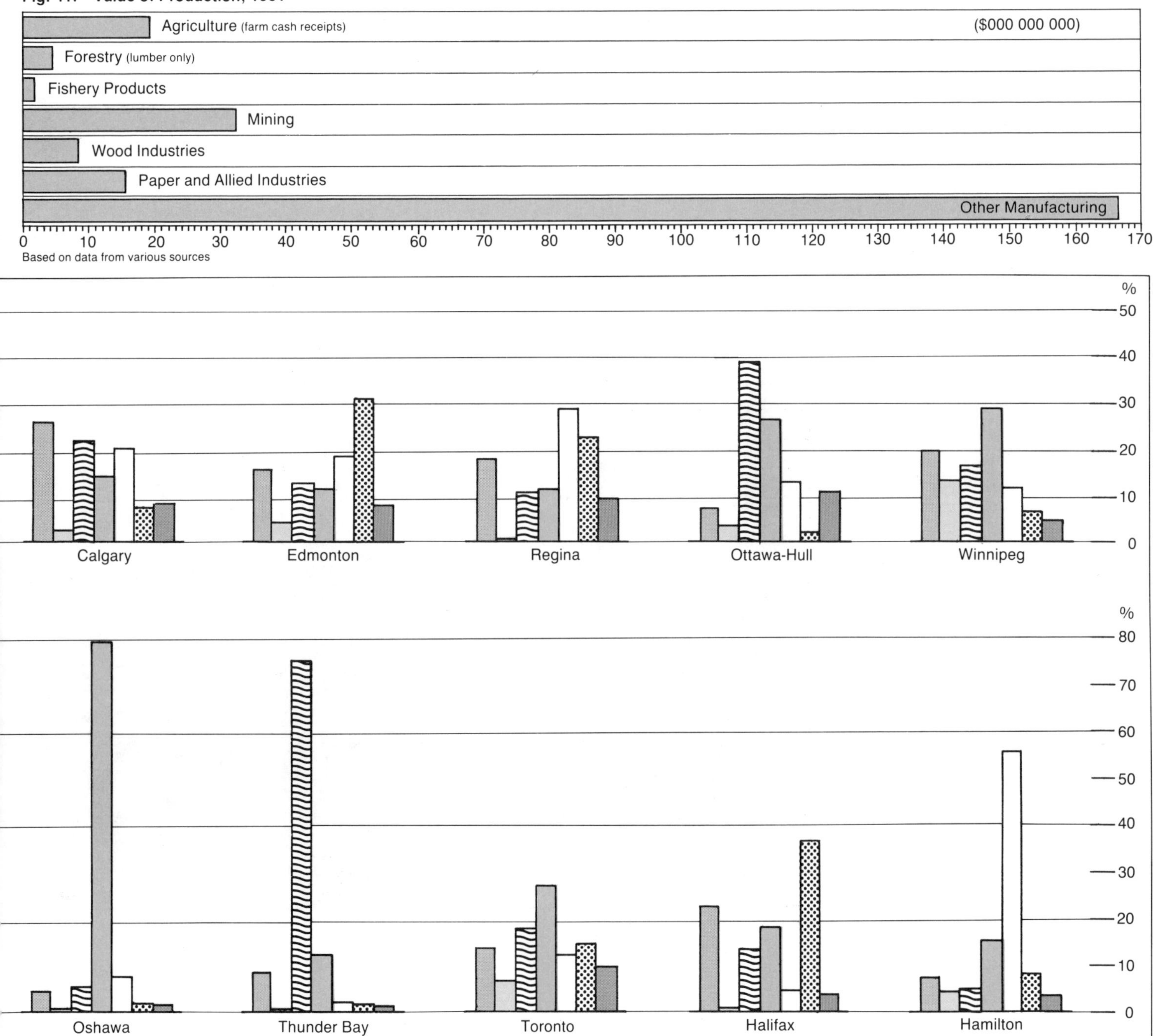

Agriculture (farm cash receipts)
($000 000 000)
Forestry (lumber only)
Fishery Products
Mining
Wood Industries
Paper and Allied Industries
Other Manufacturing
0 10 20 30 40 50 60 70 80 90 100 110 120 130 140 150 160 170
%
50
40
30
20
10
0
Calgary
Edmonton
Regina
Ottawa-Hull
Winnipeg
%
80
70
60
50
40
30
20
10
0
Oshawa
Thunder Bay
Toronto
Halifax
Hamilton

Based on data from various sources

The Labour Force

The labour force is defined as that part of the population, 15 years of age and over, either working or actively seeking employment. Clearly the age levels within the population (see the age/sex pyramids on page 5A) will have an effect on the size of the labour force.

The participation rate simply defines the percent of the population of working age in the labour force. In a developed country like Canada, the participation rate will be affected by, for example, the number of students obtaining further education beyond the age of 15 years; people staying home to raise families; etc.

The number of unemployed and the unemployment rate should be assessed in light of the increase in the total labour force; it must be noted that the labour force increases as the total population of working age increases, but the labour force will increase even faster if the participation rate goes up, and this in turn will affect the unemployment rate unless jobs can be created to match this increase.

Men have always outnumbered women in the workforce, no matter what the balance of the sexes is in the total population (see the age/sex pyramids on page 5A). New social trends within the last few decades indicate that soon this may no longer be true: while women formed less than one-third of the labour force twenty years ago, they now represent over 40%, as Fig. 43 shows. This table also shows that a major reason for the steady increase in the female labour force is the increase in the female participation rate.

As might be expected in a country where economic activity varies widely from region to region, unemployment is not uniform from province to province.

Fig. 42: The Labour Force

	Population 15 years and over	Labour Force 15 years and over	Participation Rate	Unemployed 15 years and over	Unemployment Rate
	000	000		000	
1966	13 083	7 493	57.3	251	3.4
1967	13 444	7 747	[illegible]	[illegible]	[illegible]
1968	13 805	7 951	57.6	358	4.5
1969	14 162	8 194	57.9	362	4.4
1970	14 528	8 395	57.8	476	5.7
1971	14 872	8 639	58.1	535	6.2
1972	15 186	8 897	58.6	553	6.2
1973	15 526	9 276	59.7	515	5.5
1974	15 924	9 639	60.5	514	5.3
1975	16 323	9 974	61.1	690	6.9
1976	16 701	10 203	61.1	726	7.1
1977	17 051	10 500	61.6	849	8.1
1978	17 377	10 895	62.7	908	8.3
1979	17 702	11 231	63.4	836	7.4
1980	18 053	11 573	64.1	865	7.5
1981	18 375	11 904	64.8	898	7.5
1982	18 664	11 958	64.1	1 314	11.0
1983	18 917	12 183	64.4	1 448	11.9

Based on data from *Statistics Canada, Cat. No. 71-201*

Fig. 43: Trends in the Male/Female Balance in the Workforce, 1966–1983

Labour Force

Male | Female

Year	Participation Rate Male %	Participation Rate Female %	Unemployment Rate Male %	Unemployment Rate Female %
1966	79.8	35.4	3.3	3.4
1967	79.3	36.5	3.9	3.7
1968	78.6	37.1	4.6	4.4
1969	78.3	38.0	4.3	4.7
1970	77.8	38.3	5.6	5.8
1971	77.3	39.4	6.0	6.6
1972	77.5	40.2	5.8	7.0
1973	78.2	41.9	4.9	6.7
1974	78.7	43.0	4.8	6.4
1975	78.4	44.4	6.2	8.1
1976	77.6	45.2	6.3	8.4
1977	77.7	46.0	7.3	9.4
1978	78.1	47.9	7.5	9.6
1979	78.5	49.0	6.6	8.8
1980	78.4	50.4	6.9	8.4
1981	78.4	51.7	7.0	8.3
1982	77.0	51.7	11.1	10.9
1983	76.7	52.6	12.1	11.6

Based on data from *Statistics Canada, Cat. No. 71-201*

Fig. 44 might well be considered (in light of the interprovincial migration graph on page 4a) as one of the factors in the mobility of the Canadian population.

Fig. 44: Unemployment Rates by Province, 1972–1983

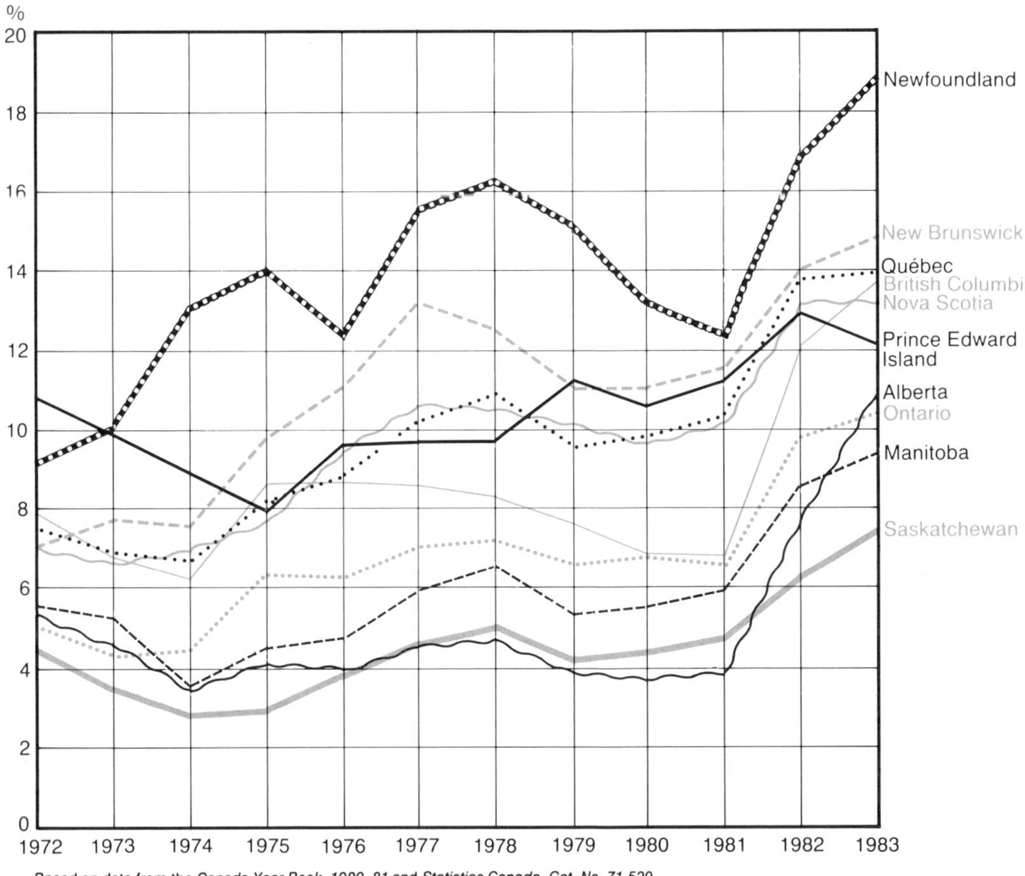
%
20
18
16
14
12
10
8
6
4
2
0
1972
1973
1974
1975
1976
1977
1978
1979
1980
1981
1982
1983
Newfoundland
New Brunswick
Québec
British Columbia
Nova Scotia
Prince Edward Island
Alberta
Ontario
Manitoba
Saskatchewan

Based on data from the *Canada Year Book, 1980–81* and *Statistics Canada, Cat. No. 71-529*

The Canadian Economy: An Overview

The gross national product—the total of all goods and services produced in Canada—is given in Fig. 45 in current dollars and 1971 dollars, together with the price index. The same treatment is accorded expenditures within Canada. This table permits comparisons of the growth of the Canadian economy without having to take the factor of inflation into account. These tables should be compared with earlier tables on the dollar value of production over a period of time.

As we have already seen, Canada is an important trading nation. Fig. 40 gave the breakdown of exports by commodities, and Fig. 46 gives a summary picture of imports on the same basis.

The U.S. is our major trading partner: in 1981, 66% of our exports went to the U.S., and we obtained 69% of our imports from the U.S.

Fig. 46: Imports to Canada by Commodities, 1981

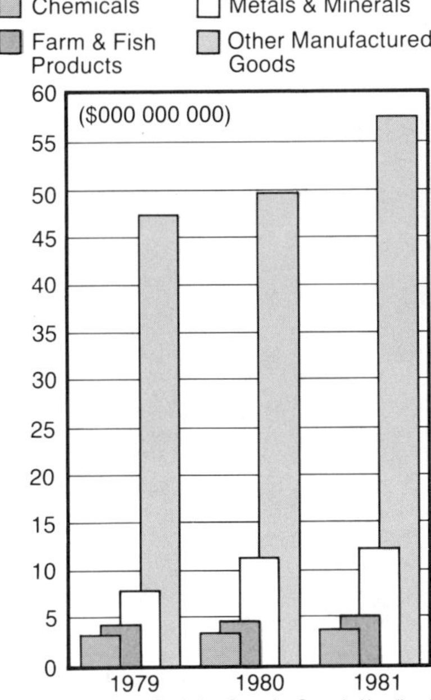
Chemicals
Metals & Minerals
Farm & Fish Products
Other Manufactured Goods
($000 000 000)
60
55
50
45
40
35
30
25
20
15
10
5
0
1979
1980
1981

Based on data from Statistics Canada, *Canada Handbook, 1982–83*

Fig. 45: Selected Economic Indicators: An Analytical Summary

Years	Gross National Product: Current Dollars	Gross National Product: 1971 Dollars	Implicit Price Indexes: Personal Expenditure on Consumer Goods and Services	Personal Expenditure on Consumer Goods and Services: Current Dollars	Personal Expenditure on Consumer Goods and Services: 1971 Dollars
			1971 = 100	$000 000	
1961	39 646	54 741	76.8	25 930	33 761
1962	42 927	58 475	77.8	27 452	35 272
1963	45 978	61 487	79.0	29 225	36 992
1964	50 280	65 610	80.0	31 389	39 218
1965	55 364	69 981	81.6	33 947	41 606
1966	61 828	74 844	84.3	36 890	43 778
1967	66 409	77 344	87.2	39 972	45 863
1968	72 586	81 864	90.8	43 704	48 138
1969	79 815	86 225	94.3	47 492	50 353
1970	85 685	88 390	97.7	50 327	51 526
1971	94 450	94 450	100.0	55 616	55 616
1972	105 234	100 248	104.0	62 208	59 841
1973	123 560	107 812	111.6	71 278	63 879
1974	147 528	111 678	124.2	83 388	67 160
1975	165 343	113 005	137.3	96 995	70 645
1976	191 857	119 612	148.5	111 657	75 180
1977	210 189	121 988	160.5	123 565	77 009
1978	232 211	126 347	172.7	136 532	79 038
1979	264 279	130 362	188.7	152 088	80 607
1980	296.555	131.675	209.1	170.236	81.431
1981	339 055	136 114	233.2	193 477	82 961
1982	356 600	130 069	258.4	209 801	81 206

Based on data from Statistics Canada, *Canadian Statistical Review*, March 1984

Electricity

Industry accounted for approximately 50% of all electricity used in Canada (see Fig. 47).

Fig. 47: Electricity Demand by Type of Use, 1978–1981

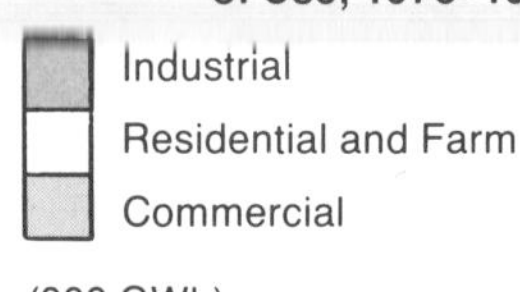
Industrial
Residential and Farm
Commercial

(000 GWh)

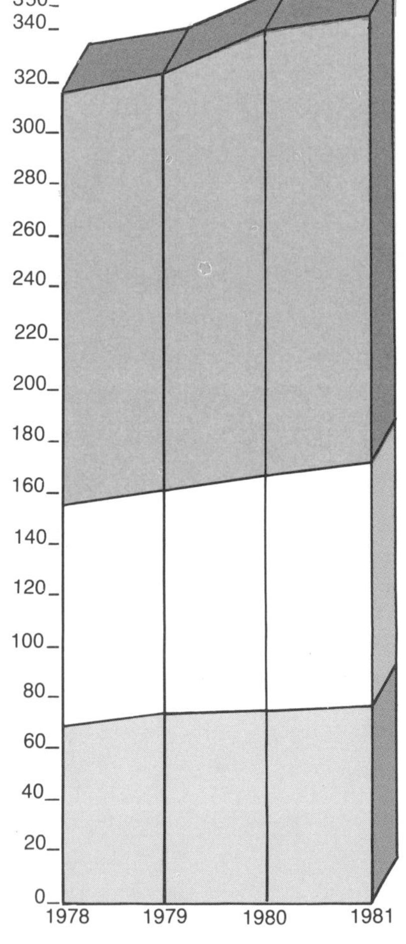
350
340
320
300
280
260
240
220
200
180
160
140
120
100
80
60
40
20
0
1978
1979
1980
1981

Based on data from *Electric Power in Canada 1982*, Energy, Mines and Resources

Fig. 48 shows that the decrease in electricity demand from 1980 to 1981 continued into 1982; however, in the period 1981–82 the real Gross National Product declined by 4.8%, a larger decrease than the decrease in electricity demand, which indicates that electricity use per dollar of GNP continued to increase.

Fig. 49 shows capacity and production by type of generation, and by province.

Fig. 48: Electricity: Statistical Summary, 1981–1982

	1982	1981	Percentage Change
Total Demand for Electricity (GWh)	344 083	346 333	–0.65
Total Generation (GWh)	375 449	380 209	–1.25
hydro	255 136	263 472	–3.16
nuclear	[illegible]	[illegible]	[illegible]
conventional thermal	83 698	78 938	6.28
Total Net Exports (GWh)	31 366	33 876	–7.41
total imports	2 848	1 496	90.37
total exports	34 214	35 372	–3.27
Total Capacity at December 31, (MW)*	84 777	83 308	1.76
hydro	49 975	49 367	1.23
nuclear	6 280	5 600	12.14
conventional thermal	28 522	28 341	0.64
Total Net Additions to Capacity During Year (MW)	1 469	2 256	–34.88
hydro	608	1 679	–63.79
nuclear	680	—	**
conventional thermal	181	577	–68.63

* Does not reflect confidential data, which is not available by province. Total confidential data for 1981: 438 MW.

**Indeterminate

Based on data from *Electric Power in Canada, 1982*, Energy, Mines and Resources

Fig. 49: Installed Capacity and Electric Energy Production by Principal Fuel Type, 1982

Percentage of Provincial Total
Newfoundland
Prince Edward Island
Nova Scotia
New Brunswick
Québec
Ontario
Manitoba
Saskatchewan
Alberta
British Columbia
Yukon
Northwest Territories
100 80 60 40 20 0
Hydro
0 20 40 60 80 100
Conventional Thermal & Nuclear
Installed Capacity
Generation
Hydro
Conventional Thermal
Nuclear

Based on data from *Electric Power in Canada 1982*, Energy, Mines and Resources

Electricity has become increasingly important as an energy source within Canada, and has continued to grow as an important export. In 1982 electricity net exports accounted for 11% of our trade balance with the United States.

Since per capita economic growth and population growth over the next twenty years is forecast to be significantly lower than that of the previous twenty-year period, electricity growth may also be lower.

Fig. 51 shows growth in the period 1960–1982 of real GNP (i.e., GNP net of inflation), population, primary energy demand (i.e., the total energy available from the energy sources in their original state) and electric energy demand, as well as the forecasts for each of these items for the period 1982–2000.

Fig. 52 predicts an enlarging role for electric energy in Canada; this growth will increasingly rely on nuclear and hydro resources.

GWh: gigawatt hour
GW: gigawatt (1 million kilowatts)
MW: megawatt (1 million watts)

Fig. 50: Electrical Energy

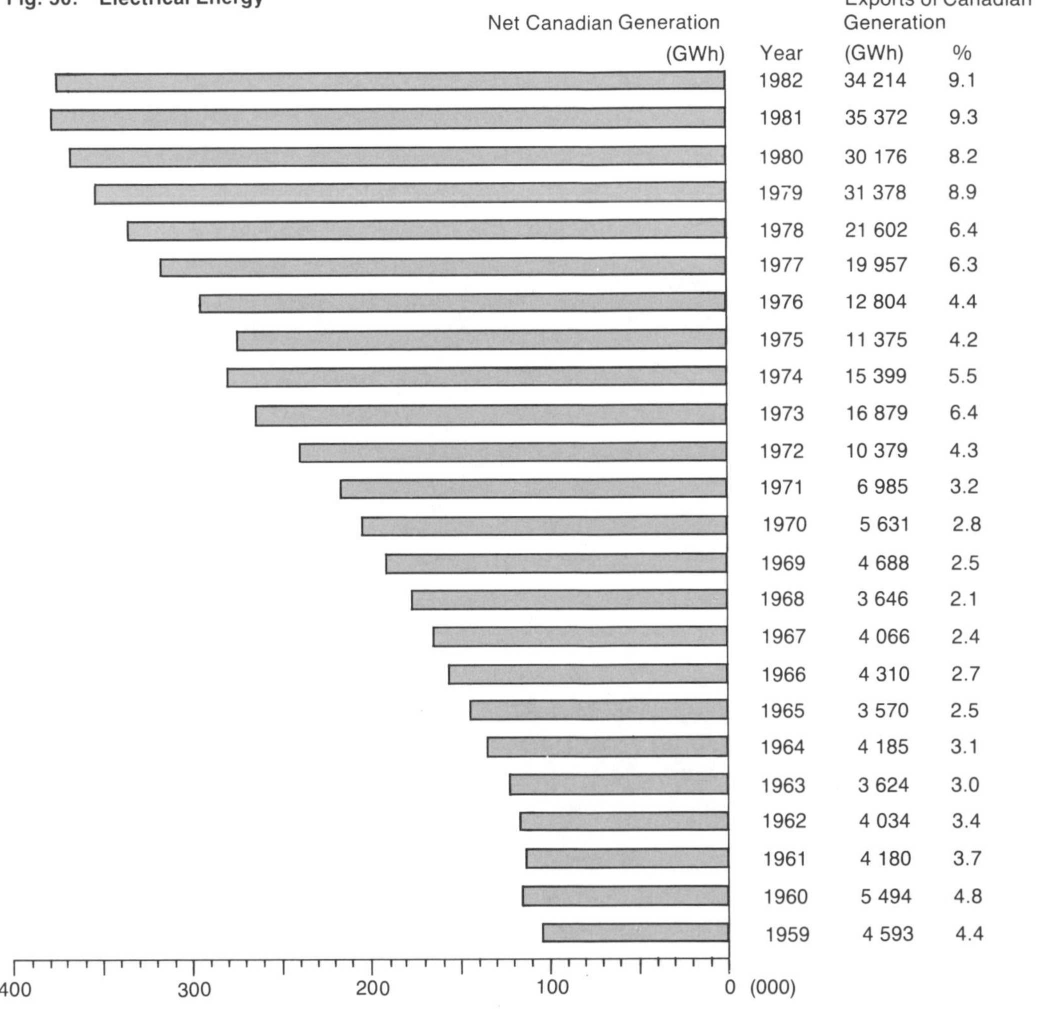
Net Canadian Generation
(GWh)
Year
Exports of Canadian Generation
(GWh) %
1982 34 214 9.1
1981 35 372 9.3
1980 30 176 8.2
1979 31 378 8.9
1978 21 602 6.4
1977 19 957 6.3
1976 12 804 4.4
1975 11 375 4.2
1974 15 399 5.5
1973 16 879 6.4
1972 10 379 4.3
1971 6 985 3.2
1970 5 631 2.8
1969 4 688 2.5
1968 3 646 2.1
1967 4 066 2.4
1966 4 310 2.7
1965 3 570 2.5
1964 4 185 3.1
1963 3 624 3.0
1962 4 034 3.4
1961 4 180 3.7
1960 5 494 4.8
1959 4 593 4.4
400
300
200
100
0 (000)

Based on data from *Electric Power in Canada 1982*, Energy, Mines and Resources

Fig. 51: Growth in Energy Demand, 1960–1982 and Forecasts to 2000

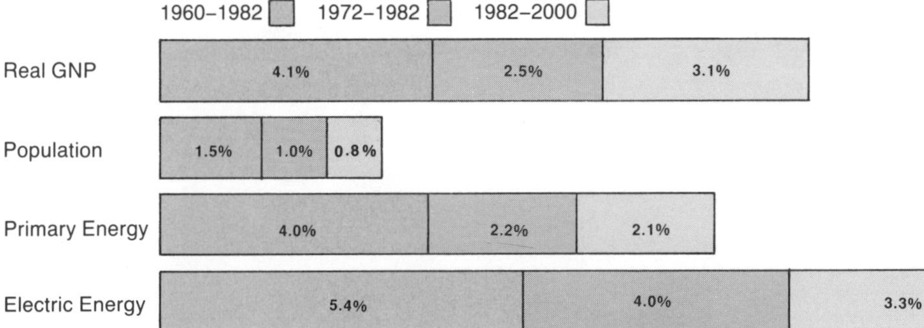
1960–1982
1972–1982
1982–2000
Real GNP
4.1%
2.5%
3.1%
Population
1.5%
1.0%
0.8%
Primary Energy
4.0%
2.2%
2.1%
Electric Energy
5.4%
4.0%
3.3%

Based on data from *Electric Power in Canada 1982*, Energy, Mines and Resources

Fig. 52: Estimates and Forecasts of Energy Generating Capacity by Type, 1983–2000

	Conventional Thermal (GW)							(%) Percentage of Total Capacity					
Year	Oil	Gas	Coal	Total	Nuclear	Hydro	**Total**	Oil	Gas	Coal	Total Conventional Thermal	Nuclear	Hydro
1983	7.8	4.2	16.8	28.8	7.0	51.9	**87.7**	9	5	19	33	8	59
1984	7.8	4.2	17.9	29.9	8.3	54.9	**93.1**	8	5	19	32	9	59
1985	7.8	4.2	18.2	30.2	10.1	56.7	**97.0**	8	4	19	31	11	58
1990	6.9	3.7	20.8	31.4	13.4	59.7	**104.5**	6	4	20	30	13	57
1995	6.8	3.8	21.7	32.3	15.2	67.9	**115.4**	6	3	19	28	13	59
2000	6.7	3.5	24.6	34.8	15.2	77.5	**127.5**	5	3	19	27	12	61

Based on data from *Electric Power in Canada 1982*, Energy, Mines and Resources

Fig. 53: Countries of the World: Selected Statistics

Countries	Area 1980 ($10^3 km^2$)	Population 1981 (millions)	Population Density 1981 (per km^2)	Arable and Permanent Pasture 1980 (% of total area)	Urban Population (%)	Birth Rate (per 1000)	Death Rate (per 1000)	Per Capita GNP 1982 ($U.S.)
Afghanistan	648	16.3	25	90	16.1	48	23	n.a.
Albania	29	2.8	97	46	33	28	7	n.a.
Algeria	2 382	19.6	8	18	52	44	11	2 350
Andorra	0.5	0.03	67	58	n.a.	17	5	n.a.
Angola	1 247	7.3	6	26	21	47	22	n.a.
Antigua	0.4	0.1	25	v.s.	34	16	6	n.a.
Antilles (Neth.)	1.0	0.3	300	8	90	27	6	5 150
Argentina	2 767	27.4	10	64	82	24	9	2 520
Australia	7 687	14.7	2	65	86	16	8	11 140
Austria	84	7.6	90	44	54.9	12	12	9 880
Bahamas, The	14	0.2	14	1	65	25	5	3 830
Bahrain	1.0	0.3	300	8	81	32	6	9 280
Bangladesh	144	90.7	630	68	10.6	49	18	140
Barbados	0.4	0.3	618	86	41	17	8	2 900
Belgium	31	9.9	323	n.a.	94.6	12	11	10 760
Belize	23	0.2	9	4	52	32	8	1 080
Benin	113	3.6	32	20	26.5	49	19	310
Bermuda	0.05	0.1	1 220	n.a.	100	15	7	
Bhutan	47	1.3	24	7	4	41	18	120
Bolivia	1 099	5.7	5	28	45.1	42	16	570
Botswana	600	0.8	1	76	16.1	50	16	900
Brazil	8 512	125.2	15	26	67.7	31	8	2 240
Brunei	5.8	0.2	33	v.s.	76	30	4	17 790
Bulgaria	111	8.9	80	56	62.8	14	11	n.a.
Burkina	274	7.1	26	46	9	48	22	210
Burma	677	36.2	53	15	29	38	14	190
Burundi	28	4.3	154	80	4	47	21	280
Cameroun	475	8.7	18	32	35	44	18	890
Canada	9 976	24.3	2	7	75.5	15	7	11 320
Cape Verde Islands	4	0.3	75	16	20	35	8	350
Central African Republic/Empire	623	2.3	4	8	35.3	46	20	310
Chad	1 284	4.5	4	38	18.4	44	23	80
Chile	757	11.3	15	23	82	24	6	2 210
China	9 597	1 007.8	105	33	21	21	8	310
Colombia	1 139	26.4	23	31	64	28	7	1 460
Comoro Islands	2	0.4	200	49	6	46	17	340
Congo	342	1.6	5	31	48	44	18	1 180
Costa Rica	51	2.3	45	40	47.5	31	4	1 280
Cuba	115	9.8	85	50	69	16	6	n.a.
Cyprus	9	0.6	67	57	53	22	8	3 840
Czechoslovakia	128	15.3	120	54	66.7	15	12	n.a.
Denmark	43	5.1	119	67	82.6	10	11	12 470
Djibouti	22	0.3	6	0.2	74	47	21	n.a.
Dominica	0.7	0.1	14	n.a.	n.a.	22	5	710
Dominican Republic	49	6.1	124	56	52	35	9	1 330
East Timor	14.9	0.6	52	0.2				
Ecuador	284	8.3	29	18	44.5	41	9	1 350
Egypt	1 001	43.0	43	3	44.3	38	11	690
El Salvador	21	4.9	235	63	39	34	8	700
Equatorial Guinea	28	0.4	14	12	54	42	18	n.a.
Ethiopia	1 222	32.2	26	49	14.4	47	23	140
Fiji	18	0.6	33	16	37.2	29	6	1 950
Finland	337	4.8	14	8	59.9	14	9	10 870
France	547	53.9	99	58	73	15	10	11 680
Gabon	268	0.6	2	19	36	35	20	4 000
Gambia	11	0.6	55	38	18.2	49	28	360
Germany, East	108	16.8	156	58	76.4	14	14	n.a.
Germany, West	249	61.7	248	49	94	10	12	12 460
Ghana	239	12.1	51	26	36	48	16	360
Greece	132	9.8	74	70	65	14	9	4 290
Greenland	342	0.05	0.146	0.15	74.7	20	7	

Countries	Area 1980 (10^3km^2)	Population 1981 (millions)	Population Density 1981 (per km^2)	Arable and Permanent Pasture 1980 (% of total area)	Urban Population (%)	Birth Rate (per 1000)	Death Rate (per 1000)	Per Capita GNP 1982 ($U.S.)
Grenada	0.3	0.1	333	50	n.a.	24	7	760
Guadeloupe	2	0.3	150	40	44	19	6	4 200
Guatemala	109	7.5	69	25	39.1	42	7	1 130
Guiana, French	91	0.1	1	0.11	30	30	7	
Guinea	246	5.2	21	19	19	47	19	310
Guinea Bissau	36	0.6	17	43	24	42	22	170
Guyana	215	0.9	4	6	30	28	8	660
Haiti	28	6.0	214	50	26	36	14	300
Honduras	112	3.8	34	46	37.4	44	10	675
Hong Kong	1	5.2	5 200	8	92	16	5	5 340
Hungary	93	10.7	115	71	53.8	12	14	2 270
Iceland	103	0.2	2	22	88.2	18	7	12 150
India	3 288	698.0	212	55	23.3	34	14	260
Indonesia	1 904	150.5	79	17	22.4	34	13	580
Iran	1 648	39.3	24	36	49	44	12	n.a.
Iraq	435	13.5	31	22	68	47	13	n.a.
Ireland	70	3.4	49	83	55.6	20	9	5 150
Israel	21	4.0	190	59	87.9	24	7	5 810
Italy	301	57.2	190	58	69	11	10	6 840
Ivory Coast	322	8.3	26	21	38	46	17	950
Jamaica	11	2.2	200	37	50	26	6	1 330
Japan	372	117.7	316	15	76.2	13	6	10 080
Jordan	98	3.4	35	15	59.2	46	9	1 690
Kampuchea	181	6.1	3	3.1	15	38	19	n.a.
Kenya	583	17.2	30	10	13	53	13	390
Korea, North	121	18.3	151	19	33	32	8	n.a.
Korea, South	99	39.1	395	23	57.3	23	7	1 910
Kuwait	18	1.4	78	8	90	35	3	19 870
Laos	237	3.8	16	7	13	42	18	n.a.
Lebanon	10	2.7	270	34	78	30	8	n.a.
Lesotho	30	1.4	47	76	5	41	12	510
Liberia	111	2.0	18	5	33	45	15	490
Libya	1 760	3.1	2	8	52	46	13	8 510
Liechtenstein	0.16	0.03	188	56	n.a.	14	7	
Luxembourg	3	0.4	141	n.a.	77.8	12	12	14 340
Macao (Port.)	0.02	0.3	15	n.a.	97	26	8	2 500
Madagascar	587	9.0	15	63	18	46	18	320
Malawi	118	6.4	54	35	8.5	51	19	210
Malaysia	330	14.4	44	13	30	31	7	1 860
Maldive Is.	0.3	0.2	527	13	20.67	43	13	470
Mali	1 240	7.1	6	26	17.2	46	22	180
Malta	0.32	0.4	1 250	44	83	14	8	3 800
Martinique	1	0.3	300	46	66	18	7	4 680
Mauritania	1 031	1.7	2	38	22.8	50	22	470
Mauritius	2	1.0	500	61	42.7	23	7	1 240
Mexico	1 973	71.8	36	50	67	32	6	2 270
Mongolia	1 565	1.7	1	80	51	36	8	n.a.
Morocco	447	21.0	47	45	42.1	41	12	870
Mozambique	802	10.8	13	59	15	45	17	n.a.
Namibia	824	1.0	1	65	45	43	14	n.a.
Nepal	141	14.6	104	29	25	43	18	170
Netherlands, The	37	14.3	386	54	88.4	12	8	10 930
New Zealand	269	3.1	12	54	83	16	8	7 920
Nicaragua	130	2.8	22	38	53.4	47	11	920
Niger	1 267	5.5	4	10	13	51	22	310
Nigeria	924	79.7	86	56	28	49	17	860
Norway	324	4.1	13	3	70.2	12	10	14 280
Oman	213	0.9	4	5	8	48	17	6 090
Pakistan	804	89.4	111	31	28.3	43	15	380
Panama	77	2.0	26	23	49.3	26	5	2 120
Papua New Guinea	462	3.2	7	1	13.1	43	14	820
Paraguay	407	3.3	8	43	38.6	35	8	1 610

Countries	Area 1980 (10^3km^2)	Population 1981 (millions)	Population Density 1981 (per km^2)	Arable and Permanent Pasture 1980 (% of total area)	Urban Population (%)	Birth Rate (per 1000)	Death Rate (per 1000)	Per Capita GNP 1982 ($U.S.)
Peru	1 285	18.1	14	24	65	37	12	1 310
Phillipines	300	50.5	168	36	37.3	32	7	820
Poland	313	35.9	115	61	59	19	9	n.a.
Polynesia	4	0.2	50	n.a.	57	32	6	7 980
Portugal	92	9.9	108	44	29.7	16	10	2 450
Puerto Rico	9	3.8	422	53	66.8	22	6	n.a.
Qatar	11	0.3	27	5	87	31	9	21 880
Réunion	3	0.5	167	24	41	23	6	4 010
Romania	238	22.4	94	63	50.1	15	10	2 560
Rwanda	26	5.0	192	55	5	49	18	260
St. Kitts-Nevis	0.4	0.04	0.1	v.s.	34	25	10	750
Saint Lucia	0.6	0.1	16	v.s.	40	33	7	720
St. Vincent and Grenadines	0.3	0.1	33	v.s.	n.a.	25	6	620
Samoa	2.8	0.2	55	v.s.	21	38	8	n.a.
Saõ Tomé e Principe	1	0.09	90	39	32	39	10	370
Saudi Arabia	2 150	9.3	4	40	70	42	12	16 000
Senegal	196	5.8	30	56	34.3	48	18	490
Seychelles	0.3	0.06	200	32	37.1	24	8	n.a.
Sierra Leone	72	3.6	50	55	25	45	19	390
Singapore	0.58	2.4	4 138	14	100	17	5	5 910
Solomon Islands	28	0.3	8	v.s	9	47	11	660
Somali Republic	638	4.9	8	47	30	47	21	290
South Africa	1 221	30.1	25	77	53	35	10	2 670
Spain	505	37.5	74	62	91.4	13	7	5 430
Sri Lanka	66	15.1	229	39	21.5	28	6	320
Sudan	2 506	18.9	8	27	21	47	17	440
Surinam	163	0.4	2	0.38	66	28	8	n.a.
Swaziland	17	0.6	35	84	15.2	48	16	940
Sweden	450	8.3	18	8	82.7	11	11	14 040
Switzerland	41	6.4	156	49	58	12	9	17 010
Syria	185	9.3	50	76	48	46	8	1 680
Taiwan	36	19.2	53	n.a.	66	23	5	n.a.
Tanzania	945	18.5	20	42	13.3	46	14	280
Thailand	514	48.1	94	36	17	26	6	790
Togo	57	2.7	47	29	17	47	18	340
Trinidad and Tobago	5	1.2	240	33	49	25	6	6 840
Tunisia	164	6.5	40	44	52	33	7	1 390
Turkey	781	46.4	59	49	44.7	31	10	1 370
Uganda	236	13.6	58	45	7	46	15	230
USSR	22 402	267.7	12	27	63.6	20	10	5 940
UAE	84	0.8	10	3	80.9	30	7	23 770
UK	245	56.3	230	75	76	13	12	9 660
USA	9 363	230.1	25	46	73.7	16	9	13 160
Uruguay	176	3.0	17	89	84	18	9	2 650
Vanuatu	14.8	0.1	8	v.s.	18	40	12	n.a.
Venezuela	912	16.2	18	23	76.4	33	5	4 140
Vietnam	329	58.3	167	7	19	34	10	n.a.
Western Sahara	266	0.08	0.30	19	45.1	21	5	
Yemen Arab Republic	195	5.9	30	50	12	48	21	500
Yemen, P.D.R.	333	1.9	6	28	38	48	19	470
Yugoslavia	256	22.5	88	56	39	16	9	2 800
Zaire	2 345	29.1	12	7	34.2	46	17	190
Zambia	753	6.0	8	53	43	48	16	640
Zimbabwe	391	7.7	20	19	23	47	13	850

Source: 1981 Statistical Yearbook U.N.
U.N. Demographic Year Book 1982
F.A.O.
World Data Sheet

Population Growth by Continent

The graph of population growth on page 114 of this atlas shows in visual form the growth of the world's population over the last six decades and projects this growth to the year 2000. The birth and death rate (see page 115) is one important factor in this growth rate; other aspects of this growth rate and some implications are depicted in Figs. 54 and 55.

Fig. 54: Population Growth by Continent

Continents	Population estimate mid-1984 (millions)	Surface area (000 km²)	Density of population per km²	Annual rate of population increase (%)	Population doubling time in years (at current rate)	Total fertility rate	Percent of population under age 15/ over age 64
Africa	531	30 312	17	2.9	24	6.4	45/3
North America	262	21 515	12	0.7	99	1.6	22/12
Latin America	397	20 555	19	2.4	30	4.2	39/4
Asia	2 782	27 574	100	1.8	38	4.0	37/4
Europe	491	4 937	99	0.3	208	1.8	22/13
Oceania	24	495	3	1.3	55	2.5	29/8
USSR	274	22 402	12	1.0	68	2.5	25/10

Based on data from the *UN Statistical Yearbook, 1983*

Notes: Population Doubling Time is based on current approximate rate of natural increase of the population; it does not forecast the actual doubling of a population, but does give some indication of the potential effect of different levels of the rate of natural increase. It must be considered in light of the actual size of the present population, and the total fertility rate.

The Total Fertility Rate indicates the average number of children that would be born to each woman through her childbearing lifetime at the present rate. A rate of 2.1 to 2.5, depending on mortality conditions, is the 'replacement level'; the rate at which a country's population would stop growing or declining assuming no net migration.

The percentage of the population under age 15 and over age 64, that is, the percentage of the 'dependent' population, indicates the economic burden that must be carried by those of working age.

Fig. 55: Spatial Implications of Population Growth

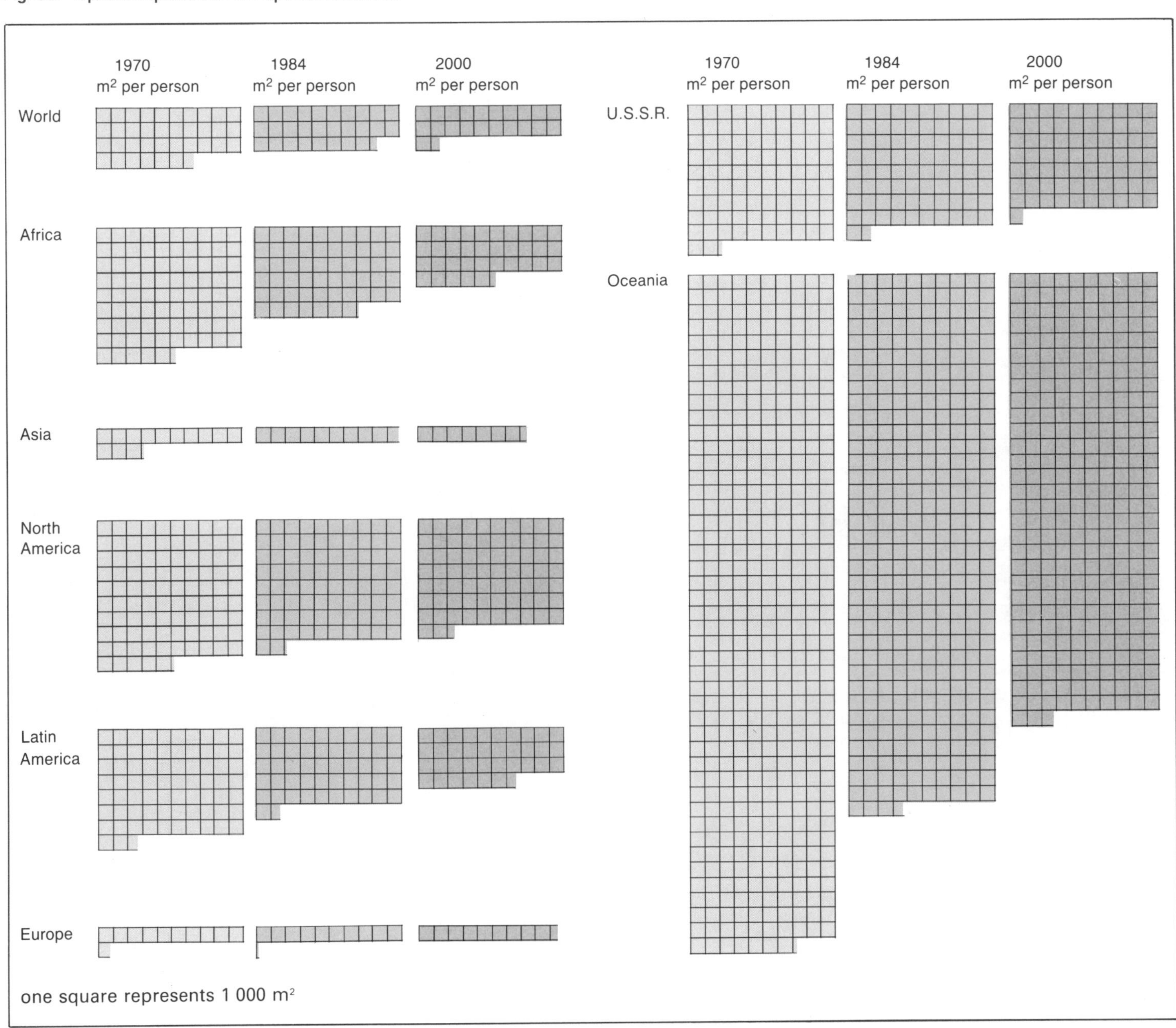
1970
m² per person
1984
m² per person
2000
m² per person
World
Africa
Asia
North America
Latin America
Europe
U.S.S.R.
Oceania
one square represents 1 000 m²

Based on data from the *UN Statistical Yearbook, 1983*

Economic Profiles

The series of graphs on page 124 highlights different economies in various parts of the world. The figures on this and the next page depict a greater range of countries, a more detailed breakdown of the economic picture, and corresponding information on employment patterns for purposes of comparison.

In North America and Europe there is a high degree of correlation between industry contribution to the Gross Domestic Product and the percentage employed in each type of industry; in other parts of the world there are some surprising discrepancies, which serve to illustrate, as two examples, the effects of subsistence agriculture, and the lack of services.

Fig. 56: Industry Contribution to the Gross Domestic Product, and Employment by Industry, Selected Countries

A Agriculture, Forestry and Fishing
B Mining
C Manufacturing
D Electricity, Gas and Water
E Construction
F Transportation and Communications
G Wholesale and Retail Trade
H Financial Institutions and Insurance
I Community and Other Services
J Government Services
K Other Producers

NOTE: The individual bars in each graph express the percentage contribution of the designated economic activity to the Gross Domestic Product; these percentages do not add up to 100, because the following adjustments have been made to calculate the value of the GDP: less imputed bank service charges, and plus import duties, value added tax and other necessary adjustments.

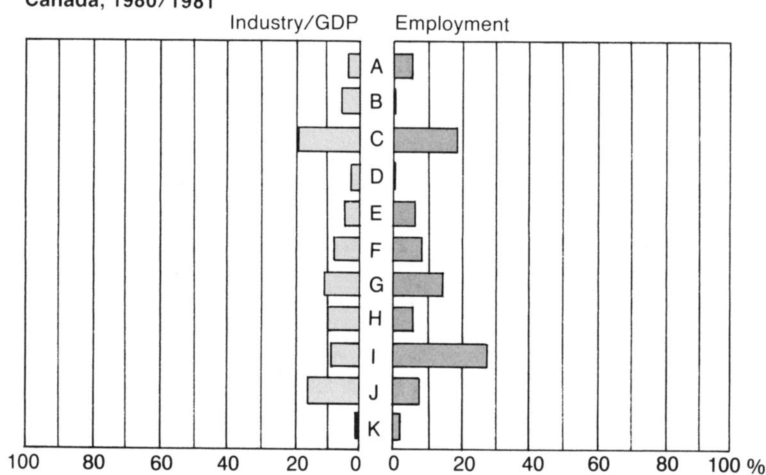
Canada, 1980/1981
Industry/GDP
Employment
A
B
C
D
E
F
G
H
I
J
K
100 80 60 40 20 0
0 20 40 60 80 100 %

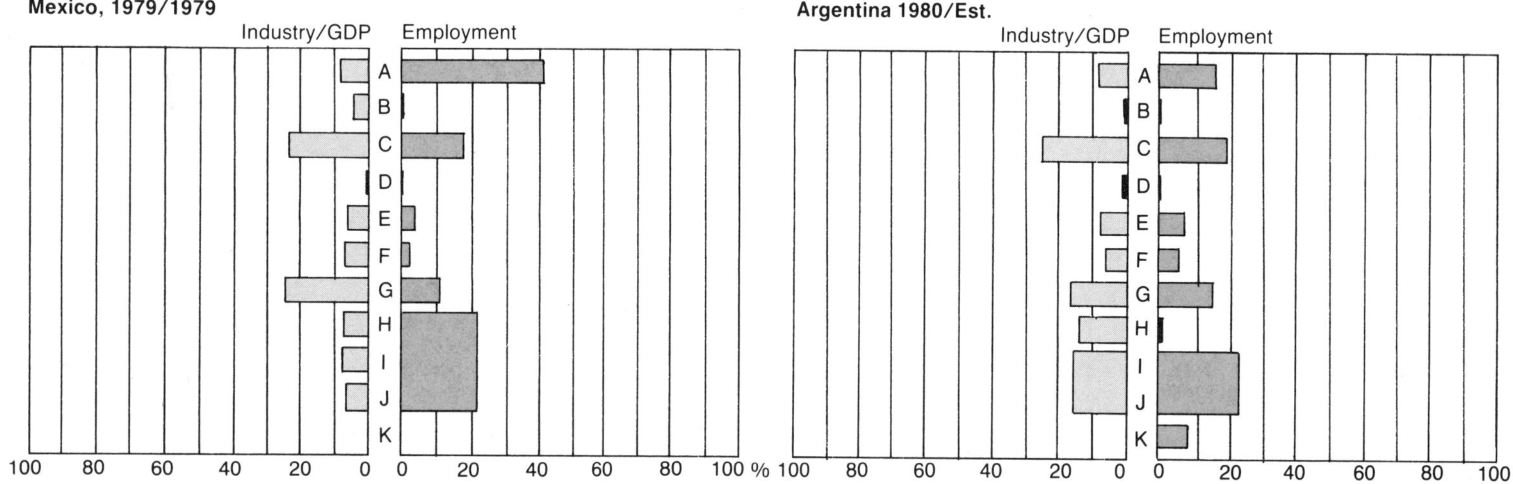
Mexico, 1979/1979
Industry/GDP
Employment
A
B
C
D
E
F
G
H
I
J
K
100 80 60 40 20 0
0 20 40 60 80 100 %
Argentina 1980/Est.
Industry/GDP
Employment
A
B
C
D
E
F
G
H
I
J
K
100 80 60 40 20 0
0 20 40 60 80 100

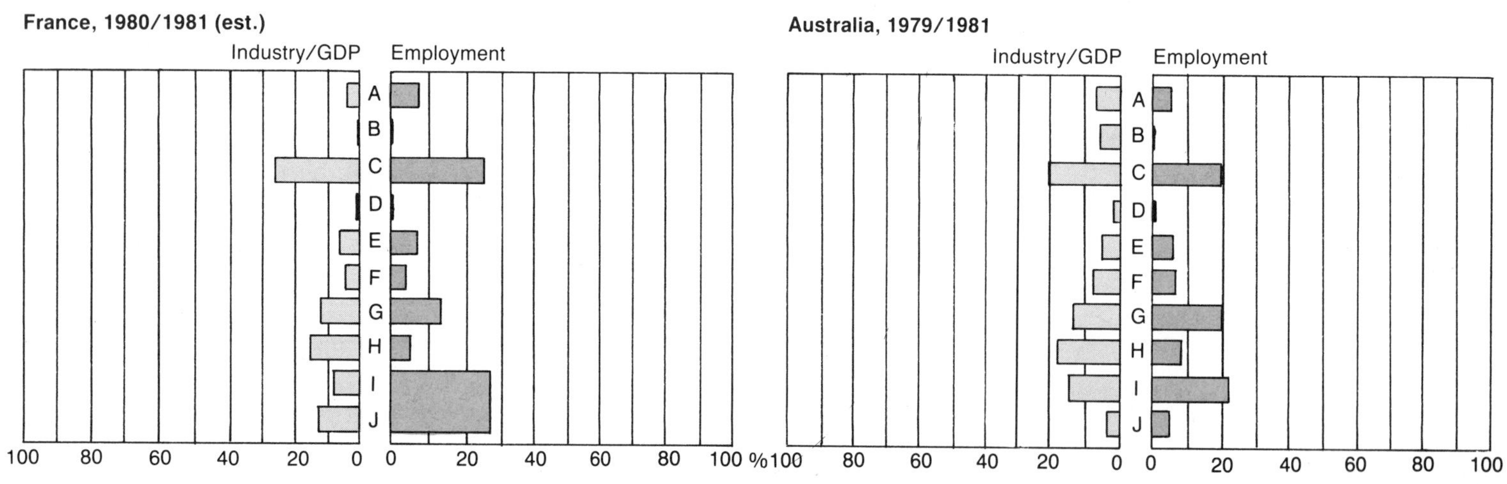
France, 1980/1981 (est.)
Industry/GDP
Employment
A
B
C
D
E
F
G
H
I
J
100 80 60 40 20 0
0 20 40 60 80 100 %
Australia, 1979/1981
Industry/GDP
Employment
A
B
C
D
E
F
G
H
I
J
100 80 60 40 20 0
0 20 40 60 80 100

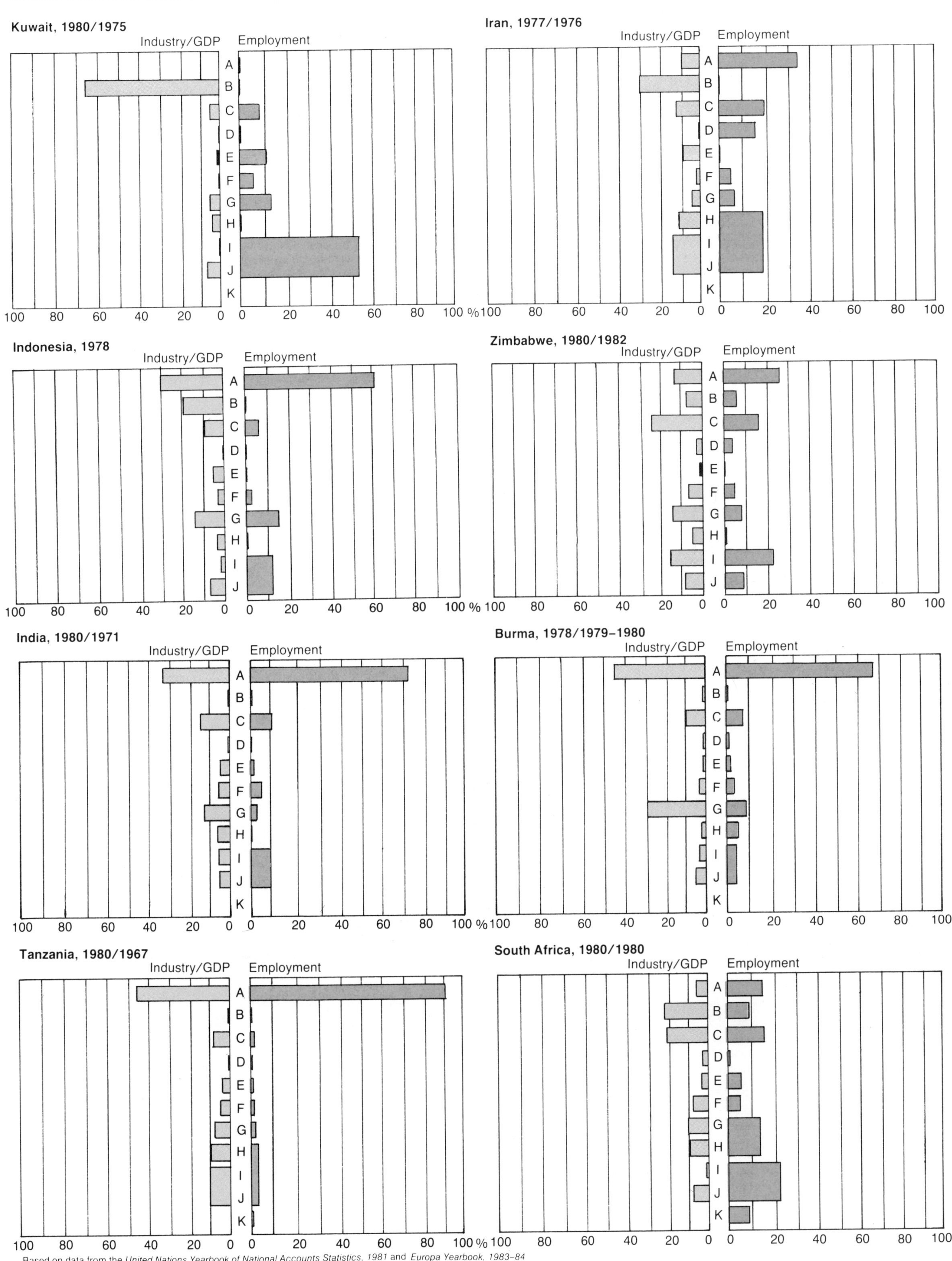
Kuwait, 1980/1975
Industry/GDP
Employment
A
B
C
D
E
F
G
H
I
J
K
100 80 60 40 20 0 0 20 40 60 80 100 %
Iran, 1977/1976
Industry/GDP
Employment
A
B
C
D
E
F
G
H
I
J
K
100 80 60 40 20 0 0 20 40 60 80 100
Indonesia, 1978
Industry/GDP
Employment
A
B
C
D
E
F
G
H
I
J
100 80 60 40 20 0 0 20 40 60 80 100 %
Zimbabwe, 1980/1982
Industry/GDP
Employment
A
B
C
D
E
F
G
H
I
J
100 80 60 40 20 0 0 20 40 60 80 100
India, 1980/1971
Industry/GDP
Employment
A
B
C
D
E
F
G
H
I
J
K
100 80 60 40 20 0 0 20 40 60 80 100 %
Burma, 1978/1979–1980
Industry/GDP
Employment
A
B
C
D
E
F
G
H
I
J
K
100 80 60 40 20 0 0 20 40 60 80 100
Tanzania, 1980/1967
Industry/GDP
Employment
A
B
C
D
E
F
G
H
I
J
K
100 80 60 40 20 0 0 20 40 60 80 100 %
South Africa, 1980/1980
Industry/GDP
Employment
A
B
C
D
E
F
G
H
I
J
K
100 80 60 40 20 0 0 20 40 60 80 100

Based on data from the *United Nations Yearbook of National Accounts Statistics, 1981* and *Europa Yearbook, 1983–84*

Urbanization

Urbanization is an increasing trend throughout the world. Figs. 57, 58, and 59 give an overview of various aspects of urbanization. Although the developed countries are among the most urbanized, the extent of urbanization by continent may cause some surprises, and should be considered in the light of size of population and areal extent.

Fig. 57: The World's 25 Most Urbanized Countries

	% urban
Belgium	94.6
W. Germany	94.0
Spain	91.4
Netherlands	88.4
Iceland	88.2
Israel	87.9
Australia	86.0
New Zealand	83.0
Uruguay	83.0
Sweden	82.7
Denmark	82.6
Argentina	82.0
Chile	81.6
UAR	80.9
Luxembourg	77.8
UK	77.7
Venezuela	76.4
GDR	76.4
Japan	76.2
Canada	75.5
Greenland	74.7
U.S.	73.7
France	73.0
Norway	70.2
Cuba	69.0

City states e.g. Hong Kong, Singapore, not included.

Fig. 58: Urbanization by Continent: Percentage of Population Living in Urban Centres

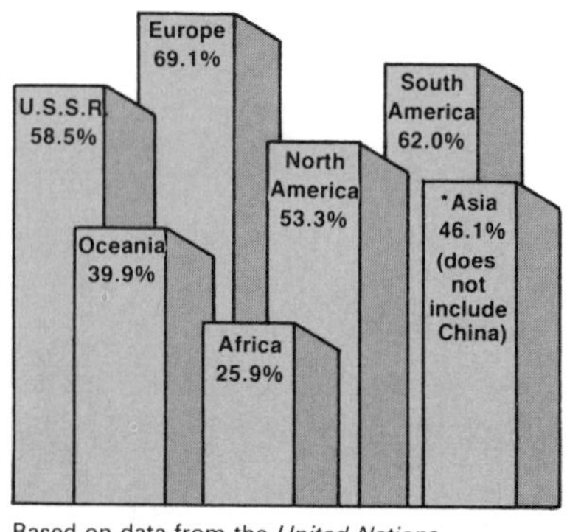
Europe 69.1%
U.S.S.R. 58.5%
South America 62.0%
North America 53.3%
Oceania 39.9%
*Asia 46.1% (does not include China)
Africa 25.9%

Based on data from the *United Nations Demographic Yearbook, 1982*

Fig. 59: World Cities

NOTE: data not always provided for both urban centre and agglomeration eg. Moscow 1961; London 1971, 1981, etc.
Moscow 1982 data as provided by source; may be owing to possibility of boundary changes (unverified).

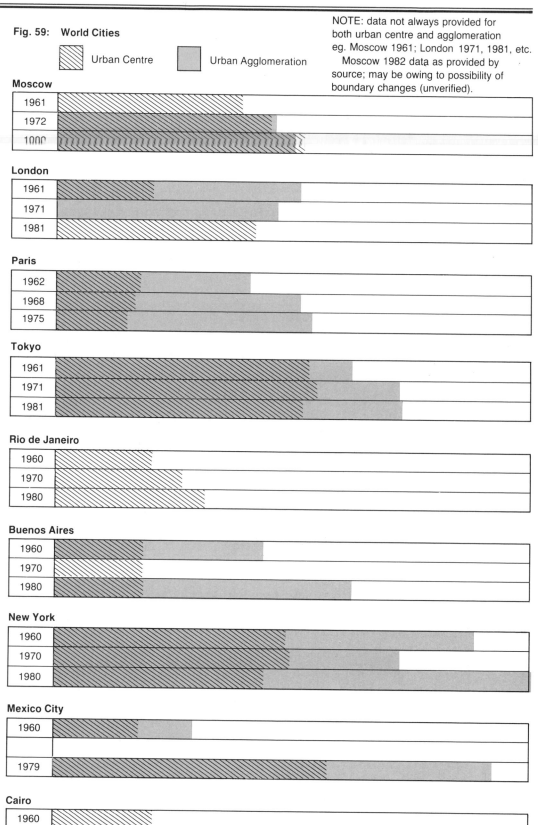

Urban Centre
Urban Agglomeration

Moscow: 1961, 1972, 1982
London: 1961, 1971, 1981
Paris: 1962, 1968, 1975
Tokyo: 1961, 1971, 1981
Rio de Janeiro: 1960, 1970, 1980
Buenos Aires: 1960, 1970, 1980
New York: 1960, 1970, 1980
Mexico City: 1960, 1979

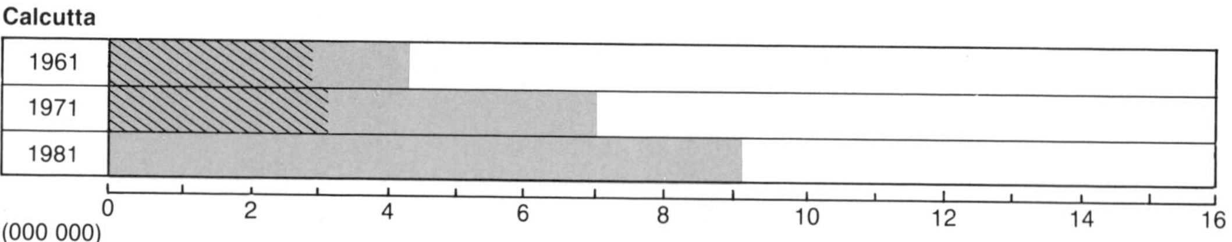
Cairo
1960
1970
1976
Calcutta
1961
1971
1981
0
2
4
6
8
10
12
14
16
(000 000)

Based on data from the *United Nations Demographic Yearbook, 1962, 1972, 1982*

International Tourism, 1980

The past twenty to thirty years has seen an enormous increase in international travel. It is estimated that in 1980 international tourists spent over 90 000 (millions of U.S. dollars) on travel, excluding air fares. Fig. 60 shows the major tourist areas of the world.

Tourists refer to persons staying at least 24 hours in a country other than their country of residence for the purposes of vacation, health, study, sport, or business. Excluded from these figures are immigrants, persons residing in one country and working in another, members of diplomatic missions and armed forces, and passengers in transit.

Data are estimates only, based on sources such as frontier checks, accommodation checks, etc., but may exclude people staying in private houses, and may duplicate people moving from one hotel to another.

Fig. 60: Patterns of International Tourism

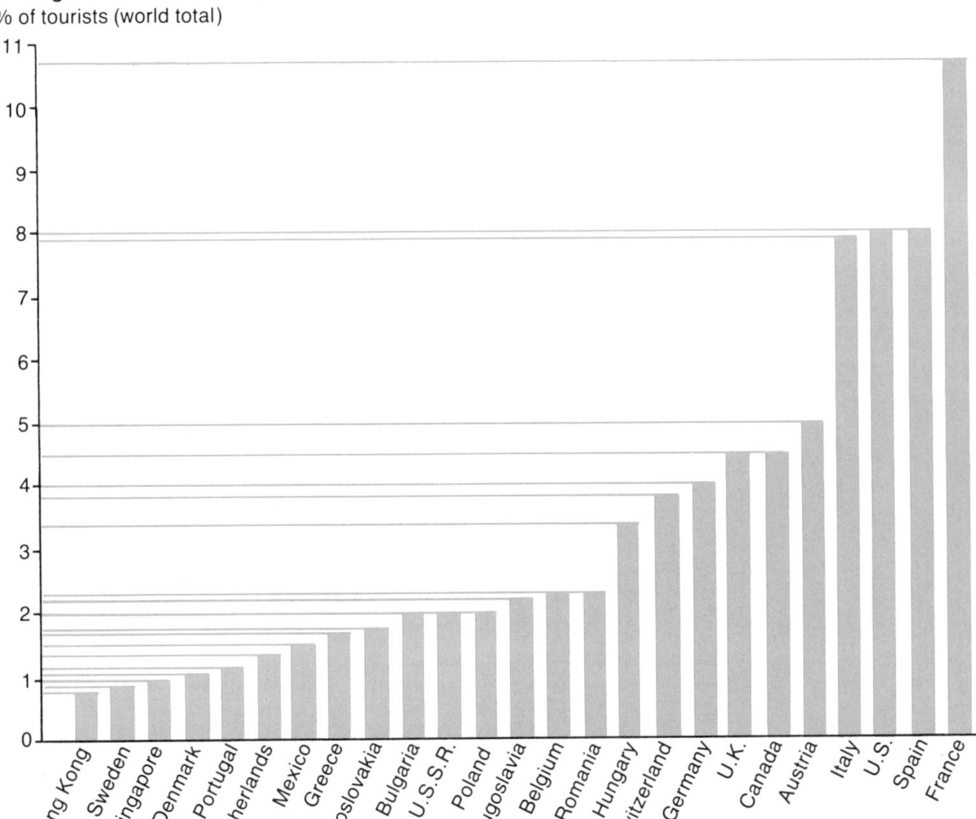
% of tourists (world total)
0
1
2
3
4
5
6
7
8
9
10
11
Hong Kong
Sweden
Singapore
Denmark
Portugal
Netherlands
Mexico
Greece
Czechoslovakia
Bulgaria
U.S.S.R.
Poland
Yugoslavia
Belgium
Romania
Hungary
Switzerland
West Germany
U.K.
Canada
Austria
Italy
U.S.
Spain
France
Country or area of destination

Based on data from the World Tourism Organization (Madrid) and the International Monetary Fund (Washington, DC) quoted in the *Statistical Yearbook of the United Nations, 1981*

Developed and Developing Countries

The maps and graphs on pages 114 to 126 provide a variety of information which can be used in determining differences between the developed and developing parts of the world. Figs. 61 and 62 provide two additional measures.

The figures on research and development serve to illustrate one of the dilemmas of the developing countries: with very little to spare for anything beyond a subsistence level, can resources be found for such things as education and research and development?

Fig. 61: Trends in the Number of R&D Scientists and Engineers

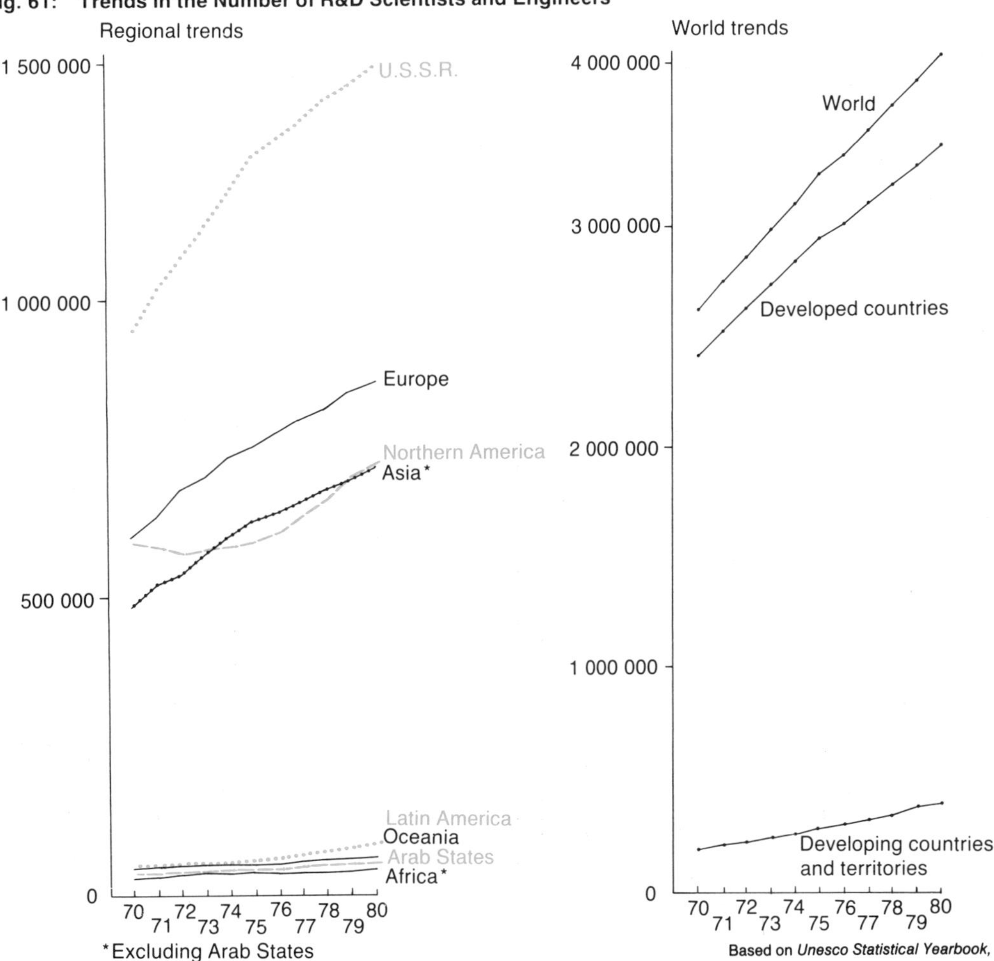
Regional trends
1 500 000
1 000 000
500 000
0
U.S.S.R.
Europe
Northern America
Asia*
Latin America
Oceania
Arab States
Africa*
70
71
72
73
74
75
76
77
78
79
80
*Excluding Arab States
World trends
4 000 000
3 000 000
2 000 000
1 000 000
0
World
Developed countries
Developing countries and territories
70
71
72
73
74
75
76
77
78
79
80

Based on *Unesco Statistical Yearbook, 1983*

Fig. 62: Number of Book Titles Published, 1955–1981

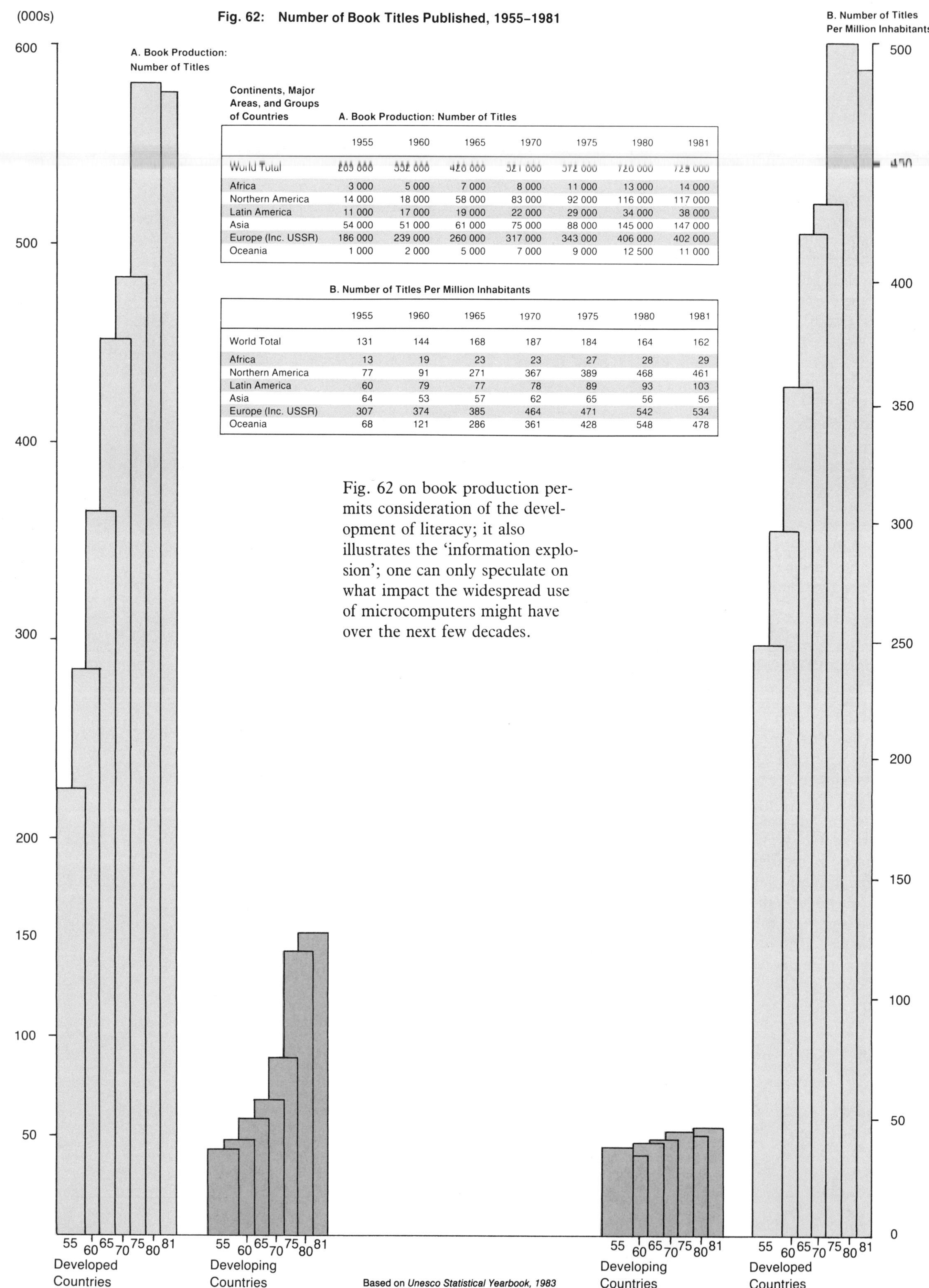
(000s)
A. Book Production: Number of Titles
B. Number of Titles Per Million Inhabitants
600
500
400
300
200
150
100
50
0
350
250
55 60 65 70 75 80 81
Developed Countries
Developing Countries
Developing Countries
Developed Countries

Continents, Major Areas, and Groups of Countries — A. Book Production: Number of Titles

	1955	1960	1965	1970	1975	1980	1981
World Total	285 000	332 000	426 000	521 000	572 000	720 000	729 000
Africa	3 000	5 000	7 000	8 000	11 000	13 000	14 000
Northern America	14 000	18 000	58 000	83 000	92 000	116 000	117 000
Latin America	11 000	17 000	19 000	22 000	29 000	34 000	38 000
Asia	54 000	51 000	61 000	75 000	88 000	145 000	147 000
Europe (Inc. USSR)	186 000	239 000	260 000	317 000	343 000	406 000	402 000
Oceania	1 000	2 000	5 000	7 000	9 000	12 500	11 000

B. Number of Titles Per Million Inhabitants

	1955	1960	1965	1970	1975	1980	1981
World Total	131	144	168	187	184	164	162
Africa	13	19	23	23	27	28	29
Northern America	77	91	271	367	389	468	461
Latin America	60	79	77	78	89	93	103
Asia	64	53	57	62	65	56	56
Europe (Inc. USSR)	307	374	385	464	471	542	534
Oceania	68	121	286	361	428	548	478

Fig. 62 on book production permits consideration of the development of literacy; it also illustrates the 'information explosion'; one can only speculate on what impact the widespread use of microcomputers might have over the next few decades.

Based on *Unesco Statistical Yearbook, 1983*

The Arctic

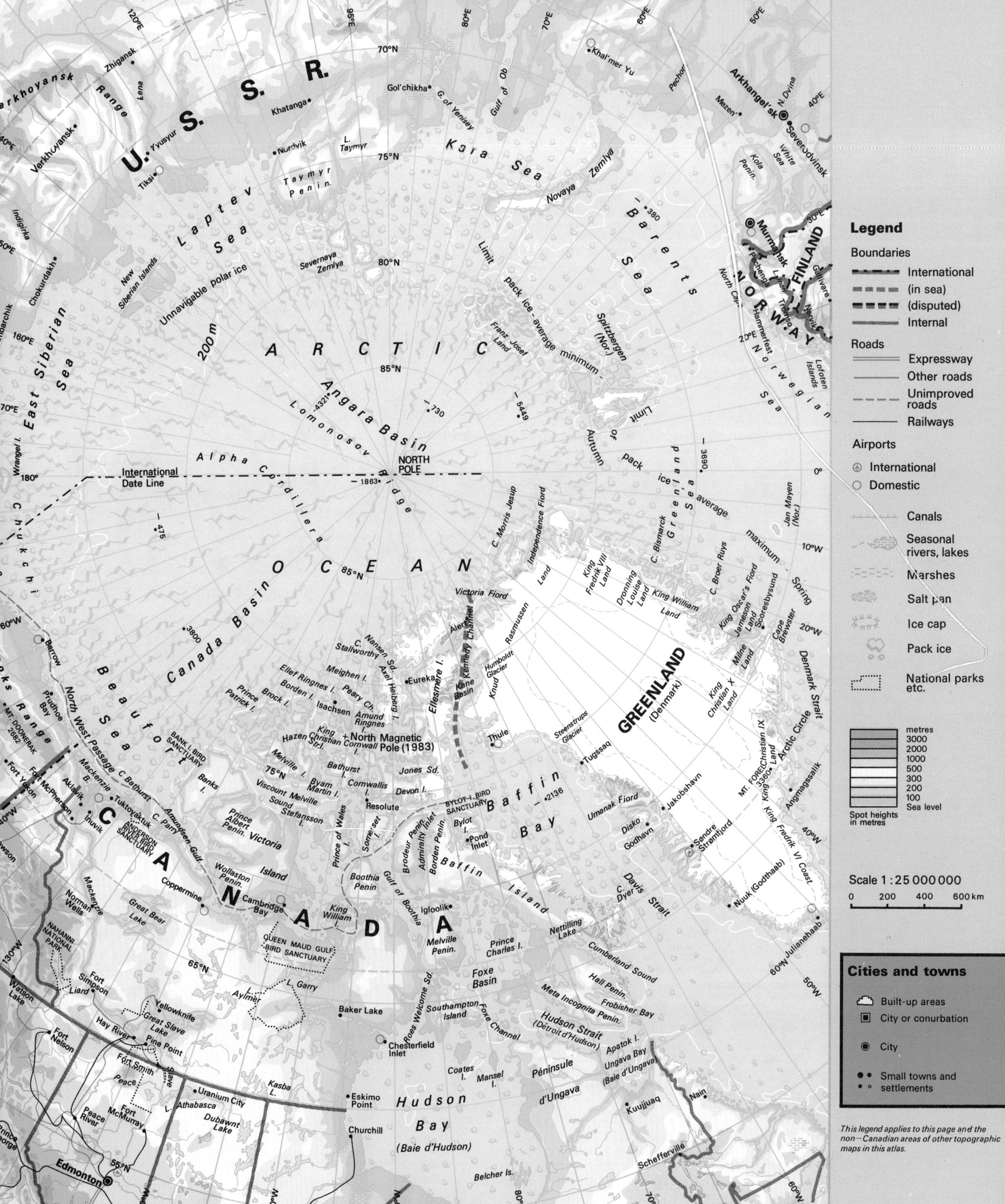
U. S. S. R.
Verkhoyansk Range
Zhigansk
Lena
Verkhoyansk
Yvusyur
Tiksi
Khatanga
Nordvik
L. Taymyr
Taymyr Penin.
Gol'chikha
G. of Yenisey
Gulf of Ob
Kara Sea
Novaya Zemlya
Khal'mer Yu
Pechora
Arkhangel'sk
Mezen
N. Dvina
Severodvinsk
Kola Penin.
White Sea
Murmansk
FINLAND
NORWAY
North Cape
Hammerfest
Lofoten Islands
Norwegian Sea
Barents Sea
Laptev Sea
Indigirka
Chokurdakh
New Siberian Islands
Unnavigable polar ice
Severnaya Zemlya
East Siberian Sea
200 m
ARCTIC OCEAN
Franz Josef Land
Spitzbergen (Nor.)
Limit of pack ice - average minimum
Limit of Autumn pack ice average maximum
Spring
Angara Basin
Lomonosov Ridge
NORTH POLE
Alpha Cordillera
International Date Line
Wrangel I.
Chukchi Sea
Canada Basin
Beaufort Sea
Greenland Sea
Jan Mayen (Nor.)
Denmark Strait
Arctic Circle
GREENLAND (Denmark)
C. Morris Jesup
Independence Fiord
Victoria Fiord
Kennedy Channel
Alert
Kane Basin
Humboldt Glacier
Thule
Tugssaq
Steenstrups Glacier
Jakobshavn
Umanak Fiord
Disko
Godhavn
Søndre Strømfjord
Nuuk (Godthaab)
Julianehaab
Angmagssalik
Scoresbysund
MT. FOREL 3360
Baffin Bay
Davis Strait
C. Dyer
Baffin Island
Ellesmere I.
Axel Heiberg I.
Eureka
Ellef Ringnes I.
Amund Ringnes I.
Borden I.
Meighen I.
Prince Patrick I.
Melville I.
Bathurst I.
Cornwallis I.
Devon I.
Resolute
Jones Sd.
North Magnetic Pole (1983)
Banks I.
Victoria Island
Prince of Wales I.
Somerset I.
Boothia Penin.
Gulf of Boothia
Pond Inlet
Bylot I.
Igloolik
Melville Penin.
Prince Charles I.
Foxe Basin
Southampton Island
Foxe Channel
Hudson Strait (Détroit d'Hudson)
Cumberland Sound
Hall Penin.
Frobisher Bay
Meta Incognita Penin.
Ungava Bay (Baie d'Ungava)
Péninsule d'Ungava
Kuujjuaq
Nain
Schefferville
Hudson Bay (Baie d'Hudson)
Belcher Is.
Churchill
Eskimo Point
Chesterfield Inlet
Baker Lake
Coates I.
Mansel I.
CANADA
Mackenzie
Inuvik
Aklavik
Tuktoyaktuk
Fort McPherson
Fort Yukon
Prudhoe Bay
Barrow
MT. DOONERAK 2682
Amundsen Gulf
Coppermine
Cambridge Bay
King William I.
QUEEN MAUD GULF BIRD SANCTUARY
Great Bear Lake
Norman Wells
NAHANNI NATIONAL PARK
Fort Simpson
Liard
Watson Lake
Fort Nelson
Yellowknife
Great Slave Lake
Hay River
Pine Point
Fort Smith
Uranium City
L. Athabasca
Fort McMurray
Edmonton
Legend
Boundaries
International
(in sea)
(disputed)
Internal
Roads
Expressway
Other roads
Unimproved roads
Railways
Airports
International
Domestic
Canals
Seasonal rivers, lakes
Marshes
Salt pan
Ice cap
Pack ice
National parks etc.
metres
3000
2000
1000
500
300
200
100
Sea level
Spot heights in metres
Scale 1 : 25 000 000
0 200 400 600 km
Cities and towns
Built-up areas
City or conurbation
City
Small towns and settlements
This legend applies to this page and the non-Canadian areas of other topographic maps in this atlas.

ithal Equidistant Projection
xford University Press

Canada : Political

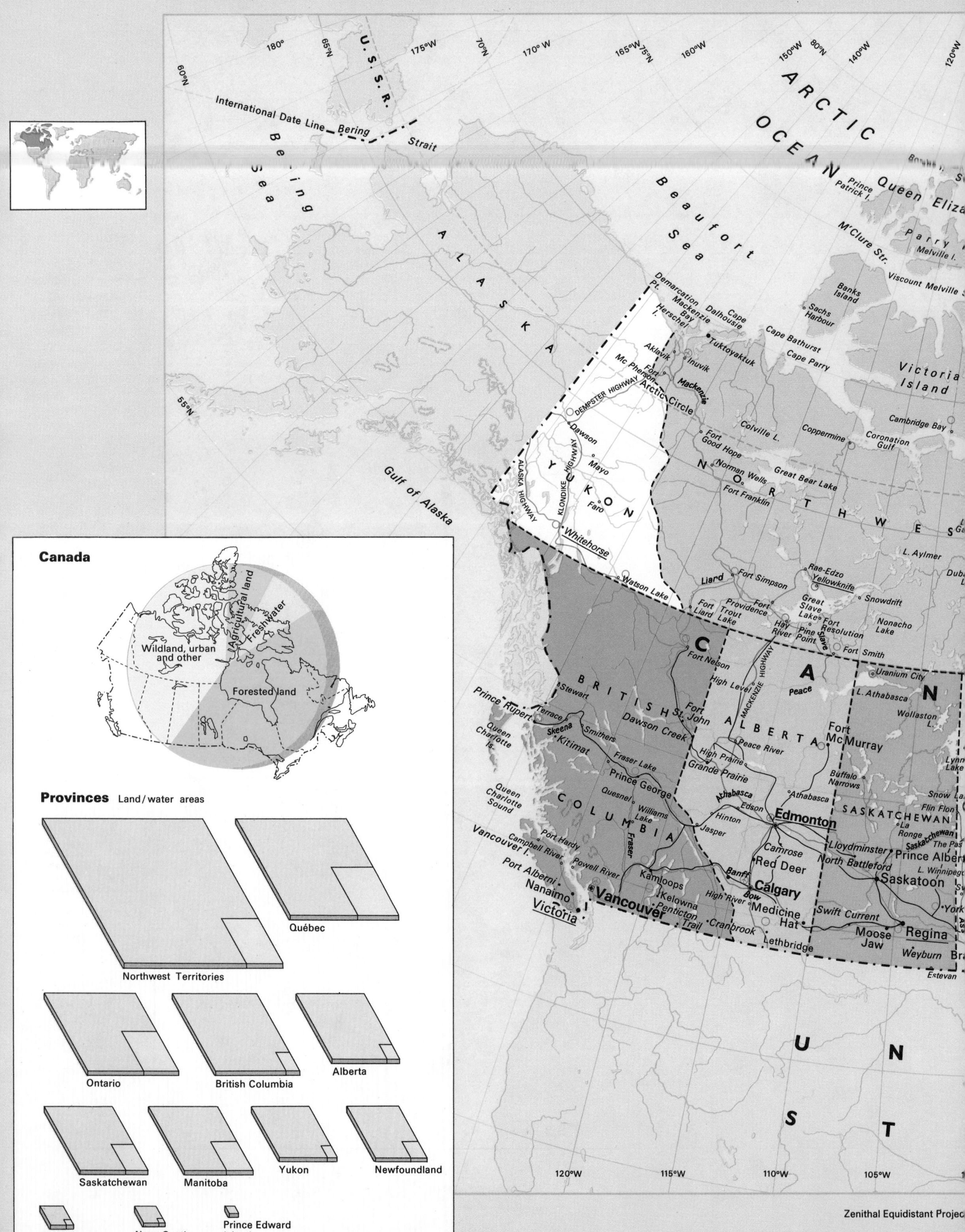

Canada
Agricultural land
Freshwater
Wildland, urban and other
Forested land
Provinces Land/water areas
Northwest Territories
Québec
Ontario
British Columbia
Alberta
Saskatchewan
Manitoba
Yukon
Newfoundland
New Brunswick
Nova Scotia
Prince Edward Island
ARCTIC OCEAN
Beaufort Sea
Bering Sea
Bering Strait
International Date Line
U.S.S.R.
ALASKA
Gulf of Alaska
YUKON
Whitehorse
Dawson
Mayo
Faro
Watson Lake
DEMPSTER HIGHWAY
KLONDIKE HIGHWAY
ALASKA HIGHWAY
BRITISH COLUMBIA
Prince Rupert
Prince George
Vancouver
Victoria
Kamloops
Kelowna
Penticton
Nanaimo
Port Alberni
Vancouver I.
Queen Charlotte Is.
Queen Charlotte Sound
ALBERTA
Edmonton
Calgary
Red Deer
Lethbridge
Medicine Hat
Fort McMurray
Grande Prairie
Peace River
SASKATCHEWAN
Saskatoon
Regina
Moose Jaw
Prince Albert
Swift Current
North Battleford
Lloydminster
Weyburn
Estevan
Uranium City
L. Athabasca
Yellowknife
Fort Smith
Hay River
Fort Simpson
Inuvik
Tuktoyaktuk
Aklavik
Fort Good Hope
Norman Wells
Great Bear Lake
Coppermine
Cambridge Bay
Victoria Island
Banks Island
Sachs Harbour
Melville I.
Prince Patrick I.
M'Clure Str.
Viscount Melville
Arctic Circle
Mackenzie
Fraser
Athabasca
Peace
Liard
120°W
115°W
110°W
105°W
55°N
60°N
65°N
70°N
75°N
80°N
180°
175°W
170°W
165°W
160°W
150°W
140°W
Zenithal Equidistant Projec

GREENLAND
(Denmark)
ICELAND
Tugssâq
3000m
2000m
Arctic Circle
Cape Columbia
Alert
Ellesmere Island
Kane Basin
Axel-Heiberg I.
Cornwall I.
Grise Fiord
Jones Sound
Devon I.
Resolute
Barrow Str.
Lancaster Sound
Bylot I.
Baffin Bay
Somerset I.
Arctic Bay
Pond Inlet
Clyde River
Baffin Island
Davis Strait
Broughton Island
Boothia Penin.
Igloolik
Hall Beach
Spence Bay
Gjoa Haven
Pangnirtung
Cumberland Sound
Foxe Basin
Repulse Bay
Iqaluit
Frobisher Bay
Resolution I.
Lake Harbour
Cape Dorset
TERRITORIES
Southampton Island
Coral Harbour
Hudson Strait
(Détroit d'Hudson)
Chesterfield Inlet
Rankin Inlet
Ungava Bay
(Baie d'Ungava)
Povungnituk
Kuujjuaq
Eskimo Point
Hudson Bay
(Baie d'Hudson)
Inukjuak
Nain
Hopedale
NEWFOUNDLAND
LABRADOR
Churchill
Schefferville
Smallwood Reservoir
Happy Valley
Strait of Belle Isle
Kuujjuarapik
Ashuanipi L.
Harrington Harbour
Nelson
Gillam
Winisk
Chisasibi
(Fort-George)
Sakami
Keyano
Labrador City
Wabush
Gagnon
Lac Allard
Natashquan
Havre-St.-Pierre
Île d'Anticosti
Windsor
Gander
Grand Falls
NEWFOUNDLAND
Wabana
St. John's
Argentia
C. Race
James Bay
(Baie James)
Corner Brook
Stephenville
Channel-Port-aux-Basques
Placentia Bay
Sept-Îles
Gulf of St. Lawrence
Attawapiskat
Lac Mistassini
QUÉBEC
Port-Cartier
Baie-Comeau
Gaspé
Îles-de-la-Madeleine (Qué.)
Cabot Strait
St-Pierre & Miquelon (Fr.)
Fort Albany
Eastmain
Rimouski
Bathurst
PRINCE EDWARD I.
Charlottetown
Glace Bay
Sydney
Cape Breton I.
Winnipeg
Berens River
Moosonee
Chibougamau
Pickle Lake
Red Lake
ONTARIO
Matagami
Dolbeau
Lac Saint-Jean
Réservoir Gouin
Roberval
Tadoussac
Campbellton
Edmundston
NEW BRUNSWICK
Chicoutimi
Moncton
New Glasgow
Hearst
Kapuskasing
L. Abitibi
Noranda
Val-d'Or
Québec
Saint-Laurent
Thetford Mines
Fredericton
Truro
NOVA SCOTIA
Halifax
Dryden
Lake Nipigon
Kenora
Lake of the Woods
Timmins
Rouyn
Kirkland Lake
Shawinigan
Trois-Rivières
Drummondville
Saint John
Bay of Fundy
Lunenburg
Rainy River
Thunder Bay
Haileybury
Maniwaki
Sherbrooke
Yarmouth
Cape Sable
North Bay
Montréal
Lake Superior
Sault Ste. Marie
Sudbury
Ottawa
Hull
Saint-Jean-sur-Richelieu
Georgian Bay
L. Huron
Kingston
Peterborough
Toronto
Lake Ontario
Hamilton
Kitchener
Niagara Falls
Lake Michigan
Sarnia
London
Windsor
Lake Erie
UNITED STATES
ATLANTIC OCEAN
80°W 60°W 50°W 40°W 35°W 30°W 25°W 20°W 15°W
75°N 70°N 65°N 60°N 55°N 50°N 45°N 40°N 35°N
95°W 90°W 85°W 80°W 75°W 70°W 65°W

Legend

Boundaries

- International
- Internal
- Roads
- Railways

Airports

- International
- Domestic

Ice cap

Population

- under 10 000
- 10–50 000
- 50–100 000
- 100–500 000
- 500–1 000 000
- over 1 000 000

Ottawa — Federal capital

Québec — Provincial capitals

Scale 1:19 000 000

0 150 300 450 km

Canada: Physical

ARCTIC OCEAN
Beaufort Sea
Bering Sea
PACIFIC OCEAN
Gulf of Alaska
Brooks Range
Alaska Range
Aleutian Range
Alaska Peninsula
St. Elias Mts.
Mackenzie Mountains
Coast Mountains
Interior Plateau
Rocky Mountains
Columbia Mountains
Cascade Range
Coast Ranges
Interior Plains
Cassiar Mts.
Blue Mts.
Bitterroot Range
Salmon River Mts.
Cypress Hills
Victoria Island
Banks Island
Melville I.
Prince Patrick I.
Great Bear Lake
Great Slave Lake
L. Athabasca
Vancouver I.
Queen Charlotte Is.
Kodiak I.
International Date Line
Unnavigable polar ice
Limit of pack ice-average min. (fall)
Arctic Circle
MT. McKINLEY 6194
MT. LOGAN 5951
MT. ST. ELIAS
MT. ROBSON 3954
MT. WADDINGTON 3994
MT. RAINIER 4392
MT. HOOD 3427
MT. SHASTA 4317
LASSEN PEAK 3186
LARAMIE PEAK 3132
YELLOWHEAD PASS
KICKING HORSE PASS
CROWSNEST PASS
PINE PASS
Yukon
Mackenzie
Liard
Peace
Athabasca
Fraser
Columbia
Snake
Saskatchewan
Missouri
Yellowstone
Great Salt Lake
Pleistocene Glaciation
Retreat of last (Wisconsin) ice sheet ice-marginal positions, years B. P.
Present-day ice cover
0
7 000
10 000
13 000
15 000 or more
Direction of temporary re-advance
Scale 1: 45 000 000
Relief Profile along 49 °N parallel
Horizontal scale 1: 19 000 000
Vertical exaggeration (land) × 98
Vertical exaggeration (sea) × 49
metres
3000
2000
1000
Sea level
1000
2000
3000
4000

Legend

Boundaries

International

(in sea/lakes)

Provincial

Pack ice

Ice cap

Escarpment

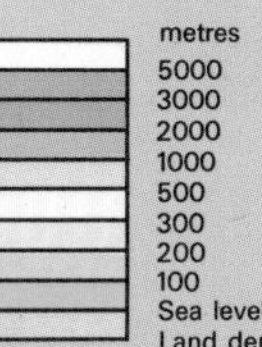
metres
5000
3000
2000
1000
500
300
200
100
Sea level
Land depression

Spot heights in metres

Scale 1:19 000 000

0 200 400 km

Zenithal Equidistant Projection

Canada: Climate

Air Masses and Winds

January

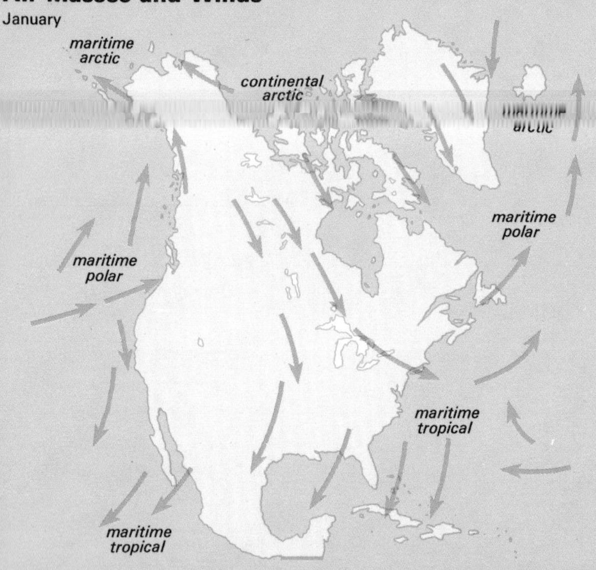
maritime
arctic
continental
arctic
arctic
maritime
polar
maritime
polar
maritime
tropical
maritime
tropical

July

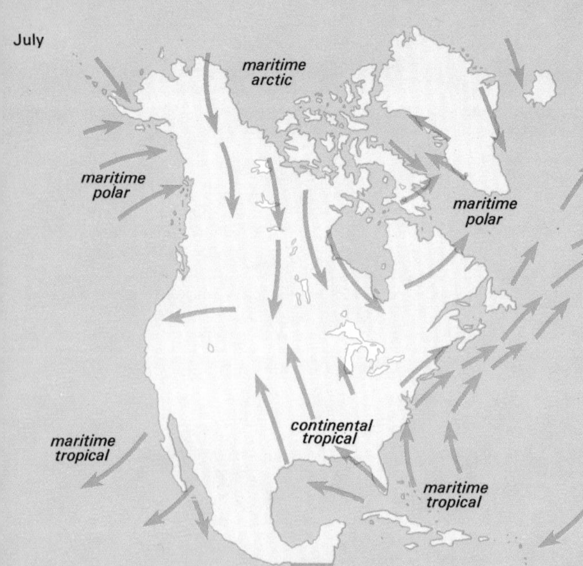
maritime
arctic
maritime
polar
maritime
polar
continental
tropical
maritime
tropical
maritime
tropical

Ocean Currents

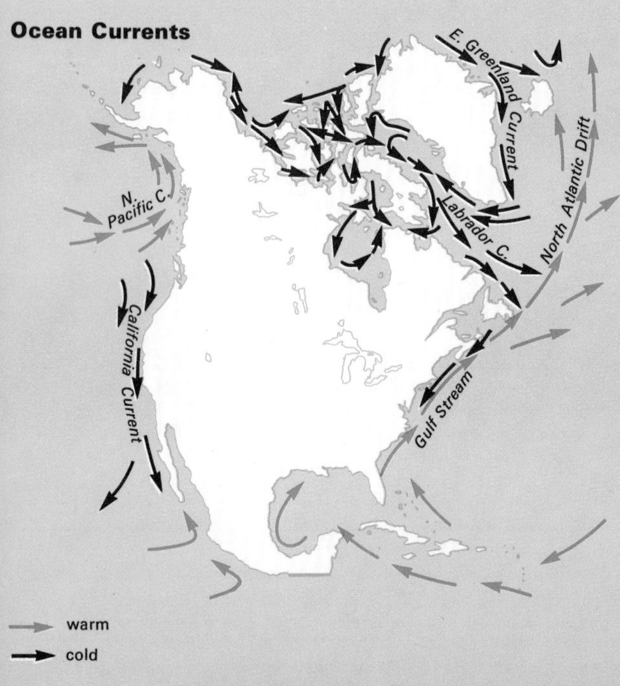
E. Greenland Current
N. Pacific C.
Labrador C.
North Atlantic Drift
California Current
Gulf Stream

warm
cold

Scale 1:108 000 000 Oblique Mercator Projection

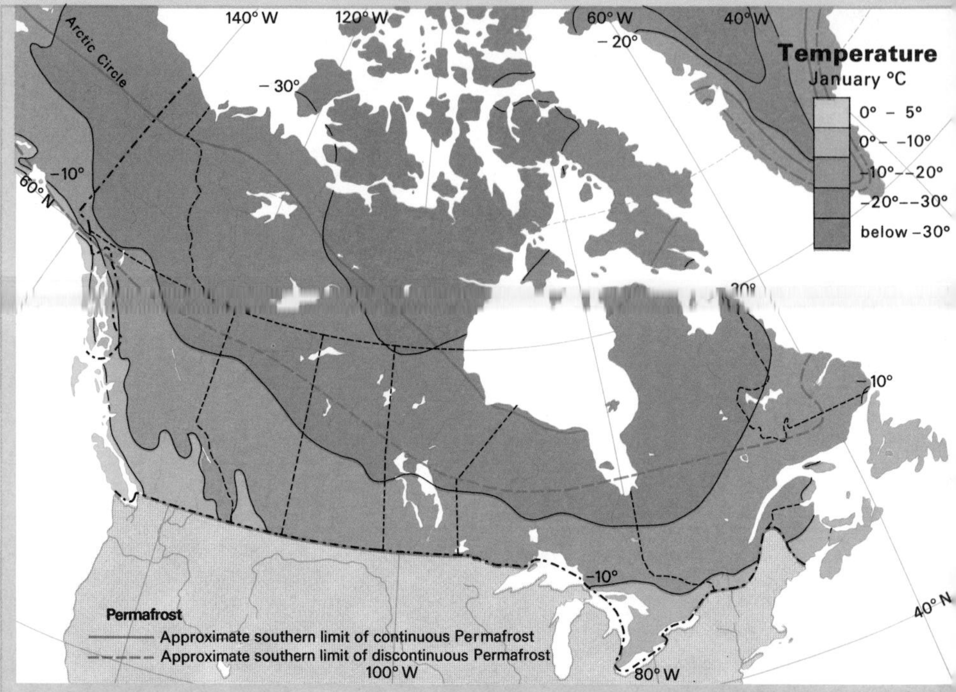

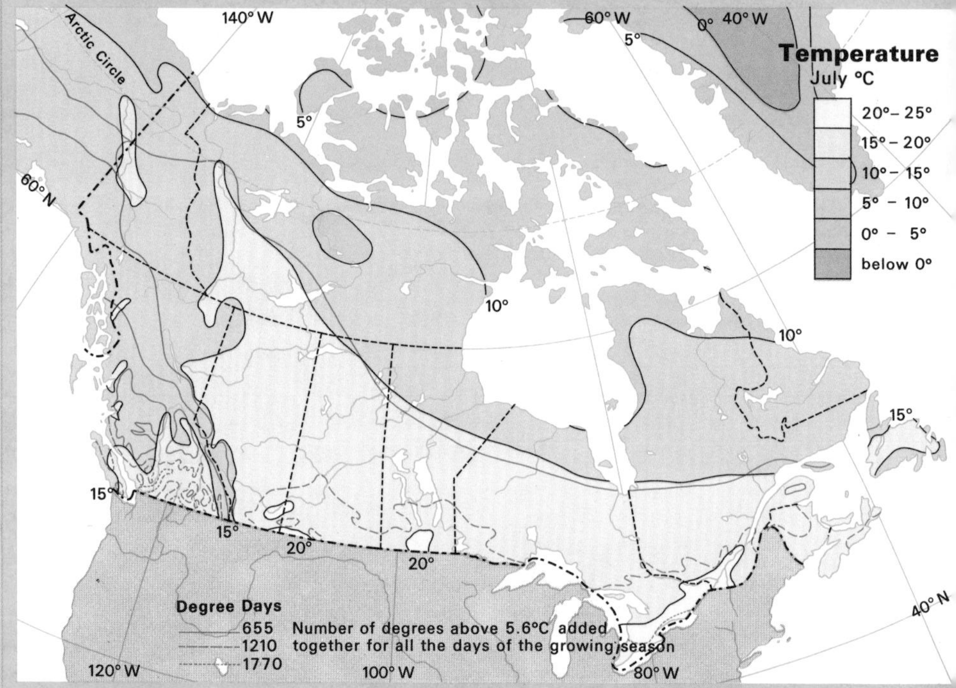

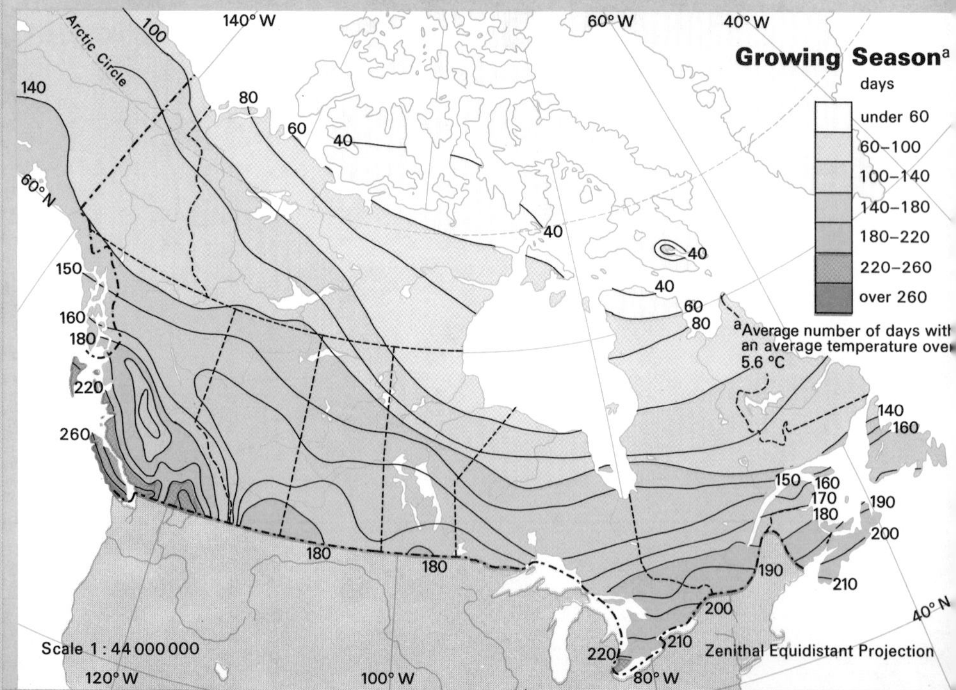

Temperature
January °C

0° – 5°
0° – −10°
−10° – −20°
−20° – −30°
below −30°

Permafrost
Approximate southern limit of continuous Permafrost
Approximate southern limit of discontinuous Permafrost

Temperature
July °C

20° – 25°
15° – 20°
10° – 15°
5° – 10°
0° – 5°
below 0°

Degree Days
655 Number of degrees above 5.6°C added
1210 together for all the days of the growing season
1770

Growing Season[a]
days

under 60
60–100
100–140
140–180
180–220
220–260
over 260

[a]Average number of days with an average temperature over 5.6 °C

Scale 1:44 000 000 Zenithal Equidistant Projection

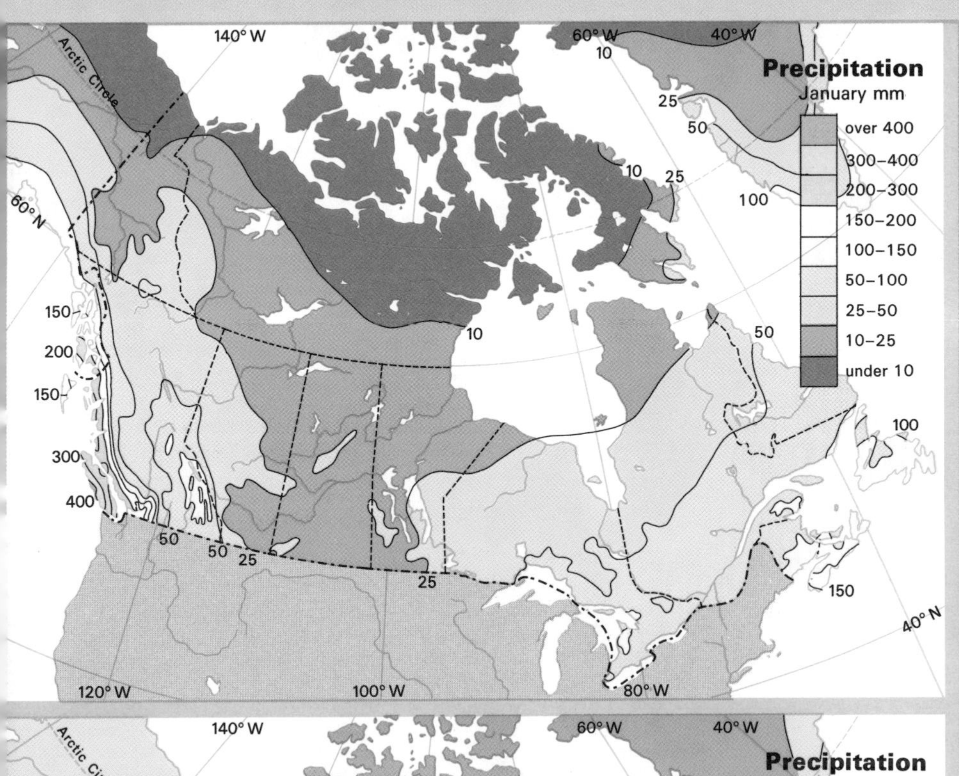
Precipitation
January mm
over 400
300–400
200–300
150–200
100–150
50–100
25–50
10–25
under 10
140° W
60° W
40° W
Arctic Circle
60° N
120° W
100° W
80° W
40° N

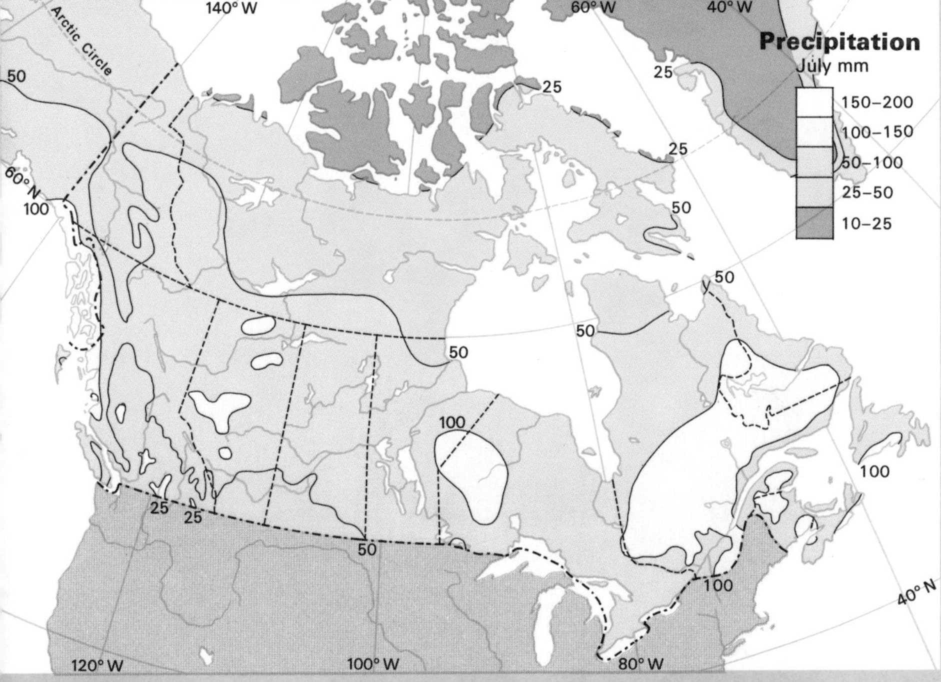
Precipitation
July mm
150–200
100–150
50–100
25–50
10–25
140° W
60° W
40° W
Arctic Circle
60° N
120° W
100° W
80° W
40° N

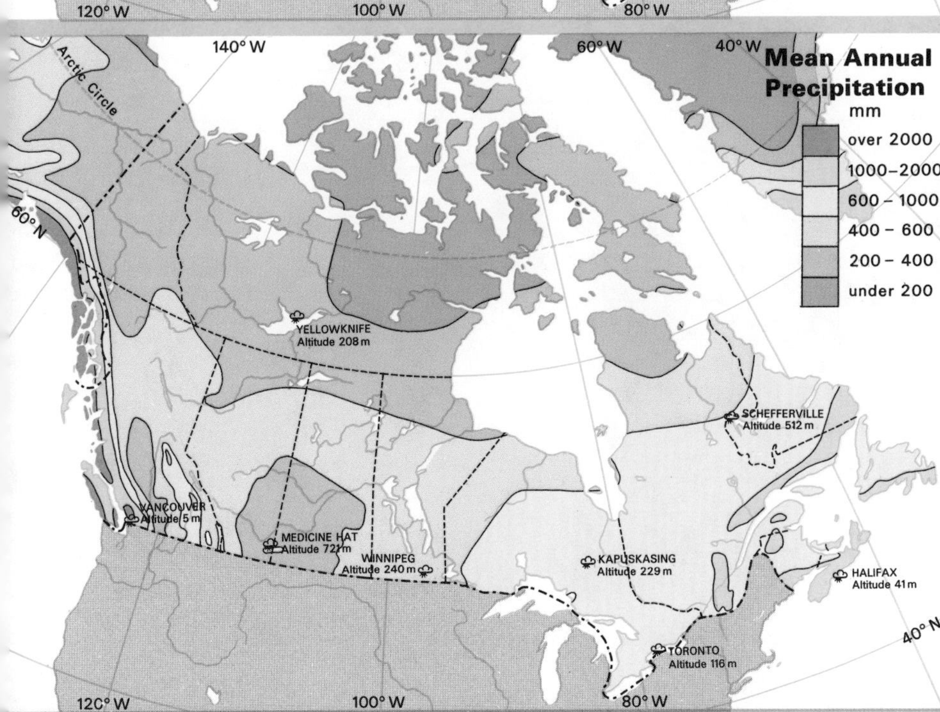
Mean Annual Precipitation
mm
over 2000
1000–2000
600 – 1000
400 – 600
200 – 400
under 200
YELLOWKNIFE Altitude 208 m
SCHEFFERVILLE Altitude 512 m
VANCOUVER Altitude 5 m
MEDICINE HAT Altitude 721 m
WINNIPEG Altitude 240 m
KAPUSKASING Altitude 229 m
HALIFAX Altitude 41 m
TORONTO Altitude 116 m
140° W
60° W
40° W
Arctic Circle
60° N
120° W
100° W
80° W
40° N

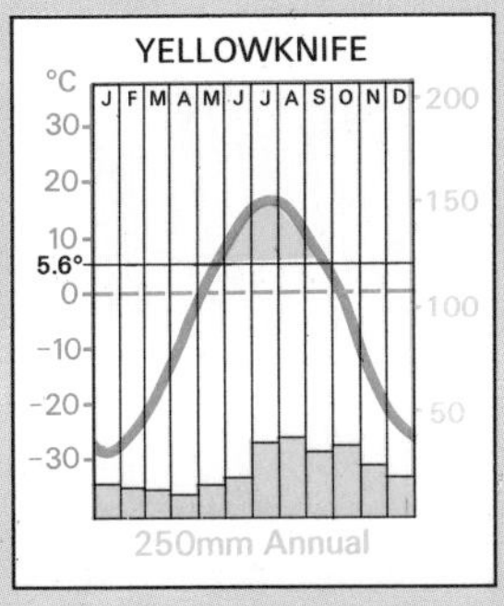
YELLOWKNIFE
°C
J F M A M J J A S O N D
5.6°
250mm Annual

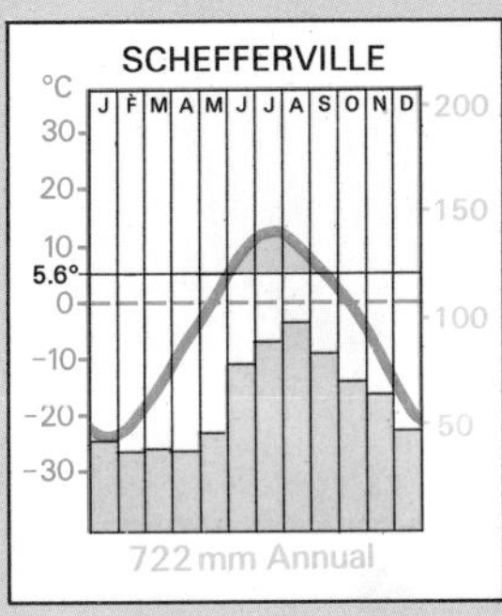
SCHEFFERVILLE
°C
J F M A M J J A S O N D
5.6°
722 mm Annual

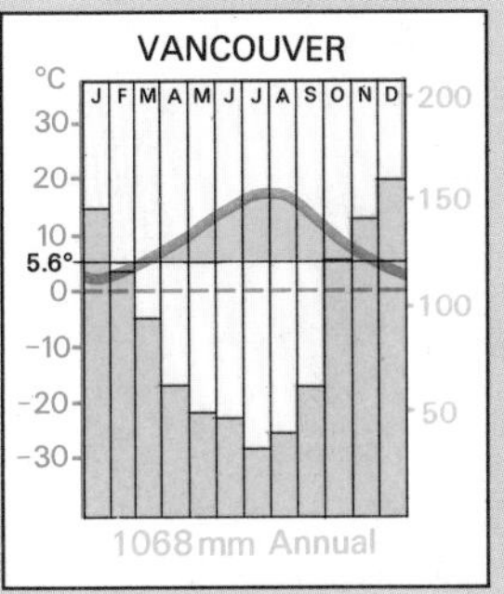
VANCOUVER
°C
J F M A M J J A S O N D
5.6°
1068 mm Annual

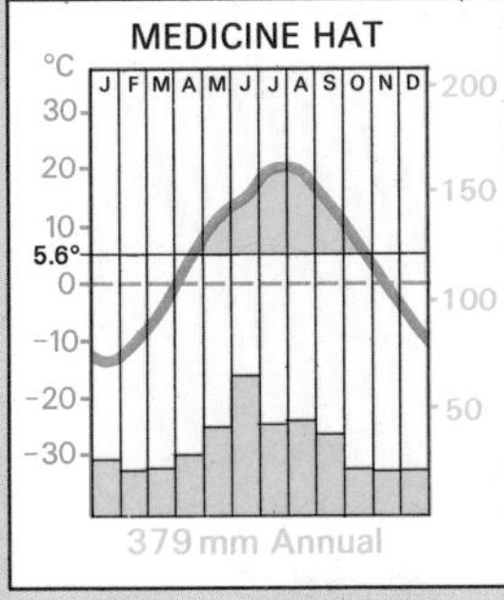
MEDICINE HAT
°C
J F M A M J J A S O N D
5.6°
379 mm Annual

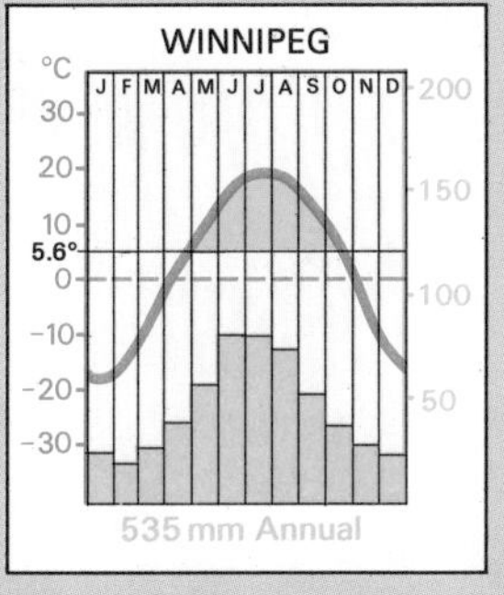
WINNIPEG
°C
J F M A M J J A S O N D
5.6°
535 mm Annual

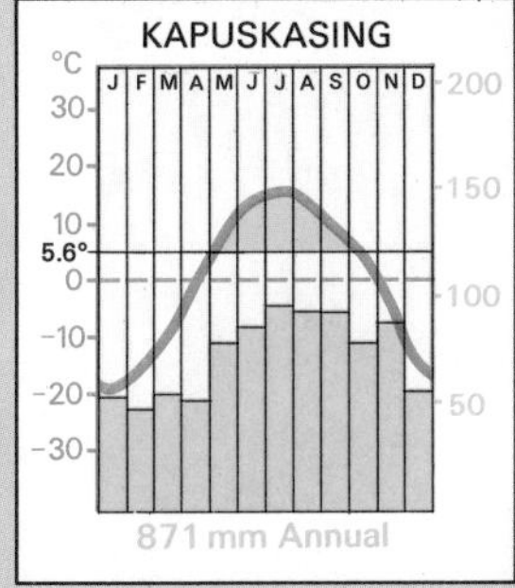
KAPUSKASING
°C
J F M A M J J A S O N D
5.6°
871 mm Annual

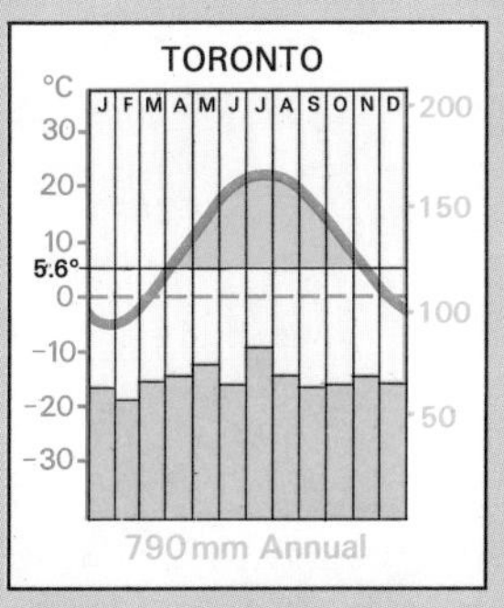
TORONTO
°C
J F M A M J J A S O N D
5.6°
790 mm Annual

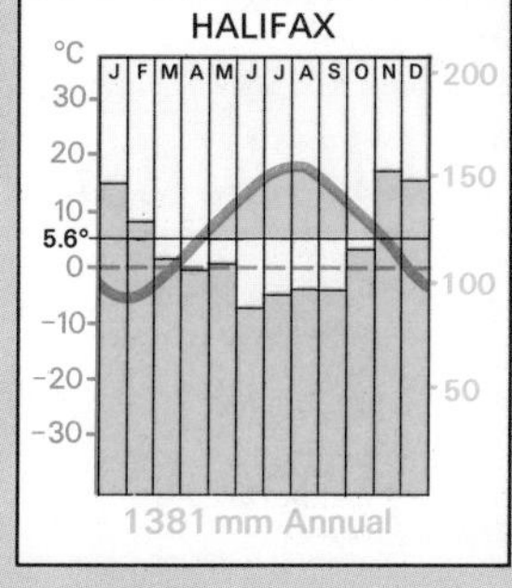
HALIFAX
°C
J F M A M J J A S O N D
5.6°
1381 mm Annual

Growing season starts when temperature rises above 5.6 °C

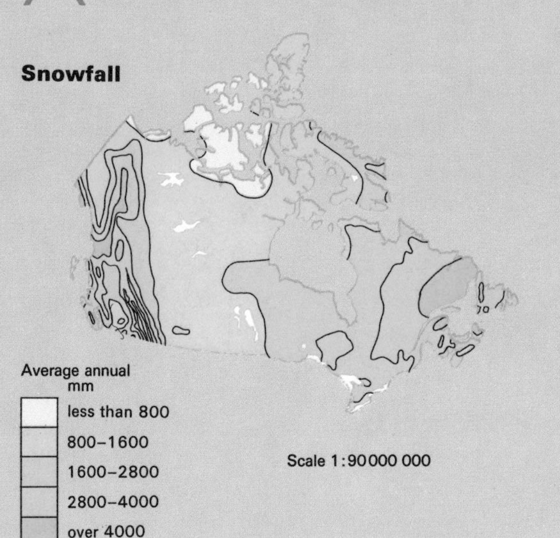
Snowfall
Average annual
mm
less than 800
800–1600
1600–2800
2800–4000
over 4000
Scale 1:90 000 000

Canada: Climate and Physiographic Regions

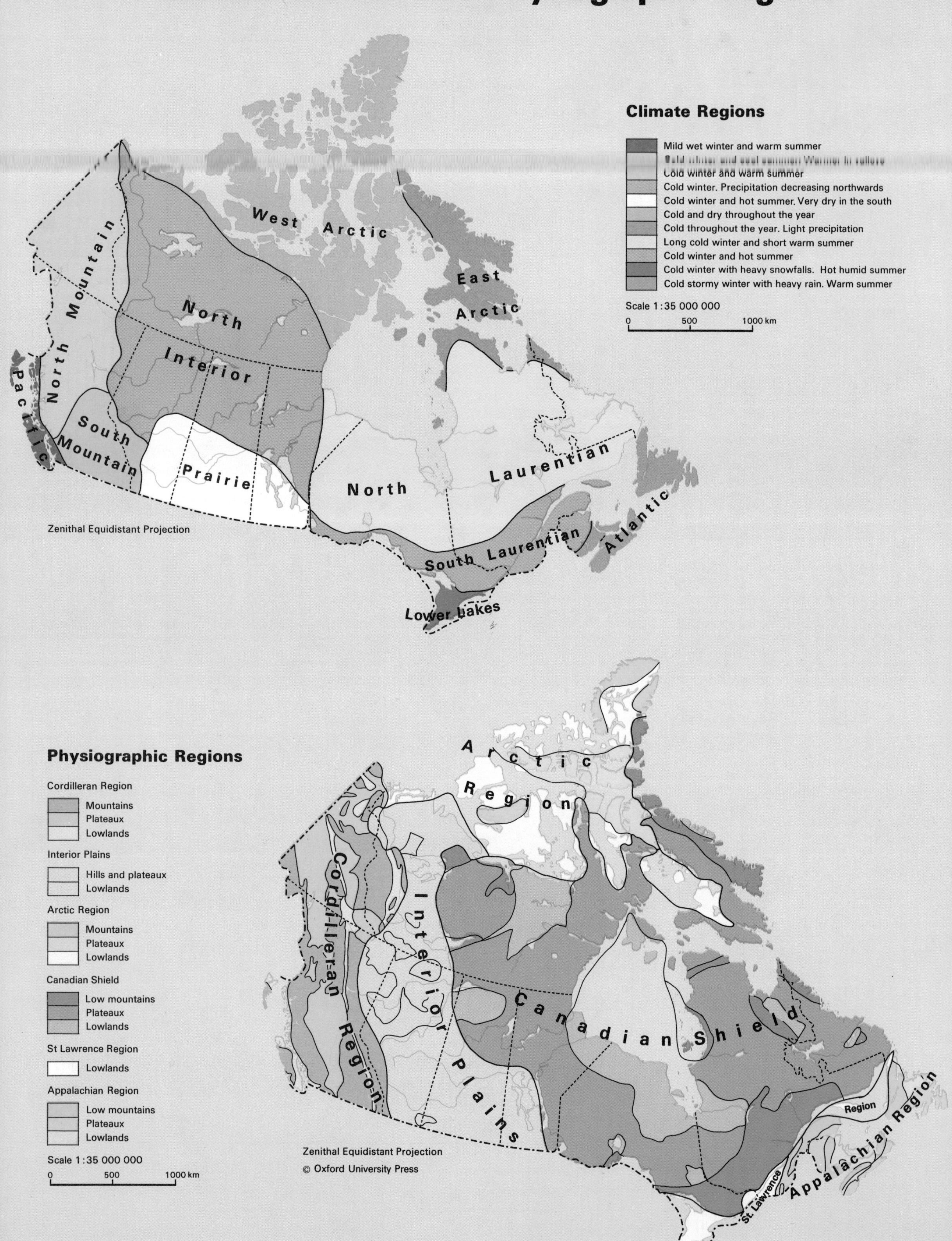
Climate Regions
Mild wet winter and warm summer
Cold winter and warm summer
Cold winter. Precipitation decreasing northwards
Cold winter and hot summer. Very dry in the south
Cold and dry throughout the year
Cold throughout the year. Light precipitation
Long cold winter and short warm summer
Cold winter and hot summer
Cold winter with heavy snowfalls. Hot humid summer
Cold stormy winter with heavy rain. Warm summer
Scale 1:35 000 000
0
500
1000 km
West Arctic
East Arctic
North Mountain
North Interior
Pacific
South Mountain
Prairie
North Laurentian
South Laurentian
Atlantic
Lower Lakes
Zenithal Equidistant Projection
Physiographic Regions
Cordilleran Region
Mountains
Plateaux
Lowlands
Interior Plains
Hills and plateaux
Lowlands
Arctic Region
Mountains
Plateaux
Lowlands
Canadian Shield
Low mountains
Plateaux
Lowlands
St Lawrence Region
Lowlands
Appalachian Region
Low mountains
Plateaux
Lowlands
Scale 1:35 000 000
0
500
1000 km
Arctic Region
Cordilleran Region
Interior Plains
Canadian Shield
St Lawrence Region
Appalachian Region
Zenithal Equidistant Projection
© Oxford University Press

Canada: Vegetation and Soils

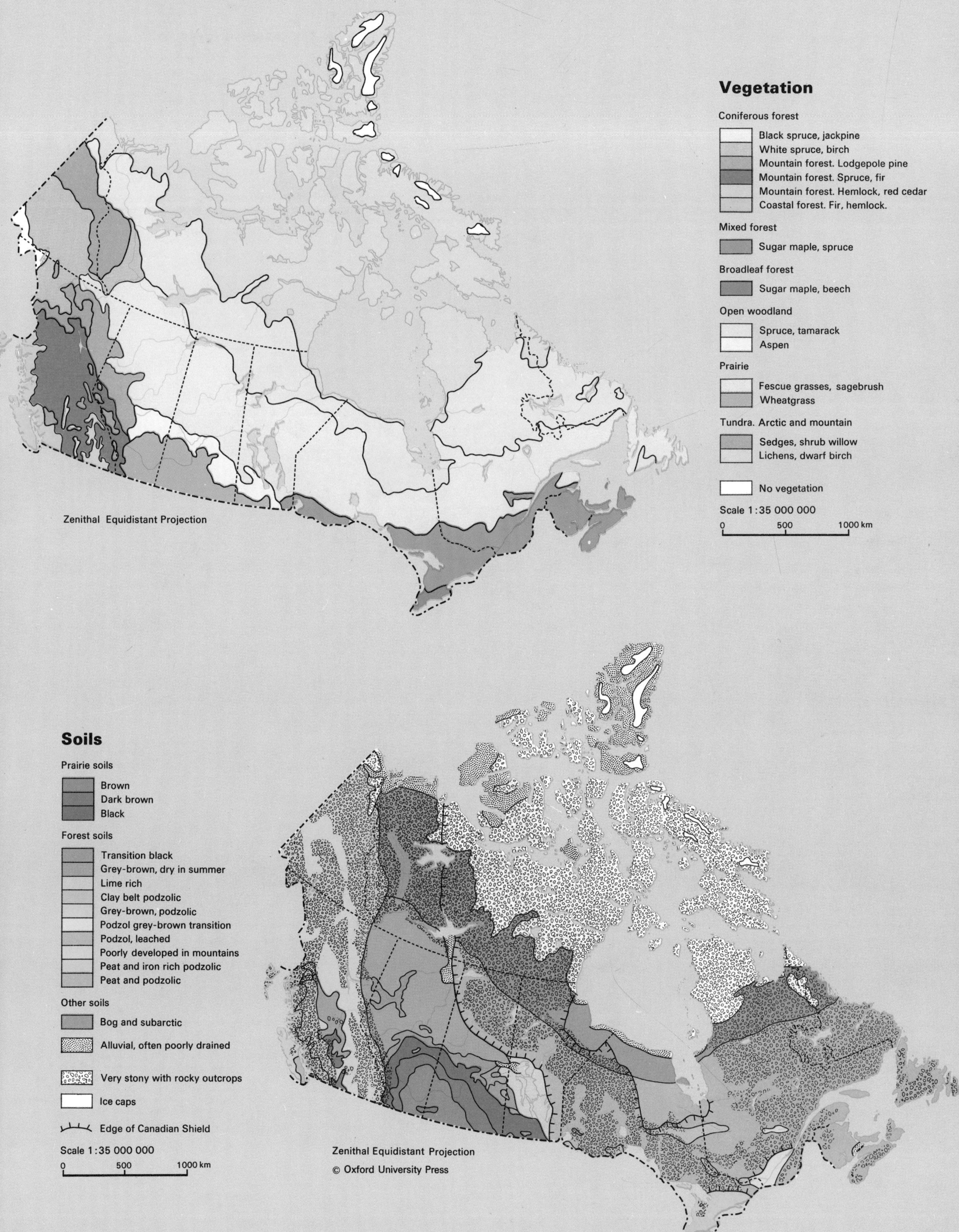
Vegetation
Coniferous forest
Black spruce, jackpine
White spruce, birch
Mountain forest. Lodgepole pine
Mountain forest. Spruce, fir
Mountain forest. Hemlock, red cedar
Coastal forest. Fir, hemlock.
Mixed forest
Sugar maple, spruce
Broadleaf forest
Sugar maple, beech
Open woodland
Spruce, tamarack
Aspen
Prairie
Fescue grasses, sagebrush
Wheatgrass
Tundra. Arctic and mountain
Sedges, shrub willow
Lichens, dwarf birch
No vegetation
Scale 1:35 000 000
0
500
1000 km
Zenithal Equidistant Projection
Soils
Prairie soils
Brown
Dark brown
Black
Forest soils
Transition black
Grey-brown, dry in summer
Lime rich
Clay belt podzolic
Grey-brown, podzolic
Podzol grey-brown transition
Podzol, leached
Poorly developed in mountains
Peat and iron rich podzolic
Peat and podzolic
Other soils
Bog and subarctic
Alluvial, often poorly drained
Very stony with rocky outcrops
Ice caps
Edge of Canadian Shield
Scale 1:35 000 000
0
500
1000 km
Zenithal Equidistant Projection

Canada: Population

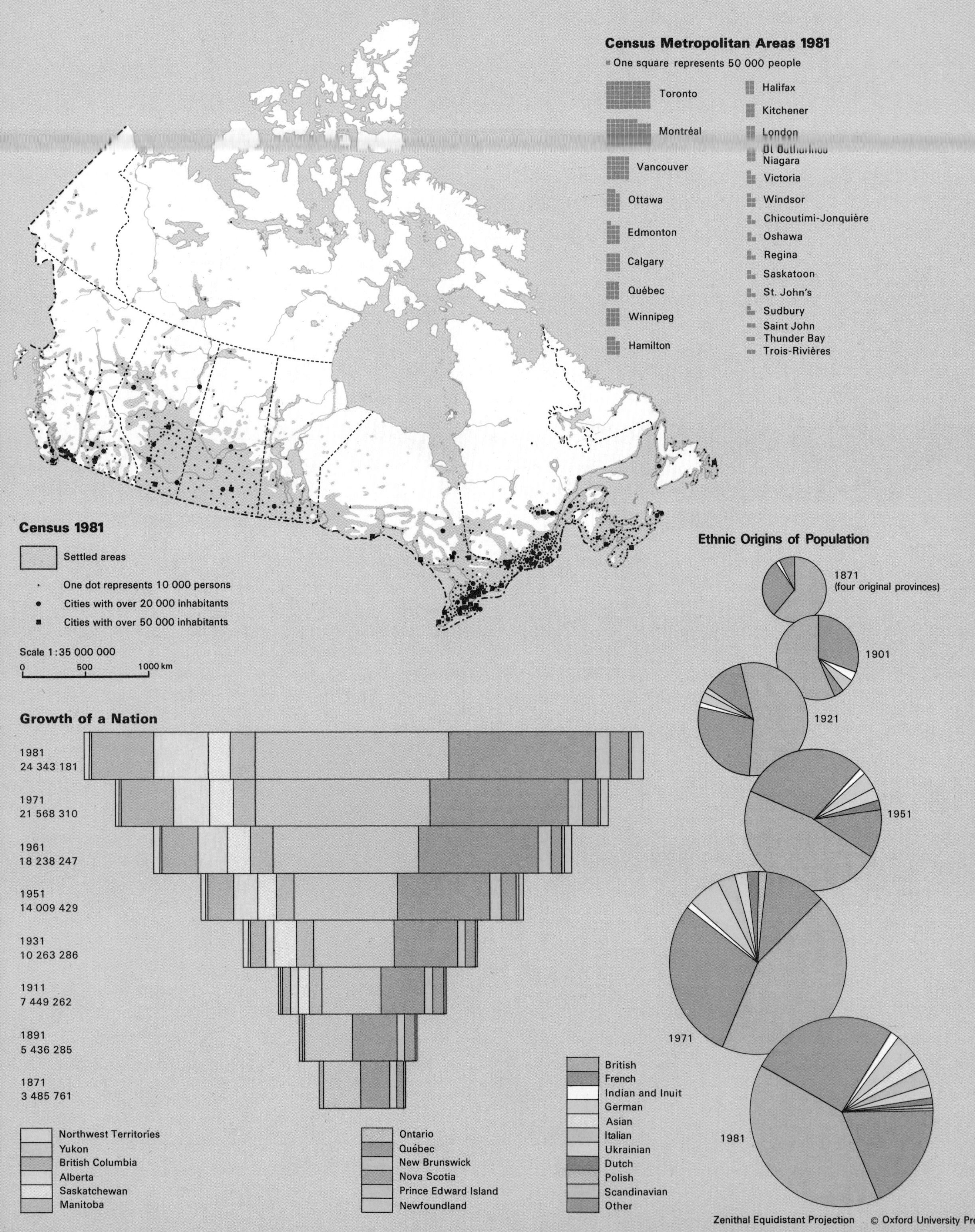

Census Metropolitan Areas 1981
One square represents 50 000 people
Toronto
Montréal
Vancouver
Ottawa
Edmonton
Calgary
Québec
Winnipeg
Hamilton
Halifax
Kitchener
London
Niagara
Victoria
Windsor
Chicoutimi-Jonquière
Oshawa
Regina
Saskatoon
St. John's
Sudbury
Saint John
Thunder Bay
Trois-Rivières
Census 1981
Settled areas
One dot represents 10 000 persons
Cities with over 20 000 inhabitants
Cities with over 50 000 inhabitants
Scale 1:35 000 000
0
500
1000 km
Growth of a Nation
1981
24 343 181
1971
21 568 310
1961
18 238 247
1951
14 009 429
1931
10 263 286
1911
7 449 262
1891
5 436 285
1871
3 485 761
Northwest Territories
Yukon
British Columbia
Alberta
Saskatchewan
Manitoba
Ontario
Québec
New Brunswick
Nova Scotia
Prince Edward Island
Newfoundland
Ethnic Origins of Population
1871
(four original provinces)
1901
1921
1951
1971
1981
British
French
Indian and Inuit
German
Asian
Italian
Ukrainian
Dutch
Polish
Scandinavian
Other
Zenithal Equidistant Projection
© Oxford University Pres

Canada: Transportation

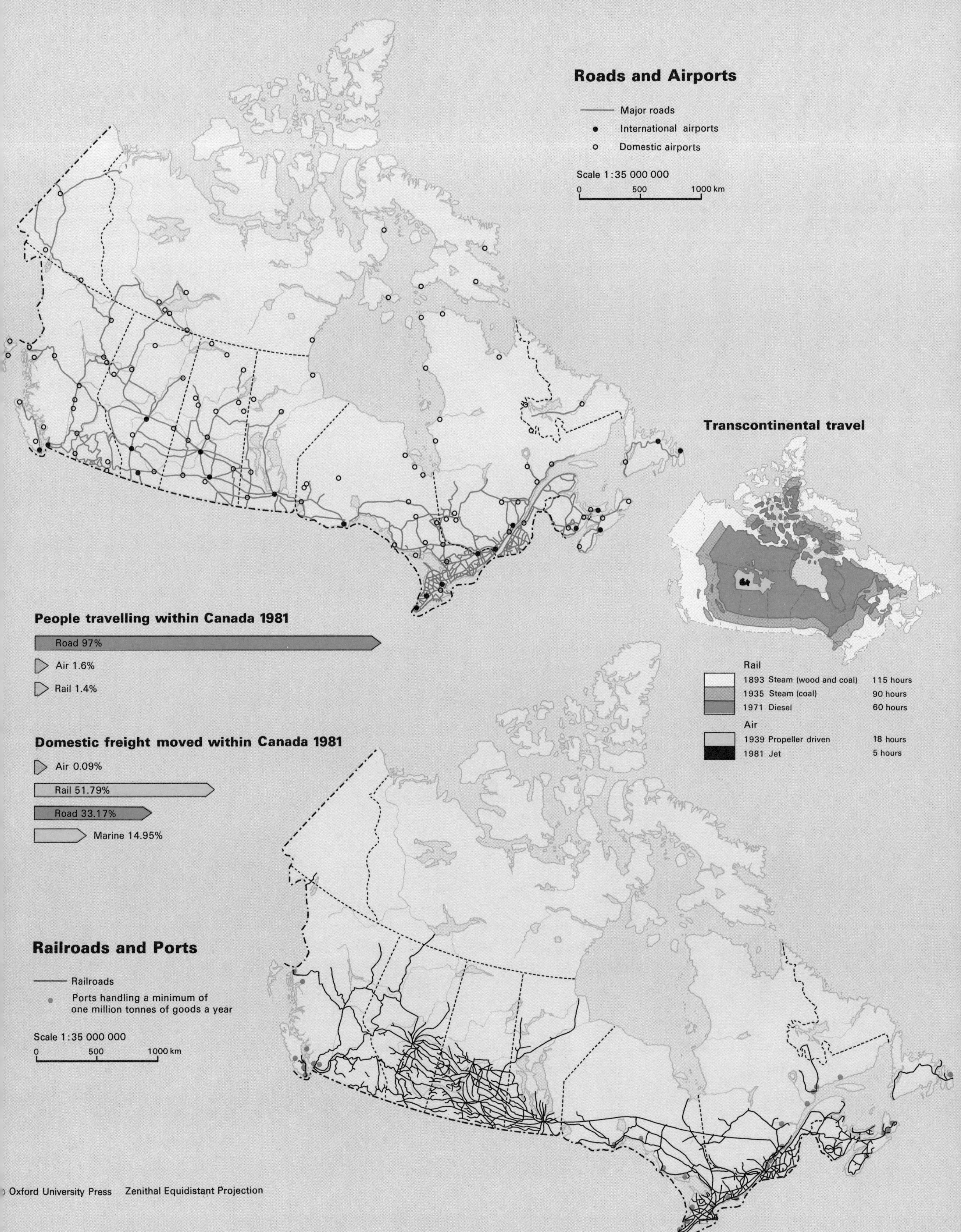
Roads and Airports
Major roads
International airports
Domestic airports
Scale 1:35 000 000
0
500
1000 km
Transcontinental travel
Rail
1893 Steam (wood and coal) 115 hours
1935 Steam (coal) 90 hours
1971 Diesel 60 hours
Air
1939 Propeller driven 18 hours
1981 Jet 5 hours
People travelling within Canada 1981
Road 97%
Air 1.6%
Rail 1.4%
Domestic freight moved within Canada 1981
Air 0.09%
Rail 51.79%
Road 33.17%
Marine 14.95%
Railroads and Ports
Railroads
Ports handling a minimum of one million tonnes of goods a year
Scale 1:35 000 000
0
500
1000 km

 Zenithal Equidistant Projection

Canada: Agriculture

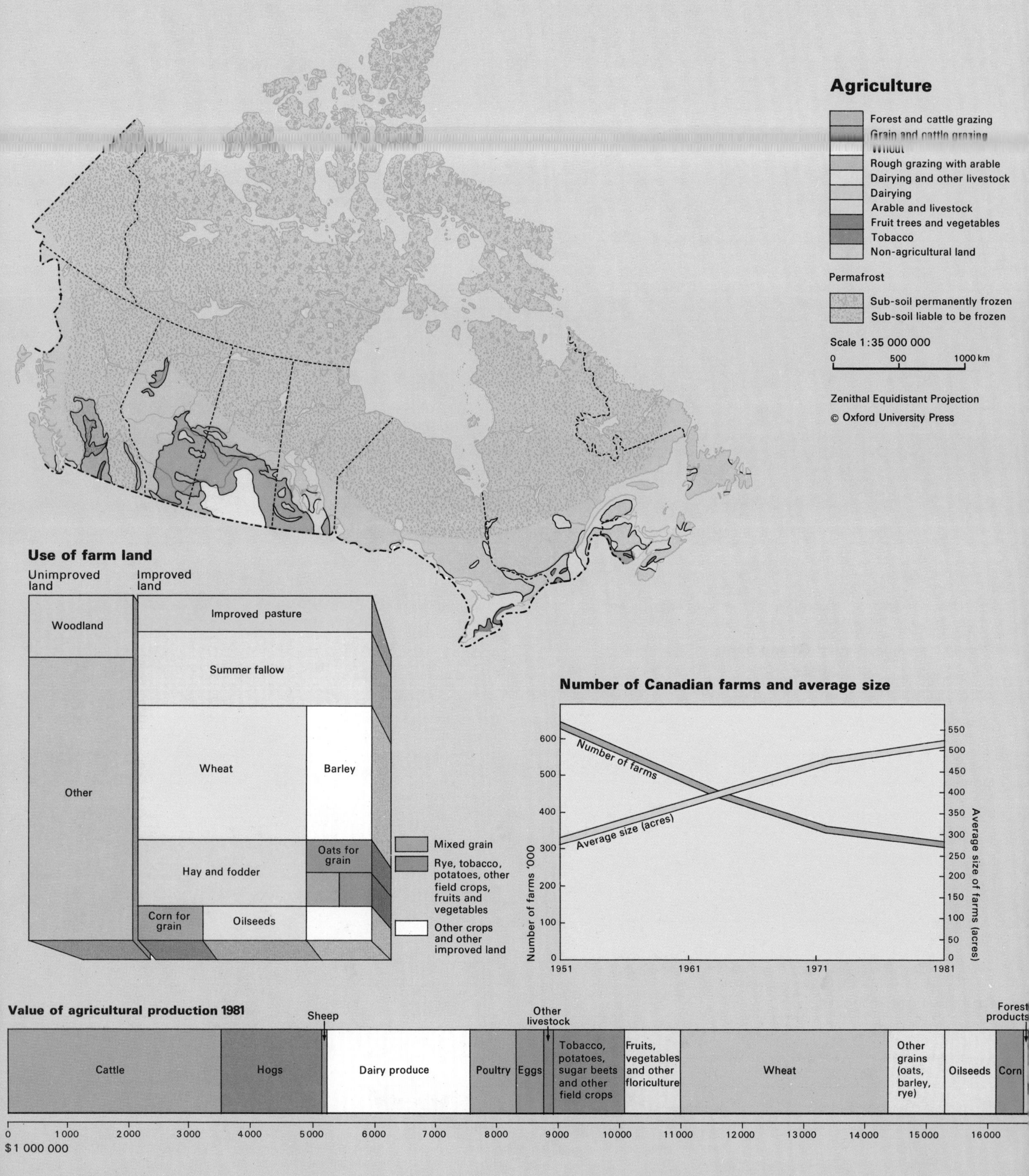
Agriculture
Forest and cattle grazing
Grain and cattle grazing
Rough grazing with arable
Dairying and other livestock
Dairying
Arable and livestock
Fruit trees and vegetables
Tobacco
Non-agricultural land
Permafrost
Sub-soil permanently frozen
Sub-soil liable to be frozen
Scale 1:35 000 000
0
500
1000 km
Zenithal Equidistant Projection
© Oxford University Press
Use of farm land
Unimproved land
Improved land
Woodland
Other
Improved pasture
Summer fallow
Wheat
Barley
Hay and fodder
Oats for grain
Corn for grain
Oilseeds
Mixed grain
Rye, tobacco, potatoes, other field crops, fruits and vegetables
Other crops and other improved land
Number of Canadian farms and average size
Number of farms
Average size (acres)
Number of farms '000
Average size of farms (acres)
600
500
400
300
200
100
0
550
500
450
400
350
300
250
200
150
100
50
0
1951
1961
1971
1981
Value of agricultural production 1981
Sheep
Other livestock
Forest products
Cattle
Hogs
Dairy produce
Poultry
Eggs
Tobacco, potatoes, sugar beets and other field crops
Fruits, vegetables and other floriculture
Wheat
Other grains (oats, barley, rye)
Oilseeds
Corn
0
1000
2000
3000
4000
5000
6000
7000
8000
9000
10000
11000
12000
13000
14000
15000
16000
$1 000 000

Land in farms

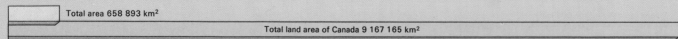

Total area 658 893 km²

Total land area of Canada 9 167 165 km²

Canada: Forestry

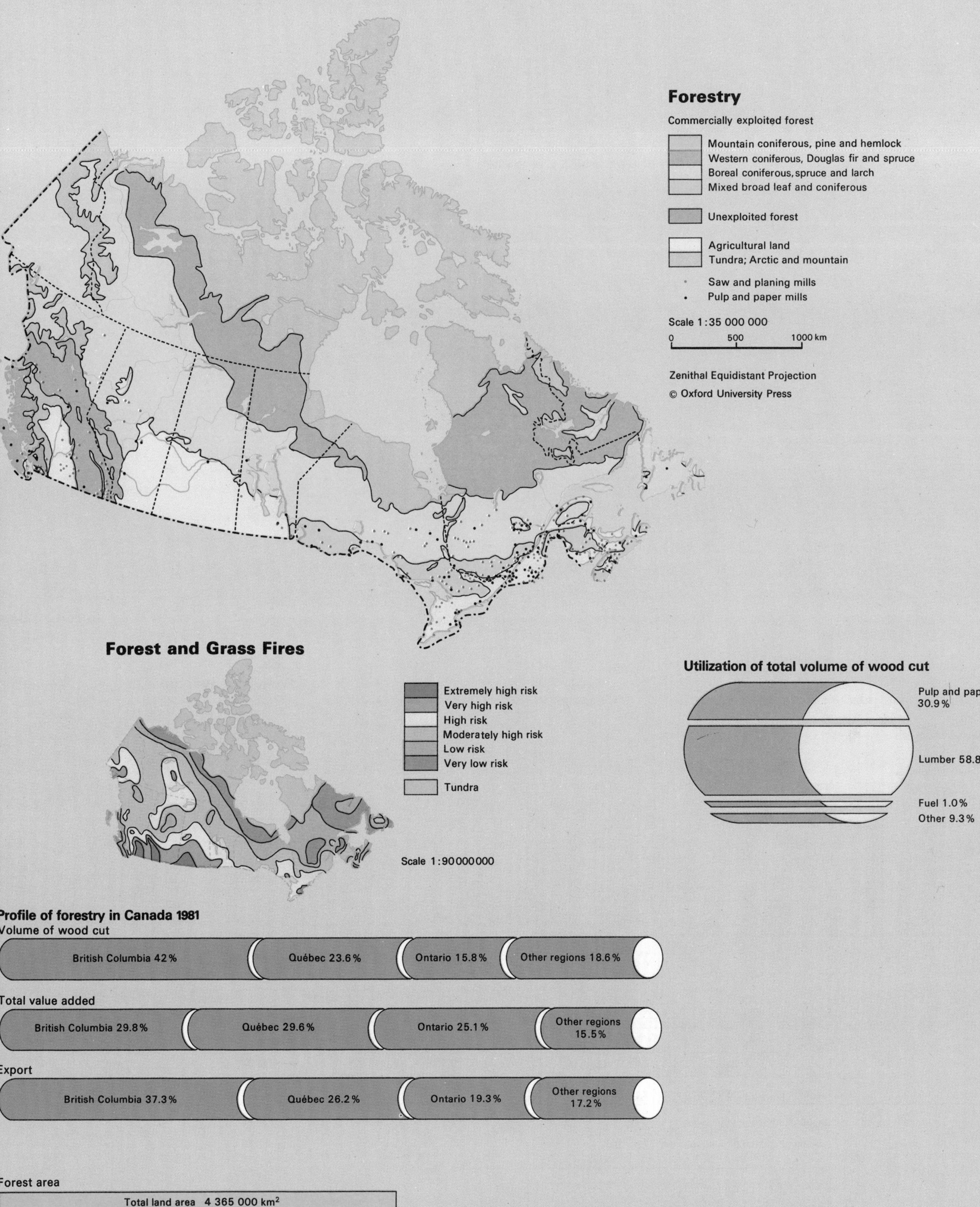
Forestry
Commercially exploited forest
Mountain coniferous, pine and hemlock
Western coniferous, Douglas fir and spruce
Boreal coniferous, spruce and larch
Mixed broad leaf and coniferous
Unexploited forest
Agricultural land
Tundra; Arctic and mountain
Saw and planing mills
Pulp and paper mills
Scale 1:35 000 000
0
500
1000 km
Zenithal Equidistant Projection
© Oxford University Press
Forest and Grass Fires
Extremely high risk
Very high risk
High risk
Moderately high risk
Low risk
Very low risk
Tundra
Scale 1:90000000
Utilization of total volume of wood cut
Pulp and paper 30.9%
Lumber 58.8%
Fuel 1.0%
Other 9.3%
Profile of forestry in Canada 1981
Volume of wood cut
British Columbia 42%
Québec 23.6%
Ontario 15.8%
Other regions 18.6%
Total value added
British Columbia 29.8%
Québec 29.6%
Ontario 25.1%
Other regions 15.5%
Export
British Columbia 37.3%
Québec 26.2%
Ontario 19.3%
Other regions 17.2%
Forest area
Total land area 4 365 000 km²
Total land area of Canada 9 167 165 km²

Canada: Fishing

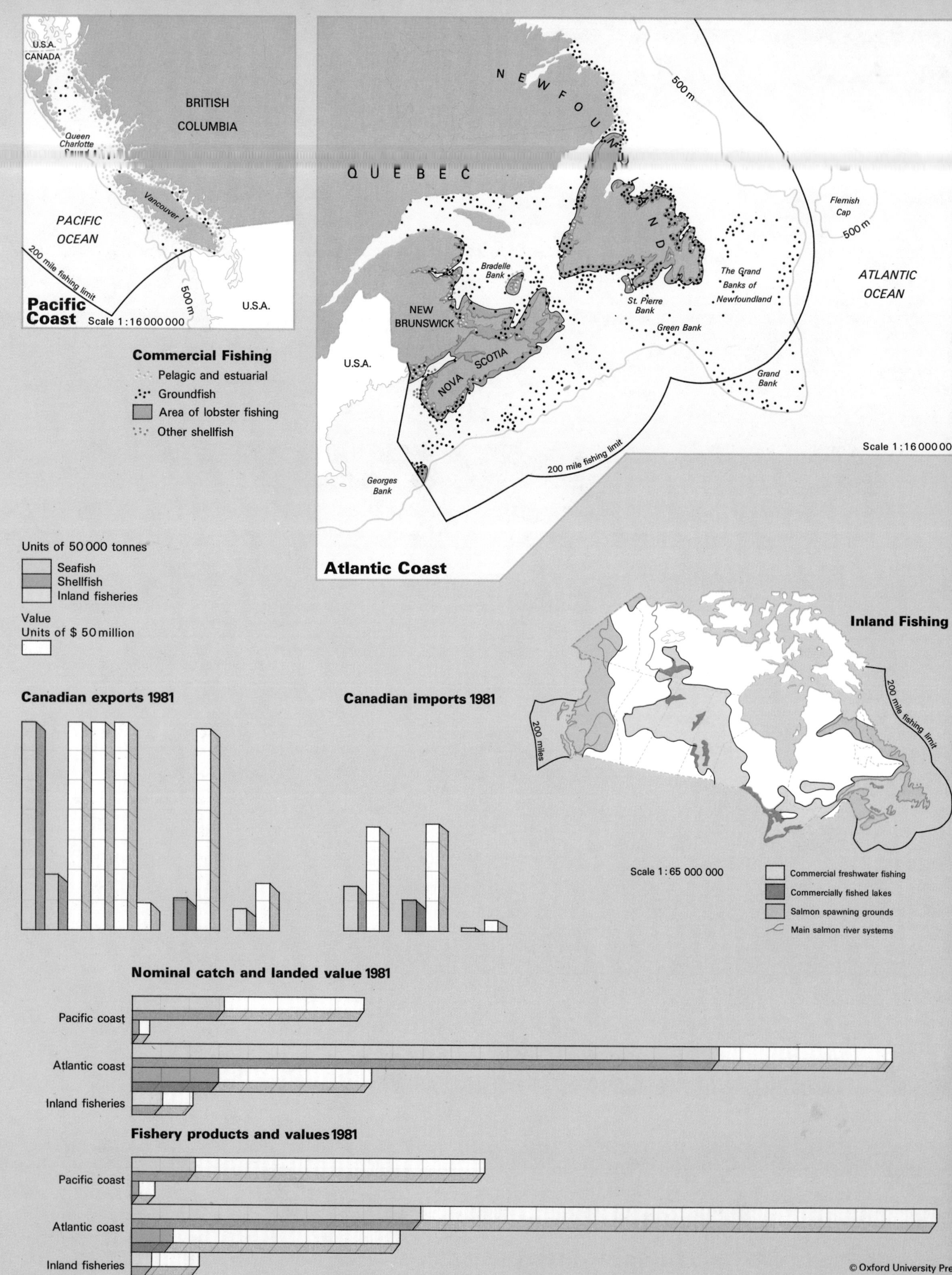
U.S.A.
CANADA
BRITISH COLUMBIA
Queen Charlotte Sound
Vancouver I.
PACIFIC OCEAN
200 mile fishing limit
500 m
U.S.A.
Pacific Coast
Scale 1:16 000 000
NEWFOUNDLAND
QUEBEC
500 m
Flemish Cap
500 m
ATLANTIC OCEAN
Bradelle Bank
The Grand Banks of Newfoundland
St. Pierre Bank
Green Bank
NEW BRUNSWICK
NOVA SCOTIA
U.S.A.
Grand Bank
Scale 1:16 000 000
200 mile fishing limit
Georges Bank
Atlantic Coast
Commercial Fishing
Pelagic and estuarial
Groundfish
Area of lobster fishing
Other shellfish
Units of 50 000 tonnes
Seafish
Shellfish
Inland fisheries
Value
Units of $ 50 million
Inland Fishing
200 mile fishing limit
200 miles
Scale 1:65 000 000
Commercial freshwater fishing
Commercially fished lakes
Salmon spawning grounds
Main salmon river systems
Canadian exports 1981
Canadian imports 1981
Nominal catch and landed value 1981
Pacific coast
Atlantic coast
Inland fisheries
Fishery products and values 1981
Pacific coast
Atlantic coast
Inland fisheries

Canada: Mining

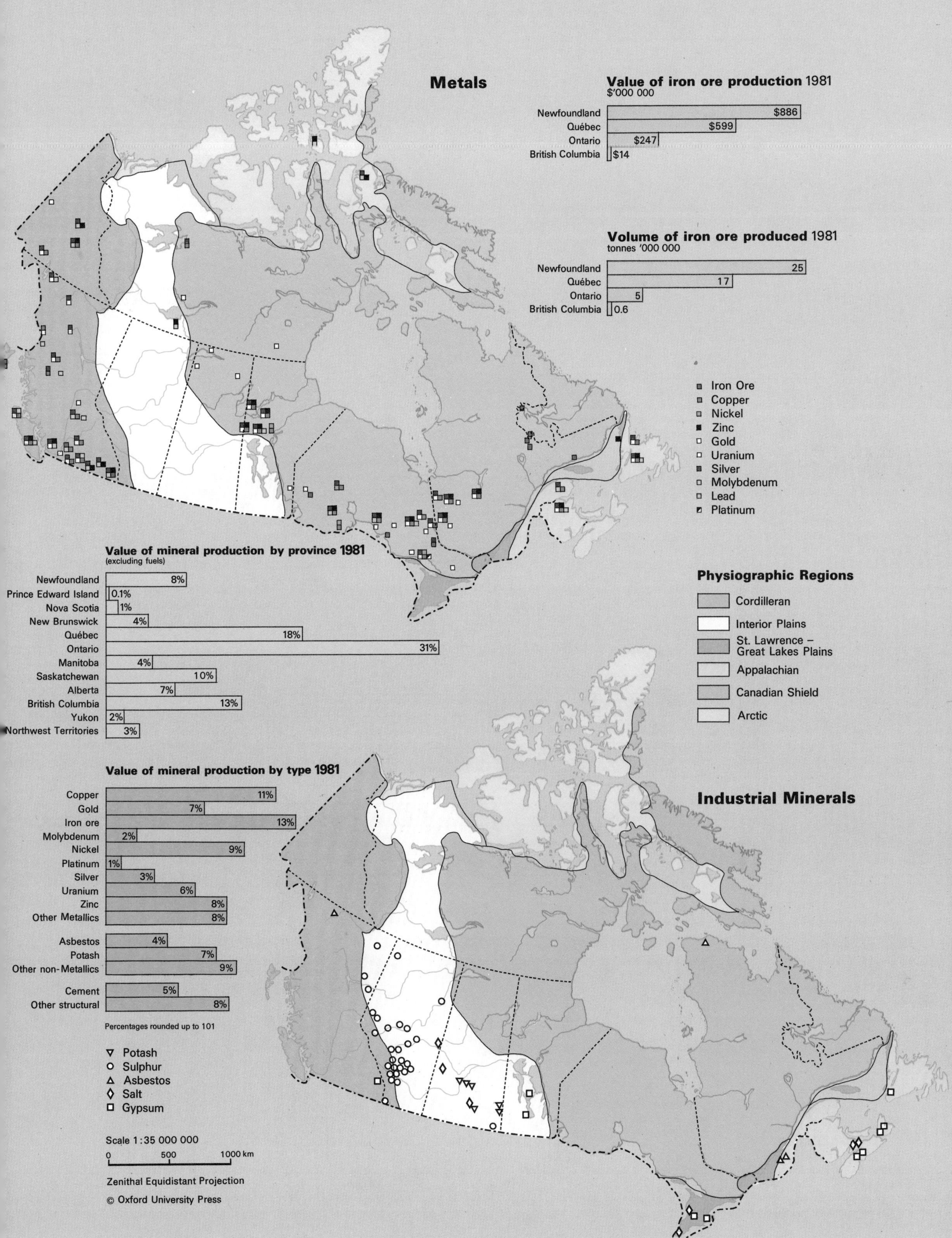
Metals
Value of iron ore production 1981
$'000 000
Newfoundland $886
Québec $599
Ontario $247
British Columbia $14
Volume of iron ore produced 1981
tonnes '000 000
Newfoundland 25
Québec 17
Ontario 5
British Columbia 0.6
Iron Ore
Copper
Nickel
Zinc
Gold
Uranium
Silver
Molybdenum
Lead
Platinum
Value of mineral production by province 1981
(excluding fuels)
Newfoundland 8%
Prince Edward Island 0.1%
Nova Scotia 1%
New Brunswick 4%
Québec 18%
Ontario 31%
Manitoba 4%
Saskatchewan 10%
Alberta 7%
British Columbia 13%
Yukon 2%
Northwest Territories 3%
Physiographic Regions
Cordilleran
Interior Plains
St. Lawrence – Great Lakes Plains
Appalachian
Canadian Shield
Arctic
Value of mineral production by type 1981
Copper 11%
Gold 7%
Iron ore 13%
Molybdenum 2%
Nickel 9%
Platinum 1%
Silver 3%
Uranium 6%
Zinc 8%
Other Metallics 8%
Asbestos 4%
Potash 7%
Other non-Metallics 9%
Cement 5%
Other structural 8%
Percentages rounded up to 101
Industrial Minerals
Potash
Sulphur
Asbestos
Salt
Gypsum
Scale 1:35 000 000
0
500
1000 km
Zenithal Equidistant Projection

Canada: Energy

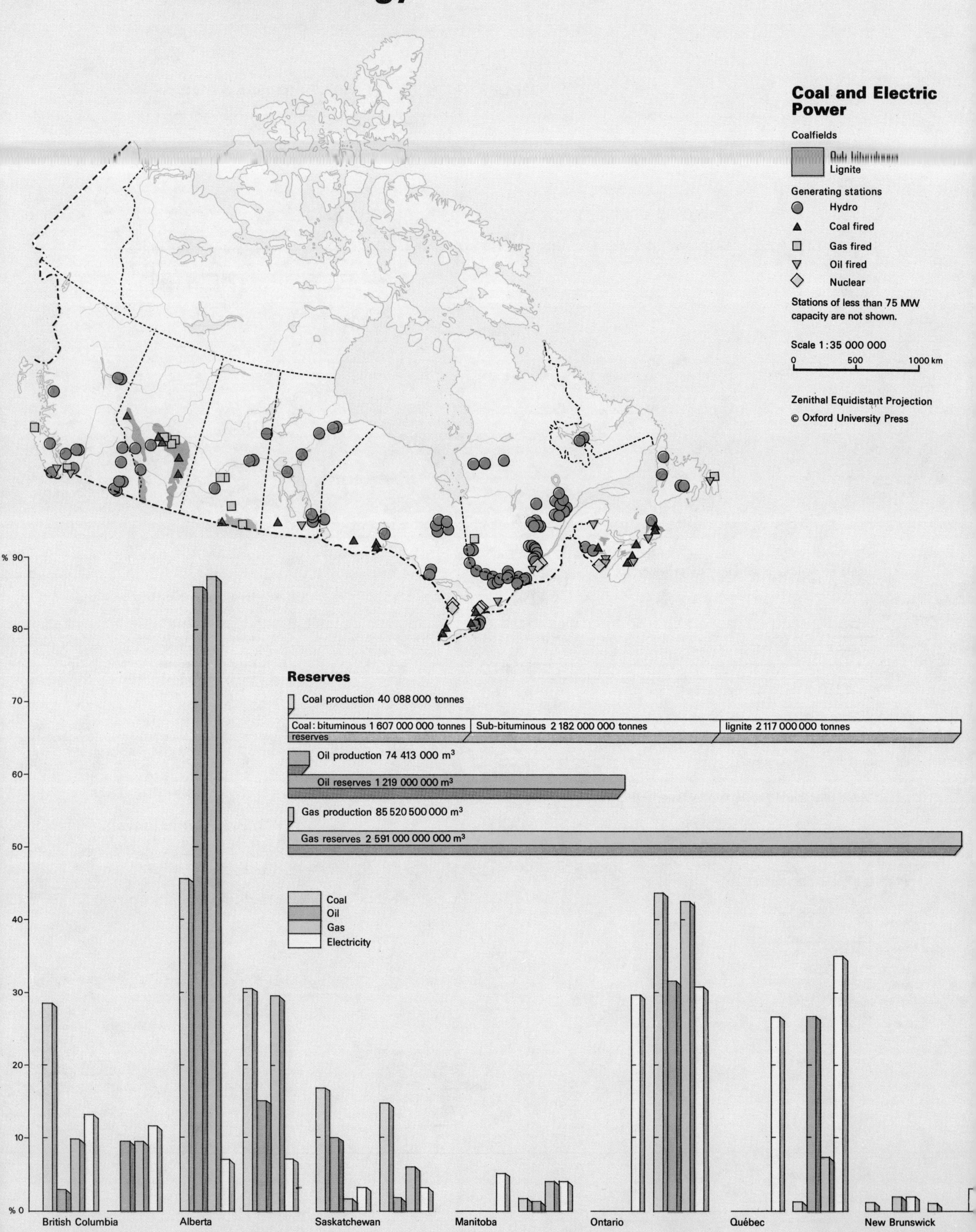
Coal and Electric Power
Coalfields
Sub-bituminous
Lignite
Generating stations
Hydro
Coal fired
Gas fired
Oil fired
Nuclear
Stations of less than 75 MW capacity are not shown.
Scale 1:35 000 000
0
500
1000 km
Zenithal Equidistant Projection
© Oxford University Press
Reserves
Coal production 40 088 000 tonnes
Coal: bituminous 1 607 000 000 tonnes
reserves
Sub-bituminous 2 182 000 000 tonnes
lignite 2 117 000 000 tonnes
Oil production 74 413 000 m³
Oil reserves 1 219 000 000 m³
Gas production 85 520 500 000 m³
Gas reserves 2 591 000 000 000 m³
Coal
Oil
Gas
Electricity
% 90
80
70
60
50
40
30
20
10
% 0
British Columbia
Alberta
Saskatchewan
Manitoba
Ontario
Québec
New Brunswick

Production and consumption 1981
includes imports

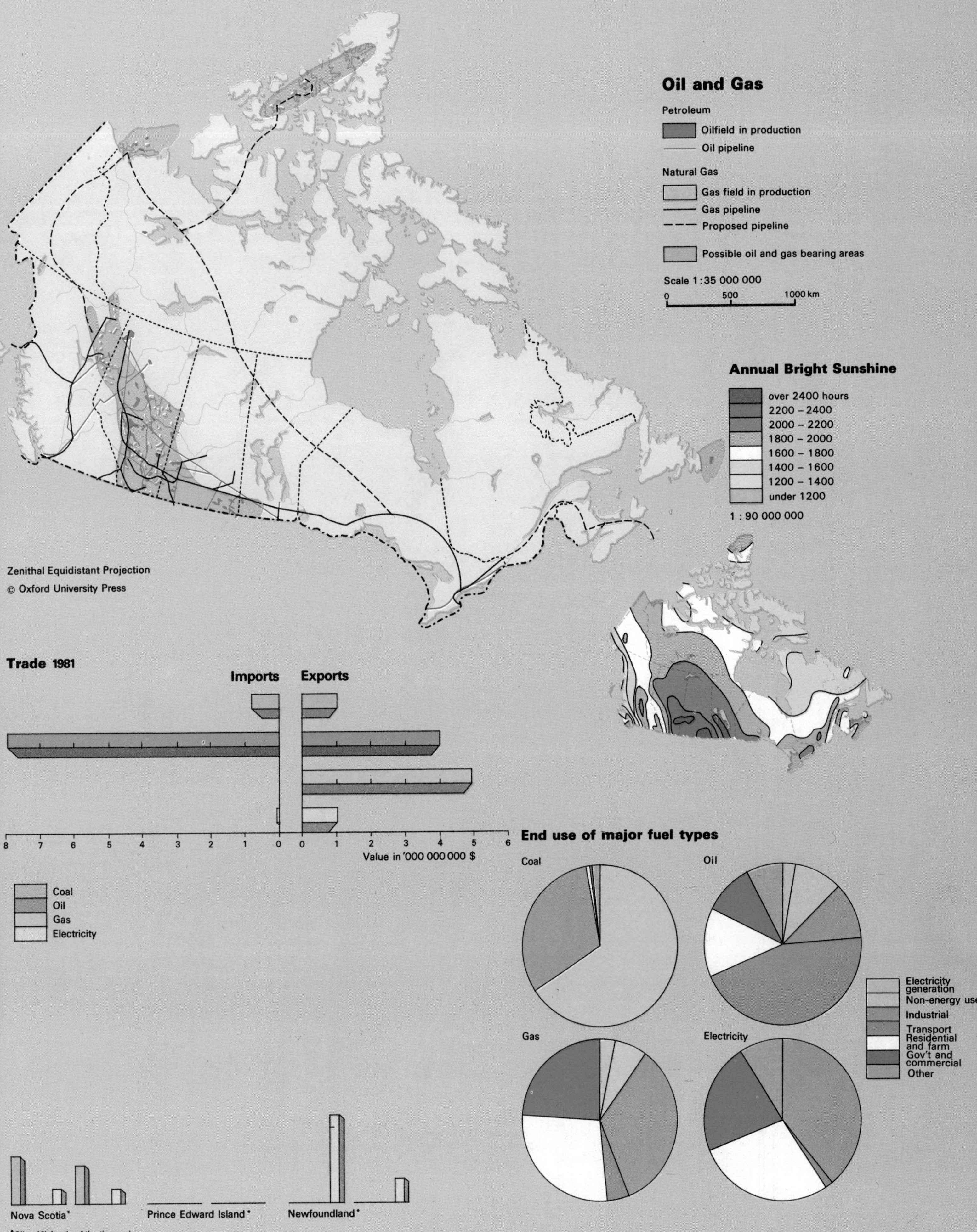

Oil and Gas
Petroleum
Oilfield in production
Oil pipeline
Natural Gas
Gas field in production
Gas pipeline
Proposed pipeline
Possible oil and gas bearing areas
Scale 1:35 000 000
0
500
1000 km
Annual Bright Sunshine
over 2400 hours
2200 – 2400
2000 – 2200
1800 – 2000
1600 – 1800
1400 – 1600
1200 – 1400
under 1200
1 : 90 000 000
Zenithal Equidistant Projection
© Oxford University Press
Trade 1981
Imports
Exports
8 7 6 5 4 3 2 1 0
0 1 2 3 4 5 6
Value in '000 000 000 $
Coal
Oil
Gas
Electricity
End use of major fuel types
Coal
Oil
Gas
Electricity
Electricity generation
Non-energy use
Industrial
Transport
Residential and farm
Gov't and commercial
Other
Nova Scotia*
Prince Edward Island*
Newfoundland*
*Oil = 1% for the Atlantic provinces

Canada: Manufacturing

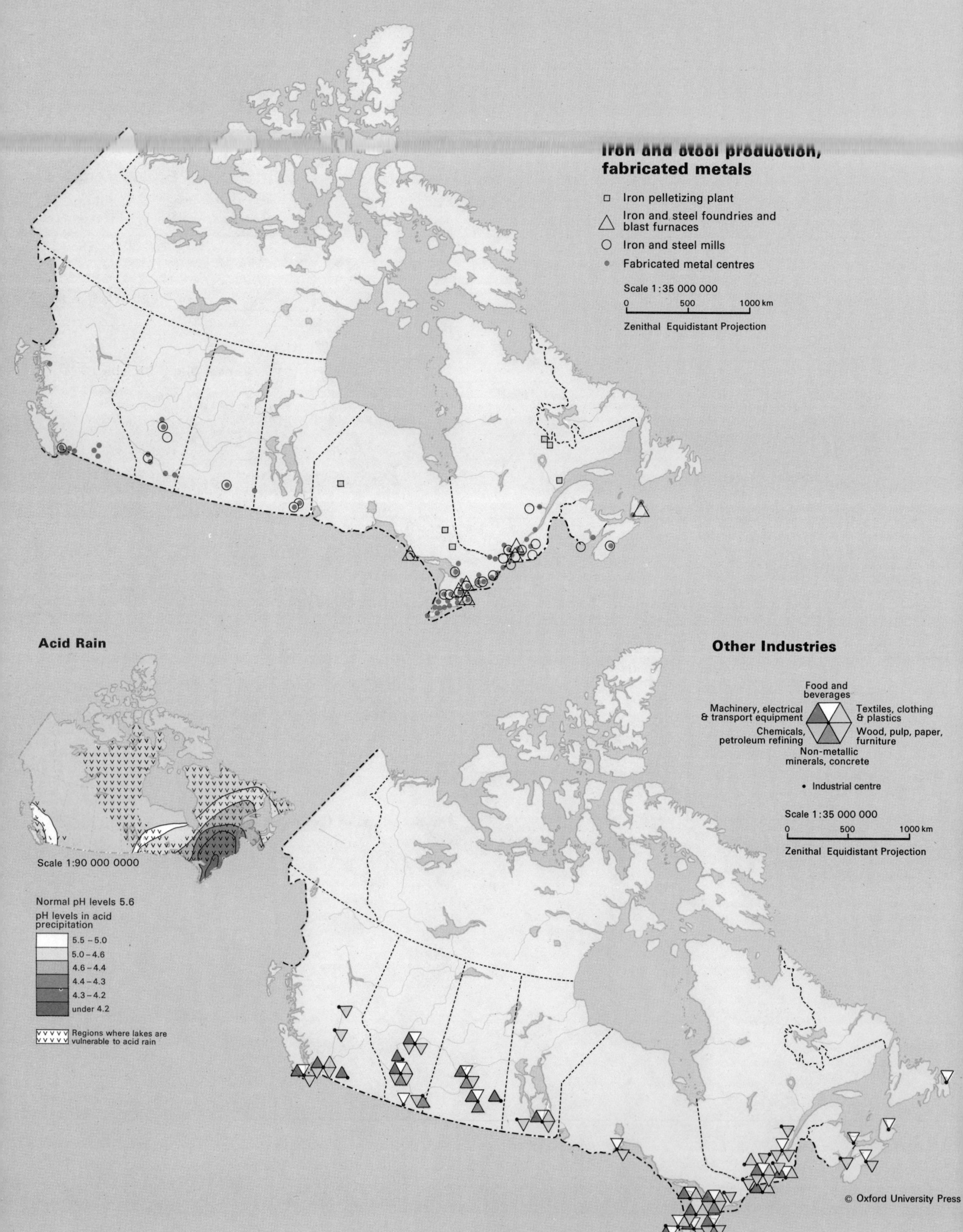
Iron and steel production, fabricated metals
Iron pelletizing plant
Iron and steel foundries and blast furnaces
Iron and steel mills
Fabricated metal centres
Scale 1:35 000 000
0 500 1000 km
Zenithal Equidistant Projection
Acid Rain
Scale 1:90 000 0000
Normal pH levels 5.6
pH levels in acid precipitation
5.5 – 5.0
5.0 – 4.6
4.6 – 4.4
4.4 – 4.3
4.3 – 4.2
under 4.2
Regions where lakes are vulnerable to acid rain
Other Industries
Food and beverages
Textiles, clothing & plastics
Wood, pulp, paper, furniture
Non-metallic minerals, concrete
Chemicals, petroleum refining
Machinery, electrical & transport equipment
Industrial centre
Scale 1:35 000 000
0 500 1000 km
Zenithal Equidistant Projection

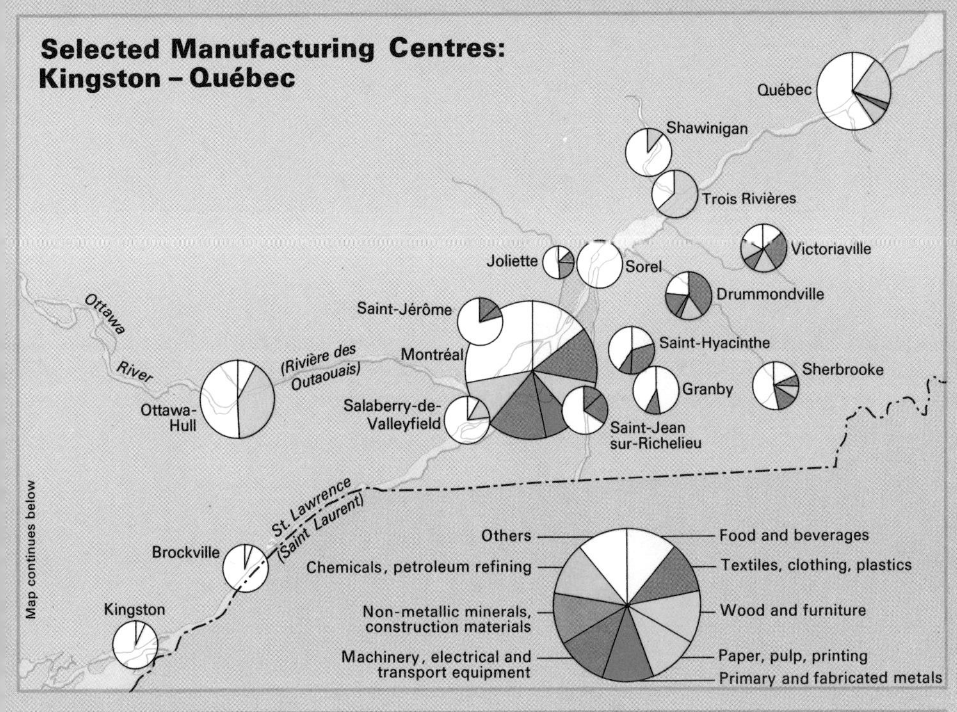

Selected Manufacturing Centres: Kingston – Québec
Québec
Shawinigan
Trois Rivières
Victoriaville
Joliette
Sorel
Drummondville
Saint-Jérôme
Saint-Hyacinthe
Ottawa River
Montréal
(Rivière des Outaouais)
Sherbrooke
Granby
Ottawa-Hull
Salaberry-de-Valleyfield
Saint-Jean sur-Richelieu
St. Lawrence (Saint Laurent)
Brockville
Kingston
Map continues below
Others
Food and beverages
Chemicals, petroleum refining
Textiles, clothing, plastics
Non-metallic minerals, construction materials
Wood and furniture
Machinery, electrical and transport equipment
Paper, pulp, printing
Primary and fabricated metals

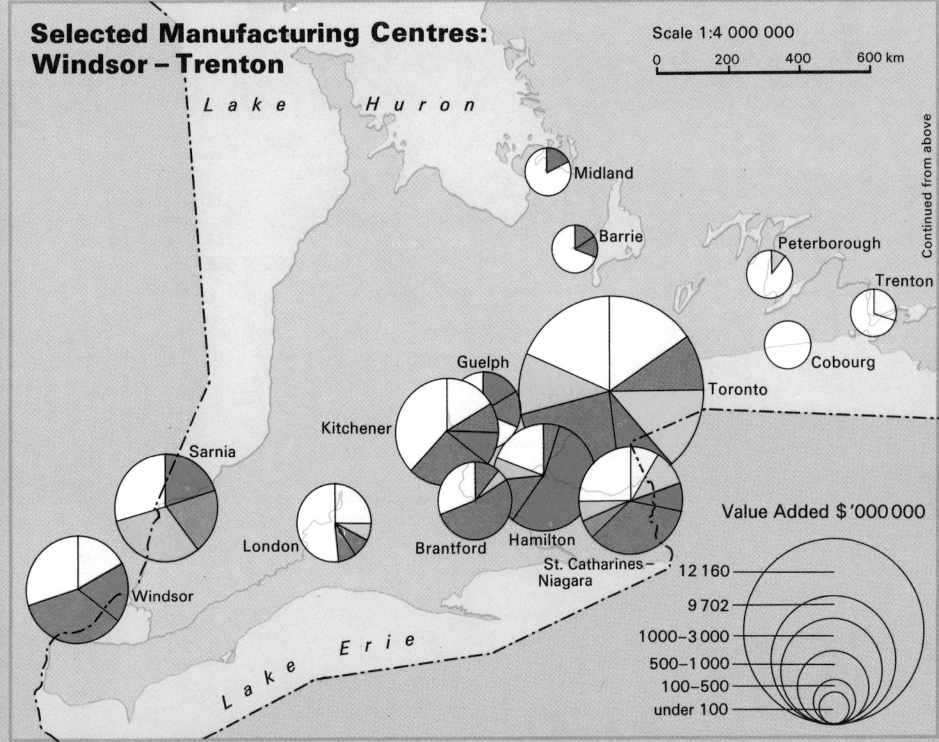

Selected Manufacturing Centres: Windsor – Trenton
Scale 1:4 000 000
0
200
400
600 km
Lake Huron
Continued from above
Midland
Barrie
Peterborough
Trenton
Cobourg
Guelph
Toronto
Kitchener
Sarnia
London
Brantford
Hamilton
St. Catharines-Niagara
Windsor
Lake Erie
Value Added $'000 000
12 160
9 702
1000–3 000
500–1 000
100–500
under 100

The top ten manufacturing industries ranked by value of shipment of goods of own manufacture 1981

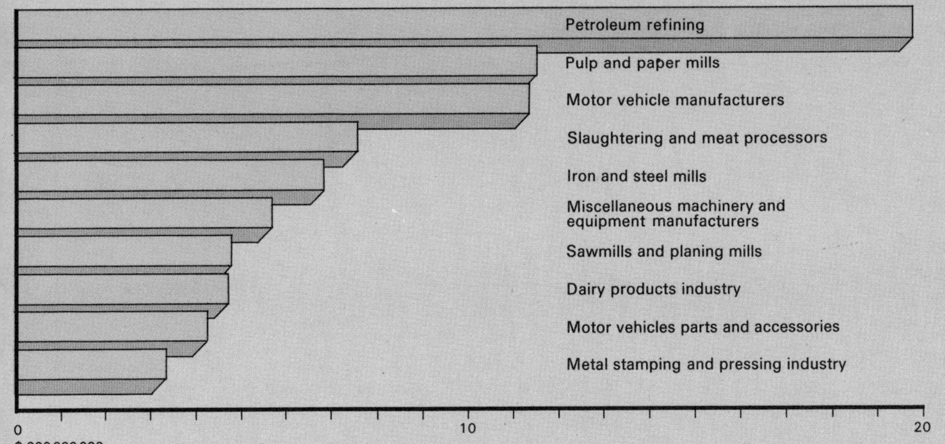

Petroleum refining
Pulp and paper mills
Motor vehicle manufacturers
Slaughtering and meat processors
Iron and steel mills
Miscellaneous machinery and equipment manufacturers
Sawmills and planing mills
Dairy products industry
Motor vehicles parts and accessories
Metal stamping and pressing industry
0
10
20
$ 000 000 000

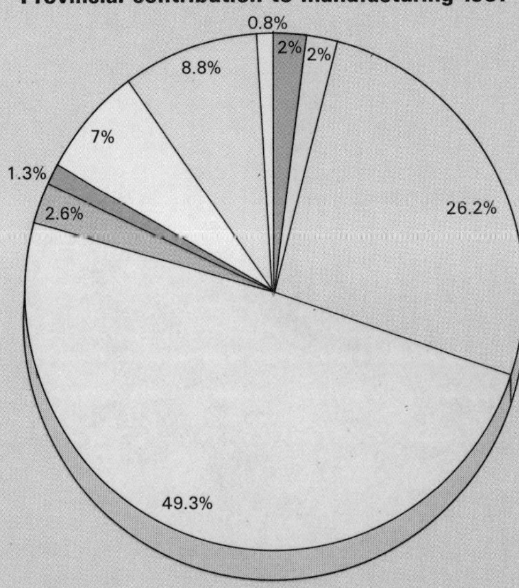

Provincial contribution to manufacturing 1981
0.8%
2%
2%
8.8%
7%
1.3%
2.6%
26.2%
49.3%
Total value of manufacturing $ 190 927 201 000

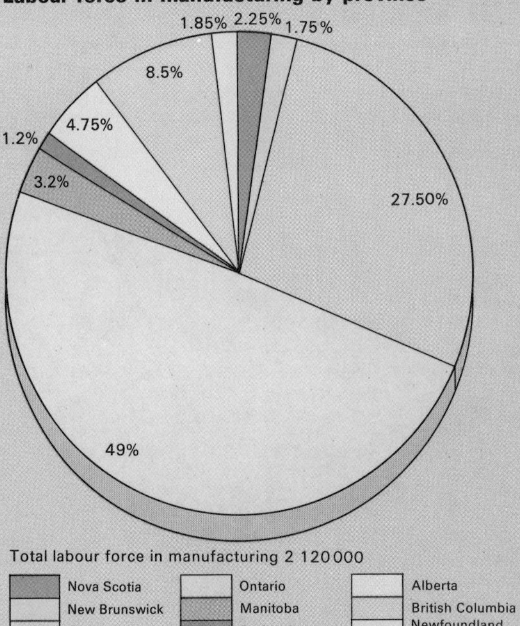

Labour force in manufacturing by province
1.85%
2.25%
1.75%
8.5%
1.2%
4.75%
3.2%
27.50%
49%
Total labour force in manufacturing 2 120 000
Nova Scotia
New Brunswick
Québec
Ontario
Manitoba
Saskatchewan
Alberta
British Columbia
Newfoundland, Prince Edward Island Yukon and Northwest Territories

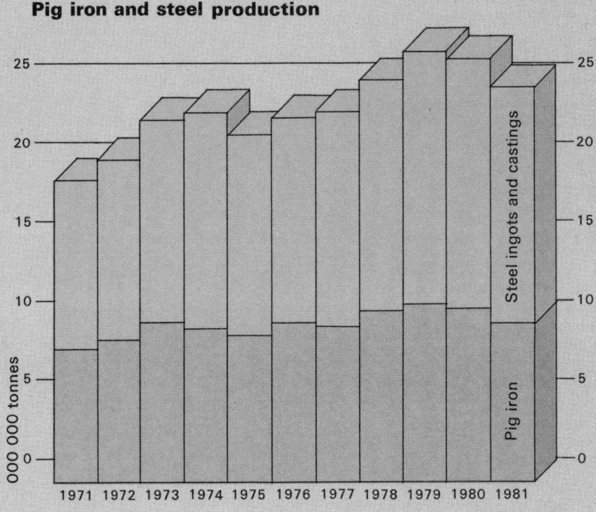

Pig iron and steel production
25
20
15
10
5
0
000 000 tonnes
Steel ingots and castings
Pig iron
1971
1972
1973
1974
1975
1976
1977
1978
1979
1980
1981

The Territories

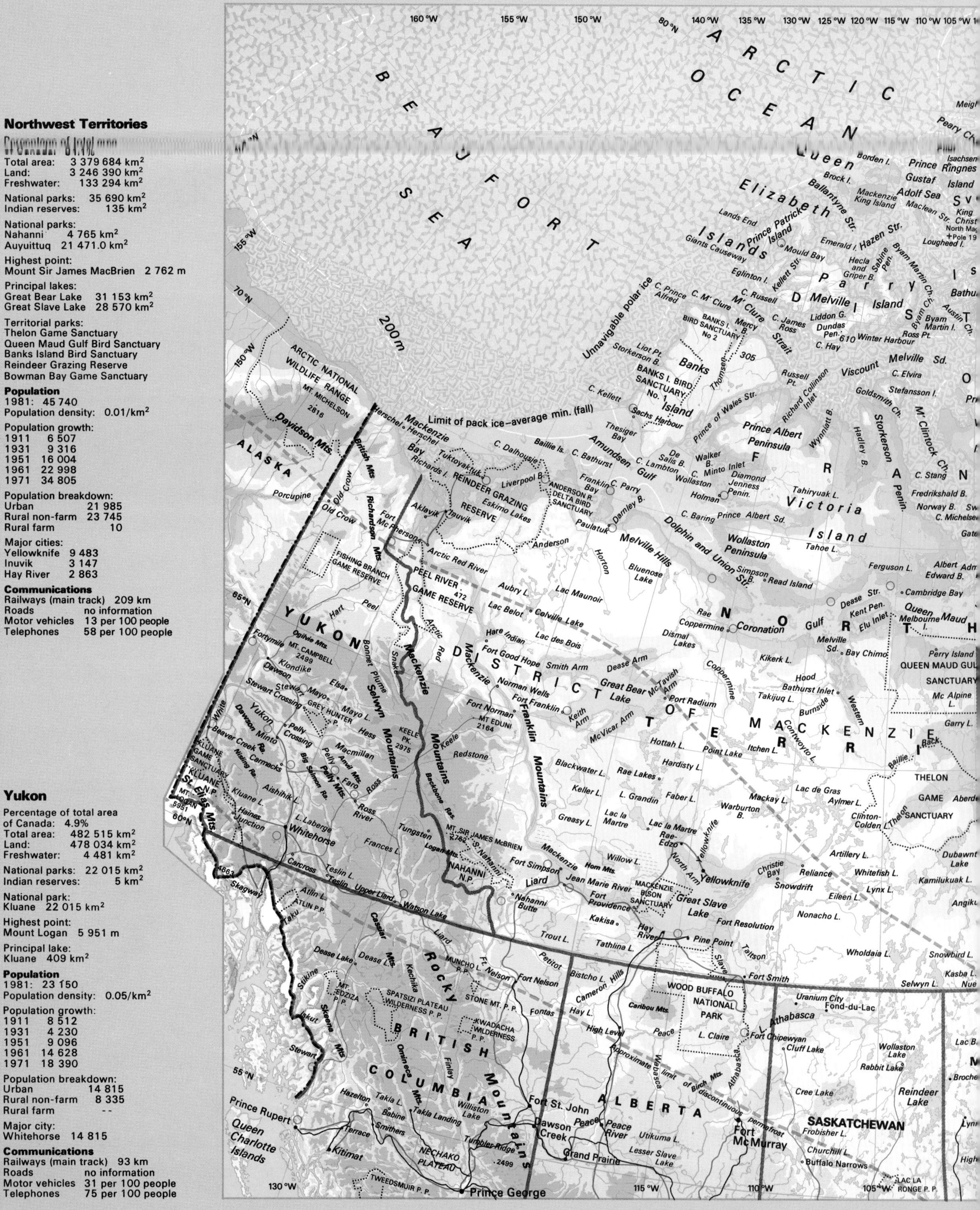
ARCTIC OCEAN
BEAUFORT SEA
Queen Elizabeth Islands
Limit of pack ice–average min. (fall)
Unnavigable polar ice
200m
ALASKA
YUKON
DISTRICT OF MACKENZIE
NORTHWEST TERRITORIES
BRITISH COLUMBIA
ALBERTA
SASKATCHEWAN
Banks Island
Victoria Island
Melville Island
Prince Patrick Island
Great Bear Lake
Great Slave Lake
Mackenzie Mountains
Selwyn Mountains
Franklin Mountains
Rocky Mountains
St. Elias Mts.
Richardson Mts.
British Mts.
Davidson Mts.
ARCTIC NATIONAL WILDLIFE RANGE
REINDEER GRAZING RESERVE
PEEL RIVER GAME RESERVE
FISHING BRANCH GAME RESERVE
KLUANE GAME SANCTUARY
KLUANE N.P.
NAHANNI N.P.
WOOD BUFFALO NATIONAL PARK
THELON GAME SANCTUARY
QUEEN MAUD GULF SANCTUARY
MACKENZIE BISON SANCTUARY
BANKS I. BIRD SANCTUARY No. 1
BANKS I. BIRD SANCTUARY No 2
ANDERSON R. DELTA BIRD SANCTUARY
MT. SIR JAMES McBRIEN 2762
MT. LOGAN 5951
MT. CAMPBELL 2499
MT. MICHELSON 2816
KEELE PK. 2975
MT EDUNI 2164
GREY HUNTER P.
Whitehorse
Dawson
Yellowknife
Inuvik
Aklavik
Tuktoyaktuk
Fort Mc Pherson
Old Crow
Mayo
Faro
Ross River
Watson Lake
Teslin
Carcross
Haines Junction
Skagway
Norman Wells
Fort Norman
Fort Good Hope
Fort Franklin
Fort Simpson
Fort Providence
Hay River
Pine Point
Fort Resolution
Fort Smith
Fort Chipewyan
Fort McMurray
Fort Nelson
Fort St. John
Dawson Creek
Grand Prairie
Peace River
High Level
Prince George
Prince Rupert
Kitimat
Stewart
Coppermine
Cambridge Bay
Sachs Harbour
Holman
Paulatuk
Port Radium
Rae-Edzo
Snowdrift
Reliance
Uranium City
Coronation Gulf
Amundsen Gulf
Dolphin and Union Str.
M'Clure Strait
Prince of Wales Str.
Viscount Melville Sd.
Queen Charlotte Islands
NECHAKO PLATEAU
SPATSIZI PLATEAU WILDERNESS P. P.
TWEEDSMUIR P. P.
160 °W
155 °W
150 °W
140 °W
135 °W
130 °W
125 °W
120 °W
115 °W
110 °W
105 °W
80 °N
70 °N
65 °N
60 °N
55 °N

Northwest Territories

Percentage of total area [illegible]
Total area: 3 379 684 km²
Land: 3 246 390 km²
Freshwater: 133 294 km²

National parks: 35 690 km²
Indian reserves: 135 km²

National parks:
Nahanni 4 765 km²
Auyuittuq 21 471.0 km²

Highest point:
Mount Sir James MacBrien 2 762 m

Principal lakes:
Great Bear Lake 31 153 km²
Great Slave Lake 28 570 km²

Territorial parks:
Thelon Game Sanctuary
Queen Maud Gulf Bird Sanctuary
Banks Island Bird Sanctuary
Reindeer Grazing Reserve
Bowman Bay Game Sanctuary

Population
1981: 45 740
Population density: 0.01/km²

Population growth:

1911	6 507
1931	9 316
1951	16 004
1961	22 998
1971	34 805

Population breakdown:

Urban	21 985
Rural non-farm	23 745
Rural farm	10

Major cities:

Yellowknife	9 483
Inuvik	3 147
Hay River	2 863

Communications

Railways (main track)	209 km
Roads	no information
Motor vehicles	13 per 100 people
Telephones	58 per 100 people

Yukon

Percentage of total area of Canada: 4.9%
Total area: 482 515 km²
Land: 478 034 km²
Freshwater: 4 481 km²

National parks: 22 015 km²
Indian reserves: 5 km²

National park:
Kluane 22 015 km²

Highest point:
Mount Logan 5 951 m

Principal lake:
Kluane 409 km²

Population
1981: 23 150
Population density: 0.05/km²

Population growth:

1911	8 512
1931	4 230
1951	9 096
1961	14 628
1971	18 390

Population breakdown:

Urban	14 815
Rural non-farm	8 335
Rural farm	--

Major city:
Whitehorse 14 815

Communications

Railways (main track)	93 km
Roads	no information
Motor vehicles	31 per 100 people
Telephones	75 per 100 people

Conical Orthomorphic Projection

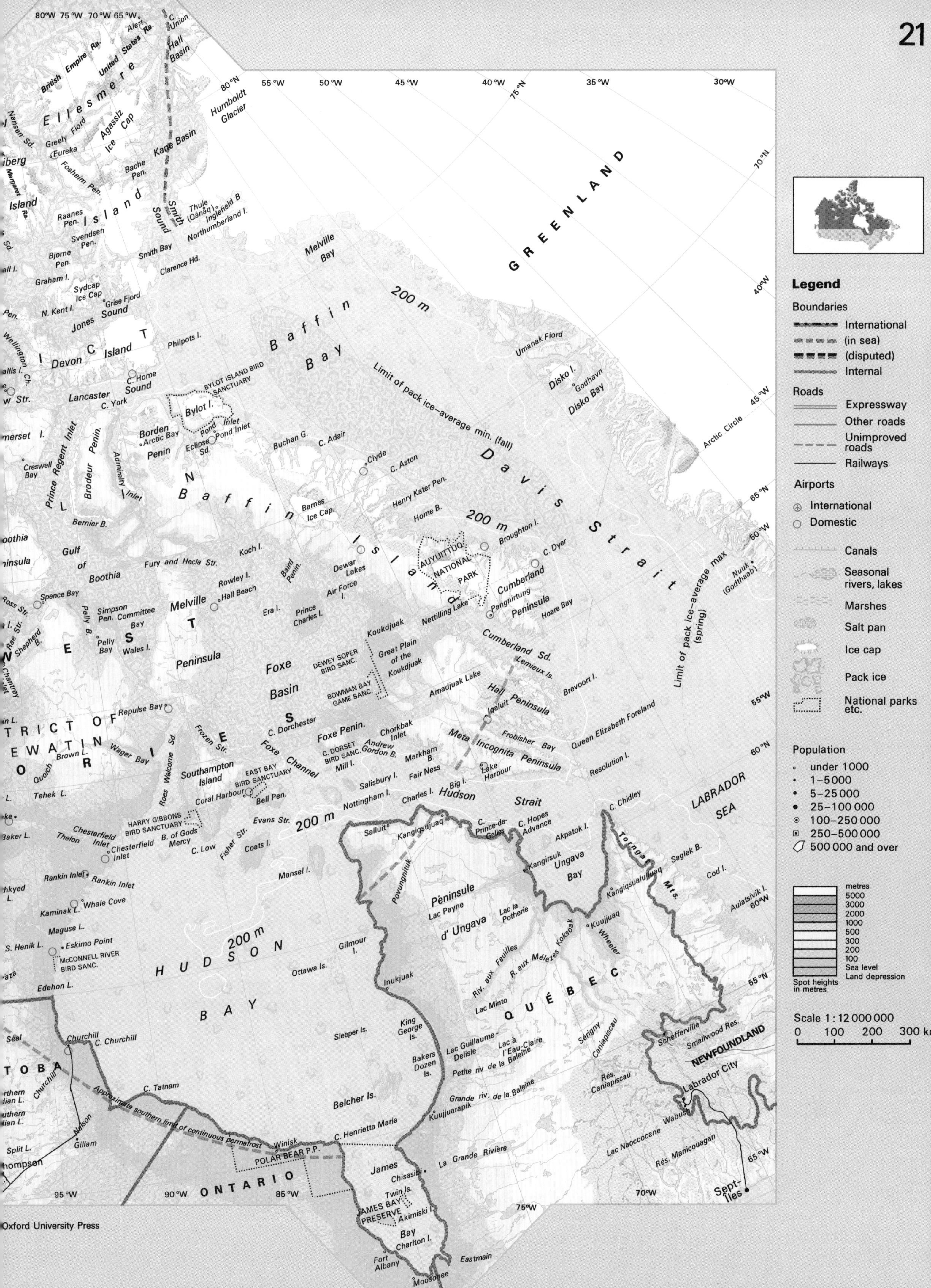
Legend
Boundaries
International
(in sea)
(disputed)
Internal
Roads
Expressway
Other roads
Unimproved roads
Railways
Airports
International
Domestic
Canals
Seasonal rivers, lakes
Marshes
Salt pan
Ice cap
Pack ice
National parks etc.
Population
under 1000
1–5000
5–25000
25–100 000
100–250 000
250–500 000
500 000 and over
metres
5000
3000
2000
1000
500
300
200
100
Sea level
Land depression
Spot heights in metres.
Scale 1 : 12 000 000
0 100 200 300 km
80°W 75°W 70°W 65°W
55°W
50°W
45°W
40°W
35°W
30°W
80°N
75°N
70°N
65°N
60°N
55°N
95°W
90°W
85°W
75°W
70°W
G R E E N L A N D
Ellesmere Island
British Empire Ra.
United States Ra.
Alert
C. Union
Hall Basin
Humboldt Glacier
Nansen Sd.
Greely Fiord
Eureka
Agassiz Ice Cap
Kane Basin
Bache Pen.
Fosheim Pen.
Margaret Ra.
Raanes Pen.
Svendsen Pen.
Bjorne Pen.
Smith Sound
Thule (Qânâq)
Inglefield B
Northumberland I.
Smith Bay
Clarence Hd.
Graham I.
Sydcap Ice Cap
Grise Fiord
N. Kent I.
Jones Sound
Melville Bay
Devon Island
Philpots I.
Wellington Ch.
C. Home
Lancaster Sound
C. York
BYLOT ISLAND BIRD SANCTUARY
Bylot I.
Pond Inlet
Borden Penin
Arctic Bay
Eclipse Sd.
Baffin Bay
200 m
Limit of pack ice–average min. (fall)
Umanak Fiord
Disko I.
Godhavn
Disko Bay
Arctic Circle
Somerset I.
Prince Regent Inlet
Brodeur Penin.
Admiralty Inlet
Creswell Bay
Buchan G.
C. Adair
Clyde
C. Aston
Henry Kater Pen.
Barnes Ice Cap.
Home B.
Davis Strait
Baffin Island
Bernier B.
Boothia Peninsula
Gulf of Boothia
Fury and Hecla Str.
Koch I.
Broughton I.
C. Dyer
AUYUITTUQ NATIONAL PARK
Cumberland Peninsula
Pangnirtung
Hoare Bay
Nuuk (Godthaab)
Limit of pack ice–average max (spring)
Dewar Lakes
Baird Penin.
Air Force I.
Rowley I.
Hall Beach
Melville Peninsula
Spence Bay
Ross Str.
Rae Str.
Shepherd B.
Simpson Pen.
Committee Bay
Pelly B.
Pelly Bay
Wales I.
Era I.
Prince Charles I.
Nettilling Lake
Koukdjuak
Great Plain of the Koukdjuak
DEWEY SOPER BIRD SANC.
BOWMAN BAY GAME SANC.
Foxe Basin
Cumberland Sd.
Lemieux Is.
Amadjuak Lake
Hall Peninsula
Brevoort I.
Iqaluit
Frobisher Bay
Queen Elizabeth Foreland
Meta Incognita Peninsula
Resolution I.
Chantrey Inlet
Repulse Bay
DISTRICT OF KEEWATIN
NORTHWEST TERRITORIES
Frozen Str.
Wager Bay
Brown L.
Quoich
Roes Welcome Sd.
Southampton Island
C. Dorchester
Foxe Penin.
Chorkbak Inlet
C. DORSET BIRD SANC.
Andrew Gordon B.
Markham B.
Foxe Channel
Mill I.
Salisbury I.
Fair Ness
Big I.
Lake Harbour
Hudson Strait
LABRADOR SEA
EAST BAY BIRD SANCTUARY
Coral Harbour
Bell Pen.
Tehek L.
Nottingham I.
Charles I.
C. Chidley
HARRY GIBBONS BIRD SANCTUARY
Evans Str.
Baker L.
Thelon
Chesterfield Inlet
B. of Gods Mercy
C. Low
Fisher Str.
Coats I.
Salluit
Kangiqsujuaq
C. Prince-de-Galles
C. Hopes Advance
Akpatok I.
Torngat Mts.
Saglek B.
Kangirsuk
Ungava Bay
Rankin Inlet
Mansel I.
Povungnituk
Péninsule d' Ungava
Lac Payne
Lac la Potherie
Kangiqsualujjuaq
Cod I.
Aulatsivik I.
Chesterfield Inlet
Whale Cove
Kaminak L.
Maguse L.
Eskimo Point
S. Henik L.
McCONNELL RIVER BIRD SANC.
HUDSON BAY
Gilmour I.
Kuujjuaq
Koksoak
Wheeler
R. aux Feuilles
R. aux Mélèzes
Edehon L.
Ottawa Is.
Inukjuak
QUÉBEC
Lac Minto
Seal
Churchill
C. Churchill
MANITOBA
Sleeper Is.
King George Is.
Bakers Dozen Is.
Lac Guillaume-Delisle
Lac à l'Eau-Claire
Petite riv de la Baleine
Sérigny
Caniapiscau
Schefferville
Smallwood Res.
NEWFOUNDLAND
Labrador City
Rés. Caniapiscau
Grande riv. de la Baleine
Kuujjuarapik
Belcher Is.
C. Tatnam
Approximate southern limit of continuous permafrost
Nelson
Gillam
Split L.
Thompson
Winisk
POLAR BEAR P.P.
C. Henrietta Maria
La Grande Rivière
Lac Naococane
Wabush
Rés. Manicouagan
ONTARIO
James Bay
Chisasibi
Twin Is.
JAMES BAY PRESERVE
Akimiski I.
Charlton I.
Fort Albany
Eastmain
Moosonee
Sept-Îles

Western Canada

British Columbia

Percentage of total area of Canada: 9.5%
Total area: 948 596 km^2
Land: 930 528 km^2
Freshwater: 18 068 km^2

National parks:* 4 690 km^2
Provincial parks:* 41 629 km^2
Provincial forests:* 303 663 km^2
Indian reserves:* 3 390 km^2
Agricultural land:* 217 860 km^2
*Includes freshwater areas

National parks:

Yoho	1 313.1 km^2
Glacier	1 349.4 km^2
Mount Revelstoke	262.6 km^2
Kootenay	1 377.9 km^2
Pacific Rim	388.5 km^2

Highest point:
Fairweather Mountain 4 663 m
Principal lake:
Williston Lake 1 660 km^2
Major provincial parks:
Mount Robson, Tweedsmuir, Wells Gray, Garibaldi, Spatsizi Plateau Wilderness, Strathcona, Atlin, Skagit Valley

Population
1981: 2 744 470
Population density: 2.9/km^2

Population growth:

1871	36 247
1891	98 173
1911	392 480
1931	694 263
1951	1 165 210
1961	1 629 082
1971	2 184 620

Population breakdown:

Urban	[illegible]
Rural non-farm	[illegible]
Rural farm	59 655

Census Metropolitan Areas:
Vancouver 1 268 183
Victoria 233 481

Major cities:

Prince George	67 559
Kamloops	64 048
Kelowna	59 196

Communications

Railways (main track)	7 292 km
Roads	62 514 km
Motor vehicles	43 per 100 people
Telephones	73 per 100 people

Alberta

Percentage of total area of Canada: 6.6%
Total area: 661 185 km^2
Land: 644 389 km^2
Freshwater: 16 796 km^2

National parks:* 54 084 km^2
Provincial parks:* 7 700 km^2
Provincial forests:* 343 098 km^2
Indian reserves:* 6 566 km^2
Agricultural land:* 191 085 km^2
*Includes freshwater areas

National parks:

Banff	6 640.8 km^2
Waterton Lakes	525.8 km^2
Jasper	10 878.0 km^2
Elk Island	194.3 km^2
Wood Buffalo (and NWT)	44 807.0 km^2

Highest point:
Mount Columbia 3 747 m
Principal lakes:
Lesser Slave Lake 1 168 km^2
Claire Lake 1 437 km^2
Major provincial parks:
Willmore Wilderness, Cypress Hills Kananaskis.

Population
1981: 2 237 725
Population density: 3.5/km^2

Population growth:

1911	374 295
1931	731 605
1951	939 501
1961	1 331 944
1971	1 627 875

Population breakdown:

Urban	1 727 545
Rural non-farm	319 425
Rural farm	[illegible]

Census Metropolitan Areas:
Edmonton 657 057
Calgary 592 743

Major cities:

Lethbridge	54 072
Red Deer	46 393
Medicine Hat	40 380

Communications

Railways (main track)	9 269 km
Roads	252 270 km
Motor vehicles	56 per 100 people
Telephones	85 per 100 people

Conical Orthomorphic Projection

Saskatchewan

Percentage of total area of Canada: 6.6%
Total area: 651 900 km^2
Land: 570 269 km^2
Freshwater: 81 631 km^2

National parks:* 3 875 km^2
Provincial parks:* 4 944 km^2
Provincial forests:* 348 887 km^2
Indian reserves:* 6 322 km^2
Agricultural land:* 259 471 km^2
*Includes freshwater areas

National park:
Prince Albert 3 875 km^2
Highest point:
Cypress Hills 1 392 m
Principal lakes:
Lake Athabasca 7 936 km^2 (spans Alberta)
Reindeer Lake 6 651 km^2 (spans Manitoba)
Wollaston Lake 2 681 km^2

Major provincial parks:
Nipawin, Meadow Lake, Lac la Ronge, Moose Mountain.

Population
1981: 968 310
Population density: 1.7/km^2

Population growth:

1911	492 432
1931	921 785
1951	831 728
1961	925 181
1971	926 240

Population breakdown:

Urban	563 165
Rural non-farm	224 890
Rural farm	180 255

Census Metropolitan Areas:
Regina 164 313
Saskatoon 154 210

Major cities:
Moose Jaw 33 941
Prince Albert 31 380

Communications

Railways (main track)	12 385 km
Roads	178 444 km
Motor vehicles	43 per 100 people
Telephones	66 per 100 people

Manitoba

Percentage of total area of Canada: 6.5%
Total area: 650 087 km^2
Land: 548 495 km^2
Freshwater: 101 592 km^2

National parks:* 2 976 km^2
Provincial parks:* 10 650 km^2
Provincial forests:* 14 025 km^2
Indian reserves:* 2 145 km^2
Agricultural land:* 76 159 km^2
*Includes freshwater areas

National park:
Riding Mountain 2 976 km^2
Highest point:
Baldy Mountain 832 m
Principal lakes:
Lake Winnipeg 24 390 km^2
Lake Winnipegosis 5 374 km^2
Lake Manitoba 4 659 km^2
Major provincial parks:
Grass River, Clearwater, Duck Mountain, Whiteshell, Nopiming, Turtle Mountain.

Population
1981: 1 026 245
Population density: 1.9/km^2

Population growth:

1871	25 228
1891	152 506
1911	461 394
1931	700 139
1951	776 541
1961	921 686
1971	988 245

Population breakdown:

Urban	730 660
Rural non-farm	199 185
Rural farm	96 390

Census Metropolitan Area:
Winnipeg 584 842

Major cities:

Brandon	36 242
Thompson	14 288
Portage la Prairie	13 086

Communications

Railways (main track)	6 430 km
Roads	83 990 km
Motor vehicles	50 per 100 people
Telephones	71 per 100 people

Legend

Boundaries
International
(in sea)
(disputed)
Internal

Roads
Expressway
Other roads
Unimproved roads
Railways

Airports
International
Domestic

Canals
Seasonal rivers, lakes
Marshes
Salt pan
Ice cap
Sand desert limits
National parks etc.

Population
under 1000
1–5 000
5–25 000
25–100 000
100–250 000
250–500 000
500 000 and over

metres: 5000, 3000, 2000, 1000, 500, 300, 200, 100, Sea level, Land depression
Spot heights in metres

Scale 1:8 000 000
0 100 200 km

See page 1 for population legend for the U.S.A.

Ontario-Québec

Ontario

Percentage of total area of Canada: 10.8%

Total area:	1 068 582 km²
Land:	891 194 km²
Freshwater:	177 388 km²

National parks:*	1 922 km²
Provincial parks:*	48 412 km²
Provincial forests:*	- -
Indian reserves:*	6 703 km²
Agricultural land:*	60 392 km²

*Includes freshwater areas

National parks:

St. Lawrence Islands	4.1 km²
Point Pelee	15.5 km²
Georgian Bay Islands	14.2 km²
Pukaskwa	1 877.8 km²

Highest point:
Timiskaming District 693 m
(47° 20′N, 80° 44′W)

Principal lakes:
(excluding Great Lakes)

Lake Nipigon	4 848 km²
Lake of the Woods (Canadian part)	3 149 km²

Major provincial parks:
Algonquin, Rondeau, Quetico, Polar Bear, Winisk River.

Population

1981:	8 625 110
Population density:	9.7/km²

Population growth:

1871	1 620 851
1891	2 114 321
1911	2 527 292
1931	3 431 683
1951	4 597 542
1961	6 236 092
1971	7 703 105

Population breakdown;

Urban	7 047 030
Rural non-farm	1 298 250
Rural farm	279 830

Census Metropolitan Areas:

Toronto	2 998 947
Ottawa	717 978
Hamilton	542 095
St. Catharines	304 353
Kitchener	287 801
London	283 668
Windsor	246 110
Oshawa	154 217
Thunder Bay	121 379

Major cities:

Sault Ste. Marie	82 697
Brantford	74 315
Guelph	71 207
Peterborough	60 620
Kingston	52 616
North Bay	51 268
Sarnia	50 892

Communications

Railways (main track)	15 367 km
Roads	161 556 km
Motor vehicles	47 per 100 people
Telephones	72 per 100 people

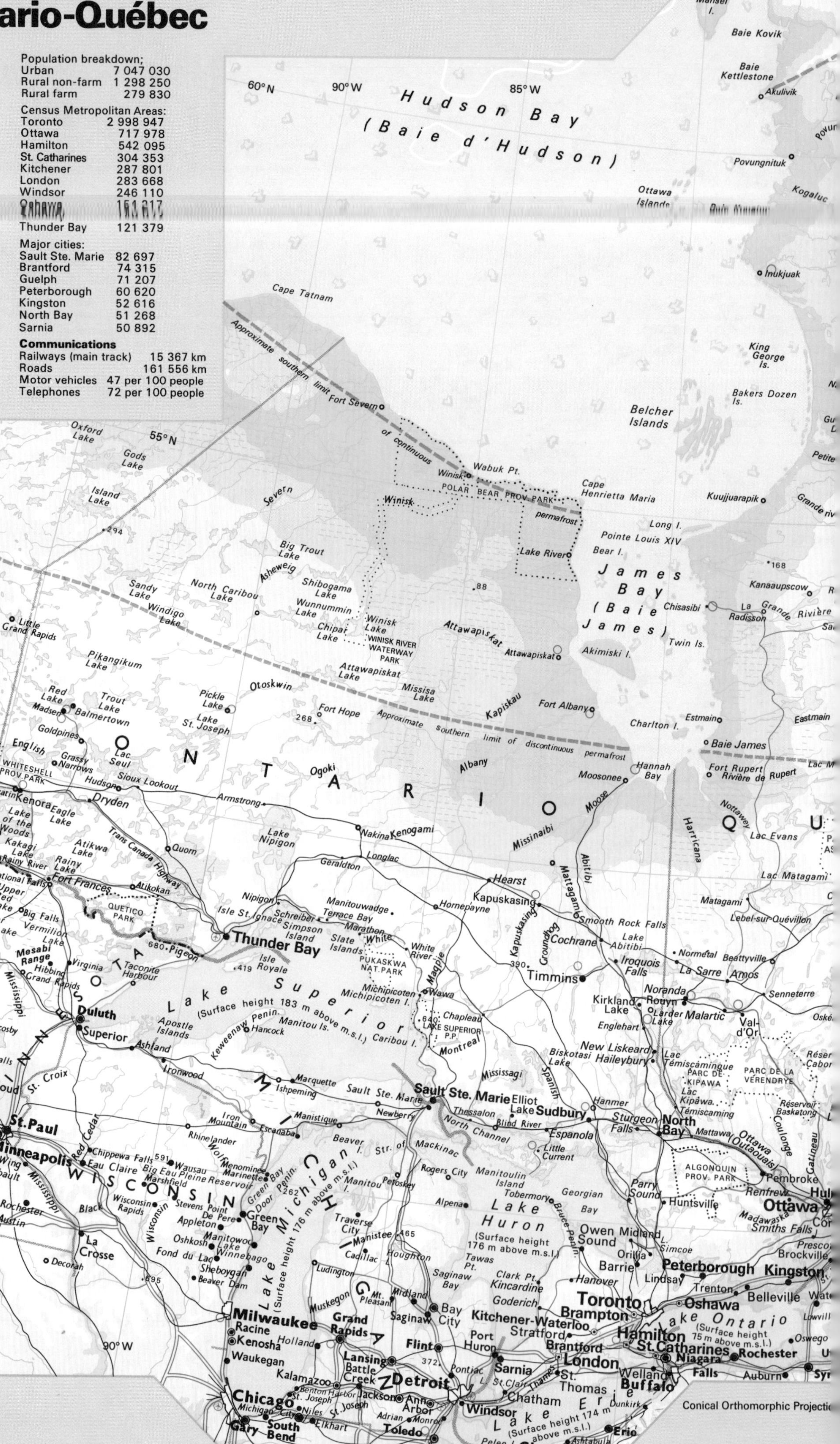

Hudson Bay
(Baie d'Hudson)
James Bay
(Baie James)
ONTARIO
Lake Superior
(Surface height 183 m above m.s.l.)
Lake Michigan
(Surface height 176 m above m.s.l.)
Lake Huron
(Surface height 176 m above m.s.l.)
Lake Erie
(Surface height 174 m above m.s.l.)
Lake Ontario
(Surface height 75 m above m.s.l.)
Approximate southern limit of continuous permafrost
Approximate southern limit of discontinuous permafrost
POLAR BEAR PROV. PARK
WINISK RIVER WATERWAY PARK
QUETICO PARK
PUKASKWA NAT. PARK
LAKE SUPERIOR P.P.
ALGONQUIN PROV. PARK
WHITESHELL PROV. PARK
Belcher Islands
Cape Tatnam
Fort Severn
Cape Henrietta Maria
Attawapiskat
Fort Albany
Moosonee
Kenora
Dryden
Sioux Lookout
Lake Nipigon
Thunder Bay
Isle Royale
Wawa
Hearst
Kapuskasing
Cochrane
Timmins
Kirkland Lake
New Liskeard
Haileybury
Sudbury
North Bay
Sault Ste. Marie
Manitoulin Island
Georgian Bay
Owen Sound
Barrie
Orillia
Peterborough
Kingston
Belleville
Oshawa
Toronto
Brampton
Kitchener-Waterloo
Stratford
Brantford
Hamilton
St. Catharines
London
Sarnia
St. Thomas
Chatham
Windsor
Ottawa
Pembroke
Smiths Falls
Brockville
Niagara Falls
Buffalo
Rochester
Detroit
Flint
Lansing
Grand Rapids
Milwaukee
Chicago
Toledo
Cleveland
Duluth
St. Paul
Minneapolis
MINNESOTA
WISCONSIN
MICHIGAN
Rouyn
Noranda
Amos
Val-d'Or
Chisasibi
60°N
55°N
50°N
45°N
90°W
85°W
80°W
Conical Orthomorphic Projection

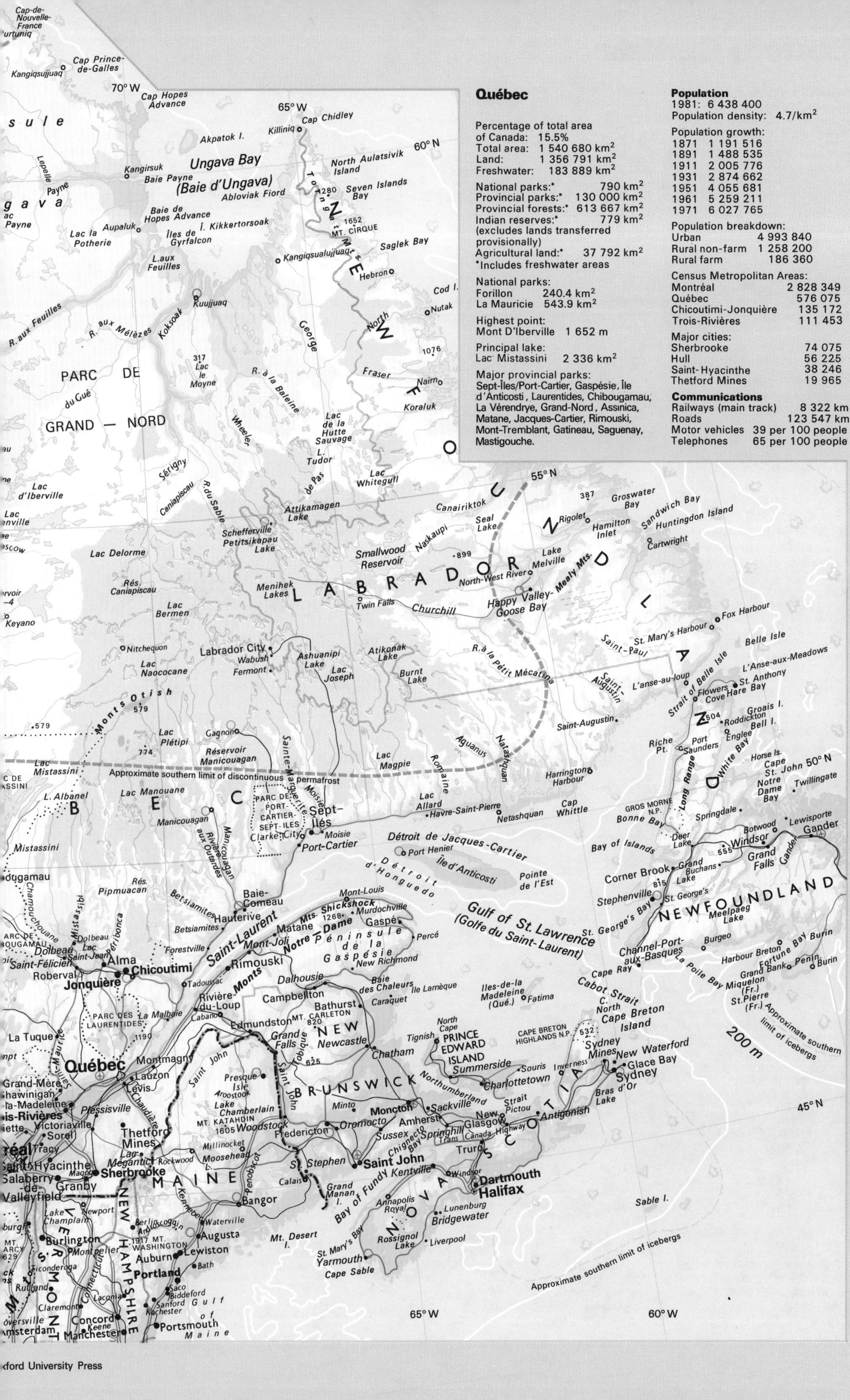

Québec

Percentage of total area of Canada: 15.5%
Total area: 1 540 680 km²
Land: 1 356 791 km²
Freshwater: 183 889 km²

National parks:* 790 km²
Provincial parks:* 130 000 km²
Provincial forests:* 613 667 km²
Indian reserves:* 779 km²
(excludes lands transferred provisionally)
Agricultural land:* 37 792 km²
*Includes freshwater areas

National parks:
Forillon 240.4 km²
La Mauricie 543.9 km²

Highest point:
Mont D'Iberville 1 652 m

Principal lake:
Lac Mistassini 2 336 km²

Major provincial parks:
Sept-Îles/Port-Cartier, Gaspésie, Île d'Anticosti, Laurentides, Chibougamau, La Vérendrye, Grand-Nord, Assinica, Matane, Jacques-Cartier, Rimouski, Mont-Tremblant, Gatineau, Saguenay, Mastigouche.

Population
1981: 6 438 400
Population density: 4.7/km²

Population growth:

Year	Population
1871	1 191 516
1891	1 488 535
1911	2 005 776
1931	2 874 662
1951	4 055 681
1961	5 259 211
1971	6 027 765

Population breakdown:

Urban	4 993 840
Rural non-farm	1 258 200
Rural farm	186 360

Census Metropolitan Areas:

Montréal	2 828 349
Québec	576 075
Chicoutimi-Jonquière	135 172
Trois-Rivières	111 453

Major cities:

Sherbrooke	74 075
Hull	56 225
Saint-Hyacinthe	38 246
Thetford Mines	19 965

Communications

Railways (main track)	8 322 km
Roads	123 547 km
Motor vehicles	39 per 100 people
Telephones	65 per 100 people

Legend

Boundaries
- International
- (in sea)
- (disputed)
- Internal

Roads
- Expressway
- Other roads
- Unimproved roads
- Railways

Airports
- International
- Domestic

- Canals
- Seasonal rivers, lakes
- Marshes
- Salt pan
- Ice cap
- Sand desert limits
- National parks etc.

Population
- under 1000
- 1–5000
- 5–25 000
- 25–100 000
- 100–250 000
- 250–500 000
- 500 000 and over

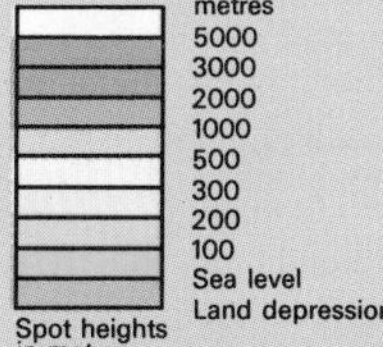
metres
5000
3000
2000
1000
500
300
200
100
Sea level
Land depression
Spot heights in metres

Scale 1 : 8 000 000
0 100 200 km

See page 1 for population legend for the U.S.A.

Eastern Canada

Newfoundland

Percentage of total area of Canada: 4.1%
Total area: 404 517 km^2
Land: 370 485 km^2
Freshwater: 34 032 km^2

National parks:* 2 339 km^2
Provincial parks:* 805 km^2
Provincial forests:* 303 km^2
Agricultural land:* 334 km^2
*Includes freshwater areas

National parks:
Terra Nova [illegible]
Gros Morne 1 942.5 km^2

Highest point:
Highest peak in Torngat Mountains 1 652 m

Principal lake:
Melville 3 069 km^2

Population
1981: 567 680
Population density: 1.5/km^2

Population growth:

1871	152 500
1891	202 040
1911	242 619
1931	281 500
1951	361 416
1961	457 853
1971	522 105

Population breakdown:

Urban	332 900
Rural non-farm	232 860
Rural farm	1 920

Census Metropolitan area:
St. John's 154 820

Major cities:
Corner Brook 24 339
Labrador City 11 538

Communications

Railways (main track)	1 458 km
Roads	12 261 km
Motor vehicles	34 per 100 people
Telephones	45 per 100 people

New Brunswick

Percentage of total area of Canada: 0.7%
Total area: 73 436 km^2
Land: 72 092 km^2
Freshwater: 1 344 km^2

National parks:* 433 km^2
Provincial parks:* 215 km^2
Provincial forests:* 2 792 km^2
Indian reserves:* 168 km^2
Agricultural land:* 4 379 km^2
*Includes freshwater areas

National parks:
Fundy 205.9 km^2
Kouchibouguac 225.3 km^2

Highest point:
Mount Carleton 820 m

Major provincial park:
Mount Carleton

Population
1981: 696 405
Population density: 9.7/km^2

Population growth:

1871	285 594
1891	321 236
1911	351 889
1931	408 219
1951	515 697
1961	597 936
1971	634 555

Population breakdown:

Urban	353 220
Rural non-farm	328 215
Rural farm	14 970

Census Metropolitan area:
Saint John 114 048

Major cities:
Moncton 54 743
Fredericton 43 723

Communications

Railways (main track)	2 628 km
Roads	20 540 km
Motor vehicles	38 per 100 people
Telephones	56 per 100 people

Nova Scotia

Percentage of total area of Canada: 0.6%
Total area: 55 491 km^2
Land: 52 841 km^2
Freshwater: 2 650 km^2

National parks:* 1 331 km^2
Provincial parks:* 126 km^2
Provincial forests:* 13 732 km^2
Indian reserves:* 114 km^2
Agricultural land:* 4 660 km^2
*Includes freshwater areas

National parks:
Cape Breton Highlands 950.5 km^2
Kejimkujik 381.5 km^2

Highest point:
Cape Breton 532 m

Principal lake:
Bras d'Or 1 098 km^2

Major provincial parks:
Tobeatic Game Sanctuary
Liscomb Game Sanctuary
Chignecto Game Sanctuary

Population
1981: 847 445
Population density: 16/km^2

Population growth:

1871	387 800
1891	450 396
1911	492 338
1931	512 846
1951	642 584
1961	737 007
1971	788 960

Population breakdown:

Urban	466 845
Rural non-farm	362 915
Rural farm	17 685

Census Metropolitan area:
Halifax 277 727

Major cities:
Sydney 29 444
Glace Bay 21 466

Communications

Railways (main track)	1 968 k
Roads	27 524 k
Motor vehicles	43 per 100 peo
Telephones	60 per 100 peo

Legend

Boundaries
International
(in sea)
(disputed)
Internal

Roads
Expressway
Other roads
Unimproved roads
Railways

Airports
International
Domestic

Canals
Seasonal rivers, lakes
Marshes
Salt pan
Ice cap
Sand desert limits
National parks etc.

Population
under 1000
1–5000
5–25000
25–100 000
100–250 000
250–500 000
500 000 and over

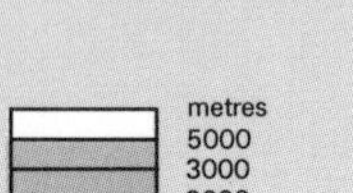

metres
5000
3000
2000
1000
500
300
200
100
Sea level
Land depression
Spot heights in metres

Scale 1:8 000 000
0 100 200 km

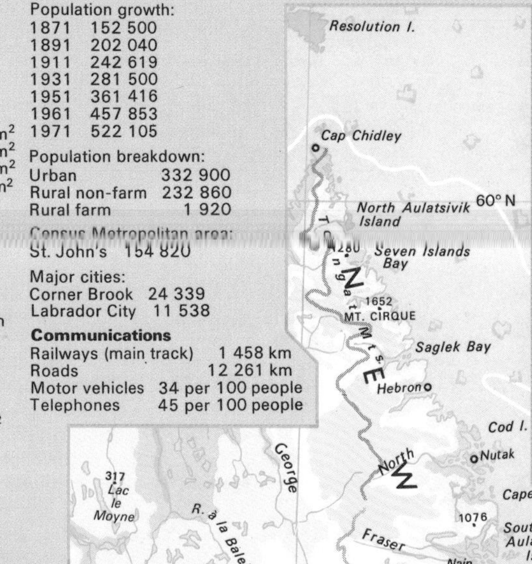

Resolution I.
Cap Chidley
North Aulatsivik Island
60° N
Seven Islands Bay
Torngat Mts
1652 MT. CIRQUE
Saglek Bay
Hebron
Cod I.
Nutak

Cape Kiglapait
South Aulatsivik Island
Nain
Paul I.
Koraluk
Tunungayualok I.
Davis Inlet
Hopedale
Makkovik
Cape Harrison
55° W
Limit of pack ice - average max.(spring)
NEWFOUNDLAND
LABRADOR
Lac le Moyne
George
R. à la Baleine
Wheeler
Lac de la Hutte Sauvage
L. Tudor
de Pas
Lac Whitegull
R. du Sable
Attikamagen Lake
Schefferville
Petitsikapau Lake
Canairiktok
Smallwood Reservoir
Naskaupi
Seal Lake
Rigolet
Groswater Bay
Hamilton Inlet
Sandwich Bay
Huntingdon Island
Cartwright
Menihek Lakes
Lake Melville
North-West River
Twin Falls
Churchill
Mealy Mts.
Happy Valley-Goose Bay
Labrador City
Wabush
Fermont
Ashuanipi Lake
Lac Joseph
Atikonak Lake
Burnt Lake
R. à la Petit Mécatina
Fox Harbour
St. Mary's Harbour
Saint-Paul
Belle Isle
Saint-Augustin
L'anse-au-loup
L'Anse-aux-Meadows
St. Anthony
Strait of Belle Isle
Flowers Cove
Hare Bay
Gagnon
Sainte-Marguerite
Approximate southern limit of discontinuous permafrost
Lac Magpie
Romaine
Aguanus
Natashquan
Groais I.
Roddickton
Bell I.
Englee
Riche Pt.
Port Saunders
White Bay
Harrington Harbour
Lac Allard
Sept-Îles
Moisie
Port-Cartier
Havre-Saint-Pierre
Netashquan
Cap Whittle
Long Range
Horse Is.
Cape St. John
Notre Dame Bay
Twillingate
Fogo Island
GROS MORNE N.P.
Bonne Bay
Springdale
Passage de Jacques-Cartier
Port Menier
Île d'Anticosti
Détroit d'Honguedo
Pointe de l'Est
Bay of Islands
Deer Lake
Botwood
Lewisporte
Windsor
Gander
Bonavista Bay
Corner Brook
Grand Lake
Buchans
Grand Falls
Stephenville
St. George's
Gulf of St. Lawrence
St. George's Bay
Meelpaeg Lake
Trinity Bay
Carbonear
Channel-Port-aux-Basques
Burgeo
Cape Ray
Harbour Breton
Fortune Bay
Marystown
Burin Penin.
Placentia Bay
Argentia
St. John's
Avalon Penin.
Iles-de-la-Madeleine (Qué.)
Fatima
Cabot Strait
La Poile Bay
Miquelon (Fr.)
St. Pierre (Fr.)
55° W
St. Mary's Bay
Cape Race

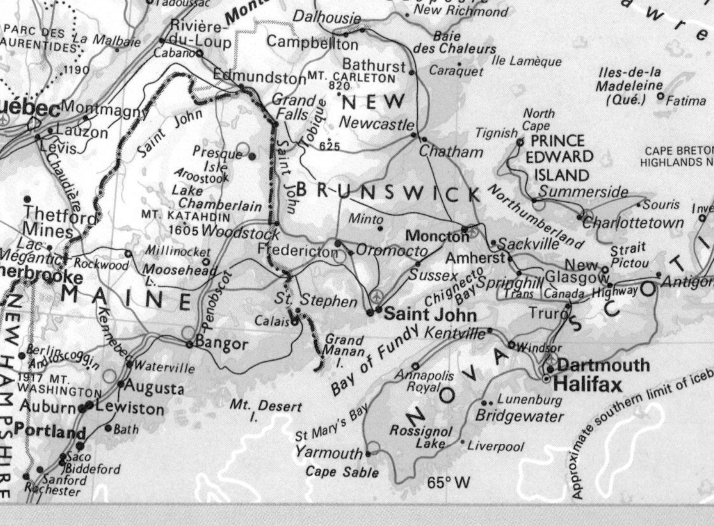

Baie-Comeau
Dolbeau
Lac Saint-Jean
Betsiamites
Hauterive
Mont-Louis
Forestville
Alma
Chicoutimi
Jonquière
Saint-Laurent
Mts. Shickshock
Murdochville
Matane
Mont-Joli
Notre-Dame
Gaspé
Péninsule de la Gaspésie
Percé
Rimouski
Tadoussac
Monts
PARC DES LAURENTIDES
Rivière-du-Loup
La Malbaie
Cabano
New Richmond
Dalhousie
Campbellton
Bathurst
Baie des Chaleurs
Île Lamèque
Caraquet
Québec
Montmagny
Edmundston
MT. CARLETON 820
NEW BRUNSWICK
Grand Falls
Newcastle
Lauzon
Lévis
Saint John
Presque Isle
Aroostook
Chatham
Tignish
North Cape
PRINCE EDWARD ISLAND
Summerside
CAPE BRETON HIGHLANDS N.P.
North C.
Cape Breton Island
Chamberlain Lake
MT. KATAHDIN 1605
Woodstock
Thetford Mines
Lac Mégantic
Millinocket
Moosehead L.
Fredericton
Oromocto
Minto
Moncton
Sackville
Northumberland Strait
Charlottetown
Souris
Inverness
Sydney Mines
New Waterford
Glace Bay
Sydney
Bras d'Or Lake
Sherbrooke
MAINE
Sussex
Amherst
Springhill
Pictou
New Glasgow
Antigonish
Trans Canada Highway
60° W
NEW HAMPSHIRE
St. Stephen
Calais
Saint John
Chignecto Bay
Truro
NOVA SCOTIA
Grand Manan I.
Bay of Fundy
Kentville
Windsor
Dartmouth
Halifax
Bangor
Waterville
Augusta
Berlin
MT. WASHINGTON 1917
Auburn
Lewiston
Portland
Bath
Mt. Desert I.
Annapolis Royal
Lunenburg
Bridgewater
Approximate southern limit of icebergs
200 m
St Mary's Bay
Rossignol Lake
Liverpool
Yarmouth
Cape Sable
65° W
Saco
Biddeford
Sanford
Rochester

Prince Edward Island

Percentage of total area of Canada: 0.1%
Total area: 5 657 km^2
Land: 5 657 km^2
Freshwater: - -

National parks: 21 km^2
Provincial parks: 32 km^2
Provincial forests: 211 km^2
Indian reserves: 8 km^2
Agricultural land: 2 830 km^2

National park:
Prince Edward Island 18.1 km^2

Highest point:
Queens County 142 m

Population
1981: 122 510
Population density: 21.7/km^2

Population growth:

1871	94 621
1891	109 078
1911	93 728
1931	88 038
1951	98 429
1961	104 629
1971	110 640

Population breakdown:

Urban	44 515
Rural non-farm	65 980
Rural farm	12 015

Major cities:
Charlottetown 15 282
Summerside 7 828

Communications

Railways (main track)	406 kr
Roads	5 612 kr
Motor vehicles	40 per 100 peo
Telephones	56 per 100 pe

Conical Orthomorphic Projection

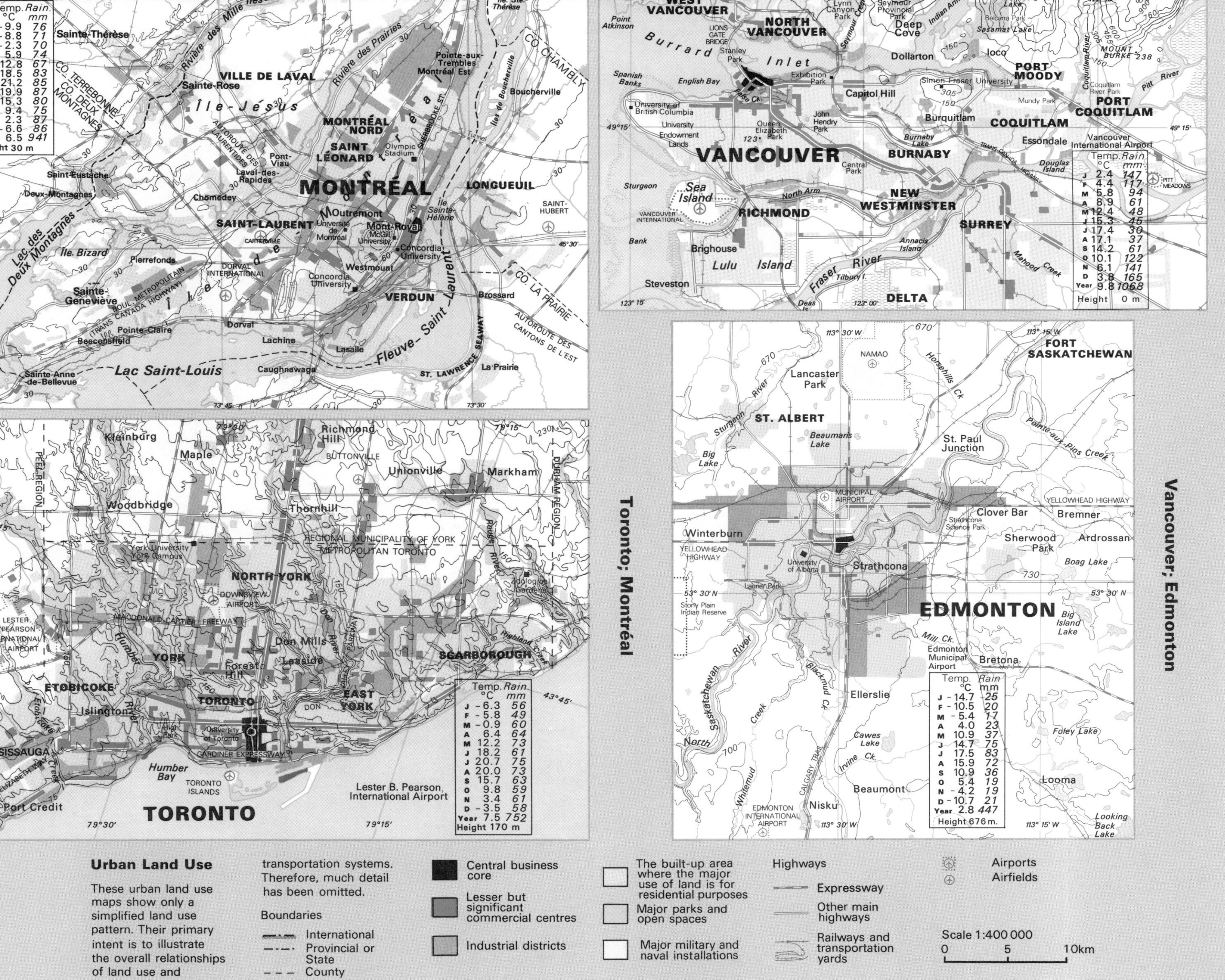

Vancouver; Edmonton
Toronto; Montréal
Urban Land Use
These urban land use maps show only a simplified land use pattern. Their primary intent is to illustrate the overall relationships of land use and transportation systems. Therefore, much detail has been omitted.
Boundaries
International
Provincial or State
County
Central business core
Lesser but significant commercial centres
Industrial districts
The built-up area where the major use of land is for residential purposes
Major parks and open spaces
Major military and naval installations
Highways
Expressway
Other main highways
Railways and transportation yards
Airports
Airfields
Scale 1:400 000
0
5
10km

Montréal

	Temp. °C	Rain. mm
J	-9.9	76
F	-8.8	71
M	-2.3	70
A	5.9	74
M	12.8	67
J	18.5	83
J	21.2	85
A	19.9	87
S	15.3	80
O	9.4	75
N	2.3	87
D	-6.6	86
Year	6.5	941
Height 30 m		

Vancouver

	Temp. °C	Rain. mm
J	2.4	147
F	4.4	117
M	5.8	94
A	8.9	61
M	12.4	48
J	15.3	45
J	17.4	30
A	17.1	37
S	14.2	61
O	10.1	122
N	6.1	141
D	3.8	165
Year	9.8	1068
Height 0 m		

Toronto

	Temp. °C	Rain. mm
J	-6.3	56
F	-5.8	49
M	-0.9	60
A	6.4	64
M	12.2	73
J	18.2	61
J	20.7	75
A	20.0	73
S	15.7	63
O	9.8	59
N	3.4	61
D	-3.5	58
Year	7.5	752
Height 170 m		

Edmonton

	Temp. °C	Rain mm
J	-14.7	25
F	-10.5	20
M	-5.4	17
A	4.0	23
M	10.9	37
J	14.7	75
J	17.5	83
A	15.9	72
S	10.9	36
O	5.4	19
N	-4.2	19
D	-10.7	21
Year	2.8	447
Height 676 m.		

British Columbia

Legend

Boundaries
- International
- (in sea)
- (disputed)
- Internal

Roads
- Expressway
- Other roads
- Unpaved roads
- Railways

Airports
- International
- Domestic

- Canals
- Seasonal rivers, lakes
- Marshes
- Salt pan
- Ice cap
- Sand desert limits
- National parks etc.

Population
- under 1000
- 1–5000
- 5–25 000
- 25–100 000
- 100–250 000
- 250–500 000
- 500 000 and over

metres: 5000, 3000, 2000, 1000, 500, 300, 200, 100, Sea level, Land depression

Spot heights in metres

Scale 1: 5 000 000
0 50 100 km

The Economy

Heavy industry
1. Oil refinery
2. Metal industries
3. Shipbuilding and repair

Lighter industry
1. Sawmills, pulp and paper
2. Fish processing
3. Fruit processing
4. Port handling
5. Tourism

Minerals
1. Gold, silver
2. Silver
3. Copper, lead, zinc
4. Copper, molybdenum
5. Iron
6. Gypsum
7. Asbestos
8. Gas

Agriculture
- Wheat and other grains
- Mixed farming
- Forest and livestock grazing
- Truck and intensive farming
- Dairying
- Fruit
- Forest and non-agricultural land

Vancouver and Vancouver Island

Scale 1: 2 500 000
0 25 50 km

Conical Orthomorphic Projection

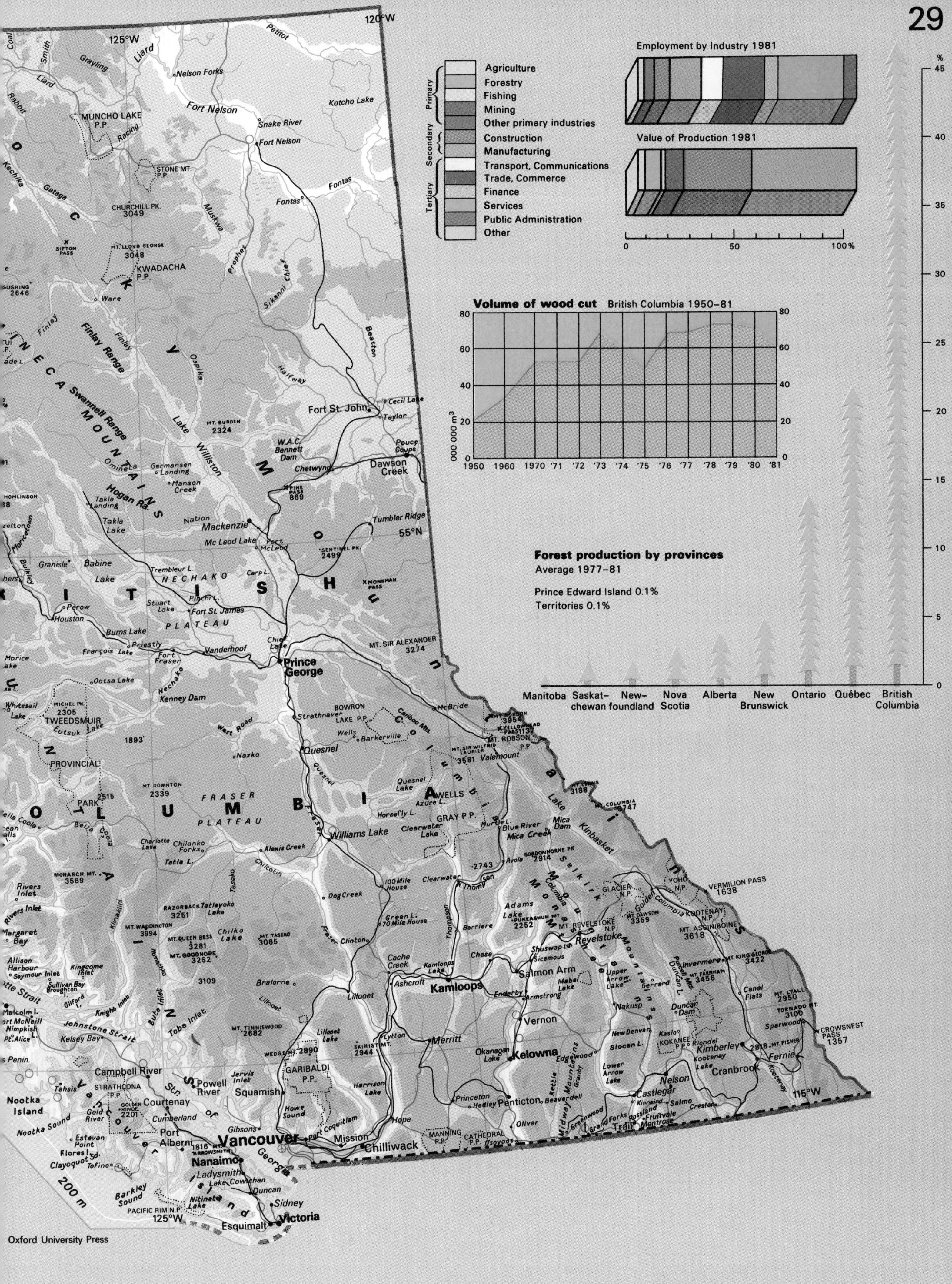

Employment by Industry 1981
Primary
Agriculture
Forestry
Fishing
Mining
Other primary industries
Secondary
Construction
Manufacturing
Tertiary
Transport, Communications
Trade, Commerce
Finance
Services
Public Administration
Other
Value of Production 1981
0
50
100%
Volume of wood cut British Columbia 1950–81
000 000 m3
0
20
40
60
80
1950
1960
1970
'71
'72
'73
'74
'75
'76
'77
'78
'79
'80
'81
Forest production by provinces
Average 1977–81
Prince Edward Island 0.1%
Territories 0.1%
%
0
5
10
15
20
25
30
35
40
45
Manitoba
Saskat-chewan
New-foundland
Nova Scotia
Alberta
New Brunswick
Ontario
Québec
British Columbia
120°W
125°W
55°N
115°W
BRITISH COLUMBIA
ROCKY MOUNTAINS
CASSIAR MOUNTAINS
COAST MOUNTAINS
NECHAKO PLATEAU
FRASER PLATEAU
Fort Nelson
Fort St. John
Dawson Creek
Mackenzie
Prince George
Quesnel
Williams Lake
Kamloops
Vernon
Kelowna
Penticton
Salmon Arm
Revelstoke
Nelson
Cranbrook
Kimberley
Fernie
Castlegar
Trail
Vancouver
Chilliwack
Mission
Squamish
Powell River
Campbell River
Courtenay
Port Alberni
Nanaimo
Ladysmith
Duncan
Victoria
Esquimalt
Sidney
Vancouver Island
Nootka Island
Strait of Georgia
200 m
MUNCHO LAKE P.P.
STONE MT. P.P.
KWADACHA P.P.
TWEEDSMUIR PROVINCIAL PARK
STRATHCONA P.P.
GARIBALDI P.P.
MANNING P.P.
CATHEDRAL P.P.
PACIFIC RIM N.P.
GLACIER N.P.
MT. REVELSTOKE N.P.
YOHO N.P.
KOOTENAY N.P.
BOWRON LAKE P.P.
WELLS GRAY P.P.
MT. ROBSON P.P.
KOKANEE P.P.
CHURCHILL PK. 3049
MT. LLOYD GEORGE 3048
MT. BURDEN 2324
PINE PASS 869
MT. SIR ALEXANDER 3274
MT. ROBSON 3954
YELLOWHEAD PASS 1137
MT. SIR WILFRID LAURIER 3581
MT. DOWNTON 2339
MONARCH MT. 3569
MT. WADDINGTON 3994
MT. QUEEN BESS 3261
MT. GOODHOPE 3252
MT. TASEKO 3065
MT. TINNISWOOD 2682
GOLDEN HINDE 2201
VERMILION PASS 1638
MT. ASSINIBOINE 3618
MT. KING GEORGE 3422
MT. FARNHAM 3456
MT. LYALL 2950
TORNADO MT. 3100
CROWSNEST PASS 1357
Williston Lake
Kinbasket Lake
Okanagan Lake
Upper Arrow Lake
Lower Arrow Lake
Kootenay Lake
Fraser
Thompson
Columbia
Liard
Peace
Selkirk Mountains
Monashee Mountains
Purcell Mts.
Cariboo Mts.
Oxford University Press

Alberta

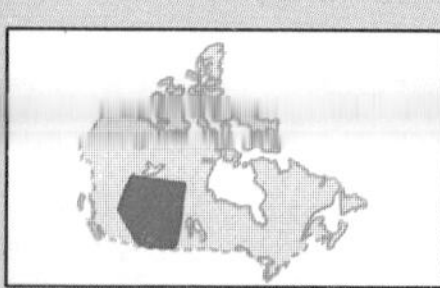

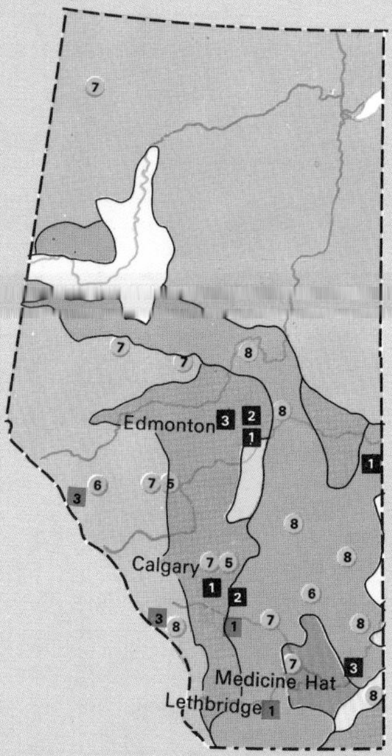

Legend

Boundaries
- International
- (in sea)
- (disputed)
- Internal

Roads
- Expressway
- Other roads
- Unpaved roads
- Railways

Airports
- International
- Domestic

- Canals
- Seasonal rivers, lakes
- Marshes
- Salt pan
- Ice cap
- Sand desert limits
- National parks etc.

Population
- under 1000
- 1–5000
- 5–25 000
- 25–100 000
- 100–250 000
- 250–500 000
- 500 000 and over

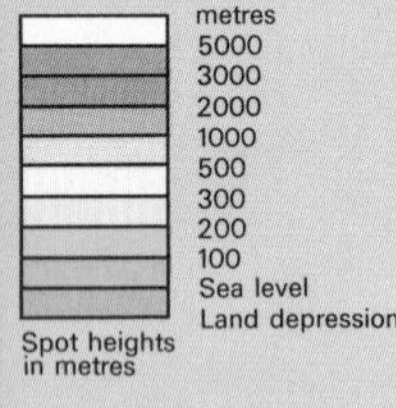

metres
5000
3000
2000
1000
500
300
200
100
Sea level
Land depression
Spot heights in metres

Scale 1:5 000 000

0 50 100 km

Provincial product per capita GDP 1981

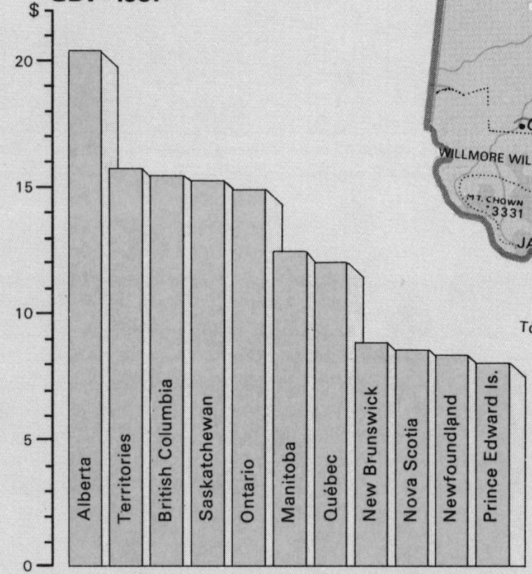

$ 0 5 10 15 20

Alberta, Territories, British Columbia, Saskatchewan, Ontario, Manitoba, Québec, New Brunswick, Nova Scotia, Newfoundland, Prince Edward Is.

Employment by Industry 1981

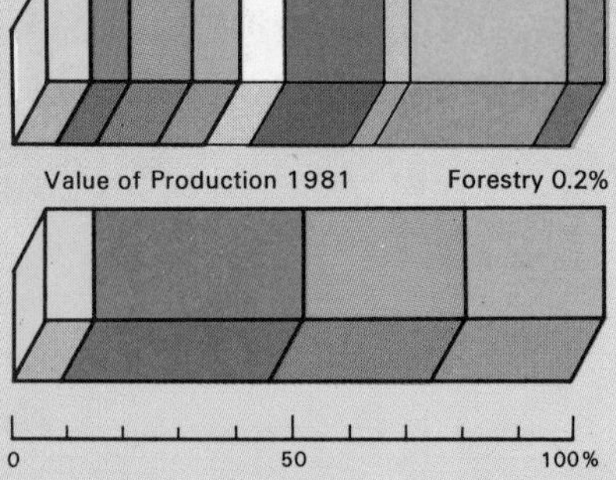

Value of Production 1981 Forestry 0.2%

0 50 100%

Primary
- Agriculture
- Forestry
- Fishing
- Mining
- Other primary industries

Secondary
- Construction
- Manufacturing

Tertiary
- Transport, Communications
- Trade, Commerce
- Finance
- Services
- Public Administration
- Other

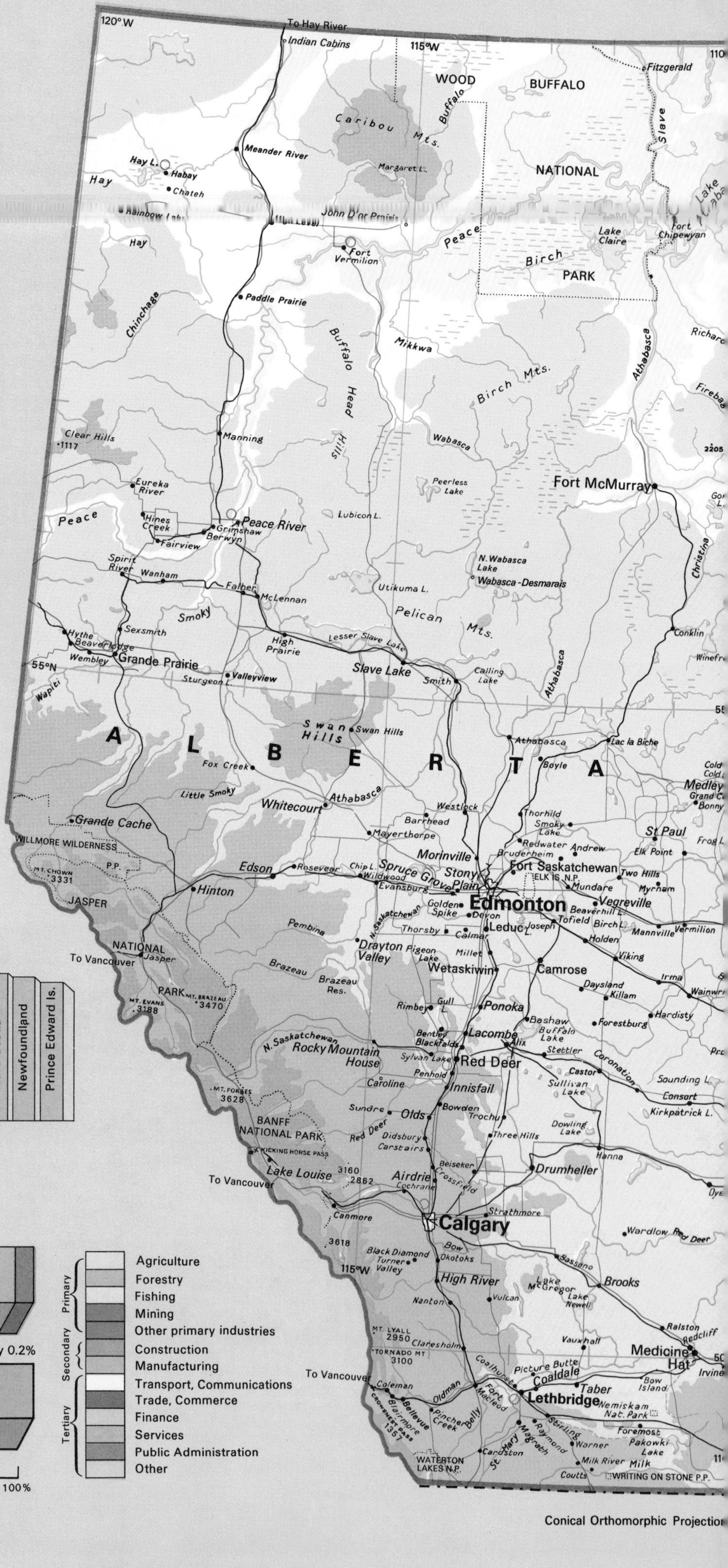

ALBERTA

Conical Orthomorphic Projection

Saskatchewan

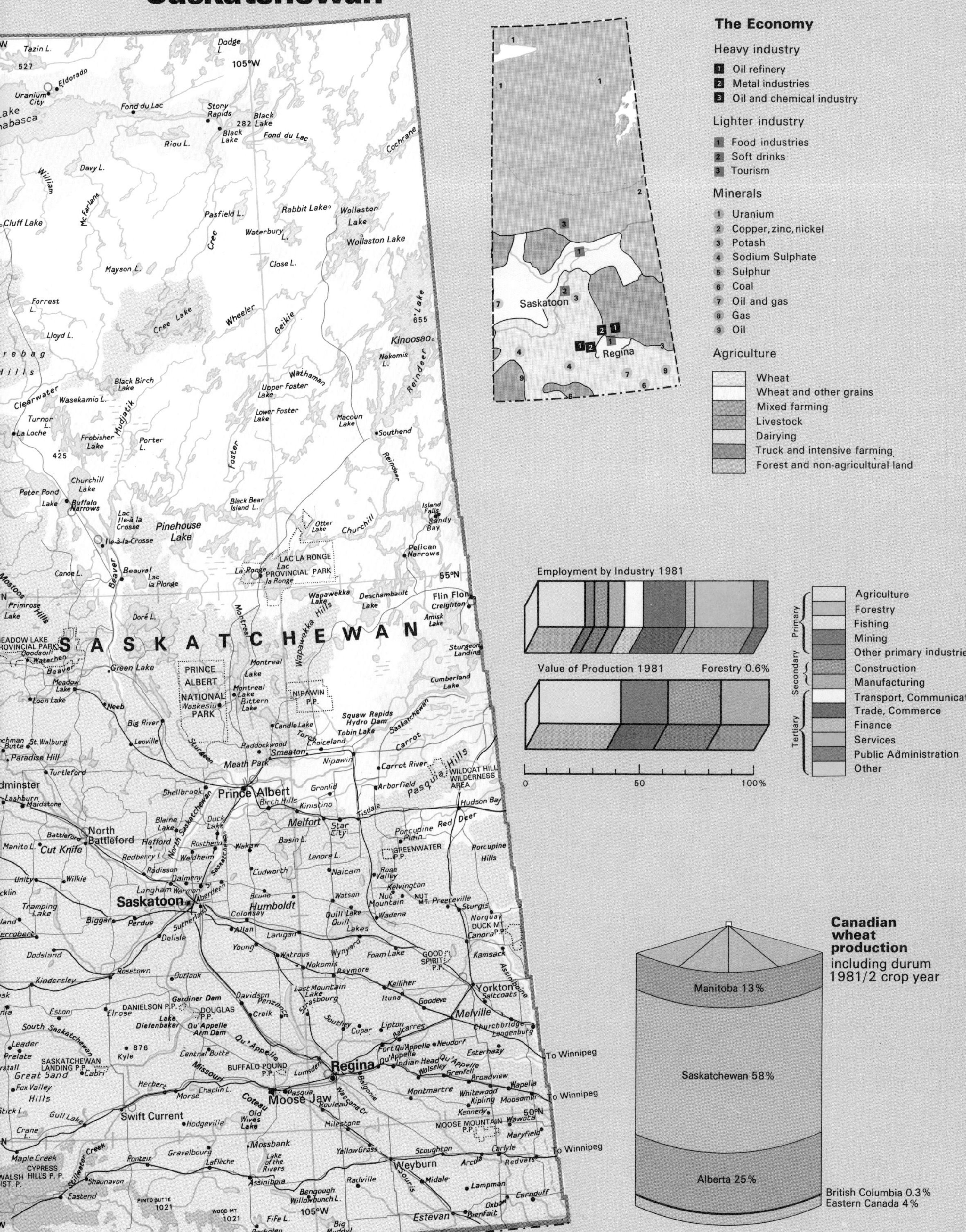
The Economy
Heavy industry
1 Oil refinery
2 Metal industries
3 Oil and chemical industry
Lighter industry
1 Food industries
2 Soft drinks
3 Tourism
Minerals
1 Uranium
2 Copper, zinc, nickel
3 Potash
4 Sodium Sulphate
5 Sulphur
6 Coal
7 Oil and gas
8 Gas
9 Oil
Agriculture
Wheat
Wheat and other grains
Mixed farming
Livestock
Dairying
Truck and intensive farming
Forest and non-agricultural land
Saskatoon
Regina
Employment by Industry 1981
Value of Production 1981
Forestry 0.6%
0
50
100%
Primary
Agriculture
Forestry
Fishing
Mining
Other primary industries
Secondary
Construction
Manufacturing
Tertiary
Transport, Communications
Trade, Commerce
Finance
Services
Public Administration
Other
Canadian wheat production
including durum
1981/2 crop year
Manitoba 13%
Saskatchewan 58%
Alberta 25%
British Columbia 0.3%
Eastern Canada 4%
SASKATCHEWAN
105°W
55°N
50°N
Tazin L.
Dodge L.
Uranium City
Eldorado
Fond du Lac
Stony Rapids
Black Lake
Riou L.
Cochrane
Davy L.
William
McFarlane
Cluff Lake
Pasfield L.
Rabbit Lake
Wollaston Lake
Waterbury L.
Cree
Close L.
Mayson L.
Forrest L.
Cree Lake
Wheeler
Geikie
Kinoosao
Lloyd L.
Nokomis L.
Reindeer Lake
Wathaman
Black Birch Lake
Upper Foster Lake
Lower Foster Lake
Clearwater
Wasekamio L.
Turnor L.
La Loche
Frobisher Lake
Mudjatik
Porter L.
Macoun Lake
Southend
Foster
Churchill Lake
Peter Pond Lake
Buffalo Narrows
Black Bear Island L.
Island Falls
Sandy Bay
Lac Île-à-la Crosse
Pinehouse Lake
Otter Lake
Churchill
Île-à-la-Crosse
Pelican Narrows
Canoe L.
Beauval
Lac la Plonge
Beaver
La Ronge
LAC LA RONGE PROVINCIAL PARK
Lac la Ronge
Wapawekka Lake
Deschambault Lake
Flin Flon
Creighton
Amisk Lake
Primrose Lake
Doré L.
Montreal
Wapawekka Hills
Sturgeon Landing
MEADOW LAKE PROVINCIAL PARK
Goodsoil
Waterhen
Beaver
Green Lake
Meadow Lake
Loon Lake
PRINCE ALBERT NATIONAL PARK
Waskesiu
Montreal Lake
Montreal Lake
Bittern Lake
NIPAWIN P.P.
Cumberland Lake
Neeb
Big River
Leoville
Candle Lake
Squaw Rapids Hydro Dam
Tobin Lake
Saskatchewan
Carrot
St. Walburg
Paradise Hill
Turtleford
Paddockwood
Smeaton
Choiceland
Torch
Sturgeon
Meath Park
Nipawin
Carrot River
Pasquia Hills
WILDCAT HILL WILDERNESS AREA
Arborfield
Shellbrook
Prince Albert
Gronlid
Birch Hills
Kinistino
Tisdale
Hudson Bay
Lashburn
Maidstone
Blaine Lake
Duck Lake
Melfort
Star City
Red Deer
North Battleford
Battleford
Hafford
Rosthern
Porcupine Plain
Manito L.
Cut Knife
Redberry L.
Waldheim
Wakaw
Basin L.
Lenore L.
GREENWATER P.P.
Porcupine Hills
Radisson
North Saskatchewan
South Saskatchewan
Unity
Wilkie
Dalmeny
Cudworth
Naicam
Rose Valley
Langham
Warman
Aberdeen
Bruno
Watson
Kelvington
Tramping Lake
Saskatoon
Humboldt
Nut Mountain
NUT MT.
Preeceville
Sturgis
Quill Lake
Quill Lakes
Wadena
Norquay
DUCK MT.
Biggar
Perdue
Sutherland
Colonsay
Allan
Canora
Delisle
Lanigan
Young
Wynyard
Dodsland
Watrous
Nokomis
Foam Lake
GOOD SPIRIT P.P.
Kamsack
Rosetown
Outlook
Raymore
Kindersley
Last Mountain Lake
Kelliher
Yorkton
Saltcoats
Assiniboine
Gardiner Dam
Davidson
Penzance
Strasbourg
Ituna
Goodeve
Melville
DANIELSON P.P.
DOUGLAS P.P.
Elrose
Eston
Craik
Lake Diefenbaker
Qu'Appelle Arm Dam
Southey
Cupar
Lipton
Balcarres
Churchbridge
Langenburg
Leader
Prelate
Kyle
876
Central Butte
Qu'Appelle
Fort Qu'Appelle
Neudorf
Esterhazy
To Winnipeg
SASKATCHEWAN LANDING P.P.
Cabri
Great Sand Hills
Missouri
BUFFALO POUND P.P.
Lumsden
Regina
Indian Head
Wolseley
Grenfell
Broadview
Wapella
Fox Valley
Herbert
Morse
Chaplin L.
Coteau
Pasqua
Moose Jaw
Balgonie
Wascana Cr
Montmartre
Whitewood
Kipling
Moosomin
Gull Lake
Swift Current
Hodgeville
Old Wives Lake
Rouleau
Kennedy
Wawota
Crane L.
Milestone
MOOSE MOUNTAIN P.P.
Maryfield
Mossbank
Yellow Grass
Stoughton
Carlyle
Maple Creek
CYPRESS HILLS P.P.
Ponteix
Gravelbourg
Laflèche
Lake of the Rivers
Weyburn
Arcola
Redvers
Stillwater Creek
Shaunavon
Assiniboia
Radville
Midale
Souris
Lampman
Eastend
Bengough
Willowbunch L.
Oxbow
Carnduff
PINTO BUTTE 1021
WOOD MT 1021
Fife L.
Big Muddy L.
Estevan
Bienfait
Rockglen
527
282
425
655

Manitoba

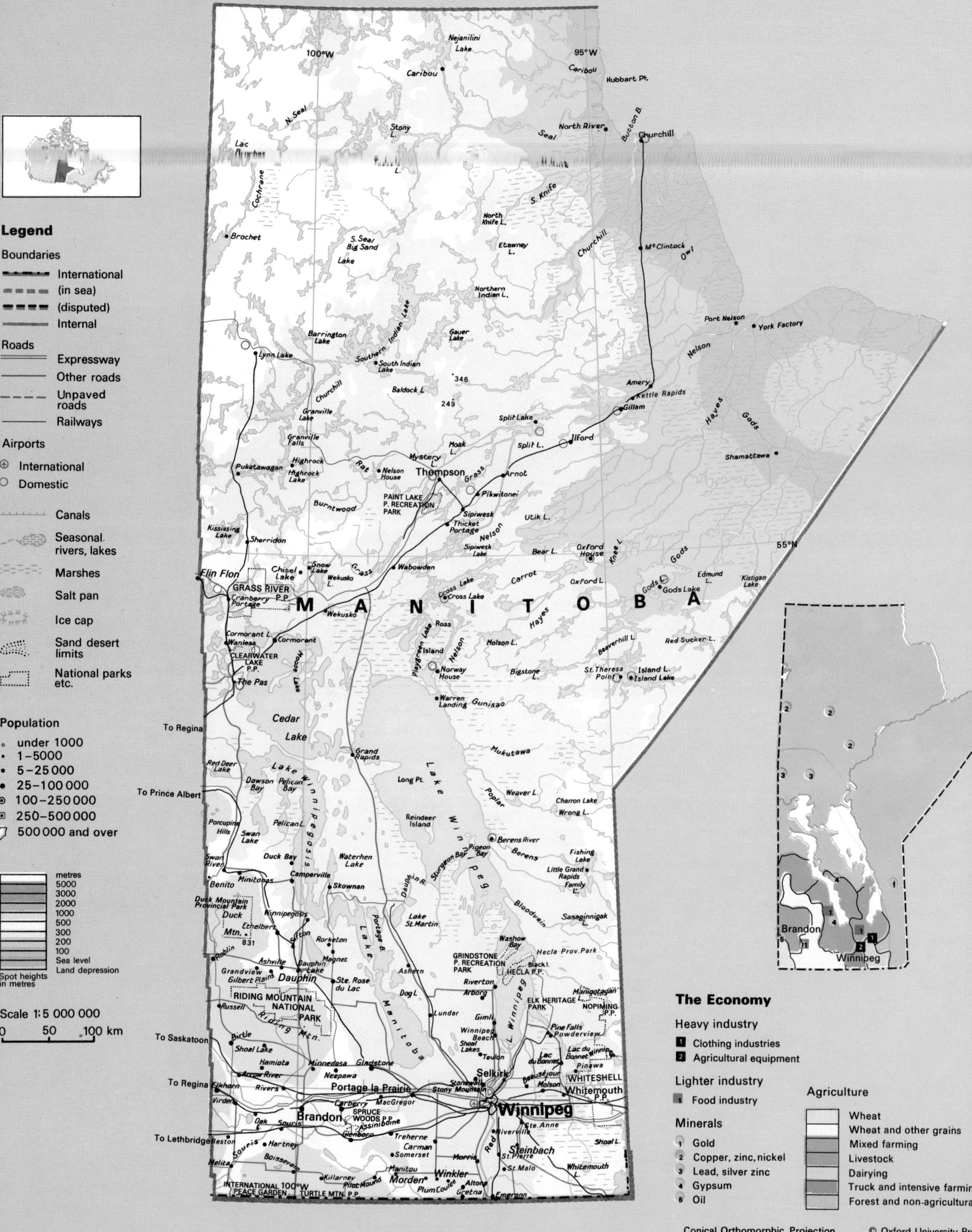
Legend
Boundaries
International
(in sea)
(disputed)
Internal
Roads
Expressway
Other roads
Unpaved roads
Railways
Airports
International
Domestic
Canals
Seasonal rivers, lakes
Marshes
Salt pan
Ice cap
Sand desert limits
National parks etc.
Population
under 1000
1–5000
5–25 000
25–100 000
100–250 000
250–500 000
500 000 and over
metres
5000
3000
2000
1000
500
300
200
100
Sea level
Land depression
Spot heights in metres
Scale 1:5 000 000
0 50 100 km
MANITOBA
Winnipeg
Brandon
Thompson
Churchill
Flin Flon
The Pas
Dauphin
Selkirk
Portage la Prairie
Lake Winnipeg
Lake Manitoba
Lake Winnipegosis
Cedar Lake
To Regina
To Prince Albert
To Saskatoon
To Lethbridge
The Economy
Heavy industry
1 Clothing industries
2 Agricultural equipment
Lighter industry
1 Food industry
Minerals
1 Gold
2 Copper, zinc, nickel
3 Lead, silver zinc
4 Gypsum
5 Oil
Agriculture
Wheat
Wheat and other grains
Mixed farming
Livestock
Dairying
Truck and intensive farming
Forest and non-agricultural

Conical Orthomorphic Projection

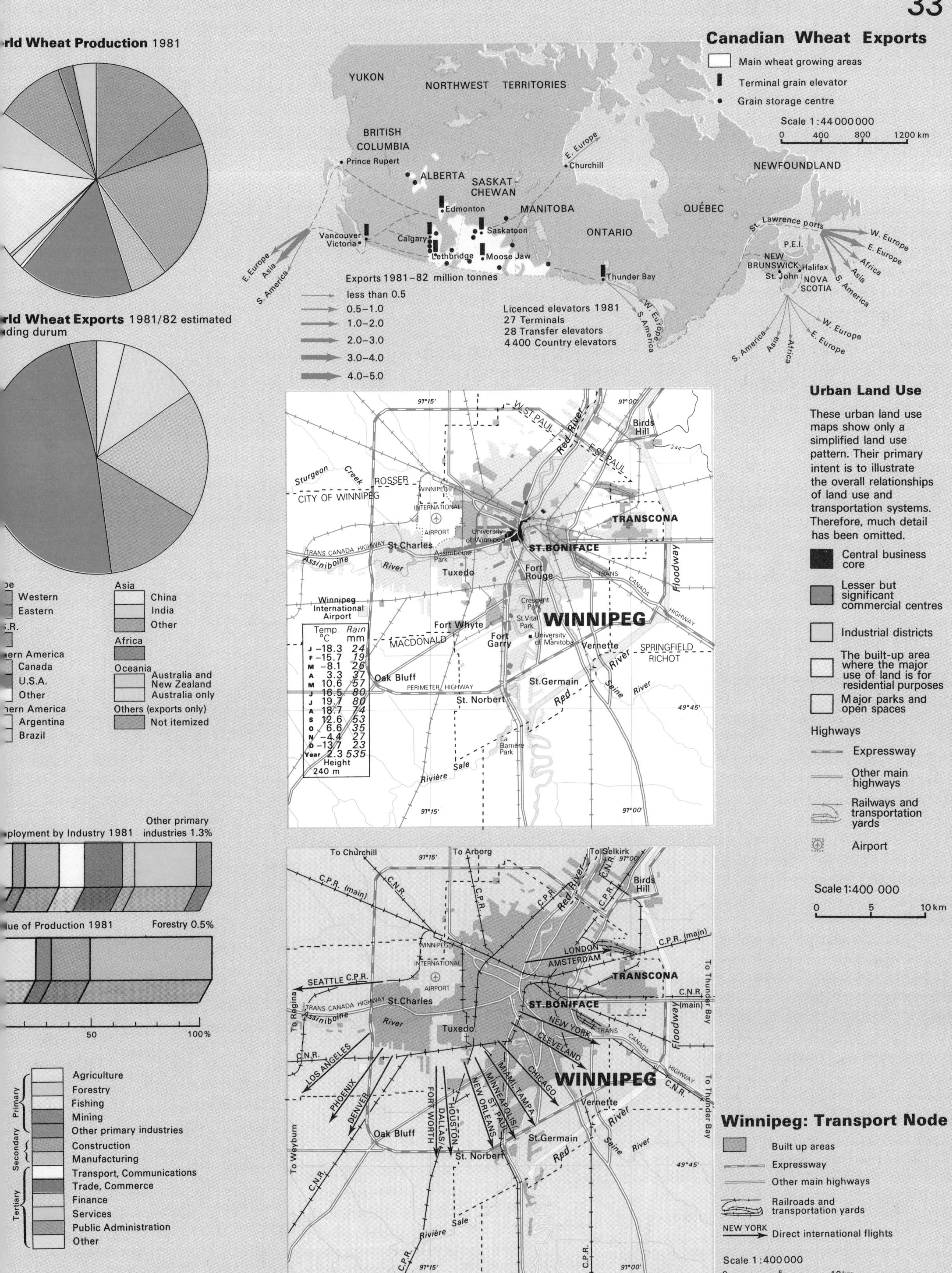
rld Wheat Production 1981
rld Wheat Exports 1981/82 estimated
ding durum
Asia
Western
China
Eastern
India
Other
Africa
Canada
Oceania
U.S.A.
Australia and New Zealand
Other
Australia only
Others (exports only)
Argentina
Not itemized
Brazil
ployment by Industry 1981
Other primary industries 1.3%
ue of Production 1981
Forestry 0.5%
50
100%
Agriculture
Forestry
Fishing
Mining
Other primary industries
Construction
Manufacturing
Transport, Communications
Trade, Commerce
Finance
Services
Public Administration
Other
Primary
Secondary
Tertiary
Canadian Wheat Exports
Main wheat growing areas
Terminal grain elevator
Grain storage centre
Scale 1:44 000 000
0 400 800 1200 km
YUKON
NORTHWEST TERRITORIES
BRITISH COLUMBIA
ALBERTA
SASKATCHEWAN
MANITOBA
ONTARIO
QUÉBEC
NEWFOUNDLAND
Prince Rupert
Churchill
E. Europe
Edmonton
Saskatoon
Vancouver
Victoria
Calgary
Lethbridge
Moose Jaw
Thunder Bay
St. Lawrence ports
W. Europe
E. Europe
Africa
Asia
S. America
P.E.I.
NEW BRUNSWICK
Halifax
St. John
NOVA SCOTIA
Exports 1981–82 million tonnes
less than 0.5
0.5–1.0
1.0–2.0
2.0–3.0
3.0–4.0
4.0–5.0
Licenced elevators 1981
27 Terminals
28 Transfer elevators
4 400 Country elevators
Urban Land Use
These urban land use maps show only a simplified land use pattern. Their primary intent is to illustrate the overall relationships of land use and transportation systems. Therefore, much detail has been omitted.
Central business core
Lesser but significant commercial centres
Industrial districts
The built-up area where the major use of land is for residential purposes
Major parks and open spaces
Highways
Expressway
Other main highways
Railways and transportation yards
Airport
Scale 1:400 000
0 5 10 km
WINNIPEG
ST. BONIFACE
TRANSCONA
Birds Hill
ROSSER
CITY OF WINNIPEG
Sturgeon Creek
St. Charles
Assiniboine River
Tuxedo
Fort Rouge
Fort Whyte
Fort Garry
MACDONALD
Oak Bluff
St. Norbert
St. Germain
Vernette
SPRINGFIELD
RICHOT
Red River
Seine River
Rivière Sale
Floodway
Winnipeg International Airport
Temp. °C Rain mm
J −18.3 24
F −15.7 19
M −8.1 26
A 3.3 37
M 10.6 57
J 16.5 80
J 19.7 80
A 18.7 74
S 12.6 53
O 6.6 35
N −4.4 27
D −13.7 23
Year 2.3 535
Height 240 m
91°15′
91°00′
49°45′
Winnipeg: Transport Node
Built up areas
Expressway
Other main highways
Railroads and transportation yards
NEW YORK Direct international flights
Scale 1:400 000
0 5 10 km
To Churchill
To Arborg
To Selkirk
C.P.R. (main)
C.N.R.
C.P.R.
SEATTLE
LONDON
AMSTERDAM
NEW YORK
CLEVELAND
CHICAGO
MIAMI-TAMPA
MINNEAPOLIS/ST. PAUL
NEW ORLEANS
HOUSTON
DALLAS/FORT WORTH
DENVER
PHOENIX
LOS ANGELES
To Regina
To Weyburn
To Thunder Bay
To North Dakota
To Minnesota

Ontario

Legend
Boundaries
International
(in lakes)
(disputed)
Internal
Roads
Expressways
Other roads
Unpaved roads
Railways
Airports
International
Domestic
Canals
Seasonal rivers, lakes
Marshes
Salt pan
Ice cap
Sand desert limits
National parks etc.
Population
under 1000
1–5000
5–25 000
25–100 000
100–250 000
250–500 000
500 000 and over
metres
5000
3000
2000
1000
500
300
200
100
Sea level
Land depression
Spot heights in metres
Scale 1: 6 500 000
0 50 100 km
Conical Orthomorphic Projection
Employment by Industry 1981
Fishing 0.2%
Forestry 0.8%
Value of Production 1981
Forestry 0.6%
0
50
100%
Primary
Agriculture
Forestry
Fishing
Mining
Other primary industries
Secondary
Construction
Manufacturing
Tertiary
Transport, Communications
Trade, Commerce
Finance
Services
Public Administration
Other
ONTARIO
Fort Severn
Approximate Southern limit of continuous permafrost
Approximate Southern limit of discontinuous permafrost
90°W
85°W
80°W
55°N
50°N
45°N
Winisk
Cape Henrietta Maria
POLAR BEAR PROV. PARK
WINISK RIVER P.P.
Severn
Big Trout Lake
Asheweig
Opasquia
Shibogama Lake
Wunnummin Lake
Winisk Lake
Chipai Lake
Kingfisher Lake
North Caribou Lake
Sandy Lake
Windigo Lake
Attawapiskat
Attawapiskat Lake
Missisa Lake
Fort Albany
Kapiskau
Pikangikum Lake
Otoskwin
Pickle Lake
Fort Hope
Red Lake
Trout Lake
Balmertown
Madsen
Lake St. Joseph
Albany
Moosonee
Ear Falls
Goldpines
Lac Seul
Ogoki
Moose
English
Grassy Narrows
Hudson
Sioux Lookout
Armstrong
Missinaibi
Coral Rapids
Abitibi
Keewatin
Kenora
Dryden
Nakina
Kenogami
Mattagami
Lake of the Woods
Eagle Lake
Dinorwic
Lake Nipigon
Longlac
Hearst
Geraldton
Island Falls
Quorn
Trans Canada Highway
Kapuskasing
Smooth Rock Falls
Atikwa Lake
Kakagi Lake
Rainy Lake
Rainy River
Fort Frances
Atikokan
Manitouwadge
Oba
Groundhog
Cochrane
To Québec
Nipigon
Terrace Bay
Iroquois Falls
Lake Abitibi
Isle St. Ignace
Simpson Island
Schreiber
Marathon
White
Porcupine
Matheson
Timmins
Kirkland Lake
QUETICO PARK
Thunder Bay
Slate Islands
White River
Magpie
PUKASKWA NAT. PARK
Michipicoten
Wawa
Englehart
Lake Superior
(Surface height 183 m above m.s.l.)
Michipicoten I.
LAKE SUPERIOR P.P.
Chapleau
Gowganda
New Liskeard
Haileybury
Cobalt
Caribou I.
Montreal
Biskotasi Lake
Temagami
Mississagi
Spanish
Sault Ste. Marie
Elliot Lake
Sudbury
Falconbridge
Sturgeon Falls
Mattawa
North Bay
Thessalon
Blind River
Espanola
North Channel
Little Current
ALGONQUIN PROV. PARK
Pembroke
Renfrew
Arnprior
Manitoulin Island
Georgian Bay
Huntsville
Madawaska
Ottawa
Tobermory
Parry Sound
Smiths Falls
Lake Huron
(Surface height 176 m above m.s.l.)
Bruce Penin.
GEORGIAN BAY IS. N. P.
Midland
L. Simcoe
Brockville
Owen Sound
Orillia
Lindsay
Peterborough
Kingston
Barrie
Trenton
Belleville
Kincardine
Hanover
Oshawa
Cobourg
Clark Pt.
Toronto
Lake Ontario
(Surface height 75 m above m.s.l.)
Goderich
Kitchener-Waterloo
Guelph
Burlington
Brantford
St. Catharines
Hamilton
Niagara Falls
London
Welland
Fort Erie
Sarnia
St. Thomas
Chatham
RONDEAU P.P.
To Chicago
Windsor
PT. PELEE N.P.
Lake Erie
(Surface height 174 m above m.s.l.)
Pelee I.
© Oxford University Press

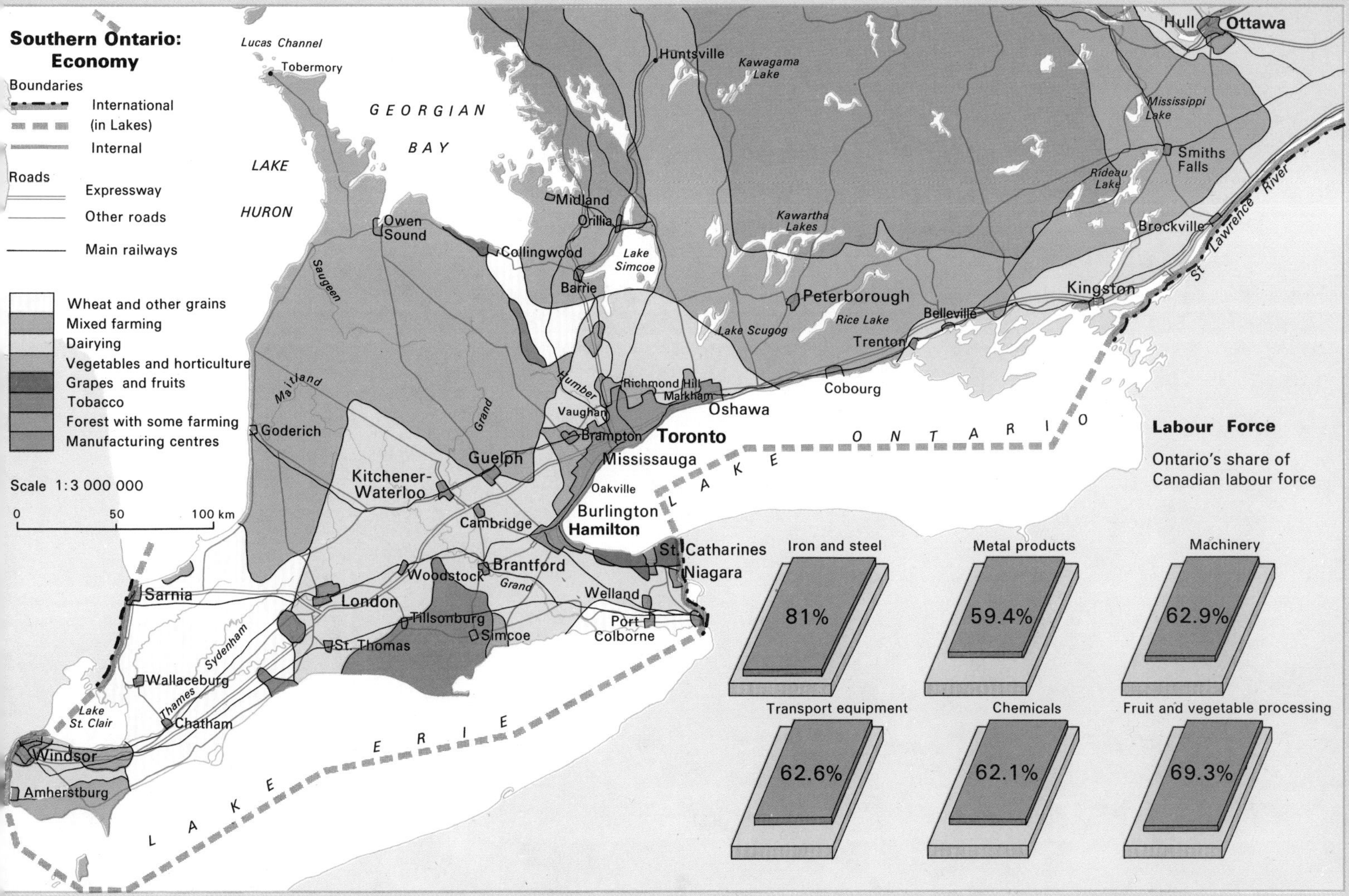

Southern Ontario: Economy

Boundaries
International
(in Lakes)
Internal
Roads
Expressway
Other roads
Main railways
Wheat and other grains
Mixed farming
Dairying
Vegetables and horticulture
Grapes and fruits
Tobacco
Forest with some farming
Manufacturing centres
Scale 1:3 000 000
0
50
100 km
Lucas Channel
Tobermory
GEORGIAN
BAY
LAKE
HURON
Huntsville
Kawagama Lake
Hull
Ottawa
Mississippi Lake
Smiths Falls
Rideau Lake
St Lawrence River
Brockville
Kingston
Midland
Orillia
Owen Sound
Collingwood
Lake Simcoe
Barrie
Kawartha Lakes
Peterborough
Rice Lake
Belleville
Trenton
Lake Scugog
Cobourg
Saugeen
Maitland
Grand
Humber
Richmond Hill
Markham
Oshawa
Vaughan
Brampton
Toronto
Mississauga
Goderich
Guelph
Kitchener-Waterloo
Oakville
Burlington
Hamilton
Cambridge
LAKE ONTARIO
St. Catharines
Niagara
Woodstock
Brantford
Grand
Welland
Sarnia
London
Tillsonburg
Simcoe
Port Colborne
St. Thomas
Sydenham
Wallaceburg
Thames
Chatham
Lake St. Clair
Windsor
Amherstburg
LAKE ERIE

Labour Force

Ontario's share of Canadian labour force

Iron and steel
81%
Metal products
59.4%
Machinery
62.9%
Transport equipment
62.6%
Chemicals
62.1%
Fruit and vegetable processing
69.3%

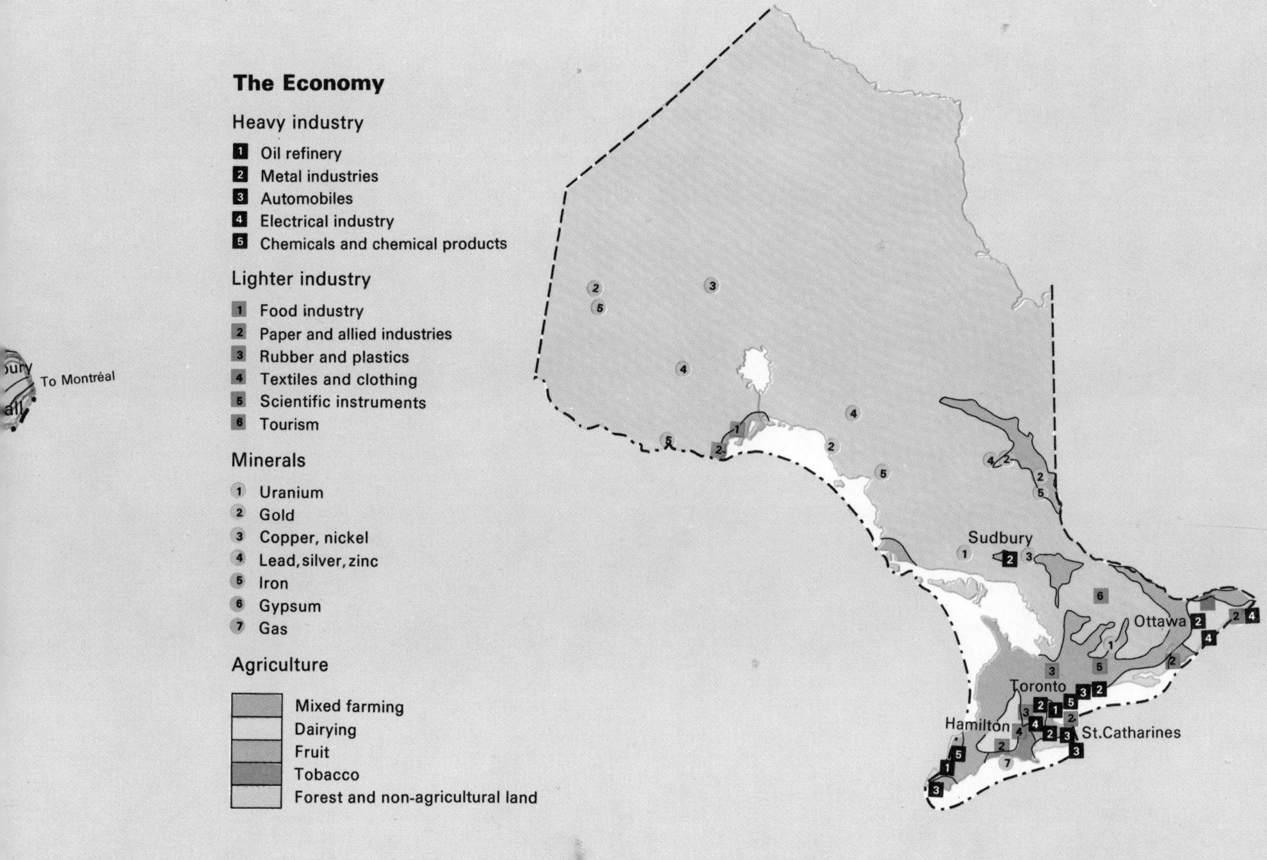

The Economy

Heavy industry
1 Oil refinery
2 Metal industries
3 Automobiles
4 Electrical industry
5 Chemicals and chemical products
Lighter industry
1 Food industry
2 Paper and allied industries
3 Rubber and plastics
4 Textiles and clothing
5 Scientific instruments
6 Tourism
Minerals
1 Uranium
2 Gold
3 Copper, nickel
4 Lead, silver, zinc
5 Iron
6 Gypsum
7 Gas
Agriculture
Mixed farming
Dairying
Fruit
Tobacco
Forest and non-agricultural land
Sudbury
Ottawa
Toronto
Hamilton
St.Catharines
To Montréal

Québec

Legend
Boundaries
International
(in sea)
(disputed)
Internal
Roads
Expressway
Other roads
Unpaved roads
Railways
Airports
International
Domestic
Canals
Seasonal rivers, lakes
Marshes
Salt pan
Ice cap
Sand desert limits
National parks etc.
Population
under 1000
1–5000
5–25 000
25–100 000
100–250 000
250–500 000
500 000 and over
metres
5000
3000
2000
1000
500
300
200
100
Sea level
Land depression
Spot heights in metres
The Economy
Heavy industry
1 Oil refinery
2 Metal industries
3 Aircraft and parts
4 Chemicals and chemical products
Lighter industry
1 Food industry
2 Wood industries
3 Textiles and clothing
4 Scientific instruments
5 Paper and allied industries
6 Tourism
Minerals
1 Gold
2 Copper, gold, silver
3 Iron
4 Asbestos
5 Silica
Agriculture
Mixed farming
Dairying
Potatoes and livestock
Forest and non-agricultural land
Chicoutimi-Jonquière
Québec
Trois-Rivières
Montréal
Ivujivik
Salluit
Déception
Purtuniq
Cap de Nouvelle-France
Cap Prince-de-Galles
Kangiqsujjuaq
Baie Kovik
Baie Kettlestone
Akulivik
Approximate southern limit of continuous permafrost
Péninsule d'Ungava
Povungnituk
Lepelle
Payne
Lac Payne
Kogaluc
Baie Kogaluc
Povungnituk
60°N
75°W
70°W
65°W
60°N
Cap Hopes Advance
Quaqtaq
Ungava Bay
Baie Payne
(Baie d'Ungava)
Kangirsuk
Killiniq
Abloviak Fiord
Baie de Hopes Advance
Î. Kikkertorsoak
Aupaluk
Îles de Gyrfalcon
Lac la Potherie
L'aux Feuilles
80°W
75°W
70°W
55°N
50°N
Caniapiscau
Îles Belcher
Petite r. de la Baleine
Grande r. de la Baleine
GB 1
GB 2
GB 3
Brisay
LA2
Réservoir Caniapiscau
Rés. LG 2
Rés. LG 3
LG 1
LG 2
LG 3
LG 4
La Grande Rivière
Baie James
Q U É B E
Rés. Opinaca
EM 1
EM 2
Eastmain
Rés EMI
R 11
R 10
Rupert
B1–6
B8
Nottaway
Broadback
Lac Mistassini
Lac Matagami
100
200
300 km
Lake or reservoir
Projected reservoir
Generating station
Dam

James Bay Project

The Société d'énergie de la Baie James (SEBJ) started to develop the hydroelectric potential of the James Bay Territory in 1971–1973.

Phase I of the project was centred on La Grande Rivière and its drainage basin. La Grande Rivière and its tributaries, which flow west into James Bay, have a flow of 1700 m³/sec, and a drop in elevation of 376 m. By diverting the flow of two adjacent rivers and their drainage basins, the Eastmain and the Cani[illegible]scau, into La Grande Rivière, an a[illegible]tional inflow of 1600 m³/sec was [illegible]tained.

Th[illegible]astmain and its tributaries flow [illegible]st into James Bay. The cons[illegible]ction of a series of dams and dike[illegible]verted 87% of the flow of thes[illegible]vers into La Grande Rivière. The [illegible]ters of the Caniapiscau flow north[illegible] to Ungava Bay; several dams and [illegible] dikes cut off 27% of the flow and [illegible]annel it into a reservoir; from ther[illegible]e water descends by gravity, into [illegible] Grande Rivière.

La Grande Complex-Phase I: Capa[illegible]ty

Jobsite	Water level max. m	Water level min. m	Active storage million m³	Reservoir area max. level km²	[illegible]mber of [illegible]erating [illegible]ts	Installed capacity MW	Guaranteed annual output TWh	Distance from river mouth km
La Grande 2	175	168	19 360	2 835	[illegible]	5 328	35.8	112
La Grande 3	256	244	25 480	2 460	[illegible]	2 304	12.3	238
La Grande 4	377	366	7 100	765	[illegible]	2 650	14.1	463
Caniapiscau	536	523	38 500	4 285	--	--	--	850 (approx.)

Phase II construction is planned to be completed by 1992. It calls for the construction of one generating station on La Grande Rivière itself, approximately 37 km from the mouth of the river (LG 1); two generating stations on the Eastmain River (EM1 and EM2); a generating station at Brisay (where the water intake structure has already been completed under Phase I); and two others in the Caniapiscau diversion area (LA1 and LA2).

The Future

A further development would be centred on a more northerly river, the Grande rivière de la Baleine, and its tributary, the Petite rivière de la Baleine, which flow into Hudson Bay. Three generating stations would be constructed on the main river, and the waters of the tributary would be diverted into the main river at the site of the second generating station.

Even longer-range plans call for the construction of seven generating stations on the Broadback River, south of La Grande Rivière, and which also flows into James Bay. Additional stations would be built on the Nottaway and Rupert Rivers, which would be diverted into the Broadback.

Employment by Industry 1981

Value of Production 1981

Fishing 0.1%
Forestry 1.3%

0 50 100%

Primary: Agriculture, Forestry, Fishing, Mining, Other primary industries
Secondary: Construction, Manufacturing
Tertiary: Transport, Communications, Trade, Commerce, Finance, Services, Public Administration, Other

Conical Orthomorphic Projection

Lake Ontario-Upper St. Lawrence

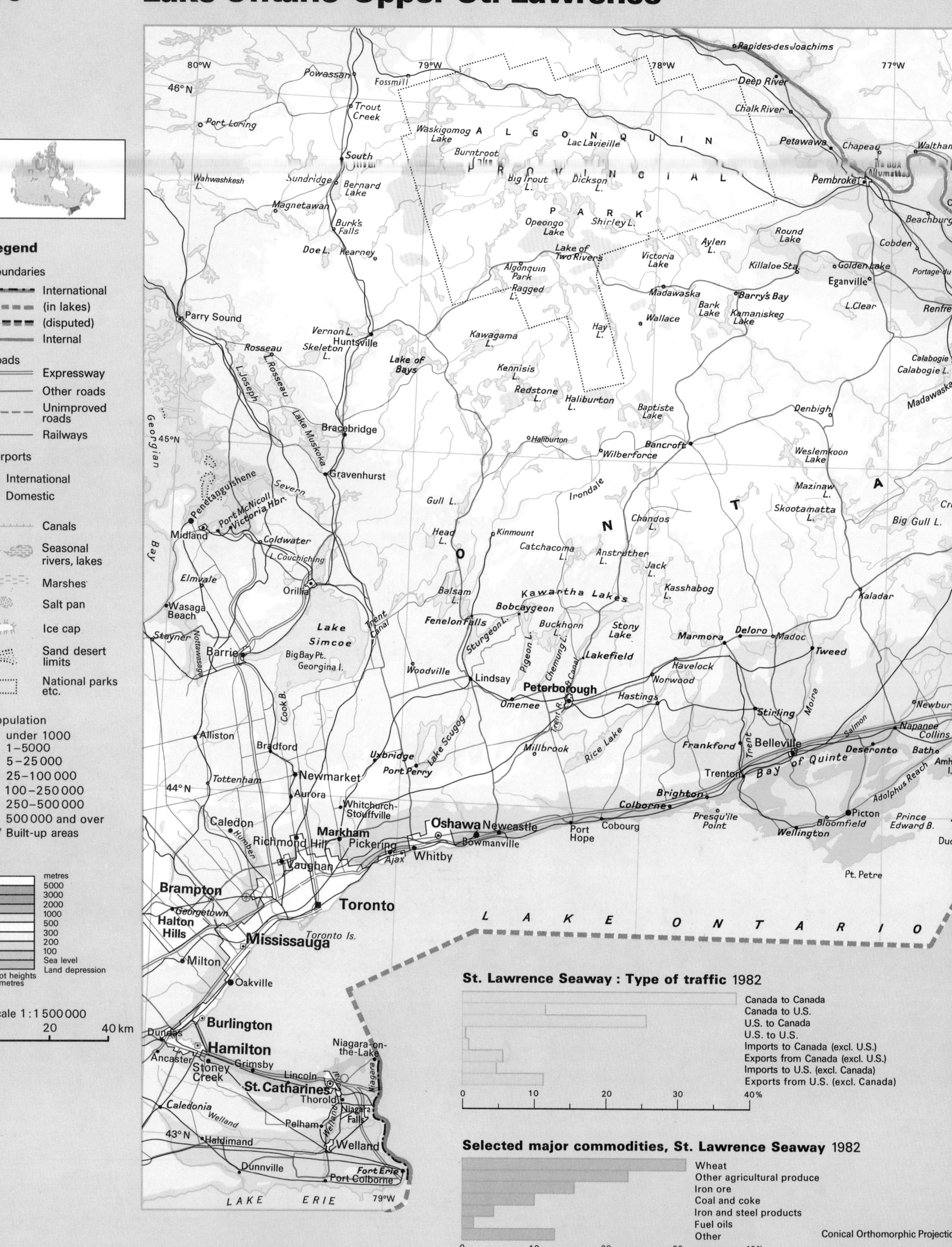
Legend
Boundaries
International
(in lakes)
(disputed)
Internal
Roads
Expressway
Other roads
Unimproved roads
Railways
Airports
International
Domestic
Canals
Seasonal rivers, lakes
Marshes
Salt pan
Ice cap
Sand desert limits
National parks etc.
Population
under 1000
1–5000
5–25 000
25–100 000
100–250 000
250–500 000
500 000 and over
Built-up areas
metres
5000
3000
2000
1000
500
300
200
100
Sea level
Land depression
Spot heights in metres
Scale 1 : 1 500 000
0
20
40 km
80°W
79°W
78°W
77°W
46° N
45°N
44° N
43° N
ALGONQUIN PROVINCIAL PARK
ONTARIO
LAKE ONTARIO
LAKE ERIE
Georgian Bay
Rapides-des-Joachims
Deep River
Chalk River
Petawawa
Chapeau
Waltham
Pembroke
Allumette
Beachburg
Cobden
Golden Lake
Eganville
Portage-du-Fort
Renfrew
L.Clear
Calabogie
Calabogie L.
Madawaska
Denbigh
Weslemkoon Lake
Mazinaw L.
Skootamatta L.
Big Gull L.
Kaladar
Tweed
Madoc
Deloro
Marmora
Havelock
Norwood
Stirling
Moira
Newburgh
Napanee
Collins B.
Bath
Deseronto
Belleville
Bay of Quinte
Trenton
Frankford
Trent
Salmon
Adolphus Reach
Amherst I.
Picton
Bloomfield
Wellington
Prince Edward B.
Duck
Pt. Petre
Brighton
Presqu'ile Point
Colborne
Cobourg
Port Hope
Newcastle
Bowmanville
Oshawa
Whitby
Ajax
Pickering
Markham
Richmond Hill
Vaughan
Toronto
Toronto Is.
Brampton
Georgetown
Halton Hills
Mississauga
Milton
Oakville
Burlington
Dundas
Hamilton
Ancaster
Stoney Creek
Grimsby
Lincoln
St. Catharines
Thorold
Niagara-on-the-Lake
Niagara Falls
Welland
Welland Canal
Pelham
Caledonia
Haldimand
Dunnville
Port Colborne
Fort Erie
Powassan
Fossmill
Trout Creek
Port Loring
South River
Sundridge
Bernard Lake
Wahwashkesh L.
Magnetawan
Burk's Falls
Doe L.
Kearney
Waskigomog Lake
Burntroot
Lac Lavieille
Big Trout L.
Dickson L.
Opeongo Lake
Shirley L.
Lake of Two Rivers
Algonquin Park
Ragged L.
Victoria Lake
Aylen L.
Round Lake
Killaloe Sta.
Madawaska
Barry's Bay
Bark Lake
Kamaniskeg Lake
Wallace
Hay L.
Kawagama L.
Kennisis L.
Redstone L.
Haliburton L.
Haliburton
Baptiste Lake
Bancroft
Wilberforce
Irondale
Chandos L.
Anstruther L.
Jack L.
Kasshabog L.
Catchacoma L.
Kinmount
Parry Sound
Vernon L.
Huntsville
Skeleton L.
Rosseau
L. Rosseau
L. Joseph
Lake of Bays
Lake Muskoka
Bracebridge
Gravenhurst
Severn
Penetanguishene
Port McNicoll
Victoria Hbr.
Midland
Coldwater
L. Couchiching
Orillia
Elmvale
Wasaga Beach
Stayner
Nottawasaga
Barrie
Lake Simcoe
Big Bay Pt.
Georgina I.
Trent Canal
Gull L.
Head L.
Balsam L.
Fenelon Falls
Kawartha Lakes
Bobcaygeon
Sturgeon L.
Pigeon L.
Buckhorn L.
Chemung L.
Stony Lake
Lakefield
Woodville
Lindsay
Omemee
Peterborough
Hastings
Trent R.
Rice Lake
Millbrook
Cook B.
Lake Scugog
Port Perry
Uxbridge
Alliston
Bradford
Newmarket
Aurora
Tottenham
Whitchurch-Stouffville
Caledon
Humber
St. Lawrence Seaway : Type of traffic 1982
Canada to Canada
Canada to U.S.
U.S. to Canada
U.S. to U.S.
Imports to Canada (excl. U.S.)
Exports from Canada (excl. U.S.)
Imports to U.S. (excl. Canada)
Exports from U.S. (excl. Canada)
0
10
20
30
40%
Selected major commodities, St. Lawrence Seaway 1982
Wheat
Other agricultural produce
Iron ore
Coal and coke
Iron and steel products
Fuel oils
Other
0
10
20
30
40%
Conical Orthomorphic Projection

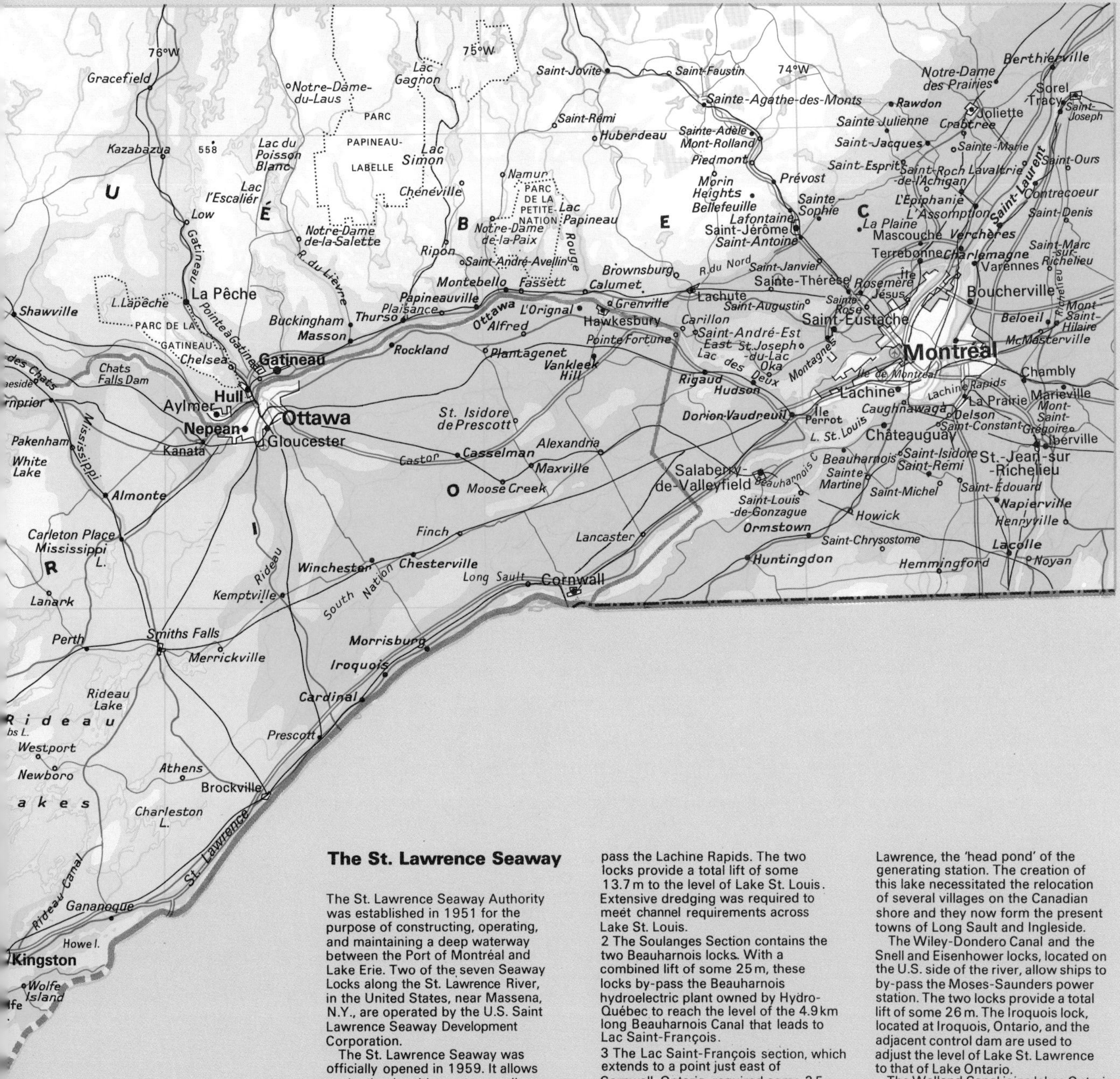

The St. Lawrence Seaway

The St. Lawrence Seaway Authority was established in 1951 for the purpose of constructing, operating, and maintaining a deep waterway between the Port of Montréal and Lake Erie. Two of the seven Seaway Locks along the St. Lawrence River, in the United States, near Massena, N.Y., are operated by the U.S. Saint Lawrence Seaway Development Corporation.

The St. Lawrence Seaway was officially opened in 1959. It allows navigation by ships not exceeding 222.5 m in length, 23.2 m in width, and loaded to a maximum draft of 7.9 m in a minimum water depth of 8.2 m.

Beginning at Montréal and progressing upstream to Lake Ontario, the Seaway naturally divides into four sections.

1 The Lachine Section required the construction of the 33 km South Shore Canal, including the St. Lambert and Côte Ste.-Catherine locks, to by-pass the Lachine Rapids. The two locks provide a total lift of some 13.7 m to the level of Lake St. Louis. Extensive dredging was required to meet channel requirements across Lake St. Louis.

2 The Soulanges Section contains the two Beauharnois locks. With a combined lift of some 25 m, these locks by-pass the Beauharnois hydroelectric plant owned by Hydro-Québec to reach the level of the 4.9 km long Beauharnois Canal that leads to Lac Saint-François.

3 The Lac Saint-François section, which extends to a point just east of Cornwall, Ontario, required some 3.5 million m^3 of excavation by dredging.

4 The International Section was developed for hydroelectric power generation and navigation simultaneously. The Hydro-Electric Power Commission of Ontario and the Power Authority of the State of New York jointly built the Moses-Saunders Power Dam, the Long Sault and Iroquois control dams, and undertook the flooding of the river above the power dam to form Lake St. Lawrence, the 'head pond' of the generating station. The creation of this lake necessitated the relocation of several villages on the Canadian shore and they now form the present towns of Long Sault and Ingleside.

The Wiley-Dondero Canal and the Snell and Eisenhower locks, located on the U.S. side of the river, allow ships to by-pass the Moses-Saunders power station. The two locks provide a total lift of some 26 m. The Iroquois lock, located at Iroquois, Ontario, and the adjacent control dam are used to adjust the level of Lake St. Lawrence to that of Lake Ontario.

The Welland Canal joins lakes Ontario and Erie and allows ships to by-pass Niagara Falls. The eight locks of the Canal provide a total lift of 99 m. The Welland Canal, completed in 1932, was deepened to ensure 7.2 m draft navigation throughout the Seaway. Modernization and improvements have been implemented on a continuing basis since the early 1960s. A new 13 km section, completed in 1973, takes the canal around, rather than through, the City of Welland.

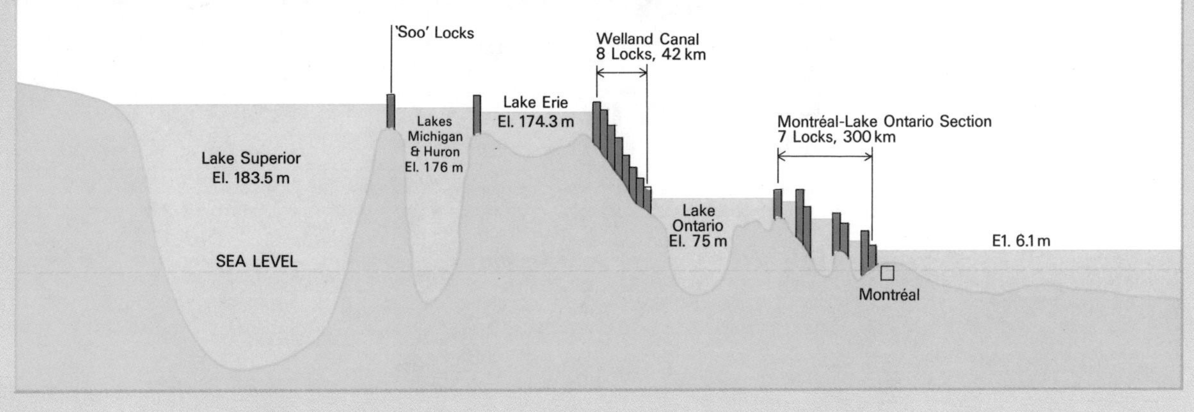
'Soo' Locks
Welland Canal
8 Locks, 42 km
Lake Erie
El. 174.3 m
Lakes
Michigan
& Huron
El. 176 m
Lake Superior
El. 183.5 m
Montréal-Lake Ontario Section
7 Locks, 300 km
Lake
Ontario
El. 75 m
El. 6.1 m
SEA LEVEL
Montréal

Atlantic Provinces

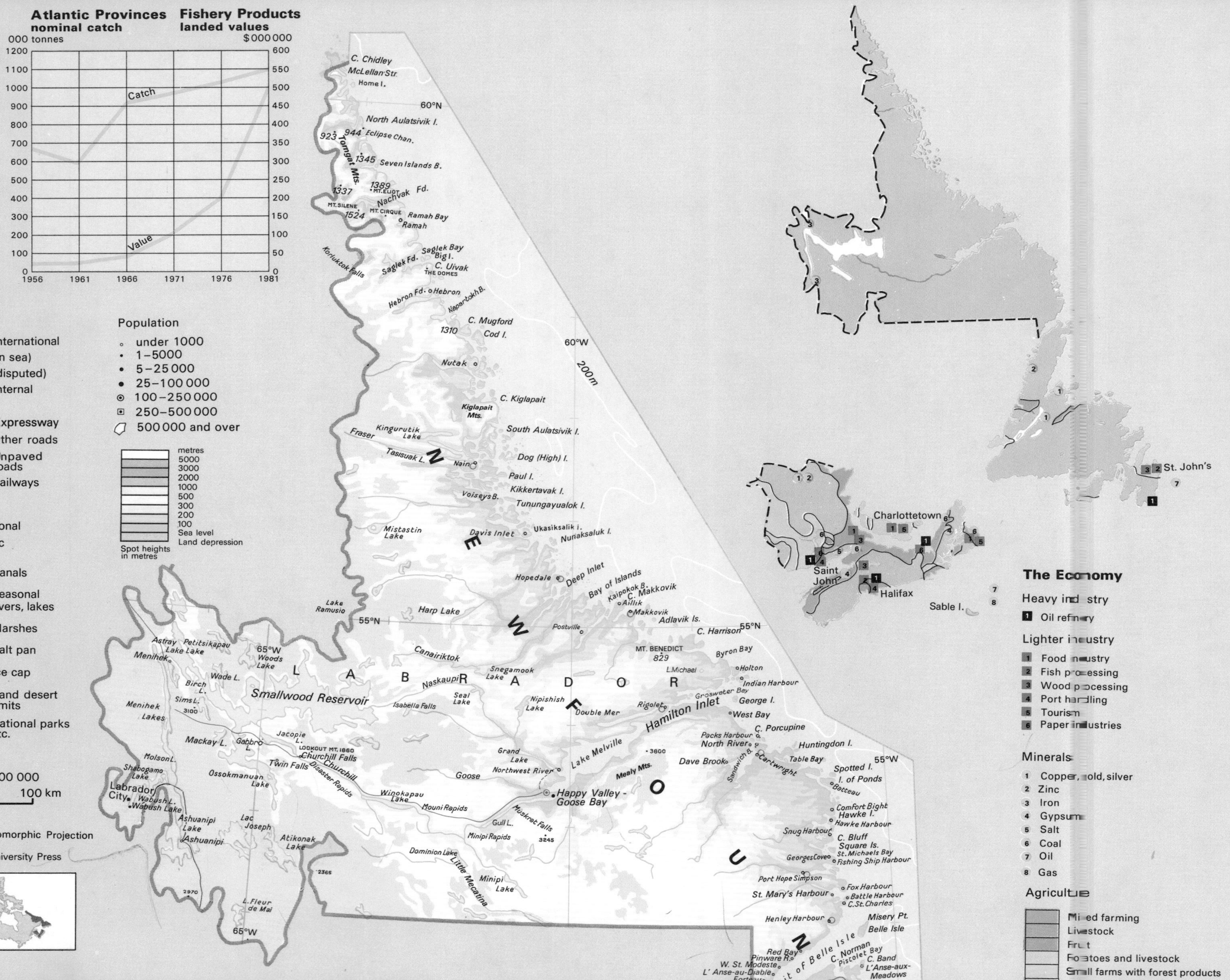

Atlantic Provinces nominal catch
Fishery Products landed values
000 tonnes
$000 000
Catch
Value
1956
1961
1966
1971
1976
1981
Legend
Boundaries
International
(in sea)
(disputed)
Internal
Roads
Expressway
Other roads
Unpaved roads
Railways
Airports
International
Domestic
Canals
Seasonal rivers, lakes
Marshes
Salt pan
Ice cap
Sand desert limits
National parks etc.
Population
under 1000
1–5000
5–25 000
25–100 000
100–250 000
250–500 000
500 000 and over
metres
5000
3000
2000
1000
500
300
200
100
Sea level
Land depression
Spot heights in metres
Scale 1: 5 000 000
0 50 100 km
Conical Orthomorphic Projection
© Oxford University Press
The Economy
Minerals
1 Copper, gold, silver
2 Zinc
3 Iron
4 Gypsum
5 Salt
6 Coal
7 Oil
8 Gas
Agriculture
LABRADOR
NEWFOUNDLAND
C. Chidley
Torngat Mts.
Nain
Hopedale
Makkovik
Smallwood Reservoir
Churchill Falls
Labrador City
Wabush
Hamilton Inlet
Lake Melville
Happy Valley - Goose Bay
Mealy Mts.
Cartwright
Strait of Belle Isle
St. John's
Charlottetown
Saint John
Halifax
Sable I.
200m
60°N
55°N
60°W
55°W
65°W

Nominal catch and fishery products. Units of 100 tonnes 1981

catch

products

Seafish

Shellfish

Landed values and product values. Units of $10 000 1981

catch

products

New Brunswick
Employment by Industry 1981

Value of Production 1981

0 50 100%

Newfoundland
Employment by Industry 1981

Value of Production 1981 Agriculture 1%

0 50 100%

Nova Scotia
Employment by Industry 1981

Value of Production 1981

0 50 100%

Prince Edward Island
Employment by Industry 1981

Value of Production 1981 Mining - structural 0.2%

0 50 100%

Primary
- Agriculture
- Forestry
- Fishing
- Mining
- Other primary industries

Secondary
- Construction
- Manufacturing

Tertiary
- Transport, Communications
- Trade, Commerce
- Finance
- Services
- Public Administration
- Other

Nominal catch
1981

NS. NB. PEI. Nfld.
Units of 50 000 tonnes

Fishery products
1981

Seafish

Shellfish

NS. NB. PEI. Nfld.
Units of 50 000 tonnes

Landed values

NS. NB. PEI. Nfld.
Units of $50 000 000

Product values

NS. NB. PEI. Nfld.
Units of $50 000 000

North and South America: Physical

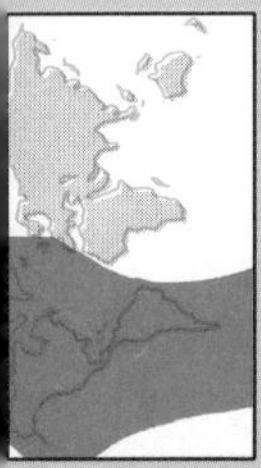

Spot heights in metres

metres 5000 3000 2000 1000 500 300 200 100 Sea level Land depression 200 3000 4000 5000 6000

Scale 1:44 000 000

0 500 1000 km

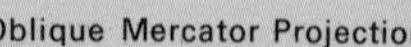

Oblique Mercator Projection

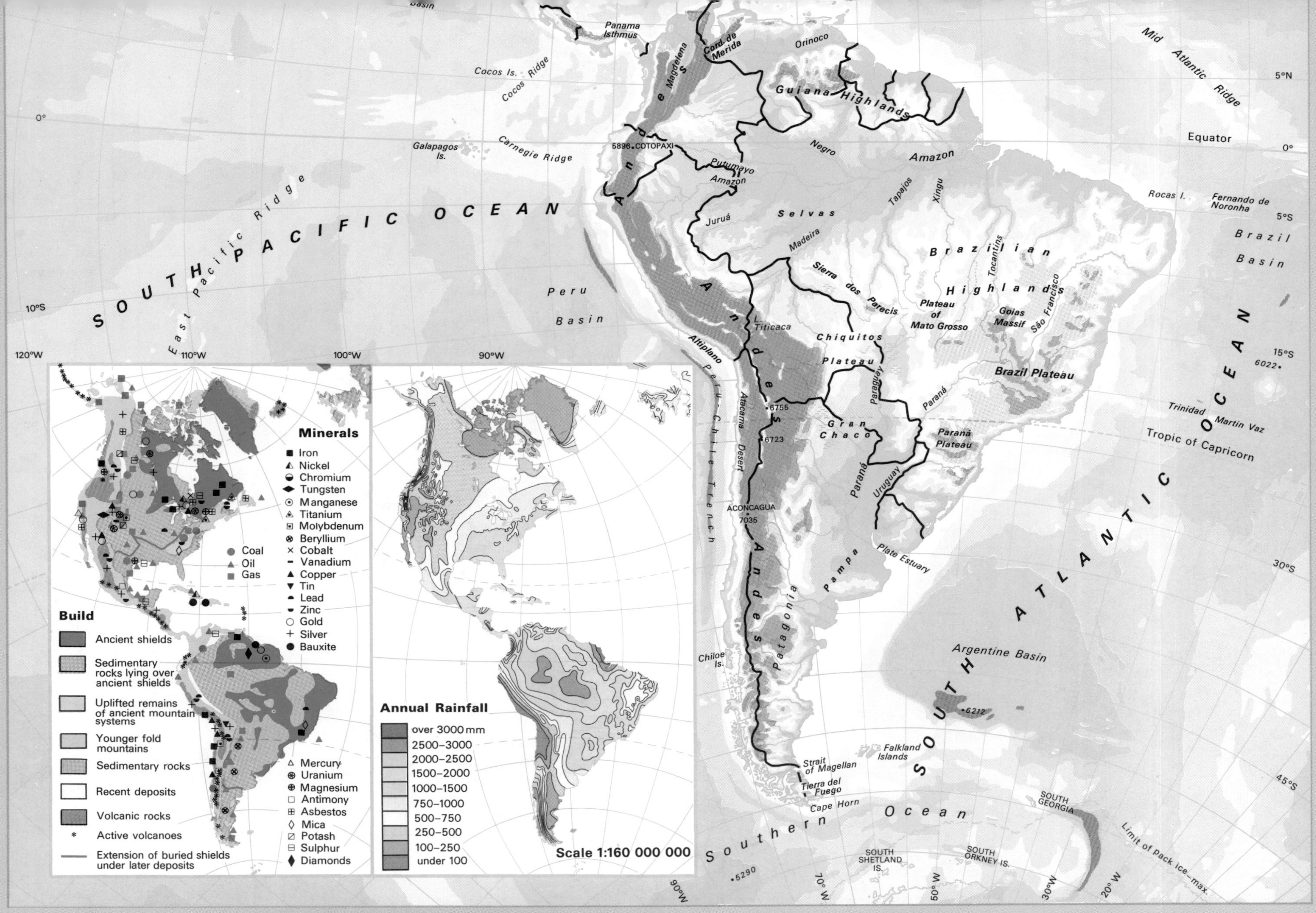

SOUTH PACIFIC OCEAN
SOUTH ATLANTIC OCEAN
Southern Ocean
Mid Atlantic Ridge
Equator
Tropic of Capricorn
Panama Isthmus
Cocos Is.
Cocos Ridge
Galapagos Is.
Carnegie Ridge
East Pacific Ridge
Peru Basin
Peru-Chile Trench
Brazil Basin
Argentine Basin
Rocas I.
Fernando de Noronha
Trinidad
Martin Vaz
6022
6212
5290
Cord. de Merida
Orinoco
Guiana Highlands
Negro
Amazon
Putumayo
Juruá
Madeira
Tapajos
Xingu
Tocantins
São Francisco
Selvas
Brazilian Highlands
Sierra dos Parecis
Plateau of Mato Grosso
Goias Massif
Brazil Plateau
Chiquitos Plateau
Gran Chaco
Paraguay
Paraná
Paraná Plateau
Uruguay
Plate Estuary
Pampa
Patagonia
Andes
5896 COTOPAXI
L. Titicaca
Altiplano
Atacama Desert
6755
6723
ACONCAGUA 7035
Chiloe Is.
Strait of Magellan
Tierra del Fuego
Cape Horn
Falkland Islands
SOUTH GEORGIA
SOUTH SHETLAND IS.
SOUTH ORKNEY IS.
Limit of pack ice–max.
5°N
0°
5°S
10°S
15°S
30°S
45°S
120°W
110°W
100°W
90°W
70° W
50° W
30°W
20° W
Minerals
Iron
Nickel
Chromium
Tungsten
Manganese
Titanium
Molybdenum
Beryllium
Cobalt
Vanadium
Copper
Tin
Lead
Zinc
Gold
Silver
Bauxite
Coal
Oil
Gas
Mercury
Uranium
Magnesium
Antimony
Asbestos
Mica
Potash
Sulphur
Diamonds
Build
Ancient shields
Sedimentary rocks lying over ancient shields
Uplifted remains of ancient mountain systems
Younger fold mountains
Sedimentary rocks
Recent deposits
Volcanic rocks
Active volcanoes
Extension of buried shields under later deposits
Annual Rainfall
over 3000 mm
2500–3000
2000–2500
1500–2000
1000–1500
750–1000
500–750
250–500
100–250
under 100
Scale 1:160 000 000

North and South America: Agriculture

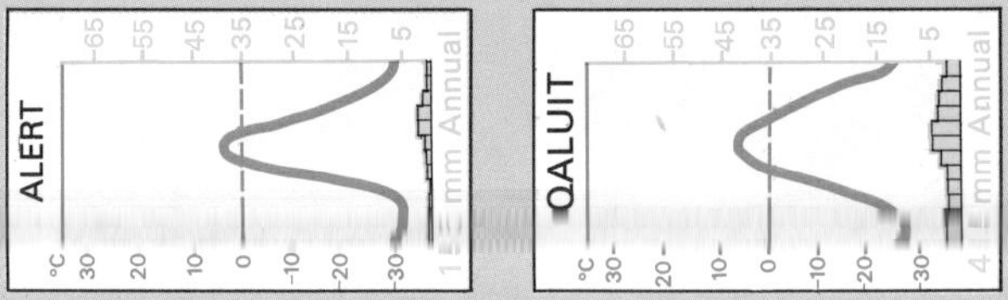

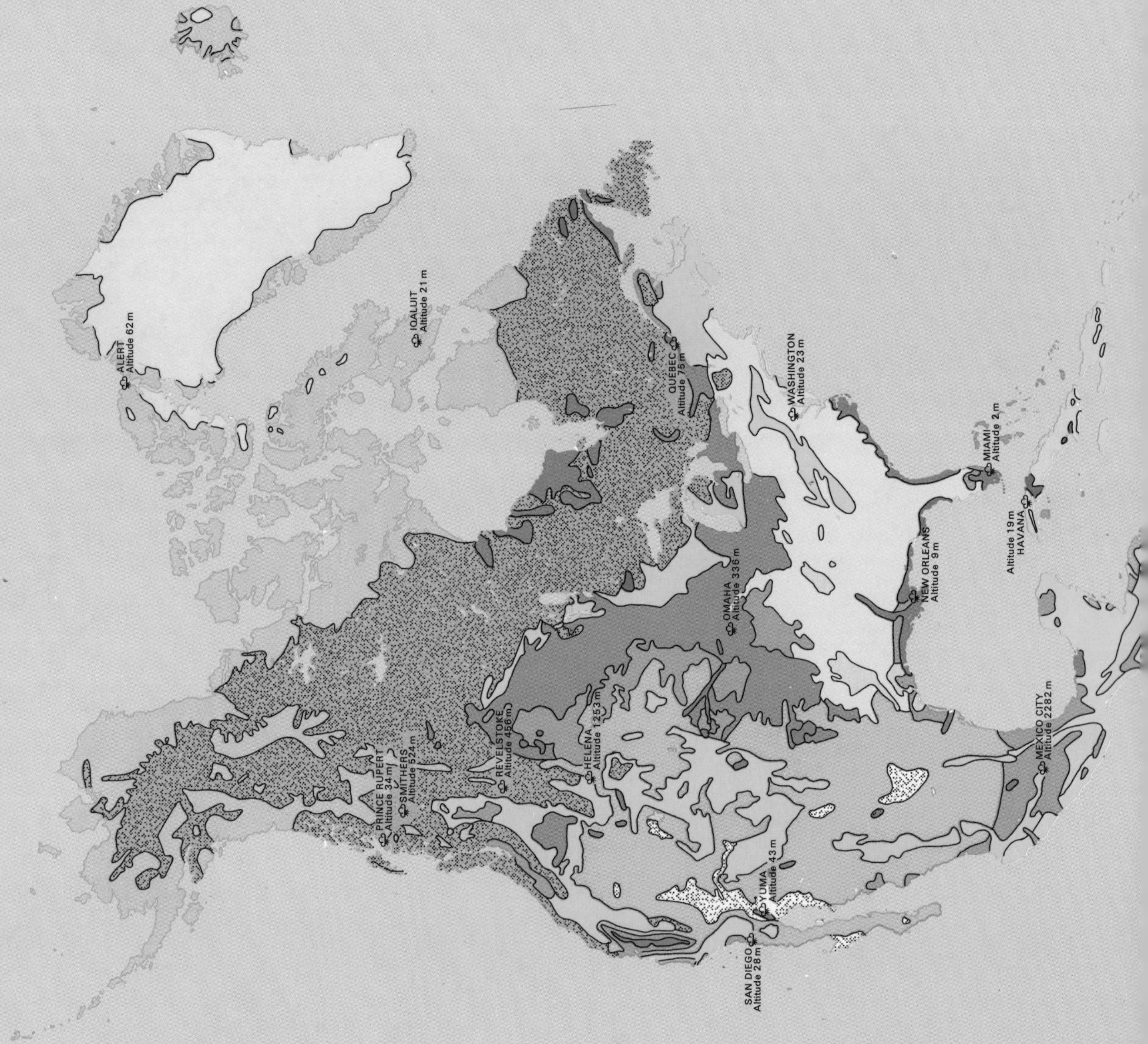

ALERT Altitude 62 m
IQALUIT Altitude 21 m
QUÉBEC Altitude 75 m
WASHINGTON Altitude 23 m
MIAMI Altitude 2 m
HAVANA Altitude 19 m
NEW ORLEANS Altitude 9 m
OMAHA Altitude 336 m
MEXICO CITY Altitude 2282 m
HELENA Altitude 1253 m
REVELSTOKE Altitude 456 m
SMITHERS Altitude 524 m
PRINCE RUPERT Altitude 34 m
YUMA Altitude 43 m
SAN DIEGO Altitude 28 m

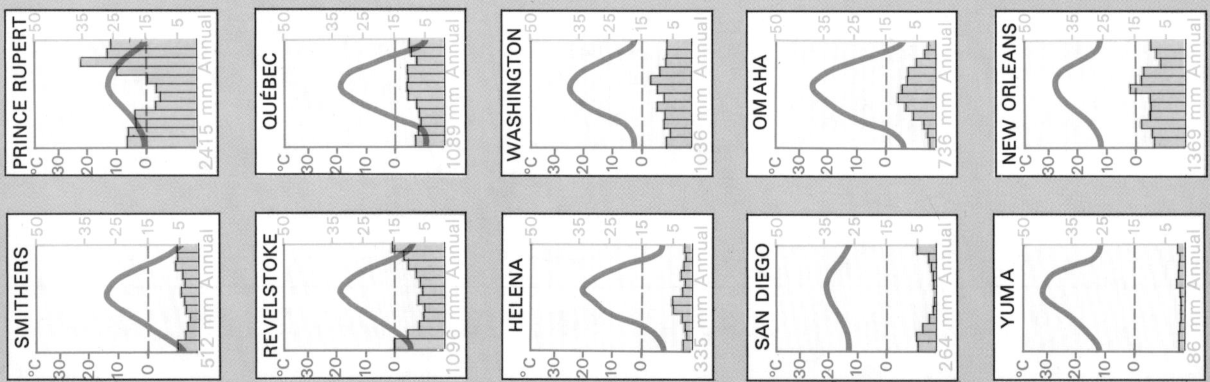

ALERT
QALUIT

Precipitation figures on graphs in 10^1 mm except annual totals

PRINCE RUPERT 2415 mm Annual
QUÉBEC 1089 mm Annual
WASHINGTON 1036 mm Annual
OMAHA 736 mm Annual
NEW ORLEANS 1369 mm Annual
SMITHERS 512 mm Annual
REVELSTOKE 1096 mm Annual
HELENA 335 mm Annual
SAN DIEGO 264 mm Annual
YUMA 86 mm Annual

Oblique Mercator Projection

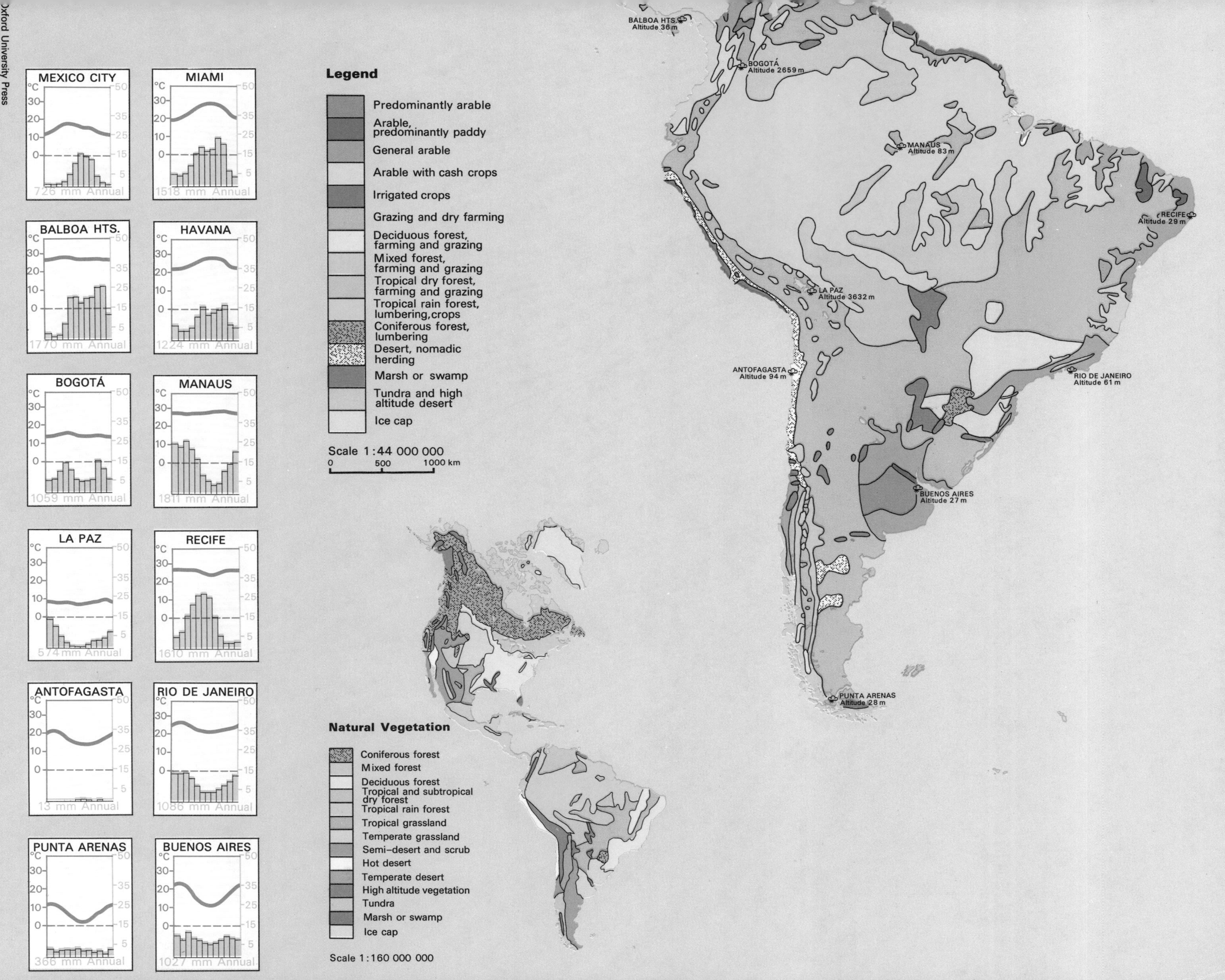

MEXICO CITY
726 mm Annual
MIAMI
1518 mm Annual
BALBOA HTS.
1770 mm Annual
HAVANA
1224 mm Annual
BOGOTÁ
1059 mm Annual
MANAUS
1811 mm Annual
LA PAZ
574 mm Annual
RECIFE
1610 mm Annual
ANTOFAGASTA
13 mm Annual
RIO DE JANEIRO
1086 mm Annual
PUNTA ARENAS
366 mm Annual
BUENOS AIRES
1027 mm Annual
°C
30
20
10
0
50
35
25
15
5
Legend
Predominantly arable
Arable, predominantly paddy
General arable
Arable with cash crops
Irrigated crops
Grazing and dry farming
Deciduous forest, farming and grazing
Mixed forest, farming and grazing
Tropical dry forest, farming and grazing
Tropical rain forest, lumbering, crops
Coniferous forest, lumbering
Desert, nomadic herding
Marsh or swamp
Tundra and high altitude desert
Ice cap
Scale 1:44 000 000
0 500 1000 km
BALBOA HTS. Altitude 36 m
BOGOTÁ Altitude 2659 m
MANAUS Altitude 83 m
RECIFE Altitude 29 m
LA PAZ Altitude 3632 m
ANTOFAGASTA Altitude 94 m
RIO DE JANEIRO Altitude 61 m
BUENOS AIRES Altitude 27 m
PUNTA ARENAS Altitude 28 m
Natural Vegetation
Coniferous forest
Mixed forest
Deciduous forest
Tropical and subtropical dry forest
Tropical rain forest
Tropical grassland
Temperate grassland
Semi-desert and scrub
Hot desert
Temperate desert
High altitude vegetation
Tundra
Marsh or swamp
Ice cap
Scale 1:160 000 000

North and South America: Population and Communications

NORTH ATLANTIC OCEAN
ICELAND
GREENLAND
Arctic Ocean
Hudson Bay
CANADA
UNITED STATES
ALASKA (U.S.A.)
MEXICO
Montreal
Ottawa
Toronto
Boston
New York
Washington
Atlanta
Miami
Chicago
St.Louis
Houston
Dallas
Denver
Winnipeg
Edmonton
Calgary
Vancouver
Seattle
San Francisco
Los Angeles
Phoenix
Monterrey
Mexico City
Guadalajara
Havana
CUBA
THE BAHAMAS
Bermuda (Br.)
HAITI
DOMINICAN REPUBLIC
Puerto Rico (U.S.A.)
ANTIGUA & BARBUDA
JAMAICA
BELIZE
Gulf of Mexico
NORTH PACIFIC OCEAN

Oblique Mercator Project

Political
Capital city
Commonwealth member
Scale 1:60 000 000
MEXICO
Mexico City
GUATEMALA
Guatemala
BELIZE*
Belmopan
HONDURAS
Tegucigalpa
San Salvador
EL SALVADOR
NICARAGUA
Managua
San José
COSTA RICA
Panamá
PANAMÁ
Havana
CUBA
Nassau
THE BAHAMAS*
Bermuda* (Br.)
JAMAICA*
Kingston
HAITI
Port-au-Prince
DOMINICAN REP.
Santo Domingo
Puerto Rico (U.S.A.)
San Juan
*ST. KITTS-NEVIS
ANTIGUA & BARBUDA*
Guadeloupe (Fr.)
DOMINICA*
Martinique (Fr.)
*ST. LUCIA
BARBADOS*
*ST. VINCENT
*GRENADA
TRINIDAD & TOBAGO*
Port of Spain
Neth. Antilles
Caracas
VENEZUELA
Georgetown
GUYANA*
Paramaribo
SURINAM
Cayenne
FRENCH GUIANA
Bogotá
COLOMBIA
Galapagos Is. (Ec.)
Quito
ECUADOR
PERU
Lima
BRAZIL
Brasília
La Paz
BOLIVIA
PARAGUAY
Asunción
CHILE
Santiago
ARGENTINA
Buenos Aires
URUGUAY
Montevideo
Port Stanley
Falkland Is. (Br.)
South Georgia (Br.)
COSTA RICA
PANAMA
Caracas
VENEZUELA
TRINIDAD AND TOBAGO
GUYANA
SURINAM
FRENCH GUIANA
Medellín
Bogotá
COLOMBIA
Galapagos Is. (Ecuador)
ECUADOR
Guayaquil
PERU
Lima
BRAZIL
Fortaleza
Recife
Salvador
Brasília
Belo Horizonte
Rio de Janeiro
São Paulo
Pôrto Alegre
La Paz
BOLIVIA
PARAGUAY
CHILE
Santiago
ARGENTINA
Buenos Aires
URUGUAY
Montevideo
SOUTH PACIFIC OCEAN
SOUTH ATLANTIC OCEAN
Southern Ocean
Falkland Is. (Br.)
South Georgia (Br.)
Legend
Population Density (/km²)
over 100
10–100
1–10
under 1
Cities (million people)
over 2
1–2
0.5–1
Communications
Principal roads
Principal railways
Principal airports
Navigable rivers
Scale 1:44 000 000
0
500
1000 km

Oxford University Press

U.S.A.: Political

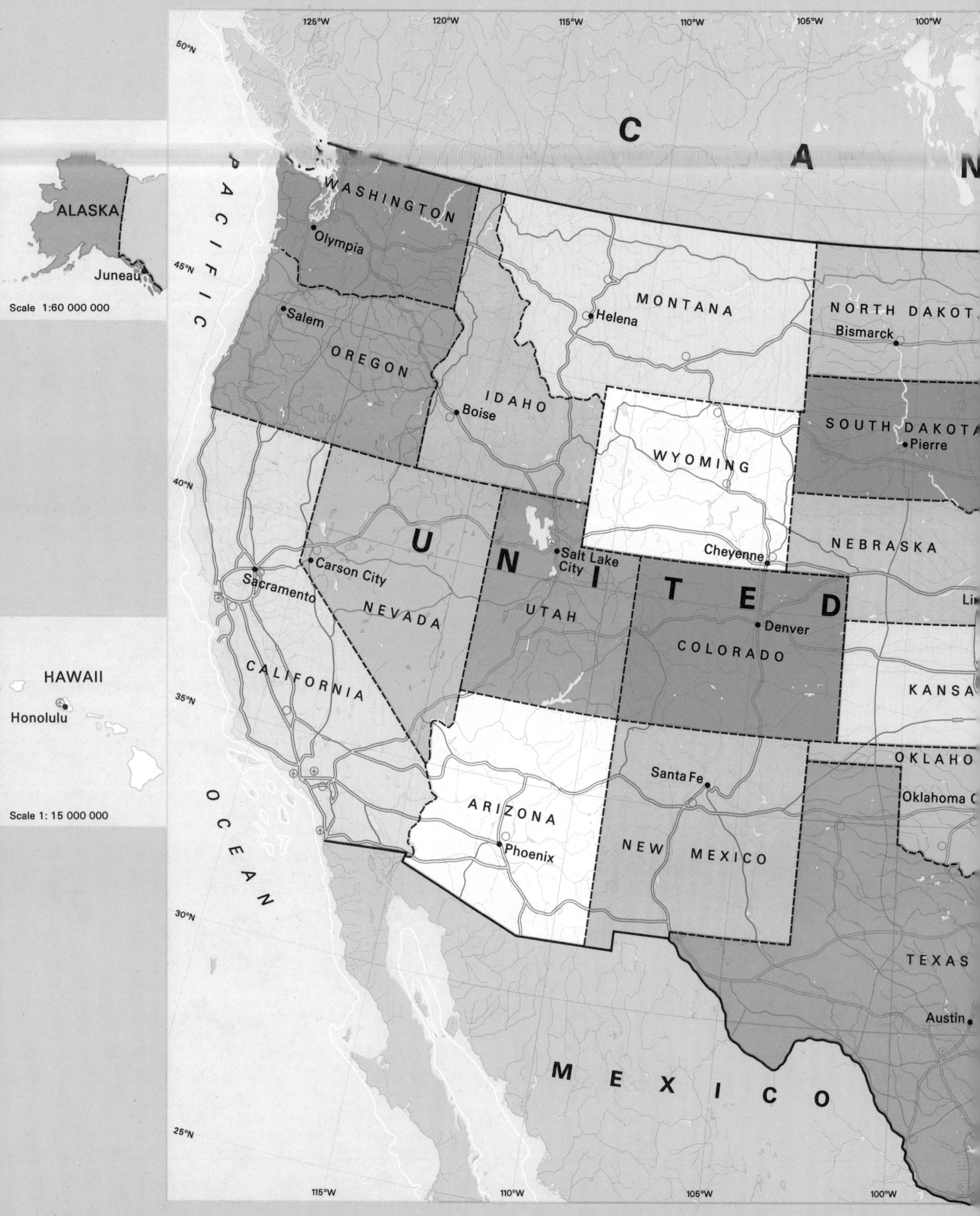

125°W
120°W
115°W
110°W
105°W
100°W
50°N
45°N
40°N
35°N
30°N
25°N
C
A
N
ALASKA
Juneau
Scale 1:60 000 000
HAWAII
Honolulu
Scale 1: 15 000 000
PACIFIC
OCEAN
WASHINGTON
Olympia
Salem
OREGON
IDAHO
Boise
MONTANA
Helena
NORTH DAKOT
Bismarck
SOUTH DAKOT
Pierre
WYOMING
Cheyenne
NEBRASKA
Li
U
N
I
T
E
D
Carson City
Sacramento
NEVADA
Salt Lake City
UTAH
Denver
COLORADO
KANSA
CALIFORNIA
OKLAHO
Oklahoma C
Santa Fe
ARIZONA
Phoenix
NEW MEXICO
TEXAS
Austin
MEXICO
Conical Orthomorphic Projec

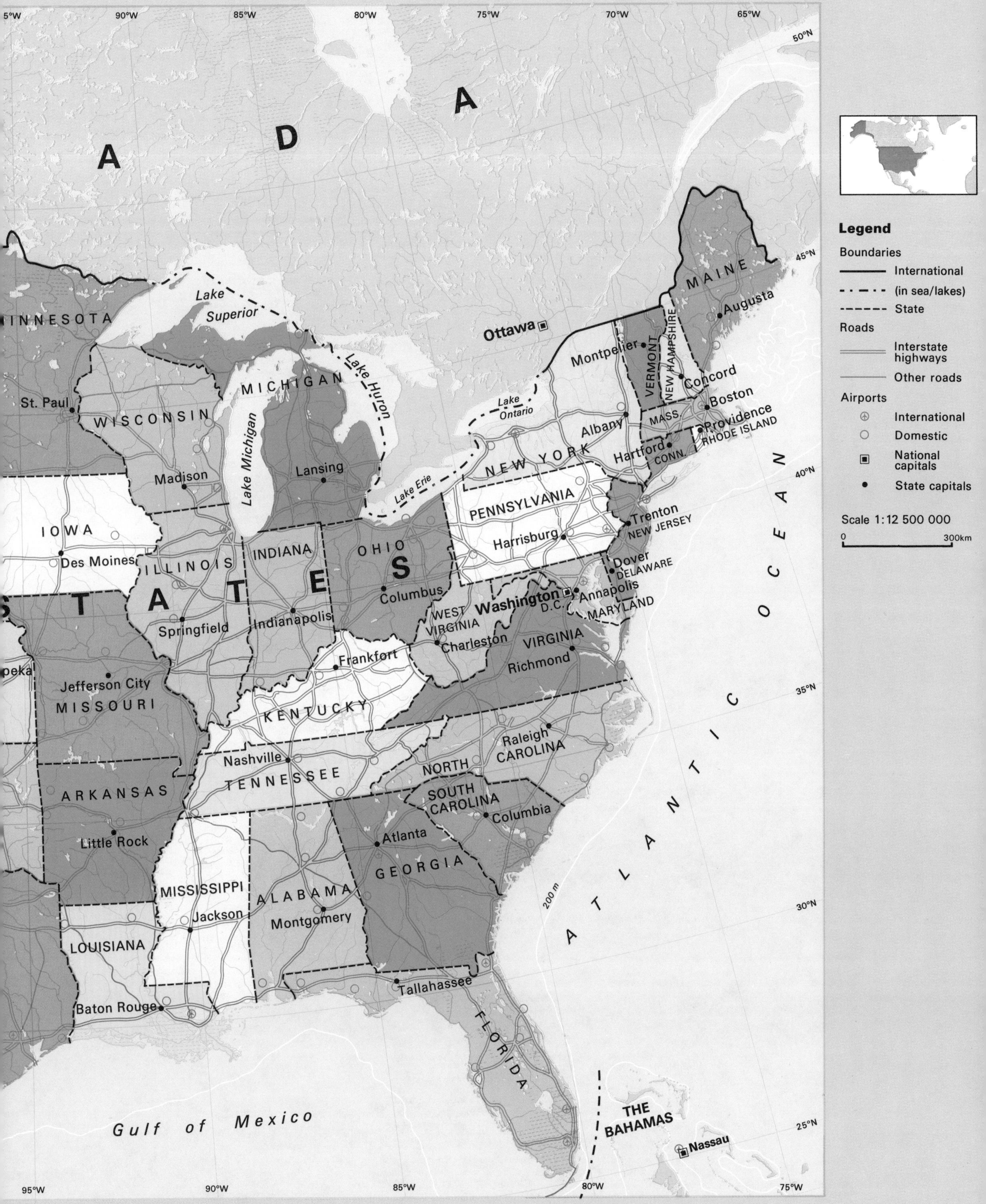

95°W 90°W 85°W 80°W 75°W 70°W 65°W

50°N 45°N 40°N 35°N 30°N 25°N

CANADA

UNITED STATES

Ottawa

MINNESOTA
St. Paul
WISCONSIN
Madison
MICHIGAN
Lansing
Lake Superior
Lake Michigan
Lake Huron
Lake Ontario
Lake Erie
IOWA
Des Moines
ILLINOIS
Springfield
INDIANA
Indianapolis
OHIO
Columbus
MISSOURI
Jefferson City
Topeka
KENTUCKY
Frankfort
TENNESSEE
Nashville
ARKANSAS
Little Rock
MISSISSIPPI
Jackson
ALABAMA
Montgomery
LOUISIANA
Baton Rouge
GEORGIA
Atlanta
FLORIDA
Tallahassee
SOUTH CAROLINA
Columbia
NORTH CAROLINA
Raleigh
VIRGINIA
Richmond
WEST VIRGINIA
Charleston
Washington D.C.
MARYLAND
Annapolis
DELAWARE
Dover
NEW JERSEY
Trenton
PENNSYLVANIA
Harrisburg
NEW YORK
Albany
CONN.
Hartford
RHODE ISLAND
Providence
MASS
Boston
VERMONT
Montpelier
NEW HAMPSHIRE
Concord
MAINE
Augusta

ATLANTIC OCEAN
200 m
Gulf of Mexico
THE BAHAMAS
Nassau

95°W 90°W 85°W 80°W 75°W

Legend

Boundaries
- International
- (in sea/lakes)
- State

Roads
- Interstate highways
- Other roads

Airports
- International
- Domestic
- National capitals
- State capitals

Scale 1:12 500 000

0 300km

Eastern U.S.A.

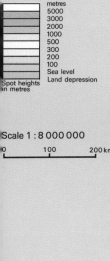

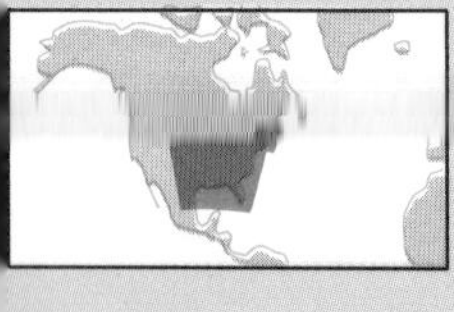

Legend

Boundaries

International

(in sea)

(disputed)

Internal

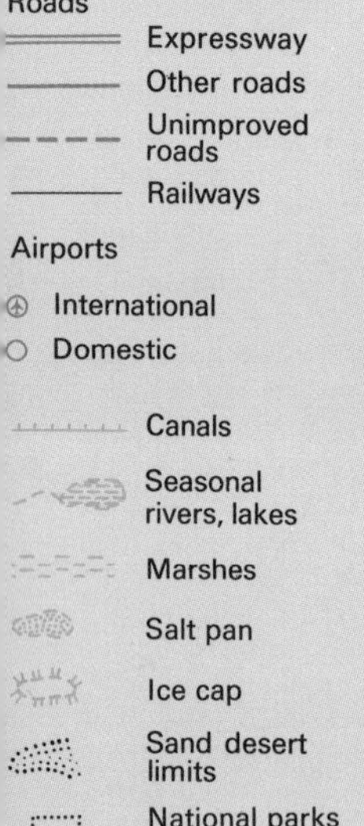

Roads
Expressway
Other roads
Unimproved roads
Railways
Airports
International
Domestic
Canals
Seasonal rivers, lakes
Marshes
Salt pan
Ice cap
Sand desert limits
National parks etc.

metres
5000
3000
2000
1000
500
300
200
100
Sea level
Land depression

Spot heights in metres

Scale 1 : 8 000 000

0 100 200 km

Conical Orthomorphic Projection

NEW YORK
PENNSYLVANIA
OHIO
INDIANA
WEST VIRGINIA
VIRGINIA
KENTUCKY
TENNESSEE
NORTH CAROLINA
SOUTH CAROLINA
GEORGIA
ALABAMA
FLORIDA
MARYLAND
DELAWARE
NEW JERSEY
Lake Erie
(Surface height 174m above m.s.l.)
ATLANTIC OCEAN
Mexico
THE BAHAMAS
Appalachian Mts.
Allegheny Mts.
Blue Ridge
Milwaukee
Chicago
Detroit
Windsor
Toledo
Cleveland
Buffalo
Erie
Pittsburgh
Columbus
Dayton
Cincinnati
Indianapolis
Louisville
Lexington
Nashville
Knoxville
Chattanooga
Atlanta
Birmingham
Montgomery
Columbus
Mobile
Pensacola
Tallahassee
Jacksonville
Savannah
Charleston
Columbia
Charlotte
Greensboro
Winston-Salem
Raleigh
Durham
Richmond
Norfolk
Washington D.C.
Baltimore
Philadelphia
New York
Trenton
Bridgeport
New Haven
Harrisburg
Tampa
St. Petersburg
Orlando
Miami
West Palm Beach
Fort Lauderdale
Hollywood
Key West
Nassau
Cape Canaveral
Cape Hatteras
Cape Fear
Cape Lookout
Cape Charles
Cape Henry
Cape May
Delaware Bay
Pamlico Sound
Albemarle Sound
Sea Islands
Florida Keys
Str. of Florida
Florida Bay
EVERGLADES NAT. PARK
Lake Okeechobee
Grand Bahama
Great Abaco Island
Andros
Eleuthera
Northwest Providence Channel
Northeast Providence Channel
Little Bahama Bank
Bimini Islands
Berry Is.
New Providence
GT.SMOKY MTNS. N.P.
CLINGMANS DOME 2024
MT. ROGERS 1743
BRASSTOWN BALD 1457
85°W
80°W
75°W
40°N
35°N
30°N
25°N
New England
Same scale as main map
CANADA
NEW BRUNSWICK
MAINE
NEW HAMPSHIRE
VERMONT
MASSACHUSETTS
CONNECTICUT
R.I.
NEW YORK
PENNSYLVANIA
L. Ontario
(Surface height 75m above m.s.l.)
Adirondack Mountains 1190
MT. MARCY 1629
MT. WASHINGTON 1917
MT. KATAHDIN 1605
Québec
Montréal
Trois Rivières
Sherbrooke
Fredericton
Boston
Providence
Worcester
Springfield
Hartford
Portland
Augusta
Bangor
Burlington
Albany
Syracuse
Rochester
Utica
Niagara Falls
Buffalo
Cape Cod
Gulf of Maine
Nantucket I.
Martha's Vineyard
70°W
45°N

Western U.S.A.

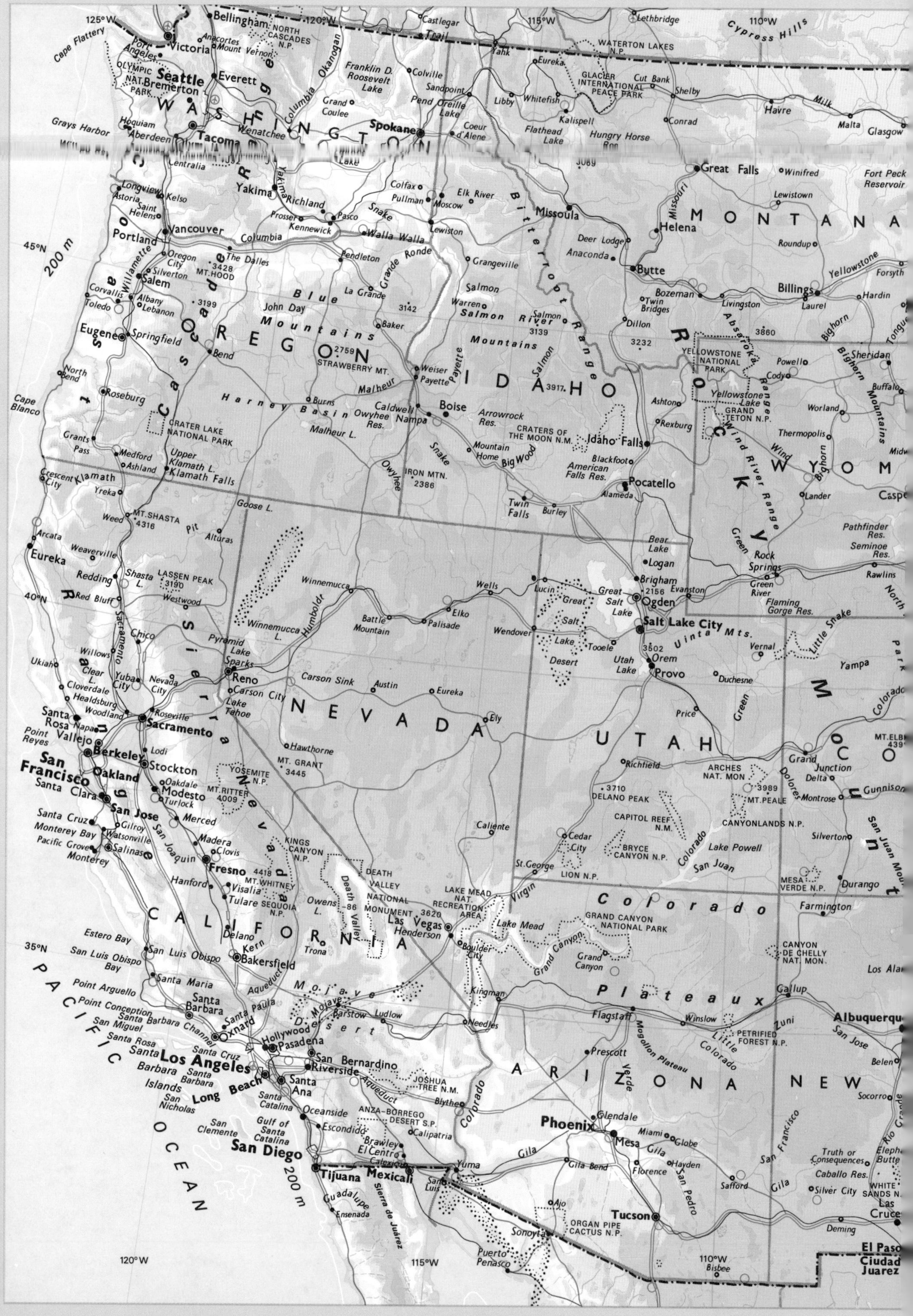

Conical Orthomorphic Projection

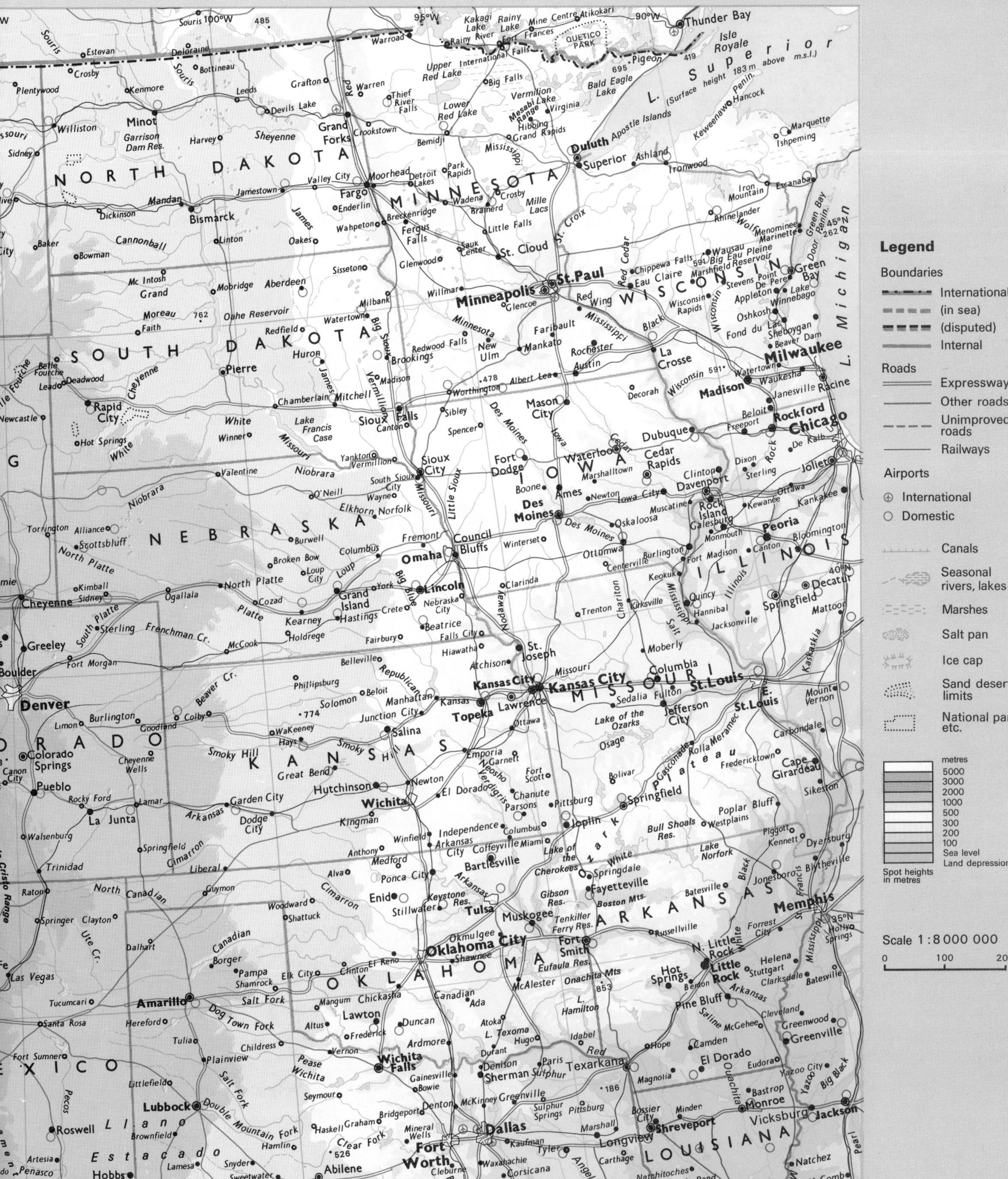

Legend
Boundaries
International
(in sea)
(disputed)
Internal
Roads
Expressway
Other roads
Unimproved roads
Railways
Airports
International
Domestic
Canals
Seasonal rivers, lakes
Marshes
Salt pan
Ice cap
Sand desert limits
National parks etc.
metres
5000
3000
2000
1000
500
300
200
100
Sea level
Land depression
Spot heights in metres
Scale 1 : 8 000 000
0
100
200 km
NORTH DAKOTA
SOUTH DAKOTA
NEBRASKA
KANSAS
OKLAHOMA
TEXAS
MINNESOTA
IOWA
MISSOURI
ARKANSAS
LOUISIANA
WISCONSIN
ILLINOIS
L. Superior
(Surface height 183 m above m.s.l.)
L. Michigan
Thunder Bay
Isle Royale
Rainy Lake
Kakagi Lake
Mine Centre
Atikokari
QUETICO PARK
Fort Frances
International Falls
Rainy River
Warroad
Souris
100°W
95°W
90°W
485
Estevan
Deloraine
Bottineau
Crosby
Plentywood
Kenmore
Leeds
Devils Lake
Grafton
Warren
Thief River Falls
Upper Red Lake
Lower Red Lake
Big Falls
Vermilion Lake
Mesabi Range
Virginia
Hibbing
Grand Rapids
Bald Eagle Lake
Pigeon
695
419
Keweenaw Penin.
Hancock
Marquette
Ishpeming
Apostle Islands
Duluth
Superior
Ashland
Tronwood
Williston
Minot
Garrison Dam Res.
Sidney
Harvey
Sheyenne
Grand Forks
Crookstown
Bemidji
Mississippi
Moorhead
Detroit Lakes
Park Rapids
Fargo
Valley City
Jamestown
Mandan
Bismarck
Dickinson
Enderlin
Wadena
Crosby
Brainerd
Mille Lacs
Iron Mountain
Escanaba
Rhinelander
Wolf
Menominee
Marinette
Green Bay Penin.
45°N
262
Baker
Bowman
Linton
Cannonball
James
Oakes
Wahpeton
Breckenridge
Fergus Falls
Little Falls
Sauk Center
St. Cloud
St. Croix
Red Cedar
Chippewa Falls
Eau Claire
Wausau
Big Eau Pleine Reservoir
Marshfield
Stevens Point
De Pere
Green Bay
Door Penin.
Sisseton
Glenwood
St. Paul
Minneapolis
Willmar
Glencoe
Red Wing
Wisconsin Rapids
Appleton
Lake Winnebago
Oshkosh
Fond du Lac
Sheboygan
Beaver Dam
Mc Intosh
Grand
Mobridge
Aberdeen
Moreau
Faith
762
Oahe Reservoir
Milbank
Watertown
Big Sioux
Redfield
Minnesota
New Ulm
Faribault
Mankato
Rochester
Austin
Black
La Crosse
Milwaukee
Waukesha
Watertown
591
Wisconsin
Madison
Janesville
Racine
Belle Fourche
Lead
Deadwood
Cheyenne
Pierre
Huron
Redwood Falls
Brookings
Madison
478
Albert Lea
Worthington
Mason City
Decorah
Beloit
Freeport
Rockford
Chicago
Rapid City
Newcastle
Hot Springs
Chamberlain
Mitchell
Vermillion
Sioux Falls
Canton
Sibley
Spencer
Des Moines
Iowa
Dubuque
Cedar
Lake Francis Case
White
Winner
Yankton
Fort Dodge
Waterloo
Cedar Rapids
Dixon
Sterling
De Kalb
Joliet
Rock
Valentine
Niobrara
Sioux City
South Sioux City
Little Sioux
Marshalltown
Clinton
Davenport
O'Neill
Wayne
Norfolk
Elkhorn
Boone
Ames
Newton
Iowa City
Muscatine
Rock Island
Kewanee
Ottawa
Kankakee
Torrington
Alliance
Scottsbluff
North Platte
Burwell
Fremont
Council Bluffs
Omaha
Winterset
Oskaloosa
Galesburg
Monmouth
Peoria
Bloomington
Canton
Broken Bow
Loup City
Columbus
Ottumwa
Centerville
Burlington
Fort Madison
Kimball
Sidney
Cheyenne
Ogallala
North Platte
Cozad
Lincoln
York
Grand Island
Kearney
Hastings
Crete
Nebraska City
Beatrice
Clarinda
Trenton
Kirksville
Keokuk
Quincy
Hannibal
Springfield
Decatur
Mattoon
40°N
Illinois
Greeley
Sterling
South Platte
Frenchman Cr.
McCook
Holdrege
Fairbury
Falls City
Hiawatha
St. Joseph
Atchison
Chariton
Salt
Moberly
Columbia
Jacksonville
Fort Morgan
Boulder
Denver
Beaver Cr.
Belleville
Republican
Phillipsburg
Beloit
Solomon
774
Manhattan
Kansas
Topeka
Lawrence
Kansas City
Missouri
Sedalia
Fulton
Jefferson City
St. Louis
E. St. Louis
Mount Vernon
Limon
Burlington
Goodland
Colby
WaKeeney
Hays
Junction City
Salina
Ottawa
Lake of the Ozarks
Osage
Gasconade
Meramec
Carbondale
Colorado Springs
Canon City
Pueblo
Cheyenne Wells
Smoky Hill
Great Bend
Emporia
Garnett
Fort Scott
Neosho
Verdigris
Chanute
Parsons
Rolla
Plateau
Fredericktown
Cape Girardeau
Sikeston
Rocky Ford
La Junta
Lamar
Garden City
Dodge City
Arkansas
Hutchinson
Newton
El Dorado
Wichita
Kingman
Pittsburg
Joplin
Springfield
Bolivar
Poplar Bluff
Westplains
Bull Shoals Res.
Walsenburg
Springfield
Cimarron
Winfield
Independence
Arkansas City
Coffeyville
Columbus
Miami
Ozark
White
Piggott
Kennett
Dyersburg
Trinidad
Liberal
Anthony
Medford
Bartlesville
Lake of the Cherokees
Springdale
Fayetteville
Lake Norfork
Black
Jonesboro
St. Francis
Blytheville
Kaskaskia
Raton
Guymon
North Canadian
Alva
Ponca City
Enid
Keystone Res.
Stillwater
Tulsa
Gibson Res.
Boston Mts.
Batesville
Memphis
Woodward
Shattuck
Muskogee
Tenkiller Ferry Res.
Russellville
Forrest City
35°N
Holly Springs
Springer
Clayton
Ute Cr.
Dalhart
Canadian
Borger
Pampa
Shamrock
Okmulgee
Oklahoma City
Shawnee
El Reno
Elk City
Clinton
Fort Smith
Eufaula Res.
N. Little Rock
Little Rock
Stuttgart
Helena
Clarksdale
Batesville
Las Vegas
Tucumcari
Amarillo
Salt Fork
Mangum
Chickasha
McAlester
Onachita Mts
853
Hot Springs
Benton
Pine Bluff
Canadian
Ada
L. Hamilton
Santa Rosa
Hereford
Dog Town Fork
Altus
Lawton
Duncan
Frederick
Atoka
L. Texoma
Saline
McGehee
Cleveland
Greenwood
Greenville
Fort Sumner
Tulia
Childress
Plainview
Pease
Vernon
Wichita Falls
Ardmore
Hugo
Idabel
Durant
Paris
Red
Texarkana
Hope
Camden
El Dorado
Eudora
Yazoo City
Big Black
Yazoo
Littlefield
Salt Fork
Seymour
Gainesville
Bowie
Denison
Sherman
Sulphur
Magnolia
186
Ouachita
Bastrop
Monroe
Pecos
Lubbock
Double Mountain Fork
Denton
McKinney
Greenville
Sulphur Springs
Pittsburg
Bossier City
Minden
Shreveport
Vicksburg
Jackson
Roswell
Llano Estacado
Brownfield
Haskell
Graham
Bridgeport
Mineral Wells
Dallas
Marshall
Longview
Hamlin
Clear Fork
526
Fort Worth
Kaufman
Tyler
Carthage
Artesia
Penasco
Snyder
Lamesa
Sweetwater
Abilene
Cleburne
Waxahachie
Corsicana
Angelina
Natchitoches
Toledo Bend Res.
Natchez
Pearl
Hobbs
McComb
97
Carlsbad
CARLSBAD CAVERNS N.P.
Big Spring
Midland
Colorado
Bayou
Brazos
Palestine
Teague
Neches
Nacogdoches
Lufkin
Sam Rayburn Res.
Alexandria
Red
Atchafalaya
Mississippi
GUADALUPE MTS. N.P.
105°W
Odessa
Concho
Brownwood
Leon
Waco
Marlin
Navasota
Trinity
95°W
Woodville
Opelousas
Eunice
Lafayette
Baton Rouge
San Angelo
100°W
Temple
Cleveland
Lake Charles
Orange
Abbeville
New Iberia
30°N

Northeastern U.S.A.

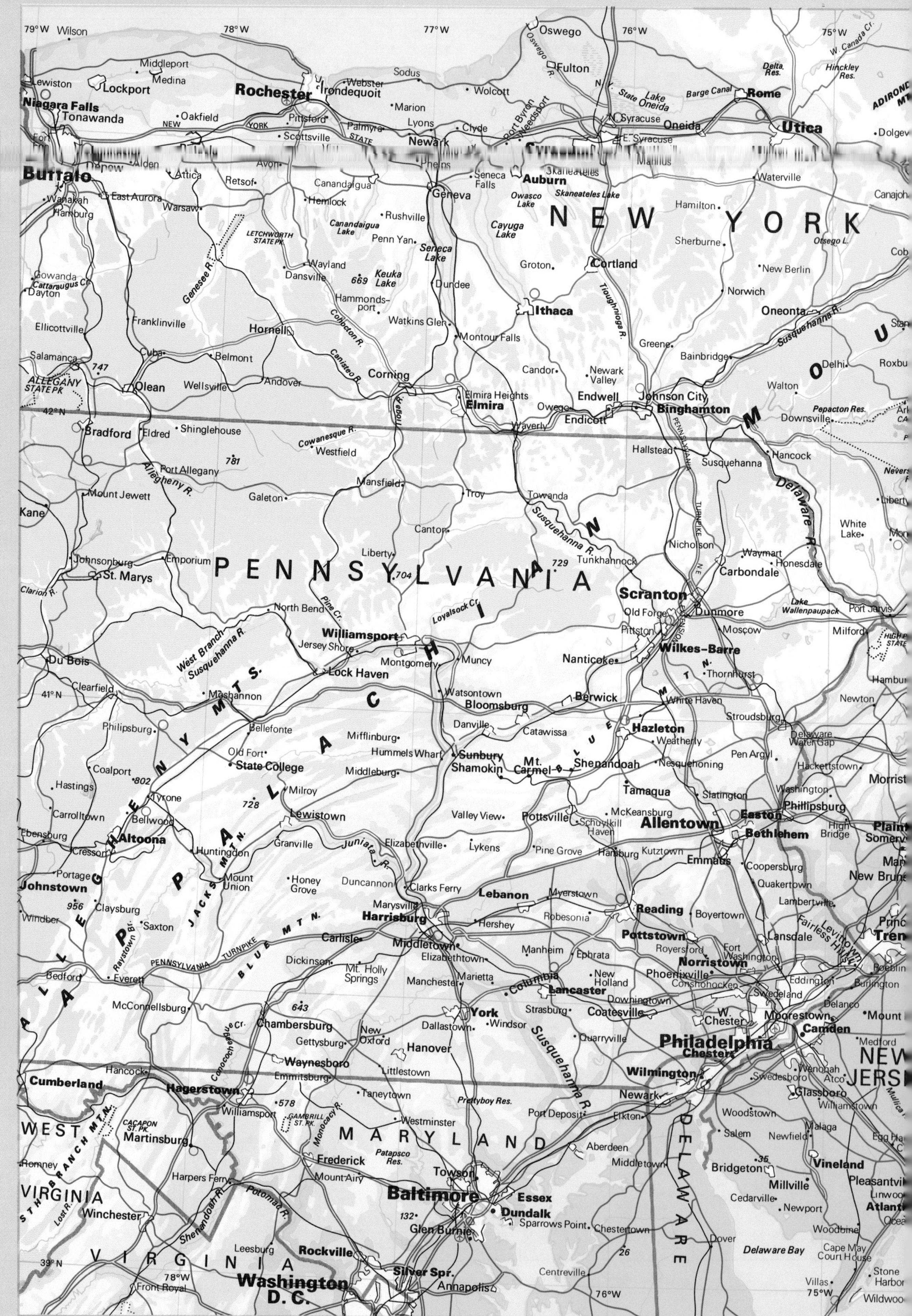
NEW YORK
PENNSYLVANIA
MARYLAND
DELAWARE
WEST VIRGINIA
VIRGINIA
NEW JERSEY
APPALACHIAN MTS.
ALLEGHENY MTS.
BLUE MTN.
Buffalo
Rochester
Syracuse
Utica
Binghamton
Scranton
Wilkes-Barre
Allentown
Bethlehem
Reading
Lancaster
Harrisburg
York
Altoona
Johnstown
Williamsport
Philadelphia
Wilmington
Baltimore
Washington D.C.
Hagerstown
Cumberland
Frederick
Camden
Trenton
Elmira
Ithaca
Cortland
Auburn
Geneva
Olean
Bradford
Lake Ontario
Delaware Bay

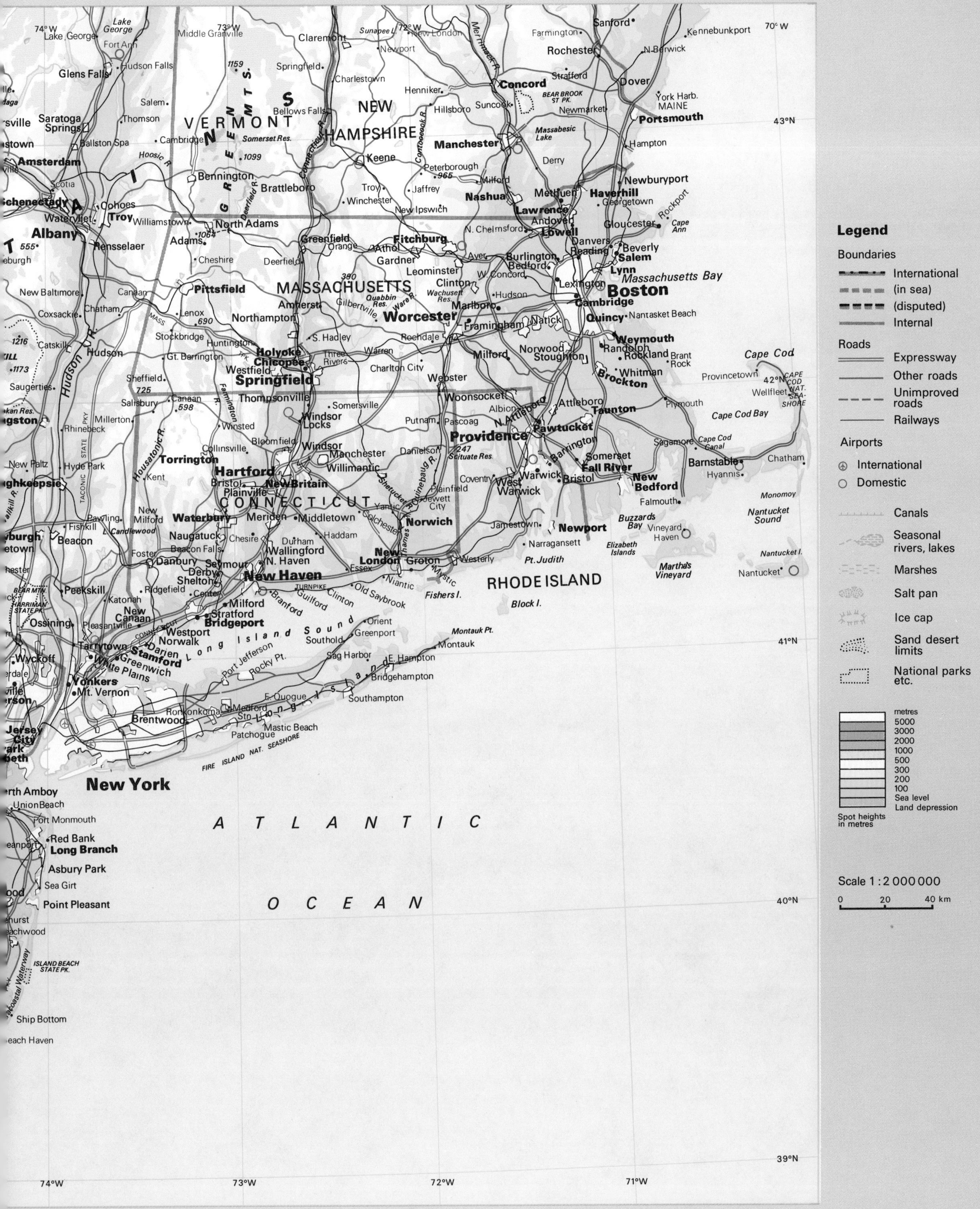

ATLANTIC OCEAN

Legend

Boundaries

- International
- (in sea)
- (disputed)
- Internal

Roads

- Expressway
- Other roads
- Unimproved roads
- Railways

Airports

- International
- Domestic

- Canals
- Seasonal rivers, lakes
- Marshes
- Salt pan
- Ice cap
- Sand desert limits
- National parks etc.

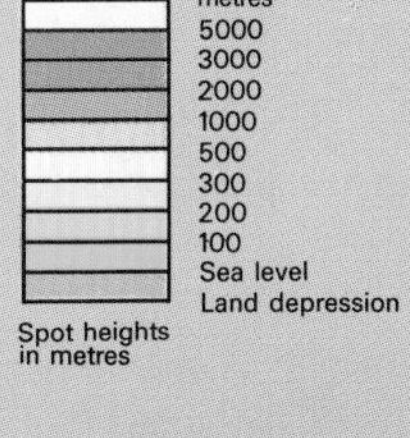

metres
5000
3000
2000
1000
500
300
200
100
Sea level
Land depression

Spot heights in metres

Scale 1 : 2 000 000

0 20 40 km

New York

Urban Land Use

These urban land use maps show only a simplified land use pattern. Their primary intent is to illustrate the overall relationships of land use and transportation systems. Therefore, much detail has been omitted.

- Central business core
- Lesser but significant commercial centres
- Industrial districts
- The built-up area where the major use of land is for residential purposes
- Major parks and open spaces
- Major military and naval installations

Boundaries

- International
- Provincial or State
- County

Highways

- Expressway
- Other main highways
- Railways and transportation yards
- Airports
- Airfields

Scale 1:400 000

0 5 10 km

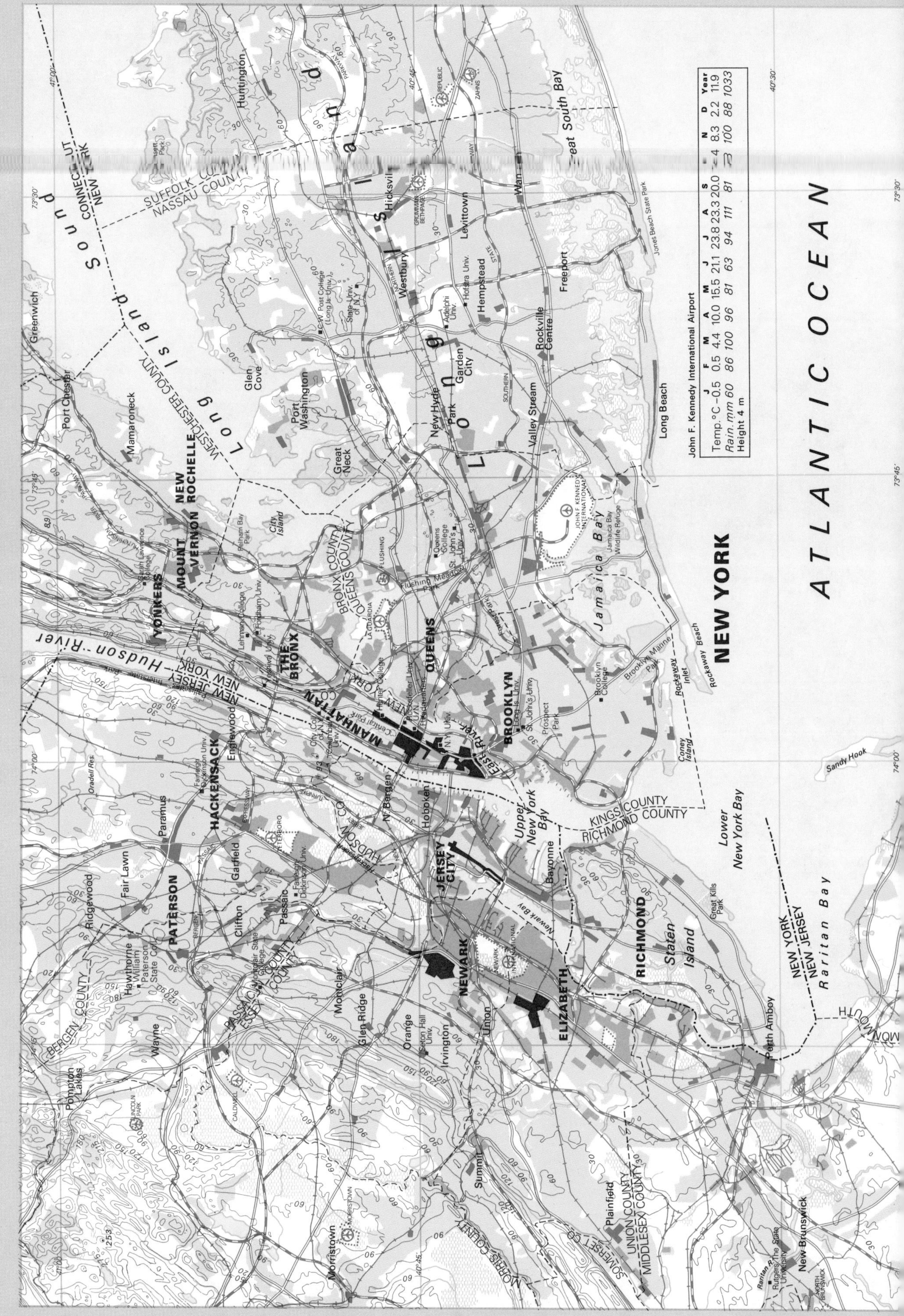

ATLANTIC OCEAN
NEW YORK
Long Island Sound
Long Island
Hudson River
East River
Upper New York Bay
Lower New York Bay
Raritan Bay
Newark Bay
Jamaica Bay
Great South Bay
Sandy Hook
MANHATTAN
BROOKLYN
QUEENS
THE BRONX
RICHMOND
Staten Island
YONKERS
MOUNT VERNON
NEW ROCHELLE
NEWARK
JERSEY CITY
ELIZABETH
PATERSON
HACKENSACK
Hoboken
Bayonne
Passaic
Clifton
Montclair
Orange
Irvington
Union
Summit
Plainfield
Morristown
New Brunswick
Perth Amboy
Wayne
Paramus
Englewood
Greenwich
Port Chester
Mamaroneck
Glen Cove
Port Washington
Great Neck
Huntington
Hicksville
Westbury
Levittown
Hempstead
Freeport
Garden City
Rockville Centre
Valley Stream
New Hyde Park
Long Beach
Rockaway Beach
Coney Island
City Island
WESTCHESTER COUNTY
BRONX COUNTY
QUEENS COUNTY
KINGS COUNTY
RICHMOND COUNTY
SUFFOLK COUNTY
NASSAU COUNTY
UNION COUNTY
MIDDLESEX COUNTY
BERGEN COUNTY
HUDSON CO.
CONNECTICUT
NEW YORK
NEW JERSEY
John F. Kennedy International Airport

John F. Kennedy International Airport

	J	F	M	A	M	J	J	A	S	O	N	D	Year
Temp. °C	−0.5	0.5	4.4	10.0	15.5	21.1	23.8	23.3	20.0	[illegible]	8.3	2.2	11.9
Rain. mm	*60*	*86*	*100*	*96*	*81*	*63*	*94*	*111*	*81*	[illegible]	*100*	*88*	*1033*

Height 4 m

WAUKEGAN
Gages Lake
Grayslake
North Chicago
Great Lakes Naval Training Center
Libertyville
Mundelein
Lake Bluff
Lake Forest
Fort Sheridan
Fairfield
Lake Zurich
HIGHLAND PARK
Deerfield
LAKE COUNTY
COOK COUNTY
Northbrook
Glencoe
Winnetka
Palatine
Arlington Heights
Prospect Heights
Mount Prospect
Glenview
WILMETTE
Northwestern University
EVANSTON
Morton Grove
SKOKIE
Schaumburg
Des Plaines
Park Ridge
Niles
Lincolnwood
Elk Grove Village
COOK COUNTY
DU PAGE COUNTY
Roselle
CHICAGO O'HARE INTERNATIONAL
Itasca
Loyola University
LAKE MICHIGAN
Harwood Heights
Montrose-Wilson Beach
Bensenville
Franklin Park
Elmwood Park
Lincoln Park
Belmont Harbor
De Paul University
Northlake
Glen Ellyn
Lombard
Elmhurst
Melrose Park
Humboldt Park
Oak Street Beach
Chicago Harbor
Berkeley
River Forest
OAK PARK
The Loop
Roosevelt University
Grant Park
Wheaton
Bellwood
Maywood
Garfield Park
Douglas Park
MEIGS
Broadview
Westchester
CICERO
CHICAGO
BERWYN
Oak Brook
Riverside
Illinois Institute of Technology
Morton Arboretum
Brookfield
Stickney
La Grange
Lyons
Downers Grove
Hinsdale
Western Springs
Washington Park
University of Chicago
Jackson Park
Lisle
Summit
CHICAGO MIDWAY
Chicago Sanitary and Ship Canal
Marquette Park
Burbank
ILLINOIS
INDIANA
Calumet Harbor
Calumet Park
DU PAGE CO.
WILL CO.
ARGONNE NATIONAL LABORATORY
Evergreen Park
Oak Lawn
Argonne Forest
Whiting
Indiana Harbor
Calumet Sag Channel
Worth
Stony Creek
Des Plaines River
Wolf Lake State Park and Conservation Area
Lemont
Blue Island
Lake Calumet Harbor
EAST CHICAGO
Duffy Preserve
GARY
COOK COUNTY
WILL COUNTY
Dolton
Calumet City
GARY MUNICIPAL
Lockport
Harvey
HAMMOND
INDIANA E-W TOLLWAY
COOK CO.
LAKE CO.
Lansing
JOLIET
Ridgewood
Little Calumet River
Homewood
Highland
Wheaton
Kensington
Beltsville
Great Falls of the Potomac
MONTGOMERY COUNTY
PRINCE GEORGE'S COUNTY
College Park
Greenbelt
Potomac
Bethesda
National Inst. of Health
Silver Spring
University of Maryland
Goddard Space Flight Center (N.A.S.A.)
MARYLAND
VIRGINIA
Chevy Chase
DISTRICT OF COLUMBIA
Hyattsville
WASHINGTON D.C.
McLean
Wolf Trap Farm N.P.
American University
Catholic University
Georgetown University
Howard Univ.
Geo. Washington Univ.
White House
The Capitol
Vienna
ARLINGTON COUNTY
Falls Church City
Arlington National Cemetery
Pentagon
Washington Airport
Capitol Heights
FAIRFAX CO.
WASHINGTON NATIONAL AIRPORT
Fairfax City
Annandale
District Heights
Suitland
Bureau of the Census
Alexandria City
Potomac River
Andrews Air Force Base
Springfield

Washington Airport

	Temp. °C	Rain. mm
J	2.2	66
F	3.3	66
M	7.2	83
A	13.3	71
M	18.9	99
J	23.3	86
J	25.6	106
A	25.0	122
S	21.1	78
O	15.0	71
N	8.9	76
D	3.3	76
Year	13.9	1101

Height 3 m

Midway Airport

	Temp. °C	Rain. mm
J	-3.3	48
F	-2.2	40
M	2.2	68
A	9.4	76
M	15.5	93
J	21.6	101
J	23.8	86
A	23.3	81
S	18.8	68
O	12.7	73
N	4.4	55
D	-1.6	73
Year	10.5	814

Height 185 m

Mexico, Central America and the Caribbean

UNITED STATES
NEVADA
UTAH
COLORADO
KANSAS
NEBRASKA
IOWA
ILLINOIS
MISSOURI
OKLAHOMA
ARKANSAS
TEXAS
LOUISIANA
MISSISSIPPI
NEW MEXICO
ARIZONA
Colorado Plateaus
Llano Estacado
Edwards Plateau
Denver
Colorado Springs
Wichita
Des Moines
Omaha
Lincoln
Peoria
St. Louis
Memphis
Nashville
Little Rock
Oklahoma City
Amarillo
Albuquerque
Santa Fe
Phoenix
Tucson
San Diego
El Paso
Ciudad Juárez
Fort Worth
Dallas
Shreveport
Jackson
Birmingham
Austin
San Antonio
Houston
Beaumont
Baton Rouge
New Orleans
Corpus Christi
Brownsville
Monterrey
Chihuahua
Torreón
Durango
Mazatlán
Guadalajara
León
San Luis Potosí
Tampico
Mexico City
Puebla
Veracruz
Acapulco
Oaxaca
Mérida
Campeche
GUATEMALA
Guatemala
BELIZE
Belize
San Salvador
EL SALVADOR
Tegucigalpa
Lower California
Gulf of California
Sierra Madre Occidental
Sierra Madre Oriental
Mexican Plateau
Southern Sierra Madre
Isthmus of Tehuantepec
Gulf of Tehuantepec
Bay of Campeche
YUCATÁN
MEXICO
GULF OF MEXICO
PACIFIC OCEAN
Tropic of Cancer
Revilla Gigedo Islands (Mex.)
Tres Marías Islands
200 m
115°W
110°W
105°W
100°W
95°W
90°W
35°N
30°N
25°N
20°N
15°N
10°N
Gaillard Cut (Culebra)
Maximum elevation 95 m
Minimum depth 12 m
ATLANTIC
PACIFIC
Sea level
0
15
30
45
60
75 km
Gatun Locks
3 pairs
Length 305 m
Width 34 m
Total Lift 26 m
Pedro Miguel Locks
1 pair
Length 305 m
Width 34 m
Total Lift 9·3 m
Miraflores Locks
2pairs
Length 305 m
Width 34 m
Total Lift 16·6 m
Panama Canal
Scale 1:1 500 000
ATLANTIC OCEAN
80°W
Colón
Gatun Locks
Gatun Lake
CANAL ZONE
PANAMÁ
Pedro Miguel Locks
Miraflores Locks
9°N
Balboa
Panama
PACIFIC OCEAN

PANAMA *The canal, opened in 1914 , is 80 km long, including approaches (actual canal 64 km). Minimum depth 12 m, minimum width 152 m (Gaillard Cut). Time of passage 8 hours. In 1982 14,009 vessels used the canal carrying 185 000 000 t of cargo. In 1979 Panama assumed control of the former Canal Zone, with the USA retaining majority representation on the Panama Commission until 1989. US military forces will remain in Panama until the year 2000 and the USA will be entitled to defend the Canal's neutrality thereafter .*

Zenithal Equidistant Projec

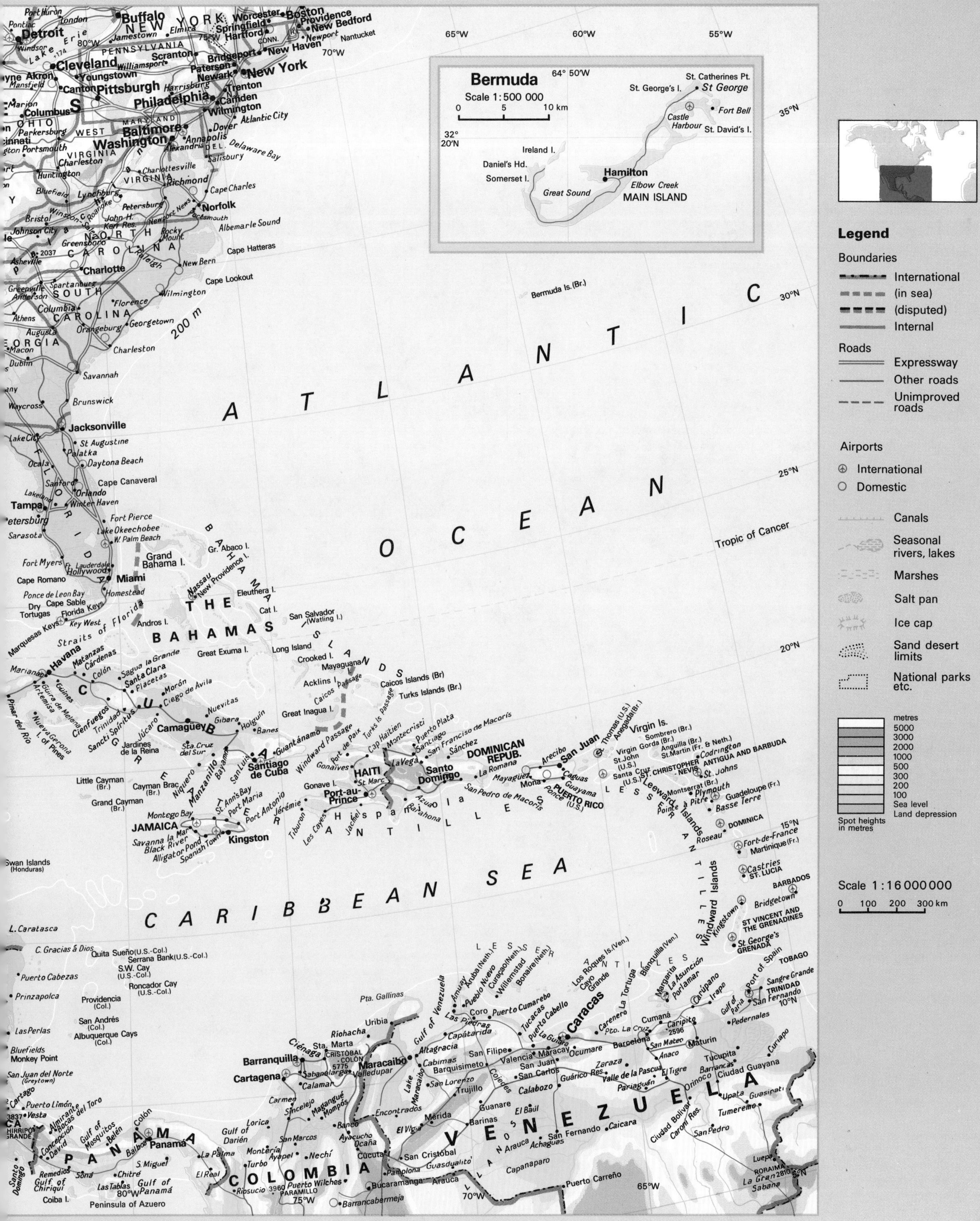

Bermuda

Scale 1:500 000

0 5 10 km

64° 50'W

32° 20'N

St. Catherines Pt.
St. George's I.
St George
Castle Harbour
Fort Bell
St. David's I.
Ireland I.
Daniel's Hd.
Somerset I.
Hamilton
Great Sound
Elbow Creek
MAIN ISLAND

ATLANTIC OCEAN

CARIBBEAN SEA

Tropic of Cancer

Bermuda Is. (Br.)

65°W 60°W 55°W 70°W 75°W 80°W

35°N 30°N 25°N 20°N 15°N 10°N

Buffalo
NEW YORK
Boston
Providence
New Bedford
Worcester
Springfield
Hartford
Newport
Nantucket
New Haven
Bridgeport
New York
Newark
Paterson
Trenton
Detroit
Lake Erie
Cleveland
Akron
Canton
Youngstown
Pittsburgh
Harrisburg
Philadelphia
Camden
Wilmington
Columbus
Baltimore
Annapolis
Dover
Atlantic City
Washington
Alexandria
Delaware Bay
Salisbury
Charleston
Huntington
Charlottesville
Richmond
Cape Charles
Lynchburg
Petersburg
Norfolk
Portsmouth
Albemarle Sound
Winston-Salem
Greensboro
Rocky Mount
NORTH CAROLINA
Raleigh
Cape Hatteras
New Bern
Cape Lookout
Charlotte
Asheville
Spartanburg
Greenville
Anderson
Columbia
SOUTH CAROLINA
Wilmington
Florence
Athens
Augusta
Orangeburg
Georgetown
200 m
Charleston
Macon
Dublin
Savannah
Brunswick
Waycross
Jacksonville
Lake City
St Augustine
Palatka
Ocala
Daytona Beach
Sanford
Orlando
Cape Canaveral
Lakeland
Winter Haven
Tampa
St Petersburg
Fort Pierce
Sarasota
Lake Okeechobee
W. Palm Beach
FLORIDA
Fort Myers
Ft. Lauderdale
Hollywood
Miami
Cape Romano
Homestead
Ponce de Leon Bay
Cape Sable
Dry Tortugas
Florida Keys
Key West
Marquesas Keys
Straits of Florida
Grand Bahama I.
Gr. Abaco I.
Nassau
New Providence I.
Eleuthera I.
Cat I.
Andros I.
THE BAHAMAS
BAHAMA ISLANDS
San Salvador (Watling I.)
Great Exuma I.
Long Island
Crooked I.
Acklins I.
Mayaguana
Caicos Passage
Caicos Islands (Br)
Turks Islands (Br.)
Great Inagua I.
Havana
Matanzas
Cárdenas
Mariano
Artemisa
Güines
Colón
Sagua la Grande
Santa Clara
Placetas
Morón
Ciego de Avila
Pinar del Río
Nueva Gerona
I. of Pines
Cienfuegos
Trinidad
Sancti Spíritus
CUBA
Nuevitas
Camagüey
Gibara
Holguín
Banes
Jardines de la Reina
Júcaro
Sta. Cruz del Sur
Bayamo
Manzanillo
Guantánamo
Santiago de Cuba
San Luis
Windward Passage
Little Cayman (Br.)
Cayman Brac (Br.)
Grand Cayman (Br.)
Montego Bay
JAMAICA
Savanna la Mar
Black River
Alligator Pond
Spanish Town
St. Ann's Bay
Port Maria
Port Antonio
Kingston
CARIBBEAN SEA
GREATER ANTILLES
Jérémie
Tiburon
Les Cayes
Jacmel
Gonaïves
Port de Paix
Cap Haïtien
Gonave I.
HAITI
St. Marc
Port-au-Prince
Hispaniola
Monte Cristi
Puerto Plata
Santiago
La Vega
San Francisco de Macorís
Sánchez
DOMINICAN REPUB.
Santo Domingo
La Romana
San Pedro de Macorís
Azua
Barahona
Mona
Mayagüez
Arecibo
San Juan
Caguas
Guayama
PUERTO RICO
Ponce (U.S.)
St. Thomas (U.S.)
Anegada (Br.)
Virgin Is.
Virgin Gorda (Br.)
St. John (U.S.)
Santa Cruz (U.S.)
Sombrero (Br.)
Anguilla (Br.)
St. Martin (Fr. & Neth.)
Codrington
ST. CHRISTOPHER-NEVIS
ANTIGUA AND BARBUDA
St. Johns
Montserrat (Br.)
Plymouth
Leeward Islands
Guadeloupe (Fr.)
Pointe à Pitre
Basse Terre
LESSER ANTILLES
DOMINICA
Roseau
Fort-de-France
Martinique (Fr.)
Castries
ST. LUCIA
BARBADOS
Bridgetown
Kingstown
ST VINCENT AND THE GRENADINES
Windward Islands
St George's
GRENADA
TOBAGO
Port of Spain
Sangre Grande
TRINIDAD
San Fernando
Swan Islands (Honduras)
L. Caratasca
C. Gracias á Dios
Quita Sueño (U.S.-Col.)
Serrana Bank (U.S.-Col.)
S.W. Cay (U.S.-Col.)
Roncador Cay (U.S.-Col.)
Puerto Cabezas
Prinzapolca
Providencia (Col.)
Las Perlas
San Andrés (Col.)
Albuquerque Cays (Col.)
Bluefields
Monkey Point
San Juan del Norte (Greytown)
Cartago
Puerto Limón
Vesta
3837
CHIRRIPÓ GRANDE
Almirante
Bocas del Toro
Gulf of Mosquitos
Colón
Belén
Concepción
David
Remedios
Soná
Gulf of Chiriquí
Coiba I.
PANAMA
Panamá
Balboa
Chitré
S. Miguel
Las Tablas
Gulf of Panamá
Peninsula of Azuero
Gulf of Darién
La Palma
El Real
Pta. Gallinas
Aruba (Neth.)
Curaçao (Neth.)
Bonaire (Neth.)
Willemstad
Los Roques Is. (Ven.)
Blanquilla (Ven.)
La Tortuga
Margarita
La Asunción
Porlamar
Carúpano
Irapa
Gulf of Paria
Riohacha
Uribia
Gulf of Venezuela
Sta. Marta
Ciénaga
CRISTÓBAL COLÓN 5775
Barranquilla
Cartagena
Sabanalarga
Valledupar
Calamar
Maracaibo
Altagracia
Cabimas
Lake Maracaibo
Coro
Puerto Cumarebo
Tucacas
Puerto Cabello
La Guaira
Caracas
Carenero
Pto. La Cruz
Cumaná
Barcelona
Caripito 2596
Maturín
Pedernales
Curiapo
Capatárida
San Felipe
Barquisimeto
Valencia
Maracay
San Juan
Ocumare
San Mateo
Anaco
Tucupita
San Lorenzo
Trujillo
Cojedes
San Carlos
Guárico Res.
Zaraza
Valle de la Pascua
El Tigre
Barrancas
Ciudad Guayana
Orinoco
Pariaguán
Calabozo
Guanare
Barinas
Upata
Guasipati
Carmen
Sincelejo
Magangué
Mompós
Lorica
Montería
San Marcos
Banco
Ayacucho
Ocaña
Encontrados
Mérida
El Vigía
El Baúl
VENEZUELA
LLANOS
Ciudad Bolívar
Caroní Res.
Tumeremo
San Pedro
Turbo
Ayapel
Nechí
Cúcuta
San Cristóbal
Guasdualito
Arauca
Achaguas
San Fernando
Caicara
Pamplona
Capanaparo
Bucaramanga
COLOMBIA
Riosucio 3960
Puerto Wilches
PARAMILLO
Barrancabermeja
Puerto Carreño
Luepa
RORAIMA 2810
La Gran Sabana
Santo Domingo

Legend

Boundaries
International
(in sea)
(disputed)
Internal

Roads
Expressway
Other roads
Unimproved roads

Airports
International
Domestic

Canals
Seasonal rivers, lakes
Marshes
Salt pan
Ice cap
Sand desert limits
National parks etc.

metres
5000
3000
2000
1000
500
300
200
100
Sea level
Land depression

Spot heights in metres

Scale 1:16 000 000

0 100 200 300 km

South America

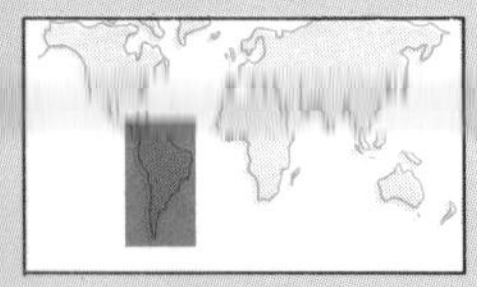

Legend

Boundaries

- International
- (in sea)
- (disputed)
- Internal

Roads

- Expressway
- Other roads
- Unimproved roads
- Railways

Airports

- ⊕ International
- ○ Domestic

- Canals
- Seasonal rivers, lakes
- Marshes
- Salt pan
- Ice cap
- Sand desert limits
- National parks etc.

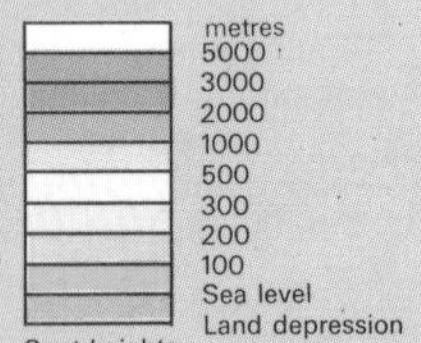
metres
5000
3000
2000
1000
500
300
200
100
Sea level
Land depression

Spot heights in metres

Scale 1:30 000 000
0 300 600 km

Transverse Mercator Projection

PARAGUAY
BRAZIL
URUGUAY
ARGENTINA
ATLANTIC OCEAN
GRAN CHACO
PAMPA
Tropic of Capricorn
Asunción
São Paulo
Rio de Janeiro
Curitiba
Florianópolis
Pôrto Alegre
Montevideo
Buenos Aires
La Plata
Córdoba
Rosario
Santa Fe
Paraná
Corrientes
Resistencia
Posadas
San Miguel de Tucumán
Santiago del Estero
Salta
Santos
Campinas
Londrina
Maringá
Ponta Grossa
Lajes
Pelotas
Rio Grande
Santa Maria
Lagoa dos Patos
Rio de la Plata
same scale
Legend
Boundaries
International
(in sea)
(disputed)
Internal
Roads
Expressway
Other roads
Unimproved roads
Railways
Airports
International
Domestic
Canals
Seasonal rivers, lakes
Marshes
Salt pan
Ice cap
Sand desert limits
National parks etc.
Spot heights in metres
metres
5000
3000
2000
1000
500
300
200
100
Sea level
Land depression
Scale 1:7 875 000
0
100
200 km

Conical Orthomorphic Projection

Europe: Physical

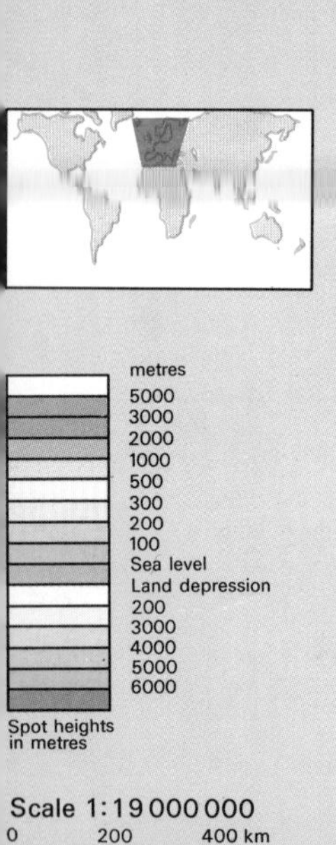
metres
5000
3000
2000
1000
500
300
200
100
Sea level
Land depression
200
3000
4000
5000
6000
Spot heights in metres
Scale 1:19 000 000
0
200
400 km

25°W 20°W 15°W 10°W 5°W 0° 5°E 10°E 15°E 20°E 25°E 30°E 40°E
65°N 60°N 55°N 50°N 45°N 40°N 35°N

North Cape
C. Kanin
Arctic Circle
Kola Peninsula
White Sea
L. Inari
Greenland Sea
Lofoten Islands
Kjølen Mountains
Lappmark
Iceland
Vatnajökull
HEKLA 1491
Lake Onega
Gulf of Bothnia
Dovrefjell
Skerriegard
Faeroe Islands
Lake Ladoga
Rybinsk Reservoir
Salpausselka
ATLANTIC OCEAN
Jostedalsbreen
Hardanger-vidda
Shetland Is
Åland Is
Gulf of Finland
Lake Peipus
L. Mälar
L. Väner
Outer Hebrides
The Minch
C. Wrath
Orkney Is
Moray Firth
Skye
Grampians
L.Vätter
G. of Riga
Gotland
West Dvina
Skagerrak
Kattegat
North Sea
Malin Hd
Southern Uplands
Öland
Baltic Sea
Jutland
Skåne
Neman
Zealand
Fyn
Bornholm
Pomeranian Bay
Central Plain
Shannon
Maximum extent of Glaciation
St George's Channel
Cambrian Mts
Pennines
The Wash
Frisian Is.
Elbe
Weser
North European Plain
Oder
Vistula
Pripet Marshes
IJeselmeer
Thames
Scheldt Est.
Waal
Maas
Harz Mts
Dneiper
Scilly Is
English Channel
Str. of Dover
Rhine
1603
Erzgebirge
Bohemian Massif
Dniestr
Bug
Channel Is
Cotentin
Ardennes
Seine
Marne
Tatry Mts
Carpathian Mountains
Brittany Pen.
Paris Basin
Vosges
Swabian Jura
Danube
Loire
Bodensee
Inn
Tisza
Tauern
Hungarian Basin
Bay of Biscay
Saône
Jura
Alps
Drava
Massif Central
MT BLANC 4810
Sava
Black Sea
C. Finnisterre
Garonne
Po
Danube
Cantabrian Mts
Rhône
Maritime Alps
Apennines
Adriatic Sea
Dinaric Alps
Balkan Mts
Pyrenees
3401
G. of Lyon
Ligurian Sea
Rhodope Mts
Bosporus
Duero
Ebro
Sea of Marmara
Central Cordilleras
Corsica
Dardanelles
Tagus
VESUVIUS 1277
Pindus Mountains
OLYMPUS 2911
Guadiana
Sardinia
Tyrrhenian Sea
G. of Taranto
Aegean Sea
Euboea
Algarve
Guadalquiver
Balearic Is.
Ionian Sea
Ionian Is.
Peloponnese
Cyclades
Betican Cordilleras
Mediterranean Sea
Sicily
MT ETNA 3340
Str. of Gibraltar
Crete
5°W 0° 5°E 10°E 20°E 25°E
Malta

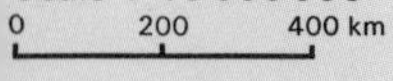

Conical Orthomorphic Projection

Precipitation figures on graphs in 10[1]mm except annual totals

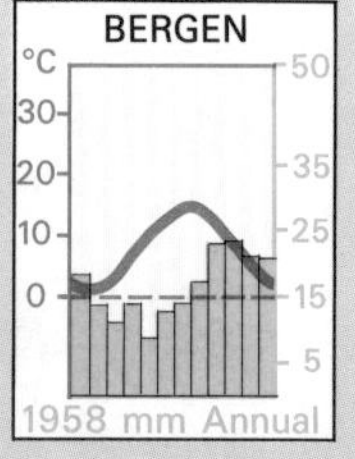
BERGEN
°C
30
20
10
0
50
35
25
15
5
1958 mm Annual

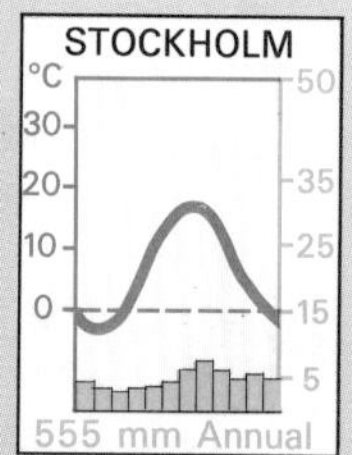
STOCKHOLM
°C
30
20
10
0
50
35
25
15
5
555 mm Annual

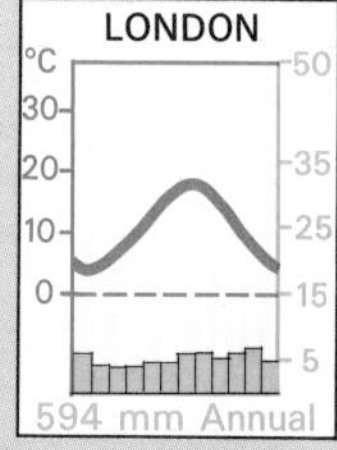
LONDON
°C
30
20
10
0
50
35
25
15
5
594 mm Annual

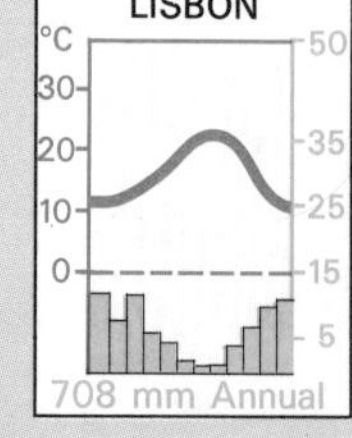
LISBON
°C
30
20
10
0
50
35
25
15
5
708 mm Annual

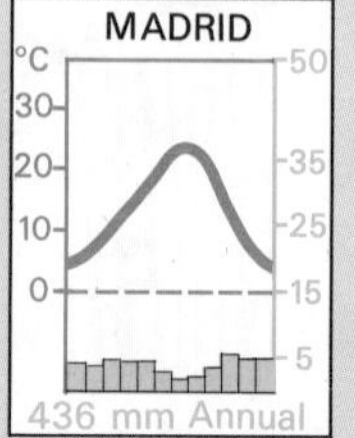
MADRID
°C
30
20
10
0
50
35
25
15
5
436 mm Annual

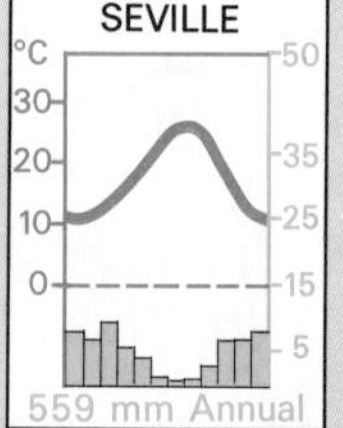
SEVILLE
°C
30
20
10
0
50
35
25
15
5
559 mm Annual

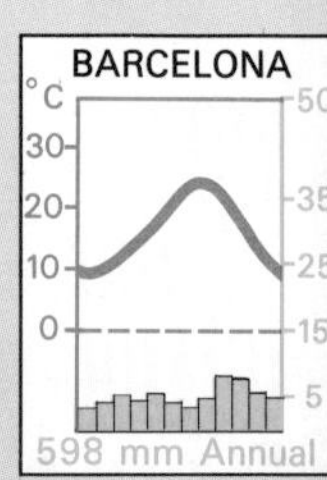
BARCELONA
°C
30
20
10
0
50
35
25
15
5
598 mm Annual

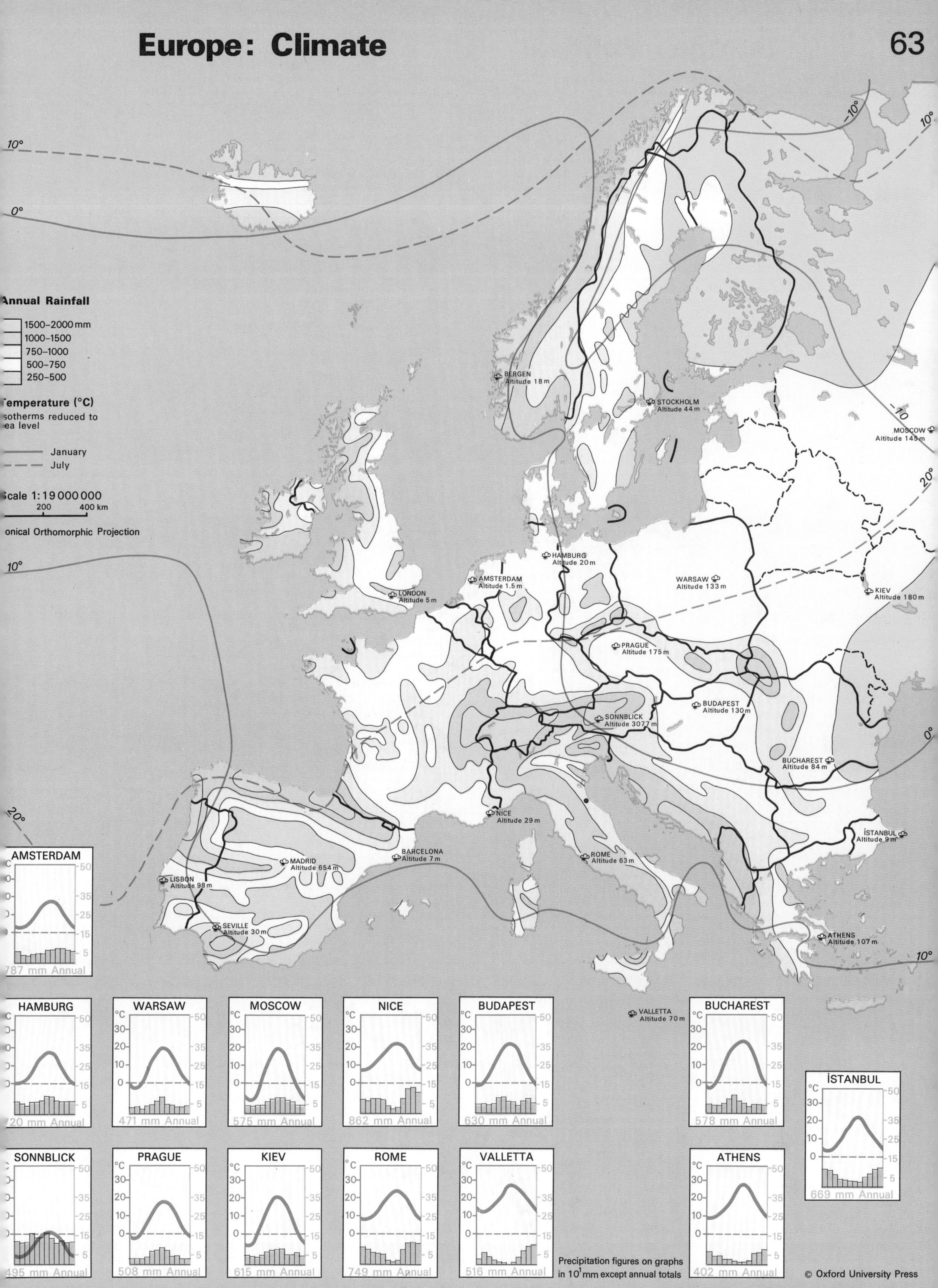
Europe: Climate
63
Annual Rainfall
1500–2000 mm
1000–1500
750–1000
500–750
250–500
Temperature (°C)
Isotherms reduced to sea level
January
July
Scale 1: 19 000 000
200
400 km
Conical Orthomorphic Projection
10°
0°
20°
-10°
-10
BERGEN Altitude 18 m
STOCKHOLM Altitude 44 m
MOSCOW Altitude 145 m
HAMBURG Altitude 20 m
AMSTERDAM Altitude 1.5 m
LONDON Altitude 5 m
WARSAW Altitude 133 m
KIEV Altitude 180 m
PRAGUE Altitude 175 m
BUDAPEST Altitude 130 m
SONNBLICK Altitude 3077 m
BUCHAREST Altitude 84 m
NICE Altitude 29 m
MADRID Altitude 654 m
BARCELONA Altitude 7 m
LISBON Altitude 98 m
SEVILLE Altitude 30 m
ROME Altitude 63 m
İSTANBUL Altitude 9 m
ATHENS Altitude 107 m
VALLETTA Altitude 70 m
AMSTERDAM
787 mm Annual
HAMBURG
720 mm Annual
WARSAW
471 mm Annual
MOSCOW
575 mm Annual
NICE
862 mm Annual
BUDAPEST
630 mm Annual
BUCHAREST
578 mm Annual
İSTANBUL
669 mm Annual
SONNBLICK
1495 mm Annual
PRAGUE
508 mm Annual
KIEV
615 mm Annual
ROME
749 mm Annual
VALLETTA
516 mm Annual
ATHENS
402 mm Annual
°C
30
20
10
0
50
35
25
15
5
Precipitation figures on graphs in 10[1] mm except annual totals
© Oxford University Press

Europe: Political

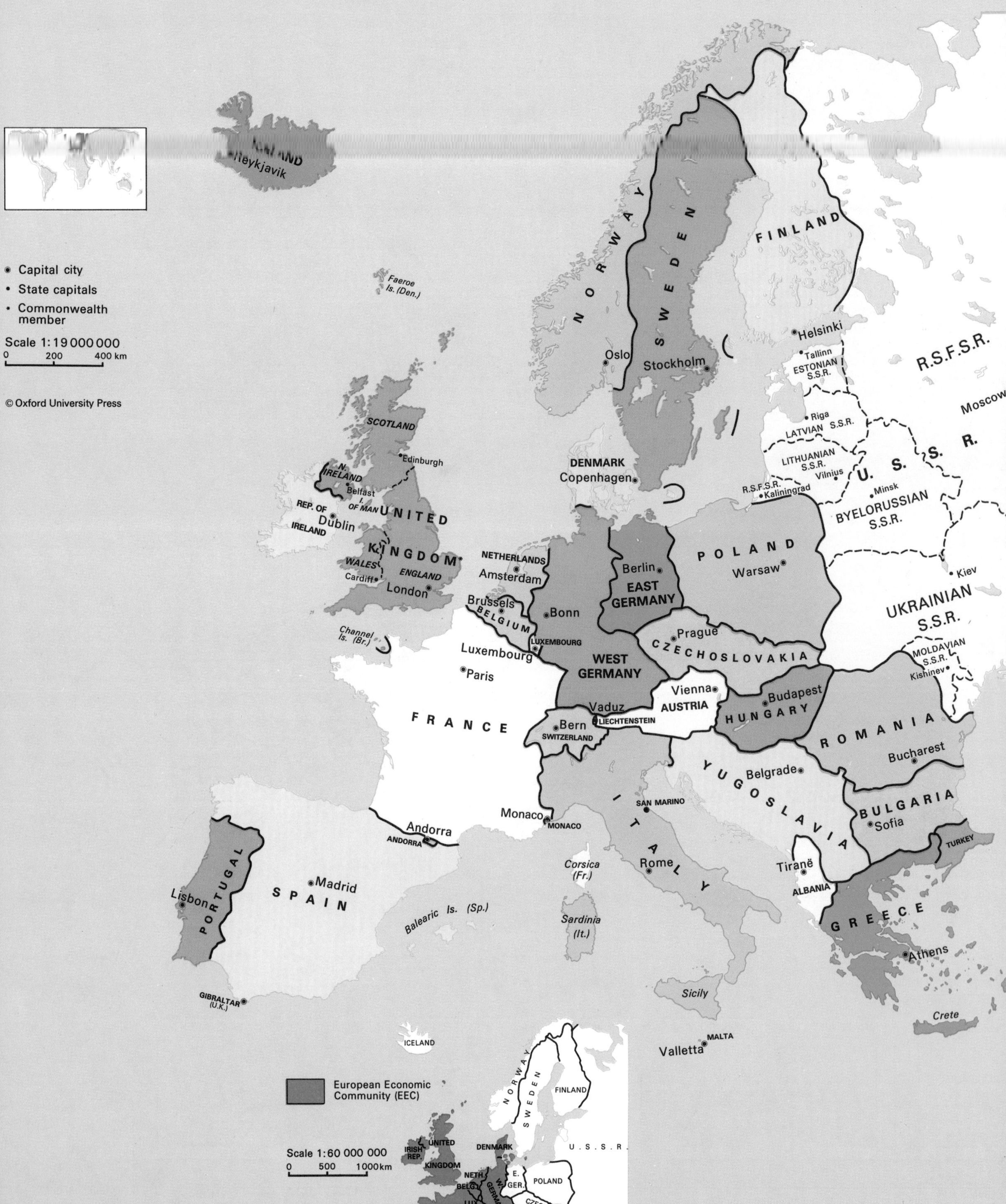

Capital city
State capitals
Commonwealth member
Scale 1:19 000 000
0 200 400 km
ICELAND
Reykjavik
Faeroe Is. (Den.)
NORWAY
SWEDEN
FINLAND
Oslo
Stockholm
Helsinki
Tallinn
ESTONIAN S.S.R.
R.S.F.S.R.
Moscow
Riga
LATVIAN S.S.R.
LITHUANIAN S.S.R.
Vilnius
U. S. S. R.
R.S.F.S.R.
Kaliningrad
Minsk
BYELORUSSIAN S.S.R.
Kiev
UKRAINIAN S.S.R.
MOLDAVIAN S.S.R.
Kishinev
SCOTLAND
Edinburgh
N. IRELAND
Belfast
I. OF MAN
REP. OF IRELAND
Dublin
UNITED KINGDOM
WALES
Cardiff
ENGLAND
London
DENMARK
Copenhagen
NETHERLANDS
Amsterdam
Brussels
BELGIUM
LUXEMBOURG
Luxembourg
Bonn
WEST GERMANY
Berlin
EAST GERMANY
POLAND
Warsaw
Prague
CZECHOSLOVAKIA
Vienna
AUSTRIA
Vaduz
LIECHTENSTEIN
Bern
SWITZERLAND
Budapest
HUNGARY
ROMANIA
Bucharest
Channel Is. (Br.)
Paris
FRANCE
Belgrade
YUGOSLAVIA
BULGARIA
Sofia
SAN MARINO
Monaco
MONACO
Andorra
ANDORRA
ITALY
Rome
Corsica (Fr.)
Sardinia (It.)
Sicily
Tiranë
ALBANIA
TURKEY
GREECE
Athens
Crete
PORTUGAL
Lisbon
SPAIN
Madrid
Balearic Is. (Sp.)
GIBRALTAR (U.K.)
MALTA
Valletta
ICELAND
European Economic Community (EEC)
Scale 1:60 000 000
0 500 1000 km
NORWAY
SWEDEN
FINLAND
U.S.S.R.
IRISH REP.
UNITED KINGDOM
DENMARK
NETH.
BELG.
LUX.
W. GERMANY
E. GER.
POLAND
CZECH.
FRANCE
SWITZ.
AUS.
HUNG.
ROMANIA
YUGOSLAVIA
BULGARIA
ITALY
ALB.
TURKEY
GREECE
PORTUGAL
SPAIN
Conical Orthomorphic Projection

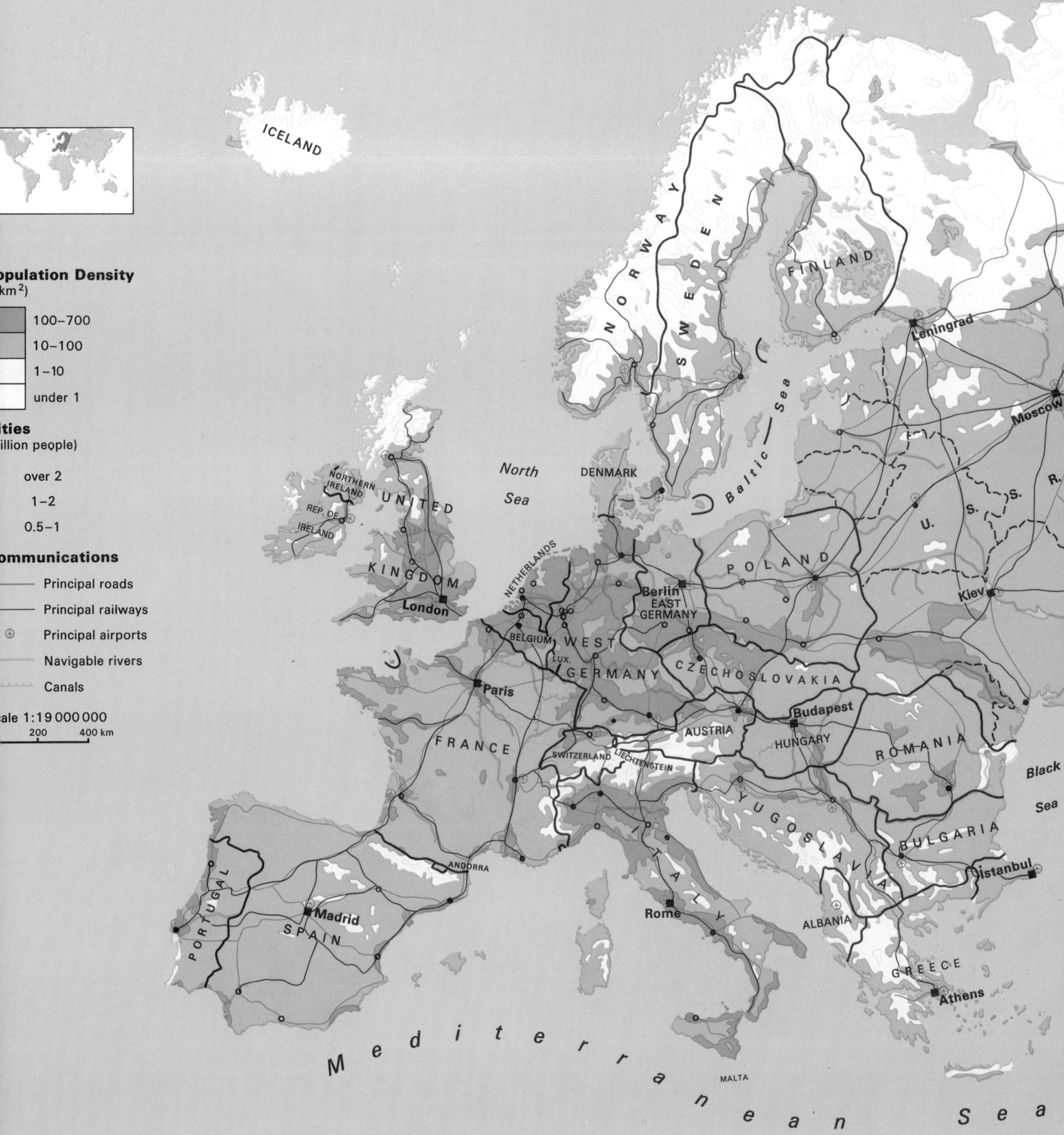
opulation Density
km²)
100–700
10–100
1–10
under 1
ities
illion people)
over 2
1–2
0.5–1
ommunications
Principal roads
Principal railways
Principal airports
Navigable rivers
Canals
ale 1:19 000 000
200
400 km
ICELAND
NORWAY
SWEDEN
FINLAND
Leningrad
Moscow
U. S. S. R.
Baltic Sea
North Sea
DENMARK
NORTHERN IRELAND
REP. OF IRELAND
UNITED KINGDOM
London
NETHERLANDS
BELGIUM
LUX.
Berlin
EAST GERMANY
WEST GERMANY
POLAND
Kiev
CZECHOSLOVAKIA
Paris
FRANCE
SWITZERLAND
LIECHTENSTEIN
AUSTRIA
Budapest
HUNGARY
ROMANIA
Black Sea
YUGOSLAVIA
BULGARIA
Istanbul
ANDORRA
PORTUGAL
Madrid
SPAIN
ITALY
Rome
ALBANIA
GREECE
Athens
MALTA
Mediterranean Sea

Europe: Agriculture

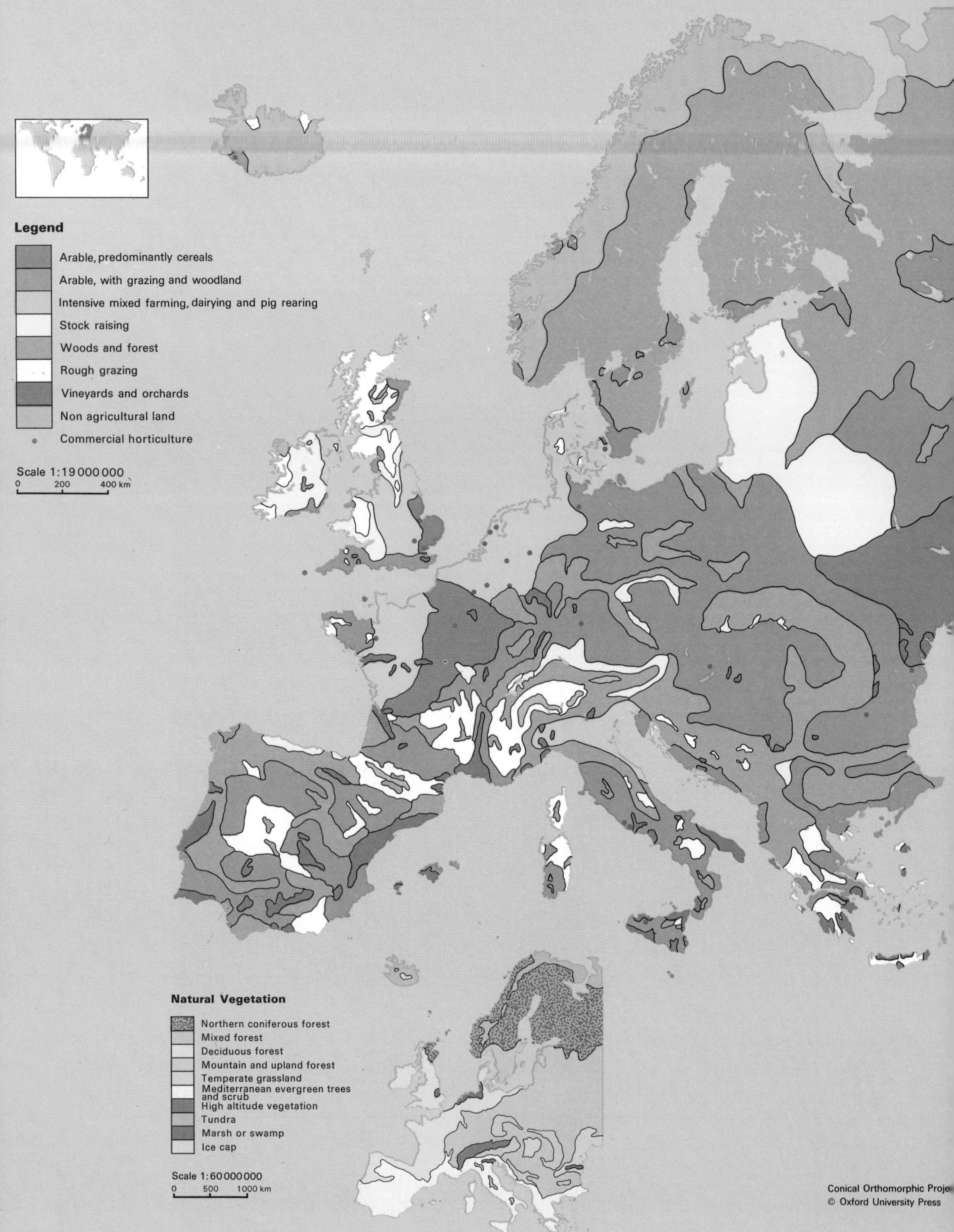
Legend
Arable, predominantly cereals
Arable, with grazing and woodland
Intensive mixed farming, dairying and pig rearing
Stock raising
Woods and forest
Rough grazing
Vineyards and orchards
Non agricultural land
Commercial horticulture
Scale 1:19 000 000
0
200
400 km
Natural Vegetation
Northern coniferous forest
Mixed forest
Deciduous forest
Mountain and upland forest
Temperate grassland
Mediterranean evergreen trees and scrub
High altitude vegetation
Tundra
Marsh or swamp
Ice cap
Scale 1:60 000 000
0
500
1000 km
Conical Orthomorphic Proje

British Isles

Population
Population Density
(/km²)
over 700
100 - 700
10 - 100
1 - 10
under 1
Central Clydeside
Tyneside
Southeast Lancashire
West Yorkshire
Merseyside
West Midlands
Greater London
Major conurbations
(million people)
over 2
1 - 2
0.5 - 1
Scale 1:12 500 000
Power
Coalfield
Oil
Gas
H.E.P. station
Nuclear power station
Shetland Is.
Orkney Is.
Outer Hebrides
S C O T L A N D
North West Highlands
The Cairngorms
Grampian Highlands
Southern Uplands
Firth of Forth
Moray Firth
Edinburgh
Glasgow
Aberdeen
Dundee
Inverness
Perth
Fort William
BEN NEVIS 1343
BEN MACDHUI 1309
BEN HOPE 927
ATLANTIC OCEAN
NORTH SEA
NORTHERN IRELAND
Belfast
Londonderry
REPUBLIC OF IRELAND
Dublin
Cork
Limerick
Galway
Wicklow Mts.
Mourne Mts.
Irish Sea
Isle of Man
St. George's Channel
Cardigan Bay
WALES
SNOWDON 1085
Cardiff
Swansea
ENGLAND
Pennines
Lake District
N. York Moors
Newcastle upon Tyne
Sunderland
Middlesbrough
York
Leeds
Hull
Manchester
Liverpool
Sheffield
Birmingham
Nottingham
Leicester
Coventry
Norwich
Cambridge
Oxford
Bristol
Bristol Channel
LONDON
Southampton
Portsmouth
Brighton
Plymouth
Exeter
Dartmoor
Exmoor
Cotswolds
Chiltern Hills
The Weald
The Fens
Isle of Wight
English Channel
Str. of Dover
Land's End
Isles of Scilly
100 m
60°N
55°N
50°N
10°W
5°W
0°

Legend

Boundaries
- International
- (in sea)
- (disputed)
- Internal

Roads
- Motorways
- Other roads
- Unimproved roads
- Railways

Airports
- International
- Domestic

- Canals
- Seasonal rivers, lakes
- Marshes
- Salt pan
- Ice cap
- Sand desert limits
- National parks etc.

metres: 5000, 3000, 2000, 1000, 500, 300, 200, 100, Sea level, Land depression

Spot heights in metres

Scale 1:4 750 000

0 50 100 150 km

al Orthomorphic Projection

Western Europe

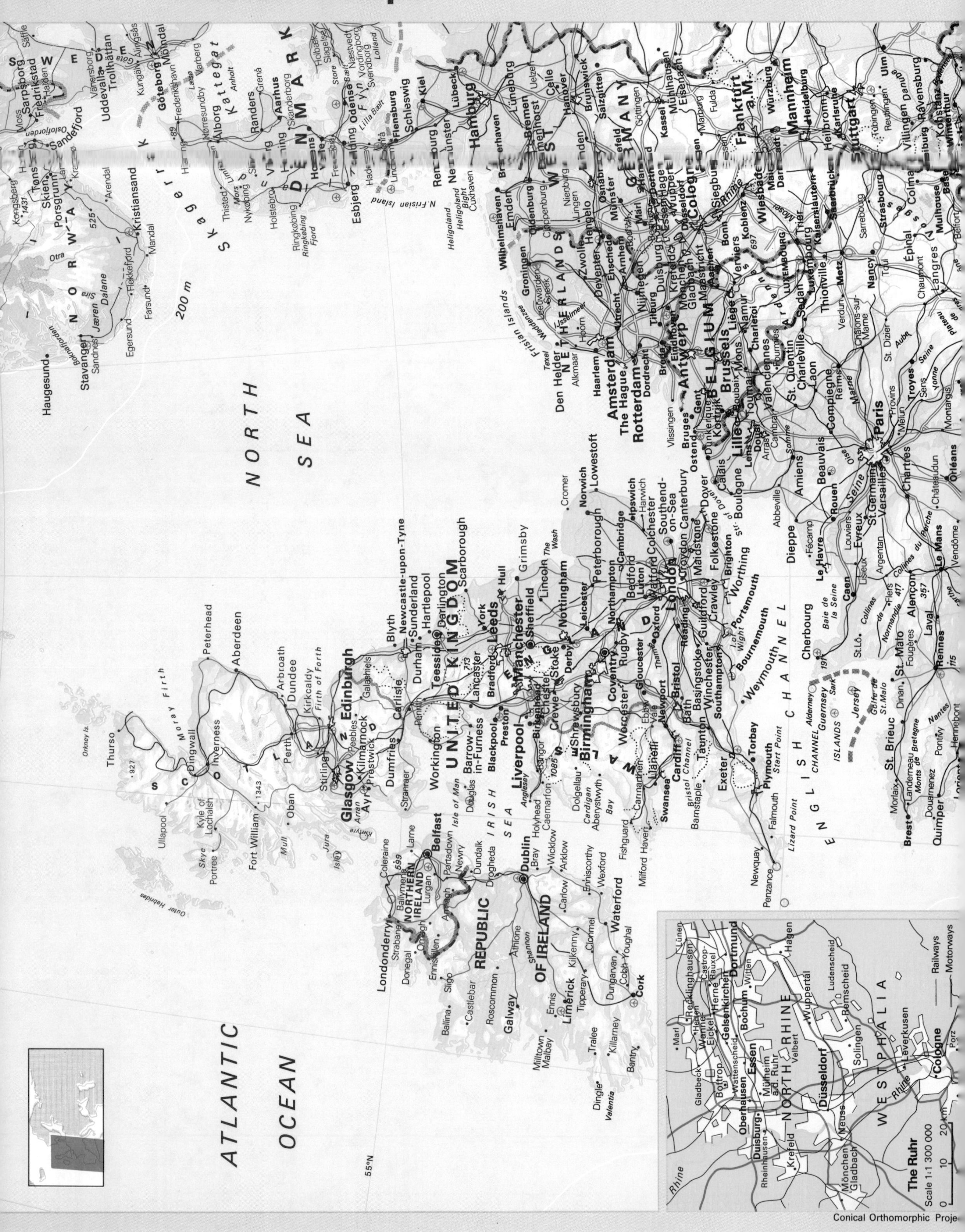

NORTH SEA
ATLANTIC OCEAN
ENGLISH CHANNEL
IRISH SEA
Skagerrak
Kattegat
UNITED KINGDOM
REPUBLIC OF IRELAND
NORTHERN IRELAND
NORWAY
SWEDEN
DENMARK
WEST GERMANY
NETHERLANDS
BELGIUM
LUXEMBOURG
SCOTLAND
ENGLAND
WALES
CHANNEL ISLANDS
Frisian Islands
N. Frisian Island
Outer Hebrides
Orkney Is.
Moray Firth
Firth of Forth
Isle of Man
Cardigan Bay
Bristol Channel
The Wash
Lizard Point
Start Point
Skye
Mull
Jura
Islay
Arran
Kintyre
Anglesey
Alderney
Guernsey
Sark
Jersey
Texel
Heligoland
Heligoland Bight
Ringkøbing Fjord
Fyn
Lolland
Seine
Rhine
Mosel
Somme
Marne
Oise
Aube
Yonne
Thames
Shannon
Otra
Cherbourg
Le Havre
Dieppe
Calais
Boulogne
Paris
Lille
Amiens
Rouen
Caen
Le Mans
Rennes
Brest
Quimper
Orléans
Chartres
Versailles
St. Germain
Reims
Laon
Troyes
Nancy
Metz
Strasbourg
Colmar
Mulhouse
Épinal
Langres
Brussels
Antwerp
Gent
Bruges
Ostend
Liège
Namur
Charleroi
Mons
Luxembourg
Amsterdam
Rotterdam
The Hague
Haarlem
Utrecht
Eindhoven
Groningen
Den Helder
Cologne
Bonn
Düsseldorf
Duisburg
Essen
Dortmund
Münster
Osnabrück
Bremen
Bremerhaven
Hamburg
Kiel
Lübeck
Flensburg
Hanover
Brunswick
Kassel
Frankfurt a.M.
Wiesbaden
Koblenz
Mainz
Mannheim
Heidelberg
Karlsruhe
Stuttgart
Würzburg
Saarbrücken
Kaiserslautern
Trier
Aachen
Esbjerg
Odense
Århus
Ålborg
Randers
Göteborg
Trollhättan
Uddevalla
Kristiansand
Stavanger
Haugesund
Mandal
Arendal
Skien
Porsgrunn
Sandefjord
Sarpsborg
Fredrikstad
London
Birmingham
Manchester
Liverpool
Leeds
Sheffield
Bradford
Nottingham
Leicester
Coventry
Oxford
Cambridge
Bristol
Cardiff
Swansea
Newport
Plymouth
Exeter
Southampton
Portsmouth
Brighton
Bournemouth
Dover
Norwich
Ipswich
Hull
York
Newcastle-upon-Tyne
Sunderland
Teesside
Carlisle
Edinburgh
Glasgow
Aberdeen
Dundee
Inverness
Perth
Belfast
Londonderry
Dublin
Cork
Limerick
Waterford
Galway
Wexford
Kilkenny
The Ruhr
Scale 1:1 300 000
NORTH RHINE-WESTPHALIA
Railways
Motorways
200 m
55°N

Conical Orthomorphic Proje

Internal
Roads
Motorways
Other roads
Canals
Seasonal rivers, lakes
Marshes
Scale 1:6 250 000
0 50 100 km
metres
5000
3000
2000
1000
500
300
200
100
Sea level
Land depression
Spot heights in metres
BAY OF BISCAY
FRANCE
SPAIN
PORTUGAL
ITALY
SWITZERLAND
MOROCCO
ALGERIA
MEDITERRANEAN SEA
Balearic Islands (Sp.)
Golfo du Lion
CÔTE D'AZUR
Golfo de Valencia
Massif Central
Pyrenees
Cordillera Cantabrica
Sistema Ibérico
Cordillera Central
Sierra Morena
Cordilleras Béticas
Meseta
Atlas Mountains
Tell Atlas
Madrid
Lisbon
Barcelona
Valencia
Seville
Bordeaux
Toulouse
Marseille
Lyon
Geneva
Turin
Milan
Genoa
Nice
Algiers
Oporto
Bilbao
Zaragoza
Málaga
Granada
Córdoba
Murcia
Alicante
Corsica (Fr.)
Sardinia (It.)
Mallorca
Menorca
Ibiza
Formentera
Ajaccio
Bastia
Cágliari
Sassari
Palma de Mallorca
Tangier
Ceuta (Sp.)
Melilla (Sp.)
Oran
Constantine
GIBRALTAR (U.K.)
Str. of Gibraltar
ANDORRA
MONACO
40°N
35°N
5°W
0°
5°E
200 m

Scandinavia
1:19 000 000
NORWAY
SWEDEN
DENMARK
POLAND
BALTIC SEA
Skagerrak
Kattegat
NORTH SEA
WEST GERMANY
EAST GERMANY
CZECHOSLOVAKIA
BYELORUSSIAN S.S.R.
UKRAINIAN S.S.R.
U.S.S.R.
Oslo
Stockholm
Copenhagen
Göteborg
Hamburg
Berlin
Warsaw
Prague
Vienna
Munich
Stuttgart
Frankfurt a.M.
Leipzig
Dresden
Gdańsk
Szczecin
Poznań
Łódź
Wrocław
Cracow
Kiev
Minsk
Brest
Pinsk
Kaliningrad
Klaipeda
Riga
Vilnius
Leningrad
Pack ice - average max. Feb. - March

Legend
Boundaries
International
(in sea)
(disputed)
Internal
Roads
Motorways
Other roads
Unimproved roads
Railways
Airports
International
Domestic
Canals
Seasonal rivers, lakes
Marshes
Salt pans
Ice cap
Sand desert limits
National parks, etc.
Scale 1:6 250 000
0 50 100 km
metres
5000
3000
2000
1000
500
300
200
100
Sea level
Land depression
Spot heights in metres
ITALY
YUGOSLAVIA
HUNGARY
ROMANIA
BULGARIA
ALBANIA
GREECE
TURKEY
BLACK SEA
ADRIATIC SEA
TYRRHENIAN SEA
IONIAN SEA
AEGEAN SEA
MEDITERRANEAN SEA
Sea of Marmara
Sea of Crete
Mirtoon Sea
Sicilian Channel
Strait of Otranto
Gulf of Taranto
Gulf of Venice
Rome
Naples
Milan
Venice
Florence
Athens
Istanbul
Belgrade
Bucharest
Sofiya
Tiranë
Sicily
Crete
Peloponnese
Dodecanese
Cyclades
Dinaric Alps
Transylvanian Alps
Balkan Mountains
Rhodope Mts
Pindus Mts
Wallachia
Danube
15°E
20°E
25°E
35°N
40°N
45°N

Paris, Moscow

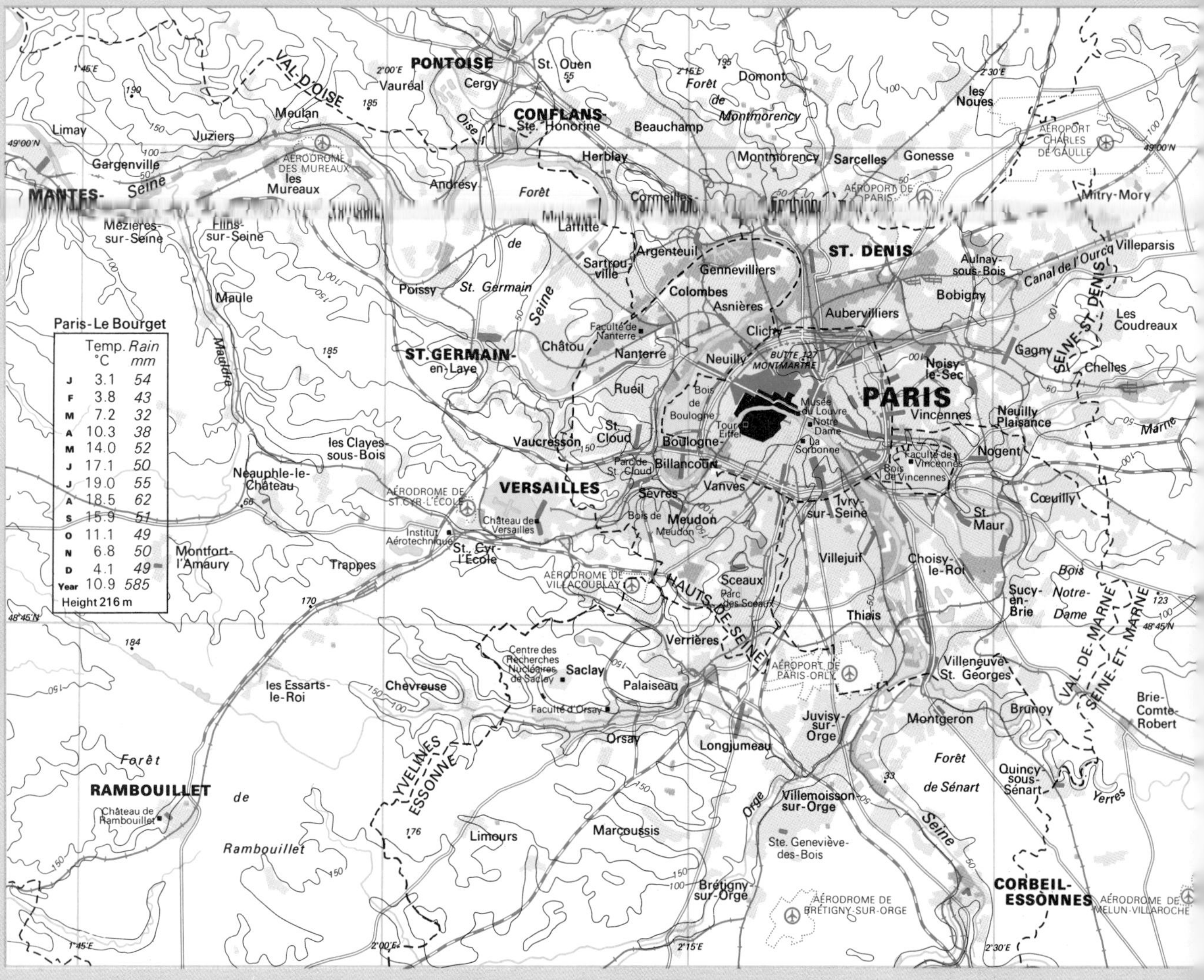

Urban Land Use

These urban land use maps show only a simplified land use pattern. Their primary intent is to illustrate the overall relationships of land use and transportation systems. Therefore, much detail has been omitted.

- Central business core
- Lesser but significant commercial centres
- Industrial districts
- The built-up area where the major use of land is for residential purposes
- Major parks and open spaces

Boundaries

- International
- Provincial or State
- County

Highways

- Limited access and rapid transit
- Other main highways
- Railways and transportation yards
- Airports
- Airfields

Scale 1:400 000

0 5 10 km

Paris - Le Bourget

	Temp. °C	Rain mm
J	3.1	54
F	3.8	43
M	7.2	32
A	10.3	38
M	14.0	52
J	17.1	50
J	19.0	55
A	18.5	62
S	15.9	51
O	11.1	49
N	6.8	50
D	4.1	49
Year	10.9	585

Height 216 m

PONTOISE
St. Ouen
Vauréal
Cergy
CONFLANS-Ste. Honorine
Forêt de Montmorency
Domont
les Noues
VAL-D'OISE
Meulan
Limay
Juziers
Gargenville
AÉRODROME DES MUREAUX
les Mureaux
Beauchamp
Herblay
Montmorency
Sarcelles
Gonesse
AÉROPORT CHARLES DE GAULLE
MANTES-
Seine
Andrésy
Forêt de St. Germain
Cormeilles
AÉROPORT DE PARIS
Mitry-Mory
Mézières-sur-Seine
Flins-sur-Seine
Laffitte
Argenteuil
ST. DENIS
Aulnay-sous-Bois
Villeparsis
Canal de l'Ourcq
Sartrouville
Gennevilliers
Colombes
Asnières
Maule
Poissy
Aubervilliers
Bobigny
Les Coudreaux
Mauldre
Faculté de Nanterre
Clichy
ST. GERMAIN-en-Laye
Châtou
Nanterre
Neuilly
BUTTE 127 MONTMARTRE
Noisy-le-Sec
Gagny
Chelles
SEINE-ST. DENIS
Rueil
Bois de Boulogne
Musée du Louvre
Notre Dame
PARIS
Vincennes
Neuilly Plaisance
Marne
les Clayes-sous-Bois
Vaucresson
St. Cloud
Tour Eiffel
Boulogne-Billancourt
La Sorbonne
Faculté de Vincennes
Bois de Vincennes
Nogent
Neauphle-le-Château
AÉRODROME DE ST. CYR-L'ÉCOLE
VERSAILLES
Parc de St. Cloud
Sèvres
Vanves
Ivry-sur-Seine
Coeuilly
Château de Versailles
Bois de Meudon
Meudon
St. Maur
Institut Aérotechnique
St. Cyr-l'École
Montfort-l'Amaury
Trappes
Villejuif
Choisy-le-Roi
AÉRODROME DE VILLACOUBLAY
Sceaux
Parc des Sceaux
Sucy-en-Brie
Bois Notre-Dame
HAUTS-DE-SEINE
Thiais
VAL-DE-MARNE
Verrières
Centre des Recherches Nucléaires de Saclay
Saclay
AÉROPORT DE PARIS-ORLY
Villeneuve-St. Georges
les Essarts-le-Roi
Chevreuse
Palaiseau
Faculté d'Orsay
Brunoy
SEINE-ET-MARNE
Brie-Comte-Robert
Juvisy-sur-Orge
Montgeron
Orsay
Longjumeau
Forêt de Sénart
YVELINES
ESSONNE
RAMBOUILLET
Château de Rambouillet
Forêt de Rambouillet
Orge
Villemoisson-sur-Orge
Quincy-sous-Sénart
Yerres
Limours
Marcoussis
Ste. Geneviève-des-Bois
Brétigny-sur-Orge
AÉRODROME DE BRÉTIGNY-SUR-ORGE
CORBEIL-ESSONNES
AÉRODROME DE MELUN-VILLAROCHE

KHIMKI
Khimki-Khovrino
Medvedkovo
Mytishchi
BABUSHKIN
NORTH PORT
Khimki Reservoir
Beskudnikovo
MOSCOW OBLAST
MOSCOW CITY
KRASNOGORSK
TUSHINO
Economic Exhibition Grounds
Kuybyshev Forest
Timiryazev Park
Ostankino
Cherkizovsky
Sokolniki Park
BALASHIKHA
CENTRAL AIRPORT
Rublevo
Moskva
Khorochevo
MOSCOW
Yauza
Izmaylovskiy Park
Mnevniki
FILI AIRFIELD
WEST PORT
REUTOV
Kremlin
PEROVO
KUNTSEVO
Matveyeskoye
Sports Stadium
Gorkiy Park
Kosino
Gagarin
Moscow University
SOUTH PORT
Kuz'minki
RAMENKI
Semenovskoye
Ochakovo
NEGATINO
LYUBERTSY AIRFIELD
Cheremushki
LYUBLINO
Z'UZINO
LYUBERTSY
Solntsevo
Moskva
Lenino
Kotel'niki
Chertanovo
Dzherzhinsky
VNUKOVO AIRPORT
Krasny Stroitel
LYTKARINO

	Temp °C	Rain mm
J	-9.9	31
F	-9.5	28
M	-4.2	33
A	4.7	35
M	11.9	52
J	16.8	67
J	19.0	74
A	17.1	74
S	11.2	58
O	4.5	51
N	-1.9	36
D	-6.8	36
Year	4.4	575

Height 156 m

Asia: Political

IRISH REP.
U.K.*
NORWAY
SWEDEN
FINLAND
FRANCE
BELG.
NETHS.
DENMARK
W. GERMANY
E. GER.
SW.
AUS.
CZECH.
POLAND
ITALY
HUNG.
YUGO.
ROMANIA
ALB.
GREECE
BULG.
LATVIAN S.S.R.
Tallinn
ESTONIAN S.S.R.
Riga
R.S.F.S.R.
LITHUANIAN S.S.R.
Vilnius
Minsk
BYELORUSSIAN S.S.R.
Moscow
Kiev
UKRAINIAN S.S.R.
MOLDAVIAN S.S.R.
Kishinev
RUSSIAN SOVIET FEDERATED SOCIALIST REPUBLIC
(R.S.F.S.R)
UNION OF SOVIET SOCIALIST REPUBLICS
(U.S.S.R.)
Ankara
TURKEY
CYPRUS*
Nicosia
GEORGIAN S.S.R.
Tbilisi
Yerevan
ARMENIAN S.S.R.
AZERBAYDZAN S.S.R.
Baku
KAZAKH S.S.R.
Beirut
LEBANON
SYRIA
Damascus
Jerusalem
ISRAEL
Amman
JORDAN
Baghdad
IRAQ
TURKMEN S.S.R.
Ashkhabad
UZBEK S.S.R.
Tashkent
Alma Ata
Frunze
KIRGHIZ S.S.R.
TADZHIZ S.S.R.
Dushambe
Tehran
IRAN
KUWAIT
Kuwait
SAUDI ARABIA
Riyadh
BAHRAIN
Manama
Doha
QATAR
UNITED ARAB EMIRATES
Abu Dhabi
OMAN
Muscat
YEMEN
San'a
YEMEN P.D.R.
Aden
Kabul
AFGHANISTAN
Islamabad
JAMMU & KASHMIR
PAKISTAN
New Delhi
NEPAL
Katmandu
Timphu
BHUTAN
BANGLADESH*
Dhaka
INDIA*
Ulan Bator
MONGOLIA
CHINA
Peking (Beijing)
NORTH KOREA
Pyongyang
Seoul
SOUTH KOREA
JAPAN
Tokyo
Taipei
TAIWAN
MACAO
HONG KONG*
Victoria
Hanoi
BURMA
LAOS
VIETNAM
Vientiane
Rangoon
THAILAND
Bangkok
KAMPUCHEA
Phnom Penh
PHILIPPINES
Manila
Lakshadweep (Ind.)
Andaman Is. (Ind.)
Nicobar Is. (Ind.)
SRI LANKA*
Colombo
Male
MALDIVES
Kota Kinabalu
SABAH
Bandar Seri Begawan
BRUNEI
MALAYSIA
MALAYA
Kuala Lumpur
SARAWAK
SINGAPORE*
Kuching
Borneo
Celebes
Sumatra
INDONESIA
Jakarta
Java
Capital city
State capitals
Commonwealth member
Scale 1:44 000 000
0 500 1000 km

Oxford University Press

Asia: Physical

North Pole
ARCTIC OCEAN
Arctic Circle
Maximum extent of Glaciation
Ural Mountains
West Siberian Plain
East Siberian Plateau
Plateau of Tibet
Gobi Desert
Tarim Depression
Takla Makan
Rub'al Khali
Syrian Desert
Thar Desert
Arabian Sea
Bay of Bengal
South China Sea
INDIAN OCEAN
Mid Indian Basin
Tropic of Cancer
Equator
EVEREST 8848
K2 8611
MT. COMMUNISM 7495
metres
5000
3000
2000
1000
500
300
200
100
Sea level
Land depression
200
3000
4000
5000
6000
Spot heights in metres
Scale 1:44 000 000
0
500
1000 km
75°E
90°E
105°E
120°E

Zenithal Equal Area Projectio

Asia: Rainfall, Vegetation, Minerals

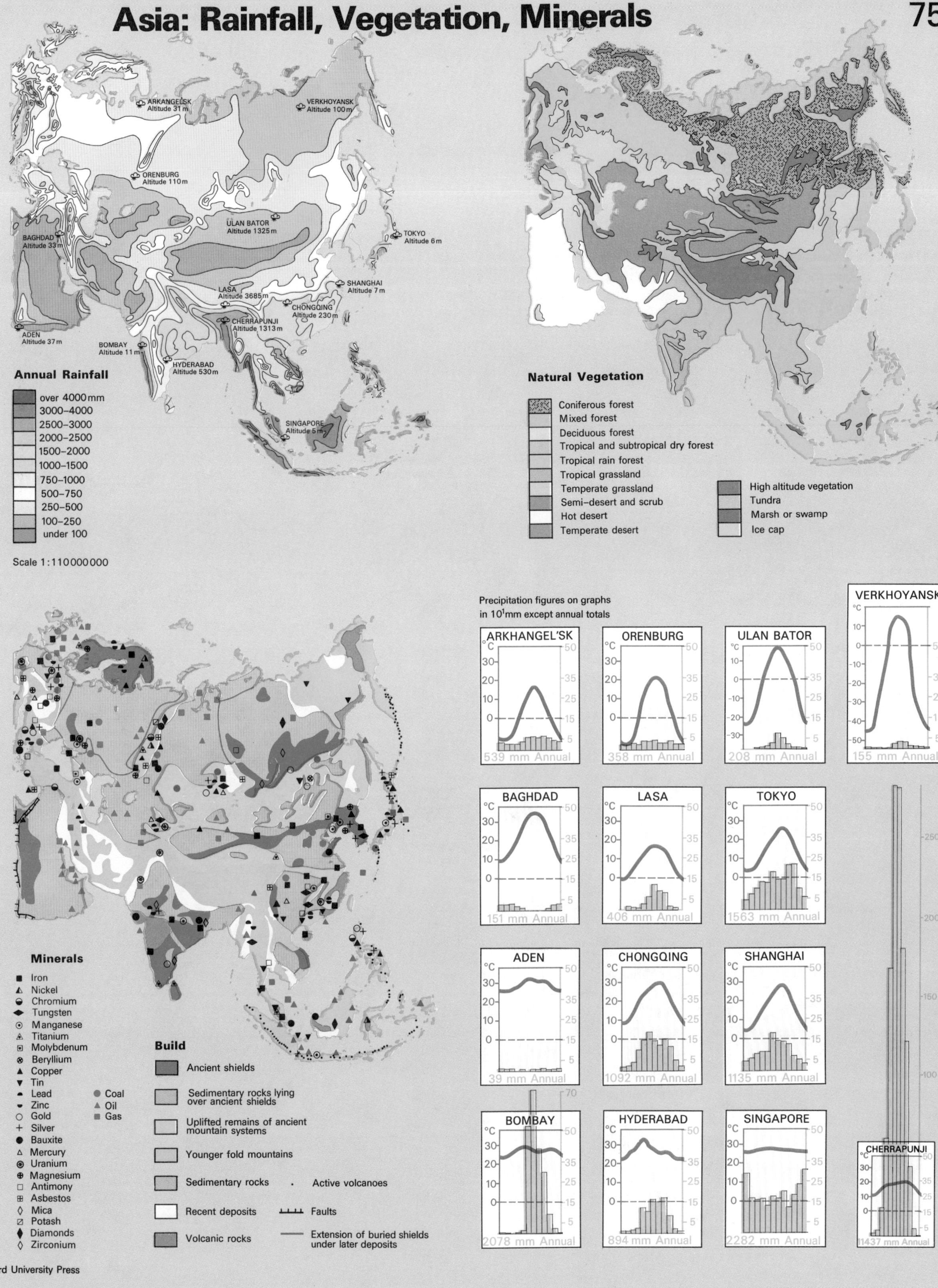
ARKHANGELSK Altitude 31 m
VERKHOYANSK Altitude 100 m
ORENBURG Altitude 110 m
ULAN BATOR Altitude 1325 m
TOKYO Altitude 6 m
BAGHDAD Altitude 33 m
SHANGHAI Altitude 7 m
LASA Altitude 3685 m
CHONGQING Altitude 230 m
CHERRAPUNJI Altitude 1313 m
ADEN Altitude 37 m
BOMBAY Altitude 11 m
HYDERABAD Altitude 530 m
SINGAPORE Altitude 5 m
Annual Rainfall
over 4000 mm
3000–4000
2500–3000
2000–2500
1500–2000
1000–1500
750–1000
500–750
250–500
100–250
under 100
Scale 1:110000000
Natural Vegetation
Coniferous forest
Mixed forest
Deciduous forest
Tropical and subtropical dry forest
Tropical rain forest
Tropical grassland
Temperate grassland
Semi-desert and scrub
Hot desert
Temperate desert
High altitude vegetation
Tundra
Marsh or swamp
Ice cap
Precipitation figures on graphs in 10¹mm except annual totals
ARKHANGEL'SK
539 mm Annual
ORENBURG
358 mm Annual
ULAN BATOR
208 mm Annual
VERKHOYANSK
155 mm Annual
BAGHDAD
151 mm Annual
LASA
406 mm Annual
TOKYO
1563 mm Annual
ADEN
39 mm Annual
CHONGQING
1092 mm Annual
SHANGHAI
1135 mm Annual
BOMBAY
2078 mm Annual
HYDERABAD
894 mm Annual
SINGAPORE
2282 mm Annual
CHERRAPUNJI
11437 mm Annual
°C
Minerals
Iron
Nickel
Chromium
Tungsten
Manganese
Titanium
Molybdenum
Beryllium
Copper
Tin
Lead
Zinc
Gold
Silver
Bauxite
Mercury
Uranium
Magnesium
Antimony
Asbestos
Mica
Potash
Diamonds
Zirconium
Coal
Oil
Gas
Build
Ancient shields
Sedimentary rocks lying over ancient shields
Uplifted remains of ancient mountain systems
Younger fold mountains
Sedimentary rocks
Recent deposits
Volcanic rocks
Active volcanoes
Faults
Extension of buried shields under later deposits

Asia: Population and Communications

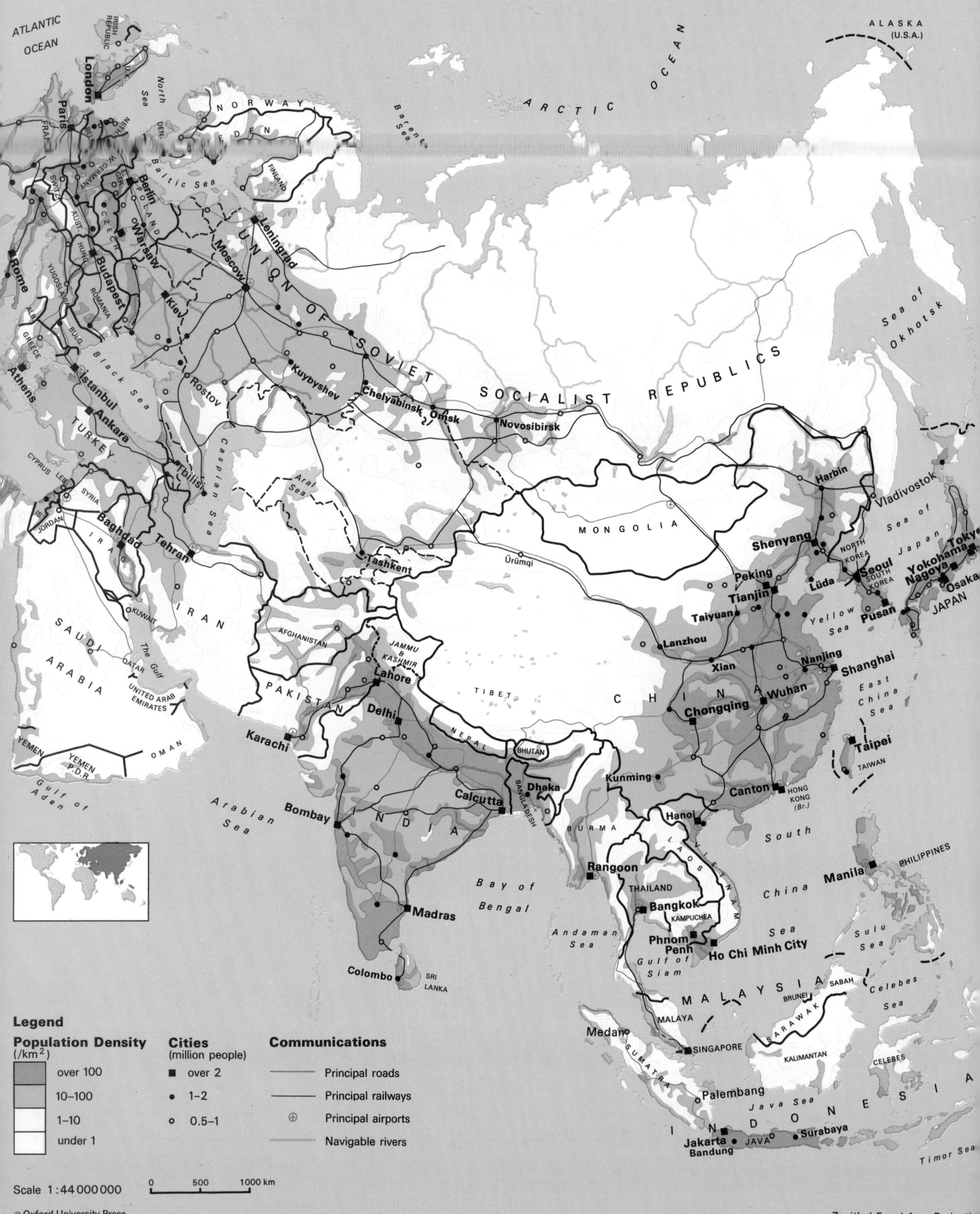
ATLANTIC OCEAN
London
Paris
Berlin
Warsaw
Leningrad
Moscow
Kiev
Budapest
Rome
Athens
Istanbul
Ankara
Rostov
Kuybyshev
Chelyabinsk
Omsk
Novosibirsk
Tbilisi
Baghdad
Tehran
Tashkent
Ürümqi
UNION OF SOVIET SOCIALIST REPUBLICS
ARCTIC OCEAN
NORWAY
FINLAND
Baltic Sea
North Sea
Black Sea
Caspian Sea
Aral Sea
TURKEY
CYPRUS
SYRIA
JORDAN
IRAQ
IRAN
KUWAIT
SAUDI ARABIA
QATAR
The Gulf
UNITED ARAB EMIRATES
OMAN
YEMEN
YEMEN P.D.R.
Gulf of Aden
AFGHANISTAN
PAKISTAN
JAMMU & KASHMIR
Lahore
Karachi
Delhi
NEPAL
BHUTAN
Dhaka
BANGLADESH
Calcutta
Bombay
INDIA
Madras
Colombo
SRI LANKA
Arabian Sea
Bay of Bengal
Andaman Sea
BURMA
Rangoon
THAILAND
Bangkok
KAMPUCHEA
Phnom Penh
Ho Chi Minh City
LAOS
VIETNAM
Hanoi
Gulf of Siam
MONGOLIA
TIBET
CHINA
Lanzhou
Xian
Chongqing
Kunming
Wuhan
Nanjing
Shanghai
Canton
HONG KONG (Br.)
Taiyuan
Peking
Tianjin
Shenyang
Harbin
Lüda
NORTH KOREA
SOUTH KOREA
Seoul
Pusan
Vladivostok
Sea of Japan
JAPAN
Tokyo
Yokohama
Nagoya
Osaka
Yellow Sea
East China Sea
Taipei
TAIWAN
Sea of Okhotsk
ALASKA (U.S.A.)
South China Sea
Manila
PHILIPPINES
Sulu Sea
Celebes Sea
MALAYSIA
SABAH
BRUNEI
SARAWAK
MALAYA
SINGAPORE
Medan
SUMATRA
KALIMANTAN
CELEBES
Palembang
Java Sea
INDONESIA
Jakarta
Bandung
JAVA
Surabaya
Timor Sea
Legend
Population Density (/km²)
over 100
10–100
1–10
under 1
Cities (million people)
over 2
1–2
0.5–1
Communications
Principal roads
Principal railways
Principal airports
Navigable rivers
Scale 1:44 000 000
0
500
1000 km
Zenithal Equal Area Projectio

Asia: Agriculture

ARKHANGEL'SK Altitude 15m
VERKHOYANSK Altitude 100m
ORENBURG Altitude 110m
ULAN BATOR Altitude 1325m
BAGHDAD Altitude 33m
TOKYO Altitude 6m
SHANGHAI Altitude 7m
CHONGQING Altitude 230m
LASA Altitude 3685m
CHERRAPUNJI Altitude 1313m
ADEN Altitude 37m
BOMBAY Altitude 11m
HYDERABAD Altitude 530m
SINGAPORE Altitude 5m
ainfall during the
ımmer Monsoon
over 2000 mm
1000-2000
500-1000
250-500
under 250 mm
LOW PRESSURE
Punjab 1st. July
Delhi 25th. June
Bengal 15th. June
Bombay 5th. June
Bay of Bengal
Main S.W. Monsoon currents
ates show the approx. rrival of the Monsoon
Arable, predominantly cereals
Arable, predominantly paddy
General arable
Arable with cash crops
Irrigated crops
Grazing and dry farming
Deciduous forest, farming and grazing
Mixed forest, farming and grazing
Tropical rain forest, lumbering, crops
Coniferous forest, lumbering
Desert, nomadic herding
Marsh or swamp
Tundra and high altitude desert
Ice cap

U.S.S.R.

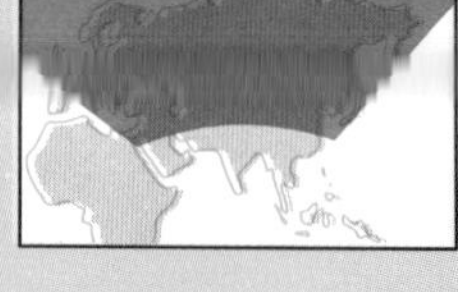

Conical Orthomorphic Projec

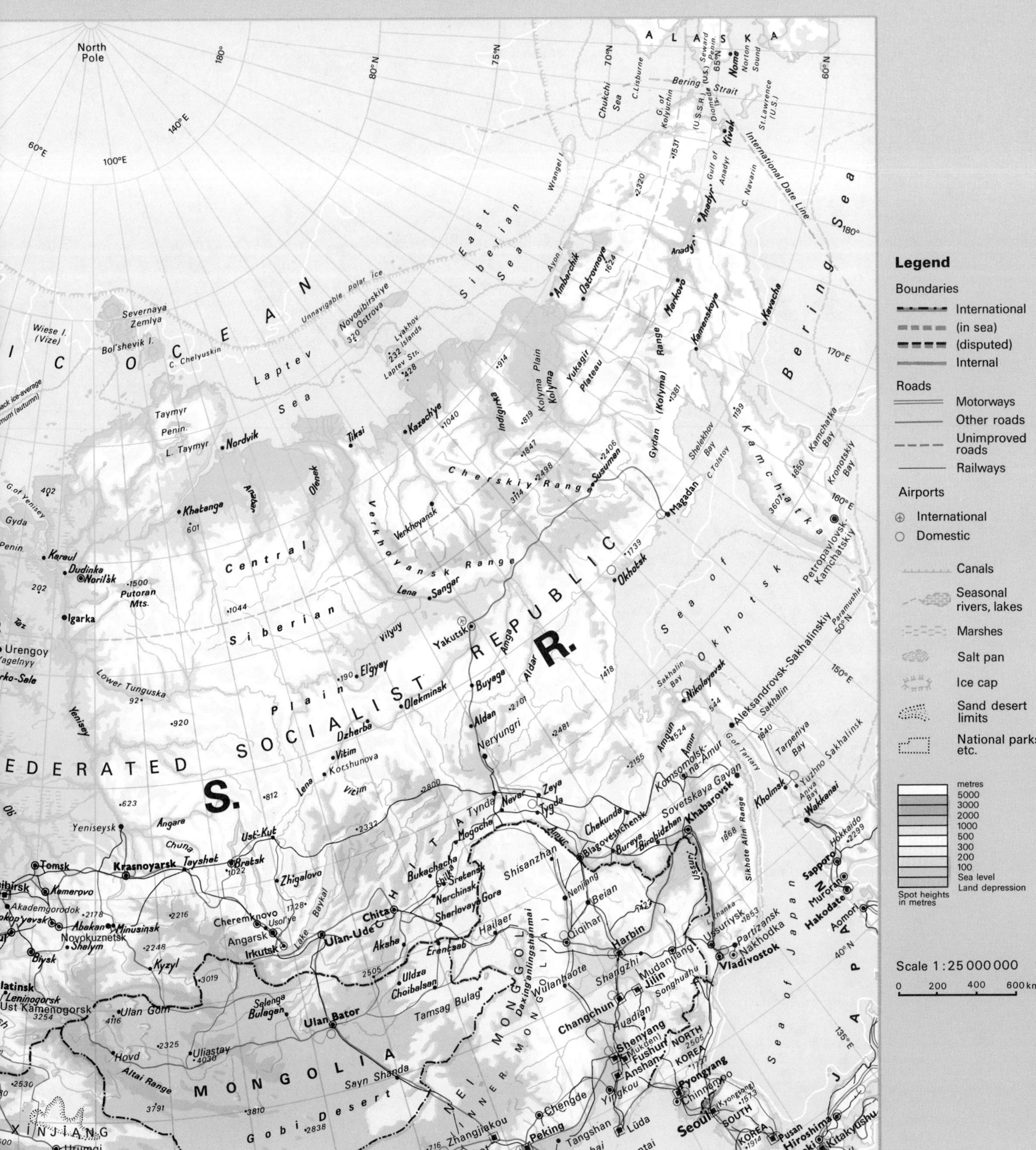

Legend
Boundaries
International
(in sea)
(disputed)
Internal
Roads
Motorways
Other roads
Unimproved roads
Railways
Airports
International
Domestic
Canals
Seasonal rivers, lakes
Marshes
Salt pan
Ice cap
Sand desert limits
National parks etc.
metres
5000
3000
2000
1000
500
300
200
100
Sea level
Land depression
Spot heights in metres
Scale 1:25 000 000
0 200 400 600 km

xford University Press

Western U.S.S.R.

Baltic Sea
Hanko
Helsinki
Vyborg
Petrozavodsk
Lake Onega
North Dvina
Ukhta
Khiumaa
Saaremaa
Gulf of Finland
Tallinn
Lake Ladoga
Gotland
Ventspils
ESTONIAN S.S.R.
Narva
Leningrad
Svir'
Gulf of Riga
Tartu
L. Peipus
Pushkin
Konosha
Vychegda
Syktyvkar
Kotlas
Liepāja
LATVIAN S.S.R.
Riga
Novgorod
Klaipeda
Kaliningrad
R.S.F.S.R.
Pskov
L. Ilmen
Cherepovets
Vologda
Kama
Rudnichnyy
Gdańsk
Sovetsk
LITHUANIAN S.S.R.
Siauliai
Vyshniy Volochek
Valdai Hills
Andropov-Rybinsk
Rybinsk Reservoir
RUSSIAN SOVIET FEDER
Kaunas
Daugavpils
W. Dvina
Velikiye Luki
Yaroslavl'
Kostroma
Kirov
Glazov
Vilnius
Vitebsk
Rzhev
Kalinin
Volga
Kineshma
Ivanovo
POLAND
Grodno
Białystok
Minsk
BYELORUSSIAN S.S.R.
Baranovichi
Smolensk
Yel'nya
Vyaz'ma
Moscow
Vladimir
Kovrov
Dzerzhinsk
Gor'kiy
Izhevsk
Warsaw
Brest
Pinsk
Pripet Marshes
Mogilev
Orekhovo-Zuyevo
Yoshkar-Ola
Kovel'
Kaluga
Kolomna
Oka
Murom
Arzamas
Kazan'
Sarny
Gomel'
Bryansk
Bezhitsa
Tula
Ryazan'
Kama
L'vov
Rovno
Chernigov
Orel'
Novomoskovsk
U
Saransk
Ul'yanovsk
S
Ivano-Frankovsk
Korosten'
Zhitomir
Berdichev
Konotop
Lipetsk
Tambov
Penza
Syzran
Togliatti
Kuybyshev
Sterlitam
UKRAINIAN S.S.R.
Kiev
Kursk
Chapayevsk
Ishimb
Chernovtsy
Dniester
Vinnitsa
Sumy
Voronezh
Samara
Buzuluk
Yermola
Botoşani
Prut
Cherkassy
Belgorod
Borisoglebsk
Balashov
Hills
Vol'sk
Bistriţa
Poltava
Khar'kov
Saratov
Orenburg
MOLD. S.S.R.
Iaşi
Dneprodzerzhinsk
Kremenchug
Don
Volga
Krasnyy Kut
Ural'sk
Sol'-Iletsk
Bacău
ROMANIA
Anan'yev
Bug
Kirovograd
Krivoy Rog
Dnepropetrovsk
Donets
Novouzensk
Kishinev
Odessa
DONBASS
Voroshilovgrad
Aleksandrov Gay
Nikolayev
Donetsk
Makeyevka
Yenakiyevo
45°N
Galaţi
Zaporozh'ye
Nikopol'
Krasnyy Luch
Tsimlyansk Reservoir
Volgograd
Kherson
Shakhty
Bucharest
Sulina
Zhdanov
Taganrog
Rostov
Novocherkassk
Baskunchak
Caspian Lowlands
K
Danube
Nogaysk
CRIMEA
Sea of Azov
Sal'sk
BULGARIA
Simferopol'
Sevastopol'
Kerch'
Yeysk
Makat
Varna
200 m
Yalta
Astrakhan'
Gur'yev
Burgas
Kuban'
Black Sea
Novorossiysk
Krasnodar
Armavir
Stavropol'
Tuapse
Maykop
Sochi
İstanbul
Zonguldak
Caucasus
Pyatigorsk
Mangyshlak Peninsula
Fort Shevchenko
Adapazarı
Pontic
Sinop
Sukhumi
EL'BRUS 5633
Nalchik
Karabük
Shevchenko
Samsun
Poti
GEORGIAN S.S.R.
Groznyy
Ordzhonikidze
Eskişehir
Kutaisi
Makhachkala
Kutahya
Ankara
Batumi
Mountains
Tbilisi
TURKEY
Afyonkarahisar
Trabzon
Derbent
Sivas
Alaverdi
Leninakan
Lake Tuz
Divriği
Erzurum
Kirovabad
Kara-Bogaz-Gol
Konya
Kayseri
L. Sevan
Yerevan
ARMENIAN S.S.R.
AZERBAYDZHAN S.S.R.
Sumgait
Caspian Sea
Surface height 28 m below m.s.l.
Malatya
Elâzığ
MT. ARARAT 5165
Baku
Taurus Mts.
Cilician Gates
Krasnovodsk
Adana
Mersin
Maraş
Diyarbakır
Muş
Nakhichevan
Araks (Araxes)
Cheleken
İskenderun
Gaziantep
Urfa
Siirt
Lake Van
Nebit-Dag
CYPRUS
Nicosia
Mardin
Tigris
Tabrīz
Astara
Latakia
Baniyās
Antakya (Antioch)
Aleppo
Euphrates
L. Urmia
Mianeh
Rasht
SYRIA
Mosul
Irbil
Elburz Mts.
Bandar-e Torkeman
Gorgān
Tripoli
Beirut
LEBANON
Homs
Palmyra
Qazvin
DAMAVAND 5610
Damascus
Kirkuk
IRAQ
IRAN
Tehrān
Semnān
Emāmrūd
ISRAEL

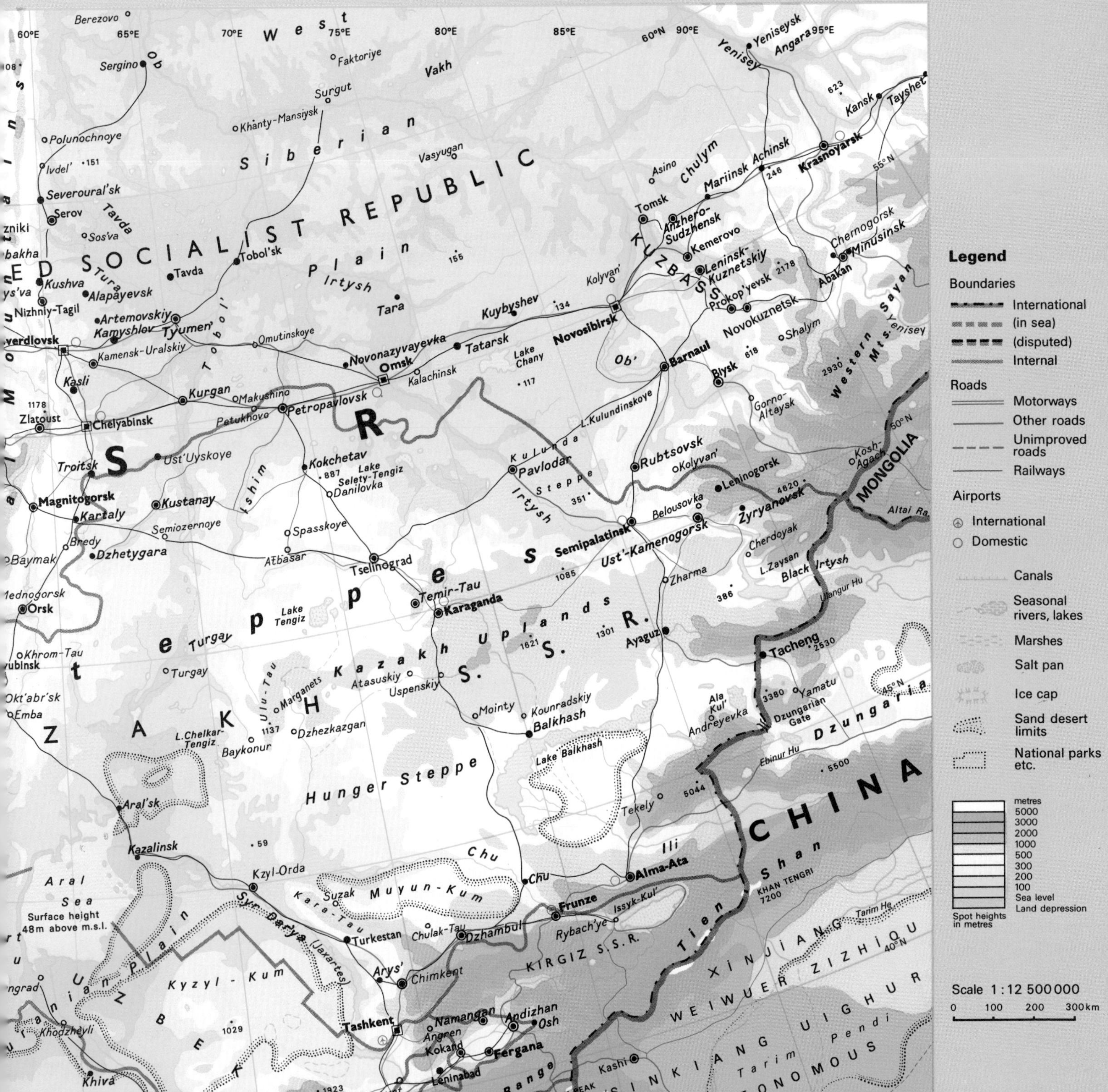

Berezovo
60°E 65°E 70°E 75°E 80°E 85°E 60°N 90°E 95°E
West Siberian Plain
Sergino Ob Faktoriye Vakh Yeniseysk Yenisey Angara
Surgut Khanty-Mansiysk Polunochnoye Ivdel' 151 Vasyugan
Severoural'sk Serov Tavda Sos'va
Asino Chulym Tomsk Mariinsk Achinsk 246 Krasnoyarsk Kansk Tayshet 623 55°N
Anzhero-Sudzhensk Kemerovo Chernogorsk Minusinsk Abakan
KUZBASS Leninsk-Kuznetskiy Prokop'yevsk 2178 Novokuznetsk Shalym
RUSSIAN SOVIET FEDERATED SOCIALIST REPUBLIC
Tobol'sk Tavda Tura Irtysh Tara 155 Kolyvan'
Kushva Alapayevsk Nizhniy-Tagil Artemovskiy Kamyshlov Tyumen' Tobol
Kuybyshev 134 Novosibirsk
Sverdlovsk Kamensk-Ural'skiy Omutinskoye Novonazyvayevka Omsk Tatarsk Kalachinsk
Lake Chany 117 Ob' Barnaul Biysk 618 Western Sayan Mts 2930
Kasli 1178 Zlatoust Chelyabinsk Kurgan Makushino Petropavlovsk Petukhovo
Gorno-Altaysk L. Kulundinskoye Kulunda Steppe
Troitsk Ust'Uyskoye Kokchetav 887 Lake Selety-Tengiz Danilovka Pavlodar 351 Rubtsovsk Kolyvan' Kosh-Agach 50°N
Magnitogorsk Kustanay Kartaly Ishim Irtysh Leninogorsk 4620 Zyryanovsk MONGOLIA Altai Ra.
Semiozernoye Spasskoye Belousovka Semipalatinsk Ust'-Kamenogorsk Cherdoyak
Baymak Bredy Dzhetygara Atbasar Tselinograd 1085 L. Zaysan Black Irtysh
Mednogorsk Orsk Temir-Tau Karaganda Zharma 386 Ulungur Hu
Lake Tengiz Turgay Kazakh Uplands 1621 1301 Ayaguz Tacheng 2530
Khrom-Tau Kazakh S.S.R. Turgay Ulu-Tau Atasuskiy Uspenskiy
Oktabr'sk Emba Marganets 1137 Dzhezkazgan Mointy Kounradskiy Balkhash Ala Kul' Andreyevka 3380 Yamatu Dzungarian Gate Dzungaria 45°N
L. Chelkar-Tengiz Baykonur Lake Balkhash Ebinur Hu 5500
Hunger Steppe Aral'sk Tekely 5044 CHINA
Kazalinsk 59 Chu Ili
Aral Sea Surface height 48m above m.s.l.
Kzyl-Orda Muyun-Kum Suzak Kara-Tau Chu Alma-Ata Tien Shan KHAN TENGRI 7200
Syr Darya (Jaxartes) Frunze Issyk-Kul' Rybach'ye Tarim He
Turan Plain Turkestan Chulak-Tau Dzhambul KIRGIZ S.S.R. XINJIANG 40°N
Kyzyl-Kum Arys' Chimkent WEIWUER ZIZHIQU
UZBEK S.S.R. Khodzheyli 1029 Tashkent Namangan Andizhan Osh SINKIANG UIGHUR AUTONOMOUS REGION
Angren Kokand Fergana Kashi Tarim Pendi
Khiva 1923 Leninabad Begovat Alai Range LENIN PEAK 7127
Samarkand Bukhara 5487 TADZHIK S.S.R. COMMUNISM PK. 7495 Shache
Kara Kum 132 Chardzhou Dushanbe Khorog Pamirs
TURKMEN S.S.R. Amu Darya (Oxus) Kerki 3342 Termez Faizabad 7010 7690 TIBET 35°N
Ashkhabad Mary (Merv) Kirovsk Mazar-i-Sharif Kishm Baghlan 5203 Chitral Hindu Kush
Kopeh Dāgh 3414 Mashhad Maimana KASHMIR
AFGHANISTAN 5075 Kabul 65°E 70°E Jalalabad PAKISTAN Indus Abbottabad 75°E 7315
60°E Kushka Peshawar

Legend

Boundaries

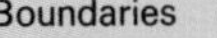
International
(in sea)
(disputed)
Internal

Roads

Motorways
Other roads
Unimproved roads
Railways

Airports

International
Domestic

Canals
Seasonal rivers, lakes
Marshes
Salt pan
Ice cap
Sand desert limits
National parks etc.

metres: 5000, 3000, 2000, 1000, 500, 300, 200, 100, Sea level, Land depression

Spot heights in metres

Scale 1:12 500 000
0 100 200 300km

Middle East

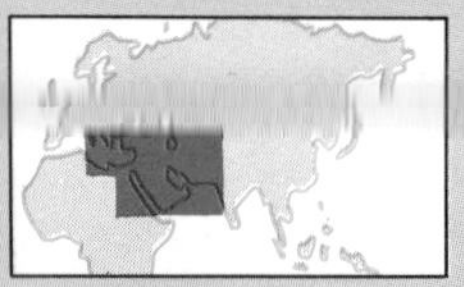

Legend

Boundaries
- International
- (in sea)
- (disputed)
- Internal

Roads
- Motorways
- Other roads
- Unimproved roads
- Railways

Airports
- ⊕ International
- ○ Domestic

- Canals
- Seasonal rivers, lakes
- Marshes
- Salt pan
- Ice cap
- Sand desert limits
- National parks etc.

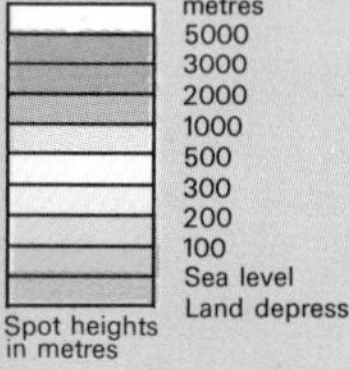

metres
5000
3000
2000
1000
500
300
200
100
Sea level
Land depression
Spot heights in metres

× Historic sites

Scale 1:12 500 000

0 100 200 300 km

Israel

Scale 1:4 000 000

0 20 40 60 km

U. S. S. R.
TURKMEN S.S.R.
AZERBAYDZHAN S.S.R.
Caspian Sea
Baku
Krasnovodsk
Ashkhabad
Bukhara
Samarkand
Chardzhou
Dushanbe
Kara Kum
Koppet Dagh
Elburz Mts.
Tehran
I R A N
Dasht-e-Kavir
Dasht-e-Lut
Khurasan
Zagros Mountains
Isfahan
Shiraz
Kerman
Mashhad
Herat
Kabul
A F G H A N I S T A N
Hindu Kush
Kandahar
Registan
Quetta
P A K I S T A N
Karachi
Hyderabad
Rawalpindi
Peshawar
Multan
Baghdad
Basra
Kuwait
The Gulf
Bahrain
Manama
Qatar
Doha
Dubai
Abu Dhabi
UNITED ARAB EMIRATES
Muscat
O M A N
Gulf of Oman
MAKRAN
Riyadh
S A U D I A R A B I A
Rub' al Khali
YEMEN P.D.R.
Hadramaut
Y E M E N
San'a
Aden
Gulf of Aden
Socotra (Yemen P.D.R.)
Salalah
Kuria Muria Is.
Arabian Sea
Tropic of Cancer
Mouths of the Indus
Rann of Kutch
50°E
55°E
60°E
65°E
70°E
75°E
45°E

Conical Orthomorphic Projection

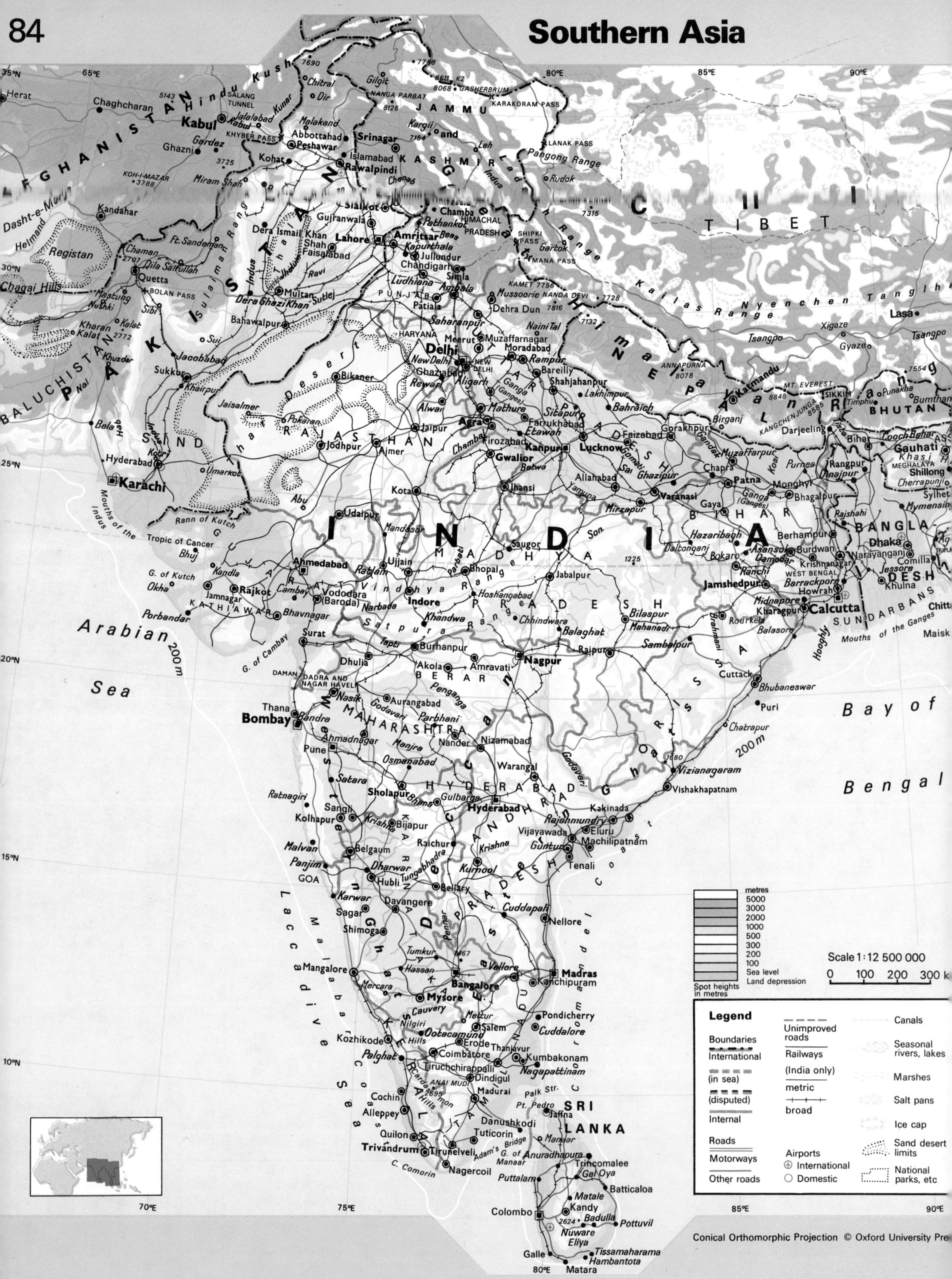
Legend
Boundaries
International
(in sea)
(disputed)
Internal
Roads
Motorways
Other roads
Unimproved roads
Railways
(India only)
metric
broad
Airports
International
Domestic
Canals
Seasonal rivers, lakes
Marshes
Salt pans
Ice cap
Sand desert limits
National parks, etc
metres
5000
3000
2000
1000
500
300
200
100
Sea level
Land depression
Spot heights in metres
Scale 1:12 500 000
Conical Orthomorphic Projection © Oxford University Pre

South East Asia Mainland

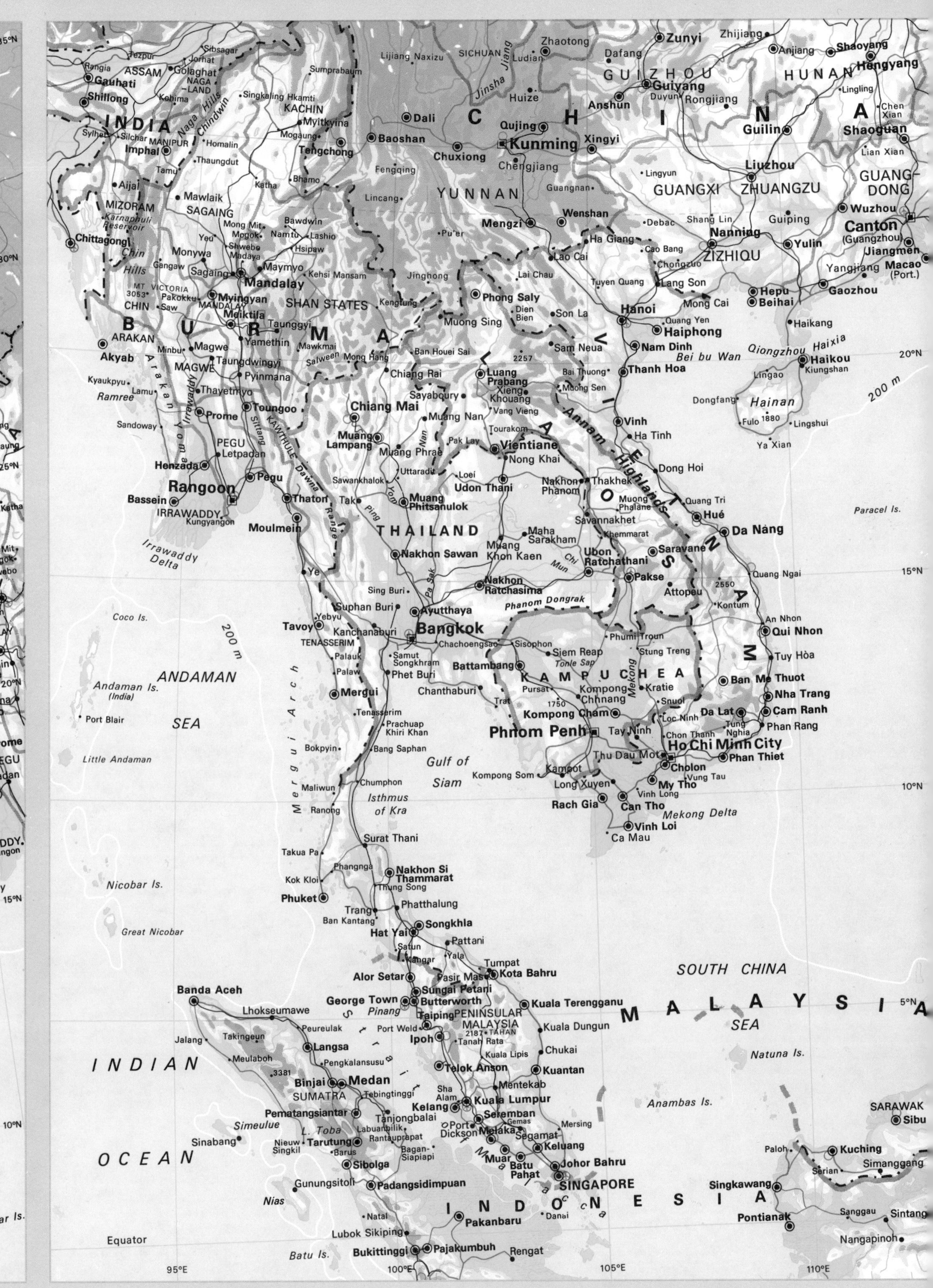

95°E
35°N
30°N
25°N
20°N
15°N
10°N
5°N
100°E
105°E
110°E
Yushu
Chang
Mekong
Qabdo
(Nujiang)
ASSAM
Gauhati
Shillong
Golaghat
Jorhat
Sibsagar
Tezpur
Rangia
NAGA LAND
Kohima
INDIA
MANIPUR
Imphal
Silchar
Sylhet
Aijal
MIZORAM
Karnaphuli Reservoir
Chittagong
Chin Hills
MT VICTORIA
3053
CHIN
ARAKAN
Akyab
Kyaukpyu
Ramree
Lamu
Sandoway
Sumprabaum
Singkaling Hkamti
KACHIN
Myitkyina
Mogaung
Homalin
Thaungdut
Tamu
Bhamo
Katha
Mawlaik
SAGAING
Mong Mit
Mogok
Bawdwin
Namtu
Lashio
Hsipaw
Shwebo
Madaya
Maymyo
Kehsi Mansam
Monywa
Gangaw
Sagaing
Mandalay
Myingyan
Pakokku
Saw
MANDALAY
Meiktila
Taunggyi
Yamethin
SHAN STATES
Kengtung
Minbu
Magwe
MAGWE
Mawkmai
Salween
Taungdwingyi
Pyinmana
Thayetmyo
Prome
Toungoo
PEGU
Letpadan
Henzada
Pegu
Rangoon
Bassein
IRRAWADDY
Kungyangon
Irrawaddy Delta
Thaton
Moulmein
Ye
Tavoy
TENASSERIM
Mergui
Tenasserim
Bokpyin
Maliwun
Ranong
B U R M A
Lijiang
Naxizu
SICHUAN
Zhaotong
Ludian
Jinsha Jiang
Huize
Dali
Baoshan
Tengchong
Fengqing
Chuxiong
Lincang
Kunming
Chengjiang
Qujing
Xingyi
YUNNAN
Pu'er
Mengzi
Wenshan
Guangnan
Jinghong
C H I N A
Zunyi
Zhijiang
Anjiang
Shaoyang
Hengyang
Dafang
GUIZHOU
Guiyang
Duyun
Rongjiang
Anshun
HUNAN
Lingling
Chen Xian
Shaoguan
Lian Xian
Guilin
Liuzhou
Lingyun
GUANGXI ZHUANGZU
GUANGDONG
Wuzhou
Guiping
Debao
Shang Lin
Nanning
Yulin
Canton
(Guangzhou)
Jiangmen
Macao (Port.)
Yangjiang
Gaozhou
ZIZHIQU
Cao Bang
Chongzuo
Hepu
Beihai
Haikang
Qiongzhou Haixia
Haikou
Kiungshan
Lingao
Hainan
Dongfang
Fulo
1880
Lingshui
Ya Xian
Bei bu Wan
200 m
Ha Giang
Lao Cai
Lai Chau
Tuyen Quang
Lang Son
Mong Cai
Hanoi
Quang Yen
Haiphong
Nam Dinh
Thanh Hoa
Vinh
Ha Tinh
Dong Hoi
Quang Tri
Hué
Da Nang
Quang Ngai
Kontum
An Nhon
Qui Nhon
Tuy Hòa
Ban Me Thuot
Nha Trang
Cam Ranh
Da Lat
Phan Rang
Phan Thiet
Ho Chi Minh City
Cholon
Vung Tau
Thu Dau Mot
My Tho
Vinh Long
Can Tho
Vinh Loi
Ca Mau
Rach Gia
Long Xuyen
Mekong Delta
V I E T N A M
Annam Highlands
Paracel Is.
Phong Saly
Dien Bien
Son La
Muong Sing
Sam Neua
2257
Ban Houei Sai
Luang Prabang
Ban Thuong
Muong Sen
Xieng Khouang
Vang Vieng
Sayaboury
Tourakom
Pak Lay
Vientiane
Nong Khai
Nakhon Phanom
Thakhek
Muong Phalane
Savannakhet
Khemmarat
Saravane
Pakse
Attopeu
2550
L A O S
Chiang Rai
Chiang Mai
Muang Nan
Muang Lampang
Muang Phrae
Nan
Uttaradit
Loei
Udon Thani
Sawankhalok
Tak
Ping
Yom
Muang Phitsanulok
THAILAND
Maha Sarakham
Muang Khon Kaen
Chi
Mun
Ubon Ratchathani
Nakhon Sawan
Pa Sak
Nakhon Ratchasima
Phanom Dongrak
Sing Buri
Suphan Buri
Yebyu
Ayutthaya
Kanchanaburi
Bangkok
Chachoengsao
Samut Songkhram
Phet Buri
Palauk
Palaw
Chanthaburi
Trat
Prachuap Khiri Khan
Bang Saphan
Chumphon
Isthmus of Kra
Gulf of Siam
Surat Thani
Takua Pa
Phangnga
Kok Kloi
Phuket
Nakhon Si Thammarat
Thung Song
Trang
Ban Kantang
Phatthalung
Songkhla
Hat Yai
Satun
Pattani
Yala
Sisophon
Siem Reap
Tonle Sap
Battambang
Phumi Troun
Stung Treng
KAMPUCHEA
Pursat
Kompong Chhnang
Kratie
Snuol
1750
Kompong Cham
Phnom Penh
Tay Ninh
Loc Ninh
Chon Thanh
Tung Nghia
Kampot
Kompong Som
Coco Is.
Andaman Is.
(India)
Port Blair
ANDAMAN SEA
Little Andaman
Mergui Arch
Nicobar Is.
Great Nicobar
Tumpat
Kota Bahru
Alor Setar
Pasir Mas
Sungai Petani
George Town
Butterworth
Pinang
Kuala Terengganu
Taiping
PENINSULAR MALAYSIA
Port Weld
Ipoh
2187
TAHAN
Tanah Rata
Kuala Dungun
Chukai
Kuala Lipis
Telok Anson
Kuantan
Mentekab
Sha Alam
Kelang
Kuala Lumpur
Seremban
Gemas
Port Dickson
Melaka
Segamat
Mersing
Keluang
Muar
Batu Pahat
Johor Bahru
SINGAPORE
M A L A Y S I A
SOUTH CHINA SEA
Natuna Is.
Anambas Is.
SARAWAK
Sibu
Kuching
Simanggang
Paloh
Serian
Singkawang
Pontianak
Sanggau
Sintang
Nangapinoh
Banda Aceh
Lhokseumawe
Peureulak
Jalang
Takingeun
Langsa
Meulaboh
Pengkalansusu
3381
Binjai
Medan
SUMATRA
Tebingtinggi
Pematangsiantar
Tanjongbalai
Labuanbilik
L. Toba
Rantauprapat
Simeulue
Sinabang
Nieuw Singkil
Tarutung
Barus
Bagan-Siapiapi
Sibolga
Gunungsitoli
Padangsidimpuan
Nias
Natal
INDONESIA
Pakanbaru
Danai
Lubok Sikiping
Bukittinggi
Pajakumbuh
Rengat
Batu Is.
INDIAN OCEAN
Equator

China

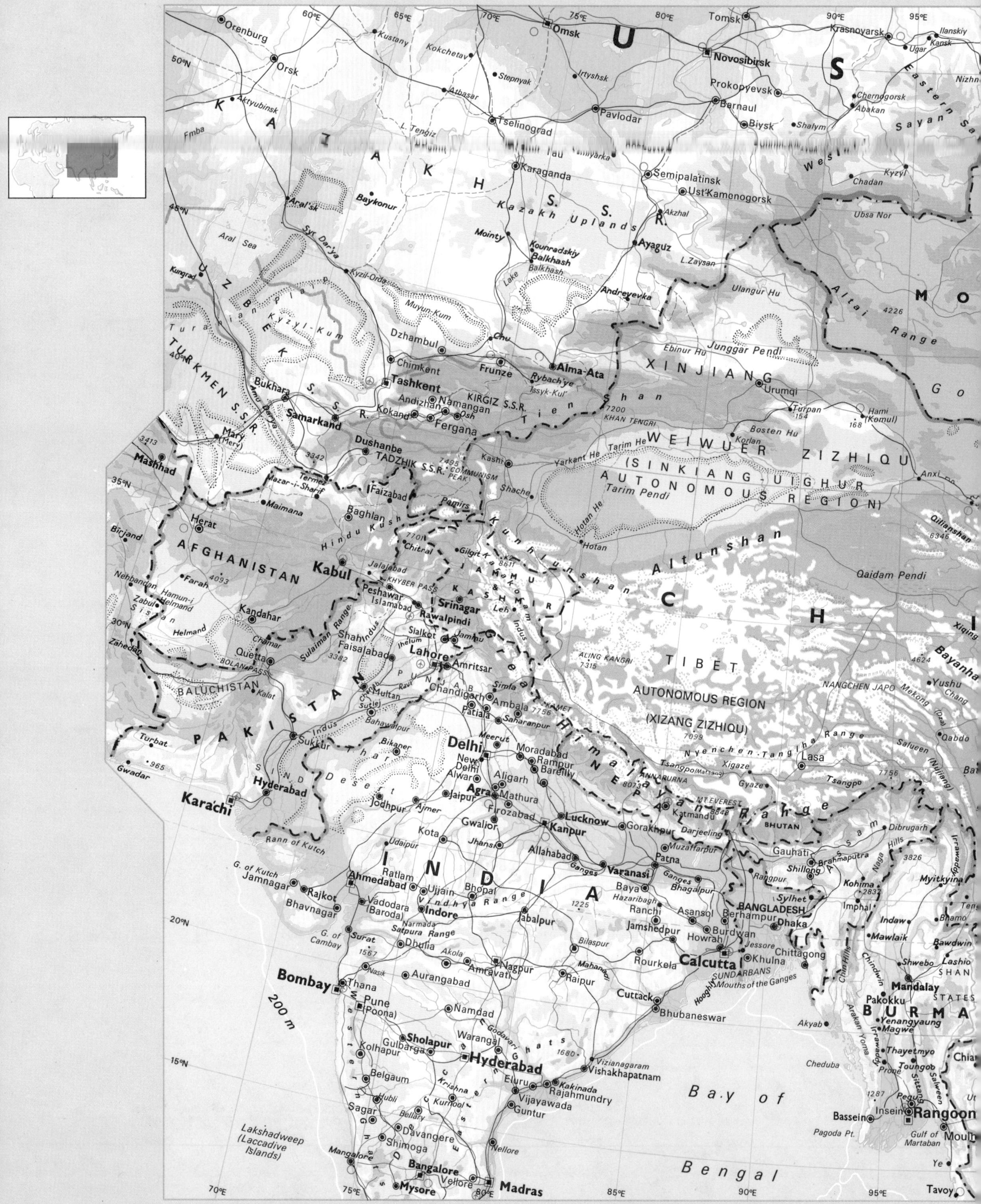
Orenburg
Orsk
Omsk
Tomsk
Novosibirsk
Krasnoyarsk
Kustany
Kokchetav
Stepnyak
Irtyshsk
Atbasar
Tselinograd
Pavlodar
Barnaul
Prokopyevsk
Biysk
Aktyubinsk
Karaganda
Semipalatinsk
Ust'Kamenogorsk
Baykonur
Aral'sk
Aral Sea
Syr Darya
Kzyl-Orda
Kazakh Uplands
Mointy
Kounradskiy
Balkhash
Lake Balkhash
Ayaguz
Akzhal
L. Zaysan
Andreyevka
Muyun-Kum
Kyzyl-Kum
Dzhambul
Chu
Frunze
Alma-Ata
Chimkent
Tashkent
Bukhara
Samarkand
Kokand
Andizhan
Namangan
Osh
Fergana
KIRGIZ S.S.R.
TURKMEN S.S.R.
UZBEK S.S.R.
KAZAKH S.S.R.
Mary (Merv)
Dushanbe
TADZHIK S.S.R.
Mashhad
Termez
Mazar-i-Sharif
Faizabad
Maimana
Baghlan
Herat
Birjand
Hindu Kush
AFGHANISTAN
Kabul
Jalalabad
KHYBER PASS
Chitral
Gilgit
Farah
Peshawar
Islamabad
Srinagar
Rawalpindi
Kandahar
Quetta
Helmand
Sialkot
Jammu
Lahore
Amritsar
Faisalabad
BALUCHISTAN
Kalat
Multan
Chandigarh
Ambala
Patiala
Simla
Saharanpur
Sukkur
Bikaner
Thar Desert
Delhi
New Delhi
Meerut
Moradabad
Rampur
Bareilly
Aligarh
Alwar
Agra
Mathura
Jaipur
Hyderabad
Karachi
PAKISTAN
Turbat
Gwadar
Jodhpur
Ajmer
Firozabad
Gwalior
Lucknow
Kanpur
Kota
Jhansi
Udaipur
Allahabad
Varanasi
Gorakhpur
Rann of Kutch
G. of Kutch
Jamnagar
Rajkot
Ahmedabad
Ratlam
Ujjain
Bhopal
Bhavnagar
Vadodara (Baroda)
Indore
Vindhya Range
Jabalpur
Surat
G. of Cambay
Satpura Range
Narmada
Dhulia
Akola
Nagpur
Amravati
Bombay
Thana
Nasik
Aurangabad
Pune (Poona)
200 m
Namdad
Sholapur
Gulbarga
Warangal
Kolhapur
Hyderabad
Belgaum
Hubli
Krishna
Kurnool
Eluru
Kakinada
Rajahmundry
Vijayawada
Guntur
Sagar
Bellary
Davangere
Shimoga
Mangalore
Nellore
Bangalore
Vellore
Mysore
Madras
Lakshadweep (Laccadive Islands)
INDIA
Bay of Bengal
Vishakhapatnam
Vizianagaram
Cuttack
Bhubaneswar
Raipur
Rourkela
Calcutta
Howrah
Burdwan
Jamshedpur
Ranchi
Asansol
Hazaribagh
Baya
Patna
Muzaffarpur
Bhagalpur
Berhampur
BANGLADESH
Dhaka
Jessore
Khulna
Chittagong
SUNDARBANS
Mouths of the Ganges
Sylhet
Gauhati
Shillong
Kohima
Imphal
Brahmaputra
Dibrugarh
BHUTAN
Darjeeling
Katmandu
MT EVEREST 8848
NEPAL
Himalaya Range
Lasa
Tsangpo
Xigaze
Gyaze
Nyenchen Tanglha Range
TIBET AUTONOMOUS REGION (XIZANG ZIZHIQU)
ALING KANGRI 7315
Kunlunshan
Altunshan
Hotan
Hotan He
Kashi
Shache
Pamirs
COMMUNISM PEAK 7495
Tarim Pendi
Tarim He
Yarkant He
WEIWUER ZIZHIQU
(SINKIANG-UIGHUR AUTONOMOUS REGION)
Tien Shan
7200 KHAN TENGRI
Korlan
Bosten Hu
Turpan
Hami (Komul)
Urumqi
XINJIANG
Junggar Pendi
Ebinur Hu
Ulangur Hu
Altai Range
Qaidam Pendi
Qilianshan
Bayanhar
Xiqing
NANGCHEN JAPO
Yushu
Mekong
Qabdo
Salween
Anxi
CHINA
MONGOLIA
Ubsa Nor
Kyzyl
Chadan
Abakan
Chernogorsk
Ugar
Kansk
Ilanskiy
Nizhneudinsk
Eastern Sayan
Western Sayan
Shalym
Myitkyina
Bhamo
Indaw
Mawlaik
Chindwin
Shwebo
Mandalay
Lashio
SHAN STATES
Pakokku
BURMA
Yenangyaung
Magwe
Akyab
Arakan Yoma
Irrawaddy
Thayetmyo
Prome
Toungoo
Sittang
Cheduba
Pegu
Bassein
Insein
Rangoon
Pagoda Pt.
Gulf of Martaban
Moulmein
Ye
Tavoy
Naga Hills
Chin Hills
Rangpur
60°E
65°E
70°E
75°E
80°E
85°E
90°E
95°E
50°N
45°N
40°N
35°N
30°N
25°N
20°N
15°N

Legend
Boundaries
International
(in sea)
(disputed)
Internal
Roads
Motorways
Other roads
Unimproved roads
Railways
Airports
International
Domestic
Canals
Seasonal rivers, lakes
Marshes
Salt pan
Ice cap
Sand desert limits
National parks etc. etc.
metres
5000
3000
2000
1000
500
300
200
100
Sea level
Land depression
Spot heights in metres
Scale 1:19 000 000
0 150 300 450 km
NORTH KOREA
SOUTH KOREA
JAPAN
Sea of Japan
Yellow Sea
East China Sea
South China Sea
THE PHILIPPINES
TAIWAN
VIETNAM
MONGGOL NEI
Tropic of Cancer
Hokkaido
Honshu
Shikoku
Kyushu
Sakhalin (U.S.S.R.)
Gulf of Tartary
Sikhote Alin Range
Limit of pack ice average maximum Jan–Mar
Ryukyu (Nansei) Islands
Formosa Strait
Qinlingshan
Nanling
Wuishan Mts
Hainan
Luzon
Gulf of Tonkin
Paracel Is. (China)
Okinawa
Sakishima Group
Izu Is.
Osumi Is.
Cheju I. (Quelpart)
Liaodong Peninsula
Shandong Peninsula
Leizhou Peninsula
Bataan Peninsula
Bohai
Tokyo
Osaka
Kyoto
Kobe
Nagoya
Yokohama
Hiroshima
Nagasaki
Sapporo
Hakodate
Sendai
Seoul (Kyongsong)
Pyongyang
Pusan
Inchon
Taegu
Taejon
Peking (Beijing)
Tianjin
Shanghai
Nanjing
Wuhan
Canton (Guangzhou)
HONG KONG (U.K.)
Victoria
Macao (Port.)
T'aipei
Kaohsiung
Manila
Quezon City
Hanoi
Haiphong
Vladivostok
Khabarovsk
Blagoveshchensk
Harbin
Shenyang
Changchun
Ulan Bator
Ulan-Ude
Chongqing
Chengdu
Xi'an
Lanzhou
Zhengzhou
Hangzhou
Qingdao
Lüda
130°E
120°E
110°E
50°N
40°N
30°N
20°N
15°N

cal Orthomorphic Projection

Eastern China

Conical Orthomorphic Projection

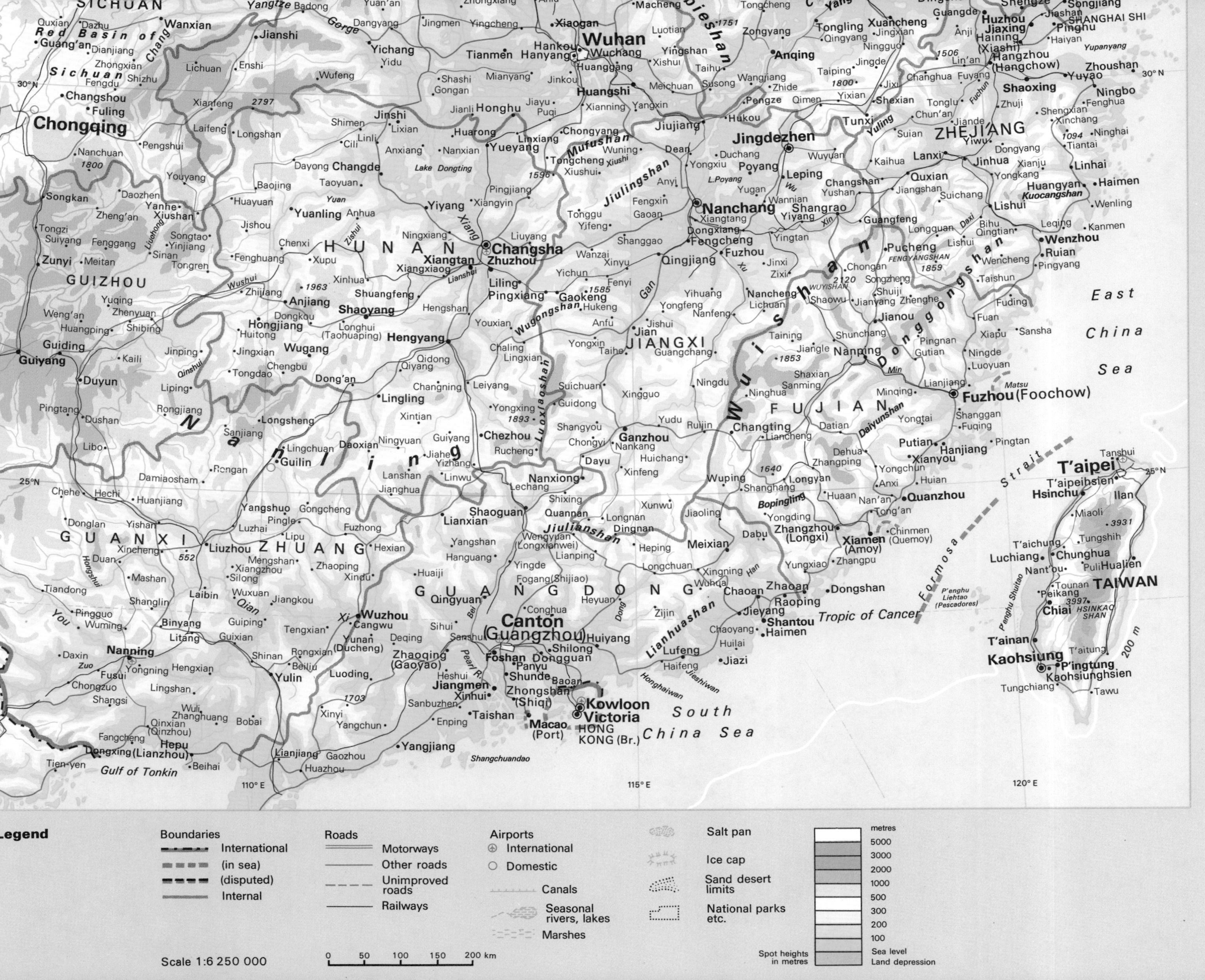

SICHUAN
Red Basin of Sichuan
Chongqing
GUIZHOU
Guiyang
HUNAN
Changsha
Wuhan
Hankou
Hanyang
Wuchang
JIANGXI
Nanchang
ZHEJIANG
Hangzhou (Hangchow)
FUJIAN
Fuzhou (Foochow)
Xiamen (Amoy)
GUANGDONG
Canton (Guangzhou)
Kowloon
Victoria
HONG KONG (Br.)
Macao (Port)
GUANGXI ZHUANG
Nanning
Guilin
Liuzhou
TAIWAN
T'aipei
Kaohsiung
T'ainan
Hsinchu
Chiai
Formosa Strait
East China Sea
South China Sea
Gulf of Tonkin
Tropic of Cancer
Yangtze
Chang
Xiang
Gan
Lake Dongting
L.Poyang
Nan Ling
Wuyishan
Daiyunshan
Jiulianshan
Luoxiaoshan
Wugongshan
Lianhuashan
Dabieshan
Jiulingshan
Mufushan
Xi
Pearl R.
Jingdezhen
Hengyang
Shaoguan
Ganzhou
Shantou
Quanzhou
Zhangzhou (Longxi)
Wenzhou
Ningbo
Shaoxing
Huzhou
Jiaxing
Anqing
Yichang
Shashi
Yueyang
Changde
Yiyang
Xiangtan
Zhuzhou
Shaoyang
Wuzhou
Yulin
Zhaoqing (Gaoyao)
Foshan
Jiangmen
Meixian
Chaoan
SHANGHAI SHI
P'enghu Liehtao (Pescadores)
HSINKAO SHAN 3997
Penghu Shuitao
Chinmen (Quemoy)
Matsu
Shangchuandao
30° N
25° N
110° E
115° E
120° E
200 m
Legend
Boundaries
International
(in sea)
(disputed)
Internal
Roads
Motorways
Other roads
Unimproved roads
Railways
Airports
International
Domestic
Canals
Seasonal rivers, lakes
Marshes
Salt pan
Ice cap
Sand desert limits
National parks etc.
Spot heights in metres
metres
5000
3000
2000
1000
500
300
200
100
Sea level
Land depression
Scale 1:6 250 000
0 50 100 150 200 km

Oxford University Press

Japan

Urban Land Use
Central business core
Lesser but significant commercial centres
Industrial districts
The built-up area where the major use of land is for residential purposes
Major parks and open spaces
Highways
Limited access and rapid transit
Other main highways
Railways and transportation yards
Airports
Airfields
Scale 1:400 000
0 5 10 km
KAWAGUCHI
SAITAMA
TOKYO
CHIBA
Mabashi
MATSUDO
Itabashi
Kita
Adachi
ICHIKAWA
Toshima
Nakano
Suginami
Shinjuku
Imperial Palace
Edogawa
Koto
Olympic Park
Shibuya
Urayasu
Ara
Edo
Setagaya
TOKYO
Shinagawa
Meguro
Shinagawa Bay
TOKYO KANAGAWA
Chitose
Ota
HAMADA AIRPORT
Tsunashima
Rokugo
Kikuna
KAWASAKI
TOKYO BAY
Kanagawa
YOKOHAMA
Isogo
139° 45′ E
35° 45′ N
35° 30′ N
Temp °C | Rain mm
J 3.7 48
F 4.3 73
M 7.6 101
A 13.1 135
M 17.6 131
J 21.1 182
J 25.1 146
A 26.4 147
S 22.8 217
O 16.7 220
N 11.3 101
D 6.1 61
Year 14.7 1563
Height 10 m
Wakkanai
SEA OF OKHOTSK
Mombetsu
Abashiri
Nayoro
Haboro
Shibetsu
Rumoi
Asahigawa
Kitami
Hokkaido
Takikawa
Sunagawa
Ishikari-wan
Bibai
Mikasa
Otaru
Ebetsu
Yoichi
Iwanai
Sapporo
Yubari
Chitose
Tomakomai
Obihiro
Kushiro
Akan
Shiranuka
Shiraoi
Noboribetsu
Muroran
Uchiura-wan
Shizunai
Urakawa
Erimo-misaki
PACIFIC OCEAN
Yakumo
Mori
Okushiri-shima
Kamiiso
Hakodate
Tsugaru-kaikyo
Tappi-zaki
Ohata
Mutsu
Mutsu-wan
Aomori
Misawa
Hachinohe
Hirosaki
Noshiro
Odate
Oga
Akita
Morioka
Miyako
Kamaishi
Yokote
Ofunato
Kesennuma
Sakata
Tsuruoka
Shinjo
Ichinoseki
Ishinomaki
Shiogama
Yamagata
Sendai
Iwanuma
Sado
Niigata
Fukushima
Honshu
Sanjo
Nagaoka
Aizu-Wakamatsu
Koriyama
Sukagawa
Kashiwazaki
Naoetsu
Shirakawa
Iwaki
Wajima
Noto-Hanto
Nanao
Himi
Toyama-wan
Uozu
Takada
Kitaibaraki
Hitachi
Takaoka
Toyama
Nagano
Utsunomiya
Kanazawa
Komatsu
Maebashi
Kiryu
Mito
Nakaminato
Matsumoto
Ashikaga
Fukui
Ueda
Okaya
Suwa
Kumagaya
Tsuchiura
Kawagoe
Tokyo
Urawa
Choshi
Chiba
Yokohama
Kisarazu
Mobara
Kofu
Yokosuka
Tateyama
Iida
Odawara
Sagami-nada
Shimizu
Numazu
Shizuoka
O-shima
Hamamatsu
Izu-Shoto
Miyake-jima
Mikura-jima
Kozu-shima
Nii-shima
Sea of Japan
Oki-gunto
SOUTH KOREA
P'ohang
Ulsan
Kyoga-saki
Tsuruga
Matsue
Sakai-minato
Tottori
Yonago
Maizuru
Nagahama
Ayabe
Hikone
Gifu
Ichinomiya
Biwa-ko
Oda
Chugoku-Sanchi
Tsuyama
Kyoto
Nagoya
Toyota
Hamada
Himeji
Otsu
Okazaki
Masuda
Okayama
Kobe
Suzuka
Yokkaichi
Handa
Toyohashi
Hagi
Nagato
Fukuyama
Kurashiki
Akashi
Osaka
Nara
Tsu
Matsuzaka
Ise
Tsushima
Tsushima-kaikyo
Hiroshima
Mihara
Kasaoka
Takamatsu
Kishiwada
Shimonoseki
Tokuyama
Kure
Iwakuni
Sumoto
Naruto
Wakayama
Daio-zaki
Kitakyushu
Ube
Imabari
Niihama
Kanonji
Tokushima
Kii-suido
Fukuoka
Iizuka
Nakatsu
Matsuyama
Anan
Tanabe
Shingu
Usa
Ozu
Kochi
Saga
Kurume
Beppu
Yawatahama
Tosa-wan
Shiono-zaki
Sasebo
Omuta
Oita
Usuki
Uwajima
Muroto-zaki
Shikoku
Nagasaki
Kumamoto
Saeki
Bungo-suido
Yatsushiro
Nobeoka
Ashizuri-zaki
Hyuga
Minamata
Kyushu
Sendai
Miyazaki
Koshiki-retto
Kagoshima
Miyakonojo
Makurazaki
Kanoya
PACIFIC OCEAN
200 m
130° E
135° E
140° E
145° E
45° N
40° N
35° N
Legend
Boundaries
International
(in sea)
(disputed)
Internal
Roads
Motorways
Other roads
Unimproved roads
Railways
Airports
International
Domestic
Canals
Seasonal rivers, lakes
Marshes
Salt pan
Ice cap
Sand desert limits
National park etc.
metres
5000
3000
2000
1000
500
300
200
100
Sea level
Land depression
Spot heights in metres
Scale 1:6 250 000
0 50 100 150

Zenithal Equidistant Project

Legend
Boundaries
International
(in sea)
(disputed)
Internal
Roads
Motorways
Other roads
Unimproved roads
Railways
Airports
International
Domestic
Canals
Seasonal rivers, lakes
Marshes
metres
5000
3000
2000
1000
500
300
200
100
Sea level
Land depression
Spot heights in metres
Scale 1:19 000 000
0 150 300 450 km
Conical Orthomorphic Projection
© Oxford University Press
THE PHILIPPINES
MALAYSIA
INDONESIA
VIETNAM
LAOS
THAILAND (Siam)
KAMPUCHEA
BURMA
SHAN STATES
TAIWAN
BRUNEI
SINGAPORE
SABAH
SARAWAK
MALAYA
JAYA PURA
AUSTRALIA
South China Sea
Sulu Sea
Celebes Sea
Java Sea
Banda Sea
Flores Sea
Sawu Sea
Bali Sea
Timor Sea
Arafura Sea
Andaman Sea
Molucca Sea
Ceram Sea
Gulf of Siam
Gulf of Tonkin
Gulf of Martaban
Gulf of Tomini
Gulf of Tolo
Gulf of Bone
Strait of Malacca
Strait of Makassar
Formosa Strait
Sunda Strait
Lombok Str.
Borneo (Kalimantan)
Celebes (Sulawesi)
Sumatra (Sumatera)
Java (Djawa)
New Guinea
Moluccas (Maluku)
Luzon
Mindanao
Mindoro
Palawan
Hainan
Timor
Ceram
Halmahera
Bangkok
Rangoon
Mandalay
Hanoi
Haiphong
Da Nang
Ho Chi Minh City (Saigon)
Phnom Penh
Vientiane
Chiang Mai
Manila
Quezon City
Cebu
Davao
Zamboanga
Kuala Lumpur
Kota Kinabalu
Bandar Seri Begawan
Kuching
Jakarta
Bandung
Surabaya
Semarang
Yogyakarta
Palembang
Medan
Ujung Pandang
Balikpapan
Banjarmasin
Samarinda
Pontianak
Manado
T'aipei
Kaohsiung
Canton (Guangzhou)
HONG KONG (U.K.)
Victoria
Macao (Port.)
Nanning (Yungning)
Kunming
Kurilskije Ostrova
Tropic of Cancer
Christmas I. (Austl.)
Paracel Is. (China)
Natuna Is. (Indon.)
Anambas Is. (Indon.)
Mentawai Is.
Melville I.
200 m
Equator
20°N
15°N
10°N
5°N
5°S
10°S
100°E
105°E
110°E
115°E
120°E
125°E
130°E
135°E

Australasia: Physical, Agriculture

Build
Ancient shields
Sedimentary rocks lying over ancient shields
Uplifted remains of ancient mountain systems
Younger fold mountains
Sedimentary rocks
Recent deposits
Volcanic rocks
Active volcanoes
Faults
Extension of buried shields under later deposits
metres
5000
3000
2000
1000
500
300
200
100
Sea level
Land depression
200
Spot heights in metres
Scale 1:44 000 000
0
500
1000 km
Borneo
Müller Mts.
G. of Tomini
Celebes
G. of Tolo
G. of Bone
Butang
Moluccas
Buru
Ceram
Banda Sea
Doberai Pen.
Berau G.
Serera B.
Schouten Is.
Nassau Mts.
5030
New Guinea
Central Ra.
Owen Stanley Ra.
Sepek
Fly
G. of Papua
Aru Is.
Tanimbar Is.
Dolak I.
Admiralty Is.
Bismarck Arch.
New Ireland
New Britain
New Britain Trench
Melanesia
Solomon Rise
Bougainville
D'Entrecasteaux Is.
Java Sea
Flores Sea
Torres Strait
Java Trench
Christmas I.
Bali
Lombok
Sumba
Timor Sea
Joseph Bonaparte Gulf
Arnhem Land
Gulf of Carpentaria
Groote Eylandt
Cape York Pen.
Roper
Wellesley I.
Great Barrier Reef
Coral Sea
Indian Ocean
Wharton Basin
Bonaparte Arch.
Kimberley
Barkly Tableland
Flinders
Great Dividing Range
Repulse Bay
Pacific Ocean
New Caledonia
Loyalty Is.
Tropic of Capricorn
Dampier Land
Eighty Mile Beach
Great Sandy Desert
Lake Mackay
Monte Bello I.
Lake Disappointment
Macdonnell Ranges
Simpson Desert
Diamantina
Cooper
Buckland Tableland
Fraser I.
Lord Howe Rise
New Caledonia Basin
N.W. Cape
Hamersley Ra.
1227
Gibson Desert
Carnarvon Ra.
Ayers Rock
1515
Musgrave Ra.
Sturt Desert
Grey Ra.
Warrego
Darling Downs
Geographe Ch.
Murchison
Great Victoria Desert
Lake Eyre
Tasman Sea
Norfolk I.
Lord Howe I.
Lake Barlee
Nullarbor Plain
Flinders Ra.
Main Barrier Ra.
Darling
Lachlan
Murray
Murrumbidgee
Great Australian Bight
Spencer G.
Lofty Ra.
The Coorong
Kangaroo I.
Australian Alps
2230
MT. KOSCIUSKO
C. Naturaliste
C. Leeuwin
Recherche Arch.
South Australian Basin
King I.
Bass Strait
Flinders I.
1593
Tasmania
Southern Ocean
North Island
Bay of Plenty
Hawke Bay
2517
Cook Str.
MT. COOK 3764
Southern Alps
South Island
Stewart I.
130°E
140°E
150°E
160°E
180°
Build
Scale 1:132 000 000
Minerals
Iron
Uranium
Ferro alloys
Copper, Tin, Gold, Lead, Zinc
Bauxite
Coal
Oil
Gas
Arable, predominantly cereals
General arable
Arable with cash crops
Grazing and dry farming
Deciduous forest, farming and grazing
Mixed forest, farming and grazing
Tropical dry forest, farming and grazing
Tropical rain forest, lumbering, crops
Desert, nomadic herding
Marsh or swamp
Natural Vegetation
Mixed forest
Tropical and subtropical dry forest
Tropical rain forest
Tropical grassland
Temperate grassland
Semi-desert and scrub
Hot desert
Marsh or swamp
Scale 1:132 000 000
Modified Zenithal Equidistant Projecti

Australasia: Rainfall, Population and Communications

nnual Rainfall

- over 3000 mm
- 2500–3000
- 2000–2500
- 1500–2000
- 1000–1500
- 750–1000
- 500–750
- 250–500
- 100–250
- under 100

ecipitation figures on graphs
10^{1}mm except annual totals

DARWIN
°C
1562 mm Annual
ALICE SPRINGS
°C
250 mm Annual
CHARLEVILLE
°C
488 mm Annual
BRISBANE
°C
1092 mm Annual
DARWIN Altitude 30 m
ALICE SPRINGS Altitude 584 m
CHARLEVILLE Altitude 294 m
BRISBANE Altitude 41 m
KALGOORLIE Altitude 361 m
PERTH Altitude 60 m
MELBOURNE Altitude 35 m

opulation Density
/km^2)

- over 100
- 10–100
- 1–10
- under 1

ities
million people)

- over 2
- 1–2
- 0.5–1

ommunications

- Principal roads
- Principal railways
- Principal airports

KALGOORLIE
°C
259 mm Annual
PERTH
°C
889 mm Annual
MELBOURNE
°C
691 mm Annual
INDONESIA
PAPUA–NEW GUINEA
SOLOMON ISLANDS
VANUATU
NEW CALEDONIA
NORTHERN TERRITORY
QUEENSLAND
WESTERN AUSTRALIA
SOUTH AUSTRALIA
NEW SOUTH WALES
A.C.T.
VICTORIA
TASMANIA
AUSTRALIA
Perth
Adelaide
Brisbane
Sydney
Melbourne
Auckland
NEW ZEALAND

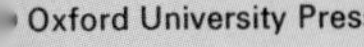

PACIFIC OCEAN
Coral Sea
Tasman Sea
Arafura Sea
Timor Sea
Banda Sea
Flores Sea
Great Australian Bight
Gulf of Carpentaria
INDONESIA
PAPUA - NEW GUINEA
New Guinea
SOLOMON ISLANDS
VANUATU
New Caledonia (Fr.)
NEW ZEALAND
NORTH ISLAND
SOUTH ISLAND
AUSTRALIA
WESTERN AUSTRALIA
NORTHERN TERRITORY
QUEENSLAND
SOUTH AUSTRALIA
NEW SOUTH WALES
VICTORIA
TASMANIA
A.C.T.
Canberra
Sydney
Melbourne
Brisbane
Adelaide
Perth
Darwin
Hobart
Auckland
Wellington
Christchurch
Port Moresby
Great Barrier Reef
Great Dividing Range
Great Victoria Desert
Gibson Desert
Great Sandy Desert
Simpson Desert
Nullarbor Plain
Tropic of Capricorn
Scale 1:22 000 000
0 250 500 km
Zenithal Equidistant Projection
© Oxford University Press

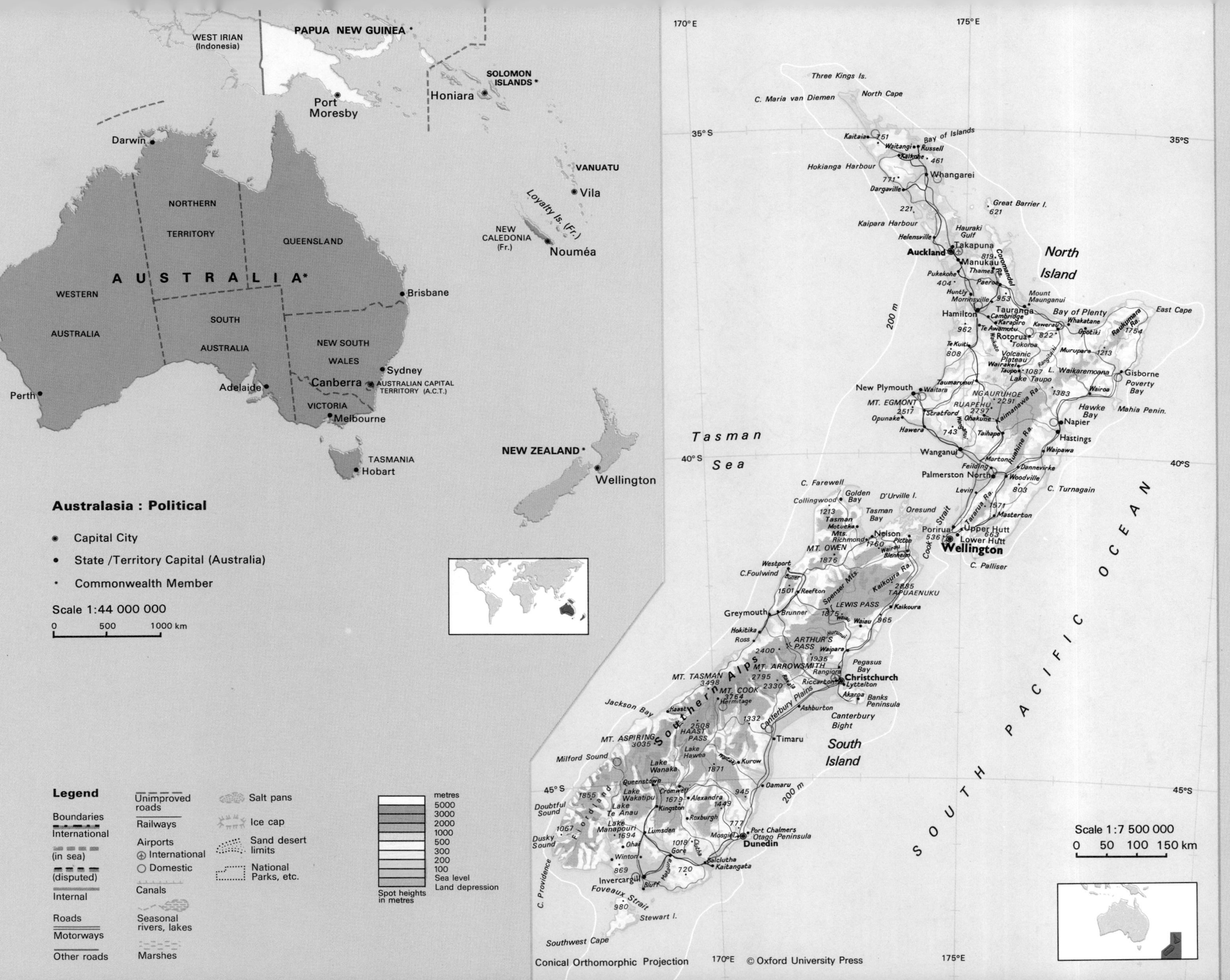

PAPUA NEW GUINEA
WEST IRIAN (Indonesia)
Port Moresby
SOLOMON ISLANDS
Honiara
VANUATU
Vila
Loyalty Is. (Fr.)
NEW CALEDONIA (Fr.)
Nouméa
AUSTRALIA*
WESTERN AUSTRALIA
NORTHERN TERRITORY
QUEENSLAND
SOUTH AUSTRALIA
NEW SOUTH WALES
VICTORIA
AUSTRALIAN CAPITAL TERRITORY (A.C.T.)
TASMANIA
Darwin
Perth
Adelaide
Brisbane
Sydney
Canberra
Melbourne
Hobart
NEW ZEALAND
Wellington
Australasia : Political
Capital City
State /Territory Capital (Australia)
Commonwealth Member
Scale 1:44 000 000
0 500 1000 km
Legend
Boundaries
International
(in sea)
(disputed)
Internal
Roads
Motorways
Other roads
Unimproved roads
Railways
Airports
International
Domestic
Canals
Seasonal rivers, lakes
Marshes
Salt pans
Ice cap
Sand desert limits
National Parks, etc.
metres
5000
3000
2000
1000
500
300
200
100
Sea level
Land depression
Spot heights in metres
Three Kings Is.
North Cape
C. Maria van Diemen
Bay of Islands
Hokianga Harbour
Whangarei
Great Barrier I.
Kaipara Harbour
Hauraki Gulf
Auckland
North Island
Hamilton
Tauranga
Bay of Plenty
East Cape
Rotorua
Lake Taupo
Gisborne
Poverty Bay
New Plymouth
MT. EGMONT 2517
RUAPEHU 2797
Hawke Bay
Napier
Hastings
Mahia Penin.
Wanganui
Palmerston North
Tasman Sea
Wellington
C. Palliser
C. Turnagain
Cook Strait
C. Farewell
Golden Bay
Tasman Bay
D'Urville I.
Nelson
Blenheim
Westport
Greymouth
LEWIS PASS
ARTHUR'S PASS
MT. ARROWSMITH
MT. TASMAN 3498
MT. COOK 3764
Southern Alps
Christchurch
Pegasus Bay
Banks Peninsula
Canterbury Plains
Canterbury Bight
Timaru
South Island
HAAST PASS
MT. ASPIRING 3035
Jackson Bay
Milford Sound
Lake Wanaka
Lake Wakatipu
Lake Te Anau
Lake Manapouri
Fiordland
Oamaru
Dunedin
Otago Peninsula
Invercargill
Foveaux Strait
Stewart I.
Southwest Cape
C. Providence
SOUTH PACIFIC OCEAN
Scale 1:7 500 000
0 50 100 150 km
Conical Orthomorphic Projection
© Oxford University Press

Africa: Physical

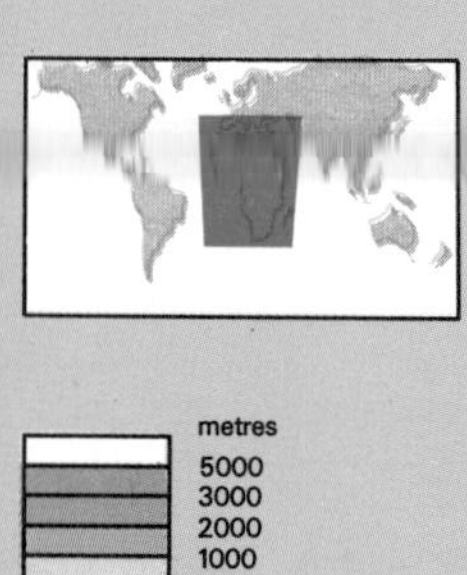

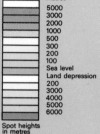

metres
5000
3000
2000
1000
500
300
200
100
Sea level
Land depression
200
3000
4000
5000
6000
Spot heights in metres

Scale 1 : 44 000 000

0
500
1000 km

20°W
15°W
NORTH ATLANTIC OCEAN
35°N
Madeira
30°N
Canary Is.
25°N
C. Blanc
20°N
Senegal
C. Verde
Fouta Djallon Mts
10°N
5°N
C. Palmas
Gulf of Guinea
Guinea Depression
Ascension I.
5°S
10°S
SOUTH ATLANTIC OCEAN
15°S
St. Helena
Angola Depression
20°S
25°S
30°S
35°S
Cape Depression
15°W
10°W
5°W
0°
10°E
15°E
30°E
35°E
45°E
50°E
Str. of Gibraltar
Mediterranean Sea
Little Atlas
Tell Atlas
High Atlas
C. Bon
Gt. Western Erg
Gt. Eastern Erg
El Hamra Hamada
G. of Sidra
Chech Erg
Sahara Desert
Tanezrouft
Ahaggar
Tibesti
3414
Kufra Oases
Libyan Desert
Quattara Depr.
Western Desert
Nile
Nile Delta
Sinai Pen.
Gulf of Suez
Red Sea Hills
Black Sea
Caspian Sea
Nafud
Tropic of Cancer
Red Sea
Asir Mtns.
L. Nasser
Nubian Desert
Niger
Bodelé Depression
Marra Mtns.
Atbara
Danakil
Bab al Mandab
C. Guardafui
White Nile
Blue Nile
L. Chad
Chari
Volta
L. Volta
Kainji Res.
Jos Plateau
Benue
Adamawa Mtns
Karé Mts.
Bight of Benin
Niger Delta
Bight of Bonny
4070
Sanaga
2829
Sudd
Bahr el Ghazal
Ethiopian Plateau
4306
East Rift Valley
Ogaden
Shibeli
L. Turkana
Juba
5°N
Boma
Uele
Sangha
Oubangui
Zaïre (Congo)
Lomami
MT. RUWENZORI 5118
L. Kyoga
Equator
C. Lopez
Mai Ndombe
Mitumba Mts
West Rift Valley
L. Victoria
Serengeti
5895
KILIMANJARO
INDIAN OCEAN
Pemba
Zanzibar
Kasai
Kuango
Lulua
Lualaba
L. Tanganyika
Aldabra Is.
10°S
L. Bangweulu
Muchinga Mts
L. Nyasa Malawi
Ruvuma
Comoro Archipelago
Angola Plateau
Zambezi
Mozambique Channel
15°
Kunene
Cuito
Kariba L.
Okovango Basin
Makariki Salt Pan
Namib Desert
Kalahari Desert
Ankaratra Mts.
Madagascar
20°S
Tropic of Capricorn
2661
25°S
Vaal
Orange
High Veld
Drakensberg
3308
30°S
Gt. Karoo
C. of Good Hope
C. Agulhas
C. St. Francis
Mozambique Depression
35°S

Zenithal Equal Area Projecti

Africa: Political

Capital city
Commonwealth member
cale 1:44 000 000
500
1000 km
CEUTA (Sp.)
Algiers
Tunis
Rabat
MELILLA (Sp.)
Madeira (Port.)
TUNISIA
Canary Is. (Sp.)
MOROCCO
Tarabulus
Cairo
ALGERIA
LIBYA
WESTERN SAHARA
EGYPT
CAPE VERDE IS.
MAURITANIA
Nouakchott
Praia
Dakar
SENEGAL
MALI
NIGER
THE GAMBIA
Banjul
Bissau
GUINEA-BISSAU
Bamako
Niamey
CHAD
Khartoum
SUDAN
DJIBOUTI
Djibouti
GUINEA
BURKINA
Ouagadougou
N'Djamena
Conakry
Freetown
SIERRA LEONE
CÔTE D'IVOIRE
GHANA
TOGO
BENIN
NIGERIA
Abuja
Addis Ababa
ETHIOPIA
SOMALI REPUBLIC
Monrovia
LIBERIA
Yamoussoukro
Accra
Lomé
Porto Novo
CENTRAL AFRICAN REPUBLIC
CAMEROUN
Bangui
Malabo
EQU. GUINEA
Yaoundé
UGANDA
KENYA
Mogadiscio
São Tomé
SAO TOME AND PRINCIPE
Libreville
GABON
CONGO
Kampala
Nairobi
ZAÏRE
Kigali
RWANDA
Bujumbura
BURUNDI
Brazzaville
Kinshasa
CABINDA (Angola)
TANZANIA
Dodoma
Luanda
Aldabra Is. (Seychelles)
Moroni
COMORO IS.
ANGOLA
MALAWI
Lilongwe
ZAMBIA
MOZAMBIQUE
Lusaka
Harare
ZIMBABWE
Antananarivo
MADAGASCAR
Windhoek
WALVIS BAY (S. Africa)
NAMIBIA
BOTSWANA
Gaborone
Pretoria
Maputo
Mbabane
SWAZILAND
REPUBLIC OF SOUTH AFRICA
Maseru
LESOTHO
Build
Ancient shields
Sedimentary rocks lying over ancient shields
Uplifted remains of ancient mountain systems
Younger fold mountains
Sedimentary rocks
Recent deposits
Volcanic rocks
Active volcanoes
Faults
Extension of buried shields under later deposits
Minerals
Scale 1:190 000 000
Iron
Chromium
Manganese
Beryllium
Cobalt
Vanadium
Copper
Tin
Lead
Gold
Silver
Bauxite
Uranium
Antimony
Mica
Phosphate
Potash
Diamonds
Coal
Oil
Gas
Annual Rainfall
Scale 1:190 000 000
over 4000 mm
3000–4000
2500–3000
2000–2500
1500–2000
1000–1500
750–1000
500–750
250–500
100–250
under 100

Oxford University Press

Africa: Population and Communications

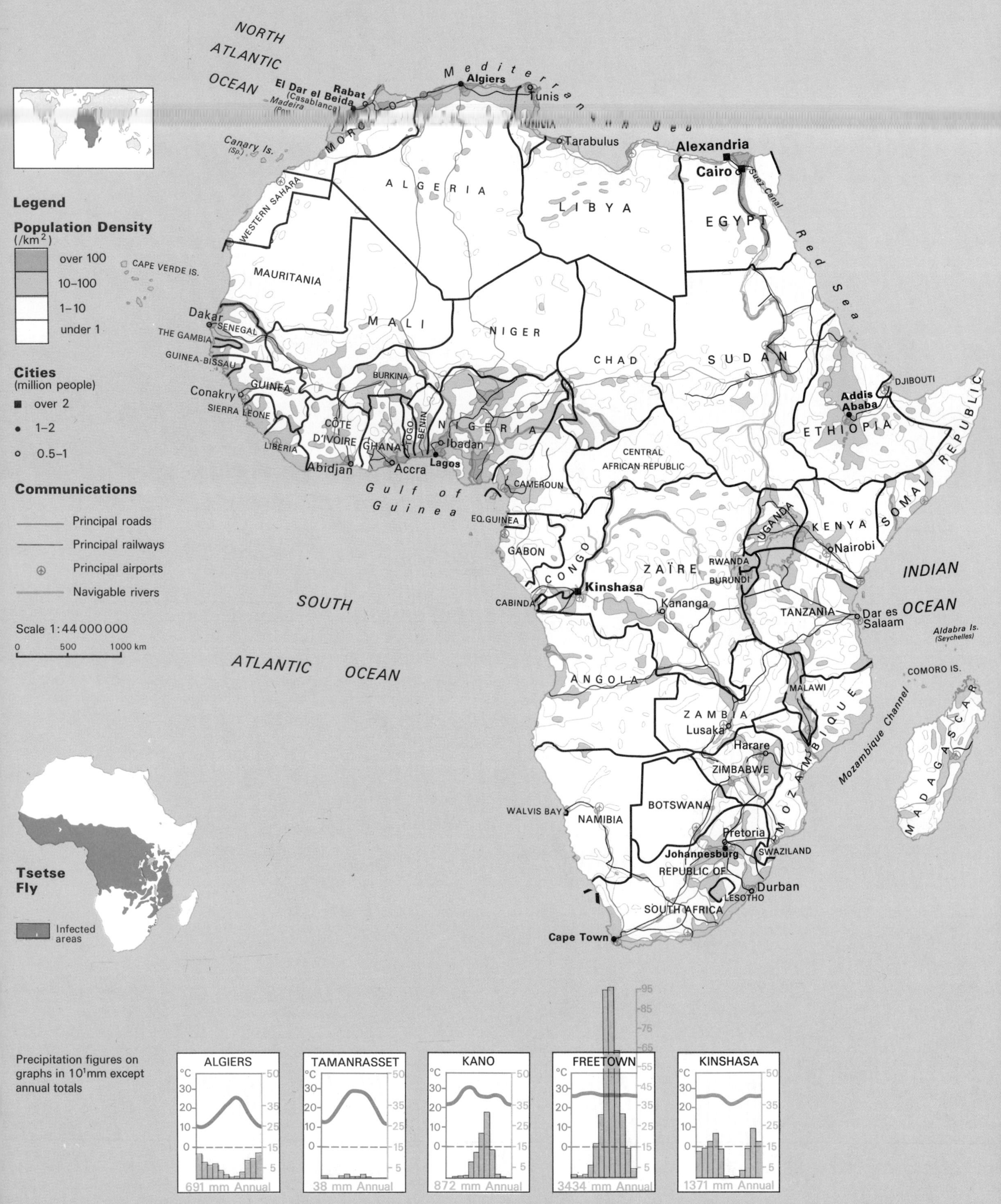
NORTH ATLANTIC OCEAN
Mediterranean Sea
Rabat
El Dar el Beida (Casablanca)
Madeira (Port.)
Canary Is. (Sp.)
Algiers
Tunis
Tarabulus
Alexandria
Cairo
Suez Canal
Red Sea
WESTERN SAHARA
ALGERIA
LIBYA
EGYPT
MAURITANIA
MALI
NIGER
CHAD
SUDAN
CAPE VERDE IS.
Dakar
SENEGAL
THE GAMBIA
GUINEA-BISSAU
GUINEA
Conakry
SIERRA LEONE
LIBERIA
CÔTE D'IVOIRE
BURKINA
GHANA
TOGO
BENIN
NIGERIA
Ibadan
Lagos
Abidjan
Accra
DJIBOUTI
Addis Ababa
ETHIOPIA
SOMALI REPUBLIC
CENTRAL AFRICAN REPUBLIC
CAMEROUN
Gulf of Guinea
EQ.GUINEA
GABON
CONGO
ZAÏRE
Kinshasa
CABINDA
Kananga
RWANDA
BURUNDI
UGANDA
KENYA
Nairobi
TANZANIA
Dar es Salaam
INDIAN OCEAN
Aldabra Is. (Seychelles)
COMORO IS.
SOUTH ATLANTIC OCEAN
ANGOLA
MALAWI
ZAMBIA
Lusaka
Harare
ZIMBABWE
MOZAMBIQUE
Mozambique Channel
MADAGASCAR
WALVIS BAY
NAMIBIA
BOTSWANA
Pretoria
Johannesburg
SWAZILAND
REPUBLIC OF SOUTH AFRICA
Durban
LESOTHO
Cape Town
Legend
Population Density (/km²)
over 100
10–100
1–10
under 1
Cities (million people)
over 2
1–2
0.5–1
Communications
Principal roads
Principal railways
Principal airports
Navigable rivers
Scale 1:44 000 000
0 500 1000 km
Tsetse Fly
Infected areas
Precipitation figures on graphs in 10¹mm except annual totals
ALGIERS
691 mm Annual
TAMANRASSET
38 mm Annual
KANO
872 mm Annual
FREETOWN
3434 mm Annual
KINSHASA
1371 mm Annual
°C
30
20
10
0
50
35
25
15
5
95
85
75
65
55
45

Zenithal Equal Area Projection

Africa: Agriculture

ALGIERS Altitude 61m
TAMANRASSET Altitude 1283m
WADI HALFA Altitude 125m
KANO Altitude 469m
FREETOWN Altitude 11m
ADDIS ABABA Altitude 2450m
NAIROBI Altitude 1646m
KINSHASA Altitude 325m
BULAWAYO Altitude 1339m
WINDHOEK Altitude 1665m
CAPE TOWN Altitude 12m

egend

- Arable, predominantly cereals
- Arable, predominantly paddy
- General arable
- Arable with cash crops
- Irrigated crops
- Grazing and dry farming
- Deciduous forest, farming and grazing
- Mixed forest, farming and grazing
- Tropical dry forest and savanna, farming and grazing
- Tropical rain forest, lumbering, crops
- Desert, nomadic herding
- Marsh or swamp

ale 1:44 000 000
500 1000 km

atural Vegetation

- Tropical and subtropical dry forest
- Tropical rain forest
- Tropical grassland and savanna
- Temperate grassland
- Semi-desert and scrub
- Hot desert
- High altitude vegetation
- Marsh or swamp

ale 1: 190 000 000

ecipitation figures on
aphs in 10[1]mm except
nual totals

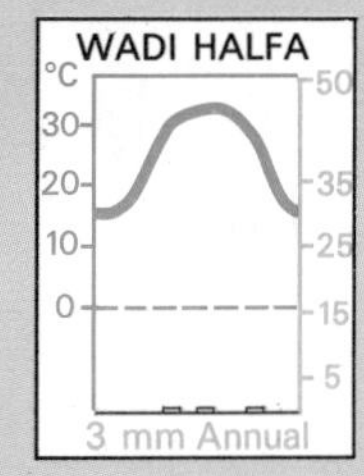
WADI HALFA
°C
30
20
10
0
50
35
25
15
5
3 mm Annual

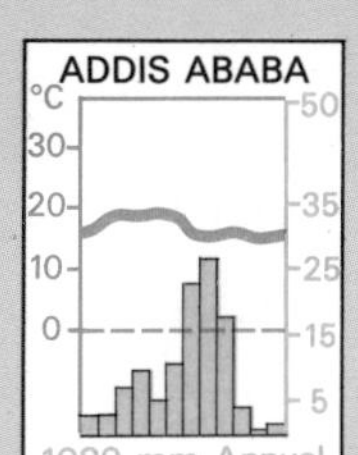
ADDIS ABABA
°C
30
20
10
0
50
35
25
15
5
1089 mm Annual

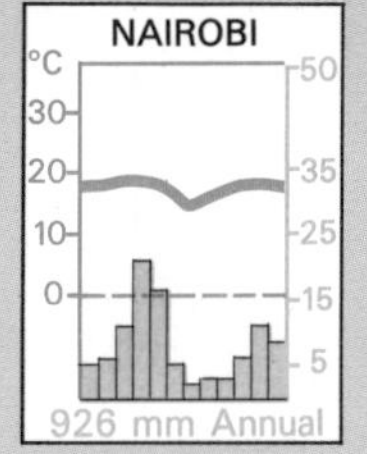
NAIROBI
°C
30
20
10
0
50
35
25
15
5
926 mm Annual

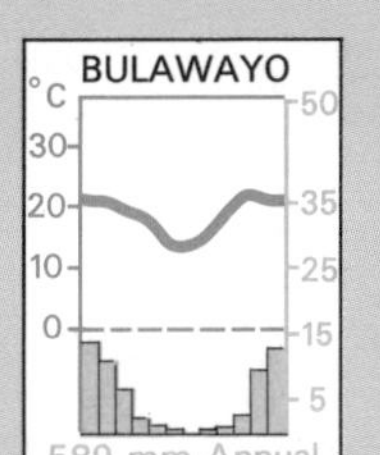
BULAWAYO
°C
30
20
10
0
50
35
25
15
5
589 mm Annual

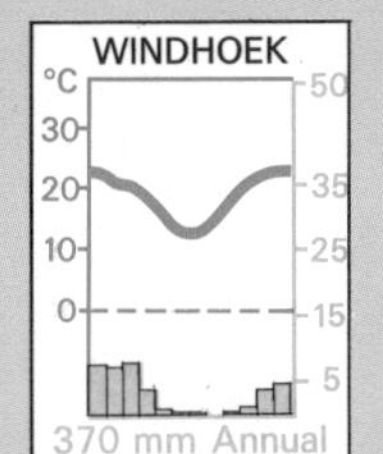
WINDHOEK
°C
30
20
10
0
50
35
25
15
5
370 mm Annual

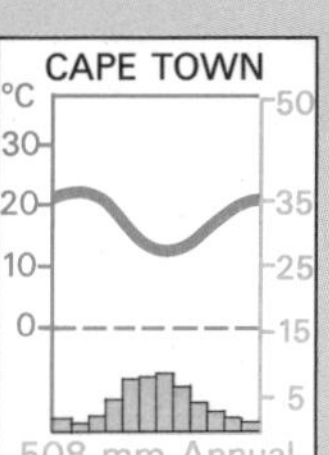
CAPE TOWN
°C
30
20
10
0
50
35
25
15
5
508 mm Annual

Northern Africa

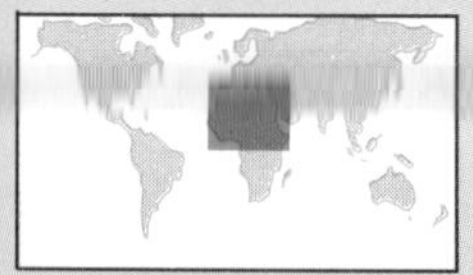

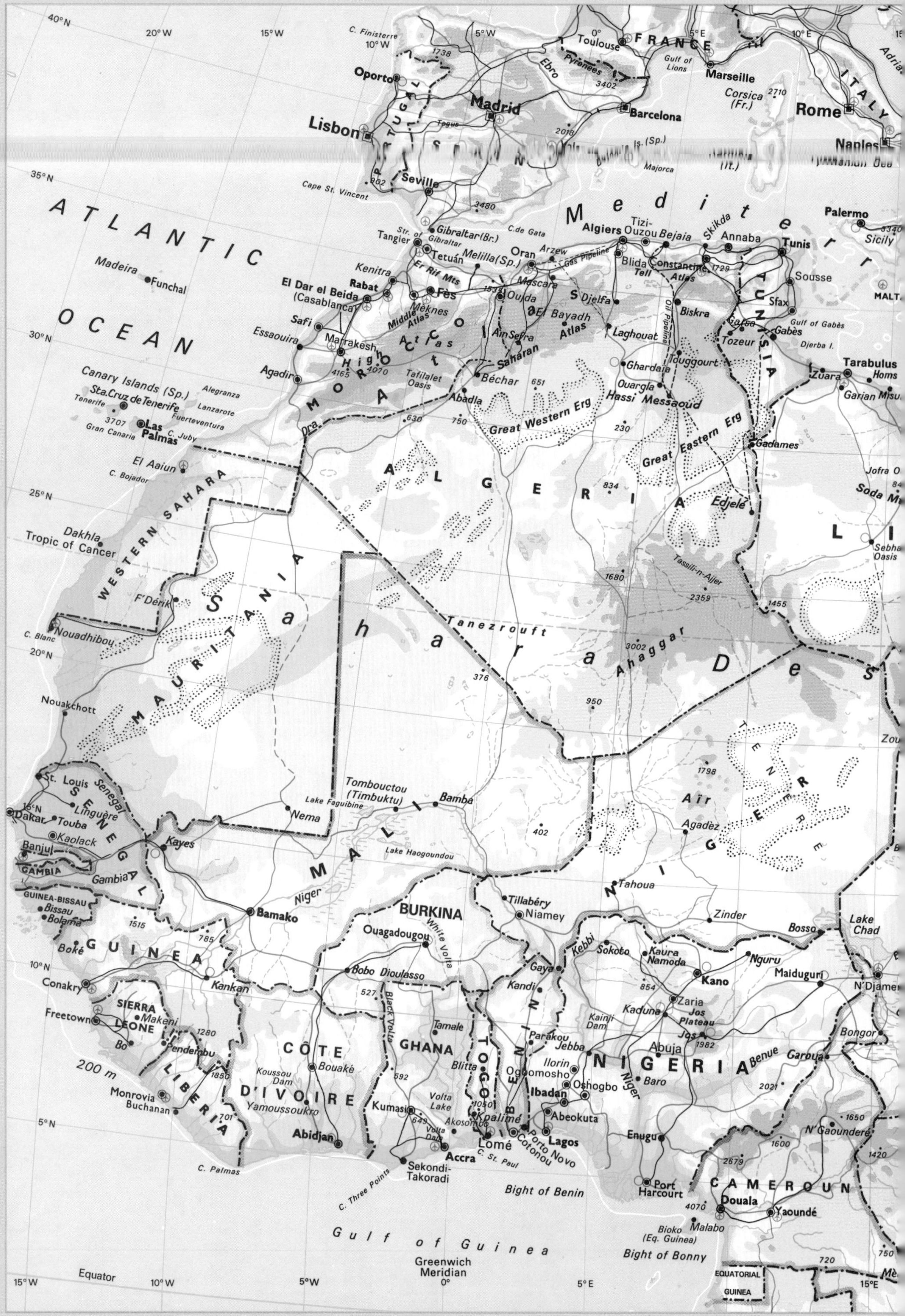

40° N
20° W
15° W
C. Finisterre
10° W
5° W
0°
5° E
10° E
Toulouse
FRANCE
Pyrenees
3402
Gulf of Lions
Marseille
Corsica (Fr.)
2710
Rome
ITALY
Adriatic
Naples
Oporto
1738
Ebro
Madrid
Barcelona
Lisbon
Tagus
2018
Is. (Sp.)
Majorca
(It.)
35° N
Cape St. Vincent
902
Seville
3480
Gibraltar (Br.)
Str. of Gibraltar
Tangier
C. de Gata
Tetuán
Melilla (Sp.)
Oran
Arzew
Algiers
Tizi-Ouzou
Bejaia
Skikda
Annaba
Tunis
Palermo
Sicily
3340
Mediterranean
ATLANTIC OCEAN
Madeira
Funchal
Kenitra
Rabat
El Dar el Beida (Casablanca)
Er Rif Mts
Fès
Mascara
Gas Pipeline
Blida
Constantine
Tell Atlas
1729
Sousse
Sfax
Gulf of Gabès
Gabès
Djerba I.
MALTA
Safi
Meknes
Middle Atlas
Oujda
El Bayadh
Djelfa
Oil Pipeline
Biskra
Gafsa
Tozeur
TUNISIA
Essaouira
Marrakesh
High Atlas
MOROCCO
Ain Sefra
Saharan Atlas
Laghouat
30° N
Agadir
4165
4070
Tafilalet Oasis
Béchar
651
Ghardaia
Touggourt
Zuara
Tarabulus
Homs
Garian
Misurata
Canary Islands (Sp.)
Sta. Cruz de Tenerife
Tenerife
3707
Las Palmas
Gran Canaria
Alegranza
Lanzarote
Fuerteventura
C. Juby
Abadla
Dra
630
750
Great Western Erg
Ouargla
Hassi Messaoud
230
Great Eastern Erg
Gadames
El Aaiun
C. Bojador
WESTERN SAHARA
ALGERIA
834
Edjelé
Jofra Oasis
Soda Mts
25° N
Dakhla
Tropic of Cancer
LIBYA
Sebha Oasis
1680
Tassili-n-Ajjer
2359
1455
F'Derik
MAURITANIA
Sahara
Tanezrouft
Ahaggar
3002
Desert
C. Blanc
Nouadhibou
20° N
376
950
Nouakchott
Ténéré
1798
Aïr
NIGER
St. Louis
Senegal
SENEGAL
15° N
Dakar
Linguère
Touba
Kaolack
Banjul
GAMBIA
Gambia
Tombouctou (Timbuktu)
Lake Faguibine
Bamba
Nema
Kayes
MALI
Lake Haogoundou
402
Agadès
Tahoua
GUINEA-BISSAU
Bissau
Bolama
Niger
Bamako
BURKINA
Tillabéry
Niamey
Zinder
Bosso
Lake Chad
1515
785
Ouagadougou
White Volta
Boké
GUINEA
10° N
Conakry
Kankan
Bobo Dioulasso
527
Black Volta
Gaya
Kandi
Kebbi
Sokoto
Kaura Namoda
854
Kano
Nguru
Maiduguri
N'Djamena
SIERRA LEONE
Freetown
Makeni
Bo
1280
Pendembu
Tamale
GHANA
TOGO
BENIN
Kainji Dam
Kaduna
Zaria
Jos Plateau
Jos
1982
Bongor
Parakou
Jebba
Abuja
200 m
LIBERIA
1850
CÔTE D'IVOIRE
Bouaké
Koussou Dam
Yamoussoukro
692
Blitta
Volta Lake
Ilorin
Ogbomosho
Oshogbo
Ibadan
NIGERIA
Baro
Benue
Garoua
2021
Monrovia
Buchanan
701
5° N
Abidjan
Kumasi
643
Volta Dam
Akosombo
1050
Kpalimé
Abeokuta
Lagos
Lomé
Cotonou
Porto Novo
Enugu
1650
N'Gaoundéré
1600
1420
Accra
C. St. Paul
Sekondi-Takoradi
C. Palmas
C. Three Points
Bight of Benin
Port Harcourt
2679
CAMEROUN
4070
Douala
Yaoundé
Bioko (Eq. Guinea)
Malabo
Gulf of Guinea
Bight of Bonny
Greenwich Meridian
0°
720
750
15° W
Equator
10° W
5° W
5° E
EQUATORIAL GUINEA
15° E

Zenithal Equal Area Projection

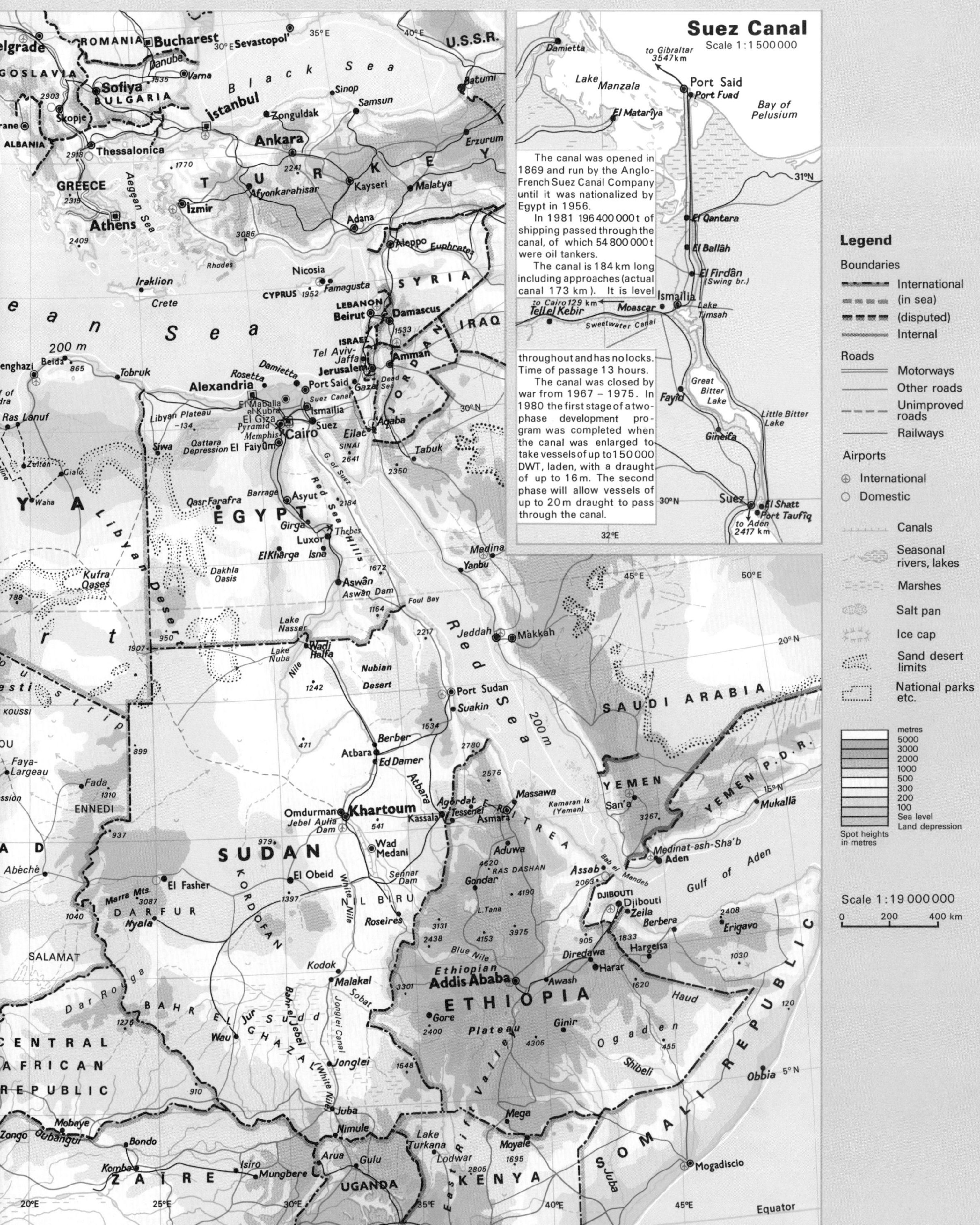
Suez Canal
Scale 1:1 500 000
The canal was opened in 1869 and run by the Anglo-French Suez Canal Company until it was nationalized by Egypt in 1956.
In 1981 196 400 000 t of shipping passed through the canal, of which 54 800 000 t were oil tankers.
The canal is 184 km long including approaches (actual canal 173 km). It is level throughout and has no locks. Time of passage 13 hours.
The canal was closed by war from 1967 – 1975. In 1980 the first stage of a two-phase development program was completed when the canal was enlarged to take vessels of up to 150 000 DWT, laden, with a draught of up to 16 m. The second phase will allow vessels of up to 20 m draught to pass through the canal.
Damietta
to Gibraltar 3547 km
Port Said
Port Fuad
Lake Manzala
El Matarîya
Bay of Pelusium
El Qantara
El Ballâh
El Firdân (Swing br.)
Ismailia
Lake Timsah
to Cairo 129 km
Tell el Kebir
Moascar
Sweetwater Canal
Great Bitter Lake
Fayid
Little Bitter Lake
Gineifa
Suez
El Shatt
Port Taufîq
to Aden 2417 km
31°N
30°N
32°E
Legend
Boundaries
International
(in sea)
(disputed)
Internal
Roads
Motorways
Other roads
Unimproved roads
Railways
Airports
International
Domestic
Canals
Seasonal rivers, lakes
Marshes
Salt pan
Ice cap
Sand desert limits
National parks etc.
metres
5000
3000
2000
1000
500
300
200
100
Sea level
Land depression
Spot heights in metres
Scale 1:19 000 000
0
200
400 km
Black Sea
TURKEY
EGYPT
SUDAN
ETHIOPIA
SAUDI ARABIA
SYRIA
IRAQ
JORDAN
LEBANON
ISRAEL
YEMEN
YEMEN P.D.R.
SOMALI REPUBLIC
DJIBOUTI
KENYA
UGANDA
ZAÏRE
CENTRAL AFRICAN REPUBLIC
CYPRUS
GREECE
BULGARIA
ROMANIA
U.S.S.R.
Red Sea
Gulf of Aden
Istanbul
Ankara
Athens
Cairo
Alexandria
Khartoum
Addis Ababa
Jeddah
Makkah
Mogadiscio

Southern Africa

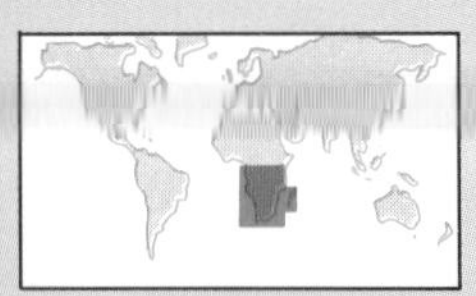

Legend

Boundaries
- International
- (in sea)
- (disputed)
- Internal

Roads
- Motorways
- Other roads
- Unimproved roads
- Railways

Airports
- International
- Domestic

- Canals
- Seasonal rivers, lakes
- Marshes
- Salt pan
- Ice cap
- Sand desert limits
- National parks etc.

metres
5000
3000
2000
1000
500
300
200
100
Sea level
Land depression

Spot heights in metres

Scale 1 : 19 000 000

0 200 400 km

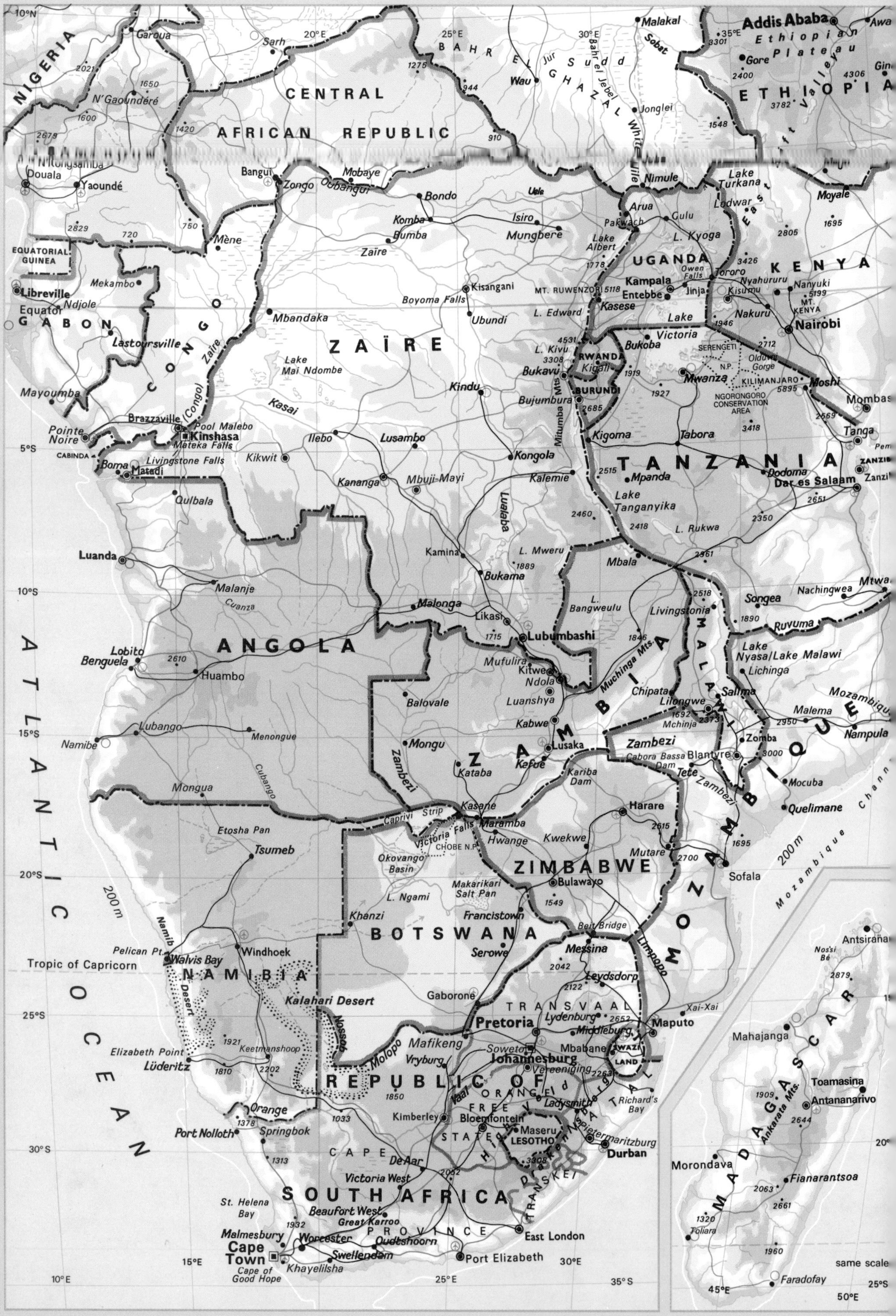

Zenithal Equal Area Project

CANADA
Hudson Bay
GREENLAND
Davis Strait
Denmark Strait
ICELAND
Arctic Circle
Norwegian Sea
Norwegian Current
Faeroe Is.
Mn. Aug.-Sept.
Feb.-March
E. Greenland Current
Labrador Current
Labrador Basin
Limit of pack ice max.
Reykjanes Ridge
Rockall Plateau
North Sea
Baltic Sea
NORWAY
SWEDEN
FINLAND
U. S. S. R.
UNITED KINGDOM
IRISH REP.
London
NETH.
BELG.
Paris
W. GERMANY
E. GERMANY
Berlin
POLAND
CZECH.
AUS.
HUNG.
ROMANIA
SWITZ.
YUGOSLAVIA
BULGARIA
Black Sea
Istanbul
TURKEY
GREECE
ITALY
FRANCE
Great Lakes
Chicago
Ottawa
Montreal
St. Lawrence
UNITED STATES
Washington
New York
Mississippi
Limit of floating ice-maximum
Newfoundland Basin
North Atlantic Drift
•5080
West European Basin
Peake Deep •5944
PORTUGAL
Lisbon
SPAIN
Mediterranean Sea
TUNISIA
LIBYA
MOROCCO
ALGERIA
Madeira
Azores
Canary Basin
Canary Islands
Canary Current
WESTERN SAHARA
NORTH ATLANTIC OCEAN
Nova Scotia Basin
Gulf Stream
Bermuda
North American Basin
Sargasso Sea
•6995
Mid-Atlantic Ridge
Gulf of Mexico
BAHAMAS
6095
Tropic of Cancer
Yucatan Basin
CUBA
HAITI
DOMINICAN REP.
Puerto Rico Trench
North Equatorial Current
JAMAICA
PUERTO RICO (U.S.A.)
ST. KITTS-NEVIS
ANTIGUA & BARBUDA
DOMINICA
ST. LUCIA
ST. VINCENT
BARBADOS
GRENADA
TRINIDAD AND TOBAGO
Caribbean Sea
Venezuelan Basin
Guiana Basin
Cape Verde Basin
CAPE VERDE ISLANDS
MAURITANIA
MALI
NIGER
CHAD
Niger
Dakar
SENEGAL
GAMBIA
GUINEA BISSAU
GUINEA
SIERRA LEONE
LIBERIA
CÔTE D'IVOIRE
BURKINA
GHANA
TOGO
BENIN
NIGERIA
Lagos
CAMEROUN
CENT. AFR. REP.
COSTA RICA
PANAMA
Panama
Caracas
VENEZUELA
COLOMBIA
Bogotá
GUYANA
SURINAM
FR. GUIANA
Equatorial Counter Current
Guinea Current
Guinea Basin
St. Paul Rocks
Bioko
Principe
Sao Tomé
EQ. GUINEA
GABON
CONGO
Zaire
Equator
ECUADOR
Amazon
Rocas I.
Fernando de Noronha
South Equatorial Current
Recife
BRAZIL
Brazil Basin
•6022
Brazil Current
Ascension I.
SOUTH ATLANTIC OCEAN
Angola Basin
•2255
ANGOLA
St. Helena
6050
Trinidad
Martin Vaz
Tropic of Capricorn
PERU
Lima
Andes
Humboldt Current
Peru Basin
Nasca Ridge
La Paz
BOLIVIA
PARAGUAY
Asunción
Rio de Janeiro
Sao Paulo
NAMIBIA
Walvis Ridge
Benguela Current
Rio Grande Rise
San Felix I.
Peru-Chile Trench
CHILE
ARGENTINA
Parana
URUGUAY
Montevideo
Buenos Aires
Santiago
Juan Fernandez Is.
SOUTH PACIFIC OCEAN
Chile Basin
Chile Rise
Tristan da Cunha
Gough I.
Cape Basin
Cape Town
REP. OF SOUTH AFRICA
Agulhas Current
Cape Rise
Argentine Basin
West Wind Drift
Limit of floating ice - maximum
Falkland Current
•6212
Falkland Is.
South Georgia
South Sandwich Trench
Scotia Sea
East Scotia Basin
West Scotia Basin
Tierra del Fuego
South Orkney Is.
Minimum Feb.-March
Limit of pack ice max. Aug.-Sept.
Bouvet I.
Atlantic - Indian Ridge
Agulhas Plateau
South East Pacific Basin
SOUTHERN OCEAN

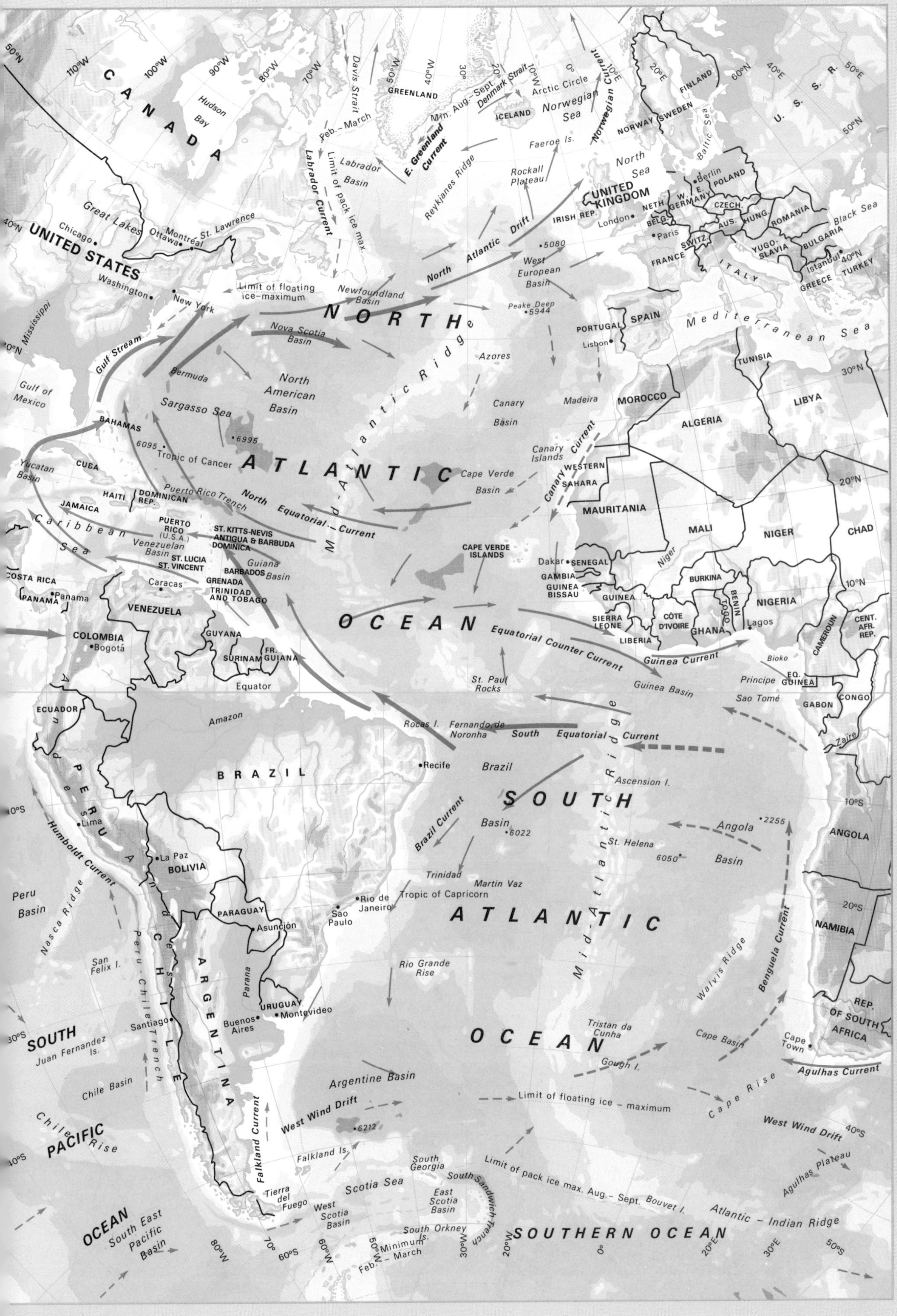

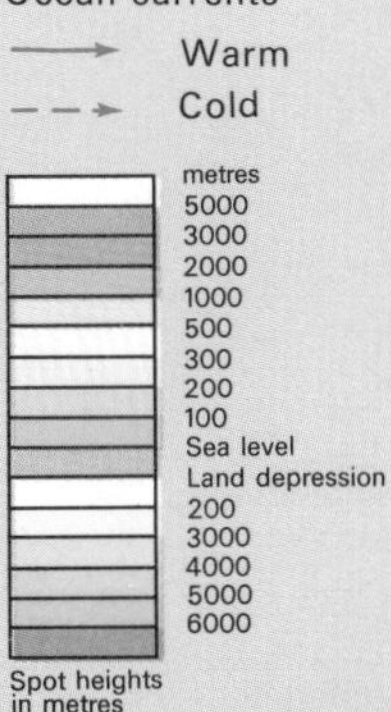

Legend
Ocean currents
Warm
Cold
metres
5000
3000
2000
1000
500
300
200
100
Sea level
Land depression
200
3000
4000
5000
6000
Spot heights in metres

Scale 1:63 000 000

0 500 1000 1500 km

odified Zenithal Equidistant Projection

Pacific Ocean

Modified Zenithal Equidistant Projection

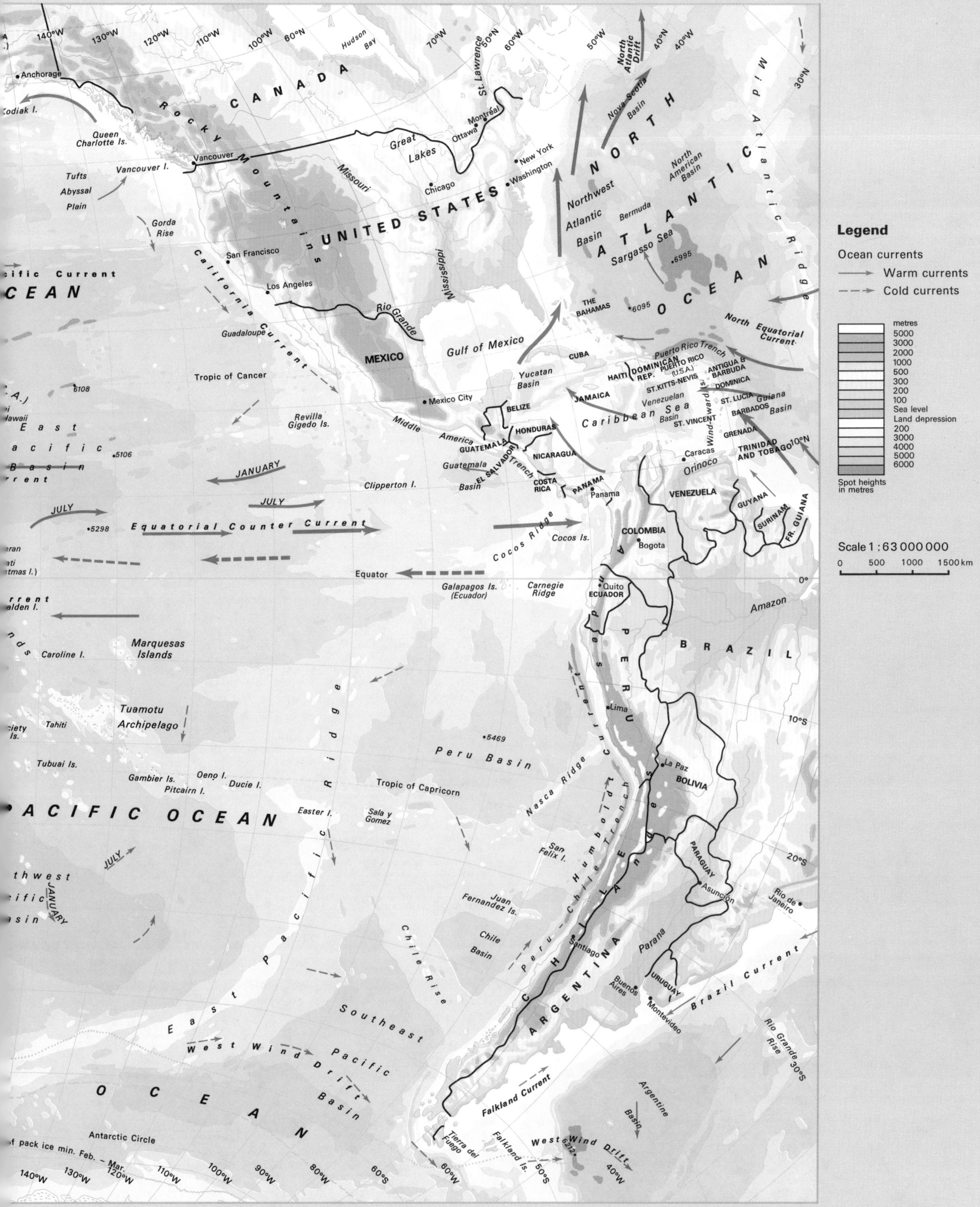

140°W 130°W 120°W 110°W 100°W 60°N 70°W 50°N 60°W 50°W 40°N 40°W 30°N

Anchorage
Kodiak I.
Queen Charlotte Is.
Tufts Abyssal Plain
Vancouver I.
Gorda Rise
CANADA
Hudson Bay
St. Lawrence
Rocky Mountains
Vancouver
Great Lakes
Ottawa
Montréal
Missouri
Chicago
New York
Washington
UNITED STATES
North Atlantic Drift
Nova Scotia Basin
NORTH ATLANTIC OCEAN
Northwest Atlantic Basin
North American Basin
Bermuda
Sargasso Sea
•6995
Mid Atlantic Ridge
San Francisco
Los Angeles
California Current
Mississippi
Rio Grande
Pacific Current
OCEAN
Guadaloupe
MEXICO
Gulf of Mexico
THE BAHAMAS
•6095
North Equatorial Current
Tropic of Cancer
•6108
Hawaii
East Pacific Basin
Current
•5106
Revilla Gigedo Is.
Mexico City
Middle America Trench
Yucatan Basin
CUBA
HAITI
DOMINICAN REP.
PUERTO RICO (U.S.A.)
Puerto Rico Trench
ANTIGUA & BARBUDA
ST. KITTS-NEVIS
DOMINICA
JAMAICA
BELIZE
Venezuelan Basin
Caribbean Sea
Windwards
ST. LUCIA
BARBADOS
Guiana Basin
ST. VINCENT
GRENADA
HONDURAS
GUATEMALA
EL SALVADOR
NICARAGUA
Guatemala Basin
JANUARY
Clipperton I.
COSTA RICA
PANAMA
Panama
Caracas
Orinoco
TRINIDAD AND TOBAGO
10°N
VENEZUELA
GUYANA
SURINAM
FR. GUIANA
JULY
•5298
Equatorial Counter Current
Cocos Ridge
Cocos Is.
COLOMBIA
Bogota
Christmas I.
Equator
Galapagos Is. (Ecuador)
Carnegie Ridge
Quito
ECUADOR
0°
Amazon
Malden I.
Marquesas Islands
Caroline I.
BRAZIL
Andes
PERU
Tuamotu Archipelago
Tahiti
Society Is.
Lima
10°S
Peru Current
•5469
Peru Basin
Tubuai Is.
Gambier Is.
Oeno I.
Ducie I.
Pitcairn I.
Tropic of Capricorn
La Paz
BOLIVIA
Nasca Ridge
PACIFIC OCEAN
Easter I.
Sala y Gomez
Humboldt Trench
San Felix I.
PARAGUAY
20°S
Southwest Pacific Basin
JULY
JANUARY
Asunción
Juan Fernandez Is.
Rio de Janeiro
Peru–Chile Trench
CHILE
Chile Rise
Chile Basin
Santiago
Parana
East Pacific Ridge
ARGENTINA
Buenos Aires
URUGUAY
Montevideo
Brazil Current
Southeast Pacific Basin
Rio Grande Rise
30°S
West Wind Drift
Falkland Current
Argentine Basin
OCEAN
Antarctic Circle
Limit of pack ice min. Feb. – Mar.
Tierra del Fuego
Falkland Is.
West Wind Drift
•6212
140°W 130°W 120°W 110°W 100°W 90°W 80°W 60°S 60°W 50°S 40°W

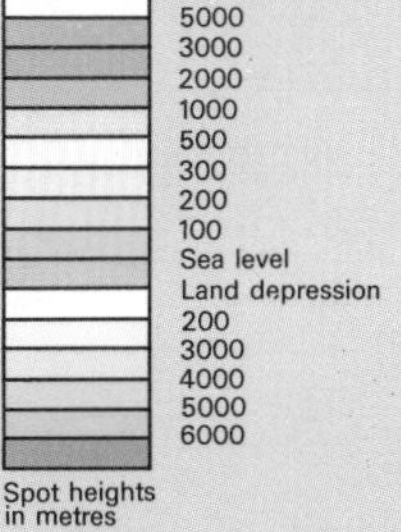
Legend
Ocean currents
Warm currents
Cold currents
metres
5000
3000
2000
1000
500
300
200
100
Sea level
Land depression
200
3000
4000
5000
6000
Spot heights in metres

Scale 1:63 000 000

0 500 1000 1500 km

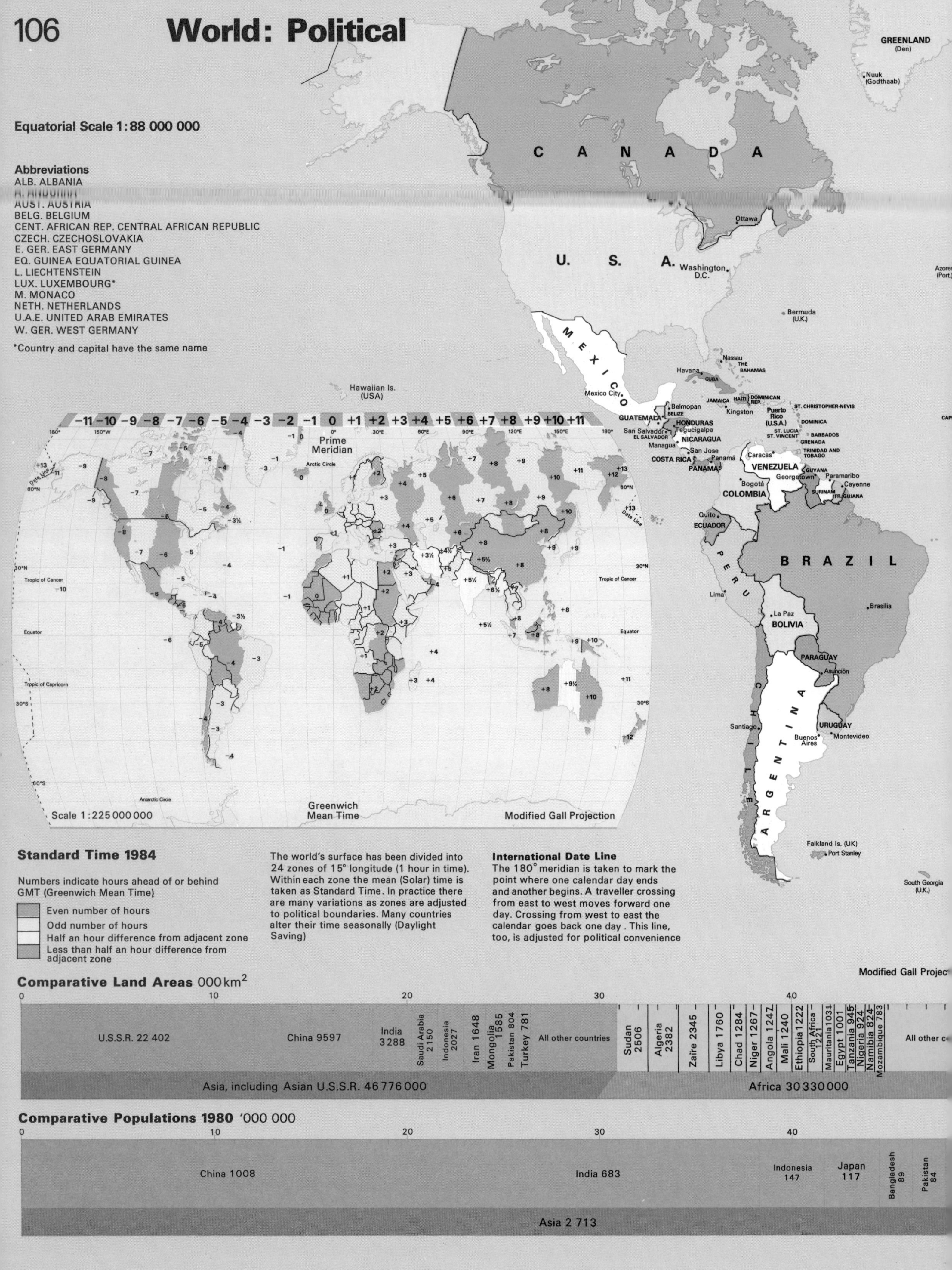
Equatorial Scale 1:88 000 000
Abbreviations
ALB. ALBANIA
AUST. AUSTRIA
BELG. BELGIUM
CENT. AFRICAN REP. CENTRAL AFRICAN REPUBLIC
CZECH. CZECHOSLOVAKIA
E. GER. EAST GERMANY
EQ. GUINEA EQUATORIAL GUINEA
L. LIECHTENSTEIN
LUX. LUXEMBOURG*
M. MONACO
NETH. NETHERLANDS
U.A.E. UNITED ARAB EMIRATES
W. GER. WEST GERMANY
*Country and capital have the same name
GREENLAND (Den)
Nuuk (Godthaab)
CANADA
Ottawa
U. S. A.
Washington, D.C.
Azores (Port.)
Bermuda (U.K.)
MEXICO
Mexico City
Nassau
THE BAHAMAS
Havana
CUBA
Hawaiian Is. (USA)
Belmopan
BELIZE
JAMAICA
HAITI
DOMINICAN REP.
Kingston
Puerto Rico (U.S.A.)
ST. CHRISTOPHER-NEVIS
DOMINICA
ST. LUCIA
ST. VINCENT
BARBADOS
GRENADA
TRINIDAD AND TOBAGO
GUATEMALA
HONDURAS
San Salvador
Tegucigalpa
EL SALVADOR
NICARAGUA
Managua
San Jose
COSTA RICA
Panamá
PANAMA
Caracas
VENEZUELA
GUYANA
Georgetown
Paramaribo
Cayenne
SURINAM
FR. GUIANA
Bogotá
COLOMBIA
Quito
ECUADOR
BRAZIL
PERU
Lima
Brasília
La Paz
BOLIVIA
PARAGUAY
Asunción
CHILE
ARGENTINA
Santiago
URUGUAY
Buenos Aires
Montevideo
Falkland Is. (UK)
Port Stanley
South Georgia (U.K.)
Modified Gall Projection
-11 -10 -9 -8 -7 -6 -5 -4 -3 -2 -1 0 +1 +2 +3 +4 +5 +6 +7 +8 +9 +10 +11
Prime Meridian
Arctic Circle
Tropic of Cancer
Equator
Tropic of Capricorn
Antarctic Circle
Date Line
Scale 1:225 000 000
Greenwich Mean Time
Modified Gall Projection
Standard Time 1984
Numbers indicate hours ahead of or behind GMT (Greenwich Mean Time)
Even number of hours
Odd number of hours
Half an hour difference from adjacent zone
Less than half an hour difference from adjacent zone
The world's surface has been divided into 24 zones of 15° longitude (1 hour in time). Within each zone the mean (Solar) time is taken as Standard Time. In practice there are many variations as zones are adjusted to political boundaries. Many countries alter their time seasonally (Daylight Saving)
International Date Line
The 180° meridian is taken to mark the point where one calendar day ends and another begins. A traveller crossing from east to west moves forward one day. Crossing from west to east the calendar goes back one day. This line, too, is adjusted for political convenience
Comparative Land Areas 000 km²
0 10 20 30 40
U.S.S.R. 22 402
China 9597
India 3288
Saudi Arabia 2150
Indonesia 2027
Iran 1648
Mongolia 1585
Pakistan 804
Turkey 781
All other countries
Sudan 2506
Algeria 2382
Zaïre 2345
Libya 1760
Chad 1284
Niger 1267
Angola 1247
Mali 1240
Ethiopia 1222
South Africa 1221
Mauritania 1031
Egypt 1001
Tanzania 945
Nigeria 924
Namibia 824
Mozambique 783
Asia, including Asian U.S.S.R. 46 776 000
Africa 30 330 000
Comparative Populations 1980 '000 000
0 10 20 30 40
China 1008
India 683
Indonesia 147
Japan 117
Bangladesh 89
Pakistan 84
Asia 2 713

U. S. S. R.
Moscow
NORWAY
SWEDEN
FINLAND
Helsinki
Oslo
Stockholm
Faeroe Is. (Den.)
DENMARK
Copenhagen
REP. OF IRELAND
Dublin
UNITED KINGDOM
London
Amsterdam
NETH.
BELG.
Brussels
LUX.
E. GER.
Berlin
Bonn
W. GER.
POLAND
Warsaw
Prague
CZECH.
Paris
FRANCE
SWITZ.
Bern
AUST.
Vienna
HUNGARY
Budapest
ROMANIA
Bucharest
Belgrade
YUGOSLAVIA
BULGARIA
Sofia
ITALY
Rome
Tirane
ALB.
GREECE
Athens
PORTUGAL
Lisbon
SPAIN
Madrid
TURKEY
Ankara
Nicosia
CYPRUS
SYRIA
Damascus
LEBANON
ISRAEL
JORDAN
Baghdad
IRAQ
KUWAIT
IRAN
Tehran
BAHRAIN
QATAR
Riyadh
SAUDI ARABIA
U.A.E.
Abu Dhabi
Muscat
OMAN
YEMEN
San'a
YEMEN P.D.R.
Aden
DJIBOUTI
AFGHANISTAN
Kabul
Islamabad
PAKISTAN
Delhi
INDIA
NEPAL
Katmandu
BHUTAN
Thimpu
Dakha
BANGLA DESH
BURMA
Rangoon
Colombo
SRI LANKA
MALDIVES
MONGOLIA
Ulan Bator
CHINA
Peking (Beijing)
NORTH KOREA
Pyongyang
SOUTH KOREA
Seoul
JAPAN
Tokyo
Taipei
TAIWAN
Hong Kong (U.K.)
Hanoi
Vientiane
LAOS
VIETNAM
THAILAND
Bangkok
KAMPUCHEA
Phnom Penh
Manila
PHILIPPINES
MALAYSIA
BRUNEI
Kuala Lumpur
SINGAPORE
INDONESIA
Jakarta
PAPUA – NEW GUINEA
Port Moresby
NAURU
SOLOMON IS.
Honiara
TUVALU
VANUATU
Port Vila
FIJI
Suva
New Caledonia (Fr.)
Noumea
AUSTRALIA
Canberra
NEW ZEALAND
Wellington
Kerguelen Is. (Fr.)
MOROCCO
Rabat
Algiers
ALGERIA
Tunis
TUNISIA
MALTA
Tarabulus
LIBYA
Cairo
EGYPT
MAURITANIA
Nouakchott
MALI
Bamako
NIGER
Niamey
Ougadougou
BURKINA
CHAD
N'Djamena
SUDAN
Khartoum
ETHIOPIA
Addis Ababa
SOMALIA
Mogadiscio
GUINEA
LIBERIA
Monrovia
CÔTE D'IVOIRE
Yamoussoukro
GHANA
Accra
TOGO
Lomé
BENIN
Cotonou
NIGERIA
Abuja
CENT. AFRICAN REP.
Bangui
CAMEROUN
Yaounde
Malabo
EQ. GUINEA
Libreville
GABON
CONGO
Brazzaville
Kinshasa
ZAÏRE
UGANDA
Kampala
KENYA
Nairobi
RWANDA
BURUNDI
TANZANIA
Dar es Salaam
SEYCHELLES
Luanda
ANGOLA
ZAMBIA
Lusaka
MALAWI
Lilongwe
COMORES
Harare
ZIMBABWE
MOZAMBIQUE
MADAGASCAR
Antananarivo
MAURITIUS
Réunion (Fr.)
NAMIBIA
Windhoek
BOTSWANA
Gaberone
Pretoria
Maputo
Mbabane
SWAZILAND
REPUBLIC OF SOUTH AFRICA
Maseru
LESOTHO
xford University Press
60
70
80
90
100%
Canada 9976
U.S.A. 9363
Greenland 2176
Brazil 8512
Argentina 2767
Mexico 1973
Colombia 1139
Bolivia 1099
Venezuela 912
Chile 757
All other countries
Australia 7687
New Zealand 269
European U.S.S.R.
France 547
Spain 505
Sweden 450
All other countries
Northern America 21 515 000
Central and South America 20 566 000
Antarctica 14 000 000
Oceania 8 510 000
Europe including European U.S.S.R. 8137000
60
70
80
90
100%
South Korea 38
Burma 33
Asian U.S.S.R. 134
All other countries
Nigeria 79
Egypt 43
Ethiopia 32
South Africa 30
Zaire 26
Morocco 20
Algeria 20
Sudan 18
Tanzania 17
All other countries
U.S.A. 229
Canada 24
Brazil 121
Mexico 71
Colombia 28
Argentina 28
Peru 17
Venezuela 14
All other countries
European U.S.S.R. 148
West Germany 61
Italy 56
United Kingdom 55
France 53
Spain 37
Poland 36
Yugoslavia 22
Romania 22
All other countries
Africa 469
Northern America 248
Central and South America 463
Oceania 22
Europe 632

World: Physical

The Moving Continents

250 million years ago — Permian

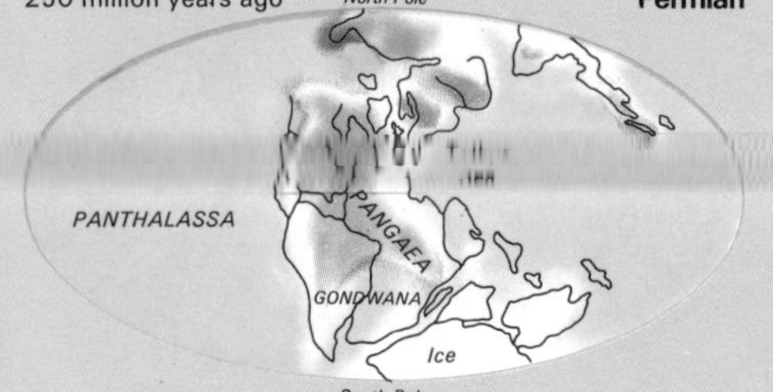

North Pole

PANTHALASSA

PANGAEA

GONDWANA

Ice

South Pole

180 million years ago — Jurassic

North Pole

LAURASIA

Tethys Sea

PANTHALASSA

PANGAEA

GONDWANA

South Pole

120 million years ago — Cretaceous

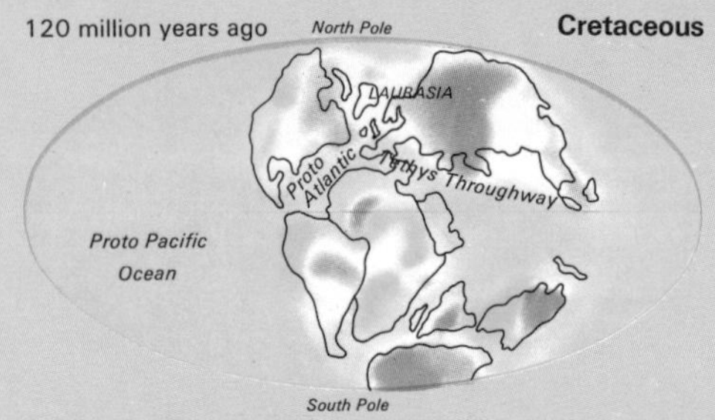

North Pole

LAURASIA

Proto Atlantic

Tethys Throughway

Proto Pacific Ocean

South Pole

60 million years ago — Tertiary

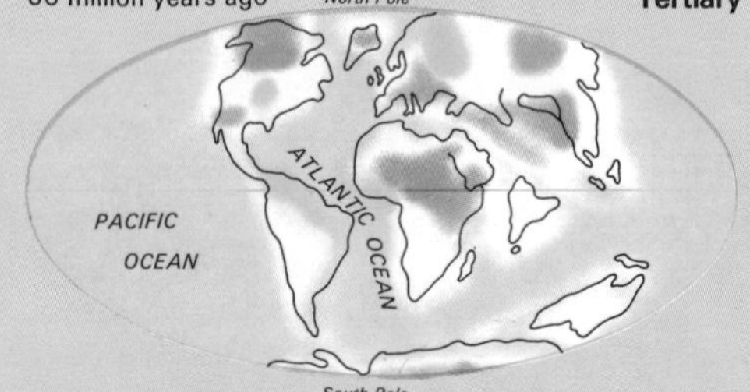

North Pole

ATLANTIC OCEAN

PACIFIC OCEAN

South Pole

Approximate distribution of land and sea

- Land
- Shallow seas
- Ocean

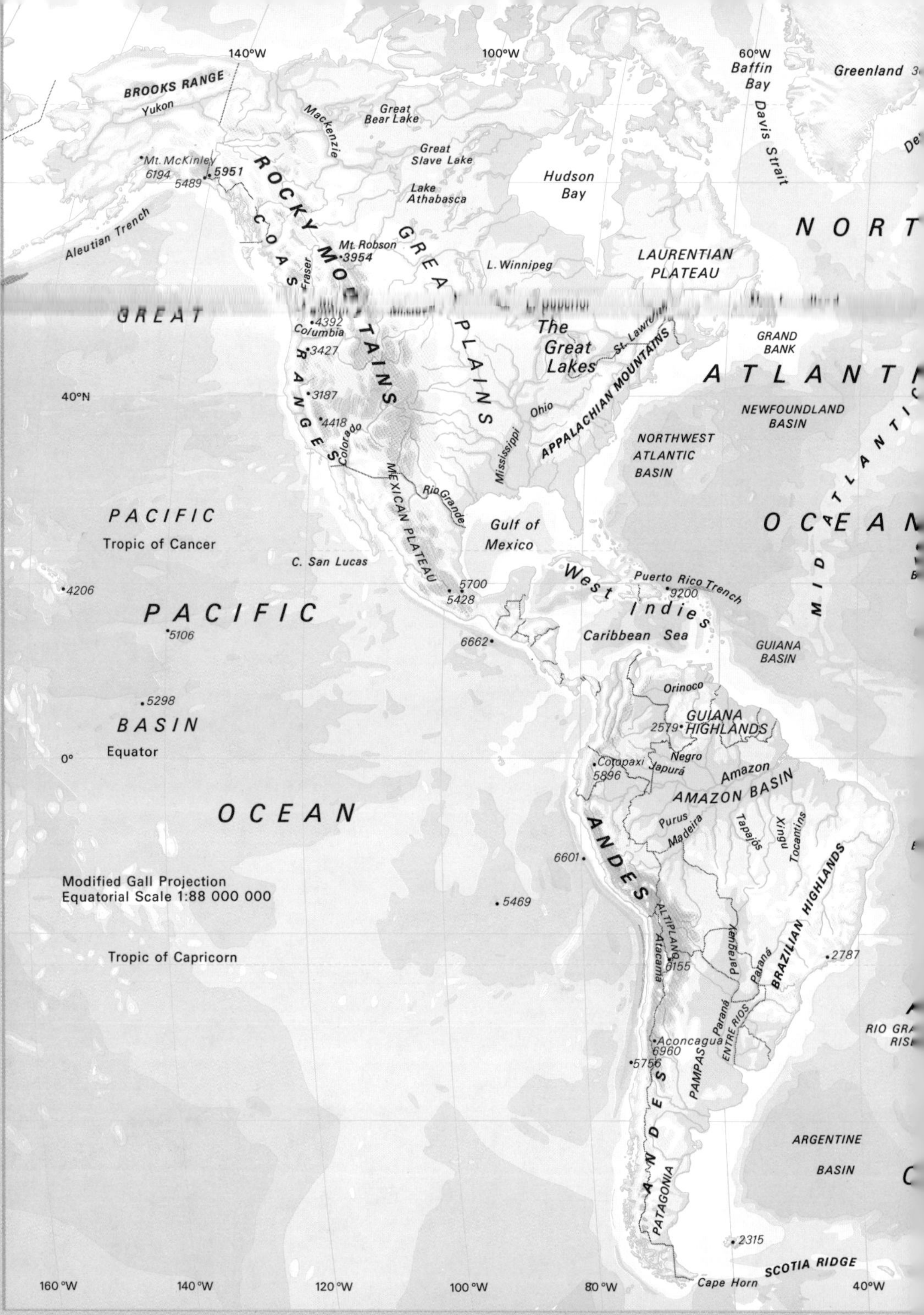

140°W 100°W 60°W

BROOKS RANGE

Yukon

Mt. McKinley 6194

5489 5951

Aleutian Trench

Mackenzie

Great Bear Lake

Great Slave Lake

Lake Athabasca

Hudson Bay

Baffin Bay

Davis Strait

Greenland

ROCKY MOUNTAINS

COAST RANGES

Mt. Robson 3954

Fraser

GREAT PLAINS

L. Winnipeg

LAURENTIAN PLATEAU

NORTH

GREAT

4392 Columbia

3427

3187

4418

Colorado

The Great Lakes

St. Lawrence

APPALACHIAN MOUNTAINS

Ohio

Mississippi

GRAND BANK

ATLANTIC

NEWFOUNDLAND BASIN

NORTHWEST ATLANTIC BASIN

40°N

MEXICAN PLATEAU

Rio Grande

Gulf of Mexico

PACIFIC

Tropic of Cancer

C. San Lucas

OCEAN

4206

PACIFIC

5106

5700 5428

West Indies

Puerto Rico Trench 9200

Caribbean Sea

6662

GUIANA BASIN

MID ATLANTIC

5298

BASIN

Equator

Orinoco

GUIANA HIGHLANDS

2579

0°

Cotopaxi 5896

Negro

Japurá

Amazon

AMAZON BASIN

OCEAN

Purus

Madeira

Tapajós

Xingu

Tocantins

ANDES

6601

Modified Gall Projection
Equatorial Scale 1:88 000 000

5469

ALTIPLANO

Atacama

6155

Paraguay

Paraná

BRAZILIAN HIGHLANDS

2787

Tropic of Capricorn

ENTRE RIOS

Aconcagua 6960

5756

PAMPAS

RIO GRANDE RISE

ANDES

ARGENTINE BASIN

PATAGONIA

2315

SCOTIA RIDGE

Cape Horn

160°W 140°W 120°W 100°W 80°W 40°W

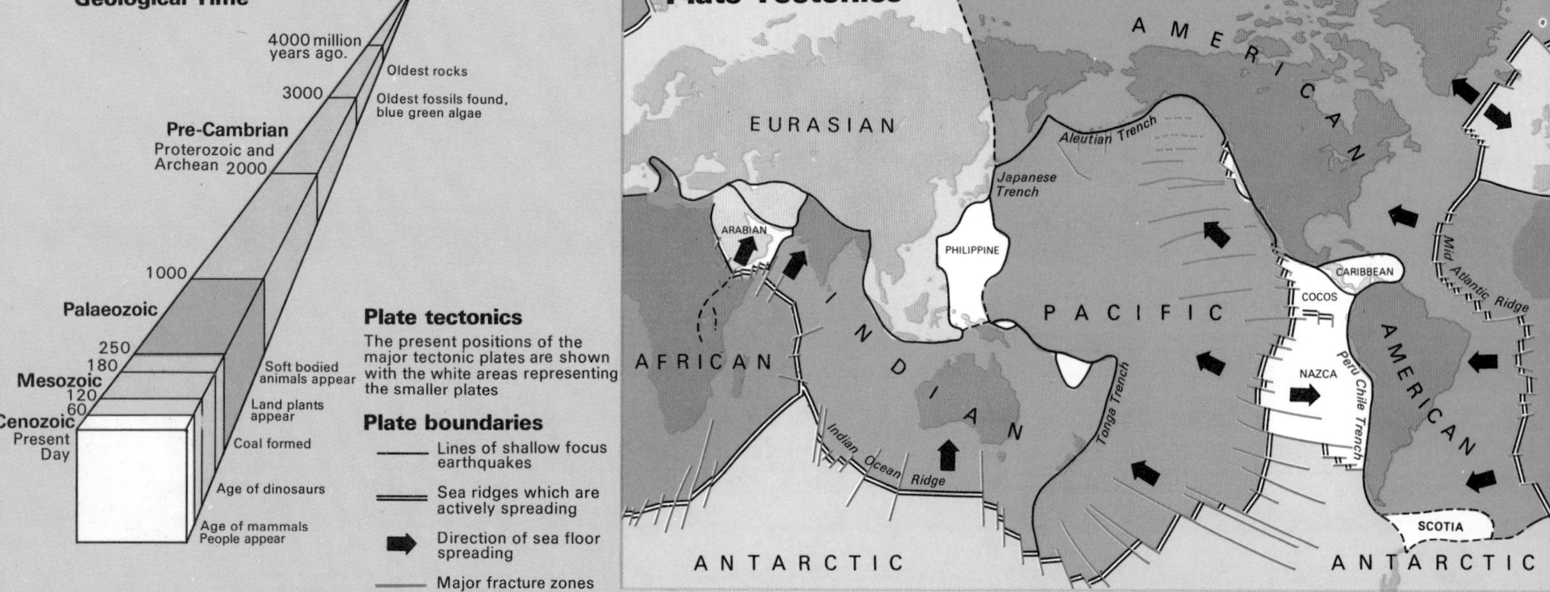

Geological Time
4000 million years ago.
Oldest rocks
3000
Oldest fossils found, blue green algae
Pre-Cambrian
Proterozoic and Archean 2000
1000
Palaeozoic
250
180
Mesozoic
120
60
Cenozoic
Present Day
Soft bodied animals appear
Land plants appear
Coal formed
Age of dinosaurs
Age of mammals
People appear
Plate Tectonics
EURASIAN
AMERICAN
Aleutian Trench
Japanese Trench
PHILIPPINE
ARABIAN
AFRICAN
INDIAN
PACIFIC
CARIBBEAN
COCOS
NAZCA
Peru Chile Trench
Mid Atlantic Ridge
AMERICAN
Tonga Trench
Indian Ocean Ridge
SCOTIA
ANTARCTIC
ANTARCTIC

Plate tectonics

The present positions of the major tectonic plates are shown with the white areas representing the smaller plates

Plate boundaries

- Lines of shallow focus earthquakes
- Sea ridges which are actively spreading
- Direction of sea floor spreading
- Major fracture zones

Arctic Circle
Norwegian Sea
Iceland
Hekla 1491
Scandinavia
Lapland
G. of Bothnia
North Sea
Baltic Sea
L. Ladoga
British Isles
Rhine
NORTH EUROPEAN PLAIN
CARPATHIANS
ALPS
Danube
BALKAN MTS.
APENNINES
PYRENEES
3404
Iberia
1186
Mediterranean Sea
Etna 3263
Dnepr
Ukraine
Black Sea
Mt. Elbrus 5633
CAUCASUS MTS.
ANATOLIAN PLATEAU
Mt. Ararat 5156
TAURUS MTS.
ELBURZ MTS.
5604
ZAGROS MTS.
MESOPOTAMIA
Caspian Sea
Volga
Ural
North Dvina
Pechora
1894
URAL MOUNTAINS
Ob
WEST SIBERIAN PLAIN
Yenisey
1701
CENTRAL SIBERIAN PLATEAU
Angara
Lena
VERKHOYANSK RANGE
CHERSKOGO RANGE
2959
KOLYMA PLAIN
YUKAGIR PLAIN
ANADYR RANGE
GYDAN RA.
KORAK RA.
KAMCHATKA PENIN.
4750
Bering Sea
Sea of Okhotsk
STANOVOY RA
L. Baykal
SAYAN MTS.
4506
ALTAI RA.
KAZAKH UPLANDS
Aral Sea
L. Balkhash
TURANIAN PLATEAU
Communism Peak 7495
PAMIRS
TIEN SHAN
Turfan Depr. −154
TARIM BASIN
ALTYN TAGH
NAN SHAN
HINDU KUSH
8611
KUNLUN SHAN
PLATEAU OF TIBET
HIMALAYAS
7728
8848 Mt. Everest
Indus
INDO-GANGETIC PLAIN
Ganges
DECCAN
Gobi
GREAT KHINGAN MTS.
Amur
MANCHURIAN PLAIN
SIKHOTE ALIN RA.
2290
Sea of Japan
Honshu
Hwang
GREAT BASIN
Yellow Sea
RED BASIN
Chang
East China Sea
NAN LING
Xi
Ryukyu Trench
Kuril-Kamchatka Trench
Aleutian Trench
Emperor Seamount Chain
NORTHWEST PACIFIC BASIN
PACIFIC OCEAN
Philippine Sea
Mariana Trench
8724
Challenger Deep 11 022
Micronesia
2928
Philippine Trench
Mekong
2598
South China Sea
Irrawaddy
Mt. Kinabalu 4101
Celebes Sea
WEST CAROLINE BASIN
EAST CAROLINE BASIN
Melanesia
Str. of Malacca
3800
Borneo
East Indies
Java Sea
Banda Sea
5030 Mt. Jaya
New Guinea
3676
Java Trench
Arafura Sea
Torres Str.
Coral Sea
Qattara Depression −133
Dead Sea −392
An Nafūd
The Gulf
Red Sea
Najd
Rub' al Khālī
Sahara
AHAGGAR
TIBESTI
3415
ATLAS MTS.
4165
4645
Nile
L. Chad
Niger
GUINEA PLATEAU
Mt. Cameroun 4070
Gulf of Guinea
GUINEA BASIN
Blue Nile
White Nile
3600
4620
G. of Aden
ETHIOPIAN HIGHLANDS
Uele
CONGO BASIN
Lualaba
Zaire
Kasai
5199
L. Victoria
Kilimanjaro 5895
L. Tanganyika
L. Nyasa (Malawi)
Zambezi
Victoria Falls
Limpopo
2610
2484
Kalahari
Orange
DRAKENSBERG
3657
Cape of Good Hope
CAPE BASIN
ANGOLA BASIN
6050
Mozambique Channel
Madagascar
2886
Arabian Sea
W. GHATS
E. GHATS
Bay of Bengal
SOMALI BASIN
5340
CHAGOS–LACCADIVE RIDGE
SEYCHELLES RIDGE
INDIAN OCEAN
MID INDIAN BASIN
6090
NINETY EAST RIDGE
COCOS BASIN
WEST AUSTRALIAN BASIN
MADAGASCAR BASIN
SOUTHWEST INDIAN RIDGE
SOUTHEAST INDIAN RIDGE
CROZET BASIN
ATLANTIC–INDIAN RIDGE
SOUTH ATLANTIC
MID ATLANTIC RIDGE
1226
1510
LAKE EYRE −12 BASIN
Great Victoria Desert
GREAT DIVIDING RANGE
Murray
Mt. Kosciusko 2230
Bass Str.
SOUTH AUSTRALIAN BASIN
Tasman Sea
LORD HOWE RISE
North I.
2795
South I.
S. ALPS
3764 Mt. Cook
7570
SOUTH FIJI BASIN
5080
20°E
40°E
60°E
80°E
100°E
120°E
140°E
160°E
60°N
40°N
20°N
0°
20°S
© Oxford University Press
Scale 1:352 000 000
Scale 1:352 000 000
Relief
metres
5000
3000
2000
1000
500
300
200
100
Sea level
Land depression
200
3000
4000
5000
6000
Spot heights in metres

Earthquakes and Volcanoes

Principal earthquake zones

- Areas with a high frequency of earthquakes
- Areas with a lower frequency of earthquakes
- · Active volcanoes

Most earthquake zones coincide with active volcanic districts but this is not always so. From these bands of high earthquake frequency can be deduced the outline of the plates, as major changes in the earth's surface occur only along the plate boundaries

Natural Hazards

- Areas where severe droughts may occur
- Major river floodplains, some partially controlled
- • High risk of cyclonic storms causing devastation and flooding
- Coasts vulnerable to tsunamis (seismic sea waves)
- Recent bush fire disasters

World: Climate

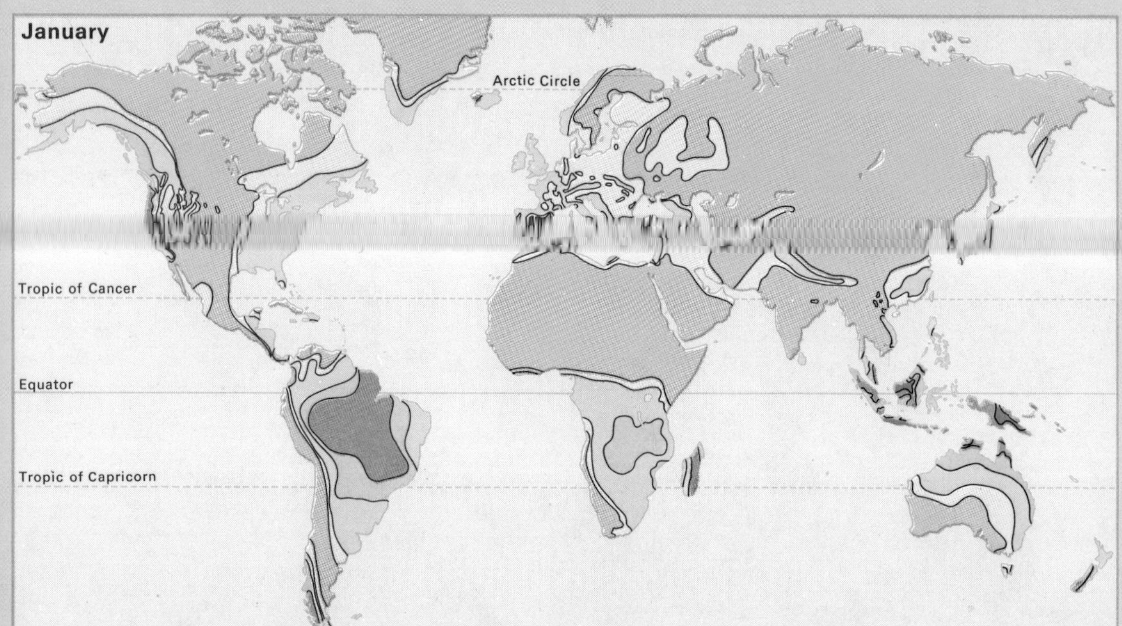
January
Arctic Circle
Tropic of Cancer
Equator
Tropic of Capricorn

Precipitation

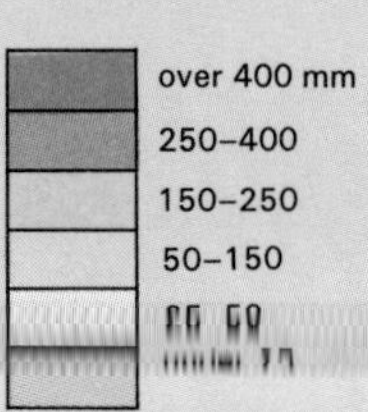
over 400 mm
250–400
150–250
50–150

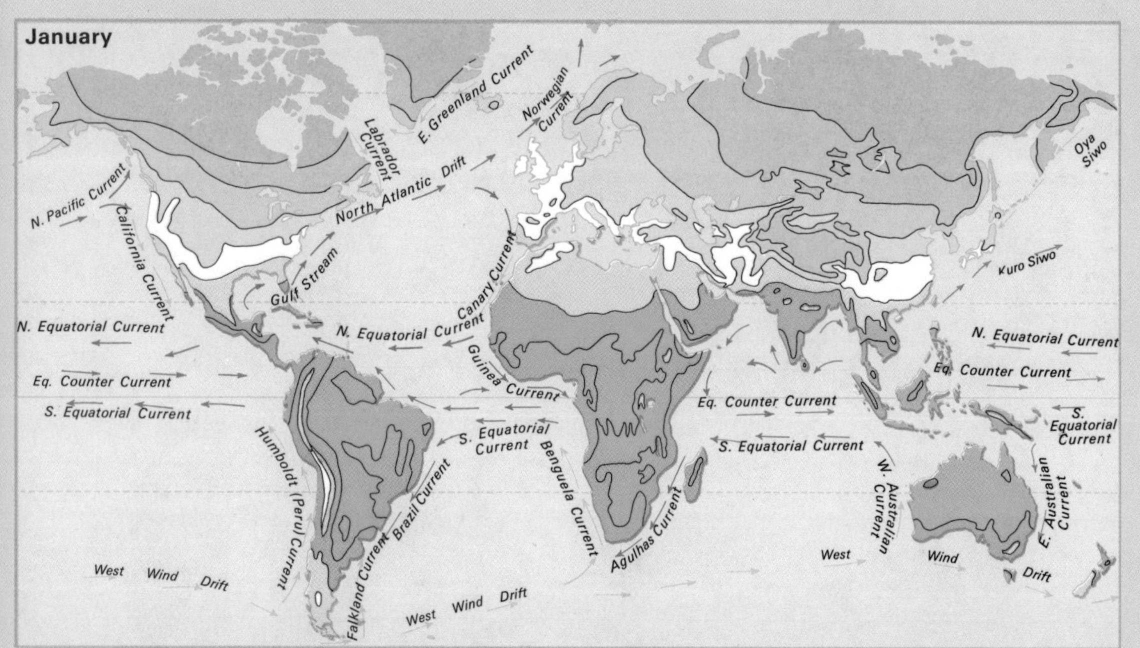
January
E. Greenland Current
Norwegian Current
Labrador Current
Oya Siwo
N. Pacific Current
North Atlantic Drift
California Current
Gulf Stream
Canary Current
Kuro Siwo
N. Equatorial Current
N. Equatorial Current
N. Equatorial Current
Eq. Counter Current
Guinea Current
Eq. Counter Current
Eq. Counter Current
S. Equatorial Current
S. Equatorial Current
S. Equatorial Current
S. Equatorial Current
Humboldt (Peru) Current
Brazil Current
Benguela Current
W. Australian Current
E. Australian Current
Agulhas Current
Falkland Current
West Wind Drift
West Wind Drift
West Wind Drift

Temperature and Ocean Currents

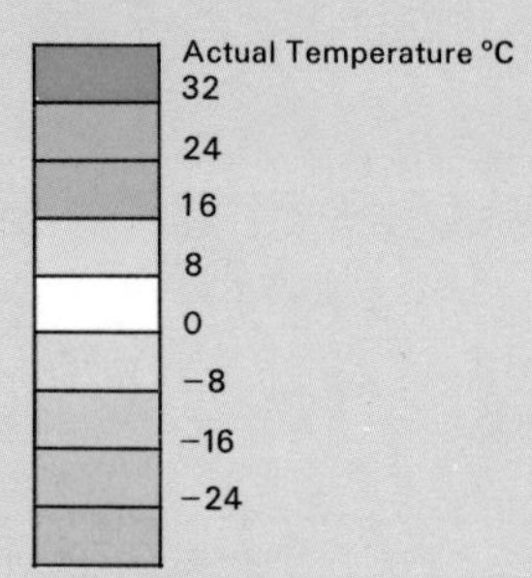
Actual Temperature °C
32
24
16
8
0
−8
−16
−24

Ocean Currents

Cold

Warm

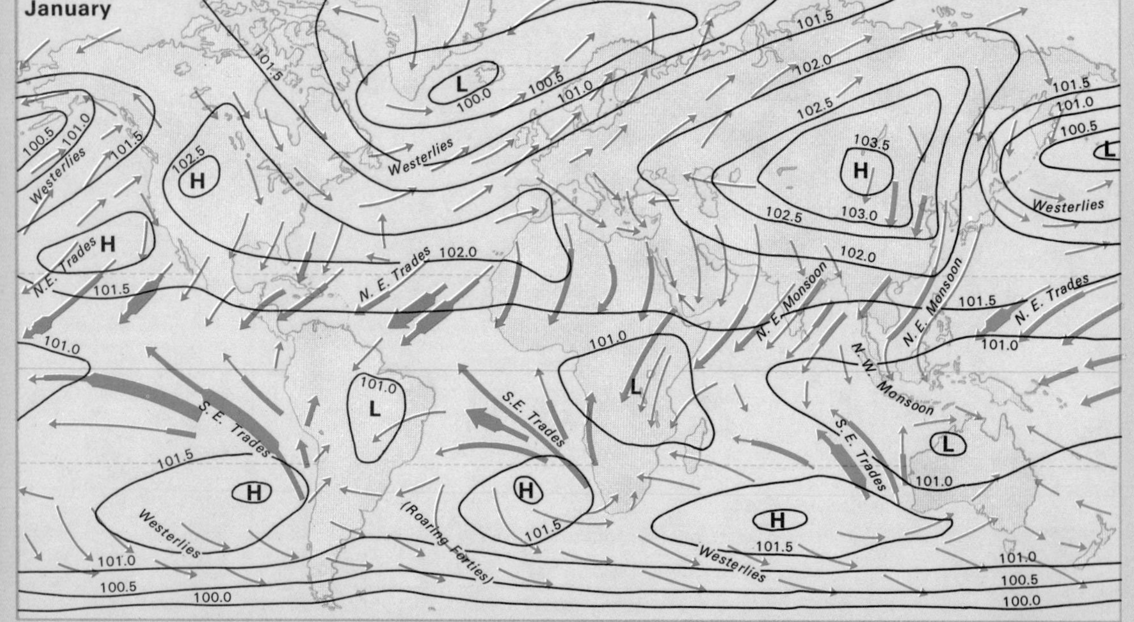
January
Westerlies
Westerlies
Westerlies
N.E. Trades
N. E. Trades
N. E. Trades
N. E. Monsoon
N. E. Monsoon
N.W. Monsoon
S. E. Trades
S.E. Trades
S.E. Trades
Westerlies
(Roaring Forties)
Westerlies
H
L
101.5
102.0
102.5
103.0
103.5
101.0
100.5
100.0

Pressure and Winds

Pressure

Kilopascals (KPa)	103.5
	103.0
	102.5
	102.0
	101.5
	101.0
	100.5
	100.0
	99.5
H	High pressure cell
L	Low pressure cell

Prevailing Winds

Arrows fly with the wind: the heavier the arrow, the more regular ('constant') the direction of the wind

Modified Gall Projection

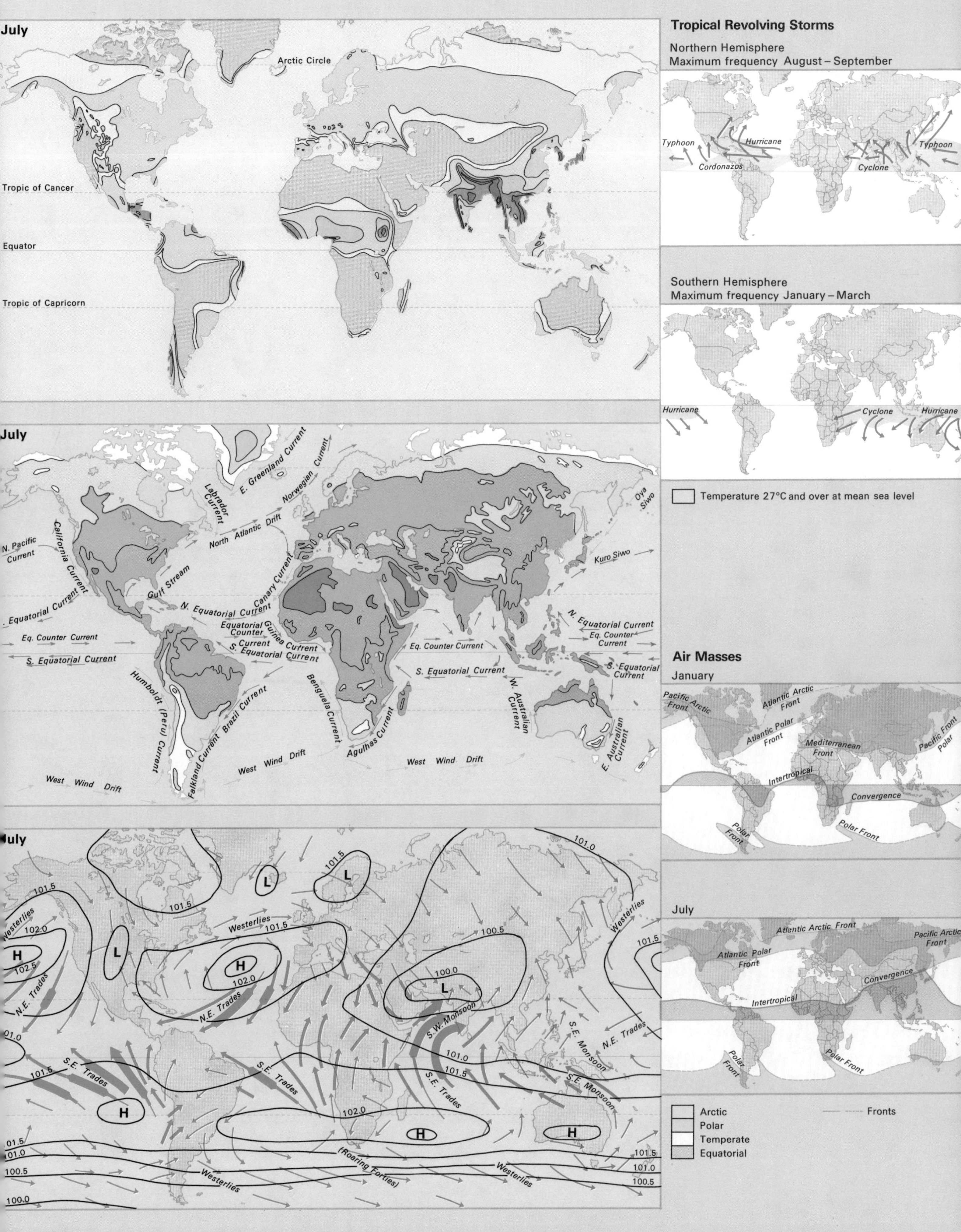
July
Arctic Circle
Tropic of Cancer
Equator
Tropic of Capricorn
July
E. Greenland Current
Norwegian Current
Labrador Current
North Atlantic Drift
Oya Siwo
N. Pacific Current
California Current
Kuro Siwo
Gulf Stream
Canary Current
N. Equatorial Current
Equatorial Counter Current
Guinea Current
S. Equatorial Current
Eq. Counter Current
S. Equatorial Current
N. Equatorial Current
Eq. Counter Current
S. Equatorial Current
Humboldt (Peru) Current
Brazil Current
Benguela Current
Agulhas Current
W. Australian Current
E. Australian Current
Falkland Current
West Wind Drift
July
Westerlies
N.E. Trades
S.E. Trades
S.W. Monsoon
S.E. Monsoon
(Roaring Forties)
H
L
101.5
102.0
102.5
101.0
100.5
100.0
Tropical Revolving Storms
Northern Hemisphere
Maximum frequency August – September
Typhoon
Hurricane
Cordonazos
Cyclone
Southern Hemisphere
Maximum frequency January – March
Hurricane
Cyclone
Temperature 27°C and over at mean sea level
Air Masses
January
Pacific Arctic Front
Atlantic Arctic Front
Atlantic Polar Front
Mediterranean Front
Pacific Polar Front
Intertropical
Convergence
Polar Front
July
Atlantic Arctic Front
Pacific Arctic Front
Atlantic Polar Front
Convergence
Intertropical
Polar Front
Arctic
Polar
Temperate
Equatorial
Fronts

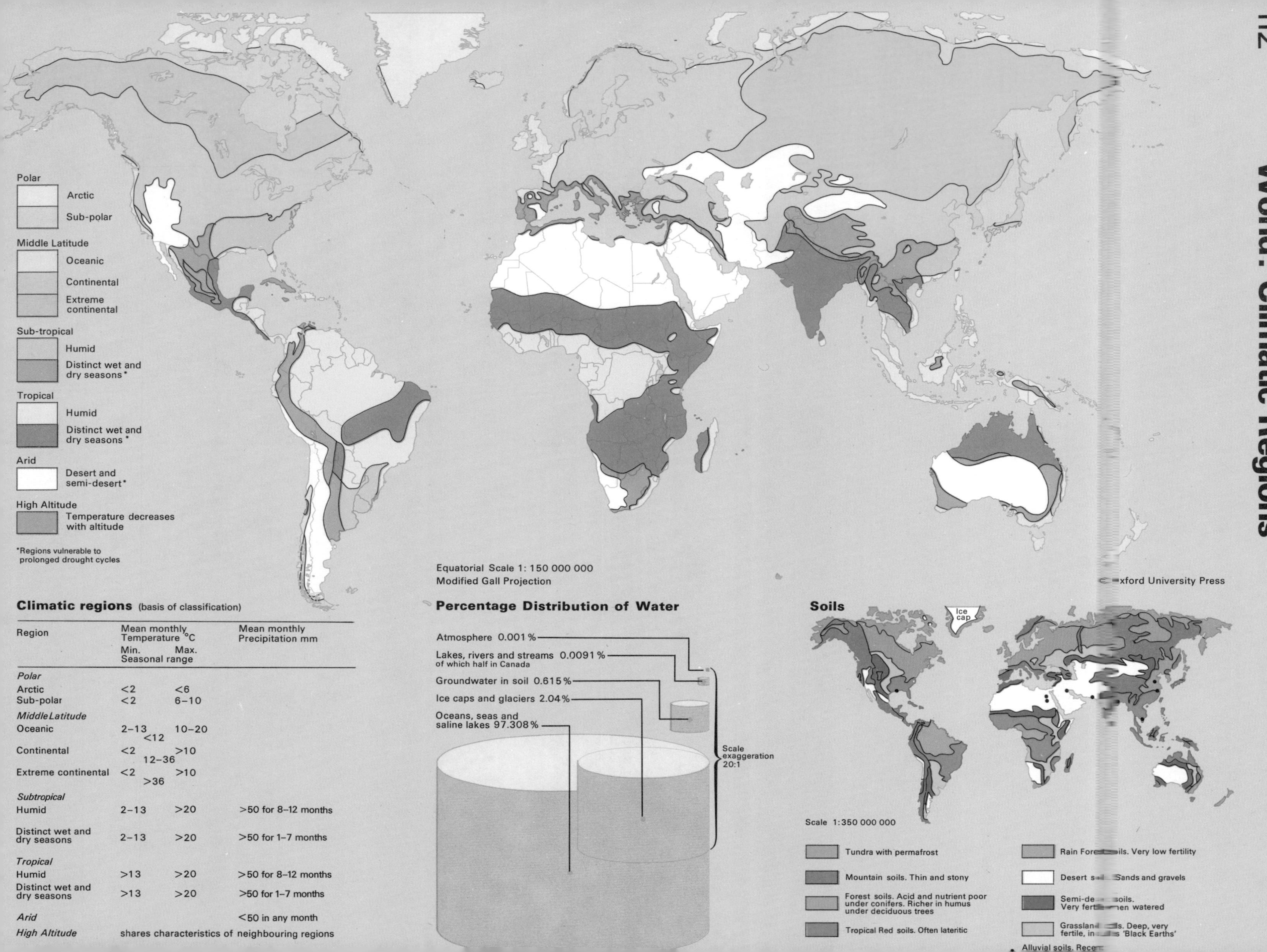

Polar
Arctic
Sub-polar
Middle Latitude
Oceanic
Continental
Extreme continental
Sub-tropical
Humid
Distinct wet and dry seasons*
Tropical
Humid
Distinct wet and dry seasons*
Arid
Desert and semi-desert*
High Altitude
Temperature decreases with altitude
*Regions vulnerable to prolonged drought cycles
Equatorial Scale 1: 150 000 000
Modified Gall Projection
xford University Press
Percentage Distribution of Water
Atmosphere 0.001%
Lakes, rivers and streams 0.0091% of which half in Canada
Groundwater in soil 0.615%
Ice caps and glaciers 2.04%
Oceans, seas and saline lakes 97.308%
Scale exaggeration 20:1
Soils
Ice cap
Scale 1:350 000 000
Tundra with permafrost
Mountain soils. Thin and stony
Forest soils. Acid and nutrient poor under conifers. Richer in humus under deciduous trees
Tropical Red soils. Often lateritic
Rain Fore ils. Very low fertility
Desert s Sands and gravels
Semi-de soils.
Very fert en watered
Deep, very fertile, 'Black Earths'
Alluvial soils. Rece

Climatic regions (basis of classification)

Region	Mean monthly Temperature °C Min.	Max.	Seasonal range	Mean monthly Precipitation mm
Polar				
Arctic	<2	<6		
Sub-polar	<2	6–10		
Middle Latitude				
Oceanic	2–13	10–20	<12	
Continental	<2	>10	12–36	
Extreme continental	<2	>10	>36	
Subtropical				
Humid	2–13	>20		>50 for 8–12 months
Distinct wet and dry seasons	2–13	>20		>50 for 1–7 months
Tropical				
Humid	>13	>20		>50 for 8–12 months
Distinct wet and dry seasons	>13	>20		>50 for 1–7 months
Arid				<50 in any month
High Altitude	shares characteristics of neighbouring regions			

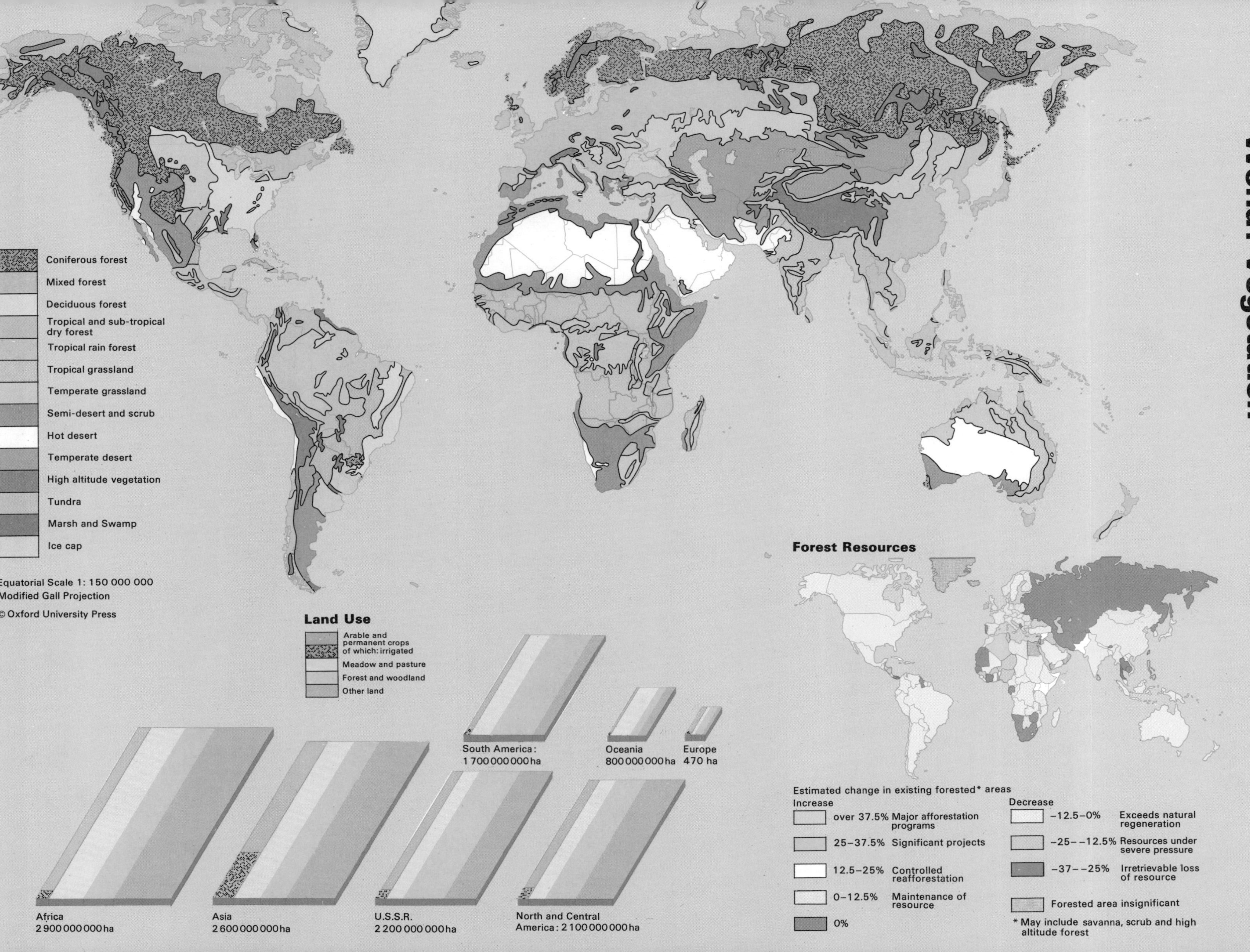

Coniferous forest
Mixed forest
Deciduous forest
Tropical and sub-tropical dry forest
Tropical rain forest
Tropical grassland
Temperate grassland
Semi-desert and scrub
Hot desert
Temperate desert
High altitude vegetation
Tundra
Marsh and Swamp
Ice cap
Equatorial Scale 1: 150 000 000
Modified Gall Projection
© Oxford University Press
Land Use
Arable and permanent crops
of which: irrigated
Meadow and pasture
Forest and woodland
Other land
Africa 2 900 000 000 ha
Asia 2 600 000 000 ha
U.S.S.R. 2 200 000 000 ha
South America: 1 700 000 000 ha
North and Central America: 2 100 000 000 ha
Oceania 800 000 000 ha
Europe 470 ha
Forest Resources
Estimated change in existing forested* areas
Increase
over 37.5% Major afforestation programs
25–37.5% Significant projects
12.5–25% Controlled reafforestation
0–12.5% Maintenance of resource
0%
Decrease
−12.5–0% Exceeds natural regeneration
−25– −12.5% Resources under severe pressure
−37– −25% Irretrievable loss of resource
Forested area insignificant
* May include savanna, scrub and high altitude forest

World: Population

Average Annual Change [illegible] Density [illegible]

Very high increase	Increase above world average	Increase below world average	Decreasing	
				Very dense rural and suburban settlement, large conurbations
				Fairly dense rural settlement, small towns
				Sparse rural settlement
				Isolated settlements only

Modified Gall Projection Equatorial Scale 1:88 000 000

Population growth 1920–1980
projected forward to 2000

thousand million
6.0
5.5
5.0
4.5
4.0
3.5
3.0
2.5
2.0
1.5
1.0
0.5
0
Africa
Northern America
Latin America
Asia
Europe
U.S.S.R.
Oceania
2000
1990
1980
1970
1960
1950
1940
1930
1920

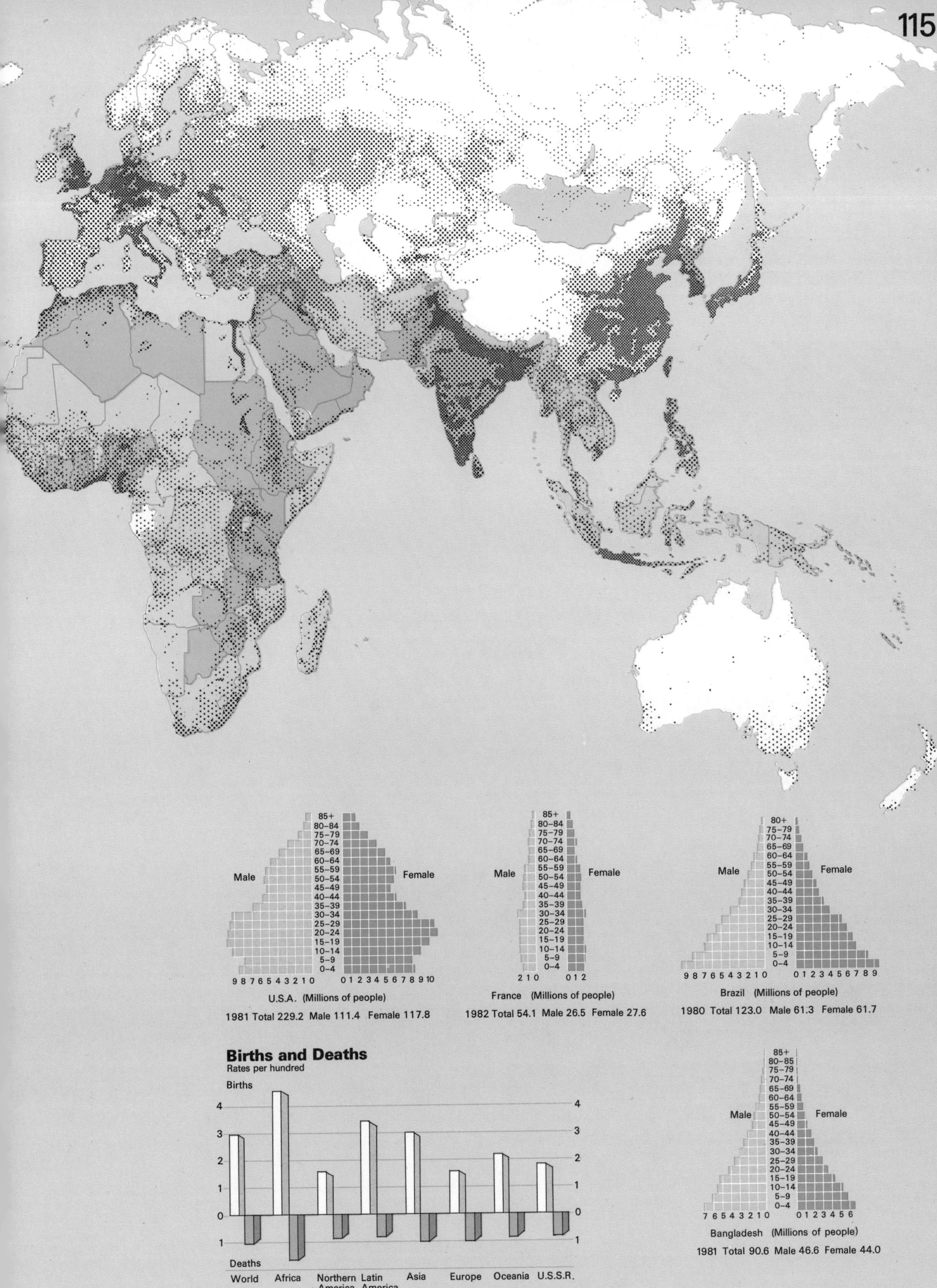

85+
80–84
75–79
70–74
65–69
60–64
55–59
50–54
45–49
40–44
35–39
30–34
25–29
20–24
15–19
10–14
5–9
0–4
Male
Female
9 8 7 6 5 4 3 2 1 0
0 1 2 3 4 5 6 7 8 9 10
U.S.A. (Millions of people)
1981 Total 229.2 Male 111.4 Female 117.8
Male
Female
2 1 0
0 1 2
France (Millions of people)
1982 Total 54.1 Male 26.5 Female 27.6
80+
Male
Female
9 8 7 6 5 4 3 2 1 0
0 1 2 3 4 5 6 7 8 9
Brazil (Millions of people)
1980 Total 123.0 Male 61.3 Female 61.7
Births and Deaths
Rates per hundred
Births
Deaths
World
Africa
Northern America
Latin America
Asia
Europe
Oceania
U.S.S.R.
85+
80–85
Male
Female
7 6 5 4 3 2 1 0
0 1 2 3 4 5 6
Bangladesh (Millions of people)
1981 Total 90.6 Male 46.6 Female 44.0

World: Demography

Life expectancy at birth

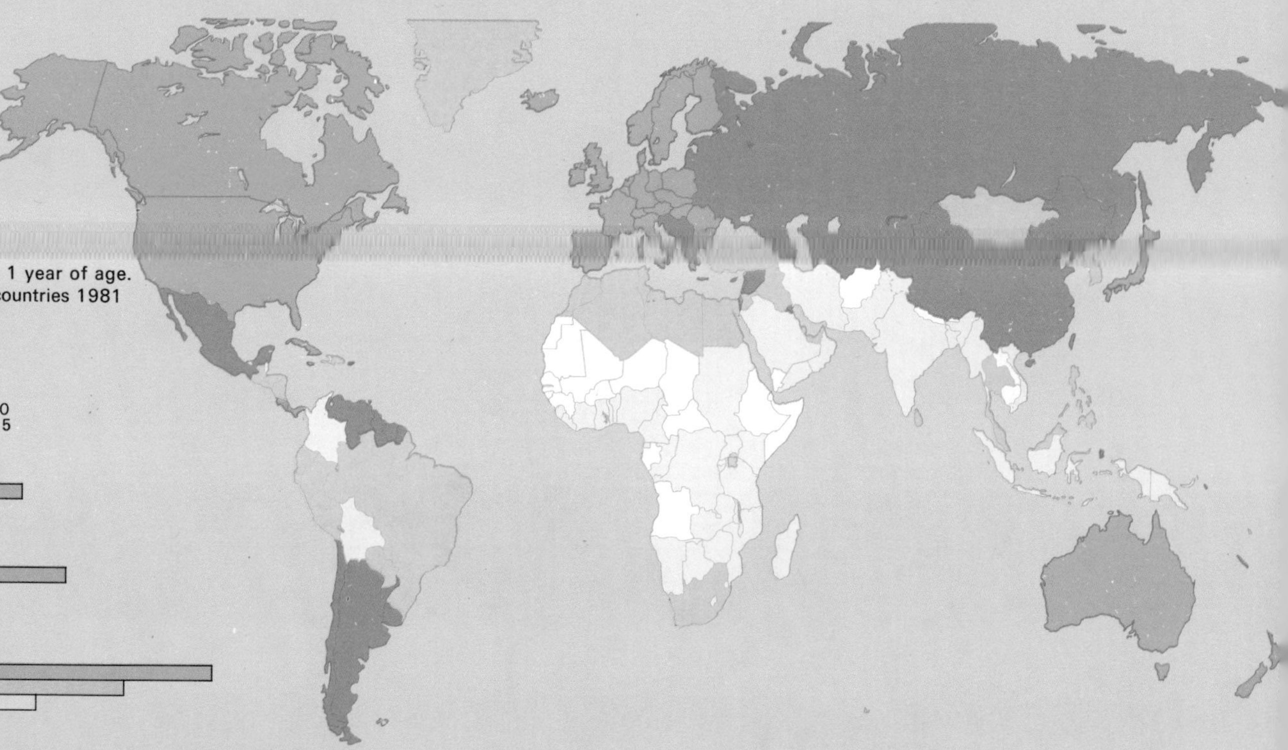

- 34–44.9 years
- 45–54.9 years
- 55–64.9 years
- 65–69.9 years
- over 70 years
- Not available

Infant mortality rates under 1 year of age.
Deaths/10000 for selected countries 1981

Oceania[1]	Australia	3.8
Europe	Yugoslavia	17
	Portugal	10
	Czechoslovakia	5
	Netherlands	2.8
North America	Mexico	26
	U. S. A.	4.3
	Canada	3.7
Asia	Philippines	32
	Iraq	18
	Thailand	8.4
	Japan	2.6
Central and South America	Guatemala	52
	Brazil	40
	Colombia	28
	Venezuela	13
Africa	Egypt	71
	South Africa	White 6 Bantu and others 69
	Kenya	40
	Angola	13

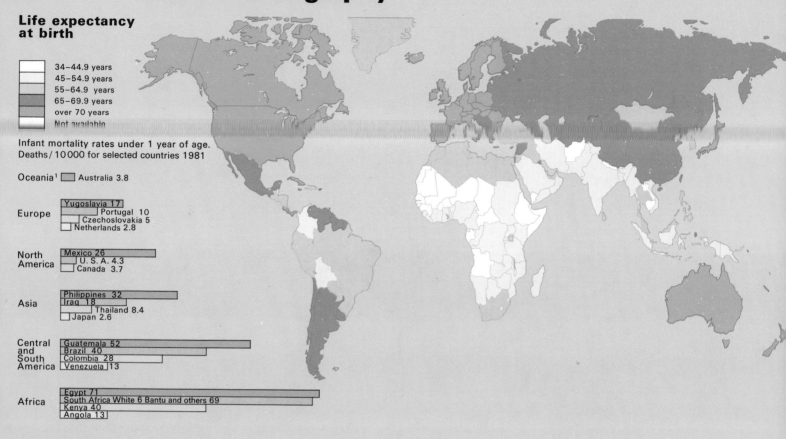

Equatorial Scale 1:180 000 000

Medical care

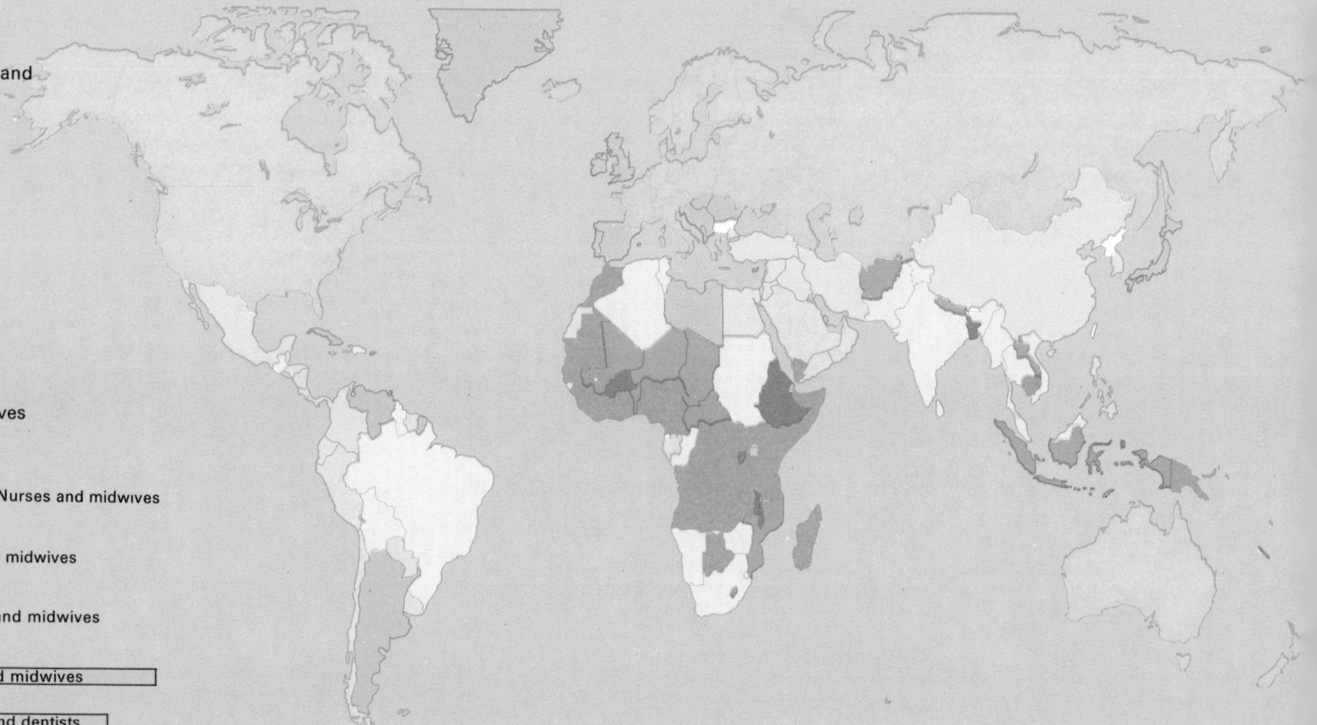

Ratio of doctors, nurses and midwives to population

N.B. Some countries exclude private practice. USSR includes dentists

One to :
- over 25 000
- 10 001 – 25 000
- 5001 – 10 000
- 2501 – 5 000
- 1001 – 2 500
- 500 – 1 000
- Under 500
- No data

Traditional healers excluded

Doctors, nurses and midwives
1:100 000 inhabitants

Region	Doctors	Nurses and midwives
Africa	1.85 Doctors	18.41 Nurses and midwives
Asia	3.48 Doctors	7.06 Nurses and midwives
Central and South America	9.49 Doctors	9.93 Nurses and midwives
Europe	18.12 Doctors	41.27 Nurses and midwives
U.S.S.R.	34.64 Doctors and dentists	61.38 Nurses and midwives
Oceania[1]	12.3 Doctors	66.28 Nurses and midwives
North America	16.89 Doctors	68.39 Nurses and midwives

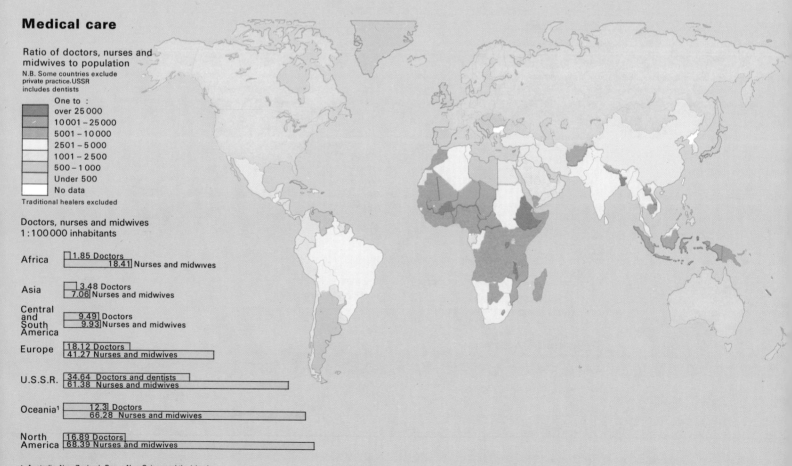

1 Australia, New Zealand, Papua New Guinea and the islands of the South Pacific Ocean

Modified Gall Project

Religion
Predominant affiliation
Christianity
Roman Catholicism
Protestant
Orthodox and Eastern Churches
Sect unspecified
Buddhism
Mahayana
Hinayana
Hinduism
Islam
Sunni
Shia
Tribal
Animist etc.
National
Chinese Confucianism, Taoism, Buddhism
Japan: Shintoism. Buddhism
Judaism
State of Israel
Major communities
(smaller communities are found in most major cities throughout the world)

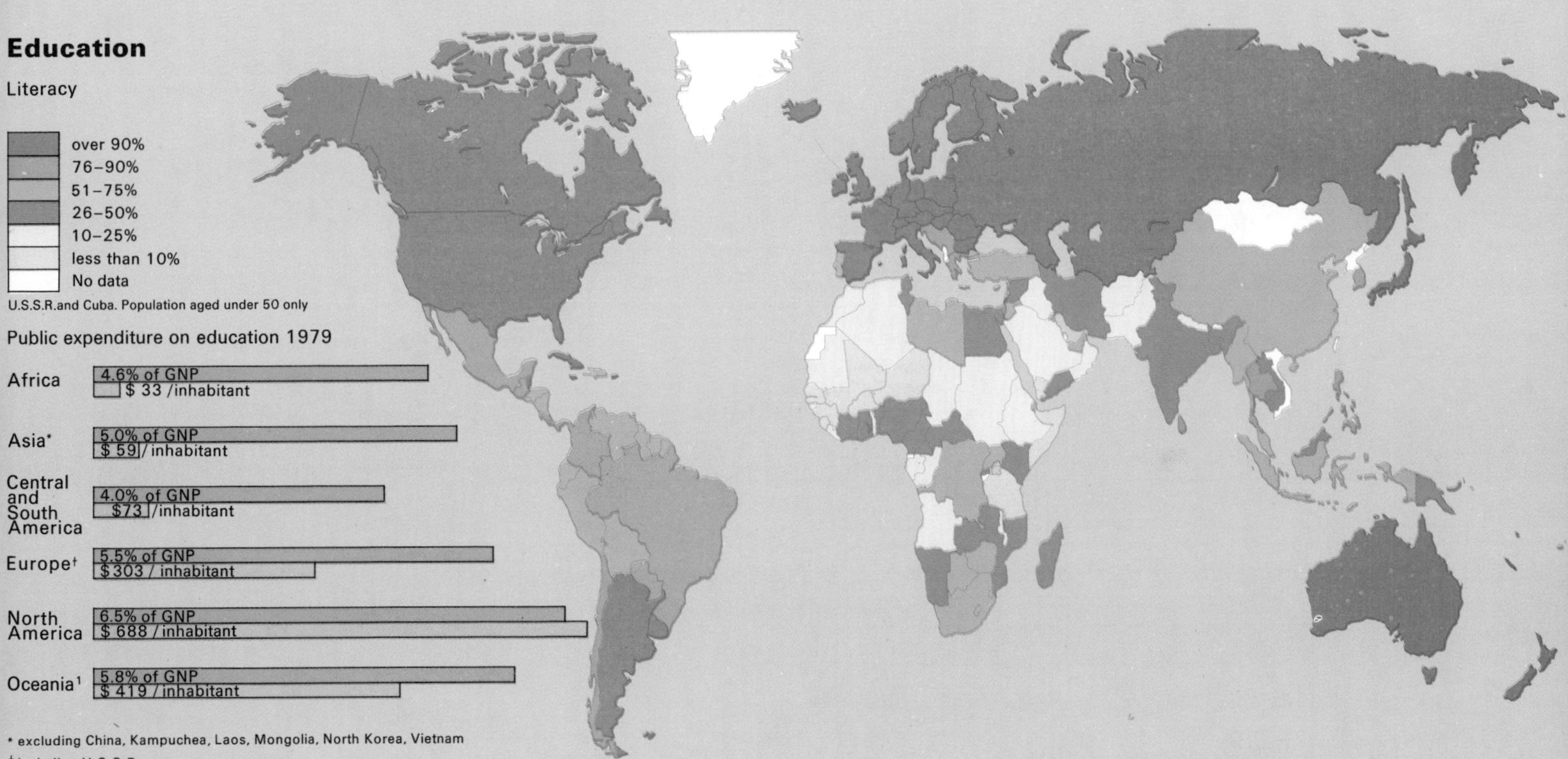
Education
Literacy
over 90%
76–90%
51–75%
26–50%
10–25%
less than 10%
No data
U.S.S.R.and Cuba. Population aged under 50 only
Public expenditure on education 1979
Africa
4.6% of GNP
$ 33 /inhabitant
Asia*
5.0% of GNP
$ 59 /inhabitant
Central and South America
4.0% of GNP
$73 /inhabitant
Europe†
5.5% of GNP
$303 / inhabitant
North America
6.5% of GNP
$ 688 / inhabitant
Oceania[1]
5.8% of GNP
$ 419 / inhabitant

* excluding China, Kampuchea, Laos, Mongolia, North Korea, Vietnam

† including U.S.S.R.

1 Australia, New Zealand, Papua New Guinea and the islands of the South Pacific Ocean

World : Agriculture and Nutrition

Cereals dominant
Mixed farming and dairy
Mixed farming, fruit and vegetables
Mixed farming, cash crops
Ranching and stockraising

Peasant (small holding) farming

Rice dominant
Other cereals dominant
Mixed farming and livestock
Mixed farming, fruit and vegetables
Mixed farming, cash crops
Stock raising

Staples : manioc, cassava, yam, potatoes
Staples : millet, sorghum, barley, rye
Nomadic herding

Forests

Commercially exploited

Non agricultural land

Ice, tundra, swamp, desert, montane and coniferous forest

Fishing

Major fishing grounds

Modified Gall Projection
Equatorial Scale 1:88 000 000

Food Production and Population

as % of world total 1981

Food production
Population

30 %
25
20
15
10
5
0

North America
Western Europe
Oceania[1]
Other

Developed countries

Africa excluding Near East
Latin America
Near and Far East and other

Developing countries

Asia
Eastern Europe and U.S.S.R.

Centrally planned economies

[1]Australia, New Zealand, Papua New Guinea and the islands of the South Pacific Ocean

Average nutritional levels by continent

Fats
Protein
Carbohydrates

0
5
10
15 MJ/day

Africa
Central America and Caribbean
Asia
South America
Oceania
Europe
U. S. A. and Canada

6.7 MJ/d
†FAO minimum requirement for active life

10.8 MJ/d
Average requirement for good health. Individual needs vary with age, sex and occupation

†FAO = Food and Agricultural Organization (of the United Nations)

Nutrition
Average consumption
Megajoules/capita/day[1]
over 12.5
10–12.5
8–9.9
Under 8
No data
Average consumption per head declining
[1] Megajoule = one million joules
Joule = a unit, in this case, for measuring the heat and other energy produced by the metabolism of food.

World: Energy

Solid fuels

Geological Structures

- Ancient shield partly covered by sedimentary rocks
- Fold mountains
- Sedimentary rocks and recent deposits
- Igneous rocks

Producing areas

Coal reserves (000 000t) estimated 1980

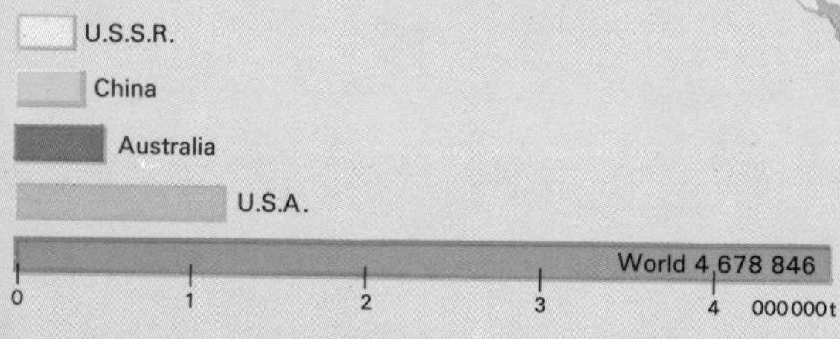

U.S.S.R.
China
Australia
U.S.A.
World 4 678 846

0 1 2 3 4 000 000t

Consumption per capita (t) 1980

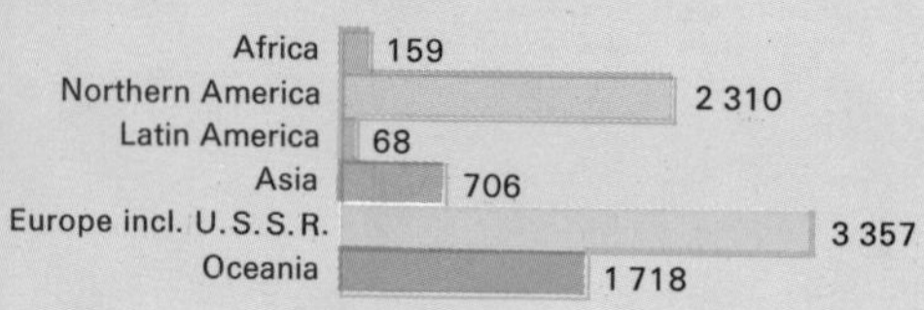

Africa	159
Northern America	2 310
Latin America	68
Asia	706
Europe incl. U.S.S.R.	3 357
Oceania	1 718

Scale 1:180 000 000

Natural Gas

Geological Structures
for key see solid fuels above

Gas fields in production

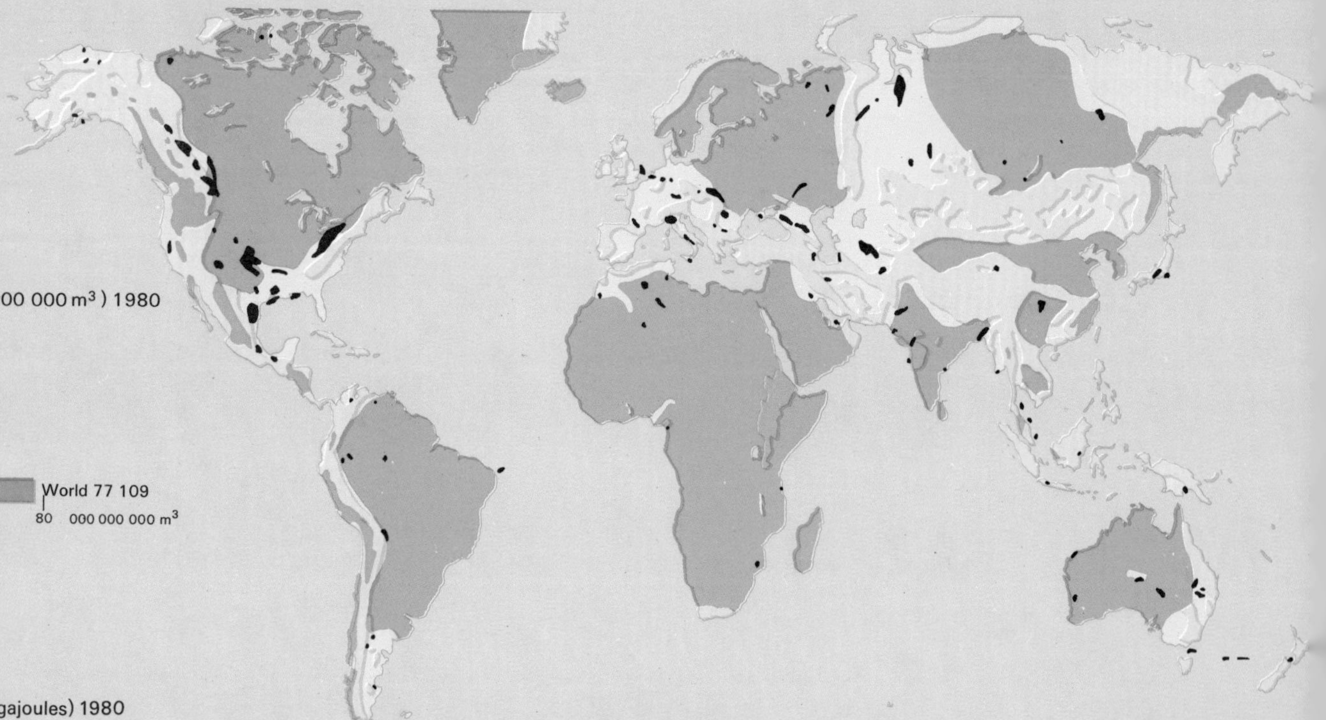

Natural gas reserves (000 000 000 m^3) 1980

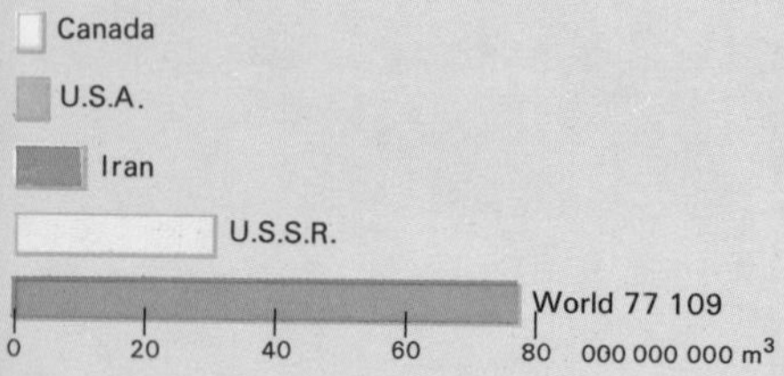

Canada
U.S.A.
Iran
U.S.S.R.
World 77 109

0 20 40 60 80 000 000 000 m^3

Consumption per capita (Megajoules) 1980

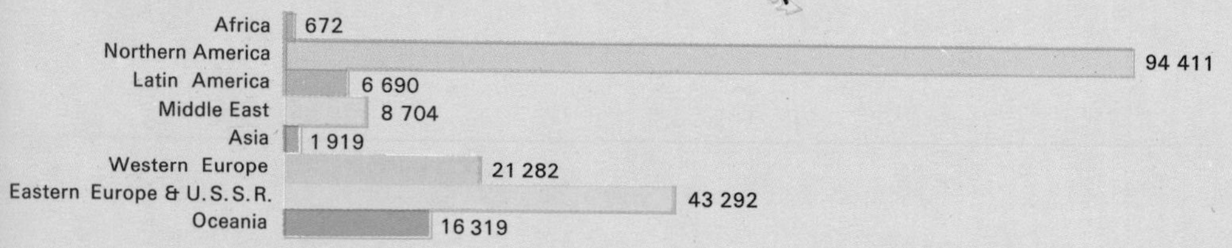

Africa	672
Northern America	94 411
Latin America	6 690
Middle East	8 704
Asia	1 919
Western Europe	21 282
Eastern Europe & U.S.S.R.	43 292
Oceania	16 319

Scale 1:180 000 000

›il

eological Structures
r key see solid fuels opposite

Oil fields in production

Major tanker routes

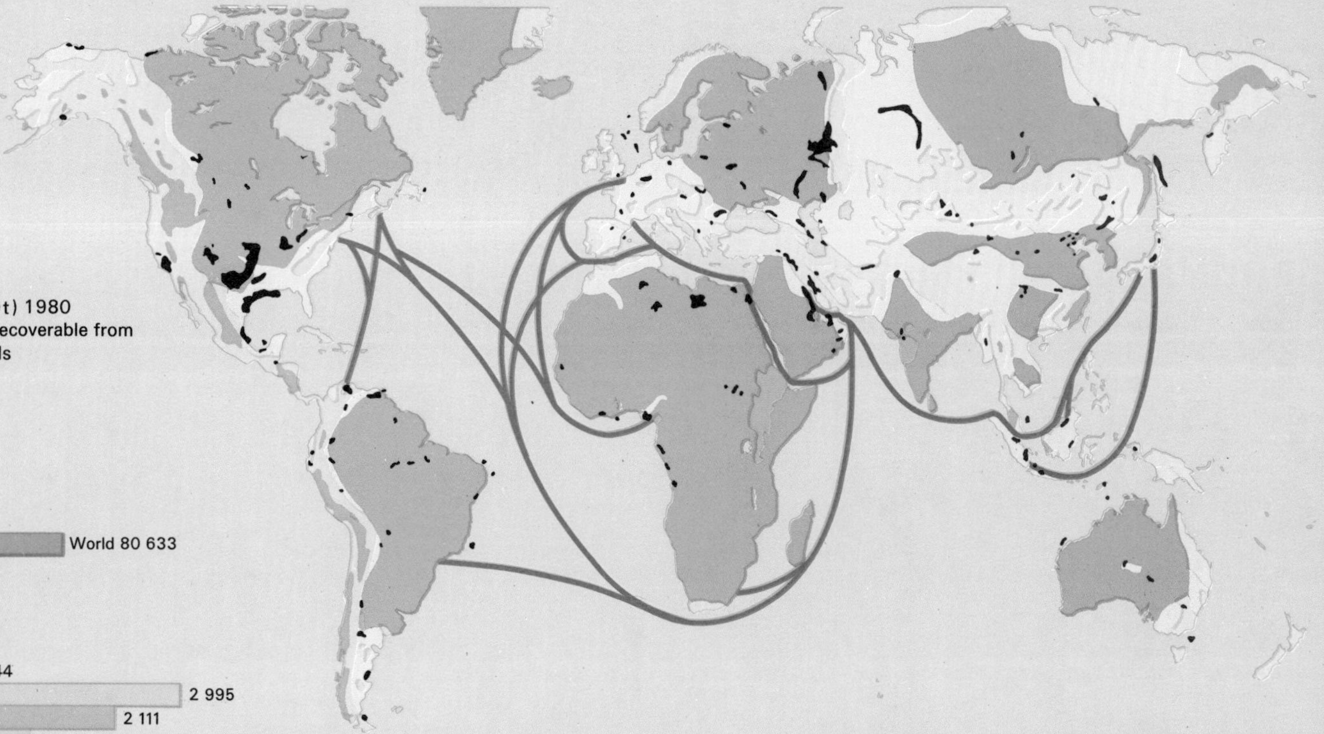

etroleum reserves (000 000t) 1980
‹cluding 81 138 000 000t recoverable from
shale and bituminous sands

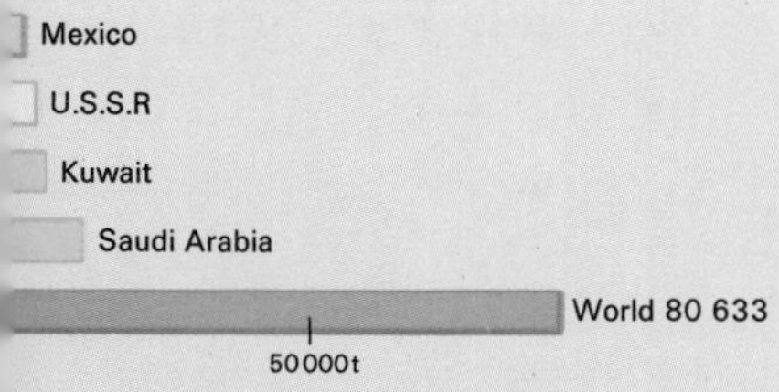

Mexico	
U.S.S.R	
Kuwait	
Saudi Arabia	
World	80 633

50 000t

›nsumption per capita (kg)

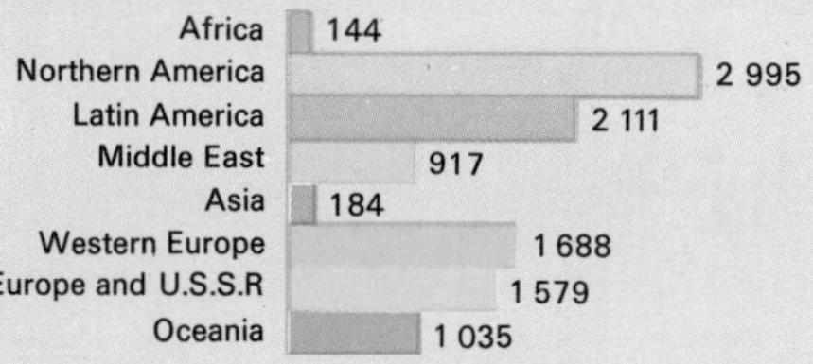

Africa	144
Northern America	2 995
Latin America	2 111
Middle East	917
Asia	184
Western Europe	1 688
›stern Europe and U.S.S.R	1 579
Oceania	1 035

Scale 1:180 000 000

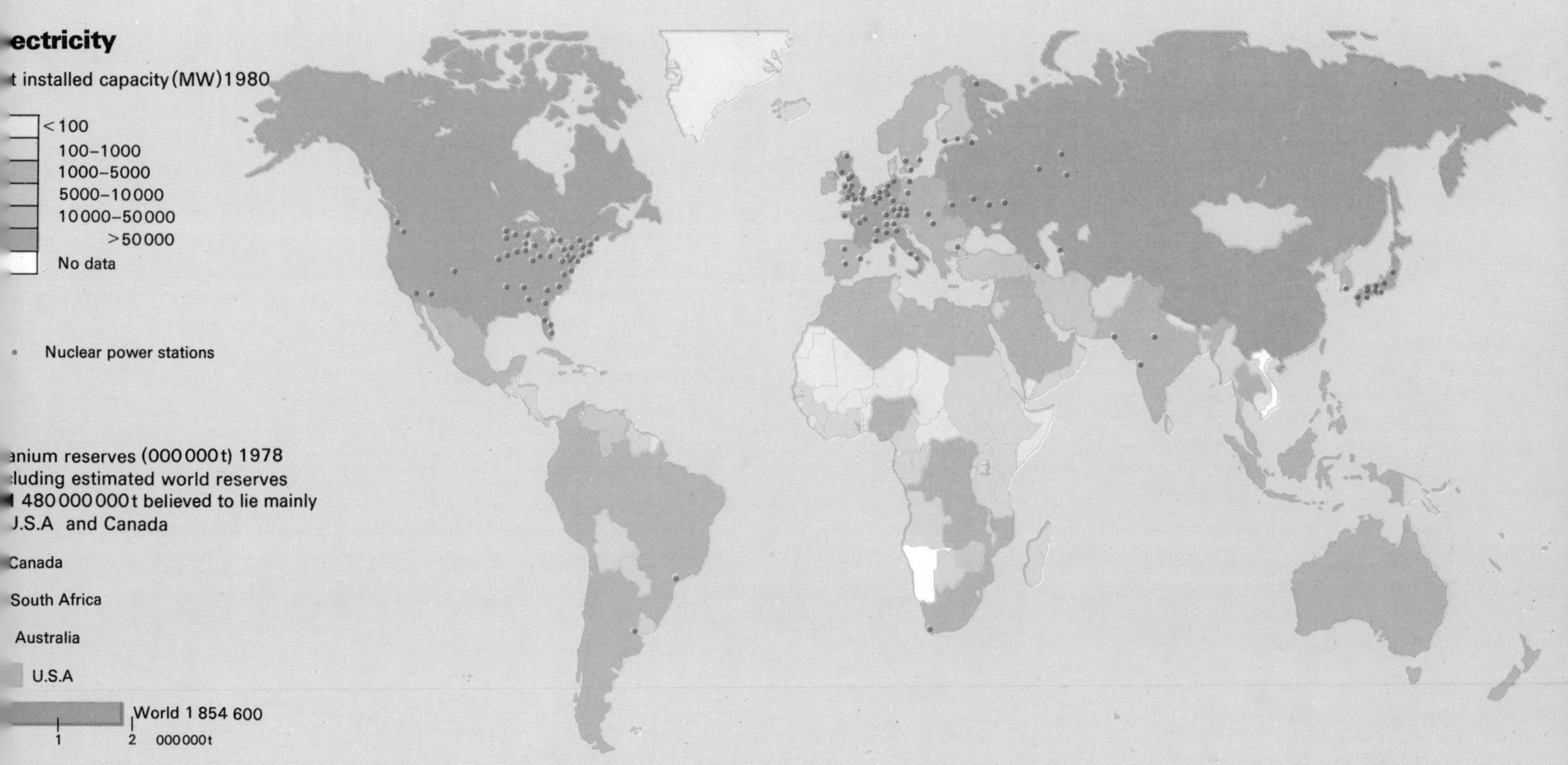
ectricity
t installed capacity (MW) 1980
< 100
100–1000
1000–5000
5000–10 000
10 000–50 000
> 50 000
No data
Nuclear power stations
anium reserves (000 000t) 1978
luding estimated world reserves
480 000 000t believed to lie mainly
J.S.A and Canada
Canada
South Africa
Australia
U.S.A
World 1 854 600
1
2 000 000t
Scale 1:180 000 000

ified Gall Projection

World: Energy Statistics 1980

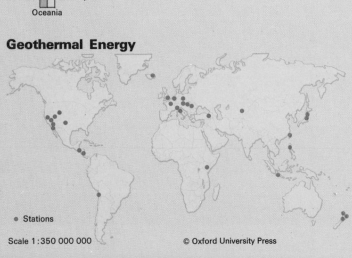

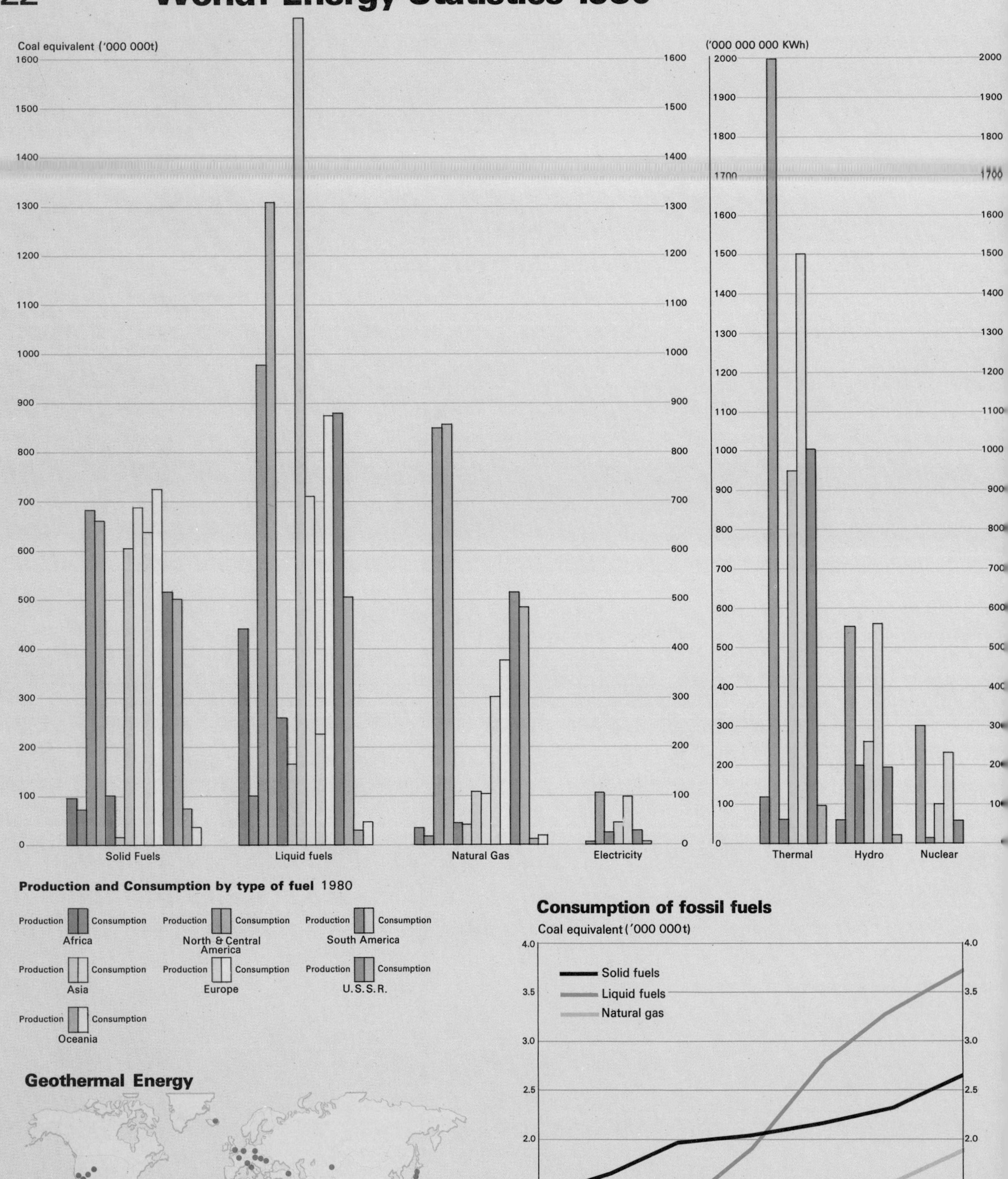

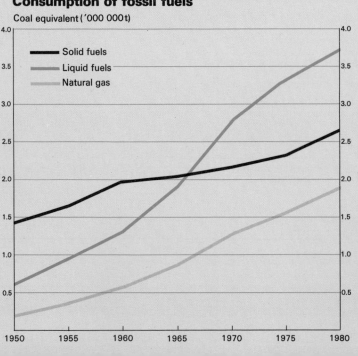

Coal equivalent ('000 000t)
('000 000 000 KWh)
Solid Fuels
Liquid fuels
Natural Gas
Electricity
Thermal
Hydro
Nuclear
Production and Consumption by type of fuel 1980
Production Consumption Africa
Production Consumption North & Central America
Production Consumption South America
Production Consumption Asia
Production Consumption Europe
Production Consumption U.S.S.R.
Production Consumption Oceania
Consumption of fossil fuels
Coal equivalent ('000 000t)
Solid fuels
Liquid fuels
Natural gas
Geothermal Energy
Stations
Scale 1:350 000 000

World: Iron and Steel, Minerals

ron and Steel 1980

- ● Mining areas
- △ Iron and steel works, including pelletizing plants

eological Structures

- Ancient shields partly covered by sedimentary rocks
- Fold mountains
- Sedimentary rocks and recent deposits
- Igneous rocks

cale 1:180 000 000
odified Gall Projection

inerals 1980
eological Structures
r key see map above
e deposits
Ferro alloys
Copper, gold, tin, molybdenum
Lead, zinc, silver
Bauxite
Uranium
Diamonds
Mica, phosphates, potash, sulphur
ale 1:180 000 000
odified Gall Projection

World: G D P and Industrialization

Gross Domestic Production 1978–80

G D P per capita $US

- 5000 and over
- 2500–4999
- 1000–2499
- 500–999
- 0–499
- No data

Manufacturing

Principal industrial areas

Equatorial Scale 1:88 000 000
Modified Gall Projection

Industry contributions to Gross Domestic Product (GDP) of selected countries 1980

Services and manufacturing emphasis

Canada: 4% · 6% · 23% · 5% · 10% · 7% · 34%

U.S.A.: 3% · 4% · 25% · 4% · 17% · 6% · 41%

Manufacturing and services emphasis

West Germany: 2% · 37% · 8% · 9% · 6% · 34%

Japan: 4% · 1% · 33% · 9% · 12% · 7% · 36%

Agricultural emphasis

India: 33% · 1% · 17% · 4% · 13% · 5% · 15%

Tanzania: 46% · 1% · 9% · 4% · 8% · 5% · 19%

Extractive emphasis

Kuwait: 68% · 6% · 3% · 6% · 2% · 14%

Saudi Arabia: 1% · 63% · 5% · 11% · 5% · 4% · 12%

GDP

Note: the individual bars in each graph express the percentage contribution of the designated economic activity to the Gross Domestic Product; these percentages do not add up to 100, because the following adjustments have been made to calculate the value of the GDP: less imputed bank service charges, and plus import duties, value added tax, and other necessary adjustments

- Agriculture, forestry, fishing
- Mining
- Manufacturing
- Construction
- Wholesale and retail trade
- Transportation and communications
- Services

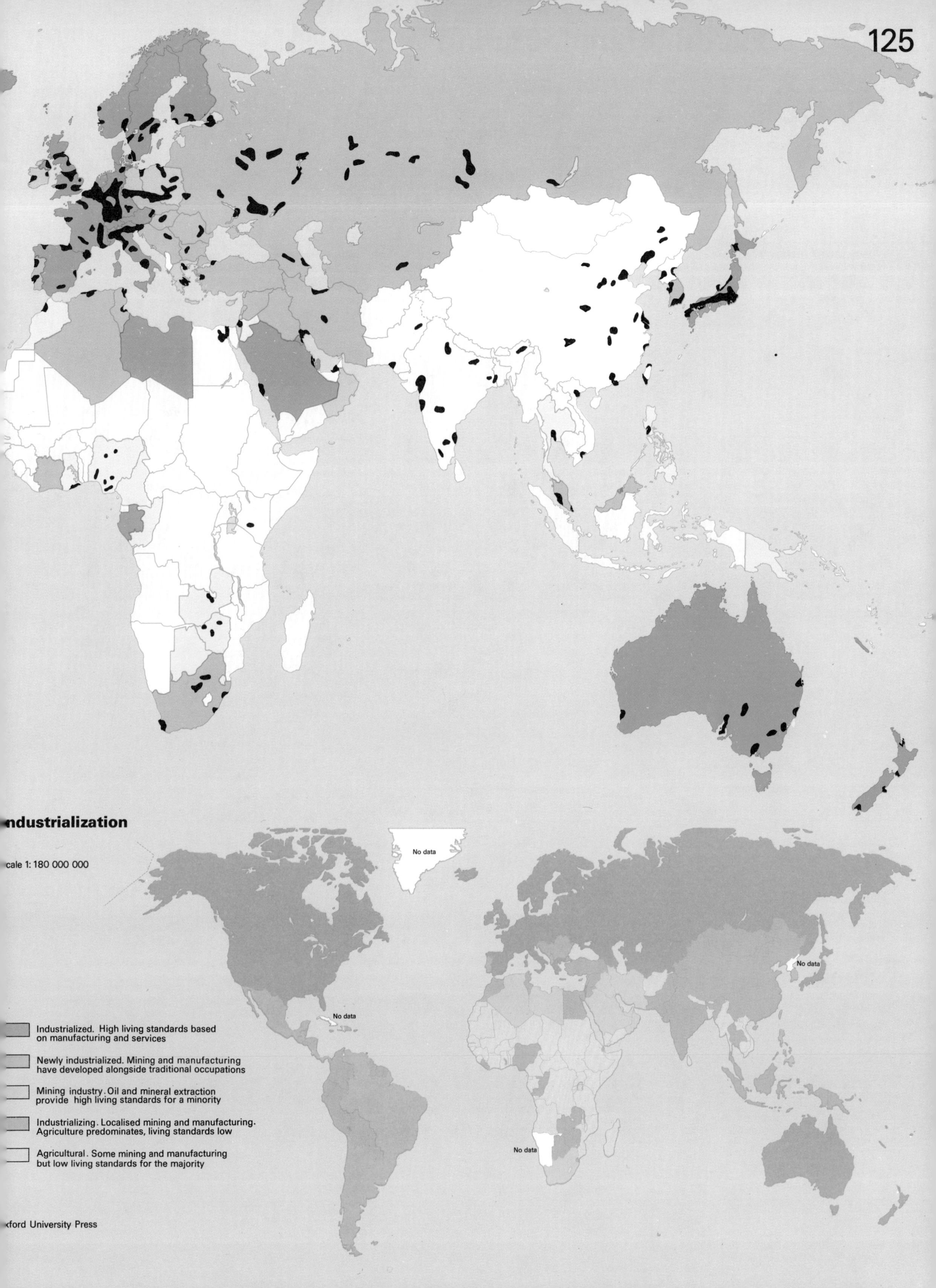
ndustrialization
cale 1: 180 000 000
No data
No data
No data
No data
Industrialized. High living standards based on manufacturing and services
Newly industrialized. Mining and manufacturing have developed alongside traditional occupations
Mining industry. Oil and mineral extraction provide high living standards for a minority
Industrializing. Localised mining and manufacturing. Agriculture predominates, living standards low
Agricultural. Some mining and manufacturing but low living standards for the majority
xford University Press

World: Manufacturing

Per capita income

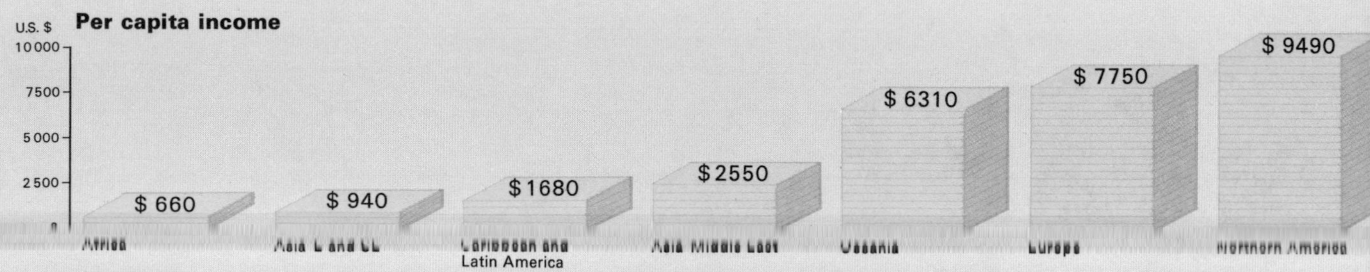
U.S. $
10 000
7500
5 000
2 500
0
$ 660
$ 940
$ 1680
$ 2550
$ 6310
$ 7750
$ 9490
Africa
Asia E and SE
Caribbean and Latin America
Asia Middle East
Oceania
Europe
Northern America

Pig iron production '000 tonnes

Raw steel production '000 tonnes

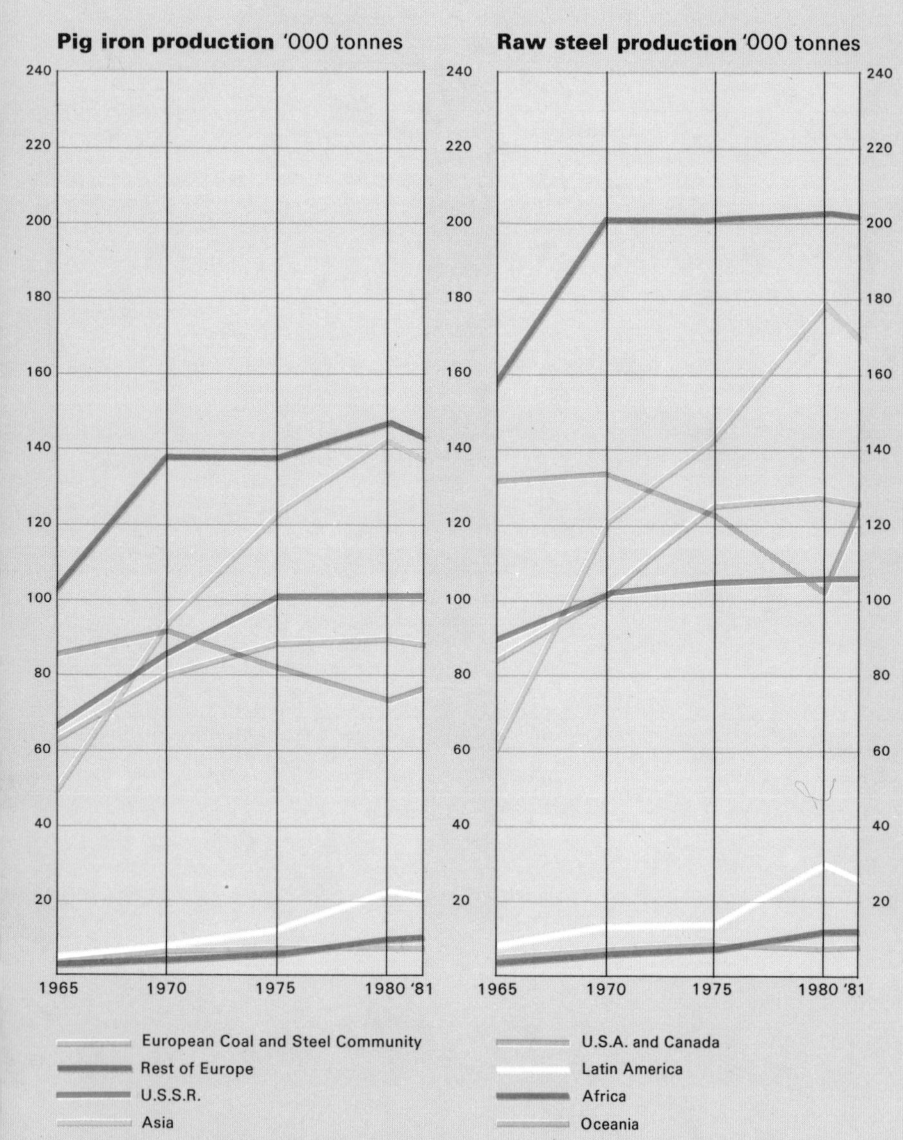
240
220
200
180
160
140
120
100
80
60
40
20
1965
1970
1975
1980 '81
European Coal and Steel Community
Rest of Europe
U.S.S.R.
Asia
U.S.A. and Canada
Latin America
Africa
Oceania

Registered vehicles per person

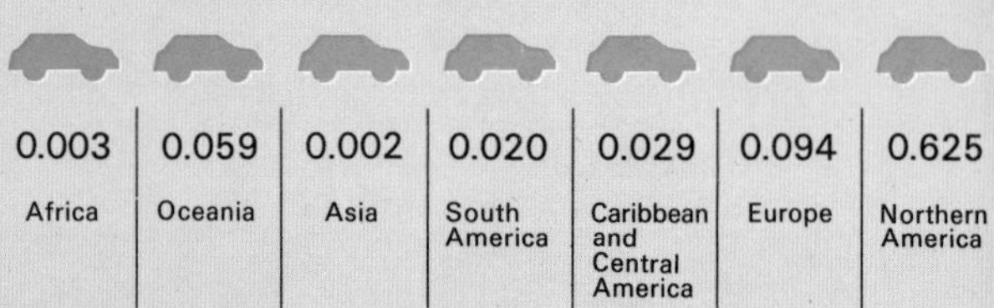
0.003
Africa
0.059
Oceania
0.002
Asia
0.020
South America
0.029
Caribbean and Central America
0.094
Europe
0.625
Northern America

No data for Bulgaria, Mongolia, North Korea, Romania, U.S.S.R.

Manufacturing production indices

1975 = 100

The differences between the centrally planned, developed and developing market economies make direct comparisons misleading. In these graphs growth rates are shown against a standard index of 100 in 1975

Centrally planned economies

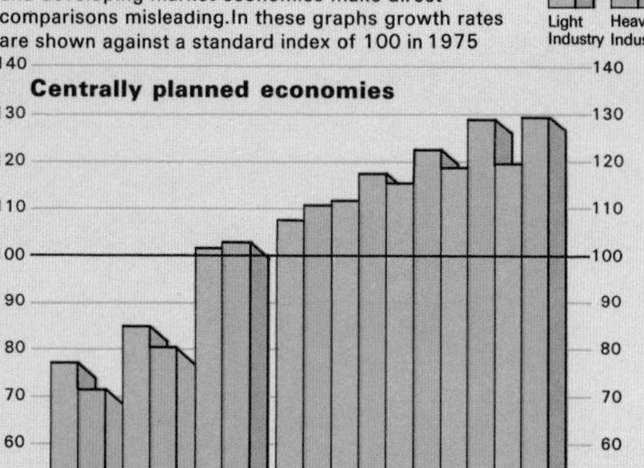
Light Industry
Heavy Industry
140
130
120
110
100
90
80
70
60
50
1968
1970
1973
1976
1977
1978
1979
1980

Developed market economies

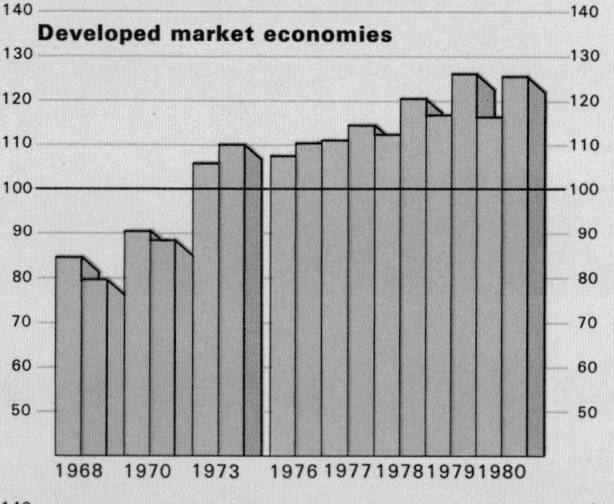
140
130
120
110
100
90
80
70
60
50
1968
1970
1973
1976
1977
1978
1979
1980

Developing market economies

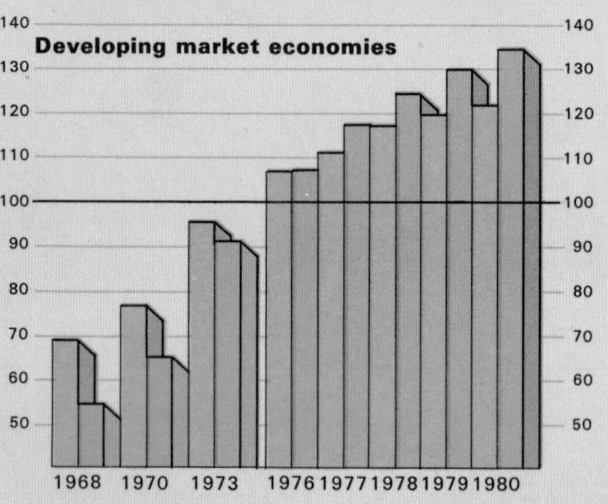
140
130
120
110
100
90
80
70
60
50
1968
1970
1973
1976
1977
1978
1979
1980

Crude steel production, 1980 (tonnes per capita)

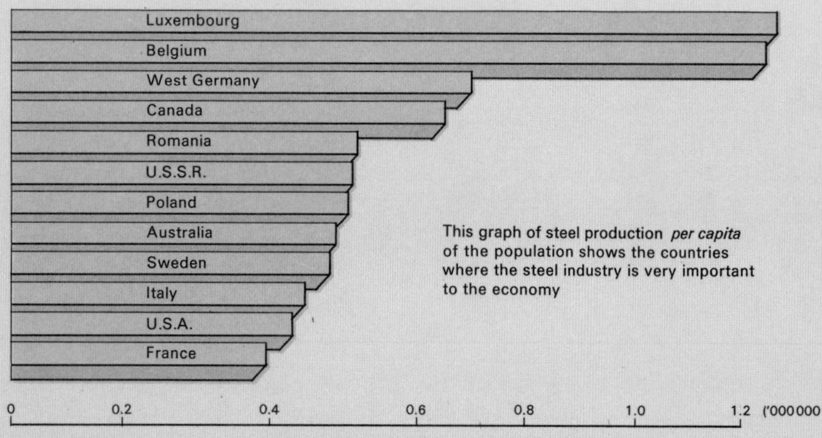
Luxembourg
Belgium
West Germany
Canada
Romania
U.S.S.R.
Poland
Australia
Sweden
Italy
U.S.A.
France
0
0.2
0.4
0.6
0.8
1.0
1.2
('000 000 t)

This graph of steel production *per capita* of the population shows the countries where the steel industry is very important to the economy

World: Air and Sea Transportation

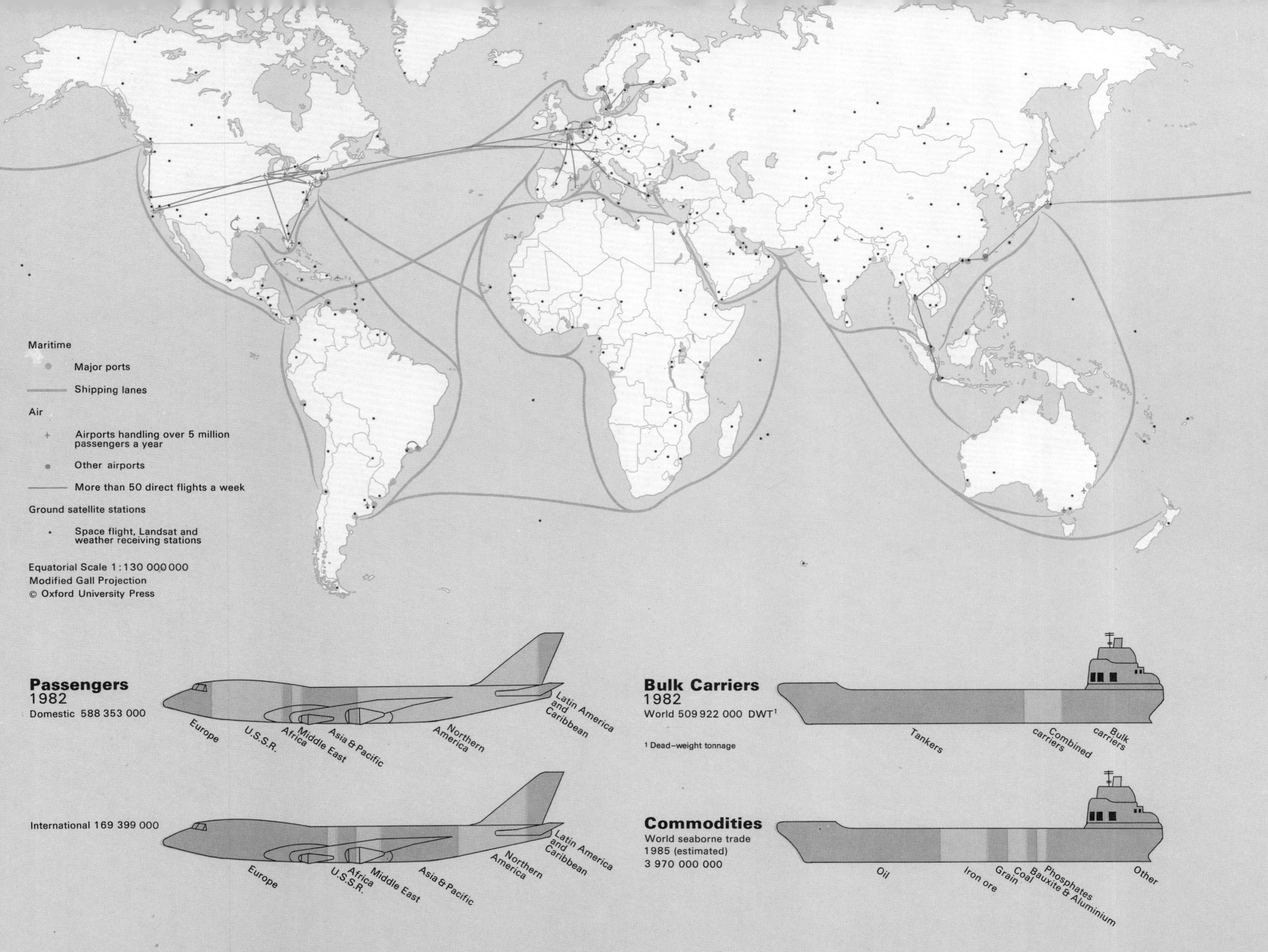

Maritime
Major ports
Shipping lanes
Air
Airports handling over 5 million passengers a year
Other airports
More than 50 direct flights a week
Ground satellite stations
Space flight, Landsat and weather receiving stations
Equatorial Scale 1:130 000 000
Modified Gall Projection
© Oxford University Press
Passengers
1982
Domestic 588 353 000
Europe
U.S.S.R.
Africa
Middle East
Asia & Pacific
Northern America
Latin America and Caribbean
International 169 399 000
Europe
U.S.S.R.
Africa
Middle East
Asia & Pacific
Northern America
Latin America and Caribbean
Bulk Carriers
1982
World 509 922 000 DWT[1]
Tankers
Combined carriers
Bulk carriers
1 Dead-weight tonnage
Commodities
World seaborne trade
1985 (estimated)
3 970 000 000
Oil
Iron ore
Grain
Coal
Bauxite & Aluminium
Phosphates
Other

The Antarctic

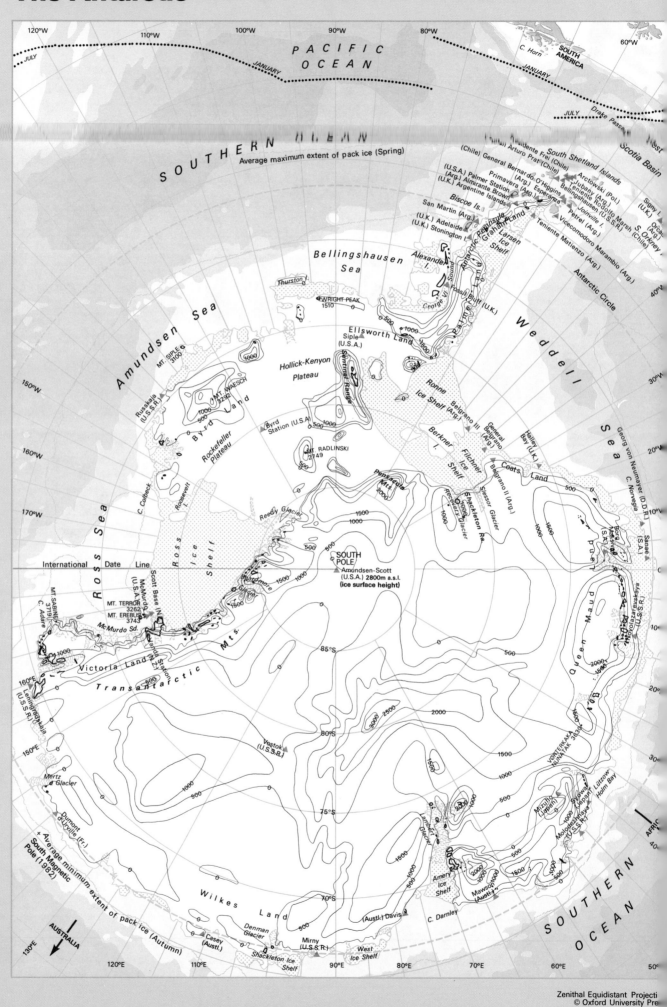

Legend

Boundaries
Historically Argentina, Australia, Chile, France, New Zealand, Norway and the United Kingdom have territorial claims in Antarctica. These were waived under the Antarctic Treaty of 1959 but this is due to expire in 1991.

▲ Research stations

•••••••• Boundary of Southern Ocean. Zones of convergence where cold Antarctic water sinks beneath warmer water

Ice shelves

—500— Sub-glacial contours

Nunataks. Rock peaks projecting above surface of an icefield

metres
land free of ice
Sea level
200
3000
4000
5000

Spot heights in metres

Scale 1 : 25 000 000

0 200 400 600 km

Zenithal Equidistant Projecti

Gazetteers

Notes

The atlas has two gazetteers. The Gazetteer of Canada, which covers the topographical maps of Canada (pages 20–41) and the urban plans of Edmonton, Montréal, Toronto and Vancouver (page 27) and Winnipeg (page 33), is exhaustive and lists all the names shown on the maps. Entries without page numbers are places which do not appear on the maps but their location may be deduced from their latitude and longitude. The World Gazetteer is selective and only lists the more important places and features so the absence of a name in the gazetteer does not necessarily mean that the place or feature is not shown on the map. All entries are gazetteered to the largest scale map on which the feature appears in its entirety. The geographical co-ordinates are given to the nearest whole degree, thus:

Åland Is.: Finland. Co-ordinates to degrees and minutes: 60°15′N 20°00′E. Gazetteered to 60N 20E.

Port Elizabeth: South Africa. Co-ordinates to degrees and minutes: 33°58′S 25°36′E. Gazetteered to 34S 26E.

Gazetteer entries in capital letters denote provincial capitals in Canada (thus: TORONTO) or country capitals in the rest of the world. Entries in bold face capitals denote countries (thus: **JAPAN**).

Several place names have been changed to Inuit forms. In northern Québec these include Kangiqsujuaq (formerly Maricourt), Kangiqsualujjuaq (formerly Port Nouveau-Québec), Kangirsuk (formerly Bellin), Kuujjuarapik (formerly Poste-de-la-Baleine), Kuujjuaq (formerly Fort Chimo), Chisasibi (formerly Fort George), Inukjuak (formerly Inoucdouac), and Salluit (formerly Saglouc). In the Northwest Territories Frobisher Bay has been changed to Iqaluit.

The Pinyin system of transliteration has been used for the Chinese names, although in some cases the Wade-Giles form is given in brackets and as a cross-reference in the gazetteer. Peking and Canton are exceptions in that these names are used as the main entry and on the map and the Pinyin form is given in brackets.

Abbreviations

The following abbreviations have been used in this atlas.

A.C.T. — Australian Capital Territory
admin. — administrative
Afghan. — Afghanistan
Afr. — Africa
Ala. — Alabama
Alb. — Albania
Alg. — Algeria
Alta. — Alberta
Antarc. — Antarctica
Arch. — Archipelago
Arab. Sea — Arabian Sea
Arg. — Argentina
Ariz. — Arizona
Ark. — Arkansas
Atl. O. — Atlantic Ocean
Aust. — Austria
Austl. — Australia
Aut. Reg. — Autonomous Region
B., b. — Baie, Bay
Bangl. — Bangladesh
B.C. — British Columbia
Belg. — Belgium
Bol. — Bolivia
Bots. — Botswana
Br. — British
Braz. — Brazil
Bulg. — Bulgaria
C., c. — Cape, Cabo
Calif. — California
Can. — Canada
cap. — capital
Carib. Sea — Caribbean Sea
Ch. — Channel
Chan. — Channel
Ck. — Creek
Co. — County
Col. — Colombia
Colo. — Colorado
Conn. — Connecticut
C.R. — Costa Rica
Cr. — Creek
Czech. — Czechoslovakia
D.C. — District of Columbia
Del. — Delaware
Den. — Denmark
dep. — depression
Derby. — Derbyshire
dist. — district
Dom. Repub. — Dominican Republic
E. — East, Eastern
Ec. — Ecuador
Eng. — England
Eq. — Equatorial
Eth. — Ethiopia
Eur. — Europe
Fd. — Fjord
Fed. — Federal, Federation
Fin. — Finland
Fla. — Florida
Fr. — France, French
Ft. — Fort
G. — Gulf
Ga. — Georgia (U.S.A.)
G.D.R. — German Democratic Republic
geog. — geographical
Ger. — German, Germany
Gl. — Glacier
Gramp. — Grampian
Grnld. — Greenland
Gt. — Great, Greater
Hd. — Head
Har., Harb. — Harbour
Hist. — Historic(al)
Hond. — Honduras
Hung. — Hungary
I.(s), i.(s) — island(s)
Ill. — Illinois
Ind. — Indiana
Ind. O. — Indian Ocean
Indon. — Indonesia
Int. — International
Irel. — Ireland
Is. — Israel
It. — Italy
Jam. — Jamaica
Kans. — Kansas
Ky. — Kentucky
L. — Lago, Lake, Loch
La. — Louisiana
Labr. — Labrador
Lag. — Lagoon
Leb. — Lebanon
Lux. — Luxembourg
Mal. — Malaysia
Man. — Manitoba
Mass. — Massachusetts
Md. — Maryland
Medit. — Mediterranean
Mex. — Mexico
Mich. — Michigan
Minn. — Minnesota
Miss. — Mississippi
Mo. — Missouri
Mong. — Mongolia
Mont. — Montana
Mor. — Morocco
Moz. — Mozambique
Mt.(n) — Mount, Mountain
Mtns. — Mountains
N. — North, Northern
Nat. — National
N.B. — New Brunswick
N.C. — North Carolina
N. Dak. — North Dakota
Nebr. — Nebraska
Neth. — Netherlands
Nev. — Nevada
Nfld. — Newfoundland
N.H. — New Hampshire
Nic. — Nicaragua
Nig. — Nigeria
N.J. — New Jersey
N.M. — New Mexico
Nor. — Norway
N.S. — Nova Scotia
N.P. — National Park
N.W.T. — Northwest Territories
N.Y. — New York
N.Z. — New Zealand
O. — Ocean
Okla. — Oklahoma
Ont. — Ontario
Oreg. — Oregon
P. — Pass
P. — Provincial
Pa. — Pennsylvania
Pac. O. — Pacific Ocean
Pak. — Pakistan
P.D.R. — People's Democratic Republic
P.E.I. — Prince Edward Island
Penin. — Peninsula
Phil. — Philippines
Pk. — Peak
Plat. — Plateau
Pol. — Poland
Port. — Portugal, Portuguese
P.P. — Provincial Park
Prov. — Province
Pt.(e) — Point(e)
Pto. — Puerto
Qué. — Québec
R., r. — River, rivière
R., Rep., Repub. — Republic
Reg. — Region
Res. — Reservoir
R.I. — Rhode Island
Rom. — Romania
R.S.F.S.R. — Russian Soviet Federative Socialist Republic
S. — South, Southern
S. Am. — South America
Sanc(t) — Sanctuary
Sask. — Saskatchewan
Sau. Arab. — Saudi Arabia
S.C. — South Carolina
Scot. — Scotland
Sd. — Sound
S. Dak. — South Dakota
sett. — settlement
Sp. — Spain, Spanish
S.S.R. — Soviet Socialist Republic
St.(e) — Saint(e)
Str. — Strait
Sud. — Sudan
Switz. — Switzerland
Tanzan. — Tanzania
Tenn. — Tennessee
Territ. — Territory
Tex. — Texas
Thai. — Thailand
Tur. — Turkey
U.A.E. — United Arab Emirates
U.A.R. — United Arab Republic
U.K. — United Kingdom
U.S.A. — United States of America
U.S.S.R. — Union of Soviet Socialist Republics
Va. — Virginia
Venez. — Venezuela
volc. — volcano
Vt. — Vermont
W. — West, Western
War. — Warwickshire
Wash. — Washington
W. Ind. — West Indies
Wilts. — Wiltshire
Wisc. — Wisconsin
W. Va. — West Virginia
Wyo. — Wyoming
Yemen A.R. — Yemen Arab Republic
Yemen P.D.R. — Yemen People's Democratic Republic
Yorks. — Yorkshire
Yugo. — Yugoslavia

DWT — dead weight tonnage
GDP — Gross Domestic Produce
GW — gigawatt
GWh — gigawatt-hour
KWh — kilowatt-hour
MJ — megajoule
MW — megawatt
pH — measure of hydrogen ion concentration

Recent Country Name Changes

BURKINA formerly Upper Volta
CENTRAL AFRICAN REPUBLIC formerly Central African Empire
KAMPUCHEA formerly Cambodia
KIRIBATI formerly Gilbert Is.
MADAGASCAR formerly Malagasy Republic
NAMIBIA formerly South West Africa
TUVALU formerly Ellice Is.
VANUATU formerly New Hebrides
ZIMBABWE formerly Rhodesia

A

Abbotsford: B.C. **28** 49N 122W
Aberdeen: Sask. **31** 52N 106W
Aberdeen Lake: N.W.T. **20** 65N 99W
Abitibi: *riv.*, Ont. **34** 50N 81W
Abitibi, Lake: Ont./Qué. **24** 49N 80W
Abloviak Fiord: Qué. **36** 59N 66W
Aconi, Point: N.S. **34** 46N 60W
Adair, Cape: N.W.T. **21** 71N 71W
Adams, Lake: B.C. **29** 51N 119W
Adelaide Penin: N.W.T. **21** 68N 98W
Adlavik Is.: Nfld. **40** 55N 59W
Admiralty Inlet: N.W.T. **21** 73N 85W
[illegible]
Agassiz: B.C. **28** 49N 121W
Agassiz Ice Cap: N.W.T. **21** 80N 75W
Aguanus: *riv.*, Qué. **37** 51N 62W
Aillik: Nfld. **40** 55N 59W
Ainslie, Lake: N.S. **41** 46N 61W
Airdrie: Alta. **30** 51N 114W
Air Force I.: N.W.T. **21** 68N 75W
Aishihik Lake: Yukon **20** 62N 138W
Ajax: Ont. **38** 44N 79W
Akimiski I.: N.W.T. **24** 53N 81W
Aklavik: N.W.T. **20** 68N 135W
Akpatok I.: N.W.T. **25** 60N 68W
Akulivik: Qué. **36** 61N 78W
Albanel: Qué. **37** 49N 72W
Albanel, Lac: Qué. **37** 51N 73W
Albany: *riv.*, Ont. **34** 51N 85W
Alberta: *Prov.* (*cap.* Edmonton) **22** — —
Albert Edward Bay: N.W.T. **20** 69N 103W
Alberton: P.E.I. **41** 47N 64W
Alert: N.W.T. **21** 83N 63W
Alexandria: Ont. **39** 45N 75W
Alexis Creek: *town*, B.C. **29** 52N 123W
Alfred: Ont. **39** 46N 75W
Alfred, Mt.: B.C. **28** 50N 124W
Algonquin Park: *town*, Ont. **38** 46N 79W
Algonquin Prov. Park: Ont. **38** 46N 78W
Alix: Alta. **30** 52N 113W
Allan: Sask. **31** 52N 105W
Allard, Lac: Qué **37** 51N 64W
Allison Harbour: B.C. **29** 51N 127W
Alliston: Ont. **38** 44N 80W
Allumettes, Île aux.: Qué. **38** 46N 77W
Alma: N.B. **41** 45N 65W
Alma: Qué. **37** 47N 72W
Almonte: Ont. **39** 45N 76W
Alouette Lake: B.C. **28** 49N 122W
Alsask: Sask. **31** 51N 110W
Alsek: *riv.*, Yukon/B.C. **28** 60N 138W
Alsek Range: B.C. **28** 59N 137W
Alta Lake: *town*, B.C. **28** 50N 123W
Altona: Man. **32** 49N 97W
Alvin: B.C. **28** 50N 122W
Amadjuak Lake: N.W.T. **21** 65N 71W
Amery: Man. **32** 56N 94W
Amherst: N.S. **41** 46N 64W
Amherst I.: Ont. **38** 44N 77W
Amisk Lake: Sask. **31** 54N 102W
Amos: Qué. **37** 48N 78W
Amund Ringnes I.: N.W.T. **21** 78N 97W
Amundsen Gulf: N.W.T. **20** 71N 123W
Ancaster: Ont. **38** 43N 80W
Anderson: *riv.*, N.W.T. **20** 69N 128W
Anderson Lake: B.C. **28** 50N 122W
Anderson River Delta Bird Sanctuary: N.W.T. **20** 70N 130W
Andrew: Alta. **30** 54N 112W
Andrew Gordon Bay: N.W.T. **21** 64N 75W
Angikuni Lake: N.W.T. **20** 62N 100W
Anguille, Cape: Nfld. **41** 48N 59W
Annacis Island: B.C. **27** 49N 123W
Annapolis Royal: N.S. **41** 45N 66W
Anstruther Lake: Ont. **38** 45N 78W
Anticosti, Île d': Qué. **37** 49N 63W
Antigonish: N.S. **41** 46N 62W
Anvil Mts.: Yukon **20** 62N 133W
Arborfield: Sask. **31** 53N 103W
Arborg: Man. **32** 51N 97W
Arcola: Sask. **31** 50N 103W
Arctic Bay: *settlement*, N.W.T. **21** 73N 84W
Arctic Red River: *town & riv.*, N.W.T. **20** 67N 134W
Ardrossan: Alta. **27** 54N 113W
Argentia: Nfld. **41** 47N 54W
Arichat: N.S. **41** 45N 61W
Aristazabal I: B.C. **28** 53N 129W
Armstrong: B.C. **29** 50N 119W
Armstrong: Ont. **34** 50N 89W
Arnot: Man. **32** 56N 97W
Arnprior: Ont. **39** 45N 76W
Arrow River: *town*, Man. **32** 50N 101W
Arrowsmith, Mt.: B.C. **28** 49N 124W
Artillery Lake: N.W.T. **20** 63N 108W
Asbestos: Qué. **37** 46N 72W
Ashcroft: B.C. **29** 51N 121W
Ashern: Man. **32** 52N 99W
Asheweig: *riv.*, Ont. **34** 54N 90W
Ashuanipi: Nfld. **40** 53N 66W
Ashuanipi Lake: Nfld. **40** 53N 66W
Ashville: Man. **32** 51N 100W
Aspy Bay: N.S. **41** 47N 60W
Assiniboia: Sask. **31** 49N 106W
Assiniboine: *riv.*, Sask./Man. **23** 50N 99W
Assiniboine, Mt. B.C./Alta. **29** 51N 116W
Assinica, Lac: Qué. **37** 50N 75W
Assinica, Parc de: Qué **37** 50N 75W
Aston, Cape: N.W.T. **21** 70N 67W
Astray Lake: Nfld. **40** 55N 67W
Athabasca: *& riv.*, Alta. **30** 55N 113W
Athabasca, Lake: Alberta/Saskatchewan **31** 59N 109W
Athens: Ont. **39** 45N 76W
Atikokan: Ont. **34** 48N 91W
Atikonak Lake: Nfld. **40** 53N 64W
Atikwa Lake: Ont. **34** 49N 93W
Atkinson, Point: B.C. **27** 49N 123W
Atlin: *& lake*, B.C. **28** 59N 134W
Atlin P.P.,: B.C. **28** 59N 134W
Atna Peak: B.C. **28** 54N 128W
Attawapiskat: *& riv.*, Ont. **34** 53N 83W
Attawapiskat Lake: Ont. **34** 52N 88W
Attikamagen Lake: Nfld. **26** 55N 66W
Aubry Lake: N.W.T. **20** 67N 126W
Aupaluk: Qué. **36** 59N 70W
Aurora: Ont. **38** 44N 79W
Austin Channel: N.W.T. **20** 75N 103W
Auyuittuq Nat. Park: N.W.T. **21** 67N 66W
Avalon Penin.: Nfld. **41** 47N 53W
Avola: B.C. **29** 52N 119W
Axel Heiberg I.: N.W.T. **21** 80N 90W
Aylen Lake: Ont. **38** 46N 78W
Aylmer: Qué. **39** 45N 76W
Aylmer Lake: N.W.T. **20** 64N 110W
Azure Lake: B.C. **29** 52N 120W

B

Babine: B.C. **22** 55N 126W
Babine Lake: B.C. **29** 55N 126W
Bache Peninsula: N.W.T. **21** 79N 76W
Back: *riv.*, N.W.T. **20** 65N 105W
Backbone Ranges: N.W.T. **20** 63N 129W
Baddeck: N.S. **41** 46N 61W
Badger: Nfld. **41** 49N 56W
Baffin Bay: Canada/Grnld. **21** 73N 70W
Baffin I.: N.W.T. **21** 70N 75W
Baie-Comeau: Qué. **37** 49N 68W
Baie des Chaleurs: Qué./N.B. **37** 48N 66W
Baie d'Ungava: Qué. **21** 59N 67W
Baie d'Hudson: **21** 60N 85W
Baie James: *town*, Qué. **37** 52N 80W
Baie Kettlestone: Qué. **36** 61N 78W
Baie Kovik: Qué. **36** 62N 78W
Baie-Saint-Paul: Qué. **37** 47N 70W
Baie Verte: Nfld. **41** 50N 56W
Baillie: *riv.*, N.W.T. **20** 65N 106W
Baillie Is.: N.W.T. **20** 71N 128W
Baker Lake: *& settlement.*, N.W.T. **21** 64N 96W
Bakers Dozen Is.: N.W.T. **24** 57N 79W
Balcarres: Sask. **31** 50N 104W
Baldock Lake: Man. **32** 56N 98W
Baldy Mt.: Man. **23** 51N 101W
Balgonie: Sask. **31** 50N 104W
Ballantyne Strait: N.W.T. **20** 78N 115W
Balmertown: Ont. **34** 51N 93W
Balsam Lake: Ont. **38** 45N 79W
Bamfield: B.C. **28** 49N 125W
Bancroft: Ont. **38** 45N 78W
Banff National Park: Alta. **30** 51N 116W
Banks I.: B.C. **28** 53N 130W
Banks I.: N.W.T. **20** 73N 120W
Banks I. Bird Sanctuary No. 1: N.W.T. **20** 73N 125W
Banks I. Bird Sanctuary No. 2: N.W.T. **20** 74N 125W
Baptiste Lake: Ont. **38** 45N 78W
Baring, Cape: N.W.T. **20** 70N 117W
Barkerville: B.C. **29** 53N 121W
Bark Lake: Ont. **38** 45N 78W
Barkley Sound: B.C. **28** 49N 125W
Barnes Ice Cap: N.W.T. **21** 70N 73W
Barrhead: Alta. **30** 54N 114W
Barrie: Ont. **38** 44N 80W
Barriere: B.C. **29** 51N 120W
Barrington Lake: Man. **32** 57N 100W
Barrow Str.: N.W.T. **21** 74N 93W
Barrys Bay: *town*, Ont. **38** 45N 78W
Bashaw: Alta. **30** 53N 113W
Basin Lake: Sask. **31** 52N 105W
Baskatong, Réservoir: Qué. **37** 47N 76W
Bassano: Alta. **30** 51N 112W
Bath: N.B. **41** 46N 67W
Bath: Ont. **38** 44N 77W
Bathurst: N.B. **41** 47N 66W
Bathurst Cape: N.W.T. **20** 71N 128W
Bathurst Inlet: *settlement*, N.W.T. **20** 67N 108W
Bathurst I.: N.W.T. **20** 76N 100W
Batteau: Nfld. **40** 53N 56W
Battle: *riv.*, Alta. **30** 53N 110W
Battleford: Sask. **31** 53N 108W
Battle Harbour: *settlement*, Nfld. **40** 52N 56W
Bauld, Cape: Nfld. **40** 51N 55W
Bay Bulls: Nfld. **41** 47N 53W
Bay Chimo: *settlement*, N.W.T. **20** 68N 108W
Bay of Islands: Nfld. **40** 55N 60W
Bay of Islands: Nfld. **41** 49N 58W
Bay Roberts: Nfld. **41** 48N 53W
Bays, Lake of: Ont. **38** 45N 79W
Beachburg: Ont. **38** 46N 77W
Beaconsfield: Qué. **27** 45N 74W
Beale, Cape: B.C. **28** 49N 125W
Bear I.: N.W.T. **24** 54N 81W
Bear Lake: Man. **32** 55N 96W
Beatton: *riv.*, B.C. **29** 57N 121W
Beattyville: Qué. **37** 49N 77W
Beauharnois: Qué. **39** 45N 74W
Beauharnois Canal: Qué. **39** 45N 74W
Beaumaris Lake: Alta. **27** 54N 114
Beaumont: Alta. **27** 53N 113W
Beauséjour: Man. **32** 50N 97W
Beauval: Sask. **31** 55N 108W
Beaver: *riv.*, Sask. **31** 55N 108W
Beaver Creek: *settlement*, Yukon **20** 62N 141W
Beaverdell: B.C. **29** 49N 119W
Beaverhill Lake: Alta. **30** 53N 112W
Beaverhill Lake: Man. **32** 54N 95W
Beaverlodge: Alta. **30** 55N 119W
Beechey Head: B.C. **28** 48N 123W
Beiseker: Alta. **30** 51N 114W
Belcher Is.: N.W.T. **24** 56N 79W
Bella Bella: B.C. **28** 52N 128W
Bella Coola: *& riv.*, B.C. **29** 52N 127W
Belle Bay: Nfld. **41** 47N 55W
Belledune: N.B. **41** 48N 66W
Belle Isle: Nfld. **40** 52N 55W
Belle Isle, Str. of: Nfld. **41** 51N 57W
Belleville: Ont. **38** 44N 77W
Bellevue: Alta. **30** 50N 114W
Bell I.: Nfld. **41** 48N 53W
Bell I.: Nfld. **41** 51N 55W
Bell Penin.: N.W.T. **21** 64N 82W
Belly: *riv.*, Alta. **30** 49N 113W
Beloeil: Qué. **39** 46N 73W
Belot, Lac: N.W.T. **20** 67N 127W
Benedict, Mt.: Nfld. **40** 55N 59W
Bengough: Sask. **31** 49N 105W
Benito: Man. **32** 52N 101W
Bennett: B.C. **28** 60N 135W
Bentley: Alta. **30** 52N 114W
Berens River: *town & riv.*, Manitoba **32** 52N 97W
Bermen, Lac: Qué. **37** 53N 69W
Bernard Lake: Ont. **38** 46N 79W
Bernier Bay: N.W.T. **21** 71N 88W
Berthierville: Qué. **39** 46N 73
Berwyn: Alta. **30** 56N 118W
Betsiamites: *& riv.*, Qué. **37** 49N 69W
[illegible]
Big Bay Point: Lake Simcoe, Ont. **38** 44N 79W
Biggar: Sask. **31** 52N 108W
Big Gull Lake: Ont. **38** 45N 77W
Big I.: Nfld. **40** 58N 62W
Big I.: Great Slave Lake, N.W.T. **22** 61N 117W
Big I.: N.W.T. **21** 63N 71W
Big Island Lake: Alta. **27** 53N 113W
Big Lake: Alta. **27** 54N 114W
Big Muddy Lake: Sask. **31** 49N 105W
Big River: *town*, Sask. **31** 54N 107W
Big Salmon Range: Yukon **20** 61N 134W
Big Sand Lake: Man. **32** 58N 99W
Big Stick Lake: Sask. **31** 50N 109W
Bigstone Lake: Man. **32** 54N 96W
Big Trout Lake: Ont. **38** 46N 79W
Big Trout Lake: Ont. **34** 54N 90W
Birch: *riv.*, Alta. **30** 58N 113W
Birch Hills: *town*, Sask. **31** 53N 105W
Birch Lake: Alta. **30** 53N 112W
Birch Lake: Nfld. **40** 54N 66W
Birch Mtns.: Alta. **30** 57N 113W
Birds Hill: *town*, Man. **33** 50N 91W
Birken: B.C. **28** 51N 123W
Birkenhead Lake P.P.: British Columbia **28** 51N 123W
Birtle: Man. **32** 50N 101W
Bishops Falls: *town*, Nfld. **41** 49N 55W
Biskotasi Lake: Ont. **34** 47N 82W
Bittern Lake: Sask. **31** 54N 106W
Bizard, I.: Qué. **27** 45N 74W
Bjorne Peninsula: N.W.T. **21** 77N 87W
Black Bear Island Lake: Saskatchewan **31** 55N 105W
Black Birch Lake: Sask. **31** 57N 108W
Black Diamond: Alta. **30** 51N 114W
Blackfalds: Alta. **30** 52N 114W
Black I.: Man. **32** 51N 96W
Black Lake: *& town*, Sask. **31** 59N 105W
Blackmund Creek: Alta. **27** 53N 114W
Blackville: N.B. **41** 47N 66W
Blackwater Lake: N.W.T. **20** 64N 123W
Blaine Lake: *town*, Sask. **31** 53N 107W
Blairmore: Alta. **30** 50N 114W
Blind River: *town*, Ont. **34** 46N 83
Bloedel: B.C. **28** 50N 125W
Bloodvein: *riv.*, Man. **32** 52N 96W
Bloomfield: Ont. **38** 44N 77W
Blubber Bay: *town*, B.C. **28** 50N 125W
Blue Mt.: Nfld. **41** 50N 57W
Bluenose Lake: N.W.T. **20** 68N 119W
Blue River: *town*, B.C. **29** 52N 119W
Bluff, Cape: Nfld. **40** 53N 56W
Boag Lake: Alta. **27** 54N 113W
Bobcaygeon: Ont. **38** 45N 79W
Bobs Lake: Ont. **39** 45N 77W
Boissevain: Man. **32** 49N 100W
Bonavista: Nfld. **41** 49N 53W
Bonavista Bay: Nfld. **41** 49N 53W
Bonne Bay: Nfld. **41** 49N 58W
Bonnet Plume: *riv.*, Yukon **20** 65N 133W
Bonnyville: Alta. **30** 54N 111W
Boothia Penin.: N.W.T. **21** 72N 95W
Boothia, G of: N.W.T. **21** 70N 90W
Borden: P.E.I. **41** 46N 64W
Borden I.: N.W.T. **20** 78N 110W
Borden Penin.: N.W.T. **21** 73N 82W
Botwood: Nfld. **41** 49N 55W
Boucherville: *& is.*, Qué. **27** 46N 73W
Bouctouche: N.B. **41** 47N 65W
Boundary: B.C. **28** 57N 132W
Boundary Range: U.S.A./Canada **28** 59N 133W
Bourne, Cape: N.W.T. **21** 82N 90W
Bow: *riv.*, Alta. **30** 51N 114W
Bowden: Alta. **30** 52N 114W
Bowen I.: B.C. **28** 49N 123W
Bow Island: *town*, Alta. **30** 50N 111W
Bowman Bay Game Sanc.: N.W.T. **21** 66N 74W
Bowmanville: Ont. **38** 44N 79W
Bowness: Alta. **30** 51N 114W
Bowron Lake Prov. Park: B.C. **29** 53N 122W
Bowser: B.C. **28** 50N 125W
Boya Lake P.P.,: B.C. **28** 59N 129W
Boyle: Alta. **30** 54N 113W
Bracebridge: Ont. **38** 45N 79W
Brackendale: B.C. **28** 50N 123W
Bradford: Ont. **38** 44N 80W
Braeside: Ont. **39** 45N 76W
Bralorne: B.C. **28** 51N 123W
Brampton: Ont. **38** 44N 80W
Branch: Nfld. **41** 47N 54W
Brandon: Man. **32** 50N 100W
Brantford: Ont. **34** 43N 80W
Bras d'Or Lake: N.S. **41** 46N 61W
Brazeau: *riv.*, Alta. **30** 53N 116W
Brazeau, Mt.: Alta. **30** 52N 117W
Brazeau Res.: Alta. **30** 53N 115W
Bremner: Alta. **27** 54N 112W
Bretona: Alta. **27** 53N 113W
Brevoort Island: N.W.T. **21** 64N 64W
Brew Mt.: B.C. **28** 51N 122W
Bridgetown: N.S. **41** 45N 65W
Bridgewater: N.S. **41** 44N 64W
Brier I.: N.S. **41** 44N 66W
Brig Bay: *town*, Nfld. **41** 51N 57W
Brighouse: B.C. **27** 49N 123W
Brighton: Ont. **38** 44N 78W
Britannia Beach: B.C. **28** 50N 123W
British Columbia: *Prov.*, (*cap.* Victoria) **22** — —
British Empire Range: N.W.T. **21** 82N 80W
British Mts.: Can/U.S.A. **20** 69N 140W
Broadview: Sask. **31** 50N 102W
Brochet: Man. **31** 58N 101W
Brochet, Lac: Man. **32** 49N 69W
Brock I.: N.W.T. **20** 78N 115W
Brockville: Ont. **39** 45N 76W
Brodeur Penin.: N.W.T. **21** 73N 87W
Brooks: Alta. **30** 50N 112W
Brooks Penin.: B.C. **29** 50N 127W
Brossard: Qué. **27** 45N 73W
Broughton I.: B.C. **29** 51N 127W
Broughton I.: N.W.T. **21** 67N 64W
[illegible]
Bruce Peninsula: Ont. **34** 45N 81W
Bruderheim: Alta. **30** 54N 113W
Bruno: Sask. **31** 52N 106W
Bryson: Qué. **38** 46N 77W
Buchan Gulf: N.W.T. **21** 72N 75W
Buchans: Nfld. **41** 49N 57W
Buckhorn Lake: Ont. **38** 44N 78W
Buckingham: Qué. **39** 46N 75W
Buffalo Head Hills: Alta. **30** 57N 116W
Buffalo Lake: Alta. **30** 52N 113W
Buffalo Lake: N.W.T. **22** 60N 116W
Buffalo Narrows: *town*, Saskatchewan **31** 57N 108W
Buffalo Pound P.P.: Sask. **31** 51N 105W
Bulkley: *riv.*, B.C. **29** 55N 127W
Buntzen Lake: B.C. **27** 49N 123W
Burden, Mt.: B.C. **29** 56N 123W
Burgeo: Nfld. **41** 48N 58W
Burin: Nfld. **41** 47N 55W
Burin Penin.: Nfld. **41** 47N 55W
Burke, Mt.: B.C. **27** 49N 123W
Burk's Falls: *town*, Ont. **38** 46N 79W
Burlington: Ont. **38** 43N 80W
Burnaby: *& lake*, B.C. **27** 49N 123W
Burnside: *riv.*, N.W.T. **20** 66N 110W
Burns Lake: *town*, B.C. **29** 54N 126W
Burnt Lake: Qué. **37** 52N 64W
Burnt Lake: Nfld. **40** 52N 64W
Burntroot Lake: Ont. **38** 46N 79W
Burntwood: *riv.*, Man. **32** 55N 100W
Burquitlam: B.C. **27** 49N 123W
Burrard Inlet: B.C. **27** 49N 123W
Burstall: Sask. **31** 51N 110W
Bute Inlet: B.C. **28** 50N 125W
Buttle Lake: B.C. **28** 50N 125W
Button Bay: Man. **32** 59N 94W
Byam Channel: N.W.T. **20** 75N 105W
Byam Martin I.: *& Chan.* N.W.T. **20** 75N 104W
Bylot I.: N.W.T. **21** 73N 78W
Bylot Island Bird Sanctuary: N.W.T. **21** 73N 78W
Byron Bay: Nfld. **40** 55N 58W

C

Cabano: Qué. **37** 48N 69W
Cabonga, Rés.: Qué. **37** 47N 76W
Cabot Strait: N.S./Nfld. **41** 47N 60W
Cabri: Sask. **31** 51N 108W
Cache Creek: *town*, B.C. **29** 51N 121W
Calabogie: Ont. **38** 45N 77W
Calabogie Lake: Ont. **38** 45N 77W
Caledon: Ont. **38** 44N 80W
Caledonia: Ont. **38** 43N 80W
Calgary: Alta. **30** 51N 114W
Calling Lake: Alta. **30** 55N 113W
Calmar: Alta. **30** 53N 114W
Calumet: Qué. **39** 46N 75W
Calvert I.: B.C. **28** 51N 128W
Cambridge Bay: *settlement*, N.W.T. **20** 69N 105W
Cameron Hills: N.W.T./Alta. **22** 60N 120W
Campbell, Mt.: Yukon **20** 64N 139W
Campbell River: *town*, B.C. **28** 50N 125W
Campbellton: N.B. **41** 48N 67W
Camperville: Man. **32** 52N 100W
Camrose: Alta. **30** 53N 113W
Canada Bay: Nfld. **41** 51N 56W
Canairiktok: *riv.*, Nfld. **40** 55N 61W
Canal Flats: B.C. **29** 50N 116W
Candle Lake: *town*, Sask. **31** 54N 105W
Caniapiscau: *res.*, Qué. **37** 54N 70W
Caniapiscau: *riv.*, Qué. **37** 55N 69W
Canmore: Alta. **30** 52N 116W
Canoe Lake: Sask. **31** 55N 108W
Canora: Sask. **31** 52N 102W
Canso: *& cape.* N.S. **41** 45N 61W
Cap-de-la-Madeleine: Qué. **37** 46N 72W
Cap de Nouvelle-France: Qué. **36** 62N 74W
Cape Breton Highlands Nat. Park: Nova Scotia **41** 47N 61W
Cape Breton I.: N.S. **41** 46N 61W
Cape Dorset Bird Sanc.: N.W.T. **21** 64N 77W
Cape Scott P.P.: B.C. **28** 51N 128W
Capitol Hill: B.C. **27** 49N 123W
Caraquet: N.B. **41** 48N 65W
Carberry: Man. **32** 50N 99W
Carbonear: Nfld. **41** 48N 53W
Carcross: Yukon **22** 60N 135W
Cardinal: Ont. **39** 45N 75W
Cardston: Alta. **30** 49N 113W
Cariboo Mtns.: B.C. **29** 53N 121W
Caribou: Man. **32** 59N 98W
Caribou: *riv.*, Man. **32** 59N 95W
Caribou I.: Ont. **34** 47N 86W
Caribou Mts.: Alta. **30** 59N 115W
Carillon: Qué. **39** 46N 74W
Carleton, Mt.: N.B. **41** 47N 67W
Carleton Mt. P.P.: N.B. **41** 47N 67W
Carleton Place: Ont. **39** 45N 76W
Carlyle: Sask. **31** 50N 102W
Carmacks: Yukon **20** 62N 137W
Carman: Man. **32** 49N 98W
Carmanville: Nfld. **41** 49N 54W
Carnduff: Sask. **31** 49N 102W
Caroline: Alta. **30** 52N 115W
Carp Lake: B.C. **29** 55N 123W

Carrot: *riv.*, Man. **32** 55N 96W
Carrot River: *& riv.*, Sask. **31** 53N 103W
Carstairs: Alta. **30** 52N 114W
Cartmel Mt.: B.C. **28** 58N 129W
Cartwright: Nfld. **40** 53N 57W
Casselman: Ont. **39** 45N 75W
Cassiar: B.C. **28** 59N 130W
Cassiar Mtns.: B.C. **28** 59N 130W
Castlegar: B.C. **29** 49N 118W
Castor: Alta. **30** 52N 112W
Castor: *riv.*, Ont. **39** 45N 75W
Catalina: Nfld. **41** 48N 53W
Catchacoma Lake: Ont. **38** 45N 78W
Cathedral P.P.: B.C. **28** 49N 120W
Caughnawaga: Qué. **27** 45N 74W
Cawes Creek: Alta. **27** 53N 113W
Cecil Lake: *town*, B.C. **29** 56N 120W
Cedar Lake: Man. **32** 53N 100W
Central Butte: Sask. **31** 51N 107W
Chalk River: *town*, Ont. **38** 46N 77W
Chambly: Qué. **39** 45N 73W
Chamouchouane: *riv.*, Qué. **37** 50N 73W
Chandler: Qué. **37** 48N 65W
Chandos Lake: Ont. **38** 45N 78W
Channel-Port-aux-Basques: Newfoundland **41** 47N 59W
Chantrey Inlet: N.W.T. **21** 67N 96W
Chapais: Qué. **37** 50N 75W
Chapeau: Qué. **38** 46N 77W
Chapleau: Ont. **34** 48N 83W
Chaplin Lake: Sask. **31** 50N 107W
Charlemagne: Qué. **39** 46N 73W
Charles I.: N.W.T. **21** 63N 74W
Charleston Lake: Ont. **39** 45N 76W
Charlotte Lake: B.C. **29** 52N 125W
CHARLOTTETOWN: Prince Edward Island **41** 46N 63W
Charlton I.: N.W.T. **24** 52N 79W
Charron Lake: Man. **32** 53N 95W
Chase: B.C. **29** 51N 120W
Châteauguay: Qué. **39** 45N 74W
Chateh: Alta. **30** 59N 119W
Chatham: N.B. **41** 47N 65W
Chatham: Ont. **34** 42N 82W
Chatham Sound: B.C. **28** 54N 130W
Chats Falls Dam: Ont./Qué. **39** 45N 76W
Chaudière: *riv.*, Qué. **37** 46N 71W
Chedabucto Bay: N.S. **41** 45N 61W
Chelsea: Qué. **39** 45N 76W
Chemainus: B.C. **28** 49N 124W
Chemung Lake: Ont. **38** 44N 78W
Chénéville: Qué. **39** 46N 75W
Chester: N.S. **41** 45N 64W
Chesterfield Inlet: *& town*, N.W.T. **21** 63N 91W
Chesterville: Ont. **39** 45N 75W
Chetwynd: B.C. **29** 56N 121W
Chibougamau: Qué. **37** 50N 75W
Chibougamau, Parc de: Qué. **37** 49N 74W
Chicoutimi: Qué. **37** 48N 71W
Chidley, C.: Nfld. **26** 60N 65W
Chief Lake: *town*, B.C. **29** 54N 123W
Chignecto Bay: New Brunswick/N.S. **41** 45N 65W
Chignecto Game Sanc.:N.S. **41** 45N 65W
Chilanko Forks: B.C. **29** 52N 124W
Chilcotin: *riv.*, B.C. **29** 52N 123W
Chilko Lake: B.C. **29** 51N 124W
Chilliwack: B.C. **28** 49N 122W
Chilliwack Lake: *& riv.*, B.C. **28** 49N 121W
Chinchaga: *riv.*, Alta. **30** 58N 119W
Chip Lake: Alta. **30** 54N 115W
Chipman: N.B. **41** 46N 66W
Chiputneticook Lakes: Canada/U.S.A. **41** 45N 67W
Chisasibi: Qué. **37** 54N 80W
Chisel Lake: *town*, Man. **32** 55N 100W
Choate: B.C. **28** 49N 121W
Choiceland: Sask. **31** 53N 104W
Chomedey: Qué. **27** 46N 74W
Chorkbak Inlet: N.W.T. **21** 65N 74W
Chown, Mt.: Alta. **30** 53N 119W
Christie Bay: N.W.T. **20** 62N 111W
Christina: *riv.*, Alta. **30** 56N 111W
Churchbridge: Sask. **31** 51N 102W
Churchill: Man. **27** 59N 94W
Churchill: *riv.*, Nfld. **40** 53N 64W
Churchill: *riv.*, Sask./Man. **23** 58N 95W
Churchill, Cape: Man. **23** 59N 93W
Churchill Falls: Nfld. **40** 53N 64W
Churchill Lake: Sask. **31** 56N 108W
Churchill Peak: B.C. **29** 58N 125W
Cirque, Mt.: Nfld. **40** 59N 64W
Claire, Lake: Alta. **30** 58N 112W
Clarence Head: N.W.T. **21** 77N 78W
Clarenville: Nfld. **41** 48N 54W
Claresholm: Alta. **30** 50N 114W
Clark Point: Ont. **34** 44N 82W
Clarke City: Qué. **37** 50N 67W
Clarks Harbour: N.S. **41** 43N 66W
Clayoquot Sound: B.C. **29** 49N 126W
Clear Lake: Ont. **38** 45N 77W
Clear Hills: Alta. **30** 57N 119W
Clearwater: *town*, B.C. **29** 52N 120W
Clearwater: *riv.*, Sask./Alta. **31** 57N 109W
Clearwater Lake: B.C. **29** 52N 120W
Clinton: B.C. **29** 51N 121W
Clinton-Colden Lake: N.W.T. **20** 64N 107W
Clo-oose: B.C. **28** 49N 125W
Close Lake: Sask. **31** 58N 105W
Clover Bar: Alta. **27** 54N 113W
Cluff Lake: *town*, Sask. **31** 58N 110W
Clyde: N.W.T. **21** 70N 68W
Coal: *riv.*, B.C./Yukon **29** 60N 127W
Coaldale: Alta. **30** 50N 113W
Coalhurst: Alta. **30** 50N 113W
Coast Mtns.: B.C. **28** 54N 128W
Coaticook: Qué. **37** 45N 72W
Coats I.: N.W.T. **21** 62N 83W
Cobalt: Ont. **34** 47N 80W
Cobden: Ont. **38** 46N 77W
Cobequid Mtns.: N.S. **41** 45N 64W
Cobourg: Ont. **38** 44N 78W
Cochrane: Alta. **30** 51N 114W
Cochrane: Ont. **34** 49N 81W
Cochrane: *riv.*, Man. **23** 58N 102W
Cod I.: Nfld. **40** 58N 62W
Colborne: Ont. **38** 44N 78W
Cold Lake: *& town*, Alta. **30** 54N 110W
Coldwater: Ont. **38** 45N 80W
Coleman: Alta. **30** 50N 115W
Collins Bay: *town*, Ont. **38** 44N 77W
Colonsay: Sask. **31** 53N 105W
Columbia: *riv.*, B.C. **29** 51N 116W
Columbia, Mt.: B.C./Alta. **29** 52N 117W
Columbia Mtns.: B.C. **29** 52N 120W
Colville Lake: *town*, N.W.T. **20** 67N 125W
Colwood: B.C. **28** 49N 123W
Comfort Bight: Nfld. **40** 53N 56W
Committee Bay: N.W.T. **21** 68N 87W
Comox: B.C. **28** 50N 125W
Comox Lake: B.C. **28** 50N 125W
Conception Harbour: Nfld. **41** 47N 53W
Conche: Nfld. **41** 51N 56W
Conklin: Alta. **30** 56N 111W
Consort: Alta. **30** 52N 111W
Contrecoeur: Qué. **39** 46N 73W
Contwoyto Lake: N.W.T. **20** 66N 111W
Cook Bay: Lake Simcoe, Ont. **38** 44N 79W
Coppermine: *& riv.*, N.W.T. **20** 67N 115W
Copper Mountain: *town*, British Columbia **28** 49N 120W
Coquitlam: *& riv.*, B.C. **27** 49N 123W
Coral Harbour: *settlement*, N.W.T. **21** 64N 83W
Coral Rapids: *town*, Ont. **34** 50N 82W
Cormack Mt.: Nfld. **41** 48N 56W
Cormorant: *& lake*, Man. **32** 54N 101W
Corner Brook: Nfld. **41** 49N 58W
Cornwall: Ont. **39** 45N 75W
Cornwall I.: N.W.T. **21** 77N 95W
Cornwallis I.: N.W.T. **21** 75N 95W
Coronation: Alta. **30** 52N 111W
Coronation Gulf: N.W.T. **20** 68N 110W
Cortes I.: B.C. **28** 50N 125W
Couchiching Lake: Ont. **38** 45N 79W
Coulonge: *riv.*, Qué. **37** 47N 77W
Courtenay: B.C. **28** 50N 125W
Coutts: Alta. **30** 49N 112W
Crabtree: Qué. **39** 46N 73W
Craik: Sask. **31** 52N 105W
Cranberry Portage: Man. **32** 55N 101W
Cranbrook: B.C. **29** 49N 116W
Crane Lake: Sask. **31** 50N 109W
Cree: *riv.*, Sask. **31** 58N 106W
Cree Lake: Sask. **31** 57N 107W
Creighton: Sask. **31** 55N 102W
Creston: B.C. **29** 49N 116W
Creswell Bay: *settlement*, N.W.T. **21** 73N 94W
Crofton: B.C. **28** 49N 124W
Crooked Lake: Nfld. **41** 48N 56W
Crossfield: Alta. **30** 51N 114W
Cross Lake: Ont. **38** 45N 77W
Cross Lake: *& town*, Man. **32** 55N 98W
Crowsnest Pass: B.C./Alta. **29** 50N 115W
Cudworth: Sask. **31** 52N 106
Cumberland: B.C. **28** 50N 125W
Cumberland: *penin. & sound*, N.W.T. **21** 66N 65W
Cumberland Lake: Sask. **31** 54N 102W
Cupar: Sask. **31** 51N 104W
Cut Knife: Sask. **31** 53N 109W
Cypress Hills: Alta./Sask. **23** 50N 110W
Cypress Hills P.P.: Sask. **31** 50N 109W

D

Dalhousie: N.B. **41** 48N 66W
Dalhousie, Cape: N.W.T. **20** 70N 130W
Dalmeny: Sask. **31** 52N 107W
Daniels Harbour: Nfld. **41** 50N 58W
Danielson P.P.: Sask. **31** 51N 107W
Darnley Bay: N.W.T. **20** 70N 124W
Dartmouth: N.S. **41** 45N 64W
Dauphin: Man. **32** 51N 100W
Dauphin: *riv.*, Man. **32** 52N 99W
Dauphin Lake: Man. **32** 51N 100W
Dave Brook: *settlement*, Nfld. **40** 54N 58W
Davidson: Sask. **31** 51N 106W
Davis Inlet: *settlement*, Newfoundland **40** 56N 61W
Davis Str.: Can./Grnld. **21** 67N 58W
Davy Lake: Sask. **31** 59N 108W
Dawson: Yukon **20** 64N 139W
Dawson Mt.: B.C. **29** 51N 117W
Dawson Bay: Man. **32** 53N 101W
Dawson Creek: *town*, B.C. **29** 56N 120W
Dawson Range: Yukon **20** 62N 139W
Daysland: Alta. **30** 53N 112W
Dease: *riv.*, B.C. **28** 59N 129W
Dease Arm: Great Bear Lake, N.W.T. **20** 67N 120W
Dease Lake: *& settlement*, British Columbia **28** 58N 130W
Dease Str.: N.W.T. **20** 69N 107W
Déception: Qué. **36** 63N 75W
Deep Cove: *town*, B.C. **27** 49N 123W
Deep Inlet: Nfld. **40** 55N 60W
Deep River: *town*, Ont. **38** 46N 77W
Deer Lake: *town*: Nfld. **41** 49N 58W
Delisle: Sask. **31** 52N 107W
Deloraine: Man. **23** 49N 100W
Deloro: Ont. **38** 44N 78W
Delson: Qué. **39** 45N 74W
Delta: B.C. **27** 49N 123W
Denbigh: Ont. **38** 45N 77W
Denman I.: B.C. **28** 50N 125W
Departure Bay: B.C. **28** 49N 124W
De Salis Bay: N.W.T. **20** 72N 122W
Deschambault Lake: Sask. **31** 55N 103W
Deseronto: Ont. **38** 44N 77W
Détroit d'Hudson: Qué./N.W.T. **21** 63N 73W
Deux Montagnes: *town*, Qué. **27** 46N 74W
Deux Montagnes, Lac des: Qué. **39** 45N 74W
Devon: Alta. **30** 53N 114W
Devon I.: N.W.T. **21** 75N 85W
Dewar Lakes: N.W.T. **21** 69N 71W
Dewey Soper Bird Sanc.: N.W.T. **21** 66N 74W
Diamond Jenness Peninsula: N.W.T. **20** 71N 116W
D'Iberville, Lac: Qué. **37** 56N 73W
Dickson Lake: Ont. **38** 46N 78W
Dickson Peak: B.C. **28** 51N 123W
Didsbury: Alta. **30** 52N 114W
Diefenbaker, Lake: Sask. **31** 51N 107W
Digby: N.S. **41** 45N 66W
Dinorwic: Ont. **34** 50N 93W
Disaster Rapids: Nfld. **40** 53N 64W
Dismal Lakes: N.W.T. **20** 67N 117W
Dixon Entrance: *str.* U.S.A./Canada **22** 54N 132W
Doaktown: N.B. **41** 46N 66W
Dodge Lake: Sask. **31** 60N 106W
Dodsland: Sask. **31** 52N 109W
Doe Lake: Ont. **38** 46N 79W
Dog Creek: *town*, B.C. **29** 52N 122W
Dog (High) Island: Nfld. **40** 57N 61W
Dog Lake: Man. **32** 51N 98W
Dolbeau: Qué. **37** 49N 72W
Dollarton: B.C. **27** 49N 123W
Dolphin & Union Str.: N.W.T. **20** 69N 115W
Dominion Lake: Nfld. **40** 53N 62W
Don: *riv.*, Ont. **27** 44N 79W
Don Mills: Ont. **27** 44N 79W
Dorchester: N.B. **41** 46N 64W
Dorchester, Cape: N.W.T. **21** 65N 78W
Doré Lake: Sask. **31** 55N 107W
Dorion-Vaudreuil: Qué. **39** 45N 74W
Dorval: Qué. **27** 45N 74W
Double Mer: *inlet*, Nfld. **40** 54N 59W
Douglas Island: B.C. **27** 49N 123W
Douglas Prov. Park: Sask. **31** 51N 107W
Dowling Lake: Alta. **30** 52N 112W
Downton, Mt.: B.C. **29** 53N 125W
Drayton Valley: *town*, Alta. **30** 53N 115W
Drumheller: Alta. **30** 51N 113W
Drummondville: Qué. **37** 46N 72W
Dryden: Ont. **34** 50N 93W
Dubawnt Lake: N.W.T. **20** 63N 102W
Duck Bay: *town*, Man. **32** 52N 100W
Duck I.: Ont. **38** 44N 77W
Duck Lake: *town*, Sask. **31** 53N 106W
Duck Mt. *& Prov. Pk.* Manitoba/Saskatchewan **32** 51N 101W
Duffey Lake: B.C. **28** 50N 122W
Du Lièvre: *riv., Qué.* **39** 46N 75W
Duncan: B.C. **28** 49N 124W
Duncan Dam: B.C. **29** 50N 117W
Duncan Lake: B.C. **29** 50N 117W
Dundas: Ont. **38** 43N 80W
Dundas I.: B.C. **28** 55N 131W
Dundas Penin.: N.W.T. **20** 75N 112W
Dunnville: Ont. **38** 43N 80W
Dyer, Cape: N.W.T. **21** 67N 61W

E

Eagle Lake: Ont. **34** 50N 93W
Ear Falls: Ont. **34** 51N 93W
East Bay Bird Sanc.: N.W.T. **21** 64N 82W
Eastend: Sask. **31** 49N 109W
Eastmain: Qué. **37** 52N 79W
Eastmain: *riv.*, Qué. **37** 52N 79W
East Point: P.E.I. **41** 46N 62W
East York: Ont. **27** 44N 79W
Eatonia: Sask. **31** 51N 110W
Eclipse Channel: Nfld. **40** 60N 64W
Eclipse Sound: N.W.T. **21** 73N 79W
Edehon Lake: N.W.T. **23** 60N 97W
Edgewood: B.C. **29** 50N 118W
EDMONTON: Alta. **30** 54N 114W
Edmund Lake: Man. **32** 55N 93W
Edmundston: N.B. **41** 47N 68W
Edson: Alta. **30** 54N 116W
Eduni, Mt.: N.W.T. **20** 64N 128W
Edziza Peak: B.C. **28** 58N 131W
Eganville: Ont. **38** 45N 77W
Eglinton I.: N.W.T. **20** 76N 118W
Egmont: B.C. **28** 50N 124W
Eileen Lake: N.W.T. **20** 62N 107W
Eldorado: Sask. **31** 58N 109W
Eliot. Mt.: Nfld. **40** 59N 64W
Elk I. Heritage Park: Man. **32** 51N 96W
Elkhorn: Man. **32** 50N 101W
Elk. Is. N.P.: Alta. **30** 54N 113W
Elk Point: *town*, Alta. **30** 54N 111W
Ellerslie: Alta. **27** 53N 113W
Ellesmere I.: N.W.T. **21** 80N 80W
Elliot Lake: *town*, Ont. **34** 46N 83W
Elmira: P.E.I. **41** 46N 62W
Elmvale: Ont. **38** 45N 80W
Elrose: Sask. **31** 51N 108W
Elsa: Yukon **20** 64N 130W
Elu Inlet. N.W.T. **20** 68N 106W
Elvira, Cape: N.W.T. **20** 74N 107W
Emerald I.: N.W.T. **20** 76N 114W
Emerson: Man. **32** 49N 97W
Empress: Alta. **23** 51N 110W
Enderby: B.C. **29** 50N 119W
Englee: Nfld. **41** 51N 56W
Englehart: Ont. **34** 48N 80W
English: *riv.*, Ont. **34** 50N 95W
English Bay: B.C. **27** 49N 123W
Era Island: N.W.T. **21** 68N 78W
Erie, Lake: Can./U.S.A. **24** 42N 81W
Escuminac, Point: N.B. **41** 47N 65W
Eskimo Lakes: N.W.T. **20** 69N 131W
Eskimo Point: *town*, N.W.T. **21** 61N 94W
Espanola: Ont. **34** 46N 82W
Esquimalt, B.C. **28** 48N 123W
Essondale: B.C. **27** 49N 123W
Esterhazy, Sask. **31** 50N 102W
Estevan: Sask. **31** 49N 103W
Estevan Point: B.C. **29** 49N 126W
Eston: Sask. **31** 51N 109W
Etawney Lake: Man. **32** 58N 96W
Ethelbert: Man. **32** 51N 100W
Etobicoke: *& creek*, Ont. **27** 44N 80W
Eureka: N.W.T. **21** 80N 86W
Eureka River: *town*, Alta. **30** 56N 119W
Eutsuk Lake: B.C. **29** 53N 126W
Evans, Lac: Qué. **37** 51N 77W
Evans, Mt.: B.C./Alta. **29** 52N 118W
Evansburg: Alta. **30** 54N 115W
Evans Strait: N.W.T. **21** 63N 82W
Exploits: *riv.*, Nfld. **41** 49N 56W

F

Faber Lake: N.W.T. **20** 63N 117W
Fair Ness: N.W.T. **21** 63N 72W
Fairview: Alta. **30** 56N 118W
Fairweather Mt.: B.C. **22** 59N 137W
Falconbridge, Ont. **34** 47N 81W
Falher: Alta. **30** 56N 117W
Family Lake: Man. **32** 52N 96W
Farnham, Mt.: B.C. **29** 50N 116W
Faro: Yukon **20** 62N 133W
Fassett: Qué. **39** 46N 75W
Fatima: Qué. **37** 46N 62W
Felix, Cape: N.W.T. **20** 70N 98W
Fenelon Falls: *town*, Ont. **27** 45N 79W
Ferguson Lake: N.W.T. **20** 70N 105W
Fermont, Qué. **37** 53N 67W
Fernie: B.C. **29** 49N 115W
Ferryland: Nfld. **41** 47N 53W
Fife Lake: Sask. **31** 49N 106W
Finch: Ont. **39** 45N 75W
Finlay: *riv.*, B.C. **29** 57N 125W
Finlay Range: B.C. **29** 57N 126W
Firebag: *riv.*, Alta./Sask. **30** 57N 110W
Firebag Hills: Sask. **31** 57N 110W
Fisher, Mt.: B.C. **29** 50N 116W
Fisher Strait: N.W.T. **21** 63N 84W
Fishing Branch Game Res.: Yukon **20** 66N 140W
Fishing Lake: Man. **32** 52N 95W
Fishing Ship Harbour: Newfoundland **40** 53N 56W
Fitzgerald: Alta. **30** 60N 111W
Fitzhugh Sound: B.C. **29** 52N 128W
Fleur de Lys: Nfld. **41** 50N 56W
Fleur de Mai, Lac: Nfld. **40** 52N 65W
Flin Flon: Man. **32** 55N 102W
Flores I.: B.C. **29** 49N 126W
Flower's Cove: *town*, Nfld. **41** 52N 57W
Foam Lake: *town*, Sask. **31** 52N 103W
Foch: B.C. **28** 50N 124W
Fogo: *& i.*, Nfld. **41** 50N 54W
Foley Lake: Alta. **27** 53N 113W
Fond du Lac: Sask. **31** 59N 107W
Fond du Lac: *riv.*, Sask. **31** 59N 105W
Fontas: *& riv.*, B.C. **29** 58N 121W
Forbes, Mt.: Alta. **30** 52N 117W
Foremost: Alta. **30** 49N 111W
Forestburg: Alta. **30** 53N 112W
Forest Hill: Ont. **27** 44N 79W
Forestville: Qué. **37** 49N 69W
Forrest Lake: Sask.: **31** 58N 109W
Fort Albany: Ont. **34** 52N 82W
Fort Chipewyan: Alta. **30** 59N 111W
Fort Coulonge: Qué. **38** 46N 77W
Forteau: *town*, Nfld. **40** 51N 57W
Fort Erie: Ont. **38** 43N 79W
Fort Franklin: N.W.T. **20** 66N 124W
Fort Fraser: B.C. **29** 54N 125W
Fort Garry: Man. **33** 50N 91W
Fort Good Hope: N.W.T. **20** 66N 128W
Fort Hope: Ont. **34** 51N 88W
Fort Liard: N.W.T. **22** 60N 124W
Fort Macleod: Alta. **30** 50N 113W
Fort McLeod: B.C. **29** 55N 123W
Fort McMurray: Alta. **30** 57N 111W
Fort McPherson: N.W.T. **20** 67N 135W
Fort Nelson: *& riv.*, B.C. **29** 59N 123W
Fort Norman: N.W.T. **20** 65N 125W
Fort Providence: N.W.T. **32** 61N 118W
Fort Qu'Appelle: Sask. **31** 51N 104W
Fort Resolution: N.W.T. **23** 61N 114W
Fort Rouge: Man. **33** 50N 91W
Fort Rupert: Qué. **37** 52N 79W
Fort St. James: B.C. **29** 54N 124W
Fort St. John: B.C. **29** 56N 121W
Fort Saskatchewan: Alta. **27** 54N 113W
Fort Severn: Ont. **34** 56N 88W
Fort Simpson: N.W.T. **20** 62N 122W
Fort Smith: N.W.T. **23** 60N 112W
Fortune: *& bay*. Nfld. **41** 47N 56W
Fort Vermilion: Alta. **30** 58N 116W
Fort Walsh Nat. Hist. P.: Sask. **31** 50N 110W
Fort William: Ont. *see* Thunder Bay
Fort Whyte: Man. **33** 50N 91W
Fortymile: *riv.*, Canada/U.S.A. **20** 64N 141W
Fosheim Peninsula: N.W.T. **21** 79N 83W
Fossmill: Ont. **38** 46N 79W
Foster: *riv.*, Sask. **31** 56N 106W
Fox Creek: *town*, Alta. **30** 54N 117W
Foxe Basin: N.W.T. **21** 68N 79W
Foxe Channel: N.W.T. **21** 65N 80W
Foxe Penin.: N.W.T. **21** 64N 77W
Fox Harbour: Nfld. **40** 52N 56W
Fox Valley: *town*, Sask. **31** 50N 109W
Frances Lake: Yukon **20** 61N 129W
François Lake: B.C. **29** 54N 126W
Frankford: Ont. **38** 44N 78W
Franklin, District of: N.W.T. **20/21** — —
Franklin Bay: N.W.T. **20** 70N 126W
Franklin Lake: N.W.T. **21** 67N 96W
Franklin Mts.: N.W.T. **20** 64N 125W
Fraser: *riv.*, B.C. **29** 51N 122W
Fraser: *riv.*, Nfld. **40** 57N 64W
Fraser Lake: *town*, B.C. **22** 54N 125W
Fraser Plateau: B.C. **29** 52N 124W
FREDERICTON: New Brunswick **41** 46N 67W
Fredrikshald Bay: N.W.T. **20** 71N 105W
Freels, Cape: Nfld. **41** 49N 53W
Frenchman Butte: Sask. **31** 54N 110W
Frobisher Bay: N.W.T. **21** 63N 68W
Frobisher Bay: Sask. **31** 56N 108W
Frog Lake: Alta. **30** 54N 110W
Frozen Strait: N.W.T. **21** 66N 85W
Fruitvale: B.C. **29** 49N 118W
Fundy, Bay of: N.B./N.S. **41** 45N 66W
Fundy Nat. Park: N.B. **41** 45N 65W
Fury & Hecla Strait: N.W.T. **21** 70N 84W

G

Gabarus Bay: N.S. **41** 46N 60W
Gabbro Lake: Nfld. **40** 54N 65W
Gabriola I.: B.C. **28** 49N 124W
Gagnon: Qué. **37** 52N 68W
Gagnon, Lac: Qué. **39** 46N 75W
Galiano I.: B.C. **28** 49N 123W
Gambier I.: B.C. **28** 49N 123W
Gambo: Nfld. **41** 49N 54W
Gananoque: Ont. **39** 44N 76W
Gander: *& lake*, Nfld. **41** 49N 55W
Gander: *riv.*, Nfld. **41** 49N 55W
Ganges: B.C. **28** 49N 123W
[illegible]
Gardner Canal: B.C. **28** 53N 128W
Garibaldi: B.C. **28** 50N 123W
Garibaldi: *mtn. & lake*, B.C. **28** 50N 123W
Garibaldi Prov. Park: B.C. **28** 50N 123W
Garry Lake: N.W.T. **20** 66N 100W
Gaspé: Qué. **37** 49N 64W
Gaspésie, Péninsule de la: Québec **37** 48N 66W
Gaspésie P.P.: Qué. **37** 48N 67W
Gateshead I.: N.W.T. **20** 71N 100W
Gatineau: Qué. **39** 45N 76W
Gatineau: *riv.*, Qué. **37** 46N 76W
Gatineau, Parc de la: Qué. **39** 46N 76W
Gauer Lake: Man. **32** 57N 98W
Geikie: *riv.*, Sask. **31** 57N 105W
George: *riv.*, Qué. **37** 58N 66W
George Island: Nfld. **40** 54N 57W
Georges Cove: *settlement*, Nfld. **40** 53N 56W
Georgetown: Ont. **38** 44N 80W
Georgetown: P.E.I. **41** 46N 62W
Georgia, Strait of: B.C. **28** 49N 124W
Georgian Bay: Ont. **34** 45N 81W
Georgian Bay Is. N.P.: Ont. **34** 45N 82W
Georgina I.: Ont. **38** 44N 79W
Geraldton: Ont. **34** 50N 87W
Germansen Landing: B.C. **29** 56N 125W
Gerrard: B.C. **29** 50N 117W
Giants Causeway: N.W.T. **20** 76N 122W
Gibsons: B.C. **28** 49N 123W
Gilbert, Mt.: B.C. **28** 51N 124W
Gilbert Plains: *town*, Man. **32** 51N 100W
Gilford I.: B.C. **29** 51N 126W
Gil I.: B.C. **28** 53N 129W
Gillam: Man. **32** 56N 95W
Gillies Bay: *town*, B.C. **28** 50N 124W
Gilmour I.: N.W.T. **21** 60N 80W
Gimli: Man. **32** 51N 97W
Gjoa Haven: N.W.T. **21** 69N 96W
Glace Bay: *town*, N.S. **41** 46N 60W
Glacier Nat. Park: B.C. **29** 51N 117W
Gladstone: Man. **32** 50N 99W
Gladys Lake: B.C. **28** 60N 133W
Glenboro: Man. **32** 50N 99W
Gloucester: Ont. **39** 45N 76W
Glovertown: Nfld. **41** 49N 54W
Goat I.: B.C. **28** 50N 124W
Goderich: Ont. **34** 44N 82W
Gods: *riv.*, Man. **32** 56N 92W
Gods Lake: *town & lake*, Man. **32** 55N 94W
God's Mercy, Bay of: N.W.T. **21** 64N 86W
Gold Bridge: B.C. **28** 51N 123W
Gold River: *town*, B.C. **29** 50N 125W
Golden: B.C. **29** 51N 117W
Golden Ears P.P.: B.C. **28** 50N 122W
Golden Hinde: *mtn.*, B.C. **29** 50N 126W
Golden Lake: *town*, Ont. **38** 46N 77W
Golden Spike: Alta. **30** 53N 114W
Gold Pines: Ont. **34** 51N 93W
Goldsmith Channel: N.W.T. **20** 73N 106W
Goodeve: Sask. **31** 51N 103W
Good Hope, Mt.: B.C. **29** 51N 124W
Goodsoil: Sask. **31** 54N 109W
Good Spirit P.P.: Sask. **31** 51N 103W
Goose: *riv.*, Nfld. **40** 53N 61W
Gordonhorne Peak: B.C. **29** 52N 119W
Gordon Lake: Alta. **30** 56N 110W
Gott Peak: B.C. **28** 50N 122W
Gouin, Réservoir: Qué. **37** 48N 75W
Gowganda: Ont. **34** 48N 81W
Gracefield: Qué. **39** 46N 76W
Graham I.: B.C. **28** 54N 132W
Graham I.: N.W.T. **21** 77N 90W
Granby: Qué. **37** 45N 73W
Granby: *riv.*, B.C. **29** 50N 118W
Grand Bank: *town*, Nfld. **41** 47N 56W
Grand Cache: Alta. **30** 54N 119W
Grand Centre: Alta. **30** 54N 110W
Grand Prairie: *town*, Alta. **30** 55N 119W
Grande rivière de la Baleine: Québec **37** 55N 77W
Grand Falls: *town*, N.B. **41** 47N 67W
Grand Falls: *town*, Nfld. **41** 49N 56W
Grand Forks: B.C. **29** 49N 118W
Grandin, Lac: N.W.T. **20** 64N 118W
Grand Lake: N.B. **41** 46N 66W
Grand Lake: Nfld. **40** 54N 61W
Grand Lake: Nfld. **41** 49N 57W
Grand Manan I.: N.B. **41** 45N 67W
Grand-Mère: Qué. **37** 47N 73W
Grand Narrows: *town*, N.S. **41** 46N 61W
Grand Rapids: *town*, Man. **32** 53N 99W
Grandview: Man. **32** 51N 101W
Granisle: B.C. **29** 55N 126W
Granite Bay: *town*, B.C. **28** 50N 125W
Granville Lake: *& falls*, Manitoba **32** 56N 100W
Grass: *riv.*, Man. **32** 56N 97W
Grass River Prov. Pk.: Man. **32** 55N 101W
Grassy Narrows: *town*, Ont. **34** 50N 94W
Gravelbourg: Sask. **31** 50N 107W
Gravenhurst: Ont. **38** 45N 79W
Grayling: *riv.*, B.C. **29** 60N 126W
Greasy Lake: N.W.T. **20** 63N 122W
Great Bear Lake: N.W.T. **20** 66N 120W
Great Central: B.C. **28** 49N 125W
Great Central Lake: B.C. **28** 49N 125W
Great Plain of the Koukdjuak: N.W.T. **21** 66N 73W
Great Sand Hills: Sask. **31** 50N 109W
Great Slave Lake: N.W.T. **20** 61N 115W
Greely Fiord: N.W.T. **21** 80N 82W
Green Lake: B.C. **29** 51N 121W
Green Lake: *town*, Sask. **31** 54N 108W
Greenville: B.C. **28** 55N 130W
Greenwater Prov. Pk.: Saskatchewan **31** 52N 104W
Greenwood: B.C. **29** 49N 119W
Grenfell: Sask. **31** 50N 103W
Grenville: Qué. **39** 46N 75W
Grenville, Mt.: B.C. **28** 51N 124W
Gretna: Man. **32** 49N 97W
Grey: *riv.*, Nfld. **41** 48N 57W
Grey Hunter Peak: Yukon **20** 63N 136W
Grey Is.: Nfld. **41** 51N 55W
[illegible]
Grimshaw: Alta. **30** 56N 118W
Grindstone Prov. Recreation Park: Man. **32** 51N 97W
Grinnell Peninsula: N.W.T. **21** 77N 95W
Grise Fiord: *settlement*, N.W.T. **21** 76N 83W
Groais I.: Nfld. **41** 51N 55W
Gronlid: Sask. **31** 53N 104W
Gros Morne: *mtn.*, Nfld. **41** 50N 58W
Gros Morne Nat. Park: Nfld. **41** 49N 58W
Groswater Bay: Nfld. **40** 54N 58W
Groundhog: *riv.*, Ont. **34** 49N 82W
Guelph: Ont. **34** 43N 80W
Guillaume-Delisle, Lac: Qué. **37** 56N 76W
Gull Lake: Alta. **30** 52N 114W
Gull Lake: Nfld. **40** 53N 61W
Gull Lake: Ont. **38** 45N 79W
Gull Lake: *town*, Sask. **31** 50N 108W
Gunisao: *riv.*, Man. **32** 54N 97W
Gun Lake: B.C. **28** 51N 123W
Gushing, Mt.: B.C. **29** 58N 127W
Gypsumville: Man. **23** 52N 99W

H

Habay: Alta. **30** 59N 119W
Hadley Bay: N.W.T. **20** 72N 109W
Hafford: Sask. **31** 107N 53W
Haileybury: Ont. **34** 47N 80W
Haldimand: Ont. **38** 43N 80W
Halfway: *riv.*, B.C. **29** 56N 122W
Haliburton: *& lake*, Ont. **38** 45N 78W
HALIFAX: Nova Scotia **41** 45N 64W
Hall Basin: Canada/Greenland **21** 82N 63W
Hall Penin.: N.W.T. **21** 63N 66W
Halton Hills: *town*, Ont. **38** 44N 80W
Hamilton: Ont. **38** 43N 80W
Hamilton Inlet: Nfld. **40** 54N 58W
Hamilton Sound: Nfld. **41** 49N 54W
Hamiota: Man. **32** 50N 100W
Hampden: Nfld. **41** 50N 57W
Hampton: N.B. **41** 46N 66W
Haney: B.C. **28** 49N 123W
Hanmer: Ont. **24** 47N 81W
Hanna: Alta. **30** 52N 112W
Hannah Bay: Ont. **24** 51N 80W
Hanover: Ont. **34** 44N 81W
Hantsport: N.S. **41** 45N 64W
Happy Valley-Goose Bay: *town*, Nfld. **40** 53N 60W
Harbour Breton: Nfld. **41** 47N 56W
Harbour Grace: Nfld. **41** 48N 53W
Harcourt: N.B. **41** 47N 65W
Hardisty: Alta. **30** 53N 111W
Hardisty Lake: N.W.T. **30** 65N 118W
Hare Bay: Nfld. **41** 51N 56W
Hare Indian: *riv.*, N.W.T. **20** 66N 127W
Harp Lake: Nfld. **40** 55N 62W
Harricana: *riv.*, Qué. **37** 51N 79W
Harrington Harbour: Qué. **37** 50N 59W
Harrison, Cape: Nfld. **40** 55N 58W
Harrison Hot Springs: B.C. **28** 49N 122W
Harrison Lake: B.C. **28** 49N 122W
Harry Gibbons Bird Sanc.: N.W.T. **21** 64N 86W
Hart: *riv.*, Yukon **20** 65N 137W
Hartland: N.B. **41** 46N 67W
Hartney: Man. **32** 49N 100W
Hastings: Ont. **38** 44N 78W
Hauterive: Qué. **26** 49N 68W
Havelock: Ont. **38** 44N 78W
Havre-Saint-Pierre: Qué. **37** 50N 64W
Hawke Harbour: Nfld. **40** 53N 56W
Hawke I.: Nfld. **40** 53N 56W
Hawkesbury: Ont. **39** 46N 75W
Hay, Cape: N.W.T. **20** 74N 112W
Hayes, *riv.*, Man. **32** 56N 93W
Hay: *riv.*, Alta./N.W.T. **22** 61N 116W
Hay Lake: Alta. **30** 59N 119W
Hay Lake: Ont. **38** 45N 78W
Hay River: *town*, N.W.T. **22** 61N 116W
Hazelton: B.C. **29** 55N 128W
Hazen Strait: N.W.T. **20** 77N 110W
Head Lake: Ont. **38** 45N 79W
Hearst: Ont. **34** 50N 84W
Hearts Content: Nfld. **41** 48N 53W
Hebron: *& fiord*, Nfld. **40** 58N 63W
Hecate Strait: B.C. **28** 53N 131W
Hecla & Griper Bay: N.W.T. **20** 76N 112W
Hecla Prov. Park: Man. **32** 52N 97W
Hedley: B.C. **28** 49N 120W
Hemmingford: Qué. **39** 45N 74W
Henley Harbour: Nfld. **40** 52N 56W
Henrietta Maria, C.: Ont. **34** 55N 82W
Henry Kater, Pen.: N.W.T. **21** 69N 67W
Henryville: Qué. **39** 45N 73W
Herbert: Sask. **31** 50N 107W
Hermitage Bay: Nfld. **41** 47N 56W
Herschel: *& i.*, Yukon **20** 69N 139W
Hess: *riv.*, Yukon **20** 63N 133W
Hickman, Mt.: B.C. **28** 57N 131W
High Level: Alta. **30** 58N 117W
High Prairie: *town*, Alta. **30** 55N 116W
High River: *town*, Alta. **30** 50N 114W
Highrock: *& lake*, Man. **32** 56N 100W
Hilliers: B.C. **28** 49N 124W
Hines Creek: *town*, Alta. **30** 56N 119W
Hinton: Alta. **30** 53N 118W
Hoare Bay: N.W.T. **21** 65N 66W
Hodgeville: Sask. **31** 50N 107W
Hodgson: Man. **23** 51N 97W
Holden: Alta. **30** 53N 112W
Holman: N.W.T. **20** 71N 117W
Holton: Nfld. **40** 54N 57W
Holyrood: Nfld. **41** 47N 53W
Homathko: *riv.*, B.C. **29** 51N 125W
Home I.: Nfld. **40** 60N 64W
Home Bay: N.W.T. **21** 69N 67W
Home, Cape: N.W.T. **21** 75N 84W
Honguedo, Détroit d': *chan.*, Qué. **37** 49N 64W
Hood: *riv.*, N.W.T. **20** 67N 110W
Hope: B.C. **28** 49N 121W
Hopedale: Nfld. **40** 55N 60W
Hope I.: B.C. **29** 50N 128W
[illegible]
[illegible]
Horn Mt.: B.C. **28** 58N 129W
Horn Mts.: N.W.T **20** 62N 120W
Horsefly Lake: B.C. **29** 52N 121W
Horsehills Creek: Alta. **27** 54N 113W
Horse Is.: Nfld. **41** 50N 55W
Horseshoe Bay: *town*, B.C. **28** 49N 123W
Horton: *riv.*, N.W.T. **20** 69N 124W
Hottah Lake: N.W.T. **20** 65N 118W
Houston: B.C. **29** 54N 126W
Howe I.: Ont. **39** 44N 76W
Howe Sound: B.C. **28** 49N 123W
Howick: Qué. **39** 45N 74W
Hubbart Point: Man. **32** 59N 95W
Huberdeau: Qué. **39** 46N 75W
Hudson: Ont. **34** 50N 92W
Hudson: Qué. **39** 45N 74W
Hudson Bay (Baie d'Hudson) **21** 60N 85W
Hudson Bay: *town*, Sask. **31** 53N 102W
Hudson's Hope: B.C. **22** 56N 122W
Hudson Strait (Détroit d'Hudson): N.W.T./Québec **21** 63N 73W
Hull: Qué. **39** 45N 75W
Humber: *riv.*, Nfld. **41** 49N 57W
Humber: *riv.*, Ont. **38** 44N 80W
Humber Bay: Ont. **27** 44N 79W
Humboldt: Sask. **31** 52N 105W
Hundred Mile House: B.C. **29** 52N 121W
Hunter I.: B.C. **28** 52N 128W
Huntingdon: Qué. **39** 45N 74W
Huntingdon I.: Nfld. **40** 54N 57W
Hunstville: Ont. **38** 45N 79W
Huron, Lake: Canada/U.S.A. **24** 45N 82W
Hutte Sauvage, Lac de la: Qué. **26** 56N 65W
Hythe: Alta. **30** 56N 120W

I

Iberville: Qué. **39** 45N 73W
Île-à-la-Crosse: Sask. **31** 55N 108W
Îles de Gyrfalcon: Qué. **36** 59N 69W
Îles-de-la-Madeleine: Qué. **37** 46N 62W
Île du Grand Calumet: Qué. **38** 46N 77W
Ilford: Man. **32** 56N 96W
Indian Cabins: Alta. **30** 60N 117W
Indian Harbour: Nfld. **40** 55N 57W
Indian Head: Sask. **31** 50N 104W
Ingonish: N.S. **41** 47N 60W
Inklin: *riv.*, B.C. **28** 59N 133W
Innisfail: Alta. **30** 52N 114W
International Peace Garden: Canada/U.S.A. **32** 49N 100W
Inukjuak: Qué. **36** 58N 78W
Inuvik: N.W.T. **20** 68N 133W
Invermere: B.C. **29** 50N 116W
Inverness: N.S. **41** 46N 61W
Ioco: B.C. **27** 49N 123W
Iqaluit: N.W.T. **21** 63N 68W
Irma: Alta. **30** 53N 111W
Irondale: *riv.*, Ont. **38** 45N 78W
Iroquois: Ont. **39** 45N 75W
Iroquois Falls: *town*, Ont. **34** 48N 81W
Irvine: Alta. **30** 50N 110W
Irvine Creek: Alta. **27** 53N 113W
Irvines Landing: B.C. **28** 50N 124W
Isabella Falls: Nfld. **40** 54N 63W
Isachsen Ringnes Island: N.W.T. **20** 79N 103W
Iskut: *riv.*, B.C. **28** 57N 131W
Island Falls: *town*, Sask. **31** 56N 102W
Island Falls: *town*, Ont. **34** 50N 81W
Island Lake: *& town*, Man. **32** 54N 95W
Island of Ponds: Nfld. **40** 54N 56W
Islands, Bay of: Nfld. **26** 49N 58W
Isle St. Ignace: Ont. **34** 48N 80W
Islington: Ont. **27** 44N 80W
Itchen Lake: N.W.T. **20** 65N 113W
Ituna: Sask. **31** 51N 104W
Ivujivik: Qué. **36** 62N 78W

J

Jack Lake: Ont. **38** 45N 78W
Jacopie Lake: Nfld. **40** 54N 64W
Jacques-Cartier P.P.: Qué. **37** 47N 71W
Jacques-Cartier, Détroit de: Québec **37** 50N 64W
James Bay (Baie James): Ont./Qué. **24** 53N 80W
James Bay Preserve: N.W.T. **21** 53N 81W
James Ross, Cape: N.W.T. **20** 75N 114W
James Ross Strait: N.W.T. **21** 70N 97W
Jasper Nat. Park: Alta. **30** 53N 118W
Jasper: Alta. **30** 53N 118W
Jean Marie River: *town*, N.W.T. **20** 62N 121W
Jennings: *riv.*, B.C. **28** 59N 131W
Jervis Inlet: B.C. **28** 50N 124W
Jésus, Île: Qué. **27** 46N 74W
John D'or Prairie: *town*, Alta. **30** 58N 115W
Joliette: Qué. **39** 46N 73W
Jones Sound: N.W.T. **21** 76N 85W
Jonquière: Qué. **37** 48N 71W
Joseph, Lac.: Nfld. **40** 53N 65W
Joseph Lake: Alta. **30** 53N 113W
Joseph, Lake: Ont. **38** 45N 80W
Juan de Fuca, Str. of: Canada/U.S.A. **22** 48N 124W

K

Kaipokok Bay: Nfld. **40** 55N 59W
Kakagi Lake: Ont. **34** 49N 94W
Kakisa: N.W.T. **20** 61N 118W
Kakisa Lake: N.W.T. **22** 61N 118W
Kaladar: Ont. **38** 45N 77W
Kamaniskeg Lake: Ont. **38** 45N 78W
Kamilukuak Lake: N.W.T. **20** 62N 102W
Kaminak Lake: N.W.T. **21** 62N 95W
Kamloops: *& lake*, B.C. **29** 51N 120W
Kamsack: Sask. **31** 52N 102W
Kanaaupscow: Qué. **37** 54N 76W
[illegible]
[illegible]
Kanata: Ont. **39** 45N 76W
Kane Basin: Can./Grnld. **21** 79N 70W
Kangiqsualujjuaq: Qué. **36** 59N 66W
Kangiqsujuaq: Qué. **36** 62N 72W
Kangirsuk: Qué. **36** 60N 70W
Kapiskau: *riv.* Ont. **34** 52N 84W
Kapuskasing: *& riv.*, Ont. **34** 49N 83W
Kasba Lake: N.W.T. **23** 60N 102W
Kaslo: B.C. **29** 50N 117W
Kasshabog Lake: Ont. **38** 45N 78W
Kates Needle: *mtn.*, Canada/U.S.A. **28** 57N 132W
Kawagama Lake: Ont. **38** 45N 79W
Kawartha Lakes: Ont. **38** 45N 78W
Kazabazua: Qué. **39** 46N 76W
Kearney: Ont. **38** 46N 79W
Kechica: *riv.*, B.C. **29** 58N 127W
Kedgwick: N.B. **41** 48N 67W
Keefers: B.C. **28** 50N 121W
Keele: *riv.*, N.W.T. **20** 64N 127W
Keele Peak: Yukon/N.W.T. **20** 63N 130W
Keewatin: Ont. **34** 50N 95W
Keewatin, District of: N.W.T. **20/21** — —
Keith Arm: Gt. Bear Lake, N.W.T. **20** 65N 122W
Kejimkujik Nat. Pk.: N.S. **41** 44N 65W
Keller Lake: N.W.T. **20** 64N 122W
Kellett, Cape: N.W.T. **20** 72N 126W
Kellett Str.: N.W.T. **20** 76N 117W
Kelliher: Sask. **31** 51N 104W
Kelowna: B.C. **29** 50N 119W
Kelsey Bay: *town*, B.C. **29** 50N 126W
Kelvington: Sask. **31** 52N 103W
Kemano: B.C. **29** 54N 128W
Kempt, Lac.: Qué. **37** 47N 74W
Kemptville: Ont. **39** 45N 76W
Kennedy: Sask. **31** 50N 102W
Kennedy Lake: B.C. **28** 49N 125W
Kenney Dam: B.C. **29** 54N 125W
Kennisis Lake: Ont. **38** 45N 79W
Kenogami: *riv.*, Ont. **34** 50N 85W
Kenora: Ont. **34** 50N 94W
Kensington: P.E.I. **41** 46N 64W
Kent Penin.: N.W.T. **20** 68N 107W
Kentville: N.S. **41** 45N 64W
Kerrobert: Sask. **31** 52N 109W
Kettle: *riv., B.C.* **29** 49N 118W
Kettle Rapids: Man. **32** 57N 95W
Keyano: Qué. **37** 54N 74W
Kicking Horse Pass: B.C./Alberta **30** 51N 116W
Kiglapait, Cape: Nfld. **40** 57N 62W
Kiglapait Mts.: Nfld. **40** 57N 62W
Kikerk Lake: N.W.T. **20** 67N 113W
Kikkertavak I.: Nfld. **40** 56N 61W
Kikkertorsoak, I.: Qué. **36** 59N 66W
Killaloe Station: Ont. **38** 46N 77W
Killam: Alta. **30** 53N 112W
Killarney: Man. **32** 49N 100W
Killiniq: Qué. **36** 60N 65W
Kimberley: B.C. **29** 50N 116W
Kinbasket, Lake: B.C. **29** 52N 118W
Kincardine: Ont. **34** 44N 82W
Kindersley: Sask. **31** 51N 109W
King Christian Island: N.W.T. **20** 78N 102W
Kingcome Inlet: *& town*, B.C. **29** 51N 126W
King George, Mt.: B.C. **29** 51N 115W
King George Is.: N.W.T. **24** 57N 79W
King I.: B.C. **29** 52N 127W
Kings Point: *town*, Nfld. **41** 50N 56W
Kingston: Ont. **39** 44N 76W
Kingurutik Lake: Nfld. **40** 57N 63W
King William I.: N.W.T. **21** 69N 97W
Kinistino: Sask. **31** 53N 105W
Kinmount: Ont. **38** 45N 79W
Kinnaird: B.C. **29** 49N 118W
Kinoosao: Sask. **31** 57N 102W
Kipawa, Lac: Qué. **37** 47N 79W
Kipawa, Parc de: Qué. **37** 47N 79W
Kipling: Sask. **31** 50N 102W
Kirkland Lake: *town*, Ont. **34** 48N 80W
Kirkpatrick Lake: Alta. **30** 52N 111W
Kississing Lake: Man. **32** 55N 101W
Kistigan Lake: Man. **32** 55N 92W
Kitchener-Waterloo: Ont. **34** 43N 80W
Kitimat: B.C. **28** 54N 129W
Klappan: *riv.*, B.C. **28** 57N 129W
Kleinburg: Ont. **27** 44N 80W
Klinaklini: *riv.*, B.C. **29** 51N 126W
Klondike, *riv.*, Yukon **20** 64N 138W
Kluane Lake: Yukon **20** 61N 138W
Kluane Game Sanc.: Yukon **20** 61N 140W
Kluane Nat. Park: Yukon **20** 61N 139W
Knee Lake: Man. **32** 55N 95W
Knight Inlet: B.C. **29** 51N 126W
Knox, Cape: B.C. **28** 54N 133W
Koch I.: N.W.T. **31** 70N 78W
Kogaluc: *riv.*, Qué. **36** 59N 77W
Kogaluc, Baie: Qué. **36** 59N 78W
Kokanee P.P.: B.C. **29** 50N 117W
Koksoak: *riv.*, Qué. **37** 58N 69W
Kootenay: *riv.*, Can/U.S.A. **29** 49N 115W
Kootenay Lake: B.C. **29** 49N 117W
Kootenay Nat. Park: B.C. **29** 51N 116W
Koraluk: *riv.* Nfld. **26** 56N 63W
Korluktok Falls: Nfld. **40** 58N 64W
Kotcho Lake: B.C. **29** 59N 121W
Kouchibouguac N.P.: N.B. **41** 47N 65W
Koukdjuak: *riv.*, N.W.T. **21** 67N 72W
Kunghit I.: B.C. **28** 52N 131W

Kuujjuaq: Qué. **36** 58N 68W
Kuujjuarapik: Qué. **37** 55N 78W
Kwadacha Wilderness Prov. Park.: B.C. **29** 58N 125W
Kyle: Sask. **31** 51N 108W

L

La Baie: Qué. **37** 48N 71W
Laberge, Lake: Yukon **20** 61N 135W
Labrador: Nfld. **26** — —
Labrador City: Nfld. **40** 53N 67W
Labrador Sea: Atl. O. **21** — —
Lac Abitibi: Qué./Ont. **24** 49N 80W
Lac à l'Eau-Claire: Qué. **37** 56N 74W
Lac aux Feuilles: Qué. **36** 59N 70W
Lac de Gras: N.W.T. **20** 65N 111W
Lac de la Hutte Sauvage: Qué. **37** 56N 65W
Lac des Bois: N.W.T. **20** 67N 126W
Lac des Chats: Ont./Qué. **39** 46N 76W
Lac du Bonnet: *& town*, Man. **32** 50N 96W
Lac Guillaume-Delisle: Qué. **37** 56N 76W
Lachine: *& rapids*, Qué. **27** 45N 74W
Lachute: Qué. **39** 46N 74W
Lac Île à-la-Crosse: Sask. **31** 56N 108W
Lac la Biche: Alta. **30** 55N 112W
Lac La Matre: *town & lake*, N.W.T. **20** 63N 117W
Lac la Plonge: Sask. **31** 55N 107W
Lac la Potherie: Qué. **36** 59N 72W
Lac la Ronge: Sask. **31** 55N 105W
Lac La Ronge Prov. Park: Sask. **31** 55N 105W
Lac-Mégantic: *town*, Qué. **37** 45N 71W
Lacolle: Qué. **39** 45N 73W
Lacombe: Alta. **30** 52N 114W
Lac Saint-Jean: Qué. **37** 48N 72W
Ladner: B.C. **28** 49N 123W
Ladysmith: B.C. **28** 49N 124W
Laflèche: Sask. **31** 50N 107W
Lafontaine: Qué. **39** 46N 74W
La Grande Rivière: Qué. **24** 54N 77W
Lahave: *riv.*, N.S. **41** 45N 65W
Lake Cowichan: *& lake*, B.C. **29** 49N 124W
Lakefield: Ont. **38** 44N 78W
Lake Harbour: N.W.T. **21** 63N 70W
Lake Louise: Alta. **30** 51N 116W
Lake of the Rivers: Sask. **31** 50N 106W
Lake of the Woods: Can./U.S.A. **23** 49N 95W
Lake River: *settlement*, Ont. **24** 54N 82W
Lake Superior Prov. Park: Ont. **34** 48N 85W
La Loche: Sask. **31** 56N 109W
La Malbaie: Qué. **37** 48N 70W
La Maurice N.P.: Qué. **37** 47N 73W
Lambton, Cape: N.W.T. **20** 71N 123W
Lamèque, Île: N.B. **41** 48N 65W
Lampman: Sask. **31** 49N 103W
Lanark: Ont. **39** 45N 76W
Lancaster: Ont. **39** 45N 75W
Lancaster Park: Alta. **27** 54N 114W
Lancaster Sound: N.W.T. **21** 74N 85W
Lands End: N.W.T. **20** 76N 122W
Langenburg: Sask. **31** 51N 101W
Langham: Sask. **31** 52N 107W
Langley: *town*, B.C. **28** 49N 123W
Lanigan: Sask. **31** 52N 105W
Lanoraie: Qué. **39** 46N 73W
L'Anse-au-Diable: Nfld. **40** 52N 57W
L'Anse au Loup: Nfld. **26** 51N 57W
L'Anse-aux-Meadows: Nfld. **40** 52N 55W
Lantzville: B.C. **28** 49N 124W
La Pêche: Qué. **39** 46N 76W
Lapêche, Lac: Qué. **39** 46N 76W
La Plaine: Qué. **39** 46N 74W
La Pocatière: Qué. **37** 47N 70W
La Poile Bay: Nfld. **41** 48N 58W
La Prairie: Qué. **27** 45N 73W
Lark Harbour: Nfld. **41** 49N 58W
La Ronge: Sask. **31** 55N 105W
Lasalle: Qué. **27** 45N 74W
La Sarre: Qué. **37** 49N 79W
La Scie: Nfld. **41** 50N 55W
Lashburn: Sask. **31** 53N 110W
Lasqueti I.: B.C. **28** 49N 124W
L'Assomption: Qué. **39** 46N 73W
Last Mountain Lake: Sask. **31** 51N 105W
La Tuque: Qué. **37** 47N 73W
Lauzon: Qué. **26** 47N 71W
Laval-des-Rapides: Qué. **27** 46N 74W
Lavaltrie: Qué. **39** 46N 73W
Lavieille, Lac: Ont. **38** 46N 78W
Leader: Sask. **31** 51N 110W
Leaside: Ont. **27** 44N 79W
Lebel-sur-Quévillon: Qué. **37** 49N 77W
Leduc: Alta. **30** 53N 114W
Lemieux Is.: N.W.T. **21** 64N 65W
Le Moyne, Lac: Qué. **37** 57N 68W
Lenore Lake: Sask. **31** 52N 105W
Leoville: Sask. **31** 54N 108W
Lepelle: *riv.*, Qué. **36** 60N 73W
L'Epiphanie: Qué. **39** 46N 73W
L'Escalier, Lac: Qué. **39** 46N 76W
Lesser Slave Lake: Alta. **30** 55N 115W
Lethbridge: Alta. **30** 50N 113W
Level Mt.: B.C. **28** 58N 131W
Lévis: Qué. **37** 47N 71W
Lewisporte: Nfld. **41** 49N 55W
Liard: *riv.*, B.C./N.W.T. **22** 61N 123W
Liard Range: N.W.T. **22** 61N 123W
Liddon Gulf: N.W.T. **20** 75N 114W
Lillooet: B.C. **28** 51N 122W
Lillooet: *riv.*, B.C. **28** 50N 122W
Lillooet Lake: B.C. **28** 50N 122W
Lincoln: Ont. **38** 43N 79W
Lindsay: Ont. **38** 44N 79W
Liot Point: N.W.T. **20** 74N 125W
Lipton: Sask. **31** 51N 104W
Liscomb Game Sanc.: N.S. **41** 45N 62W
Little Current: Ont. **34** 46N 82W
Little Grand Rapids: *town*, Man. **32** 52N 95W
Little Mecatina River (Rivière du Petit Mécatina): Nfld./Qué. **40** 52N 62W
Little Smoky: *riv.*, Alta. **30** 54N 117W
Liverpool: N.S. **41** 44N 65W
Liverpool Bay: N.W.T. **20** 70N 130W
Lloyd George, Mt.: B.C. **29** 58N 125W
Lloyd Lake: Sask. **31** 57N 109W
Lloydminster: Alta./Sask. **31** 53N 110W
Logan, Mt.: Yukon **20** 60N 140W
Logan Mts.: Yukon/N.W.T. **20** 62N 128W
London: Ont. **34** 43N 81W
Long I.: N.W.T. **24** 55N 80W
Long I.: N.S. **41** 44N 66W
Longlac: Ont. **34** 50N 86W
Long Lake: N.B. **41** 47N 67W
Long Point: Man. **32** 53N 98W
Long Range: Nfld. **41** 48N 59W
Long Range: Nfld. **41** 50N 57W
Long Sault: Ont. **39** 45N 75W
Longueuil: Qué. **27** 46N 73W
Looking Back Lake: Alta. **27** 53N 113W
Lookout Mt.: Nfld. **40** 53N 64W
Looma: Alta. **27** 53N 113W
Loon Lake: *town*, Sask. **31** 54N 109W
L'Orignal: Ont. **39** 46N 75W
Loughborough Inlet: B.C. **28** 50N 125W
Lougheed I.: N.W.T. **20** 77N 105W
Louisbourg: N.S. **41** 46N 60W
Louise I.: B.C. **28** 53N 132W
Low: Qué. **39** 46N 76W
Low, Cape: N.W.T. **21** 63N 85W
Lower Arrow Lake: B.C. **29** 50N 118W
Lower Foster Lake: Sask. **31** 57N 105W
Lower Post: B.C. **28** 60N 128W
Lubicon Lake: Alta. **30** 56N 116W
Lulu I.: B.C. **27** 49N 123W
Lumsden: Sask. **31** 51N 105W
Lund: B.C. **28** 50N 125W
Lundar: Man. **32** 51N 98W
Lunenberg: N.S. **41** 44N 64W
Luseland: Sask. **31** 52N 109W
Lyall, Mt.: B.C./Alta. **29** 50N 115W
Lynn Lake: Man. **32** 57N 101W
Lynx Lake: N.W.T. **20** 62N 106W
Lytton: B.C. **28** 50N 122W

M

Mabel Lake: B.C. **29** 50N 119W
Mabou: N.S. **41** 46N 61W
McAdam: N.B. **41** 45N 67W
MacAlpine Lake: N.W.T. **20** 67N 103W
McClintock: Man. **32** 58N 94W
M'Clintock Chan.: N.W.T. **20** 73N 104W
M'Clure, Cape: N.W.T. **20** 75N 121W
M'Clure Str.: N.W.T. **20** 75N 118W
McConnell River Bird Sanc.: N.W.T. **21** 61N 95W
McFarlane: *riv.*, Sask. **31** 58N 108W
McGillivray: B.C. **28** 51N 122W
McGivney: N.B. **41** 46N 66W
MacGregor: Man. **32** 50N 99W
McGregor, Lake: Alta. **30** 50N 113W
McGuire: B.C. **28** 50N 123W
MacKay Lake: N.W.T. **20** 64N 112W
Mackay Lake: Nfld. **40** 54N 66W
Mackenzie: B.C. **29** 55N 123W
Mackenzie: *riv.*, N.W.T. **20** 67N 128W
Mackenzie, District of: N.W.T. **20** — —
Mackenzie Bay: Yukon **20** 69N 138W
Mackenzie Bison Sanctuary: N.W.T. **20** 62N 117W
Mackenzie King Island: N.W.T. **20** 78N 112W
Mackenzie Mtns.: Yukon/N.W.T. **20** 64N 130W
Macklin: Sask. **31** 52N 110W
McLellan Strait: Nfld. **40** 60N 64W
McLennan: Alta. **30** 55N 117W
Maclean Str.: N.W.T. **20** 78N 105W
McBride: B.C. **29** 53N 120W
McLeod Lake: B.C. **29** 55N 123W
McMasterville: Qué. **39** 46N 73W
Macmillan: *riv.*, Yukon **20** 63N 133W
Macoun Lake: Sask. **31** 56N 104W
McTavish Arm: Great Bear Lake, N.W.T. **20** 66N 118W
McVicar Arm: Great Bear Lake, N.W.T. **20** 65N 120W
Madame I.: N.S. **41** 45N 61W
Madawaska: Ont. **38** 45N 78W
Madawaska: *riv.*, Ont. **34** 45N 78W
Madoc: Ont. **38** 45N 77W
Madsen: Ont. **34** 51N 94W
Magnet: Man. **32** 51N 99W
Magnetawan: Ont. **38** 46N 80W
Magog: Qué. **37** 45N 72W
Magpie: *riv.*, Ont. **34** 48N 84W
Magpie, Lac: Qué. **37** 51N 65W
Magrath: Alta. **30** 49N 113W
Maguse Lake: N.W.T. **21** 62N 95W
Mahone Bay: *town*, N.S. **41** 44N 64W
Maidstone: Sask. **31** 53N 109W
Main Brook: *town*, Nfld. **41** 51N 56W
Makkovik: *& cape*, Nfld. **40** 55N 59W
Malartic: Qué. **37** 48N 78W
Malaspina Strait: B.C. **28** 50N 124W
Malcolm I.: B.C. **29** 51N 127W
Malpeque Bay: P.E.I. **41** 47N 64W
Manicouagan: Qué. **37** 51N 69W
Manicouagan: *riv.* Qué. **37** 50N 68W
Manicouagan, Réservoir: Qué. **37** 51N 68W
Manigotagan Lake: Man. **32** 51N 95W
Manitoba: *Prov. (cap. Winnipeg)* **23** — —
Manitoba, Lake: Man. **32** 51N 99W
Manito Lake: Sask. **31** 53N 110W
Manitou: Man. **32** 49N 98W
Manitoulin I.: Ont. **34** 46N 82W
Manitouwadge: Ont. **34** 49N 86W
Maniwaki: Qué. **37** 46N 76W
Manning: Alta. **30** 57N 118W
Manning P.P.: B.C. **28** 49N 121W
Mannville: Alta. **30** 54N 112W
Manouane, Lac: Qué. **37** 51N 70W
Mansel I.: N.W.T. **21** 62N 80W
Manson Creek: *town*, B.C. **29** 56N 124W
Maple: Ont. **27** 44N 79W
Maple Creek: *town*, Sask. **31** 50N 109W
Marathon: Ont. **34** 49N 86W
Margaret Bay: *town*, B.C. **29** 51N 127W
Margaret Lake: Alta. **30** 59N 115W
Marieville: Qué. **39** 45N 73W
Markham: Ont. **27** 44N 79W
Markham Bay: N.W.T. **21** 63N 72W
Marmora: Ont. **38** 44N 78W
Maryfield: Sask. **31** 50N 102W
Marystown: Nfld. **41** 47N 55W
Mascouche: Qué. **39** 46N 74W
Masset: B.C. **28** 54N 132W
Masset Inlet: B.C. **28** 54N 132W
Massey Sound: N.W.T. **21** 79N 95W
Masson: Qué. **39** 46N 75W
Mastigouche P.P.: Qué. **37** 47N 73W
Matagami: *& lake*, Qué. **37** 50N 78W
Matane: Qué. **37** 49N 68W
Matane P.P.: Qué. **37** 49N 67W
Matheson: Ont. **34** 48N 80W
Mattagami: *riv.*, Ont. **34** 50N 82W
Mattawa: Ont. **34** 46N 79W
Maunoir, Lac: N.W.T. **20** 67N 126W
Maxville: Ont. **39** 45N 75W
Mayerthorpe: Alta. **30** 54N 115W
Mayo: Yukon **20** 63N 136W
Mayo Lake: Yukon **20** 64N 135W
Mayson Lake: Sask. **31** 58N 107W
Mazinaw Lake, Ont. **38** 45N 77W
Meadow Lake: *town*, Sask. **31** 54N 108W
Meadow Lake Prov. Park: Sask. **31** 54N 109W
Mealy Mtns.: Nfld. **40** 53N 59W
Meander River: *town*, Alta. **30** 59N 118W
Meath Park: *town*, Sask. **31** 53N 105W
Medicine Hat: Alta. **30** 50N 111W
Medley: Alta. **30** 54N 110W
Meelpaeg Lake: Nfld. **41** 48N 57W
Meighen Island: N.W.T. **20** 80N 100W
Melbourne I.: N.W.T. **20** 68N 104W
Melfort: Sask. **31** 53N 105W
Melita: Man. **32** 49N 101W
Melville: Sask. **31** 51N 103W
Melville, Lake: Nfld. **40** 54N 59W
Melville Hills: N.W.T. **20** 68N 120W
Melville I.: N.W.T. **20** 75N 110W
Melville Penin.: N.W.T. **21** 68N 84W
Melville Sound: N.W.T. **20** 68N 108W
Menihek: Nfld. **40** 54N 66W
Menihek Lakes: Nfld. **40** 54N 66W
Mercy Bay: N.W.T. **20** 74N 119W
Merrickville: Ont. **39** 45N 76W
Merritt: B.C. **29** 50N 121W
Mesgouez, Lac: Qué. **37** 51N 75W
Meta Incognita Penin.: N.W.T. **21** 63N 68W
Metchosin: B.C. **28** 48N 124W
Mica Creek: B.C. **29** 52N 118W
Mica Dam: B.C. **29** 52N 118W
Michael, Lake: Nfld. **40** 55N 58W
Michaud Point: N.S. **41** 46N 61W
Michel Peak: B.C. **29** 54N 126W
Michelson, Cape: N.W.T. **20** 71N 103W
Michipicoten: Ont. **34** 48N 85W
Michipicoten I.: Ont. **34** 48N 86W
Midale: Sask. **31** 49N 103W
Middleton: N.S. **41** 45N 65W
Midland: Ont. **38** 45N 80W
Midway Mts.: B.C. **29** 49N 119W
Mikkwa: *riv.*, Alta. **30** 58N 115W
Milbanke Sound: B.C. **28** 51N 128W
Milestone: Sask. **31** 50N 104W
Milk: *riv.*, Alta. **30** 49N 111W
Milk River: *town*, Alta. **30** 49N 112W
Millbrook: Ont. **38** 44N 78W
Mill Creek: Alta. **27** 53N 113W
Mille Îles, R.des: Qué. **27** 46N 74W
Millet: Alta. **30** 53N 113W
Mill I.: N.W.T. **21** 64N 78W
Milton: N.S. **41** 44N 65W
Milton: Ont. **38** 43N 80W
Minas Basin: N.S. **41** 45N 64W
Minipi Lake: Nfld. **40** 52N 61W
Minipi Rapids: Nfld. **40** 53N 62W
Minitonas: Man. **32** 52N 101W
Minnedosa: Man. **32** 50N 100W
Minto: N.B. **41** 46N 66W
Minto: Yukon **20** 63N 137W
Minto, Lac: Qué. **37** 57N 74W
Minto Inlet: N.W.T. **20** 71N 117W
Miramichi, N.W.: *riv.*, N.B. **41** 47N 66W
Miramichi, S.W.: *riv.*, N.B. **41** 46N 67W
Miramichi Bay: N.B. **41** 47N 65W
Miscou: *i. & point*: N.B. **41** 48N 64W
Misery Point: Nfld. **40** 52N 55W
Missinaibi Lake: Ont. **34** 48N 84W
Mission: B.C. **28** 49N 122W
Missisa Lake: Ont. **34** 52N 85W
Mississagi: *riv.*, Ont. **34** 46N 83W
Mississauga: Ont. **27** 44N 80W
Mississippi: *riv. & lake*, Ont. **39** 45N 76W
Missouri Coteau: *plateau*, Sask. **31** 50N 106W
Mistassibi: *riv.*, Qué. **37** 49N 72W
Mistassini: Qué. **37** 49N 72W
Mistassini, Lac: Qué. **37** 51N 74W
Mistassini, Parc de: Qué. **37** 50N 74W
Mistastin Lake: Nfld. **40** 56N 63W
Moak Lake: Man. **32** 56N 97W
Moira: *riv.*, Ont. **38** 44N 77W
Moisie: *& riv.*, Qué. **37** 50N 66W
Molson: Man. **32** 50N 96W
Molson Lake: Nfld. **40** 53N 66W
Molson Lake: Man. **32** 54N 97W
Monarch Mt.: B.C. **29** 52N 126W
Monashee Mts.: B.C. **29** 51N 118W
Moncton: N.B. **41** 46N 65W
Monkman Pass: B.C. **29** 55N 121W
Montebello: Qué. **39** 46N 75W
Mont-Joli: Qué. **37** 48N 68W
Mont-Laurier: Qué. **37** 47N 75W
Mont-Louis: Qué. **37** 49N 66W
Montmagny: Qué. **37** 47N 70W
Montmartre: Sask. **31** 50N 103W
Montréal: Qué. **39** 46N 74W
Montreal: *riv.*, Ont. **34** 47N 84W
Montreal: *riv.*, Sask. **31** 55N 106W
Montréal Est: Qué. **27** 46N 74W
Montréal, Île de: Qué. **27** 46N 74W
Montreal Lake: *& town*, Sask. **31** 54N 106W
Montréal Nord: Qué. **27** 46N 74W
Mont-Rolland: *town*, Qué. **39** 46N 74W
Montrose: B.C. **29** 49N 118W
Mont-Royal: Montréal, Qué. **27** 46N 74W
Mont-Saint-Grégoire: Qué. **39** 45N 73W
Mont-Saint-Hilaire: Qué. **39** 46N 73W
Mont-Tremblant P.P.: Québec **37** 46N 74W
Moose: *riv.*, Ont. **34** 51N 81W
Moose Creek: *town*, Ont. **39** 45N 75W
Moose Jaw: Sask. **31** 50N 106W
Moose Lake: Man. **32** 54N 100W
Moose Mtn. P.P.: Sask. **31** 50N 102W
Moosonee: Ont. **34** 51N 81W
Moosomin: Sask. **31** 50N 102W
Morden: Man. **32** 49N 98W
Moresby I.: B.C. **28** 52N 132W
Moriarty, Mt.: B.C. **28** 49N 124W
Morice Lake: B.C. **29** 54N 127W
Moricetown: B.C. **29** 55N 127W
Morin Heights: *town*, Qué. **39** 46N 74W
Morinville: Alta. **30** 54N 114W
Morris: Man. **32** 49N 97W
Morrisburg: Ont. **39** 45N 75W
Morse: Sask. **31** 50N 107W
Mossbank: Sask. **31** 50N 106W
Mould Bay: *settlement*, N.W.T. **20** 71N 119W
Mouni Rapids: Nfld. **40** 53N 62W
Mount Edziza Prov. Park: B.C. **28** 58N 131W
Mount Revelstoke N.P.: B.C. **29** 51N 118W
Mount Robson Prov. Park: B.C. **29** 53N 119W
Mudjatik: *riv.*, Sask. **31** 57N 107W
Mugford, Cape: Nfld. **40** 58N 62W
Mukutawa: *riv.*, Man. **32** 53N 97W
Mulgrave: N.S. **41** 46N 61W
Muncho Lake P.P.: B.C. **29** 59N 125W
Mundare: Alta. **30** 54N 112W
Murdochville: Qué. **37** 49N 65W
Murtle Lake: B.C. **29** 52N 120W
Muskoka, Lake: Ont. **38** 45N 79W
Muskrat Falls: Nfld. **40** 53N 61W
Muskwa: *riv.*, B.C. **29** 58N 123W
Myrnam: Alta. **30** 54N 111W
Mystery Lake: Man. **31** 56N 98W

N

Nachvak Fiord: Nfld. **40** 59N 63W
Nackawic: N.B. **41** 46N 67W
Nahanni Butte: N.W.T. **20** 61N 123W
Nahanni Nat. Park: N.W.T. **20** 62N 125W
Naicam: Sask. **31** 52N 104W
Nain: Nfld. **40** 56N 62W
Nakina: Ont. **34** 50N 87W
Nakcon P.P.: B.C. **28** 54N 132W
Nakusp: B.C. **29** 50N 118W
Namur: Qué. **39** 46N 75W
Nanaimo: B.C. **28** 49N 124W
Nansen Sound: N.W.T. **21** 81N 90W
Nanton: Alta. **30** 50N 114W
Naococane, Lac: Qué. **37** 53N 77W
Napanee: Ont. **38** 44N 77W
Napartokh Bay: Nfld. **40** 58N 62W
Napierville: Qué. **39** 45N 73W
Naskaupi: *riv.*, Nfld. **40** 54N 63W
Nass; *riv.*, B.C. **28** 55N 129W
Nastapoka: *riv.*, Qué. **37** 57N 76W
Natashquan: Qué. **37** 50N 62W
Natashquan: *riv.*, Qué. **37** 51N 62W
Nation: *riv.*, B.C. **29** 55N 124W
Nazko: B.C. **29** 53N 124W
Nechako: *riv.*, B.C. **29** 54N 125W
Nechako Plateau: B.C. **29** 54N 124W
Neeb: Sask. **31** 54N 108W
Neepawa: Man. **32** 50N 99W
Neguac: N.B. **41** 48N 66W
Nejanilini Lake: Man. **32** 60N 98W
Nelson: B.C. **29** 49N 117W
Nelson: *riv.*, Man. **32** 57N 93W
Nelson Forks: B.C. **29** 59N 124W
Nelson House: Man. **32** 56N 99W
Nelson I.: B.C. **32** 51N 124W
Nelson-Miramichi: N.B. **41** 48N 66W
Nemiskam Nat. Park: Alta. **30** 49N 111W
Nepean: Ont. **39** 45N 76W
Nettilling Lake: N.W.T. **21** 66N 70W
Neudorf: Sask. **31** 51N 103W
Newboro: Ont. **39** 45N 76W
New Brunswick: *Prov. (cap.* Fredericton) **26** 46N 66W
Newburgh: Ont. **38** 44N 77W
Newcastle: N.B. **41** 47N 65W
Newcastle: Ont. **38** 44N 79W
New Denver: B.C. **29** 50N 117W
Newell, Lake: Alta. **30** 50N 112W
Newfoundland: *Prov. (cap.* St. John's) **26** — —
Newfoundland: *i.*, Canada **26** 49N 56W
New Glasgow: N.S. **41** 46N 63W
New Liskeard: Ont. **34** 47N 80W
Newmarket: Ont. **38** 44N 79W
New Richmond: Qué. **37** 48N 66W
New Waterford: N.S. **41** 46N 60W
New Westminster: B.C. **27** 49N 123W
Niagara: *riv.*, Can./U.S.A. **38** 43N 79W
Niagara Falls: *& town*, Ont. **38** 43N 79W
Niagara-on-the-Lake: Ont. **38** 43N 79W
Nigei I.: B.C. **29** 51N 127W
Niksu: Alta. **27** 53N 114W
Nimpkish Lake: B.C. **29** 50N 127W
Nipawin: Sask. **31** 53N 104W
Nipawin Prov. Park: Sask. **31** 54N 105W
Nipigon: Ont. **34** 48N 88W
Nipigon, Lake: Ont. **34** 50N 88W
Nipishish Lake: Nfld. **40** 54N 60W
Nisling Range: Yukon **20** 62N 139W
Nitchequon: Qué. **37** 53N 71W
Nitinat Lake: B.C. **28** 49N 125W
Niverville: Man. **32** 50N 97W
Nokomis: Sask. **31** 51N 105W
Nokomis Lake: Sask. **31** 57N 103W
Nonacho Lake: N.W.T. **20** 62N 109W
Nootka: *i. & sound*, B.C. **29** 50N 127W
Nopiming P.P.: Man. **32** 51N 95W
Noranda: Qué. **37** 48N 79W
Norman, Cape: Nfld. **40** 52N 56W
Norman Wells: N.W.T. **20** 65N 126W
Normétal: Qué. **37** 49N 79W

Norquay: Sask. **31** 52N 102W
Norris Arm: Nfld. **41** 49N 55W
Norris Point: *settlement*, Nfld. **41** 49N 58W
North: *riv.*, Nfld. **26** 57N 63W
North, Cape: N.S. **41** 47N 60W
North Arm: B.C. **27** 49N 123W
North Arm, Great Slave Lake: N.W.T. **20** 62N 115W
North Aulatsivik I.: Nfld. **40** 60N 64W
North Battleford: Sask. **31** 53N 108W
North Bay: *town*, Ont. **34** 46N 79W
North Bend: B.C. **28** 50N 121W
North Cape: P.E.I. **41** 47N 64W
North Caribou Lake: Ont. **34** 53N 90W
North Channel: Ont. **34** 46N 83W
[illegible]
[illegible]
North Knife: *riv.*, Man. **32** 59N 96W
North Knife Lake: Man. **32** 58N 97W
North Magnetic Pole 1984: N.W.T. **20** 77N 101W
North River: *settlement*, Nfld. **40** 54N 57W
North River: *town*, Man. **32** 59N 95W
North Saskatchewan: *riv.*, Alberta/Saskatchewan **31** 53N 107W
North Seal: *riv.*, Man. **32** 59N 100W
North Sydney: N.S. **41** 46N 60W
North Thompson: *riv.*, B.C. **29** 52N 120W
Northumberland Strait: Canada **41** 46N 64W
North Vancouver: B.C. **27** 49N 123W
North Wabasca Lake: Alberta **30** 56N 114W
North West River: *settlement*, Nfld. **40** 53N 60W
Northwest Territories: (*seat of Govt.*: Yellowknife) **20/21** ——
North York: Ont. **27** 44N 79W
Norton: N.B. **41** 46N 66W
Norway Bay: N.W.T. **20** 71N 105W
Norway House: Man. **32** 54N 98W
Norwood: Ont. **38** 44N 78W
Notre Dame Bay: Nfld. **41** 50N 55W
Notre-Dame-de-la-Paix: Québec **39** 46N 75W
Notre-Dame-de-la-Salette: Québec **39** 46N 76W
Notre-Dame-des-Prairies: Qué. **39** 46N 73W
Notre-Dame-du-Laus: Québec **39** 46N 76W
Notre-Dame, Monts: Qué. **37** 48N 67W
Nottawasaga: *riv.*, Ont. **38** 44N 80W
Nottingham I.: N.W.T. **21** 63N 78W
Nouveau-Comptoir: Qué. **37** 53N 78W
Nova Scotia: *Prov.* (*cap.* Halifax) **41** ——
Noyan: Qué. **39** 45N 73W
Nueltin Lake: N.W.T/Man. **23** 60N 100W
Nunaksaluk Island: Nfld. **40** 56N 60W
Nutak: Nfld. **40** 58N 62W
Nut Mountain: *town & mt.*, Sask. **31** 52N 103W

O

Oak Bluff: Man. **33** 50N 91W
Oak Lake: Man. **32** 50N 101W
Oakville: Ont. **38** 43N 80W
Oba: Ont. **34** 49N 84W
Observatory Inlet: B.C. **28** 55N 130W
Ocean Falls: *town*, B.C. **29** 52N 128W
Ogilvie Mtns.: Yukon **20** 65N 138W
Ogoki: *riv.*, Ont. **34** 51N 88W
Oka: Qué. **39** 45N 74W
Okanagan Lake: B.C. **29** 50N 120W
Okotoks: Alta. **30** 51N 114W
Old Crow: *& riv.*, Yukon **20** 68N 140W
Oldman: *riv.*, Alta. **30** 50N 114W
Olds: Alta. **30** 52N 114W
Old Wives Lake: Sask. **31** 50N 106W
Oliver: B.C. **29** 49N 120W
Omemee: Ont. **38** 44N 79W
Omineca: *riv.*, B.C. **29** 56N 125W
Omineca Mtns.: B.C. **29** 57N 127W
Ontario: *Prov.* (*cap.* Toronto) **24/25** ——
Ontario, Lake: Can./U.S.A. **24** 44N 78W
Ootsa Lake: *town*, B.C. **29** 54N 126W
Opasquia: Ont. **34** 53N 94W
Opeongo Lake: Ont. **38** 46N 78W
Opiscotéo, Lac: Qué. **37** 53N 68W
Orange Bay: Nfld. **41** 50N 56W
Orillia: Ont. **38** 45N 79W
Ormstown: Qué. **39** 45N 74W
Oromocto: N.B. **41** 46N 66W
Oshawa: Ont. **38** 44N 79W
Oskélanéo: Qué. **37** 48N 75W
Osoyoos: B.C. **29** 49N 120W
Ospika: *riv.*, B.C. **29** 57N 124W
Ossokmanuan Lake: Nfld. **40** 53N 65W
Otish, Monts: Qué. **37** 52N 70W
Otoskwin: *riv.*, Ont. **34** 51N 89W
OTTAWA: Ontario **39** 45N 75W
Ottawa River (Rivière des Outaouais): Qué./Ont. **24** 46N 75W
Ottawa Is.: N.W.T. **24** 59N 80W
Otter Lake: Sask. **31** 55N 104W
Outlook: Sask. **31** 51N 107W
Outremont: Qué. **27** 46N 74W
Owen Sound: *town*, Ont. **34** 45N 81W
Owl: *riv.*, Man. **32** 58N 93W
Oxbow: Sask. **31** 49N 102W
Oxford: N.S. **41** 46N 64W
Oxford House: Man. **32** 55N 95W
Oxford Lake: Man. **32** 55N 95W
Oyen: Alta. **30** 51N 110W

P

Pacific: B.C. **28** 55N 128W
Pacific Rim N.P.: B.C. **28** 49N 125W
Packs Harbour: Nfld. **40** 54N 57W
Pacquet: Nfld. **41** 50N 56W
Paddle Prairie: *town*, Alta. **30** 58N 117W
Paddockwood: Sask. **31** 53N 105W
Paint Lake Prov. Recreation Park: Man. **32** 56N 98W
Pakenham: Ont. **39** 45N 76W
Pakowki Lake: Alta. **30** 49N 111W
Pangnirtung: N.W.T. **21** 66N 66W
Papineau-Labelle, Parc: Qué. **39** 46N 75W
Papineau, Lac: Qué **39** 46N 75W
Papineauville: Qué. **39** 46N 75W
Paradise Hill: *town*, Sask. **31** 53N 109W
Parc de Grand-Nord: Qué **37** 57N 70W
Parc de la Vérendrye: Qué. **37** 47N 77W
Parc des Laurentides: Qué. **37** 48N 71W
Parc d'Île-Anticosti: Qué. **37** 49N 62W
Parc National de Forillon: Qué. **37** 49N 64W
Parent: Qué. **37** 48N 75W
Parksville: B.C. **28** 49N 124W
Parrsboro: N.S. **41** 45N 64W
Parry, Cape: N.W.T. **20** 70N 125W
Parry Is.: N.W.T. **20** 76N 110W
[illegible]
[illegible]
Pasqua: Sask. **31** 50N 105W
Pasquia Hills: Sask. **31** 53N 103W
Passamaquoddy Bay: N.B. **41** 45N 67W
Patullo, Mt.: B.C. **28** 56N 130W
Paulatuk: N.W.T. **20** 69N 123W
Paul I.: Nfld. **40** 56N 62W
Payne: *riv.*, Qué. **36** 60N 72W
Payne, Baie: Qué. **36** 60N 70W
Payne, Lac: Qué. **36** 59N 74W
Peace: *riv.*, B.C./Alta. **22** 58N 114W
Peace River: *town*, Alta. **30** 56N 117W
Peary Chan.: N.W.T. **20** 79N 100W
Peel: *riv.*, Yukon **20** 67N 134W
Peel River Game Reserve: Yukon/N.W.T. **20** 67N 133W
Peel Sound: N.W.T. **21** 73N 97W
Peerless Lake: Alta. **30** 57N 114W
Pelee Island: Ont. **34** 42N 83W
Pelham: Ont. **38** 43N 79W
Pelican Bay: Man. **32** 53N 100W
Pelican Lake: Man. **32** 52N 100W
Pelican Mtns.: Alta. **30** 56N 114W
Pelican Narrows: *town*, Sask. **31** 55N 103W
Pelly: *riv.*, Yukon **20** 62N 133W
Pelly Bay: *& settlement*, N.W.T. **21** 69N 90W
Pelly Crossing: Yukon **20** 63N 137W
Pelly Mtns.: Yukon **20** 62N 133W
Pemberton: B.C. **28** 50N 123W
Pembina: *riv.*, Alta. **30** 53N 116W
Pembroke: Ont. **38** 46N 77W
Penetanguishene: Ont. **38** 45N 80W
Penhold: Alta. **30** 52N 114W
Péninsule de la Gaspésie: Qué. **37** 48N 66W
Penticton: B.C. **29** 49N 120W
Penzance: Sask. **31** 51N 105W
Percé: Qué. **37** 49N 64W
Perdue: Sask. **31** 52N 108W
Péribonca: *riv.*, Qué. **37** 49N 71W
Perow: B.C. **29** 54N 126W
Perrot, Île: Qué. **39** 45N 74W
Perry Island: *town*, N.W.T. **20** 67N 103W
Perth: Ont. **39** 45N 76W
Perth-Andover: N.B. **41** 47N 68W
Petawawa: Ont. **38** 46N 78W
Peterborough: Ont. **38** 44N 78W
Peter Pond Lake: Sask. **31** 56N 109W
Petit Mécatina, Rivière du: Qué./Nfld. **40** 52N 62W
Petite-Nation, Parc de la: Qué. **39** 46N 75W
Petite rivière de la Baleine: Qué. **37** 56N 76W
Petit Nord Penin.: Nfld. **41** 51N 57W
Petitot: *riv.*, B.C. **29** 60N 121W
Petitsikapau Lake: Nfld. **40** 54N 66W
Petre, Point: Ont. **38** 44N 77W
Philpots I.: N.W.T. **21** 75N 80W
Pickering, Ont. **38** 44N 79W
Pickle Lake: Ont. **34** 51N 90W
Picton: Ont. **38** 44N 77W
Pictou: *& i.*, N.S. **41** 46N 63W
Picture Butte: Alta. **30** 50N 113W
Piedmont: Qué. **39** 46N 74W
Pierrefonds: Qué. **27** 45N 74W
Pigeon Bay: Man. **32** 52N 97W
Pigeon Lake: Alta. **30** 53N 114W
Pigeon Lake: Ont. **38** 44N 78W
Pikangikum Lake: Ont. **34** 52N 94W
Pikwitonei: Man. **32** 56N 97W
Pilot Mound: Man. **32** 49N 99W
Pinawa: Man. **32** 51N 96W
Pincher Creek: *town*, Alta. **30** 49N 114W
Pinchi Lake: B.C. **29** 55N 124W
Pine, Cape: Nfld. **41** 47N 54W
Pine Falls: *town*, Man. **32** 51N 96W
Pinehouse Lake: Sask. **31** 56N 107W
Pine Pass: B.C. **29** 55N 122W
Pine Point: N.W.T. **22** 61N 114W
Pinto Butte: *mtn.* Sask. **31** 49N 107W
Pinware River: *settlement*, Nfld. **40** 52N 57W
Pipmuacan, Rés.: Qué. **37** 49N 70W
Pistolet Bay: Nfld. **40** 51N 56W
Pitman: *riv*, B.C. **28** 58N 128W
Pitt: *riv. & lake*, B.C. **28** 49N 123W
Pitt I.: B.C. **28** 53N 130W
Placentia: *& bay*, Nfld. **41** 47N 54W
Plaisance: Qué. **39** 46N 75W
Plantagenet: Ont. **39** 45N 75W
Plaster Rock: N.B. **41** 47N 67W
Playgreen Lake: Man. **32** 54N 98W
Plessisville: Qué. **25** 46N 72W
Plétipi, Lac: Qué. **37** 51N 70W
Plonge, Lac la: Sask. **31** 55N 107W
Plum Coulee: Man. **32** 49N 98W
Plum Point: *settlement*, Nfld. **41** 51N 57W
Pointe à Gatineau: Qué. **39** 45N 76W
Pointe-aux-Pins Creek: Alta. **27** 54N 113W
Pointe-aux-Trembles: Qué. **27** 46N 74W
Pointe-Claire: Qué.: **27** 45N 74W
Pointe de l'Est: Qué. **37** 49N 62W
Pointe Fortune: Ont. **39** 46N 74W
Pointe Louis XIV: Qué. **37** 55N 80W
Point Lake: N.W.T. **20** 65N 113W
Point Pelee N.P.: Ont. **34** 42N 83W
Poisson Blanc, Lac du: Qué. **39** 46N 76W
Polar Bear P.P.: Ont. **34** 55N 85W
Pond Inlet: *& settlement*, N.W.T. **21** 73N 78W
Ponoka: Alta. **30** 53N 114W
Ponteix: Sask. **31** 50N 108W
Pont-Viau: Qué. **27** 46N 74W
Poplar: *riv.*, Man./Ont. **32** 53N 97W
Porcher I.: B.C. **28** 54N 130W
Porcupine: Ont. **34** 48N 81W
Porcupine, Cape: Nfld. **40** 54N 57W
Porcupine Hills: Sask./Man. **31** 52N 101W
Porcupine Plain: *town*, Sask. **31** 53N 103W
Portage Bay: Man. **32** 51N 99W
Portage-du-Fort: Qué. **38** 46N 77W
Portage la Prairie: Man. **32** 50N 98W
Port Alberni: B.C. **28** 49N 125W
Port Alice: B.C. **29** 50N 127W
Port Arthur: Ont. *see* Thunder Bay
Port-au-Port: *penin. & bay*, Newfoundland **41** 49N 59W
Port-Cartier: Qué. **37** 50N 67W
[illegible]
[illegible]
Port Clements: B.C. **28** 53N 132W
Port Colborne: Ont. **38** 43N 79W
Port Coquitlam: B.C. **27** 49N 123W
Port Credit: Ont. **27** 44N 80W
Port Edward: B.C. **28** 54N 130W
Porter Lake: Sask.: **31** 56N 107W
Port Frances: Ont. **34** 49N 93W
Port Hardy: B.C. **29** 51N 128W
Port Hawkesbury: N.S. **41** 46N 61W
Port Hood: N.S. **41** 46N 62W
Port Hope, Ont. **38** 44N 78W
Port Hope Simpson: Nfld. **40** 53N 56W
Portland Canal: B.C. **28** 55N 130W
Portland Inlet: B.C. **28** 55N 130W
Port Loring: Ont. **38** 46N 80W
Port McNeill: B.C. **29** 51N 128W
Port McNicoll: Ont. **38** 45N 80W
Port Mellon: B.C. **28** 49N 123W
Port Menier: Qué. **37** 50N 64W
Port Moody: B.C. **27** 49N 123W
Port Nelson: Man. **32** 57N 93W
Port Perry: Ont. **38** 44N 79W
Port Radium: N.W.T. **20** 66N 118W
Port Renfrew: B.C. **28** 49N 124W
Port Saunders: Nfld. **41** 51N 57W
Port Simpson: B.C. **28** 55N 130W
Port Stanley: Ont. **51** 43N 81W
Postville: Nfld. **40** 55N 60W
Pouce Coupé: B.C. **29** 56N 120W
Povungnituk *& riv.*,: Qué. **36** 60N 76W
Powassan: Ont. **38** 46N 79W
Powderview: Man. **32** 51N 96W
Powell Lake: B.C. **28** 50N 124W
Powell River: *town*, B.C. **28** 50N 125W
Prairies, R.des: Qué. **27** 46N 74W
Preeceville: Sask. **31** 52N 103W
Prelate: Sask. **31** 51N 109W
Prescott: Ont. **39** 45N 76W
Presqu'ile Point: *town*, Ont. **22** 44N 78W
Prévost: Qué. **39** 46N 74W
Priestly: B.C. **29** 54N 125W
Primrose Lake: Sask. **31** 55N 110W
Prince Albert: Sask. **31** 53N 106W
Prince Albert Nat. Park: Saskatchewan **31** 54N 106W
Prince Albert Penin.: N.W.T. **20** 72N 117W
Prince Albert Sound: N.W.T. **20** 70N 115W
Prince Alfred, Cape: N.W.T. **20** 75N 121W
Prince Charles I.: N.W.T. **21** 67N 76W
Prince-de-Galles, Cap: Qué. **36** 62N 72W
Prince Edward Bay: Ont. **38** 44N 77W
Prince Edward I.: *Prov.* (*cap.* Charlottetown) **41** 46N 63W
Prince Edward I. Nat. Park: P.E.I. **41** 46N 63W
Prince George: B.C. **29** 54N 123W
Prince Gustaf Adolf Sea: N.W.T. **20** 78N 107W
Prince of Wales I.: N.W.T. **20** 72N 100W
Prince of Wales Str.: N.W.T. **20** 73N 118W
Prince Patrick I.: N.W.T. **20** 77N 120W
Prince Regent Inlet: N.W.T. **21** 74N 90W
Prince Rupert: B.C. **28** 54N 130W
Princess Margaret Range: N.W.T. **21** 80N 92W
Princess Royal I.: B.C. **28** 53N 129W
Princeton: B.C. **28** 49N 120W
Prophet: *riv.*, B.C. **29** 58N 123W
Provost: Alta. **30** 52N 110W
Pukaskwa Nat. Park: Ont. **34** 48N 86W
Pukatawagan: Man. **32** 56N 101W
Pukeashun Mt.: B.C. **29** 51N 119W
Purcell Mtns.: B.C. **29** 50N 117W
Purtuniq: Qué. **36** 62N 74W

Q

Quadra I.: B.C. **28** 50N 125W
Qualicum Beach: B.C. **28** 49N 124W
Qu'Appelle: Sask. **31** 51N 104W
Qu'Appelle: *riv.*, Sask. **31** 51N 104W
Qu'Appelle Arm Dam: Saskatchewan **31** 51N 107W
Quaqtaq: Qué. **36** 61N 70W
Quatsino Sound: B.C. **28** 50N 128W
QUÉBEC: Québec **37** 47N 71W
Québec: *Prov.* (*cap* Québec) **24/25** ——
Queen Bess, Mt.: B.C. **29** 51N 124W
Queen Charlotte: *& is.*, British Columbia **28** 53N 132W
Queen Charlotte Sd.: B.C. **28** 52N 129W
Queen Charlotte Str.: B.C. **28** 50N 128W
Queen Elizabeth Foreland: N.W.T. **21** 62N 65W
Queen Elizabeth Is.: N.W.T. **20** 78N 100W
Queen Maud Gulf: N.W.T. **20** 67N 102W
Queen Maud Gulf Bird Sanctuary: N.W.T. **20** 67N 105W
Quesnel: *& riv.*, B.C. **29** 53N 122W
Quesnel Lake: B.C. **29** 53N 121W
Quetico P. Park: Ont. **34** 48N 90W
Quill Lake: *town*, Sask. **31** 52N 104W
Quill Lakes: Sask. **31** 52N 104W
Quinte, Bay of: Ont. **38** 44N 77W
Quispamsis: N.B. **41** 46N 67W
Quoich: *riv.*, N.W.T. **21** 65N 95W
Quorn: Ont. **34** 49N 91W

R

Raanes Peninsula: N.W.T. **21** 78N 86W
Rabbit: *riv.*, B.C. **29** 59N 127W
Rabbit Lake: *town*, Sask. **31** 58N 104W
Race, Cape: Nfld. **41** 47N 53W
Racing: *riv.*, B.C. **29** 59N 125W
Radisson: Qué. **37** 54N 78W
Radisson: Sask. **31** 52N 107W
Radville: Sask. **31** 49N 104W
Rae-Edzo: N.W.T. **20** 63N 116W
Rae: *riv.*, N.W.T. **20** 68N 117W
Rae Lakes: N.W.T. **20** 64N 116W
Rae Strait: N.W.T. **21** 69N 95W
[illegible]
[illegible]
Rainy Lake: Ont. **34** 49N 93W
Rainy River: *town*, Ont. **34** 49N 95W
Ralston: Alta. **30** 51N 112W
Ramah: *& bay.*, Nfld. **40** 59N 63W
Ramea Is.: Nfld. **41** 48N 57W
Rankin Inlet: N.W.T. **21** 63N 92W
Rapides-des-Joachims: Qué. **38** 46N 78W
Rat: *riv.*, Man. **32** 56N 99W
Ratz, Mt.: B.C. **28** 57N 132W
Rawdon: Qué. **39** 46N 74W
Ray, Cape: Nfld. **41** 48N 59W
Raymond: Alta. **30** 49N 113W
Raymore: Sask. **31** 52N 105W
Razorback: *mt.*, B.C. **29** 51N 124W
Read I.: B.C. **28** 50N 125W
Read Island: *settlement*, N.W.T. **20** 69N 114W
Red: *riv.*, Can./U.S.A. **32** 49N 97W
Red Bay: *settlement*, Nfld. **40** 52N 57W
Redberry Lake: Sask. **31** 53N 107W
Redcliff: Alta. **30** 50N 111W
Red Deer: Alta. **30** 52N 114W
Red Deer: *riv.*, Alta. **30** 51N 111W
Red Deer: *riv.*, Sask. **31** 53N 102W
Red Deer Lake: Man. **32** 53N 101W
Red Indian Lake: Nfld. **41** 49N 57W
Red Lake: *& town*, Ont. **34** 51N 94W
Redonda Bay: *town*, B.C. **28** 50N 125W
Redonda Is.: B.C. **28** 50N 125W
Redstone: *riv.*, N.W.T. **20** 63N 126W
Redstone Lake: Ont. **38** 45N 78W
Red Sucker Lake: Man. **32** 54N 94W
Redvers: Sask. **31** 50N 102W
Redwater: Alta. **30** 54N 113W
Refuge Cove: *town*, B.C. **28** 50N 125W
REGINA: Saskatchewan **31** 50N 105W
Reindeer: *riv.* Sask. **31** 56N 103W
Reindeer Grazing Reserve: N.W.T. **20** 69N 133W
Reindeer I.: Man. **32** 52N 98W
Reindeer Lake: Sask./Man. **23** 58N 102W
Reliance: N.W.T. **20** 63N 109W
Renews: Nfld. **41** 47N 53W
Renfrew: Ont. **38** 45N 77W
Repulse Bay: *settlement*, N.W.T. **21** 67N 86W
Resolute: N.W.T. **21** 75N 95W
Resolution I.: N.W.T. **21** 61N 65W
Reston: Man. **32** 50N 102W
Revelstoke: B.C. **29** 51N 118W
Rice Lake: Ont. **38** 44N 78W
Richard Collinson Inlet: N.W.T. **20** 72N 114W
Richards I.: N.W.T. **20** 69N 135W
Richardson: *riv.*, Alta./Sask. **30** 58N 110W
Richardson Mtns.: Yukon **20** 67N 136W
Richelieu: *riv.*, Qué. **39** 46N 73W
Riche Pt.: Nfld. **26** 51N 57W
Richibucto: N.B. **41** 47N 65W
Richmond: B.C. **27** 49N 123W
Richmond Hill: Ont. **27** 44N 79W
Rideau: *riv.*, Ont. **39** 45N 76W
Rideau Canal: Ont. **39** 44N 76W
Rideau Lake: Ont. **39** 45N 76W
Rideau Lakes: Ont. **39** 45N 76W
Riding Mt.: *& Nat. Park*, Manitoba **32** 51N 100W
Rigaud: Qué. **39** 45N 74W
Rigolet: Nfld. **40** 54N 58W
Rimbey: Alta. **30** 53N 114W
Rimouski: Qué. **37** 48N 68W
Rimouski P.P.: Qué. **37** 48N 68W
Riondel: B.C. **29** 50N 117W
Riou Lake: Sask. **31** 59N 106W
Ripon: Qué. **39** 46N 75W
Rivers: Man. **32** 50N 100W
Rivers Inlet: *& town*, B.C. **28** 52N 127W
Riverton: Man. **32** 51N 97W
Rivière à la Baleine: Qué. **37** 57N 67W
Rivière aux Feuilles: Qué. **37** 57N 73W
Rivière aux Graines: Qué. **37** 50N 65W
Rivière aux Mélèzes: Qué. **37** 58N 70W
Rivière aux Outardes: Qué. **37** 50N 69W
Rivière de Pas: Qué. **37** 55N 65W
Rivière de Rupert: Qué. **37** 51N 77W
Rivière des Mille Îles: Qué. **27** 46N 74W
Rivière des Outaouais (Ottawa River): Qué./Ont. **24** 46N 75W
Rivière des Prairies: Qué. **27** 46N 74W
Rivière du Gué: Qué. **37** 57N 72W
Rivière-du-Loup: *town*, Qué. **37** 48N 70W
Rivière du Nord: Qué. **39** 46N 74W
Rivière du Sable: Qué. **37** 55N 68W
Roberts Bank: B.C. **28** 49N 123W
Roberts Creek: *town*, B.C. **28** 49N 124W
Roberval: Qué. **37** 48N 72W
Roblin: Man. **32** 51N 101W
Robson, Mt.: B.C. **29** 53N 119W
Rock Bay: *town*, B.C. **29** 50N 125W
Rockglen: Sask. **31** 49N 106W
Rockland: Ont. **39** 46N 75W
Rocky Harbour: Nfld. **41** 50N 58W
Rocky Mt. House: Alta. **30** 52N 115W
Rocky Mtns.: Can./U.S.A. **22/23** ——
Rocky Saugeen: *riv.*, Ont. **20** 44N 81W
Roddickton: Nfld. **41** 51N 56W
Roes Welcome Sound: N.W.T. **21** 65N 87W
Rogersville: N.B. **41** 47N 65W
Romaine: *riv.*, Qué. **37** 51N 63W
Rondeau P.P.: Ont. **34** 42N 82W
Rorketon: Man. **32** 51N 100W

Rose Blanche: Nfld. **41** 48N 59W
Rosemère: Qué. **39** 46N 74W
Rose Point: B.C. **28** 54N 131W
Rosetown: Sask. **31** 51N 108W
Rose Valley: *town*, Sask. **31** 52N 104W
Rosevear: Alta. **30** 54N 116W
Rosseau: *& lake*, Ont. **38** 45N 80W
Rossignol, Lake: N.S. **41** 44N 65W
Ross I.: Man. **32** 54N 98W
Rossland: B.C. **29** 49N 118W
Ross Point: N.W.T. **20** 75N 107W
Ross River: *& river.*, Yukon **20** 62N 132W
Rosthern: Sask. **31** 53N 106W
Rothesay: N.B. **41** 45N 66W
Rouge: *riv.*, Ont. **27** 44N 79W
Rouge: *riv.*, Ont. **39** 46N 75W
Rouleau: Sask. **31** 50N 105W
Round Lake: Ont. **38** 46N 78W
Round Pond: Nfld. **41** 48N 56W
Rouyn: Qué. **37** 48N 79W
Rowley I.: N.W.T. **21** 69N 79W
Roy: B.C. **28** 50N 125W
Ruby Creek: *town*, British Columbia **28** 49N 122W
Russell: Man. **32** 51N 101W
Russell, Cape: N.W.T. **20** 75N 117W
Russell Point: N.W.T. **20** 73N 116W

S

Sabine Penin.: N.W.T. **20** 76N 109W
Sable, Cape: N.S. **26** 43N 66W
Sachs Harbour: N.W.T. **20** 72N 126W
Sackville: N.B. **41** 46N 64W
Saglek Bay: *& fiord*, Nfld. **40** 58N 63W
Saguenay P.P.: Qué. **37** 48N 70W
Sainte-Adèle: Qué. **39** 46N 74W
Sainte-Agathe-des-Monts: Qué. **39** 46N 74W
St. Albans: Nfld. **41** 48N 56W
St. Albert: Alta. **27** 54N 114W
Saint-André-Avellin: Qué. **39** 46N 75W
Saint-André-Est: Qué. **39** 46N 74W
Ste. Anne: Man. **32** 50N 97W
Sainte-Anne-de-Bellevue: Qué. **27** 45N 74W
Sainte-Anne-des-Monts: Qué. **37** 49N 66W
St. Anthony: Nfld. **41** 51N 55W
St. Antoine: N.B. **17** 47N 64W
Saint-Antoine: Qué. **39** 46N 74W
Saint-Augustin: Qué. **39** 46N 74W
Saint-Augustin: & *riv.*, Qué. **37** 51N 59W
St. Boniface: Man. **33** 50N 91W
St. Catharines: Ont. **38** 43N 79W
St. Charles: Man. **33** 50N 91W
St. Charles, Cape: Nfld. **40** 52N 56W
Saint-Chrysostome: Qué. **39** 45N 74W
St. Clair, Lake: Can./U.S.A. **35** 42N 83W
Saint-Constant: Qué. **39** 45N 74W
St. Croix: *riv.*, Can./U.S.A. **41** 45N 67W
Saint-Denis: Qué. **39** 46N 73W
Saint-Edouard: Qué. **39** 45N 74W
St. Elias Mtns.: Yukon/B.C. **20** 60N 140W
Saint-Esprit: Qué. **39** 46N 74W
Saint-Eustache: Qué. **27** 46N 74W
Saint-Faustin: Qué. **39** 46N 74W
Saint-Félicien: Qué. **37** 48N 72W
Sainte-Foy: Qué. **37** 47N 71W
St. Francis, Cape: Nfld. **41** 48N 53W
Saint-François: *riv.*, Qué. **37** 46N 72W
Saint-François, Lac: Qué. **39** 45N 74W
Sainte-Geneviève: Qué. **27** 45N 74W
St. Germain: Man. **33** 50N 91W
St. George: N.B. **41** 45N 67W
St. George, Cape: Nfld. **41** 48N 59W
St. George's: Nfld. **41** 48N 58W
Saint-George's: Qué. **37** 46N 71W
St. George's Bay: Nfld. **41** 48N 59W
St. George's Bay: N.S. **41** 46N 62W
St. Gregory: *mt.*, Nfld. **41** 49N 58W
Sainte-Hélène, Î.: Qué. **27** 45N 74W
Saint-Hyacinthe: Qué. **37** 46N 73W
Saint-Isidore: Qué. **39** 45N 74W
St. Isidore de Prescott: Ont. **39** 45N 75W
Saint-Jacques: Qué. **39** 46N 74W
St. James, Cape: B.C. **28** 52N 131W
Saint-Janvier: Qué. **39** 46N 74W
Saint-Jean-sur-Richelieu: Qué. **39** 45N 73W
Saint-Jean, Lac: Qué. **37** 48N 72W
Saint-Jérôme: Qué. **39** 46N 74W
Saint John: N.B. **41** 45N 66W
Saint John: *riv.*, Canada/U.S.A. **41** 46N 67W
St. John Bay: Nfld. **41** 51N 58W
St. John, Cape: Nfld. **41** 50N 56W
ST. JOHN'S: Nfld. **41** 48N 53W
Saint-Joseph: Qué. **39** 46N 73W
St. Joseph, Lake: Ont. **34** 51N 91W
Saint-Joseph-du-Lac: Qué. **39** 46N 74W
Saint-Jovite: Qué. **39** 46N 75W
Sainte-Julienne: Qué. **39** 46N 74W
Saint-Laurent: Qué. **27** 46N 74W
Saint-Laurent, Fleuve (St. Lawrence River): Canada/U.S.A. **24/25** — —
Saint-Laurent, Golfe du: Qué. **37** 49N 68W
St. Lawrence: Nfld. **41** 47N 55W
St. Lawrence River (Fleuve Saint-Laurent): Canada/U.S.A. **24/25** — —
St. Lawrence (Upper): *riv. & seaway*, Canada/U.S.A. **39** — —
St. Lawrence, Gulf of: Can. **26** 48N 62W
St. Lawrence Is. N.P.: Ont. **34** 44N 76W
St. Leonard: N.B. **41** 47N 68W
Saint-Leonard: Qué. **27** 46N 74W
Saint-Louis, Lac: Qué. **27** 45N 74W
Saint-Louis-de-Gonzague: Québec **39** 45N 74W
St. Malo: Man. **32** 49N 97W
Saint-Marc-sur-Richelieu: Qué. **39** 46N 73W
Sainte-Marguerite: *riv.*, Qué. **37** 51N 67W
Sainte-Marie: Qué. **39** 46N 73W
St. Martin, Lake: Man. **32** 52N 98W
Sainte-Martine: Qué. **39** 45N 74W
St. Martins: N.B. **41** 45N 66W
St. Mary: *riv.*, Alta. **30** 49N 113W
St. Mary's Bay: N.S. **41** 44N 66W
St. Mary's Bay: Nfld. **41** 47N 54W
St. Mary's: *riv.*, N.S. **41** 45N 62W
St. Mary's Harbour: Nfld. **40** 52N 56W
Saint-Maurice: *riv.*, Qué. **37** 47N 73W
St. Michael's Bay: Nfld. **40** 53N 56W
Saint-Michel: Qué. **39** 45N 74W
St. Norbert: Man. **33** 50N 91W
Saint-Ours: Qué. **39** 46N 73W
Saint-Pacôme: Qué. **37** 47N 70W
St. Paul: Alta. **30** 54N 111W
Saint-Paul: *riv.*, Qué./Nfld. **26** 52N 58W
St. Paul Junction: Alta. **27** 54N 113W
St. Pierre: Man. **32** 50N 97W
St. Quentin: N.B. **41** 47N 67W
Saint-Rémi: Qué. **39** 45N 74W
Saint-Rémi: Qué. **39** 46N 75W
Saint-Roch: Qué. **39** 46N 73W
Saint-Roch-de-l'Achigan: Qué. **39** 46N 74W
Sainte-Rose: Qué. **27** 46N 74W
Ste. Rose du Lac: Man. **32** 51N 99W
Sainte-Sophie: Qué. **39** 46N 74W
St. Stephen: N.B. **41** 45N 67W
St. Theresa Point: Man. **32** 54N 95W
Sainte-Thérèse: Qué. **27** 46N 74W
Sainte-Thérèse, Ile: Qué. **27** 46N 73W
St. Thomas: Ont. **34** 43N 81W
St. Walburg: Sask. **31** 54N 109W
Sakami: *riv.*, Qué. **37** 53N 76W
Sakami: Qué. **37** 53N 77W
Salaberry-de-Valleyfield: Qué. **39** 45N 74W
Sale: *riv.* Man. **33** 50N 91W
Salisbury: N.B. **41** 46N 65W
Salisbury I.: N.W.T. **21** 63N 77W
Salluit: Qué. **36** 62N 75W
Salmo: B.C. **29** 49N 118W
Salmon: *riv.*, N.B. **41** 46N 66W
Salmon: *riv.*, Ont. **38** 44N 77W
Salmon Arm: B.C. **29** 51N 119W
Saltcoats: Sask. **31** 51N 102W
Saltspring I.: B.C. **28** 49N 123W
Sandspit: B.C. **28** 53N 132W
Sandwich Bay: Nfld. **40** 53N 57W
Sandy Bay: *town*, Sask. **31** 56N 103W
Sandy Cove: *settlement*, Nfld. **41** 51N 56W
Sandy Lake: Nfld. **41** 49N 57W
Sandy Lake: Ont. **34** 53N 93W
Sardis: B.C. **28** 49N 122W
Sarnia: Ont. **34** 43N 82W
Sasaginnigak Lake: Man. **32** 52N 96W
Sasamat Lake: B.C. **27** 49N 123W
Saskatchewan: *Prov (cap.* Regina) **23** — —
Saskatchewan: *riv.*, Sask./Manitoba **23** 54N 103W
Saskatchewan Landing P.P.: Saskatchewan **31** 51N 108W
Saskatoon: Sask. **31** 52N 107W
Sault Ste. Marie: Ont. **34** 46N 84W
Scarborough: Ont. **27** 44N 79W
Scatarie I.: N.S. **41** 46N 60W
Schefferville: Qué. **37** 55N 66W
Schreiber: Ont. **34** 49N 87W
Schultz Lake: N.W.T. **21** 65N 97W
Scott Chan.: B.C. **28** 51N 128W
Scott Is.: B.C. **28** 51N 129W
Scugog, Lake: Ont. **38** 44N 79W
Sea Island: B.C. **27** 49N 123W
Seal: *riv.*, Man. **32** 59N 96W
Seal Lake: Nfld. **40** 54N 62W
Sechelt: B.C. **28** 49N 124W
Sechelt Penin.: B.C. **28** 49N 124W
Seine: *riv.* Man. **33** 50N 91W
Selkirk: Man. **32** 50N 97W
Selkirk Mtns.: B.C. **29** 51N 118W
Selwyn Lake: Sask./N.W.T. **23** 60N 104W
Selwyn Mtns.: Yukon **20** 63N 130W
Senneterre: Qué. **37** 48N 77W
Sentinel Peak: B.C. **29** 55N 122W
Sept-Îles: *town*, Qué. **37** 50N 66W
Sérigny: *riv.*, Qué. **37** 55N 69W
Seton Lake: B.C. **28** 51N 122W
Seul, Lac: Ont. **34** 50N 92W
Seven Islands Bay: Nfld. **40** 59N 64W
Seventy Mile House: B.C. **29** 51N 121W
Severn: *riv.*, Ont. **34** 55N 88W
Severn: *riv.*, Ont. **38** 45N 80W
Sexsmith: Alta. **30** 55N 119W
Seymour Creek: B.C. **27** 49N 123W
Seymour Inlet: B.C. **29** 51N 127W
Shabogamo Lake: Qué. **40** 53N 67W
Shalalth: B.C. **28** 51N 122W
Shamattawa: Man. **32** 56N 92W
Shaunavon: Sask. **31** 50N 108W
Shawville: Qué. **39** 46N 76W
Shawinigan: Qué. **37** 46N 73W
Shawnigan Lake: *town*, B.C. **28** 49N 124W
Shediac: N.B. **41** 46N 65W
Sheet Harbour: N.S. **41** 45N 63W
Shelburne: N.S. **41** 44N 65W
Shellbrook: Sask. **31** 53N 106W
Shepherd Bay: N.W.T. **21** 68N 95W
Sherbrooke: Qué. **37** 45N 72W
Sherridon: Man. **32** 55N 101W
Sherwood: P.E.I. **41** 46N 63W
Sherwood Park: Alta. **27** 54N 113W
Sheslay: *riv.*, B.C. **28** 58N 132W
Shibogama Lake: Ont. **34** 54N 88W
Shickshock, Monts: Qué. **37** 49N 66W
Shippagan: N.B. **41** 48N 65W
Shirley Lake: Ont. **38** 46N 78W
Shoal Lake: *town*, Man. **32** 50N 101W
Shoal Lake: Man./Ont. **32** 49N 95W
Shoal Lakes: Man. **32** 50N 97W
Shuswap Lake: B.C. **29** 51N 119W
Sicamous: B.C. **29** 51N 119W
Sidney: B.C. **28** 49N 123W
Sifton: Man. **32** 51N 100W
Sifton Pass: B.C. **29** 58N 126W
Sikanni Chief: *riv.*, B.C. **29** 57N 123W
Silene, Mt.: Nfld. **40** 59N 64W
Silvertip Mt.: B.C. **28** 49N 121W
Simcoe Lake: Ont. **38** 44N 79W
Simon, Lac: Qué. **39** 46N 75W
Simpson Bay: N.W.T. **20** 69N 114W
Simpson I.: Ont. **34** 48N 88W
Simpson Penin.: N.W.T. **21** 68N 89W
Simpson Strait: N.W.T. **20/21** 68N 98W
Sims Lake: Nfld. **40** 54N 66W
Sioux Lookout: Ont. **34** 50N 92W
Sipiwesk: Man. **32** 56N 97W
Sipiwesk Lake: Man. **32** 55N 97W
Sir Alexander, Mt.: B.C. **29** 54N 120W
Sir Francis Drake, Mt.: B.C. **28** 51N 125W
Sir James Macbrien, Mt.: N.W.T. **20** 62N 127W
Sir Wilfrid Laurier, *mt.*, B.C. **29** 53N 120W
Siwhe Mt.: B.C. **28** 50N 122W
Skagit Valley P.P.: B.C. **22** 49N 120W
Skeena: *riv.*, B.C. **28** 54N 129W
Skeena Mtns.: B.C. **28** 57N 130W
Skeleton Lake: Ont. **38** 45N 79W
Skihist Mt.: B.C. **28** 50N 122W
Skootamatta Lake: Ont. **38** 45N 77W
Skownan: Man. **32** 52N 99W
Slate Is.: Ont. **34** 49N 87W
Slave: *riv.*, Alta./N.W.T. **23** 60N 112W
Slave Lake: *town*, Alta. **30** 55N 115W
Sleeper Is.: N.W.T. **21** 57N 80W
Slocan Lake: B.C. **29** 50N 117W
Smallwood Reservoir: Nfld. **40** 54N 65W
Smeaton: Sask. **31** 53N 105W
Smith: Alta. **30** 55N 114W
Smith: *riv.*, B.C./Yukon **29** 60N 126W
Smith Arm: Great Bear Lake, N.W.T. **20** 66N 123W
Smith Bay: N.W.T. **21** 77N 80W
Smithers: B.C. **29** 55N 127W
Smiths Falls: *town*, Ont. **39** 45N 76W
Smith Sound: Canada/Greenland **21** 78N 74W
Smokey: *riv.*, Alta. **30** 55N 118W
Smoky, Cape: N.S. **41** 47N 60W
Smoky Lake: *town*, Alta. **30** 54N 112W
Smooth Rock Falls: *town*, Ont. **34** 49N 82W
Snake: *riv.*, Yukon **20** 66N 133W
Snake River: *town*, B.C. **29** 59N 122W
Snegamook Lake: Nfld. **40** 55N 61W
Snowbird Lake: N.W.T. **23** 61N 103W
Snowdrift: N.W.T. **20** 63N 111W
Snow Lake: *town*, Man. **32** 55N 100W
Snowy Mt.: B.C. **28** 49N 120W
Snug Harbour: Nfld. **40** 53N 56W
Somerset: Man. **32** 50N 99W
Somerset I.: N.W.T. **21** 73N 93W
Sooke: B.C. **28** 48N 124W
Sops I.: Nfld. **41** 50N 57W
Sorel: Qué. **39** 46N 73W
Soulanges: Qué. **39** 45N 74W
Sounding Lake: Alta. **30** 52N 110W
Souris: Man. **32** 50N 100W
Souris: P.E.I. **41** 46N 62W
Souris: *riv.*, Man./Sask. **32** 49N 101W
Southampton Island: N.W.T. **21** 64N 83W
South Aulatsivik I.: Nfld. **40** 57N 61W
Southend: Sask. **31** 56N 103W
Southern Indian Lake: Man. **32** 57N 99W
Southey: Sask. **31** 51N 104W
South Henik Lake: N.W.T. **21** 61N 97W
South Indian Lake: *town*, Man. **32** 57N 99W
South Knife: *riv.*, Man. **32** 58N 96W
South Nahanni: *riv.*, N.W.T. **20** 61N 126W
South Nation: *riv.*, Ont. **21** 45N 75W
South River: *town*, Ont. **38** 46N 79W
South Saskatchewan: *riv.*, Sask./Alta. **31** 51N 109W
South Seal: *riv.*, Man. **32** 58N 99W
Spanish: *riv.*, Ont. **34** 47N 82W
Spanish Banks: B.C. **27** 49N 123W
Sparwood: B.C. **29** 50N 115W
Spatsizi Plat Wilderness Prov. Park: B.C. **28** 58N 129W
Spear, Cape: Nfld. **41** 47N 53W
Spence Bay: *settlement*, N.W.T. **21** 69N 93W
Spirit River: *town*, Alta. **30** 56N 119W
Split Lake: *& town*, Man. **32** 56N 96W
Spotted I.: Nfld. **40** 54N 56W
Springdale: Nfld. **41** 49N 56W
Springhill: N.S. **41** 46N 64W
Sproat Lake: B.C. **28** 49N 125W
Spruce Grove: Alta. **30** 53N 114W
Spruce Woods Prov. Park.: Man. **33** 50N 99W
Spuzzum: B.C. **28** 50N 121W
Squamish: B.C. **28** 50N 123W
Squamish: *riv.*, B.C. **28** 50N 123W
Square Is.: Nfld. **40** 53N 56W
Squaw Rapids Dam.: Sask. **31** 54N 103W
Stang, Cape: N.W.T. **20** 71N 105W
Star City: Sask. **31** 53N 104W
Stave Falls: *town*, B.C. **28** 49N 122W
Stave Lake: B.C. **28** 49N 122W
Stayner: Ont. **38** 44N 80W
Stefansson I.: N.W.T. **20** 73N 107W
Steinbach: Man. **32** 49N 97W
Stellarton: N.S. **41** 46N 63W
Stephenville: Nfld. **41** 49N 69W
Stettler: Alta. **30** 52N 113W
Steveston: B.C. **27** 49N 123W
Stewart: B.C. **28** 56N 130W
Stewart: *riv.*, Yukon **20** 63N 138W
Stewart Crossing: Yukon **20** 64N 136W
Stikine: *riv.*, B.C. **28** 57N 131W
Stikine Range: B.C. **28** 59N 130W
Stillwater: B.C. **28** 50N 124W
Stillwater Creek: Sask. **31** 50N 108W
Stirling: Alta. **30** 50N 113W
Stirling: Ont. **38** 44N 78W
Stone Mountain P.P.: B.C. **29** 59N 125W
Stonewall: Man. **32** 50N 97W
Stoney Creek: *town*, Ont. **38** 43N 80W
Stony Lake: Man. **32** 59N 99W
Stony Lake: Ont. **38** 45N 78W
Stony Mountain: *town*, Man. **32** 50N 97W
Stony Plain: *town*, Alta. **30** 54N 114W
Stony Rapids: *town*, Sask. **31** 59N 106W
Storkerson Bay: N.W.T. **20** 73N 125W
Storkerson Penin: N.W.T. **20** 72N 107W
Stoughton: Sask. **31** 50N 103W
Strasbourg: Sask. **31** 51N 105W
Strathcona: Alta. **27** 54N 113W
Strathcona Prov. Park: B.C. **29** 50N 126W
Strathmore: Alta. **30** 51N 113W
Strathnaver: B.C. **29** 53N 123W
Stuart Lake: B.C. **29** 55N 124W
Sturgeon: *riv.*, Sask. **31** 53N 106W
Sturgeon Bank: B.C. **27** 49N 123W
Sturgeon Bay: Man. **32** 52N 98W
Sturgeon Creek: Man. **33** 50N 91W
Sturgeon Falls: *town*, Ont. **34** 46N 80W
Sturgeon Lake: Alta. **30** 55N 117W
Sturgeon Lake: Ont. **38** 44N 79W
Sturgeon Landing: Sask. **31** 54N 102W
Sturgis: Sask. **31** 52N 102W
Sudbury: Ont. **34** 46N 81W
Sullivan Bay: *town*, B.C. **29** 51N 127W
Sullivan Lake: Alta. **30** 52N 112W
Summerside: P.E.I. **41** 46N 64W
Sundre: Alta. **30** 52N 115W
Sundridge: Ont. **38** 46N 79W
Superior, Lake: Canada/U.S.A. **24** 48N 88W
Surrey: B.C. **27** 49N 123W
Sussex: N.B. **41** 46N 66W
Sutherland: Sask. **31** 52N 107W
Svendsen Peninsula: N.W.T. **21** 78N 84W
Sverdrup Is.: N.W.T. **20-21** 78N 100W
Swan Hills: Alta. **30** 55N 116W
Swan Hills: *town*, Alta. **30** 55N 115W
Swan Lake: Man. **32** 52N 101W
Swannell Range: B.C. **29** 56N 126W
Swan River: *town*, Man. **32** 52N 101W
Swift Current: Sask. **31** 50N 108W
Swinburne, Cape: N.W.T. **20** 71N 99W
Sydney: N.S. **41** 46N 60W
Sydney Ice Cap: N.W.T. **21** 77N 85W
Sydney Mines: N.S. **41** 46N 60W
Sylvan Lake: *town*, Alta. **30** 52N 114W

T

Taber: Alta. **30** 50N 112W
Table Bay: Nfld. **40** 54N 56W
Tadoule Lake: Man. **32** 59N 98W
Tadoussac: Qué. **26** 48N 70W
Tahiryuak Lake: N.W.T. **20** 71N 112W
Tahoe Lake: N.W.T. **20** 70N 109W
Tahsis: B.C. **29** 50N 126W
Tahtsa Lake: B.C. **29** 54N 127W
Takijuq Lake: N.W.T. **20** 66N 113W
Takla Lake: B.C. **29** 55N 126W
Takla Landing: B.C. **29** 56N 126W
Taku: *riv.*, B.C. **28** 59N 133W
Taku Arm: *lake*, B.C. **28** 60N 134W
Taltson: *riv.*, N.W.T. **23** 60N 111W
Tar Island: Alta. **23** 57N 111W
Taseko: *riv. & mtn.*, B.C. **29** 51N 123W
Tasisuak Lake: Nfld. **40** 57N 63W
Tathlina Lake: N.W.T. **22** 60N 118W
Tatla Lake: B.C. **29** 52N 124W
Tatlatui Prov. Park: B.C. **29** 57N 128W
Tatlayoka Lake: B.C. **29** 52N 124W
Tatnam, Cape: Man. **23** 57N 91W
Tatshenshini: *riv.* B.C./Yukon **30** 60N 137W
Taylor: B.C. **29** 56N 121W
Tazin Lake: Sask. **31** 60N 109W
Tehek Lake: N.W.T. **21** 65N 95W
Telegraph Creek: *town*, B.C. **28** 58N 131W
Temagami: Ont. **34** 47N 80W
Témiscaming: Qué. **37** 47N 79W
Témiscamingue, Lac (Lake Timiskaming): Ont./Qué. **37** 47N 79W
Terrace: B.C. **28** 55N 129W
Terrace Bay: *town*, Ont. **34** 49N 87W
Terra Nova Nat. Park: Nfld. **41** 48N 54W
Terrebone: Qué. **39** 46N 74W
Teslin: *& lake*, Yukon **20** 60N 132W
Teslin: *riv.*, Yukon/B.C. **20** 61N 134W
Teulon: Man. **32** 50N 97W
Texada I.: B.C. **28** 50N 124W
The Domes: *mt.*, Nfld. **40** 58N 63W
Thelon: *riv. & game sanctuary*, N.W.T. **20** 64N 104W
The Pas: Man. **32** 54N 101W
Thesiger Bay: N.W.T. **20** 72N 125W
Thessalon: Ont. **34** 46N 84W
Thetford Mines: Qué. **37** 46N 71W
Thicket Portage: Man. **32** 55N 98W
Thlewiaza: *riv.*, N.W.T. **21** 61N 97W
Thomlinson, Mt.: B.C. **29** 56N 128W
Thompson: Man. **32** 56N 98W
Thompson: *riv.*, B.C. **29** 51N 121W
Thomsen: *riv.*, N.W.T. **20** 74N 120W
Thorhild: Alta. **30** 54N 113W
Thornhill: Ont. **27** 44N 79W
Thorold: Ont. **38** 43N 79W
Thorsby: Alta. **30** 53N 114W
Three Hills: *town*, Alta. **30** 52N 113W
Thunder Bay: Ont. **34** 48N 89W
Thurlow: B.C. **28** 50N 125W
Thurso: Qué. **39** 46N 75W
Thutade Lake: B.C. **29** 57N 127W
Tidehead: N.B. **41** 48N 67W
Tignish: P.E.I. **41** 47N 64W
Tilbury Island: B.C. **27** 49N 123W
Tilt Cove: Nfld. **41** 50N 56W
Timiskaming, Lake (Lac Témiscamingue): Ont./Qué. **37** 47N 79W
Timmins: Ont. **34** 48N 81W
Tinniswood, Mt.: B.C. **28** 50N 124W
Tisdale: Sask. **31** 53N 104W
Toba: *inlet & riv.*, B.C. **28** 50N 124W
Tobeatic Game Sanc.: N.S. **41** 44N 66W
Tobermory: Ont. **34** 45N 82W
Tobin Lake: Sask. **31** 54N 103W
Tobique: *riv.*, N.B. **41** 47N 67W
Tofield: Alta. **30** 53N 113W
Tofino: B.C. **29** 49N 126W
Torbay: Nfld. **41** 48N 53W
Torch: *riv.*, Sask. **31** 54N 105W
Tormentine, Cape: N.B. **41** 46N 64W
Tornado Mt.: B.C./Alta. **29** 50N 115W
Torngat Mountains (Monts Torngat): Nfld./Qué. **40** 60N 64W
TORONTO: Ont. **38** 44N 79W
Toronto Islands: Ont. **38** 44N 79W
Tottenham: Ont. **38** 44N 80W
Tracadie: N.B. **41** 47N 65W
Tracy: Qué. **39** 46N 73W
Trail: B.C. **29** 49N 118W

Tramping Lake: Sask. **31** 52N 109W
Transcona: Man. **33** 50N 91W
Treherne: Man. **32** 50N 99W
Trembleur Lake: B.C. **29** 55N 125W
Trent: *riv.*, Ont. **38** 44N 78W
Trent Canal: Ont. **38** 44N 79W
Trenton: Ont. **38** 44N 78W
Trepassey: Nfld. **41** 47N 53W
Trinity; *& bay*, Nfld. **41** 48N 53W
Trochu: Alta. **30** 52N 113W
Trois-Rivières: Qué. **37** 46N 73W
Trout Creek: *town*, Ont. **38** 46N 79W
Trout Lake: N.W.T. **22** 60N 121W
Trout Lake: Ont. **34** 51N 93W
Trout River: *town*, Nfld. **41** 50N 58W
[illegible]
[illegible]
Tuktoyaktuk: N.W.T. **20** 69N 133W
Tumbler Ridge: *town*, B.C. **29** 55N 121W
Tungsten: N.W.T. **20** 62N 128W
Tunungayualuk I.: Nfld. **40** 56N 61W
Turnagain: *riv.*, B.C. **29** 59N 128W
Turner Valley: *town*, Alta. **30** 51N 114W
Turnor Lake: Sask. **31** 57N 109W
Turtle Mountain P.P.: Man. **32** 49N 100W
Turtleford: Sask. **31** 53N 109W
Tuxedo: Man. **33** 50N 91W
Tweed: Ont. **38** 44N 77W
Tweedsmuir Prov. Park: B.C. **29** 53N 126W
Twillingate: Nfld. **41** 50N 55W
Twin Falls: Nfld. **40** 53N 65W
Twin Is.: N.W.T. **24** 53N 80W
Two Hills: *town*, Alta. **30** 54N 112W
Two Rivers, Lake of: Ont. **38** 46N 78W

U

Uivak, Cape: Nfld. **40** 58N 63W
Ukasiksalik I.: Nfld. **40** 56N 61W
Ungava Bay (Baie d'Ungava): Qué. **21** 59N 67W
Ungava, Péninsule d': Qué. **36** 61N 75W
Union Bay: *town*, B.C. **28** 50N 125W
Union, Cape: N.W.T. **21** 82N 61W
Unionville: Ont. **27** 44N 79W
United States Range: N.W.T. **21** 83N 80W
Unity: Sask. **31** 52N 109W
Upper Arrow Lake: B.C. **29** 50N 118W
Upper Foster Lake: Sask. **31** 57N 105W
Upper Liard: Yukon **20** 60N 129W
Uranium City: Sask. **31** 60N 109W
Utik Lake: Man. **32** 55N 96W
Utikuma Lake: Alta. **30** 56N 115W
Uxbridge: Ont. **38** 44N 79W

V

Valdes I.: B.C. **28** 49N 124W
Val-d'Or: Qué. **37** 48N 78W
Valemount: B.C. **29** 53N 119W
Valleyview: Alta. **30** 55N 117W
Vancouver: B.C. **36** 49N 123W
Vancouver I.: B.C. **29** 50N 126W
Vanderhoof: B.C. **29** 54N 124W
Vankleek Hill: *town*, Ont. **39** 45N 75W
Varennes: Qué. **39** 46N 73W
Vaughan: Ont. **38** 44N 79W
Vauxhall: Alta. **30** 50N 112W
Vegreville: Alta. **30** 53N 112W
Verchères: Qué. **39** 46N 73W
Verdun: Qué. **27** 45N 74W
Vermilion: Alta. **30** 53N 111W
Vermilion Pass: Alta./B.C. **29** 51N 116W
Vernette: Man. **33** 50N 91W
Vernon: B.C. **29** 50N 119W
Vernon Lake: Ont. **38** 45N 79W
VICTORIA: B.C. **28** 48N 123W
Victoria: Nfld. **41** 48N 53W
Victoria Harbour: Ont. **38** 45N 80W
Victoria I.: N.W.T. **20** 70N 110W
[illegible]
[illegible]
Viking: Alta. **30** 53N 112W
Ville de Laval: Qué. **27** 46N 74W
Virden: Man. **32** 50N 101W
Viscount Melville Sound: N.W.T. **20** 74N 110W
Voiseys Bay: Nfld. **40** 56N 62W
Vulcan: Alta. **30** 50N 113W

W

Wabana: Nfld. **41** 48N 53W
Wabasca: *riv.*, Alta. **30** 57N 114W
Wabasca-Desmarais: Alta. **30** 56N 114W
Wabowden: Man. **32** 55N 99W
Wabuk Point: Ont. **34** 55N 85W
Wabush Lake: *town*, Nfld. **40** 53N 67W
Wabush Lake: Nfld. **40** 53N 67W
W.A.C. Bennett Dam: B.C. **29** 56N 122W
Waddington, Mt.: B.C. **29** 51N 125W
Wade Lake:Nfld. **40** 54N 66W
Wadena: Sask. **31** 52N 104W
Wager Bay: N.W.T. **21** 66N 90W
Wahwashkesh Lake: Ont. **38** 46N 80W
Wainwright: Alta. **30** 53N 111W
Wakaw: Sask. **31** 53N 106W
Waldheim: Sask. **31** 53N 107W
Wales I.: N.W.T. **21** 68N 87W
Walker Bay: N.W.T. **20** 71N 119W
Wallace: Ont. **38** 45N 78W
Waltham: Ont. **38** 46N 77W
Wanham: Alta. **30** 56N 118W
Wanless: Man. **32** 54N 101W
Wapawekka Hills: *& lake*, Sask. **31** 54N 105W
Wapella: Sask. **31** 50N 102W
Wapiti: *riv.*, B.C./Alta. **30** 55N 120W
Warburton Bay: *lake*, N.W.T. **20** 64N 112W
Wardlow: Alta. **30** 51N 112W
Ware: B.C. **29** 58N 126W
Warman: Sask. **31** 52N 106W
Warner: Alta. **30** 49N 112W
Warren Landing: Man. **32** 54N 98W
Wasaga Beach: Ont. **38** 45N 80W
Wascana Creek: Sask. **31** 50N 105W
Wasekamio Lake: Sask. **31** 57N 109W
Washow Bay: Man. **32** 51N 97W
Waskesiu: Sask. **31** 54N 106W
Waskigomog Lake: Ont. **38** 46N 79W
Waterbury Lake: Sask. **31** 58N 104W
Waterhen: *riv.*, Sask. **31** 54N 109W
Waterhen Lake: Man. **32** 52N 99W
Waterton Lakes Nat. Park: Alta. **30** 49N 114W
Wathaman: *riv.*, Sask. **31** 57N 104W
Watrous: Sask. **31** 52N 105W
Watson: Sask. **31** 52N 104W
Watson Lake: *town*, Yukon **22** 60N 129W
Wawa: Ont. **34** 48N 85W
Wawota: Sask. **31** 50N 102W
Weaver Lake: Man. **32** 53N 97W
Wedge Mt.: B.C. **28** 50N 123W
Wekusko: *& lake*, Man. **32** 55N 100W
Welland: *& canal*, Ont. **38** 43N 79W
Welland: *riv.*, Ont. **38** 43N 80W
Wellington: Ont. **38** 44N 77W
Wellington Chan.: N.W.T. **21** 75N 93W
Wells: B.C. **29** 53N 122W
[illegible]
[illegible]
Wernecke Mts.: Yukon **20** 65N 133W
Weslemkoon Lake: Ont. **38** 45N 77W
Wesleyville: Nfld. **41** 49N 54W
West Bay: *settlement*, Nfld. **40** 54N 57W
Western: *riv.*, N.W.T. **20** 66N 107W
Westlock: Alta. **30** 54N 114W
Westmount: Qué. **27** 45N 74W
Westport: Ont. **39** 45N 76W
West Road: *riv.*, B.C. **29** 53N 123W
West St. Modest: Nfld. **40** 52N 57W
West Vancouver: B.C. **27** 49N 123W
Westville: N.S. **41** 46N 63W
Wetaskiwin: Alta. **30** 53N 113W
Weyburn: Sask. **31** 50N 104W
Weymouth: N.S. **41** 44N 66W
Whale Cove: *settlement*, N.W.T. **21** 63N 92W
Wheeler: *riv.*, Qué. **37** 56N 67W
Wheeler: *riv.*, Sask. **31** 57N 105W
Whitby: Ont. **38** 44N 79W
Whitchurch-Stouffville: Ont. **38** 44N 79W
White: *riv.*, Ont. **34** 48N 85W
White: *riv.*, Yukon **20** 63N 140W
White Bay: Nfld. **41** 50N 57W
Whitecap Mtn.: B.C. **28** 51N 123W
Whitecourt: Alta. **30** 54N 116W
Whitefish Lake; N.W.T. **20** 63N 107W
Whitegull, Lac: Qué. **37** 55N 64W
WHITEHORSE: Yukon **20** 61N 135W
White Lake: Ont. **39** 45N 76W
Whitemouth: Man. **32** 50N 96W
Whitemouth Lake: Man. **32** 49N 96W
Whitemund Creek: Alta. **27** 53N 114W
White Pass: *town*, B.C. **28** 60N 135W
White River: *town*, Ont. **34** 49N 85W
White Rock: B.C. **28** 49N 123W
Whitesail Lake: B.C. **29** 53N 127W
Whiteshell Prov. Park: Man. **32** 50N 95W
Whitewood: Sask. **31** 50N 102W
Whittle, Cap: Qué. **37** 50N 60W
Wholdaia Lake: N.W.T. **23** 60N 104W
Wilberforce: Ont. **38** 45N 78W
Wildcat Hill Wilderness Area: Sask. **31** 53N 102W
Wilderness Area: *park*, Nfld. **41** 47N 53W
Wilderness Area: *park*, Nfld. **41** 48N 57W
Wildwood: Alta. **30** 54N 115W
Wilkie: Sask. **31** 52N 109W
Will, Mt.: B.C. **28** 58N 129W
William: *riv.*, Sask. **31** 59N 109W
Williams Lake: *town*, B.C. **29** 52N 122W
Williston Lake: B.C. **29** 56N 124W
Willmore Wilderness Prov. Park: Alta. **30** 53N 118W
Willowbunch Lake: Sask. **31** 49N 106W
Willow Lake: N.W.T. **20** 62N 119W
Winchester: Ont. **39** 45N 75W
Windigo Lake: Ont. **34** 53N 92W
Windsor: Nfld. **41** 49N 56W
Windsor: N.S. **41** 45N 64W
Windsor: Ont. **34** 42N 83W
Winefred Lake: Alta. **30** 55N 111
Winisk: *& riv.*, Ont. **34** 55N 85W
Winisk Lake: Ont. **34** 53N 87W
Winisk River P.P.: Ont. **34** 53N 87W
[illegible]
[illegible]
Winnipeg: *riv.*, Man. **32** 50N 95W

Winnipeg, Lake: Man. **32** 52N 98W
Winnipeg Beach: Man. **32** 51N 97W
Winnipegosis: Man. **32** 52N 100W
Winnipegosis: Lake: Man. **32** 52N 100W
Winokapau Lake: Nfld. **40** 53N 63W
Winterburn: Alta. **27** 54N 114W
Winter Harbour: N.W.T. **20** 75N 110W
Wolfe Island: *& i.*, Ont. **39** 44N 76W
Wolfville: N.S. **41** 45N 64W
Wollaston, Cape: N.W.T. **20** 71N 118W
Wollaston Lake: *& town*, Sask. **31** 58N 103W
Wollaston Penin.: N.W.T. **20** 70N 115W
Wolseley: Sask. **31** 50N 103W
Wood Buffalo National Park: N.W.T./Alberta **22** 59N 113W
Woodbridge: Ont. **27** 44N 80W
Woodfibre: B.C. **28** 50N 123W
Wood Mt.: Sask. **31** 49N 106W
Woods, Lake of the: Canada/U.S.A. **23** 49N 94W
Woods Lake:Nfld. **40** 54N 65W
Woodstock: N.B. **41** 46N 68W
Woodville: Ont. **38** 44N 79W
Writing on Stone P.P.: Alta. **30** 49N 112W
Wrong Lake: Man. **32** 53N 96W
Wunnummin Lake: Ont. **34** 53N 89W
Wynniatt Bay: N.W.T. **20** 72N 111W
Wynyard: Sask. **31** 52N 104W

Y

Yale: B.C. **28** 50N 121W
Yarmouth: N.S. **41** 44N 66W
Yathkyed Lake: N.W.T. **21** 63N 98W
Yellow Grass: Sask. **31** 50N 104W
Yellowhead Pass: B.C./Alta. **29** 53N 119W
YELLOWKNIFE: N.W.T. **20** 62N 114W
Yellowknife: *riv.*, N.W.T. **20** 63N 114W
Yoho Nat. Park: B.C. **29** 51N 117W
York: Ont. **27** 44N 79W
York, Cape: N.W.T. **21** 74N 87W
York Factory: Man. **32** 57N 92W
Yorkton: Sask. **31** 51N 102W
Youbou: B.C. **28** 49N 124W
Young: Sask. **31** 52N 106W
Yukon: *riv.*, U.S.A./Can. **20** 62N 137W
Yukon Territories (*seat of gov't*: Whitehorse) **20** — —

Gazetteer of the World

A

Aachen: W. Germany **68** 51N 6E
Ābādān: Iran **83** 30N 48E
Abadla: Algeria **100** 31N 2W
Abakan: U.S.S.R. **81** 54N 91E
Abashiri: Japan **90** 44N 144E
Abéché: Chad **101** 14N 21E
Åbenrå (Aabenraa): Denmark **70** 55N 9E
Abbeville: France **68** 50N 2E
Abbeville: U.S.A. **50** 30N 92W
Abbottabad: Pak. **84** 34N 73E
Abd al Kuri: *i.*, Indian O. **83** 12N 52E
Abeokuta: Nigeria **100** 7N 3E
Aberdeen: Scotland **67** 57N 2W
Aberdeen: S. Dak., U.S.A. **53** 45N 99W
Aberdeen: Wash., U.S.A. **52** 47N 124W
Aberystwyth: Wales **67** 52N 4W
Abidjan: Côte D'Ivoire **100** 5N 4W
Abilene: U.S.A. **50** 32N 100W
Absaroka Range: U.S.A. **52** 45N 110W
Abu: India **84** 25N 73E
ABU DHABI: United Arab Emirates **83** 24N 54E
Abuja: Nigeria **100** 9N 7E
Academgorodok: U.S.S.R. **87** 52N 104E
Acapulco: Mexico **58** 17N 99W
ACCRA: Ghana **100** 5N 0
Achill I.: R. of Ireland **67** 54N 10W
Achinsk: U.S.S.R. **81** 56N 90E
Acklins I.: The Bahamas **59** 22N 74W
Aconcagua: *mtn.*, Argentina **60** 33S 70W
Acre: *see* Akko
Ada: U.S.A. **53** 35N 97W
Adam's Bridge: India/Sri Lanka **84** 9N 80E
Adana: Turkey **82** 37N 35E
Adapazarı: Turkey **82** 41N 30E
ADDIS ABABA: Ethiopia **101** 9N 39E
Adelaide: Australia **94** 35S 139E
Adelaide I.: Antarctica **128** 67S 68W
ADEN: Yemen P.D.R. **83** 13N 45E
Aden: *gulf*, Arabian Sea **83** 13N 47E
Adirondack Mts.: U.S.A. **54** 43N 75W
Admiralty Is.: Papua New Guinea **94** 2S 147E
Adour: *r.*, France **69** 44N 1W
Adrian: U.S.A. **51** 42N 84W
Adriatic Sea **71** 43N 15E
Aduwa: Ethiopia **101** 14N 39E
Aegean Sea: **71** 38N 26E
AFGHANISTAN: *cap.* Kabul **83** — —
Afyonkarahisar: Turkey **82** 39N 30E
Agadèz: Niger **100** 17N 8E
Agadir: Morocco **100** 30N 10W
Agartala: India **84** 24N 91E
Agen: France **69** 44N 1E
Agordat: Ethiopia **101** 15N 37E
Agra: India **84** 27N 78E
Agrigento: Sicily **71** 37N 14E
Agrínion: Greece **71** 39N 21E
Aguascalientes: Mexico **58** 22N 102W
Ahaggar: *mtns.*, Algeria **100** 23N 6E
Ahmadnagar: India **84** 19N 75E
Ahmedabad: India **84** 23N 73E
Ahvāz: Iran **83** 31N 49E
Aïn Sefra: Algeria **100** 33N 1W
Aïn Témouchement: Algeria **69** 35N 1W
Aïr: *mtns.*, Niger **100** 18N 8E
Aire: *r.*, England **67** 54N 1W
Aitape: Papua New Guinea **94** 3S 142E
Aix-en-Provence: Fr. **69** 44N 5E
Aizu-Wakamatsu: Japan **90** 34N 135E
Ajaccio: Corsica **69** 42N 9E
Ajmer: India **84** 27N 75E
Ajo: U.S.A. **52** 32N 113E
Akan:Japan **90** 43N 144E
Akaroa: N.Z. **95** 44S 173E
Akashi: Japan **90** 35N 135E
Akhisar: Turkey **71** 39N 28E
Akita: Japan **90** 40N 140E
Akkeshi: Japan **90** 43N 145E
Akko (Acre): Israel **82** 32N 35E
Akola: India **84** 21N 77E
Akritas, C.: Greece **71** 37N 22E
Akron: U.S.A. **51** 41N 82W
Aksha: U.S.S.R. **79** 50N 113E
Aktyubinsk: U.S.S.R. **81** 50N 57E
Akyab: Burma **85** 20N 92E
Alabama: *r.*, U.S.A. **51** 32N 88W
Alabama: *State*, U.S.A. **51** 33N 87W
Alai Range: U.S.S.R. **81** 39N 71E
Ala Kul': *l.*, U.S.S.R. **81** 46N 82E
Alameda: U.S.A. **52** 43N 112W
Alamogordo: U.S.A. **53** 33N 106W
Alamosa: U.S.A. **50** 37N 106W
Åland Is.: Finland **70** 60N 20E
Alapayevsk: U.S.S.R. **81** 58N 62E
Ala Shan: *desert*, China **87** 40N 103E
Alaska: *State*, U.S.A. **105** 65N 150W
Alaverdi: U.S.S.R. **80** 41N 45E
Albacete: Spain **69** 39N 2W
ALBANIA: *cap.* Tiranë **71** 41N 20E
Albany: Australia **94** 35S 118E
Albany: Ga., U.S.A. **51** 32N 84W
Albany: N.Y., U.S.A. **55** 43N 74W
Albany: Oregon, U.S.A. **52** 45N 123W
Albemarle Sound: U.S.A. **51** 36N 76W
Alberche: *r.*, Spain **69** 40N 5W
Albert, Lake: Uganda **102** 2N 31E
Albert Lea: U.S.A. **53** 44N 93W
Albi: France **69** 44N 2E
Ålborg (Aalborg): Denmark **70** 57N 10E
Albuquerque: U.S.A. **52** 35N 107W
Albury: Australia **94** 36S 147E
Alcalá: Spain **69** 40N 3W
Alcázar de San Juan: Spain **69** 39N 3W
Alcira: Spain **69** 39N 0
Alcoy: Spain **69** 39N 0
Aldan: U.S.S.R. **79** 58N 125E
Alderney: *i.*, Channel Is. **68** 50N 2W
Aldershot: England **67** 51N 1W
Alegranza: *i.*, Canary Islands **100** 29N 13W
Alegrete: Brazil **61** 30S 56W
Aleksandrov Gay: U.S.S.R. **80** 50N 49E
Aleksandrovsk-Sakhalinskiy: U.S.S.R. **79** 51N 142E
Alençon: France **68** 48N 0
Aleppo: Syria **82** 36N 37E
Alès: France **69** 44N 4E
Alessandria: Italy **69** 45N 9E
Ålesund: Norway **70** 62N 6E
Aleutian Abyssal Plain: Pacific Ocean **104** 43N 165W
Aleutian Is.: Bering Sea **104** 50N 170W
Aleutian Trench: Pacific Ocean **104** 45N 165W
Alexander Arch.: U.S.A. **22** 57N 137W
Alexander City: U.S.A. **51** 33N 86W
Alexander Island: Antarctica **128** 70S 70W
Alexandra: N.Z. **95** 45S 169E
Alexandria: Egypt **82** 31N 30E
Alexandria: U.S.A. **50** 31N 93W
Alexandria City: U.S.A. **57** 39N 77W
Algarve: *Prov.*, Port. **69** 37N 8W
Algeciras: Spain **69** 36N 5W
Alghero: Sardinia **69** 41N 8E
ALGIERS: Algeria **69** 37N 3E
ALGERIA: *cap.* Algiers **100** — —
Al Hoceima: Morocco **69** 35N 4W
Alicante: Spain **69** 38N 0
Alice: U.S.A. **50** 28N 98W
Alice Springs: Australia **94** 24S 134E
Aligarh: India **84** 28N 78E
Aling Kangri: *mtn.*, China **86** 33N 81E
Alingsås: Sweden **70** 58N 12E
Alkmaar: Neth. **68** 53N 5E
Al Kut: Iraq **83** 33N 46E
Allahabad: India **84** 25N 82E
Allegheny: *r.*, U.S.A. **51** 42N 80W
Allegheny Mts.: U.S.A. **51** 40N 79W
Allentown: U.S.A. **54** 41N 76W
Alleppey: India **84** 9N 76E
Alliance: U.S.A. **53** 42N 103W
Allier: *r.*, France **69** 47N 3E
Alma-Ata: U.S.S.R. **81** 43N 77E
Almada: Portugal **69** 39N 9W
Almadén: Spain **69** 39N 5W
Almeria: Spain **69** 37N 2W
Alnwick: England **67** 55N 2W
Alor Setar: Malaysia **85** 6N 100E
Alps, The: *mtns.*, Europe **71** 46N 7E
Altai Range: Mong. **86** 46N 93E
Altamaha: *r.*, U.S.A. **51** 32N 82W
Altamura: Italy **71** 41N 17E
Altoona: U.S.A. **54** 40N 78W
Altun Shan: *mtns.*, China **86** 37N 85E
Alturas: U.S.A. **52** 41N 121W
Altus: U.S.A. **50** 35N 99W
Alva: U.S.A. **50** 37N 99W
Alwar: India **84** 27N 77E
Amara: Iraq **83** 32N 47E
Amarillo: U.S.A. **53** 35N 102W
Amazon: *r.*, Brazil **60** 3S 60W
Ambala: India **84** 31N 77E
Ambarchik: U.S.S.R. **79** 70N 162E
Amboina: Indonesia **91** 4S 128E
Ambon: *i.*, Indon. **91** 4S 128E
Americus: U.S.A. **51** 32N 84W
Ames: U.S.A. **53** 42N 94W
Amiens: France **68** 50N 2E
'AMMAN: Jordan **82** 32N 36E
Amoy: *see* Xiamen
Amravati: India **84** 21N 78E
Amritsar: India **84** 32N 75E
AMSTERDAM: Netherlands **68** 52N 5E
Amsterdam: U.S.A. **55** 43N 74W
Amu Dar'ya (Oxus): *r.*, U.S.S.R. **81** 38N 64E
Amur: *r.*, U.S.S.R./China **79** 52N 138E
Anabar: *r.*, U.S.S.R. **79** 72N 112E
Anaconda: U.S.A. **52** 46N 113W
Anacortes: U.S.A. **52** 48N 122W
Anadyr': *& gulf*, U.S.S.R. **79** 65N 178W
Anai Mudi *mtn.*, India **84** 10N 77E
Anaiza: *see* Unayzah
Anambas Is.: Indon. **85** 3N 106E
Anan: Japan **90** 34N 135E
Anan' yev: U.S.S.R. **80** 48N 30E
Anchorage: U.S.A. **105** 61N 150W
Ancona: Italy **71** 44N 14E
Andalsnes: Norway **70** 62N 8E
Andalusia: U.S.A. **51** 31N 86W
Andaman Is.: Indian Ocean **85** 12N 93E
Andaman Sea: S.E. Asia **85** 12N 95E
Anderson: Indiana, U.S.A. **51** 40N 86W
Anderson: S.C., U.S.A. **51** 34N 83W
Andes: *range*, S. Am. **60** — —
Andhra Pradesh: *State*, India **84** 17N 79E
Andizhan: U.S.S.R. **81** 41N 73E
ANDORRA: *cap.*, Andorra **69** 43N 2E
Andover: U.S.A. **55** 43N 71W
Andreyevka: U.S.S.R. **81** 46N 81E
Andropov-Rybinsk (*formerly* Rybinsk) **80** 58N 38E
Andros: *i.*, The Bahamas **59** 24N 78W
Andros: *i.*, Greece **71** 38N 25E
Andújar: Spain **69** 38N 4W
Anegada: *i.*, W. Indies **59** 19N 64W
Angara: *r.*, U.S.S.R. **79** 58N 97E
Angel de la Guardia: *i.*, Mexico **58** 30N 113W
Angers: France **68** 47N 1W
Angical: Brazil **60** 12S 45W
Angkor: *ruins*, Kampuchea **91** 13N 104E
Anglesey: *i.*, Wales **67** 53N 4W
ANGOLA: *cap.* Luanda **102** — —
Angola Basin: Atl. O. **103** 15S 14E
Angoulême: France **69** 46N 0
Angren: U.S.S.R. **81** 41N 70E
Anguilla: *i.*, W. Indies **59** 18N 63W
Anhui (Anhwei): *Prov.*, China **88** 32N 117E
Aniva Bay: U.S.S.R. **79** 46N 143E
Anjiang: China **89** 27N 110E
Ankang: China **88** 33N 109E
ANKARA: Turkey **82** 40N 33E
Ankarata Mts.: Madagascar **102** 20S 47E
Annaba: Algeria **69** 37N 8E
Annam Highlands: *range*, S.E. Asia **85** 18N 105E
Annandale: U.S.A. **57** 39N 77W
Annapolis: U.S.A. **54** 39N 76W
Ann Arbor: U.S.A. **51** 42N 84W
Annecy: France **69** 46N 6E
Anniston: U.S.A. **51** 34N 86W
Anqing: China **89** 31N 117E
Ansbach: W. Germany **70** 49N 11E
Anshan: China **88** 41N 123E
Anshun: China **85** 26N 106E
Antakya (Antioch): Turkey **82** 37N 36E
Antalya: *& Gulf.*, Tur. **82** 37N 31E
ANTANANARIVO (TANANARIVE): Madagascar **102** 18S 47E
Antarctic, The **128** — —
Antequera: Spain **69** 37N 4W
Anthony: U.S.A. **50** 37N 98W
Antibes: France **69** 44N 7E
Antifer, Cap d': Fr. **67** 50N 0
Antigua: Guatemala **58** 15N 91W
ANTIGUA AND BARBUDA: *cap.* St. John's **59** 17N 62W
Antipodes Is.: Pacific Ocean **104** 50S 179E
Antofagasta: Chile **60** 23S 70W
Antsirañana (Diego Suarez): Madagascar **102** 12S 49E
Antung: *see* Dandong
Antwerp (Anvers): Belgium **68** 51N 4E
Anuradhapura: Sri Lanka **84** 8N 80E
Anyang: China **88** 36N 114E
Anzhero-Sudzhensk: U.S.S.R. **81** 56N 86E
Aomori: Japan **90** 41N 141E
Aosta: Italy **69** 46N 7E
Apalachicola: *r.*, U.S.A. **51** 30N 85W
Aparri: Philippines **91** 18N 122E
Apennines: *mtns.*, Italy **71** 43N 12E
Appalachian Mts.: U.S.A. **51** 37N 80W
Appleby: England **67** 55N 3W
Appleton: U.S.A. **53** 44N 88W
Aqaba: Jordan **82** 29N 35E
Arabian Sea: **83** 15N 55E
Aracajú: Brazil **60** 11S 37W
Arad: Romania **71** 46N 21E
Arafura Sea: Indonesia **94** 10S 135E
Araguaia: *r.*, Brazil **60** 12S 51W
Arak: Iran **82** 34N 50E
Arakan Yoma: *mtns.*, Burma **85** 19N 94E
Araks (Araxes): *r.*, U.S.S.R./Iran **80** 39N 47E
Aral Sea: U.S.S.R. **81** 45N 60E
Aral'sk: U.S.S.R. **81** 47N 62E
Aran Is.: R. of Ireland **67** 53N 10W
Ararat, Mt.: Turkey **83** 40N 44E
Arauca: Colombia **59** 7N 71W
Arbroath: Scotland **67** 57N 3W
Arcachon: France **69** 45N 1W
Arcata: U.S.A. **50** 41N 124W
Arctic Ocean: **1** — —
Ardabil: Iran **83** 38N 48E
Ardennes: *mtns.*, Belgium **68** 50N 5E
Ardmore: U.S.A. **50** 34N 97W
Ardrossan: Scotland **67** 56N 5W
Arendal: Norway **70** 58N 9E
Arequipa: Peru **60** 16S 72W
Arezzo: Italy **71** 43N 12E
Argentan: France **68** 49N 0
Argenteuil: France **72** 49N 2E
ARGENTINA: *cap.* Buenos Aires **60** — —
Argentine Basin: Atl. O. **103** 45S 45W
Århus (Aarhus): Denmark **70** 56N 10E
Arica: Chile **60** 18S 70W
Arizona: *State*, U.S.A. **52** 34N 112W
Arkansas: *r. & State*, U.S.A. **50** 36N 93W
Arkansas City: U.S.A. **50** 37N 97W
Arkhangel'sk: U.S.S.R. **78** 64N 40E
Arles: France **69** 44N 5E
Arlington Heights: U.S.A. **57** 42N 88W
Armagh: N. Ireland **67** 54N 7W
Armavir: U.S.S.R. **80** 45N 41E
Armenian S.S.R.: U.S.S.R. **80** 40N 45E
Arnhem: Neth. **68** 52N 6E
Arnhem Land: Australia **94** 14S 133E
Arno: *r.*, Italy **71** 44N 11E
Arran: *i.*, Scotland **67** 56N 5W
Arras: France **68** 50N 3E
Arrowrock Res.: U.S.A. **52** 44N 116W
Arrowsmith, Mt.: New Zealand **95** 43S 171E
Arta: Greece **71** 39N 21E
Artemovskiy: U.S.S.R. **81** 57N 62E
Artesia: U.S.A. **53** 33N 104W
Arthur's Pass: N.Z. **95** 43S 172E
Arua: Uganda **102** 7S 31E
Aruba: *i.*, Carib. Sea **59** 13N 70W
Aru Is.: Indonesia **91** 6S 134E
Arun: *r.*, England **67** 51N 1W
Arunachal Pradesh: *State*, India **85** 28N 95E
Arvika: Sweden **70** 60N 13E
Arys': U.S.S.R. **81** 42N 69E
Arzamas: U.S.S.R. **80** 56N 44E
Asahigawa: Japan **90** 44N 142E
Asansol: India **84** 24N 87E
Ascension I.: Atlantic Ocean **103** 8S 15W
Ascoli Piceno: Italy **71** 43N 14E
Asenovgrad: Bulg. **71** 42N 25E
Ashburton: N.Z. **95** 44S 172E
Ashburton: *r.*, Austl. **94** 23S 116E
Asheville: U.S.A. **51** 35N 83W
Ashford: England **67** 51N 1E
Ashikaga: Japan **90** 36N 139E
Ashkelon: Israel **82** 32N 34E
Ashkhabad: U.S.S.R. **81** 38N 58E
Ashland: Ky., U.S.A. **51** 38N 83W
Ashland: Oregon, U.S.A. **52** 42N 123W
Ashland: Wisconsin, U.S.A. **53** 47N 91W
Ashtabula: U.S.A. **51** 42N 81W
Ashton: U.S.A. **52** 44N 111W
Asino: U.S.S.R. **81** 57N 86E
Asir: *reg.*, Saudi Arabia **83** 20N 42E
Asmara: Ethiopia **101** 15N 39E
Aspiring, Mt.: N.Z. **95** 44S 169E
Assab: Ethiopia **101** 13N 42E
Assam: *State*, India **84** 27N 93E
Assisi: Italy **71** 43N 13E
Astara: U.S.S.R. **80** 39N 49E
Asti: Italy **69** 45N 8E
Astipálaia: *i.*, Greece **71** 37N 26E
Astoria: U.S.A. **52** 46N 124W
Astrakhan': U.S.S.R. **80** 46N 48E
ASUNCIÓN: Paraguay **61** 25S 58W
Aswân: *& dam.* Egypt **101** 24N 33E
Asyut: Egypt **101** 27N 31E
Atacama Desert: Chile **60** 22S 69W
Atasuskiy: U.S.S.R. **81** 49N 72E
Atbara: *& r.*, Sudan **101** 18N 34E
Atbasar: U.S.S.R. **81** 52N 68E
Atchafalaya: *r.*, U.S.A. **50** 31N 92W
Atchison: U.S.A. **53** 40N 95W
ATHENS: Greece **71** 38N 24E
Athens: Ga., U.S.A. **51** 34N 83W
Athens: Tenn., U.S.A. **51** 35N 85W
Athlone: R. of Irel. **67** 53N 8W
Athos: *mtn.*, Greece **71** 40N 24E
Atlanta: U.S.A. **51** 34N 84W
Atlantic City: U.S.A. **54** 39N 75W
Atlantic Ocean **103** — —
Atoka: U.S.A. **50** 34N 96W
Attopeu: Laos **85** 15N 107E
Atrak: *r.*, Iran **83** 38N 57E
At Ta'if: Saudi Arabia **82** 21N 40E
Aube: *r.*, France **68** 48N 4E
Auburn: Ala., U.S.A. **51** 33N 85W
Auburn: Maine, U.S.A. **51** 44N 70W
Auburn: N.Y., U.S.A. **54** 43N 77W
Auckland: N.Z. **95** 37S 175E
Auckland Is.: Pacific Ocean **104** 50S 166E
Augsberg: W. Germany **70** 48N 11E
Augusta: Sicily **71** 37N 15E
Augusta: Ga., U.S.A. **51** 33N 82W
Augusta: Maine, U.S.A. **51** 44N 70W
Aurangabad: India **84** 20N 75E
Aurillac: France **69** 45N 2E
Austin: Minnesota, U.S.A. **53** 44N 93W
Austin: Nev., U.S.A. **52** 40N 117W
Austin: Texas, U.S.A. **50** 30N 98W
AUSTRALIA: *cap.* Canberra **94** — —
Australian Alps: Australia **94** 37S 148E
Australian Capital Territory: Austl. **94** 35S 149E
AUSTRIA: *cap.* Vienna **71** 47N 15E
Auxerre: France **68** 48N 4E
Aveiro: Portugal **69** 41N 9W
Avellaneda: Arg. **61** 35S 58W
Aveyron: *r.*, France **69** 44N 2E
Avignon: France **69** 44N 5E
Avila: Spain **69** 41N 5W
Avilés: Spain **69** 44N 6W
Avon: *r.*, War., Eng. **67** 52N 2W
Avon: *r.*, Wilts., Eng. **67** 51N 2W
Avezzano: Italy **71** 42N 13E
Awash: Ethiopia **101** 9N 40E
Ayabe: Japan **90** 35N 135E
Ayaguz: U.S.S.R. **81** 48N 80E
Aydin: Turkey **71** 38N 28E
Ayers Rock: *mtn.*, Australia **94** 25S 131E
Aylesbury: England **67** 51N 0
Ayon I.: U.S.S.R. **79** 70N 168E
Ayr: Scotland **67** 55N 5W
Ayutthaya: Thailand **85** 14N 101E
Azerbaydzhan S.S.R.: U.S.S.R. **80** 41N 47E
Azores: *is.*, Atlantic Ocean **103** 39N 29W
Azov, Sea of: U.S.S.R. **80** 46N 37E

B

Babar Is.: Indonesia **91** 8S 130E
Bab el Mandeb: *str.*, Ethiopia/Arabia **101** 13N 43E
Babushkin: U.S.S.R. **72** 55N 38E
Babylon: *hist.*, Iraq **83** 33N 44E
Bacău: Romania **71** 47N 27E
Bacolod: Philippines **91** 11N 123E
Badajoz: Spain **69** 39N 7W
Badulla: Sri Lanka **84** 7N 81E
Bagdarin: U.S.S.R. **87** 55N 114E
Bagé: Brazil **61** 31S 54W
BAGHDÀD: Iraq **83** 33N 44E
Bagheria: Sicily **71** 38N 14E
Baghlan: Afghanistan **83** 36N 69E
Baguio: Philippines **91** 16N 121E
BAHAMAS, THE: *cap.* Nassau **59** 25N 75W
Bahawalpur: Pak. **84** 29N 72E
Bahia: *see* Salvador
Bahia Blanca: Arg. **60** 39S 62W
Bahraich: India **84** 28N 82E
BAHRAIN: *cap.* Manama **83** 26N 51E
Bahr el Ghazal: *r.*, Chad **100** 14N 17E
Bahr el Ghazal: *Prov.*, Sudan **101** 10N 27E
Bahr el Jebel: *see* White Nile

Baia-Mare: Rom. **71** 48N 24E
Baihe: China **88** 33N 110E
Bainbridge: U.S.A. **51** 31N 85W
Baja: Hungary **71** 46N 19E
Baker: Mont., U.S.A. **53** 46N 104W
Baker: Oreg., U.S.A. **52** 45N 118W
Bakersfield: U.S.A. **52** 35N 119W
Baku: U.S.S.R. **80** 40N 50E
Balaghat: India **84** 22N 80E
Bala Lake: Wales **67** 53N 4W
Balashikha: U.S.S.R. **72** 55N 38E
Balashov: U.S.S.R **80** 51N 43E
Balasore: India **84** 21N 87E
Balatón L.: Hungary **71** 47N 18E
Balboa: Panama **59** 9N 80W
Balclutha: N.Z. **95** 46S 170E
[illegible]
Balearic. Is.: Spain **69** 39N 3E
Bali: *i.*, Indonesia **91** 8S 115E
Balikesir: Turkey **71** 40N 28E
Balikpapan: Indon. **91** 1S 117E
Balkan Mts.: Bulgaria **71** 43N 25E
Balkhash: *& l.*, U.S.S.R. **81** 46N 75E
Ballarat: Australia **94** 38S 144E
Ballina: R. of Ireland **67** 54N 9W
Ballymena: N. Ireland **67** 55N 6W
Balovale: Zambia **102** 14S 23E
Balsas: *& r.*, Mexico **58** 18N 100W
Balta: U.S.S.R. **70** 48N 30E
Baltic Sea **70** — —
Baltimore: U.S.A. **54** 39N 77W
Baluchistan: *reg.*, Pakistan **84** 27N 65E
BAMAKO: Mali **100** 13N 8W
Bamba: Mali **100** 17N 2W
Bamberg: W. Germany **70** 50N 11E
Banda Aceh: Indon. **85** 5N 95E
Bandar Abbās: Iran **83** 27N 56E
Bandar-e Khomeyni (*formerly* Bandar-e Shāpūr): Iran **83** 30N 49E
Bandar-e Torkman: (*formerly* Bandar-e Shāh): Iran **83** 37N 54E
BANDAR SERI BEGAWAN: Brunei **91** 5N 115E
Banda Sea: Indon. **91** 6S 127E
Banderas Bay: Mexico **58** 21N 106W
Bandırma: Turkey **71** 40N 28E
Ban Me Thuot: Vietnam **85** 12N 108E
Bandjarmasin: Indon. **91** 3S 115E
Bandra: India **84** 19N 73E
Bandung: Indonesia **91** 7S 107E
Banff: Scotland **67** 58N 3W
Bangalore: India **84** 13N 78E
Bangbu: China **88** 33N 117E
Bangka: *i.*, Indonesia **91** 2S 106E
BANGKOK (KRUNG THEP): Thailand **85** 14N 100E
BANGLADESH: *cap.*, Dhaka **84** — —
Bangor: N. Ireland **67** 55N 6W
Bangor: U.S.A. **51** 45N 69W
BANGUI: Central African Republic **101** 4N 18E
Bangweulu, L.: Zambia **102** 11S 31E
Ban Houei Sai: Laos **85** 20N 100E
Baniâs: Syria **82** 35N 36E
Banja Luka: Yugo. **71** 45N 17E
BANJUL: The Gambia **100** 13N 17W
Banks Penin.: N.Z. **95** 44S 173E
Bann: *r.*, N. Ireland **67** 55N 7W
Bannu: Pakistan **84** 33N 71E
Banská Bystrica: Czech. **70** 49N 19E
Bantry: *& bay*, R. of Ireland **67** 52N 9W
Baoan: China **89** 23N 114E
Baoding: China **88** 39N 115E
Baoji: China **88** 34N 107E
Baoshan: China **85** 25N 99E
Baotou: China **88** 41N 110E
Baoying: China **88** 33N 119E
Baranof I.: U.S.A. **22** 57N 135W
Baranovichi: U.S.S.R. **70** 53N 26E
Barataria Bay: U.S.A. **51** 29N 90W
BARBADOS: *cap.* Bridgetown **59** 13N 60W
Barbuda: *i.*, Antigua and Barbuda **59** 18N 62W
Barcaldine: Austl. **94** 24S 145E
Barce: Libya **82** 33N 21E
Barcellona: Sicily **71** 38N 15E
Barcelona: Spain **69** 41N 2E
Barcelona: Venezuela **59** 10N 65W
Barcoo: *r.*, Australia **94** 24S 144E
Bardawil, Lake: Egypt **82** 31N 33E
Bardia: Libya **82** 32N 25E
Bareilly: India **84** 28N 80E
Barents Sea: U.S.S.R. **78** 73N 40E
Bari: Italy **71** 41N 17E
Barkly Tableland: Australia **94** 18S 136E
Barletta: Italy **71** 41N 16E
Barnaul: U.S.S.R. **81** 53N 84E
Barnstaple: England **67** 51N 4W
Baro: Nigeria **100** 9N 6E
Baroda: *see* Vododara
Barquisimeto: Venez. **59** 10N 69W
Barra: *i. & Hd.*, Scot. **67** 57N 7W
Barrackpore: India **84** 23N 88E
Barra do Piraí: Brazil **61** 22S 44W
Barra Mansa: Brazil **61** 22S 44W
Barranquilla: Colombia **59** 11N 75W
Barreiro: Portugal **69** 39N 9W
Barrow-in-Furness: England **67** 54N 3W
Barrow: U.S.A. **1** 71N 157W
Barry: Wales **67** 51N 3W
Barstow: U.S.A. **52** 35N 117W
Bartlesville: U.S.A. **52** 37N 96W
Basel (Bâle): Switzerland **68** 48N 7E
Básilán: *i.*, Phil. **91** 7N 122E
Baskunchak: U.S.S.R. **80** 48N 47E
Basra: Iraq **83** 30N 48E
Bassein: Burma **85** 17N 95E
BASSE-TERRE: Guadeloupe **59** 16N 62W
Bass Strait: Australia **94** 40S 146E
Bastia: Corsica **69** 43N 9E
Bastrop: U.S.A. **50** 33N 92W
Bataan Penin.: Phil. **91** 15N 120E
Batang: China **86** 30N 99E
Batangas: Phil. **91** 14N 121E
Batesville: Arkansas, U.S.A. **50** 36N 92W
Batesville: Miss., U.S.A. **51** 34N 90W
Bath: England **67** 51N 2W
Bathurst I.: Australia **94** 12S 130E
Baton Rouge: U.S.A. **50** 31N 91W
Battambang: Kampuchea **85** 13N 103E
Batticaloa: Sri Lanka **84** 8N 82E
Battle Creek: *city*, U.S.A. **51** 42N 85W
Battle Mountain: *city*, U.S.A. **52** 41N 117W
Batu Is.: Indonesia **91** 0 99E
Batu Pahat: Malaysia **85** 2N 103E
Batumi: U.S.S.R. **80** 42N 42E
Bautzen: E. Germany **70** 51N 14E
Bawdwin: Burma **85** 23N 97E
Bayamo: Cuba **59** 20N 77W
Bayanharshan: *mtns.*, China **86** 34N 99E
Bayan Obo: China **88** 42N 110E
Bay City: Mich., U.S.A. **24** 44N 84W
Bay City: Texas, U.S.A. **50** 29N 96W
Baykal, L.: U.S.S.R. **79** 53N 107E
[illegible]
Baymak: U.S.S.R. **81** 53N 58E
Bayonne: France **69** 43N 1W
Bayonne: U.S.A. **56** 41N 74W
Bayreuth: W. Germany **70** 50N 12E
Baytown: U.S.A. **50** 29N 95W
Baza: Spain **69** 37N 3W
Beachy Head: Eng. **67** 51N 0
Beardmore Glacier: Antarctica **128** 84S 170E
Bear I.: U.S.S.R. **78** 74N 20E
Beas: *r.*, India **84** 32N 76E
Beatrice: U.S.A. **53** 40N 97W
Beaufort: U.S.A. **51** 32N 81W
Beaufort Sea **1** 73N 140W
Beaufort West: S. Africa **102** 32S 23E
Beaumont: U.S.A. **50** 30N 94W
Beauvais: France **68** 49N 2E
Beaver Dam: *city*, U.S.A. **53** 43N 89W
Beaver I.: U.S.A. **24** 45N 85W
Béchar: Algeria **100** 32N 2W
Beckley: U.S.A. **51** 38N 81W
Bedford: England **67** 52N 0
Bedford: Ind., U.S.A. **51** 39N 86W
Bedford: Pa., U.S.A. **54** 40N 79W
Beersheba: Israel **82** 31N 35E
Beeville: U.S.A. **50** 28N 98W
Begovat: U.S.S.R. **81** 40N 69E
Bei: *r.*, China **89** 24N 113E
Beian: China **87** 48N 127E
Bei bu Wan (Gulf of Tonkin): S.E. Asia **85** 21N 108E
BEIJING (PEKING): China **88** 40N 116E
Beipiao: China **88** 42N 121E
Beira: *see* Sofala
BEIRUT: Lebanon **82** 34N 34E
Beit Bridge: Zimbabwe **102** 22S 30E
Beizhen: China **88** 42N 122E
Beja: Portugal **69** 38N 8W
Bejaia: Algeria **69** 36N 5E
Békéscsaba: Hungary **71** 47N 21E
Bela: Pakistan **84** 26N 66E
Belaya: *r.*, U.S.S.R. **80** 54N 56E
Belaya Tserkov: U.S.S.R. **70** 50N 30E
Belém: Brazil **60** 1S 48W
Belen: U.S.A. **52** 35N 107W
BELFAST: N. Ireland **67** 55N 6W
Belfast L.: N. Ireland **67** 55N 6W
Belfort: France **68** 48N 7E
Belgaum: India **84** 16N 75E
BELGIUM: *cap.* Brussels **68** 51N 4E
Belgorod: U.S.S.R. **80** 51N 36E
BELGRADE: Yugoslavia **71** 45N 20E
Belitung: *i.*, Indon. **91** 3S 108E
BELIZE: *cap.* Belmopan **58** 17N 88W
Belize: Belize **58** 17N 88W
Bellary: India **84** 15N 77E
Belle Fourche: *& r.*, U.S.A. **53** 45N 104W
Belle Glade: U.S.A. **51** 27N 81W
Belle-Île-en-Mer: Fr. **68** 47N 3W
Belleville: Kansas, U.S.A. **53** 40N 98W
Bellingham: U.S.A. **52** 49N 122W
Bellingshausen Sea: Antarctica **128** 71S 85W
Belluno: Italy **71** 46N 12E
Bellwood: U.S.A. **57** 42N 88W
BELMOPAN: Belize **58** 17N 88W
Belo Horizonte: Brazil **60** 20S 44W
Beloit: Kans., U.S.A. **53** 39N 98W
Beloit: Wisc., U.S.A. **53** 43N 89W
Belousovka: U.S.S.R. **81** 50N 83E
Bel'tsy: U.S.S.R. **70** 47N 28E
Beltsville: U.S.A. **57** 39N 77W
Belyy I.: U.S.S.R. **79** 73N 70E
Bemidji: U.S.A. **53** 47N 95W
Bend: U.S.A. **52** 44N 121W
Bendery: U.S.S.R. **71** 47N 30E
Bendigo: Australia **94** 37S 144E
Bengal, Bay of: Bangl./India **84** 17N 87E
Benghazi: Libya **101** 32N 20E
Benguela: Angola **102** 13S 13E
Ben Hope: *mtn.*, Scotland **67** 58N 5W
BENIN: *cap.* Cotonou **100** 10N 3E
Benin, Bight of: Africa **100** 4N 3E
Beni Saf: Algeria **69** 35N 1W
Ben Macdhui: *mtn.*, Scotland **67** 57N 4W
Ben Nevis: *mtn.*, Scot. **67** 57N 5W
Bennington: U.S.A. **51** 43N 74W
Bensenville: U.S.A. **57** 42N 88W
Benton: U.S.A. **50** 35N 93W
Benton Harbor: U.S.A. **51** 43N 86W
Benue: *r.*, Africa **100** 9N 12E
Beppu: Japan **90** 33N 132E
Berber: Sudan **101** 18N 34E
Berbera: Somali Republic **101** 10N 45E
Berdichev: U.S.S.R. **70** 50N 29E
Beregovo: U.S.S.R. **70** 48N 23E
Berezovo: U.S.S.R. **81** 64N 65E
Bergama: Turkey **71** 39N 27E
Bergamo: Italy **71** 46N 10E
Bergen: Norway **70** 60N 5E
Berhampore: India **84** 24N 88E
Bering Sea **104** 61N 170W
Bering Strait: U.S.S.R./U.S.A. **79** 65N 170W
Berkeley: Calif. U.S.A. **52** 38N 122W
Berkeley: Ill., U.S.A. **57** 42N 88W
BERLIN: **E. & W. Ger.** (*cap of* E. Germany) **70** 52N 13E
Berlin: U.S.A. **51** 45N 71W
Bermejo: *r.*, Arg. **61** 26S 60W
Bermuda: *i.*, Atlantic Ocean **59** 32N 65W
BERN: Switzerland **69** 47N 7E
Berry Is.: The Bahamas **51** 26N 78W
Berwick upon Tweed: England **67** 56N 2W
Berwyn: U.S.A. **57** 41N 88W
Besançon: France **68** 47N 6E
Bessemer: U.S.A. **51** 33N 87W
Bethesda: U.S.A. **57** 39N 77W
Bethlehem: U.S.A. **54** 41N 75W
Béticas, Cordilleras: *mtns.*, Spain **69** 38N 2W
Betwa: *r.*, India **84** 26N 80E
Beverley: England **67** 54N 0
Beverly: U.S.A. **55** 42N 71W
Bezhitsa: U.S.S.R. **80** 53N 34E
Béziers: France **69** 43N 3E
Bhagalpur: India **84** 25N 88E
Bhamo: Burma **85** 24N 97E
[illegible]
Bhima: *r.*, India **84** 17N 76E
Bhopal: India **84** 23N 77E
Bhubaneswar: India **84** 20N 86E
Bhuj: India **84** 23N 70E
BHUTAN: *cap.* Timphu (Thimphu) **84** 27N 90E
Biak: *i.*, Indon. **91** 1S 136E
Białystok: Poland **70** 53N 23E
Biarritz: France **69** 43N 1W
Biddeford: U.S.A. **51** 43N 70W
Biel: Switzerland **68** 47N 7E
Biella: Italy **69** 46N 8E
Bielsko Biała: Poland **70** 50N 19E
Big Black: *r.*, U.S.A. **50** 33N 90W
Big Blue: *r.*, U.S.A. **50** 41N 97W
Big Falls: *city.*, U.S.A. **53** 48N 94W
Bighorn Mts.: *r.*, U.S.A. **52** 45N 108W
Big Spring: U.S.A. **53** 32N 102W
Big Wood: *r.*, U.S.A. **52** 43N 115W
Bihać: Yugoslavia **71** 45N 16E
Bihar: *State*, India **84** 25N 85E
Bijapur: India **84** 17N 76E
Bikaner: India **84** 28N 73E
Bilaspur: India **84** 22N 82E
Bilbao: Spain **69** 43N 3W
Billings: U.S.A. **52** 46N 109W
Bilo Gora: *dist.*, Yugo. **71** 46N 17E
Biloxi: U.S.A. **51** 30N 89W
Bimini Is.: The Bahamas **51** 26N 79W
Binghamton: U.S.A. **54** 42N 76W
Binhai (Dongkan): China **88** 34N 120E
Binjai: Indonesia **85** 3N 98E
Binyang: China **89** 23N 109E
Bioko: *i.*, Eq. Guinea **100** 4N 9E
Birdum: Australia **94** 16S 133E
Birganj: Nepal **84** 27N 85E
Birjand: Iran **83** 33N 59E
Birkenhead: England **67** 53N 3W
Birlad: Romania **71** 46N 28E
Birmingham: England **67** 52N 2W
Birmingham: Ala., U.S.A. **51** 33N 87W
Birobidzhan: U.S.S.R. **79** 49N 133E
Birr: R. of Irel. **67** 53N 8W
Bisbee: U.S.A. **52** 31N 110W
Biscay, Bay of: Atl. Ocean **69** 45N 5W
Biskra: Algeria **100** 35N 6E
Bismarck: U.S.A. **53** 47N 101W
Bismarck Arch.: Papua New Guinea **94** 5S 150E
BISSAU: Guinea-Bissau **100** 12N 16W
Bistrita: *r.*, Romania **71** 47N 26E
Bitolă: Yugoslavia **71** 41N 21E
Bitterroot Range: U.S.A. **52** 46N 115W
Biwa-ko: *l.*, Japan **90** 35N 136E
Biysk: U.S.S.R. **81** 53N 85E
Black: *r.*, Ark., U.S.A. **50** 36N 91W
Black: *r.*, N.Y., U.S.A. **51** 43N 75W
Black: *r.*, Wisc., U.S.A. **53** 44N 91W
Blackburn: England **67** 54N 2W
Blackfoot: U.S.A. **52** 43N 112W
Black Irtysh: *r.*, U.S.S.R./China **81** 48N 85E
Blackpool: England **67** 54N 3W
Black Sea: U.S.S.R. **80** 43N 35E
Black Volta: *r.*, West Africa **100** 10N 2W
Blackwater: *r.*, R. of Ireland **67** 52N 8W
Blagoveshchensk: U.S.S.R. **79** 50N 127E
Blanc, C.: W. Sahara **100** 20N 17W
Blanc, Mt.: Fr./Italy **69** 46N 7E
Blantyre: Malawi **102** 16S 35E
Blenheim: N.Z. **95** 42S 174E
Blida: Algeria **69** 36N 3E
Blitta: Togo **100** 8N 1E
Bloemfontein: S. Africa **102** 29S 26E
Blois: France **68** 48N 1E
Bloody Foreland: R. of Ireland **67** 55N 8W
Bloomington: Ill., U.S.A. **51** 40N 89W
Bloomington: Ind., U.S.A. **51** 39N 86W
Bluefield: U.S.A. **51** 37N 81W
Blue Island: *town*, U.S.A. **57** 42N 88W
Blue Mts.: U.S.A. **52** 45N 120W
Blue Nile: *r.*, Africa **101** 10N 37E
Blue Ridge: *mtns.*, U.S.A. **51** 36N 81W
Bluff: N.Z. **95** 46S 168E
Blumenau: Brazil **61** 27S 49W
Blythe: U.S.A. **52** 34N 115W
Blytheville: U.S.A. **51** 36N 90W
Bo: Sierra Leone **100** 8N 12W
Boai: China **88** 35N 113E
Boa Vista: Brazil **60** 3N 61W
Bobo Dioulasso: Burkina **100** 12N 4W
Bobruysk: U.S.S.R. **70** 53N 29E
Bocholt: W. Germany **68** 52N 7E
Bochum: W. Germany **68** 51N 7E
Bodelé Depression: Chad **100/101** 17N 17E
Bodensee (L. Constance): *l.*, Switz./W. Ger. **68** 48N 9E
Bodmin: England **67** 50N 5W
Bodø: Norway **70** 67N 14E
Bogalusa: U.S.A. **51** 31N 90W
Bogor: Indonesia **91** 7S 107E
BOGOTA: Colombia **60** 5N 74W
Bohai (Gulf of Chihli): China **88** 39N 120E
Bohol: *i.*, Phil. **91** 10N 124E
Boise: U.S.A. **52** 44N 116W
Bojador, C.: W. Sahara **100** 26N 15W
Boké: Guinea **100** 11N 14W
Boknafjorden: Norway **68** 59N 6E
Bolama: Guinea-Bissau **100** 12N 15W
Bolan Pass: Pakistan **84** 30N 68E
Bolesławiec: Poland **70** 51N 16E
Bolivar: U.S.A. **50** 38N 93W
BOLIVIA: *cap.* La Paz (government), Sucre (legal) **60** 17S 65W
Bologna: Italy **71** 44N 11E
Bol'shevik I.: U.S.S.R. **79** 78N 102E
Bolton: England **67** 53N 2W
Bolzano: Italy **71** 47N 11E
Boma: Zaire **102** 6S 13E
Bombay: India **84** 19N 73E
Bonaire: *i.*, Caribbean Sea **59** 12N 98W
Bondo: Zaire **102** 4N 24E
Bone, G. of: Indon. **91** 4S 121E
Bongor: Chad **100** 10N 15E
Bonifacio: Corsica **69** 41N 9E
[illegible]
Bonn: W. Germany **68** 51N 7E
Bonny, Bight of: Gulf of Guinea **100** 3N 8E
Borås: Sweden **70** 58N 13E
Bordeaux: France **69** 45N 1W
Borger: U.S.A. **53** 36N 101W
Borgholm: Sweden **70** 57N 17E
Borislav: U.S.S.R. **70** 49N 23E
Borisoglebsk: U.S.S.R. **80** 51N 42E
Borlänge: Sweden **70** 60N 15E
Borneo: *i.*, S.E. Asia **91** 0 115E
Bornholm: *i.*, Denmark **70** 55N 15E
Bornova: Turkey **71** 38N 27E
Boshan: China **88** 37N 118E
Bosporus: *str.*, Tur. **62** 41N 29E
Bossier City: U.S.A. **50** 33N 94W
Bosso: Niger **100** 14N 13E
Boston: England **67** 53N 0
Boston: U.S.A. **51** 42N 71W
Bothnia, Gulf of: Baltic Sea **70** 63N 20E
Botosani: Romania **70** 47N 26E
BOTSWANA: *cap.* Gaborone **102** 22S 24E
Boltineau: U.S.A. **53** 49N 100W
Bottrop: W. Germany **68** 51N 7E
Bouaké: Côte D'Ivoire **100** 8N 5E
Bougainville: *i.*, Papua New Guinea **94** 6S 155E
Boulder: U.S.A. **53** 40N 105W
Boulder City: U.S.A. **52** 36N 115W
Boulogne: France **68** 51N 2E
Boulogne-Billancourt: France **72** 49N 2E
Bourg: France **69** 46N 5E
Bourges: France **69** 47N 2E
Bourke: Australia **94** 30S 146E
Bournemouth: Eng. **67** 51N 2W
Bou Saâda: Algeria **69** 35N 4E
Bowling Green: U.S.A. **51** 37N 86W
Bowman: U.S.A. **53** 46N 103W
Boxian: China **88** 34N 116E
Boyoma Falls: Zaire **102** 0 25E
Boyne: *r.*, R. of Irel. **67** 54N 6W
Bozeman: U.S.A. **52** 46N 111W
Bozhen: China **88** 38N 117E
Brač: *i.*, Yugoslavia **71** 43N 16E
Bradenton: U.S.A. **51** 28N 83W
Bradford: England **67** 54N 1W
Braga: Portugal **69** 42N 8W
Bragança: Portugal **69** 42N 7W
Bragança Paulista: Brazil **61** 23S 47W
Brahmani: *r.*, India **84** 22N 85E
Brahmaputra: *r.*, Bangl./India **86** 26N 93E
Braila: Romania **71** 45N 28E
Brainerd: U.S.A. **53** 46N 94W
Branco: *r.*, Brazil **60** 1N 62W
Brandenburg: E. Ger. **70** 52N 13E
BRASÍLIA: Brazil **60** 16S 48W
Braşov: Romania **71** 46N 26E
Brasstown Bald: *mtn.*, U.S.A. **51** 35N 84W
Bratislava: Czech. **70** 48N 17E
Bratsk: U.S.S.R. **79** 56N 102E
Braunschweig: *see* Brunswick, W. Ger.
Brawley: U.S.A. **52** 33N 115W
Bray: R. of Ireland **67** 53N 6W
BRAZIL: *cap.* Brasília **60** — —
Brazil Basin: Atl. O. **103** 10S 25W
Brazilian Highlands: Brazil **60** 15S 50W
Brazos: *r.*, U.S.A. **50** 29N 95W
Brazo Sur del Rio Pilcomay: *r.*, Arg./Paraguay **61** 24S 59W
BRAZZAVILLE: Congo **102** 4S 15E
Breckenridge: U.S.A. **53** 46N 97W
Brecon: Wales **67** 52N 3W
Brecon Beacons: *mtns.*, Wales **67** 52N 3W
Breda: Netherlands **68** 52N 5E
Bredy: U.S.S.R. **81** 52N 60E
Bremen: W. Germany **68** 53N 9E
Bremerhaven: W. Germany **68** 54N 9E
Bremerton: U.S.A. **52** 47N 123W
Brenner Pass: Austria/Italy **71** 47N 12E
Brescia: Italy **71** 46N 10E
Brest: France **68** 48N 4W
Brest: U.S.S.R. **70** 52N 24E
Breton Sound: U.S.A. **51** 30N 90W
Bridgeport: Conn., U.S.A. **55** 41N 73W
Bridgeport: Texas, U.S.A. **50** 33N 99W
BRIDGETOWN: Barbados **59** 13N 60W
Bridlington: England **67** 54N 0
Brigham: U.S.A. **52** 42N 112W
Brighton: England **67** 51N 0
Brindisi: Italy **71** 41N 18E
Brisbane: Australia **94** 27S 153E
Bristol: England **67** 51N 3W
Bristol: U.S.A. **51** 37N 82W
Bristol Channel: Eng./Wales **67** 51N 4W
British Isles: Europe **67** — —
Brive-la-Gaillarde: France **69** 45N 2E
Brno: Czech. **70** 49N 17E
Broadview: U.S.A. **57** 42N 88W
Brockton: U.S.A. **55** 42N 71W
Brockway: U.S.A. **53** 47N 106W
Brod: Yugoslavia **71** 42N 21E
Broken Bow: U.S.A. **53** 41N 100W
Broken Hill: Australia **94** 32S 141E
Bronx, The: U.S.A. **56** 41N 74W
Brookfield: U.S.A. **57** 43N 83W
Brookings: U.S.A. **53** 44N 97W
Brooklyn: U.S.A. **56** 41N 74W
Brooks Range: U.S.A. **1** 68N 150W
Brooksville: U.S.A. **51** 29N 82W
Broome: Australia **94** 18S 122E

Brough Head: Scotland 67 59N 3W
Brownsville: U.S.A. 50 26N 97W
Brownwood: U.S.A. 50 32N 99W
Bruges (Brugge): Belgium 68 51N 3E
BRUNEI: *cap.* Bandar Seri Begawan 91 5N 115E
Brunswick: U.S.A. 51 31N 81W
Brunswick (Braunschweig): W. Ger. 70 52N 10E
BRUSSELS: Belgium 68 51N 4E
Bryan: U.S.A. 50 30N 96W
Bryansk: U.S.S.R. 80 53N 34E
Bucaramanga: Colombia 59 7N 73W
Buchanan: Liberia 100 6N 10E
Buchan Ness: Scotland 67 57N 2W
BUCHAREST: Romania 71 44N 26E
BUDAPEST: Hungary 71 48N 19E
Bude: England 67 51N 5W
Buenaventura: Columbia 60 4N 77W
BUENOS AIRES: Argentina 61 35S 58W
Buffalo: N.Y., U.S.A. 54 43N 79W
Buffalo: Wyo., U.S.A. 52 44N 107W
Bug: *r.*, Pol./U.S.S.R. 70 51N 24E
BUJUMBURA: Burundi 102 3S 30E
Bukachacha: U.S.S.R. 79 53N 117E
Bukama: Zaïre 102 9S 26E
Bukavu: Zaïre 102 2S 29E
Bukhara: U.S.S.R. 81 40N 65E
Bukittinggi: Indon. 85 0 100E
Bukoba: Tanzania 102 1S 32E
Bulagan: Mongolia 87 49N 103E
Bulawayo: Zimbabwe 102 20S 29E
BULGARIA: *cap.* Sofiya (Sofia) 71 42N 25E
Buller: *r.*, N.Z. 104 42S 172W
Bull Shoals Res.: U.S.A. 50 37N 93W
Bumba: Zaïre 102 2N 23E
Bumthang: Bhutan 84 27N 91E
Bunbury: Australia 94 33S 116E
Bundaberg: Austl. 94 25S 152E
Bunguran Is. *see* Natuna Is.
Buraimi: United Arab Emirates 83 24N 56E
Buraydah: Saudi Arabia 83 27N 44E
Burbank: U.S.A. 57 42N 88W
Burdur: Turkey 82 38N 30E
Burdwan: India 84 23N 88E
Bureya: U.S.S.R. 79 50N 130E
Burgas: Bulgaria 71 42N 27E
Burgos: Spain 69 42N 4W
Burhanpur: India 84 21N 76E
BURKINA (*formerly* UPPER VOLTA): *cap.*, Ouagadougou 100 — —
Burley: U.S.A. 52 42N 114W
Burlington: Colo., U.S.A. 53 39N 103W
Burlington: Iowa, U.S.A. 53 41N 91W
Burlington: Mass., U.S.A. 55 42N 71W
Burlington: N.C., U.S.A. 51 36N 80W
Burlington: Vt., U.S.A. 51 44N 73W
BURMA: *cap.*, Rangoon 85 — —
Burnie: Tasmania 94 41S 146E
Burns: U.S.A. 52 44N 119W
Bursa: Turkey 82 40N 29E
Burton upon Trent: England 67 53N 2W
Buru: *i.*, Indonesia 91 4S 126E
BURUNDI: *cap.*, Bujumbura 102 3S 30E
Bury St. Edmonds: England 67 52N 1E
Bushire (Büshehr): Iran 83 29N 51E
Butler: U.S.A. 51 41N 80W
Butte: U.S.A. 52 46N 113W
Butterworth: Malaysia 85 5N 100E
Butt of Lewis: Scotland 67 58N 6W
Butuan: Philippines 91 9N 126E
Butung *i.*, Indon. 91 5S 123E
Buyaga: U.S.S.R. 79 60N 127E
Buzău: Romania 71 45N 27E
Buzuluk: U.S.S.R. 80 53N 52E
Bydgoszcz: Poland 70 53N 18E
Byelorussian S.S.R.: U.S.S.R. 80 53N 27E
Byrd Land: Antarctica 128 80S 130W
Bytom: Poland 70 50N 19E

C

Caballo Res.: U.S.A. 52 33N 107W
Cabantuan: Phil. 91 16N 121E
Cabimas: Venezuela 59 10N 71W
Cabinda: *Prov.*, Angola 102 5S 12E
Cabora Bassa Dam: Mozambique 102 16S 33E
Čačak: Yugoslavia 71 44N 20E
Cáceres: Brazil 60 15S 58W
Cáceres: Spain 69 39N 6W
Cachoeira do Sul: Brazil 61 30S 53W
Cadilac: U.S.A. 24 44N 85W
Cádiz: *& Golfo de*, Spain 69 37N 6W
Caen: France 68 49N 0
Caernarfon: Wales 67 53N 4W
Cagayan: Philippines 91 8N 125E
Cágliari: Sardinia 69 39N 9E
Cahors: France 69 44N 1E
Caicos Is.: Caribbean Sea 59 22N 72W
Cairngorms: *mtns.*, Scotland 67 57N 4W
Cairns: Australia 94 17S 146E
CAIRO: Egypt 82 30N 31E
Calabozo: Venezuela 59 9N 67W
Calais: France 68 51N 2E
Calais: U.S.A. 51 45N 67W
Calamian Group: Philippines 91 12N 120E
Călăraşi: Romania 71 44N 27E
Calbayog: Philippines 91 12N 125E
Calcutta: India 84 22N 88E
Caldas da Rainha: Portugal 69 39N 9W
Caldera: Chile 60 27S 71W
Caldwell: U.S.A. 52 44N 117W
Calexico: U.S.A. 52 33N 115W
Calf of Man: I. of Man 67 54N 5W
Cali: Colombia 60 3N 77W
Calicut: *see* Kozhikode
Caliente: U.S.A. 52 38N 115W
California: *State*, U.S.A. 52 — —
California, Gulf of: Mexico 58 27N 112W
Calipatria: U.S.A. 52 33N 115W
Callao: Peru 60 12S 77W
Caltanissetta: Sicily 71 37N 14E
Calumet City: U.S.A. 57 41N 87W
Calvi: Corsica 69 43N 9E
Camagüey: Cuba 59 21N 78W
Camargo: Mexico 58 28N 105W
Cambay: *& Gulf*, India 84 22N 73E
CAMBODIA: *now* KAMPUCHEA
Cambrai: France 68 50N 3E
Cambridge: England 67 32N 0
Cambridge: Del., U.S.A. 51 39N 76W
Cambridge: Mass., U.S.A. 55 42N 71W
Camden: U.S.A. 50 34N 93W
Cameron: U.S.A. 50 31N 97W
CAMEROUN: *cap.*Yaoundé 102 5N 12E
Camocim: Brazil 60 3S 41W
Camooweal: Australia 94 20S 138E
Campeche: *& Bay*, Mexico 58 20N 93W
Campina Grande: Brazil 60 7S 36W
Campinas: Brazil 61 23S 47W
Campo Grande: Brazil 60 20S 55W
Campos: Brazil 60 22S 41W
Cam Ranh: Vietnam 85 11N 109E
Canadian: *r.*, U.S.A. 50 35N 97W
Çanakkale: Turkey 71 40N 26E
Canary Basin: Atl. O. 103 32N 25W
Canary Islands: Atlantic Ocean 100 28N 15W
Canaveral, Cape: U.S.A. 51 29N 81W
CANBERRA: Australia 94 35S 149E
Canea: *see* Khaniá
Canna: *i.*, Scotland 67 57N 7W
Cannes: France 69 44N 7E
Cannonball: *r.*, U.S.A. 53 46N 102W
Canoas: Brazil 61 30S 51W
Canon City: U.S.A. 53 38N 105W
Cantábrica, Cordillera (Cantabrian Mts.): Spain 69 43N 5W
Canterbury: England 67 51N 1E
Canterbury Bight: New Zealand 95 44S 172E
Canterbury Plains: New Zealand 95 43S 172E
Can Tho: Vietnam 85 10N 105E
Canton (Guangzhou): China 89 23N 113E
Canton: Ill., U.S.A. 50 41N 90W
Canton: Ohio, U.S.A. 51 41N 81W
Canton: S. Dakota, U.S.A. 53 43N 97W
Canudos: Brazil 60 7S 57W
Caoxian: China 88 35N 116E
Cape Girardeau: *city*, U.S.A. 51 37N 90W
Cape Province: South Africa 102 32S 23E
Cape Rise: Atl. O. 103 45S 12E
Cape Town: S. Africa 102 34S 18E
Cape Verde Basin: Atl. Ocean 103 25N 25W
Cape Verde Is.: Atlantic Ocean 103 18N 25W
Cape York Penin.: Australia 94 13S 143E
Cap Haïtien: *town*, Haiti 59 20N 72W
Capitol Heights: U.S.A. 57 39N 77W
Capri: *i.*, Italy 71 40N 14E
Caprivi Strip: Namibia 102 18S 23E
CARACAS: Venezuela 59 10N 67W
Caravelas: Brazil 60 18S 39W
Carbondale: U.S.A. 51 38N 89W
Carbonia: Sardinia 69 39N 8E
Carcassonne: France 69 43N 2E
Cardamon Hills: India 84 10N 77E
Cárdenas: Cuba 59 21N 83W
CARDIFF: Wales 67 51N 3W
Cardigan: Wales 67 52N 5W
Cardigan Bay: Wales 67 52N 4W
Caribbean Sea 59 15N 75W
Carlisle: England 67 55N 3W
Carlow: R. of Ireland 67 53N 7W
Carlsbad: U.S.A. 53 32N 104W
Carmarthen: Wales 67 52N 4W
Carmen: Mexico 58 19N 92W
Carnarvon: Australia 94 25S 114E
Carnic Alps: Austria/Italy 71 47N 13E
Carolina: Brazil 60 7S 47W
Caroline I.: Pacific O. 105 10S 150W
Caroline Is.: Pac. O. 104 2N 145W
Caroni: *r.*, Venezuela 60 6N 63W
Carpathians: *mtns.*, Europe 70/71 47N 25E
Carpentaria, Gulf of: Australia 94 15S 138E
Carrauntuohill: *mtn.*, R. of Ireland 67 52N 10W
Carrick on Shannon: R. of Ireland 67 54N 8W
Carson City: U.S.A. 52 39N 120W
Carson Sink: *dep.*, U.S.A. 52 40N 118W
Cartagena: Columbia 59 10N 75W
Cartagena: Spain 69 38N 1W
Carthage: U.S.A. 50 32N 94W
Casablanca: *see* El Dar el Beida
Cascade Range: Canada/U.S.A. 52 46N 121W
Cascavel: Brazil 60 5S 38W
Caserta: Italy 71 41N 14E
Casiquiare: *r.*, Venezuela 60 2N 66W
Casper: U.S.A. 52 43N 106W
Caspian Lowlands: U.S.S.R. 80 47N 51E
Caspian Sea: U.S.S.R./Iran 80 42N 51E
Cassino: Italy 71 41N 14E
Castellón de la Plana: Spain 69 40N 0
Castelo Branco: Portugal 69 40N 7W
Castlebar: R. of Ireland 67 54N 9W
Castrop-Rauxel: W. Germany 68 51N 7E
Catamarca: Arg. 61 28S 66W
Catania: Sicily 71 37N 15E
Catanzaro: Italy 71 39N 17E
Catastrophe, C.: Australia 94 35S 136E
Cat I.: The Bahamas 59 24N 76W
Catoche, Cape: Mex. 58 21N 87W
Catskill Mts.: U.S.A. 55 42N 74W
Cauca: *r.*, Colombia 60 7N 76W
Caucasus Mts.: U.S.S.R. 80 43N 45E
Cauvery: *r.*, India 84 12N 77E
Cavan: R. of Ireland 67 54N 7W
Caxias do Sul: Brazil 61 29S 51W
CAYENNE: Fr. Guiana 60 5N 52W
Cayman Is.: Carib. Sea 59 19N 81W
Cayuga Lake: U.S.A. 54 43N 77W
Cebu: *& i.*, Phil. 91 10N 124E
Cedar City: U.S.A. 52 38N 114W
Cedar Rapids: U.S.A. 53 42N 92W
Ceduna: Australia: 94 32S 134E
Cegléd: Hungary 71 47N 20E
Celebes (Sulawesi): *i & sea*, Indonesia 91 3S 120E
Celje: Yugoslavia 71 46N 15E
Celle: W. Germany 70 53N 10E
Centerville: U.S.A 53 41N 93W
Central, Cordillera: *mtns.*, Spain 69 40N 5W
CENTRAL AFRICAN REPUBLIC: *cap.* Bangui 100/101 7N 20E
Centralia: Ill., U.S.A. 51 38N 89W
Centralia: Wash., U.S.A. 52 47N 123W
Central Pacific Basin: Pacific Ocean 104 10N 180
Central Siberian Plain: U.S.S.R. 79 65N 110E
Cephalonia: *i.*, Greece 71 38N 21E
Ceram: *i., & sea*, Indonesia 91 3S 130E
Cero de Pasco: Peru 60 11S 76W
Ceské Budejovice: Czechoslovakia 70 49N 14E
Ceuta: Spain 69 36N 5W
Cévennes: *mtns.*, Fr. 69 44N 4E
Chaco Central: *geog. reg.*, Argentina 61 25S 60W
CHAD: *cap.* N'Djamena 100/101 — —
Chad, Lake: Africa 100 13N 14E
Chalon-sur-Saône: France 69 47N 3E
Châlons-sur-Marne: France 68 49N 4E
Chaman: Pakistan 84 31N 66E
Chamba: India 84 32N 76E
Chambal: *r.*, India 84 26N 77E
Chamberlain, L.: U.S.A. 51 46N 69W
Chambersburg: U.S.A. 54 40N 78W
Chambéry: France 69 46N 6E
Champaign: U.S.A. 51 40N 88W
Champlain, L.: U.S.A. 51 45N 74W
Chañaral: Chile 60 26S 71W
Chandigarh: India 84 31N 77E
Changchun: China 87 44N 125E
Changde: China 89 29N 112E
Changjiang: China 87 25N 103E
Changkiakow: *see* Zhangjiakou
Changli: China 88 40N 119E
Changsha: China 89 28N 113E
Changshan: China 89 29N 118E
Changshou: China 89 30N 107E
Changshu: China 88 32N 121E
Changting: China 89 26N 116E
Changwu: China 88 35N 108E
Changzhi: China 88 36N 113E
Changzhou: China 88 32N 120E
Channel Is.: U.K. 68 49N 2W
Chanthaburi: Thai. 85 13N 102E
Chanute: U.S.A. 53 38N 95W
Chany, L: U.S.S.R. 81 55N 77E
Chaoan: China 89 24N 116E
Chaoyang: China 88 42N 120E
Chaoyangchen: *see* Huadian
Chapala Lake: Mex. 58 20N 103W
Chapayevsk: U.S.S.R. 80 53N 50E
Chapra: India 84 26N 85E
Chardzhou: U.S.S.R. 81 39N 64E
Chari: *r.*, Chad 100 11N 16E
Charleroi: Belgium 68 50N 4E
Charleston: Indiana, U.S.A. 51 39N 88W
Charleston: S.C., U.S.A. 51 33N 80W
Charleston: W. Va., U.S.A. 51 38N 81W
Charleville: Australia 94 26S 146E
Charleville: France 68 50N 5E
Charlotte: U.S.A. 51 35N 81W
Charlotte Harbour: *bay*, U.S.A. 51 27N 82W
Charlottesville: U.S.A. 51 38N 79W
Charters Towers: Australia 94 20S 146E
Chartres: France 68 48N 1E
Châteaudun: France 68 48N 1E
Châteauroux: France 69 47N 2E
Châtellerault: France 68 47N 1E
Chatham Is.: Pac. O. 104 44S 177W
Chatham Strait: U.S.A. 22 57N 135W
Chatrapur: India 84 19N 85E
Chattahoochee: *& r.*, U.S.A. 51 31N 85W
Chattanooga: U.S.A. 51 35N 85W
Chaumont: France 68 48N 5E
Chefoo: *see* Yantai
Cheju: *i.*, S. Korea 87 33N 126E
Chekiang: *Prov.*, *see* Zhejiang
Chekunda: U.S.S.R 79 51N 132E
Cheleken: U.S.S.R. 80 39N 54E
Chéliff: *r.*, Algeria 69 36N 1E
Chelkar-Tengiz, L.: U.S.S.R. 81 48N 63E
Chełm: Poland 70 51N 24E
Chelmsford: England 67 52N 0
Cheltenham: England 67 52N 2W
Chelyabinsk: U.S.S.R. 81 55N 61E
Chelyuskin, Cape: U.S.S.R. 79 77N 105E
Chenab: *r.*, India/Pakistan 84 33N 75E
Chengchow: *see* Zhengzhou
Chengde: China 88 41N 118E
Chengdu: China 87 31N 104E
Cheraw: U.S.A. 51 35N 80W
Cherbourg: France 68 50N 2W
Cheremkhovo: U.S.S.R. 79 53N 103E
Cherepovets: U.S.S.R. 80 59N 38E
Cherkassy: U.S.S.R. 80 49N 32E
Chernigov: U.S.S.R. 80 52N 31E
Chernogorsk: U.S.S.R. 81 54N 91E
Chernovtsy: U.S.S.R. 70 48N 26E
Chernyakhovsk: U.S.S.R. 70 55N 22E
Cherokees, Lake of the: U.S.A. 50 37N 95W
Cherrapunji: India 84 25N 92E
Cherskiy Range: U.S.S.R. 79 65N 145E
Chervonograd: U.S.S.R. 70 50N 24E
Chesapeake Bay: U.S.A. 51 38N 76W
Chester: England 67 53N 3W
Chester: U.S.A. 54 40N 76W
Chesterfield: England 67 53N 1W
Cheviot Hills: England/Scotland 67 55N 2W
Chevy Chase: U.S.A. 57 39N 77W
Cheyenne: U.S.A. 53 41N 105W
Cheyenne: *r.*, U.S.A. 53 44N 102W
Chezhou: China 89 26N 113E
Chhindwara: India 84 22N 79E
Chiai: Taiwan 89 23N 120E
Chiang Mai: Thai 85 19N 99E
Chiang Rai: Thai. 85 20N 100E
Chiba: Japan 90 36N 140E
Chicago: U.S.A. 57 42N 88W
Chicagof I.: U.S.A. 22 58N 136W
Chichester: England 67 51N 1W
Chickasha: U.S.A. 53 35N 98W
Chiclayo: Peru 60 7S 80W
Chico: U.S.A. 52 40N 122W
Chieti: Italy 71 42N 14E
Chihli, G. of: *see* Bohai
Chihuahua: Mexico 58 29N 106W
CHILE: *cap.* Santiago 60 — —
Chile Rise: Pacific O. 105 35S 95W
Chillán: Chile 60 36S 72W
Chillicothe: U.S.A. 51 39N 83W
Chiloé I.: Chile 60 43S 64W
Chilpancingo: Mex. 58 17N 100W
Chilterns: *hills*, England 67 52N 0
Chimbote: Peru 60 9S 79W
Chimkent: U.S.S.R. 81 42N 70E
CHINA: *cap.* Peking (Beijing) 86/7 — —
Chindwin: *r.*, Burma 85 25N 95E
Chin Hills: Burma 85 22N 93E
Chinmen (Quemoy): China 89 24N 118E
Chinnampo: N. Korea 87 39N 125E
Chios: *i. & town*, Greece 71 38N 26E
Chippewa Falls: *city* U.S.A. 53 45N 91W
Chita: *& Prov.*, U.S.S.R. 79 52N 113E
Chitose: Japan 90 43N 142E
Chitral: Pakistan 84 36N 72E
Chittagong: Bangladesh 84 22N 92E
Chivilcoy: Argentina 61 35S 60W
Choctawhatchee: *r.*, U.S.A. 51 31N 86W
Choibalsan: Mong. 87 48N 114E
Cholet: France 69 47N 1W
Cholon: Vietnam 85 10N 107E
Chongjin: N. Korea 87 42N 130E
Chongqing (Chungking): China 89 30N 107E
Choshi: Japan 90 36N 141E
Christchurch: N.Z. 95 43S 173E
Christmas I.: Indian Ocean 91 11S 106E
Christmas I., Pac. O: *now* Kirimati
Christmas Ridge: Pacific Ocean 104 10N 167W
Chu: *& r.*, U.S.S.R. 81 44N 74E
Chuanchow: *see* Quazhou
Chobe Nat. Park: Botswana 102 19S 24E
Chubut: *r.*, Arg. 60 43S 66W
Chuchow: *see* Zhuzhou
Chugoku-Sanchi: *mtns.* Japan 90 35N 133E
Chuguchak: *see* Tacheng
Chuho: *see* Shangzhi
Chukai: Malaysia 85 4N 103E
Chukchi Sea: U.S.S.R. 79 70N 170W
Chulym: *r.*, U.S.S.R. 81 57N 87E
Chumphon: Thailand 85 10N 99E
Chunghua: Taiwan 89 24N 121E
Chungking: *see* Chongqing
Chuquicamata: Chile 60 22S 69W
Chur (Coire): Switz. 71 47N 9E
Chuxiong (Tsuyung): China 85 26N 101E
Cicero: U.S.A. 57 42N 88W
Ciego de Avila: Cuba 59 22N 79W
Cienfuegos: Cuba 59 22N 80W
Cilician Gates: Turkey 82 37N 35E
Cimarron: *r.*, U.S.A. 50 37N 99W
Cincinnati: U.S.A. 51 39N 84W
Cirebon: Indonesia 91 7S 109E
City Island: U.S.A. 56 41N 74W
Ciudad Acuña: Mexico 50 29N 101W
Ciudad Bolívar: Venezuela 59 8N 64W
Ciudad Guzmán: Mex. 58 20N 103W
Ciudad Juarez: Mex. 58 32N 107W
Ciudad Madero: Mex. 58 22N 98W
Ciudad Obregon: Mex. 58 27N 110W
Ciudad Real: Spain 69 39W 4W
Ciudad Victoria: Mex. 58 24N 99W
Civitavecchia: Italy 71 42N 12E
Claremont: U.S.A. 51 43N 73W
Clarinda: U.S.A. 53 41N 95W
Clark Hill Res.: U.S.A. 51 34N 82W
Clarksburg: U.S.A. 51 39N 80W
Clarksdale: U.S.A. 50 34N 90W
Clarksville: U.S.A. 51 36N 87W
Clayton: U.S.A. 53 36N 103W
Clear L.: U.S.A. 52 39N 123W
Clearwater: U.S.A. 51 28N 83W
Cleburne: U.S.A. 50 32N 97W
Clermont-Ferrand: France 69 46N 3E
Cleveland: Ark., U.S.A. 50 34N 91W
Cleveland: Ohio, U.S.A. 51 42N 82W
Cleveland: Tenn., U.S.A. 51 35N 85W
Cleveland: Texas: U.S.A. 50 30N 95W
Clew Bay: R. of Irel. 67 54N 9W
Clifden: R. of Irel. 67 53N 10W
Clifton: U.S.A. 56 41N 74W
Clingmans Dome: *mtn.*, U.S.A. 51 36N 84W
Clinton: Iowa, U.S.A. 53 42N 90W
Clinton: Mass. U.S.A. 55 42N 72W
Clipperton I.: Pacific O. 105 10N 110W
Cloncurry: Australia 94 21S 140E
Clonmel: R. of Irel. 67 52N 8W
Cloppenburg: W. Ger. 68 53N 8E
Cluj: Romania 71 47N 24E
Clyde: *r.*, Scotland 67 55N 4W
Clyde, Firth of: Scot. 67 56N 5W
Coast Range: U.S.A. 52 45N 124W
Coats Land: Antarc. 128 78S 30W
Coatzacoalcos: Mexico 58 18N 94W
Cobar: Australia 94 31S 146E
Cobh: R. of Ireland 67 52N 8W
Coburg: W. Germany 70 50N 11E
Cochabamba: Bolivia 60 17S 66W
Cochin: India 84 10N 76E
Cocoa: U.S.A. 51 28N 81W
Cocos Is.: Indian O. 104 11S 97E
Cocos Is.: Pacific O. 105 6N 87W
Cocos Ridge: Pacific O. 105 4N 85W
Cod, Cape: U.S.A. 55 42N 70W
Cody: U.S.A. 52 45N 109W
Coeur d'Alene: U.S.A. 52 48N 117W
Coffeyville: U.S.A. 53 37N 96W
Coff's Harbour: Australia 94 30S 153E
Cognac: France 69 46N 0
Coimbatore: India 84 11N 77E
Coimbra: Portugal 69 40N 8W
Colatina: Brazil 60 20S 40W
Colby: U.S.A. 53 39N 101W
Colchester: England 67 52N 1E
Coleraine: N. Ireland 67 55N 7W
Colfax: U.S.A. 52 47N 117W
Colima: Mexico 58 19N 104W
Coll: *i.*, Scotland 67 57N 7W
College Park: *town*, U.S.A. 57 39N 77W
Colmar: France 68 48N 7E
Cologne (Köln): W. Germany 68 51N 7E

COLOMBIA: *cap.* Bogotá **60** 5N 72W
COLOMBO: Sri Lanka **84** 7N 80E
Colón: Cuba **59** 23N 81W
Colón: Panama **58** *Inset*
Colonsay: *i.*, Scotland **67** 56N 6W
Colorado: *R.*, Arg. **60** 37S 69W
Colorado: *r.*, Texas U.S.A. **50** 29N 96W
Colorado: *r.*, U.S.A./Mexico **52** 33N 114W
Colorado: *State*, U.S.A. **52/3** 39N 106W
Colorado Plateaux: U.S.A. **52** 37N 111W
Colorado Springs: U.S.A. **53** 39N 105W
Columbia: Mo., U.S.A. **53** 39N 92W
Columbia: S.C., U.S.A. **51** 34N 81W
Columbia: *r.*, U.S.A. **52** 46N 120W
Columbia: Tenn., U.S.A. **51** 36N 87W
[illegible]
Columbus: Ind., U.S.A. **51** 39N 86W
Columbus: Miss., U.S.A. **51** 33N 89W
Columbus: Nebr., U.S.A. **50** 41N 97W
Columbus: Ohio, U.S.A. **51** 40N 83W
Colville: U.S.A. **52** 49N 118W
Comilla: Bangladesh **84** 23N 91E
Communism, Pk.: U.S.S.R. **81** 39N 72E
Como: *& lake*, Italy **69** 46N 9E
Comodoro Rivadavia: Argentina **60** 46S 67W
Comorin, C.: India **84** 8N 77E
Compiègne: France **68** 49N 3E
CONAKRY: Guinea **100** 10N 14W
Concepción: Chile **60** 37S 73W
Concepción: Paraguay **61** 23S 57W
Concepción del Uruguay: Argentina **61** 32S 58W
Concord: N.C., U.S.A. **51** 35N 80W
Concord: N.H., U.S.A. **55** 43N 71W
Concordia: Argentina **61** 31S 58W
Conecuh: *r.*, U.S.A. **51** 31N 87W
Coney Island: U.S.A. **56** 41N 74W
CONGO: *cap*, Brazzaville **102** 0 15E
Congo: *r.*, *see* Zaïre
Conn, L.: R. of Ireland **67** 54N 9W
Connecticut: *r.*, U.S.A. **51** 43N 73W
Connecticut: *State* U.S.A. **55** 41N 72W
Connemara: *reg.*, R. of Ireland **67** 54N 10W
Connersville: U.S.A. **51** 40N 85W
Conrad: U.S.A. **52** 48N 112W
Consett: England **67** 55N 2W
Constance, Lake: *see* Bodensee
Constanta: Rom. **71** 44N 29E
Constantine: Algeria **69** 37N 7E
Conway: U.S.A. **51** 34N 79W
Cooch Behar: India **84** 26N 90E
Cook Is.: Pacific O. **104** 20S 160W
Cook, Mt.: N.Z. **95** 44S 170E
Cook Strait: N.Z. **95** 41S 174E
Cooktown: Australia: **94** 15S 145E
Coolgardie: Australia: **94** 31S 121E
Cooper Creek: Austl. **94** 27S 140E
COPENHAGEN: Den **70** 56N 13E
Coral Gables: U.S.A. **51** 26N 80W
Coral Sea: Pacific O. **94** 15S 152E
Corbeil-Essonnes: France **72** 49N 3E
Cordele: U.S.A. **51** 32N 84W
Córdoba: Argentina **61** 31S 64W
Córdoba: Mexico **58** 19N 97W
Córdoba: Spain **69** 38N 5W
Corfu (Kérkira): *i.*, Greece **71** 40N 20E
Corinth: *& gulf*, Greece **71** 38N 23E
Corinth: U.S.A. **51** 35N 89W
Cork: R. of Ireland **67** 52N 8W
Corlu: Turkey **71** 41N 28E
Coromandel Ra.: New Zealand **95** 37S 176E
Coromandel Coast: India **84** 13N 81E
Corpus Christi: *& bay*, U.S.A. **50** 28N 79W
Corrib, L.: R. of Ireland **67** 53N 9W
Corrientes: Arg. **61** 27S 59W
Corsica: *i.*, Medit. Sea **69** 42N 9E
Corsicana: U.S.A. **50** 32N 96W
Corte: Corsica **69** 42N 9E
Corumbá: Brazil **60** 19S 57W
Corunna: *see* La Coruña
Corvallis: U.S.A. **52** 45N 123W
Cosenza: Italy **71** 39N 16E
Costa Brava: *coast*, Spain **69** 42N 3E
Costa del Sol: *coast*, Spain **69** 36N 4W
COSTA RICA: *cap.* San José **58/9** 10N 84W
Côte d'Azur: France **69** 43N 7E
CÔTE D'IVOIRE: *cap.* Yamoussoukro **100** 7N 6W
COTONOU: Benin **100** 6N 2E
Cotswolds: *hills*, Eng. **67** 52N 2W
Cottbus: E. Germany **70** 52N 14E
Council Bluffs: U.S.A. **53** 41N 96W
Coventry: England **67** 53N 2W
Covilhã: Portugal **69** 40N 7W
Covington: U.S.A. **51** 37N 80W
Cozumel I.: Mex. **58** 20N 87W
Cracow (Kraków): Poland **70** 50N 20E
Craiova: Romania **71** 44N 24E
Crater L. Nat. Park: U.S.A. **52** 43N 122W
Crawfordsville: U.S.A. **51** 40N 88W
Cremona: Italy **71** 45N 10E
Cres: *i.*, Yugoslavia **71** 45N 14E
Crescent City: U.S.A. **52** 42N 124W
Crestview: U.S.A. **51** 31N 87W
Crete: *i, & sea*, Greece **71** 35N 25E
Crete: U.S.A. **53** 41N 97W
Crewe: England **67** 53N 2W
Criciuma: Brazil **61** 29S 50W
Crimea: *penin.*, U.S.S.R. **80** 45N 34E
Cromarty: Scotland **67** 58N 4W
Cromer: England **67** 53N 1E
Cromwell: N.Z. **95** 45S 169E
Crookstown: U.S.A. **53** 47N 96W
Crosby: Minn., U.S.A. **53** 46N 94W
Crosby: N. Dakota, U.S.A. **53** 49N 103W
Cross Sound: U.S.A. **22** 58N 136W
Crotone: Italy **71** 39N 17E
Croydon: England **68** 51N 0
Cruz Alta: Brazil **61** 29S 54W
Cruzeiro: Brazil **61** 23S 45W
Cruzeiro do Sul: Brazil **60** 8S 73W
CUBA: *cap* Havana **59** 21N 80W
Cubango: *r.*, Angola **102** 17S 18E
Cucuta: Colombia **60** 8N 73W
Cuernavaca: Mexico **58** 19N 99W
Cuddalore: India **84** 12N 80E
Cuddapah: India **84** 15N 79E
Cuenca: Spain **69** 40N 2W
Cuiabá: Brazil **60** 16S 56W
Culiacán: Mexico **58** 23N 106W
Cullman: U.S.A. **51** 34N 87W
Cumana: Venezuela **59** 10N 64W
Cumberland: U.S.A. **54** 40N 79W
Cumberland, L.: U.S.A. **51** 37N 85W
Cuneo: Italy **69** 44N 8E
Cunnamulla: Austl. **94** 28S 146E
Cupar: Scotland **67** 56N 3W
Curaçao: *i.*, Carib. Sea **59** 12N 69W
Curitiba: Brazil **61** 25S 49W
Cut Bank: U.S.A. **52** 48N 113W
Cuttack: India [illegible] 20N 86E
Cuxhaven: W. Germany **68** 54N 9E
Cuzco: Peru **60** 14S 72W
Cyclades: *is.*, Greece **71** 37N 25E
CYPRUS: *cap.* Nicosia **82** 35N 33E
CZECHOSLOVAKIA: *Cap.* Prague **70** 49N 17E
Czestochowa: Poland **70** 51N 19E

D

Dabashan (Tapa Shan): *mts.*, China **88** 32N 108E
Dabieshan (Taipeh Shan): *ra.*, China **89** 31N 116E
DACCA: *see* DHAKA
Dadra and Nagar Haveli: *Union Territ*, India **84** 20N 73E
Dagupan: Philippines **91** 16N 120E
Dahlak Arch.: Red Sea **82** 16N 40W
Dajarra: Australia **94** 22S 140E
DAKAR: Senegal **100** 15N 17W
Dakhla: W. Sahara **100** 24N 16W
Dakhla Oasis: Egypt **101** 25N 29E
Daking: China **88** 40N 116E
Dalaman: Turkey **82** 37N 29E
Da Lat: Vietnam **85** 12N 108E
Dalhousie: India **84** 33N 76E
Dali: China **88** 35N 110E
Dall I.: U.S.A. **22** 55N 133W
Dallas: U.S.A. **50** 33N 97W
Dalton: U.S.A. **51** 35N 85W
Daltonganj: India **84** 24N 84E
Daly: *r.*, Australia **94** 14S 132E
Daly Waters: *town*, Australia **94** 16S 133E
Daman: *Union Territ.*, India **84** 20N 73E
DAMASCUS: Syria **82** 34N 36E
Damāvand: *mtn.*, Iran **83** 36N 52E
Damietta: Egypt **82** 31N 32E
Damodar: *r.*, India **84** 24N 86E
Dampier: Austl. **94** 21S 117E
Dampier Land: Australia **94** 17S 123E
Da Nang: Vietnam **85** 16N 108E
Dandong (Antung): China **87** 40N 124E
Danilovka: U.S.S.R. **81** 53N 71E
Danlinganjing (Gt. Khingan Mts.): China **87** 47N 119E
Dannevirke: N.Z. **95** 40S 176E
Danube: *r.*, Europe **70/1** — —
Danushkodi: India **84** 9N 80E
Danville: Ill., U.S.A. **51** 40N 88W
Danville: Va., U.S.A. **51** 37N 79W
Danxian: China **88** 35N 116E
Danyang: China **88** 32N 120E
Dardanelles: *str.*, Turkey **82** 40N 26E
DAR ES SALAAM: Tanzania **102** 7S 40E
Darfur: *Prov.*, Sudan **101** 13N 25E
Dargaville: N.Z. **95** 36S 174E
Darién, Gulf of: Colombia **58** 9N 77W
Darjeeling: India **84** 27N 88E
Darling: *r.*, Australia **94** 31S 145E
Darling Downs: Australia **94** 27S 150E
Darlington: England **67** 55N 2W
Darmstadt: W. Ger. **68** 50N 9E
Dar Rouga: *Reg.*, Central African Rep. **101** 10N 23E
Dart: *r.*, England **67** 50N 4W
Dartmoor: England **67** 51N 4W
Dartmouth: England **67** 50N 4W
Darwin: Australia **94** 12S 131E
Dasht-e Kavir: *desert*, Iran **83** 34N 55E
Dasht-e Lūt: *desert*. Iran **83** 32N 57E
Datong: China **88** 40N 113E
Daugava: *r.*, *see* West Dvina
Daugavpils: U.S.S.R. **80** 56N 26E
Davangere: India **84** 14N 76E
Davao: Philippines **91** 7N 126E
Davenport: U.S.A. **50** 41N 90W
Davidson Mts.: U.S.A. **20** 69N 142E
Davis: Antarc. **128** 64S 92E
Davos: Switzerland **71** 47N 10E
Dawna Range: Burma/Thailand **85** 13N 99E
Daxian: China **89** 31N 108E
Dayton: U.S.A. **51** 40N 84W
Daytona Beach: U.S.A. **51** 29N 81W
De Aar: S. Africa **102** 31S 24E
Dead Sea: Israel/Jordan **82** 32N 35E
Deadwood: U.S.A. **53** 44N 104W
Death Valley: & *Nat. Monument*, U.S.A. **52** 37N 117W
Debrecen: Hungary **71** 48N 22E
Decatur: Albama, U.S.A. **51** 35N 87W
Decatur: Ill. U.S.A. **51** 40N 89W
Deccan: *reg.*, India **84** 17N 77E
Dee: *r.*, Eng./Wales **67** 53N 3W
Dee: *r.*, Gramp., Scot. **67** 57N 3W
Deerfield: U.S.A. **57** 42N 88W
Deer Lodge: U.S.A. **52** 46N 113W
Dehra Dun: India **84** 30N 78E
Deir ez Zor: Syria **82** 35N 40E
De Kalb: U.S.A. **51** 42N 89W
Delano: U.S.A. **52** 36N 119W
Delano Peak: U.S.A. **52** 38N 112W
Delaware: *State, & bay*, U.S.A. **51** 39N 75W
Delmenhorst: W. Ger. **68** 53N 9E
Delray Beach: *city*. U.S.A. **51** 26N 80W
Del Rio: U.S.A. **50** 29N 101W
DELHI: India **84** 29N 77E
Deming: U.S.A. **52** 32N 108W
Denbigh: Wales **67** 53N 3W
Den Helder: Neth. **68** 53N 5E
Denison: U.S.A. **50** 34N 97W
Denizli: Turkey **82** 38N 29E
DENMARK: *cap.* Copenhagen **70** 56N 10E
Denton: U.S.A. **50** 33N 98W
D'Entrecasteaux Is.: Papua New Guinea **94** 10S 151E
Denver: U.S.A. **53** 40N 105W
Denville: U.S.A. **55** 41N 74W
De Pere: U.S.A. **53** 44N 88W
Dera'a: Syria **82** 32N 36E
Dera Ghazi Khan: Pakistan **84** 30N 70E
Dera Ismail Khan: Pakistan **84** 32N 71E
Derbent: U.S.S.R. **80** 42N 48E
Derby: Australia **94** 17S 123E
Derby: [illegible]
Derg, L.: R. of Ireland **67** 53N 8W
Derna: Libya **82** 33N 22E
Derwent: *r.*, Derby, England **67** 53N 2W
Derwent: *r.*, N. Yorks., England **67** 54N 1W
Des Moines: & *r.*, U.S.A. **50** 42N 94W
Des Plaines: U.S.A. **57** 42N 88W
Dessau: E. Germany **70** 52N 12E
Detroit: U.S.A. **51** 42N 83W
Deva: Romania **71** 46N 23E
Deventer: Neth **68** 52N 6E
Devils Lake: *town* U.S.A. **53** 48N 98W
Dexter: U.S.A. **51** 45N 69W
Dezhou: China **88** 37N 116E
Dhahran: Saudi Arabia **83** 26N 50E
DHAKA: Bangladesh **84** 24N 90E
Dharwar: India **84** 15N 75E
Dhulia: India **84** 21N 75E
Diamantina: Brazil **60** 18S 44W
Dibrugarh: India **85** 28N 95E
Dieciocho de Marzo: Mexico **50** 26N 98W
Diego Suarez: *see* Antsirañana
Dieppe: France **68** 50N 1E
Digboi: India **85** 27N 96E
Digne: France **69** 44N 6E
Dijon: France **68** 47N 5E
Dili: Indon. **91** 8S 126E
Dimitrovgrad: Bulgaria **71** 42N 26E
Dinajpur: Bangladesh **84** 26N 89E
Dinan: France **68** 48N 2W
Dinaric Alps: Yugo. **71** 44N 16E
Dindigul: India **84** 10N 78E
Dingshan: China **89** 31N 120E
Dingwall: Scotland **67** 58N 4W
Dingxian: China **88** 39N 115E
Diomede Is.: Bering Strait **79** 66N 169W
Dir: Pakistan **84** 35N 72E
Diredawa: Ethiopia **101** 10N 42E
Dirk Hartog I.: Australia **94** 26S 113E
Disappointment, L.: Australia **94** 23S 123E
Disko: *i.*, Greenland **1** 69N 54W
District Heights: U.S.A. **57** 39N 77W
Divriği: Turkey **82** 40N 38E
Dixon: U.S.A. **51** 42N 90W
Diyarbakir: Turkey **82** 38N 40E
DJAKARTA *see* JAKARTA
Djelfa: Algeria **100** 35N 3E
Djerba I.: Tunisia **100** 34N 11E
DJIBOUTI: cap. Djibouti **101** 12N 43E
Dneprodzerzhinsk: U.S.S.R. **80** 48N 34E
Dnepropetrovsk: U.S.S.R. **80** 48N 35E
Dnestr: *r.*, U.S.S.R. **70** 49N 25E
Doberai Penin.: Indon. **91** 2S 132E
Dodecanese: *is.*, Greece **71** 37N 27E
Dodge City: U.S.A. **50** 38N 100W
Dodoma: Tanzania **102** 6S 36E
DOHA: Qatar **83** 26N 51E
Dolak I.: Indonesia **94** 8S 138E
Dolgellau: Wales **67** 53N 4W
Dolomites: *mtns.*, Italy **71** 46N 12E
Dolton: U.S.A. **57** 42N 88W
DOMINICA: *cap.* Roseau **59** 15N 61W
DOMINICAN REPUBLIC: *cap.* Santo Domingo **59** 19N 70W
Don: *r.*, England **67** 54N 1W
Don: *r.*, Scotland **67** 57N 2W
Don: *r.*, U.S.S.R. **80** 50N 40E
Donbass: *reg.*, U.S.S.R. **80** 48N 38E
Doncaster: England **67** 54N 1W
Donegal: R. of Ireland **67** 55N 8W
Donegal Bay: R. of Ireland **67** 55N 8W
Donets: *r.*, U.S.S.R. **80** 49N 37E
Donetsk: U.S.S.R. **80** 48N 37E
Dongguan: China **89** 23N 114E
Donghai (Haizhou): China **88** 35N 119E
Dong Hoi: Vietnam **85** 17N 107E
Dongkan: *see* Binhai
Dongshan: China **89** 24N 117E
Dongtai: China **88** 33N 120E
Dongting, L: China **89** 29N 112E
Doonerak, Mt.: U.S.A. **1** 68N 152W
Dorchester: Dorset, England **67** 51N 2W
Dordogne: *r.*, France **69** 45N 0
Dordrecht: Neth. **68** 52N 5E
Dornoch: Scotland **67** 58N 4W
Dortmund: W. Ger. **68** 52N 7E
Dothan: U.S.A. **51** 31N 85W
Douai: France **68** 50N 3E
Douala: Cameroun **100** 4N 10E
Douarnenez: France **68** 48N 4W
Doubtful Sound: New Zealand **95** 45S 167E
DOUGLAS: I. of Man **67** 54N 4W
Dounreay: Scotland **67** 59N 4W
Douro (Duero): *r.*, Spain/Portugal **69** 41N 8W
Dover: England **67** 51N 1E
Dover: U.S.A. **54** 39N 76W
Dover, Strait of: England/France **67** 51N 1E
Dovrefjell: *mtns.*, Norway **70** 62N 10E
Downers Grove: U.S.A. **57** 42N 88W
Downpatrick: N. Ireland **67** 54N 6W
Dra: *r.*, Mor./Alg. **100** 29N 8W
Draguignan: France **69** 44N 6E
Drakensberg: *mtns.*, S. Africa **102** 31S 28E
Dráma: Greece **71** 41N 24E
Drammen: Norway **70** 60N 10E
Drava (Drau or Drave): *r.*, Europe **71** 46N 16E
Dresden: E. Germany **70** 51N 14E
Drogheda: R. of Irel. **67** 54N 6W
Drogobych: U.S.S.R. **70** 50N 24E
Dubai: United Arab Emirates **83** 25N 55E
Dubbo: Australia **94** 32S 149E
DUBLIN: R. of Ireland **67** 53N 6W
Dublin: U.S.A. **51** 32N 83W
Dubno: U.S.S.R. **70** 50N 26E
Dubrovnik: Yugo. **71** 43N 18E
Dubuque: U.S.A. **53** 42N 91W
Ducie I.: Pacific O. **105** 25S 125W
Dudinka: U.S.S.R. **79** 70N 86E
Duisburg: W. Gemany **68** 51N 7E
Dulce: *r.*, Arg. **61** 29S 64W
Duluth: U.S.A. **53** 47N 92W
Dumfries: Scotland **67** 55N 4W
Dunaújváros: Hungary **71** 47N 19E
Duncan: U.S.A. **50** 34N 98W
Duncansby Head: Scotland **67** 59N 3W
[illegible]
Dundee: Scotland **67** 56N 3W
Dunedin: N.Z. **95** 46S 171E
Dunkerque (Dunkirk): France **68** 51N 2E
Dunkirk: U.S.A. **51** 42N 79W
Dun Laoghaire: R. of Ireland **67** 53N 6W
Duns: Scotland **67** 56N 2W
Durance: *r.*, France **69** 44N 6E
Durango: Mexico **58** 24N 105W
Durango: U.S.A. **52** 37N 108W
Durant: U.S.A. **50** 34N 96W
Durban: S. Africa **102** 30S 31E
Durham: England **67** 55N 2W
Durham: U.S.A. **51** 36N 79W
Durrës: Albania **71** 41N 19E
D'Urville I.: N.Z. **95** 41S 174E
Dushanbe: U.S.S.R. **81** 39N 69E
Duyun: China **89** 26N 107E
Düsseldorf: W. Ger. **68** 51N 7E
Dyersburg: U.S.A. **51** 36N 89W
Dyfi: *r.*, Wales **67** 53N 4W
Dzerzhinsk: U.S.S.R. **80** 56N 43E
Dzhambul: U.S.S.R. **81** 43N 71E
Dzherba: U.S.S.R. **79** 60N 116E
Dzhetygara: U.S.S.R. **81** 52N 61E
Dzhezkazgan: U.S.S.R. **81** 48N 68E
Dzungarian Gate: *pass*, China/U.S.S.R. **81** 45N 82E

E

Eagle Pass: *city*. U.S.A. **50** 29N 100W
Earn: *r.*, Scotland **67** 56N 4W
East: *r.*, U.S.A. **56** 41N 74W
East Anglia: *reg.*, Eng. **67** 52N 1E
East Cape: N.Z. **95** 38S 178E
East Chicago: U.S.A. **57** 42N 87W
East China Sea: **87** 30N 123E
Easter I: Pacific O. **105** 27S 110W
Eastern Desert: Egypt **82** 27N 32E
Eastern Ghats: *mtns.*, India **84** 16N 80E
Eastern Sierra Madre *see* Sierra Madre, Eastern
East Liverpool: U.S.A. **51** 41N 81W
East London: S. Africa **102** 33S 28E
East Pacific Basin: Pacific Ocean **105** 15N 155W
East Pacific Ridge: Pacific Ocean **105** 20S 110W
East Rift Valley: Kenya/Ethiopia **102** 5N 37E
East Siberian Sea: U.S.S.R. **79** 73N 160E
Eau Claire: U.S.A. **53** 45N 92W
Eauripik Ridge: Pacific Ocean **104** 5N 142E
Eberswalde: E. Ger. **70** 53N 14E
Ebetsu: Japan **90** 43N 142E
Ebinur Hu (Ebi Nor): *l.*, China **81** 45N 83E
Ebro: *r.*, Spain **69** 42N 1W
Écija: Spain **69** 38N 5W
ECUADOR: *cap.* Quito **60** 2S 77W
Ed Damer: Sudan **101** 17N 34E
Eden: *r.*, England **67** 55N 3W
Edhessa: Greece **71** 41N 22E
EDINBURGH: Scotland **67** 56N 3W
Edirne (Adrianople): Turkey **71** 42N 26E
Edjelé: Algeria **100** 28N 9E
Edremit: Turkey **71** 40N 27E
Edward, Lake: Africa **102** 0 30E
Edwards Plateau: U.S.A. **50** 30N 100W
Eger: Hungary **70** 48N 20E
Egersund: Norway **68** 58N 6E
Egmont, Mt.: N.Z. **95** 39S 174E
EGYPT: *cap.* Cairo **102** 27N 30E
Eigg: *i.*, Scotland **67** 57N 6W
Eighty Mile Beach: Australia **94** 21S 121E
Eilat: Israel **82** 30N 35E
Eindhoven: Neth. **68** 51N 5E
Eisenach: E. Germany **70** 51N 10E
EL AAIÚN: Western Sahara **100** 27N 14W
El Alamein: Egypt **82** 31N 29E
El Asnam: Algeria **69** 36N 1E
Elâziğ: Turkey **82** 39N 39E
Elba: *i.*, Italy **71** 43N 10E
El Ballâh: Egypt **101** *Inset*
Elbasan: Albania **71** 41N 20E
El Bayadh: Algeria **100** 34N 2E
Elbe: *r.*, E. & W. Ger. **70** 53N 11E
Elbert, Mt.: U.S.A. **52** 39N 107W
Elbląg: Poland **70** 54N 20E
El'brus: *mtn.*, U.S.S.R. **80** 43N 42E
El Centro: U.S.A. **52** 33N 116W
Elche: Spain **69** 38N 1W
El Dar el Beida (Casablanca): Morocco **100** 34N 8W
El Dorado: Ark., U.S.A. **50** 33N 93W
El Dorado: Kansas, U.S.A. **50** 38N 97W
Elephant Butte Res.: U.S.A. **52** 33N 107W
Eleuthera: *i.*, The Bahamas **59** 25N 76W
El Faiyûm: Egypt **82** 29N 31E
El Fasher: Sudan **101** 14N 25E
El Ferrol del Caudillo: Spain **69** 43N 8W
El Firdân: Egypt **101** *Inset*
Elgin: Scotland **67** 58N 3W
El'gyay: U.S.S.R. **79** 62N 117E
Elizabeth: Australia **94** 35S 139E
Elizabeth: U.S.A. **56** 41N 74W
Elizabeth City: U.S.A. **51** 36N 76W
Elizabeth Point: Namibia **102** 27S 15E
Elizabethton: U.S.A. **51** 36N 82W
Elizabethtown: U.S.A. **51** 38N 86W
Elk: Poland **70** 54N 22E

Elk City: U.S.A. **50** 35N 99W
Elk Grove Village: U.S.A. **57** 42N 88W
El Kharga: Egypt **82** 25N 30E
Elkhart: U.S.A. **51** 42N 86W
Elkins: U.S.A. **51** 39N 80W
Elko: U.S.A. **52** 41N 116W
Elk River: *city*, U.S.A. **52** 47N 116W
Ellensburg: U.S.A. **52** 47N 121W
Ellice Is.: *now* **TUVALU**
Ellsworth Land: Antarctica **128** 77S 90W
El Matarîya: Egypt **101** *Inset*
Elmhurst: U.S.A. **57** 42N 88W
El Minya: Egypt **82** 28N 31E
Elmira: U.S.A. **54** 42N 77W
Elmwood Park: U.S.A. **57** 42N 88W
El Obeid: Sudan **101** 13N 30E
El Paso: U.S.A. **52** 32N 106W
El Qantara: Egypt **101** *Inset*
El Reno: U.S.A. **50** 36N 98W
EL SALVADOR: *cap.* San Salvador **58** 14N 89W
El Shatt: Egypt **101** *Inset*
Eluru: India **84** 17N 81E
Ely: England **67** 52N 0
Ely: U.S.A. **52** 39N 115W
Emba: & *r.*, U.S.S.R. **80/1** 49N 58E
Emden: W. Germany **68** 53N 7E
Emi Koussi: *mtn.*, Chad **101** 20N 19E
Emamrud (*formerly* Shahrûd): Iran **83** 36N 55E
Emory Peak: U.S.A. **50** 29N 104W
Enderlin: U.S.A. **53** 47N 98W
Enggano: *i.*, Indon. **91** 5S 102E
ENGLAND: *cap.* London **67** — —
Englewood: U.S.A. **56** 41N 74W
English Channel: Eng./Fr. **68** 50N 2W
Enid: U.S.A. **50** 36N 98W
Enna: Sicily **71** 38N 14E
Ennis: R. of Irel. **67** 53N 9W
Enniscorthy: R. of Ireland **67** 53N 7W
Enniskillen: N. Ireland **67** 54N 8W
Enschede: Netherlands **68** 52N 7E
Ensenada: Argentina **61** 35S 58W
Ensenada: Mexico **58** 32N 117W
Entebbe: Uganda **102** 0 33E
Enterprise: U.S.A. **51** 31N 86W
Enugu: Nigeria **100** 6N 8E
Épinal: France **68** 48N 6E
EQUATORIAL GUINEA: *cap.* Malabo **100** 2N 10E
Erbil: Iraq **83** 36N 44E
Erentsab: Mongolia **87** 50N 115E
Erfurt: E. Germany **70** 51N 11E
Erie: U.S.A. **51** 42N 80W
Erie, Lake: U.S.A./Canada **51** 42N 81W
Erigavo: Somali Republic **101** 11N 47E
Eritrea: *Prov.*, Eth. **101** 15N 40E
Erne, Lough: N. Ireland **67** 55N 8W
Erode: India **84** 11N 78E
Er Rif Mtns.: Morocco **69** 35N 5W
Erzgebirge: E. Ger./Czech. **70** 50N 13E
Erzincan: Turkey **82** 40N 40E
Erzurum: Turkey **82** 40N 41E
Esbjerg: Denmark **70** 55N 8E
Escanaba: U.S.A. **53** 46N 87W
Escondido: U.S.A. **52** 33N 117W
Eskilstuna: Sweden **70** 59N 17E
Eskisehir: Turkey **82** 40N 30E
Esperance: Australia **94** 34S 122E
Espirito Santo: *State*, Brazil **60** 20S 40W
Essaouira: Morocco **100** 32N 10W
Essen: W. Germany **68** 51N 7E
Essequibo: *r.*, Guyana **60** 5N 58W
Estonian S.S.R.: U.S.S.R. **80** 59N 26E
Etawah: India **84** 27N 79E
ETHIOPIA: *cap.* Addis Ababa **101** — —
Ethiopian Plat.: E. Africa **101** 10N 37E
Etna, Mt.: *volc.*, Sicily **71** 38N 15E
Etosha Pan: Namibia **102** 19S 16E
Euboea: *i.*, Greece **71** 38N 24E
Eucla: Australia **94** 32S 129E
Eudora: U.S.A. **50** 33N 91W
Eugene: U.S.A. **52** 44N 123W
Eunice: U.S.A. **50** 30N 92W
Euphrates: *r.*, Asia **82/3** 35N 40E
Eureka: California, U.S.A. **52** 41N 124W
Eureka: Montana, U.S.A. **52** 49N 115W
Eureka: Nev., U.S.A. **52** 40N 116W
Evanston: Ill., U.S.A. **57** 42N 88W
Evanston: Wyo., U.S.A. **52** 41N 111W
Evansville: U.S.A. **51** 38N 88W
Everest: *mtn.*, Himalayas **84** 28N 87E
Everett: U.S.A. **52** 48N 122W
Everglades: *swamp*, U.S.A. **51** 26N 81W
Evergreen Park: *town*, U.S.A. **57** 42N 88W
Evora: Portugal **69** 39N 8W
Evreux: France **68** 49N 1E
Exe: *r.*, England **67** 51N 4W
Exeter: England **67** 51N 4W
Exmoor: England **67** 51N 4W
Exmouth Gulf: Austl. **94** 22S 114E
Eyre, Lake: Australia **94** 28S 137E

F

Fada: Chad **101** 17N 22E
Fäeroe Is.: Atl. O. **103** 62N 7W
Fagersta: Sweden **70** 60N 16E
Faguibine, L.: Mali. **100** 16N 4W
Fairfax City: U.S.A. **57** 39N 77W
Fairfield: U.S.A. **57** 42N 88W
Fair Isle: Scotland **67** 59N 2W
Fair Lawn: U.S.A. **56** 41N 74W
Fairmont: U.S.A. **51** 40N 80W
Faith: U.S.A. **53** 45N 102W
Faizabad: Afghan. **83** 37N 71E
Faizabad: India **84** 27N 82E
Falkirk: Scotland **67** 56N 4W
Falkland Is.: Atl. O. **60** 52S 60W
Falköping: Sweden **70** 58N 13E
Fall River: *city*, U.S.A. **55** 42N 71W
Falls Church City: U.S.A. **57** 39N 77W
Falmouth: England **67** 50N 5W
Famagusta: Cyprus **82** 35N 34E
Fangcheng: China **88** 33N 113E
Fangxian: China **88** 32N 111E
Fanning I.: *now* Tabaueran
Faradofay: Madagascar **102** 25S 47E
Farasan Is.: Red Sea **82** 17N 42E
Farewell, Cape: Greenland **13** 60N 44W
Farewell, Cape: N.Z. **95** 40S 173E
Fargo: U.S.A. **53** 47N 97W
Faribault: U.S.A. **53** 44N 93W
Farmington: U.S.A. **52** 37N 108W
Faro: Portugal **69** 37N 8W
Farrukhabad: India **84** 27N 80E
Fars: *reg.*, Iran **83** 29N 51E
Fastov: U.S.S.R. **70** 50N 30E
Faya-Largeau: Chad **101** 18N 19E
Fayette: U.S.A. **51** 34N 88W
Fayetteville: Ark., U.S.A. **50** 36N 94W
Fayetteville: N.C., U.S.A. **51** 35N 79W
Fayid: Egypt **101** *Inset*
F'Dérik: Mauritania **100** 23N 13W
Fear, C.: U.S.A. **51** 34N 78W
Fécamp: France **68** 50N 0
Feilding: N.Z. **95** 40S 176E
Feira de Santana: Brazil **60** 12S 39W
Feldkirch: Austria **71** 47N 10E
Fen: *r.*, China **88** 36N 112E
Fengcheng: China **89** 28N 116E
Fengzehn: China **88** 40N 113E
Fens, The: *reg.* Eng. **67** 53N 0
Fenyang: China **88** 37N 112E
Fergana: U.S.S.R. **81** 40N 72E
Fergus Falls: *city*, U.S.A. **53** 46N 96W
Ferrara: Italy **71** 45N 12E
Fès: Morocco **100** 34N 5W
Fethiye: Turkey **82** 36N 29E
Fianarantsoa: Madagascar **102** 22S 47E
Fife Ness: Scotland **67** 56N 3W
FIJI:*cap.* Suva **104** 18S 178E
Filchner Ice Shelf: Antarctica **128** 78S 50W
Findlay: U.S.A. **51** 41N 84W
Finisterre, Cape: Sp. **69** 43N 9W
FINLAND:*cap.* Helsinki **70** — —
Finschhafen: Papua New Guinea **94** 7S 148E
Fiordland: *district*, N.Z. **95** 46S 167E
Firenze: *see* Florence
Firozabad: India **84** 27N 78E
Fishguard: Wales **67** 52N 5W
Fitchburg: U.S.A. **55** 43N 72W
Fitzroy: *r.*, W. Austl. **94** 18S 124E
Flagstaff: U.S.A. **52** 35N 112W
Flamborough Head: England **67** 54N 0
Flathead L.: U.S.A. **52** 48N 114W
Flattery, C.: U.S.A. **52** 48N 125W
Fleetwood: England **67** 54N 3W
Flensburg: W. Germany **70** 55N 9E
Flers: France **68** 49N 1W
Flinders: *r.*, Australia **94** 20S 141E
Flinders Range: Australia **94** 31S 139E
Flint: U.S.A. **51** 43N 84W
Flint: *r.*, U.S.A. **51** 31N 85W
Florence (Firenze): Italy **71** 44N 11E
Florence: Alabama, U.S.A. **51** 35N 88W
Florence: Arizona, U.S.A. **52** 33N 111W
Florence: S.C., U.S.A. **51** 34N 80W
Florencia: Colombia **60** 2N 76W
Flores: *i. & sea*, Indonesia **91** 9S 121E
Floreshty: U.S.S.R. **70** 48N 28E
Floriano: Brazil **60** 7S 43W
Florianópolis: Brazil **61** 27S 48W
Florida: *State*, U.S.A. **51** 28N 82W
Florida, Straits of: U.S.A. **51** 24N 81W
Florida Keys: *is.*, U.S.A. **51** 25N 81W
Flórina: Greece **71** 41N 21E
Flushing: *see* Vlissingen
Fly: *r.*, Papua New Guinea **94** 8S 142E
Focşani: Romania **71** 46N 27E
Foggia: Italy **71** 41N 16E
Foligno: Italy **71** 43N 13E
Folkestone: England **67** 51N 1E
Fond du Lack: U.S.A. **53** 44N 88W
Foochow: *see* Fuzhou
Forel, Mt.: Greenland **1** 67N 37W
Forfar: Scotland **67** 57N 3W
Forli: Italy **71** 44N 12E
Formentera: *i.*, Balearic Is. **69** 38N 1E
Formosa: Argentina **61** 26S 58W
Formosa Strait **89** 24N 121E
Forrest: Australia **94** 31S 128E
Forrest City: U.S.A. **50** 35N 91W
Forsayth: Australia **94** 19S 144E
Forsyth: U.S.A. **52** 46N 107W
Fortaleza: Brazil **60** 4S 38W
Fort Collins: U.S.A. **52** 41N 105W
Fort Dauphin: *see* Faradofay
FORT-DE-FRANCE: Martinique **59** 15N 61W
Fort Dodge: U.S.A. **53** 43N 94W
Fortescue: *r.*, Austl. **94** 22S 118E
Forth, Firth of: Scot. **67** 56N 3W
Fort Lauderdale: U.S.A. **51** 26N 80W
Fort Madison: U.S.A. **50** 41N 91W
Fort Morgan: U.S.A. **53** 40N 104W
Fort Myers: U.S.A. **51** 27N 82W
Fort Peck Res.: U.S.A. **52** 47N 107W
Fort Pierce: U.S.A. **51** 27N 80W
Fort Sandeman: Pakistan **84** 31N 70E
Fort Shevchenko: U.S.S.R. **80** 45N 50E
Fort Smith: U.S.A. **50** 35N 94W
Fort Sumner: U.S.A. **53** 34N 104W
Fort Wayne: U.S.A. **51** 41N 85W
Fort William: Scotland **67** 57N 5W
Fort Worth: U.S.A. **50** 33N 97W
Fort Yukon: U.S.A. **1** 67N 145W
Foshan: China **89** 23N 113E
Fougères: France **68** 48N 1W
Foul Bay: Red Sea **82** 23N 36E
Foulwind, C.: N.Z. **95** 42S 172E
Fourmies: France **68** 50N 4E
Foveaux Strait: N.S. **95** 47S 168E
Foyle, L.: Ireland **67** 55N 7W
Framingham: U.S.A. **55** 42N 71W
FRANCE: *cap.* Paris **68/9** — —
Francistown: Bots. **102** 21S 27E
Frankfort: Indiana, U.S.A. **51** 40N 86W
Frankfort: Kentucky, U.S.A. **51** 33N 85W
Frankfurt am Main: W. Germany **68** 50N 9E
Frankfurt an der Oder: E. Germany **70** 52N 15E
Franklin D. Roosevelt Lake: U.S.A. **52** 48N 118W
Franklin Park: U.S.A. **57** 42N 88W
Franz Josef Land: U.S.S.R. **78/9** 80N 55E
Fraserburgh: Scotland **67** 58N 2W
Fray Bentos: Uruguay **61** 33S 58W
Frederick: U.S.A. **50** 34N 99W
Fredericksburg: U.S.A. **51** 38N 78W
Frederikshavn: Den. **70** 57N 11E
Frederikstad: Norway **70** 59N 11E
Freeport: N.Y., U.S.A. **56** 41N 74W
Freeport: Texas, U.S.A. **50** 29N 97W
FREETOWN: Sierra Leone **100** 7N 13W
Freiburg: W. Germany **68** 48N 8E
Freising: W. Germany **70** 48N 12E
Fremantle: Australia **94** 32S 116E
Fremont: U.S.A. **53** 41N 97W
FRENCH GUIANA: *cap.* Cayenne **60** 4N 53W
Frenchman Creek: U.S.A. **53** 40N 102W
Fresnillo: Mexico **58** 23N 103W
Fresno: U.S.A. **52** 37N 120W
Frisian Is., North: W. Germany **68** 55N 8E
Frisian Is.: Neth. **68** 53N 5E
Frome, Lake: Austl. **94** 31S 140E
Frosinone: Italy **71** 42N 13E
Frunze: U.S.S.R. **81** 43N 75E
Frýdek Mistek: Czech. **70** 50N 18E
Fuerteventura: *i.*, Canary Islands **100** 29N 14W
Fujian (Fukien): *Prov.*, China **89** 26N 118E
Fuji San: *mtn.*, Japan **90** 35N 139E
Fukien: *Prov.*, *see* Fujian
Fukui: Japan **90** 36N 136E
Fukuoka: Japan **90** 34N 130E
Fukushima: Japan **90** 38N 140E
Fukuyama: Japan **90** 34N 133E
Fulda: W. Ger. **70** 50N 10E
Fuling: China **89** 30N 107E
Fulton: U.S.A. **53** 39N 92W
Funchal: Madeira **100** 33N 17W
Furneaux Group: *is.*, Australia **94** 40S 148E
Fushun: China **87** 42N 124E
Fuyang: China **88** 33N 116E
Fuzhou (Foochow): China **89** 26N 118E
Fyn: *i.*, Denmark **68** 55N 10E
Fyne, L.: Scotland **67** 56N 5W

G

Gabès: *& gulf*, Tunisia **100** 34N 11E
GABON: *cap.* Libreville **102** 2N 12E
GABORONE: Botswana **102** 24S 26E
Gabrovo: Bulgaria **71** 43N 25E
Gadames: Libya **100** 30N 10E
Gadsden: U.S.A. **51** 34N 86W
Gaffney: U.S.A. **51** 35N 81W
Gages Lake: *town*, U.S.A. **57** 42N 88W
Gaillard Cut: Panama Canal **58** *Inset*
Gainesville: Georgia, U.S.A. **51** 34N 84W
Gainesville: Texas, U.S.A. **50** 34N 97W
Gainsville: Florida, U.S.A. **51** 30N 82W
Gairdner, L: Austl. **94** 32S 136E
Gaixian: China **88** 40N 122E
Galápagos Is.: Pacific O: **105** 1S 91W
Galashiels: Scotland **67** 56N 3W
Galati: Romania **71** 45N 28E
Galesburg: U.S.A. **50** 41N 90W
Galilee, Sea of: Israel **82** 33N 36E
Galle: Sri Lanka **84** 6N 80E
Gallinas, Pta: *cape.*, Colombia **59** 13N 72W
Gällivare: Sweden **70** 67N 21E
Gallup: U.S.A. **52** 36N 109W
Gal Oya: Sri Lanka **84** 8N 81E
Galveston: *& bay*, U.S.A. **50** 30N 95W
Galway: *& bay*, R. of Ireland **67** 53N 9W
GAMBIA, THE: *cap.* Banjul **100** 13N 15W
Gambier: *r.*, Gambier **100** 13N 13W
Gambier Is.: Pac. O. **105** 22S 135W
Gand: *see* Gent
Gandak: *r.*, India **84** 27N 85E
Ganga (Ganges): *r.*, Bangl./India **84** 25N 86E
Gansu (Kansu): *Prov.*, China **88** 36N 108E
Ganzhou: China **89** 26N 115E
Gaokeng: China **89** 27N 114E
Gacyao: *see* Zhaoqing
Gap: France **69** 45N 6E
Garden City: N.Y., U.S.A. **56** 41N 74W
Gardez: Afghan. **83** 34N 69E
Gardner I.: *now* Nikumaroro
Garfield: U.S.A. **56** 41N 74W
Gargano, C.: Italy **70** 42N 16E
Garian: Libya **100** 2N 13E
Garnett: U.S.A. **53** 38N 95W
Garonne: *r.*, France **69** 45N 0
Garoua: Cameroun **100** 9N 13E
Gartok: China **84** 32N 80E
Gary: U.S.A. **57** 42N 86W
Gastonia: U.S.A. **51** 35N 81W
Gata, C. de: Spain **69** 37N 2W
Gateshead: England **67** 55N 2W
Gatun Lake: *& locks*, Panama Canal **58** *Inset*
Gauhati: India **84** 26N 92E
Gävle: Sweden **70** 61N 17E
Gaya: India **84** 25N 85E
Gaya: Niger **100** 12N 4E
Gaza: Egypt **82** 31N 34E
Gaziantep: Turkey **82** 37N 37E
Gdánsk: *& Gulf*, Poland **70** 54N 19E
Gdynia: Poland **70** 55N 18E
Geelong: Australia **94** 38S 144E
Geissen: W. Germany **68** 51N 9E
Gela: Sicily **71** 37N 14E
Gelibolu: Turkey **71** 10N 27E
Gelsenkirchen: W. Ger. **68** 51N 7E
Geneva: *& l.*, Switz. **69** 46N 6E
Genoa: Italy **69** 44N 9E
Gent (Gand, Ghent): Belgium **68** 51N 4E
GEORGETOWN: Guyana **60** 7N 58W
George Town: Mal. **85** 5N 100E
Georgetown: U.S.A. **51** 33N 79W
Georgia: *State*, U.S.A. **51** 33N 84W
Georgian S.S.R.: U.S.S.R. **80** 43N 45E
Gera: E. Germany **70** 51N 12E
Geraldton: Australia **94** 29S 115E
GERMANY, EAST *cap.* Berlin **70** — —
GERMANY, WEST:*cap.* Bonn **68/70** — —
Gerona: Spain **69** 42N 3E
Gettysburg: U.S.A. **51** 40N 77W
GHANA: *cap.* Accra **100** 7N 0
Ghardaïa: Algeria **100** 33N 4E
Ghaziabad: India **84** 29N 77E
Ghazipur: India **84** 26N 83E
Ghent: *see* Gent
Gheorghe Gheorghiu-Dej: Rom. **71** 46N 27E
GIBRALTAR: *& strait* **69** 36N 5W
Gibson Desert: Austl. **94** 24S 124E
Gifu: Japan **90** 35N 137E
Gijón: Spain **69** 44N 6W
Gila: *r.*, U.S.A. **52** 33N 113W
Gila Bend: U.S.A. **52** 33N 113W
Gilbert: *r.*, Australia **94** 17S 142E
Gilbert Is.: *now* **KIRIBATI**
Gilgit: India **84** 36N 74E
Gineifa: Egypt **101** *Inset*
Ginir: Ethiopia **101** 7N 41E
Gippsland: *reg.*, Austl. **94** 38S 148E
Girga: Egypt **82** 26N 32E
Gironde: *r.*, France **69** 45N 1W
Gisborne: N.Z. **95** 39S 178E
Giurgiu: Romania **71** 44N 26E
Giza: Egypt **82** 30N 31E
Gjinokastër: Albania **71** 40N 20E
Gladbeck: W. Germany **68** 52N 7E
Gladstone: Australia **94** 24S 151E
Glasgow: Ky., U.S.A. **51** 37N 86W
Glasgow: Montana, U.S.A. **52** 48N 107W
Glasgow: Scotland **67** 56N 4W
Glazov: U.S.S.R. **80** 58N 53E
Glencoe: Ill., U.S.A. **57** 42N 88W
Glencoe: Minn., U.S.A. **53** 45N 94W
Glen Cove: U.S.A. **56** 41N 74W
Glen Ellyn: U.S.A. **57** 42N 88W
Glen Ridge: U.S.A. **56** 41N 74W
Glenview: U.S.A. **57** 42N 88W
Glenwood: U.S.A. **53** 46N 95W
Gliwice: Poland **70** 50N 19E
Globe: U.S.A. **52** 33N 111W
Gloucester: England **67** 52N 2W
Gloucester: U.S.A. **55** 43N 71W
Gloversville: U.S.A. **55** 43N 74W
Gniezno: Poland **70** 53N 18E
Goa: *Union Territ.*, India **84** 15N 74E
Gobi Desert: Mong. **86/87** 43N 105E
Godavari: *r.*, India **84** 18N 81E
GODTHAAB: *now* NUUK
Goiânia: Brazil **60** 17S 49W
Goiás Massif: Brazil **60** 15S 48W
Gold Coast: Austl. **94** 28S 153E
Golden Bay: N.Z. **95** 41S 173E
Gomati: *r.*, India **84** 26N 82E
Gomel: U.S.S.R. **80** 53N 31E
Gómez Palacio: Mexico **58** 26N 103W
Gondar: Ethiopia **100** 13N 37E
Good Hope, C. of: S. Africa **102** 34S 18E
Goodland: U.S.A. **53** 39N 103W
Goondiwindi: Austl. **94** 29S 150E
Goose L.: U.S.A. **52** 42N 120W
Gorakhpur: India **84** 27N 83E
Gore: Ethiopia **101** 8N 36E
Gore: N.Z. **95** 46S 169E
Gorizia: Italy **71** 46N 14E
Gor'kiy: U.S.S.R. **80** 56N 44E
Görlitz: E. Germany **70** 51N 15E
Gorno-Altaysk: U.S.S.R. **81** 52N 86E
Gorzów Wielkopolski: Poland **70** 53N 15E
Göta: *r.*, Sweden **70** 58N 12E
Göteborg: Sweden **70** 58N 12E
Gotha: E. Germany **70** 51N 11E
Gotland: *i.*, Sweden **70** 57N 19E
Göttingen: W. Germany **70** 52N 10E
Gottwaldov: Czech. **70** 49N 18E
Goulburn: Australia **94** 35S 150E
Gouverneur: U.S.A. **51** 44N 76W
Governador Valadores: Brazil **60** 19S 42W
Goya: Argentina **61** 29S 59W
Gozo: *i.*, Medit. Sea **71** 36N 14E
Gracias á Dios, C.: Nicaragua **59** 15N 83W
Grafton: Australia **94** 30S 153E
Grafton: U.S.A. **53** 48N 98W
Graham: U.S.A. **50** 33N 99W
Grampians: *mtns.*, Scotland **67** 57N 4W
Granada: Spain **69** 37N 4W
Gran Canaria: *i.*, Canary Is. **100** 28N 15W
Gran Chaco: *reg.*, Arg./Paraguay **60** 25S 61W
Grand: *r.*, U.S.A. **53** 46N 102W
Grand Bahama I.: The Bahamas **59** 27N 79W
Grand Canyon: *& city*, U.S.A. **52** 36N 112W
Grand Coulee: U.S.A. **52** 48N 119W
Grande Ronde: *r.*, U.S.A. **52** 46N 118W
Grand Forks: U.S.A. **53** 48N 97W
Grand Island: *city*, U.S.A. **53** 41N 98W
Grand Junction: U.S.A. **52** 39N 109W
Grand Rapids: *city*, Mich., U.S.A. **51** 43N 86W
Grand Rapids: *city*, Minn., U.S.A. **53** 47N 94W
Grant, Mt.: U.S.A. **52** 38N 119W
Grantham: England **67** 53N 1W
Grants Pass: *city*, U.S.A. **52** 42N 123W
Grasse: France **69** 44N 7E
Grays Harbor: *bay*, U.S.A. **52** 47N 124W
Grayslake: U.S.A. **57** 42N 88W
Graz: Austria **71** 47N 15E
Great Abaco I.,: The Bahamas **59** 27N 11W
Great Australian Bight **94** 33S 130E
Great Barrier I.: New Zealand **95** 36S 175E
Great Barrier Reef: Australia **94** 17S 147E
Great Bend: U.S.A. **53** 38N 99W
Great Bitter Lake: Egypt **101** *Inset*
Great Dividing Range: Australia **94** — —
Greater Antilles: W. Indies **59** 18N 75W
Great Eastern Erg: *desert*. Algeria **100** 30N 8E
Great Falls: *city*, U.S.A. **52** 47N 111W
Great Himalayan Range: Asia **84** — —
Great Inagua I.,: The Bahamas **59** 21N 74W
Great Karroo: *plat.*, S. Africa **102** 33S 23E
Great Khingan Mts.: *see* Danlinganjing
Great Neck: U.S.A. **56** 41N 74W
Great Salt Lake: *& Desert*, U.S.A. **52** 41N 113W

Great Sandy Desert: Australia **94** 21S 124E
Great South Bay: U.S.A. **56** 41N 74W
Great Victoria Desert: Australia **94** 28S 130E
Great Wall: China **87** 41N 114E
Great Western Erg: *desert*, Algeria **100** 30N 0
Great Yarmouth: England **67** 53N 2E
GREECE: *cap.* Athens **71** 40N 23E
Greeley: U.S.A. **53** 40N 105W
Green: *r.*, U.S.A. **52** 40N 110W
Greenbelt: U.S.A. **57** 39N 77W
Greenock: Scotland **67** 56N 5W
Green Bay: *& city*, U.S.A. **53** 45N 88W
GREENLAND: *cap.* Nuuk **1** 70N 40W
Green Mts.: U.S.A. **55** 43N 73W
Green River: *city*, U.S.A. **52** 42N 110W
[illegible]
Greenville: Ala., U.S.A. **51** 32N 87W
Greenville: Miss., U.S.A. **50** 33N 91W
Greenville: S.C., U.S.A. **51** 35N 82W
Greenville: Tenn., U.S.A. **51** 36N 83W
Greenville: Texas, U.S.A. **50** 33N 96W
Greenwich: U.S.A. **56** 41N 74W
Greenwood: Miss., U.S.A. **50** 34N 90W
Greenwood: S.C., U.S.A. **51** 34N 82W
GRENADA: *cap.* St. George's **59** 12N 62W
Grenadines, The: *is.*, *see* St. Vincent and the Grenadines
Grenoble: France **69** 45N 6E
Gretna Green: Scotland **67** 55N 3W
Greymouth: N.Z. **95** 42S 171E
Griffin: U.S.A. **51** 33N 84W
Grimsby: England **67** 54N 0
Grodno: U.S.S.R. **70** 54N 24E
Groningen: Neth. **68** 53N 7E
Groote Eylandt: *i.*, Australia **94** 14S 137E
Grosseto: Italy **71** 43N 11E
Groznyy: U.S.S.R. **80** 43N 46E
Grudziądz: Poland **70** 53N 18E
Guadalajara: Mexico **58** 21N 103W
Guadalajara: Spain **69** 41N 3W
Guadalcanal: *i.*, Solomon Is. **104** 10S 160E
Guadalquivir: *r.*, Spain **69** 37N 6W
Guadalupe: *i.*, Pac. O. **105** 29N 118W
Guadalupe: *r.*, U.S.A. **50** 29N 97W
Guadeloupe: *i.*, W. Indies **59** 16N 61W
Guadiana: *r.*, Spain/Portugal **69** 38N 8W
Gualeguaychu: Argentina **61** 33S 58W
Guam: *i.*, Pacific O. **104** 14N 145E
Guanajuato: Mexico **58** 21N 101W
Guang'an: China **89** 30N 107E
Guangdong (Kwangtung): *Prov.*, China **89** 23N 113E
Guangfeng: China **89** 28N 118E
Guanghua: China **88** 32N 112E
Guangzhou (Canton): China **89** 23N 113E
Guantánamo: Cuba **59** 20N 75W
Guanxi Zhuang (Kwangsi Chuang): *Prov.*, China **89** 24N 108E
Guarapuava: Brazil **61** 25S 52W
Guarda: Portugal **69** 41N 7W
GUATEMALA: *cap.* Guatemala **59** 15N 91W
Guayaquil: *& gulf*, Ecuador **60** 2S 80W
Guaymas: Mexico **58** 28N 111W
Gubakha: U.S.S.R. **81** 58N 57E
Guéret: France **69** 46N 2E
Guernsey: *i.*, Channel Islands **68** 50N 2W
Guiding: China **89** 26N 107E
Guildford: England **67** 51N 1W
Guilin: China **89** 25N 110E
GUINEA: *cap.* Conakry **100** 11N 1W
Guinea, G. of **100** 3N 0
GUINEA-BISSAU: *cap.* Bissau **100** 12N 15W
Guiyang: China **89** 26N 107E
Guizhou (Kweichow): *Prov.*, China **89** 26N 107E
Gujarat: *State*, India **84** 23N 72E
Gujranwala: Pakistan **84** 32N 74E
Gulbarga: India **84** 17N 77E
Gulf, The (Persian Gulf) **83** 27N 52E
Gulfport: U.S.A. **51** 30N 89W
Gulu: Uganda **102** 7S 32E
Guntersville L.: U.S.A. **51** 34N 86W
Guntur: India **84** 16N 80E
Gunungsitoli: Indon. **85** 1N 98E
Gurgan: Iran **83** 37N 55E
Gur'yev: U.S.S.R. **80** 47N 52E
Gushi: China **88** 32N 116E
GUYANA: *cap.* Georgetown **60** 5N 58W
Guyana Highlands: S. America **60** 3N 60W
Guymon: U.S.A. **50** 37N 101W
Gwalior: India **84** 26N 78E
Gyaze: China **84** 29N 90E
Gyda Peninsula: U.S.S.R. **79** 71N 77E
Gydan Range (Kolyma Ra.): U.S.S.R. **79** 62N 160E
Gympie: Australia **94** 26S 153E
Gyöngyös: Hungary **71** 48N 20E

H

Haarlem: Neth. **68** 52N 5E
Haast: *& Pass*, N.Z. **95** 44S 169E
Hab: *r.*, Pakistan **84** 25N 67E
Habbaniyah: Iraq **83** 34N 43E
Hachinohe: Japan **90** 40N 141E
Hackensack: *& r.*, U.S.A. **56** 41N 74W
Haddington: Scotland **67** 56N 3W
Hadhramaut: *valley*, Yemen P.D.R. **83** 16N 48E
Hadibu: Socotra **83** 13N 54E
Hadithah: Iraq **82** 34N 42E
Hagen: W. Germany **68** 51N 7E
Hagi: Japan **90** 34N 131E
Ha Giang: Vietnam **85** 23N 105E
HAGUE, THE (S'Gravenhage) Netherlands **68** 52N 4E
Haifa: Israel **82** 33N 35E
Haikou: China **85** 20N 110E
Hail: Saudi Arabia **82** 27N 42E
Hailar: China **87** 49N 120E
Haimen: China **89** 29N 121E
Hainan: *i.*, China **85** 19N 110E
Haines: U.S.A. **22** 59N 135W
Haining (Xiashi): China **89** 31N 121E
Haiphong: Vietnam **85** 21N 107E
HAITI: *cap.* Port-au-Prince **59** 19N 73W
Haizhou: *see* Donghai
Hajara: *desert*, Sau. Arabia **82** 31N 42E
Hajnówka: Poland **70** 53N 24E
Hakodate: Japan **90** 42N 141E
Halaib: Sudan **82** 22N 36E
Halberstadt: E. Ger. **70** 52N 11E
Halifax: England **67** 54N 2W
Halle: E. Germany **70** 51N 12E
Hall's Creek: *town*, Australia **94** 18S 128E
Halmahera: *i.*, Indon. **91** 1N 128E
Halmstad: Sweden **70** 57N 13E
Hälsingborg: Sweden **70** 56N 13E
Hama: Syria **82** 35N 37E
Hamada: Japan **91** 35N 132E
[illegible]
Hamamatsu: Japan **90** 35N 138E
Hambantota: Sri Lanka **84** 7N 81E
Hamburg: W. Ger. **70** 54N 10E
Hamersley Range: Australia **94** 22S 118E
Hami (Komul): China **86** 43N 93E
Hamilton: N.Z. **95** 38S 175E
Hamilton: Scotland **67** 56N 4W
Hamilton: U.S.A. **51** 39N 85W
Hamlin: U.S.A. **50** 33N 100W
Hammerfest: Norway **70** 71N 24E
Hammond: U.S.A. **57** 42N 86W
Hampton: U.S.A. **51** 37N 76W
Hancock: U.S.A. **53** 47N 88W
Handa: Japan **90** 35N 137E
Handan: China **88** 37N 114E
Hanford: U.S.A. **52** 36N 120W
Hangzhou (Hangchow): China **89** 30N 120E
Hanjiang: China **89** 26N 119E
Hanko: Finland **70** 60N 23E
Hankou: China **89** 31N 114E
Hannibal: U.S.A. **53** 40N 91W
HANOI: Vietnam **85** 21N 106E
Hanover (Hannover): W. Germany **70** 52N 10E
Hanyang: China **89** 31N 114E
Hanzhong: China **88** 33N 107E
Haogoundou, L.: Mali **100** 15N 3W
Haradh: Saudi Arabia **83** 24N 49E
Harar: Ethiopia **101** 9N 42E
HARARE: (*formerly* Salisbury) Zimbabwe **102** 18S 31E
Harbin: China **87** 46N 127E
Hargeisa: Somali Republic **101** 10N 44E
Harlingen: U.S.A. **50** 26N 98W
Harney Basin: U.S.A. **52** 43N 120W
Harris: *i.*, Scotland **67** 58N 7W
Harrisburg: U.S.A. **54** 40N 77W
Harrisonburg: U.S.A. **51** 39N 79W
Harrogate: England **67** 54N 2W
Hartford: U.S.A. **55** 42N 73W
Hartland Pt.: England **67** 51N 5W
Hartlepool: England **67** 55N 1W
Harvey: Ill. U.S.A. **57** 41N 88W
Harvey: N. Dak. U.S.A. **57** 47N 100W
Harwell: England **67** 52N 1W
Harwich: England **67** 52N 1E
Harwood Heights: U.S.A. **57** 42N 88W
Haryana: *State*, India **84** 29N 76E
Harz: *mtns.*, E & W Germany **70** 52N 11E
Hasa: *reg.*, Saudi Arabia **83** 27N 48E
Haskovo: Bulgaria **71** 42N 26E
Hassan: India **84** 13N 76E
Hassi Messaoud: Alg. **100** 32N 6E
Hastings: England **67** 51N 1E
Hastings: N.Z. **95** 40S 177E
Hastings: U.S.A. **53** 41N 98W
Ha Tinh: Vietnam **85** 18N 106E
Hatteras, C.: U.S.A. **51** 35N 75W
Hattiesburg: U.S.A. **51** 31N 89W
Hat Yai: Thailand **85** 7N 100E
Haugesund: Norway **68** 59N 5E
Hauraki Gulf: N.Z. **95** 37S 175E
Hauta: Saudi Arabia **83** 23N 47E
HAVANA (LA HABANA): Cuba **59** 23N 82W
Havre: U.S.A. **52** 48N 110W
Hawaii: *i.* & *State*., Pacific O., U.S.A. **105** 20N 155W
Hawaiian Is.: *arch.*, Pacific Ocean **104/105** 20N 160W
Hawera: N.Z. **95** 40S 174E
Hawke Bay: N.Z. **95** 39S 177E
Hawthorne: Nev., U.S.A. **52** 38N 119W
Hawthorne: N.J., U.S.A. **56** 41N 74W
Hayden: U.S.A. **52** 33N 111W
Hays: U.S.A. **53** 39N 99W
Hazaribagh: India **84** 24N 85E
Hazleton: U.S.A. **54** 41N 76W
Hebei (Hopeh): *Prov.*, China **88** 39N 116E
Hefei: China **88** 32N 117E
Hegang: China **87** 47N 130E
Heidelberg: W. Ger. **68** 49N 9E
Heilbronn: W. Germany **70** 49N 9E
Helena: Ark., U.S.A. **51** 35N 91W
Helena: Montana, U.S.A. **52** 47N 112W
Helensville: N.Z. **95** 37S 174E
Heligoland (Helgoland): *i.*, W. Germany **68** 54N 8E
Heligoland Bight: W. Germany **68** 54N 8E
Hellin: Spain **69** 39N 2W
Helmsdale: *r.*, Scotland **67** 58N 4W
HELSINKI (Helsingfors): Finland **70** 60N 25E
Hempstead: U.S.A. **56** 41N 74W
Henan (Honan): *Prov.*, China **88** 34N 113E
Henderson: Ky., U.S.A. **51** 38N 88W
Henderson: Nv., U.S.A. **52** 36N 115W
Henderson: N.C., U.S.A. **51** 36N 78W
Hengelo: Netherlands **68** 52N 7E
Hengyang: China **89** 27N 112E
Henlopen, C.: U.S.A. **51** 39N 75W
Hennebont: France **68** 48N 3W
Henry, C.: U.S.A. **51** 37N 76W
Henzada: Burma **85** 17N 95E
Hepu (Lianzhou): China **89** 22N 109E
Herat: Afghanistan **83** 34N 62E
Hereford: England **67** 52N 3W
Hereford: U.S.A. **50** 35N 102W
Hermitage: N.Z. **95** 44S 170E
Herning: Denmark **70** 56N 9E
Hertford: England **67** 52N 0
Hexian: China **89** 24N 112E
Heysham: England **67** 54N 3W
Heze: China **88** 35N 115E
Hiawatha: U.S.A. **53** 40N 96W
Hibbing: U.S.A. **53** 47N 93W
Hicksville: U.S.A. **56** 41N 74W
Hidalgo del Parral: Mexico **58** 27N 106W
High Atlas: *mtns.*, Morocco **100** 31N 7W
Highland: Ind., U.S.A. **57** 42N 87W
Highland Park: Ill., U.S.A. **57** 42N 87W
Highlands, The: *reg.*, Scotland **67** 57N 5W
High Point: *city*, U.S.A. **51** 36N 80W
High Veld: *plat.*, S. Africa **102** 30S 28E
Hiiumaa (Khiumaa): *i.*, U.S.S.R. **70** 59N 23E
Hijaz: *reg.*, Saudi Arabia **82** 25N 39E
Hikone: Japan **90** 35N 136E
[illegible]
Hillah: Iraq **83** 32N 44E
Himachal Pradesh: *State*, India **84** 32N 77E
Himeji: Japan **90** 35N 135E
Himi: Japan **90** 37N 137E
Hindu Kush: *mtns.*, Afghanistan **83** 36N 70E
Hinsdale: U.S.A. **57** 42N 88W
Hirosaki: Japan **90** 41N 140E
Hiroshima: Japan **90** 34N 132E
Hispaniola: *i.*, W. Indies **59** 20N 70W
Hitachi: Japan **90** 37N 141E
Hjørring: Denmark **70** 57N 10E
Hobart: Australia **94** 43S 147E
Hobbs: U.S.A. **50** 32N 103W
Hoboken: U.S.A. **56** 41N 74W
Ho Chi Minh City (Saigon): Vietnam **85** 11N 107E
Hodeida: Yemen **82** 15N 43E
Hódmezövásárhely: Hungary **71** 46N 20E
Hof: W. Germany **70** 50N 12E
Hofi: *see* Hefei
Hokianga Harbour: *bay*, New Zealand **95** 36S 173E
Hokitika: N.Z. **95** 43S 171E
Hokkaido: *I.*, Japan **90** 43N 143E
Holbaek: Denmark **70** 56N 12E
Holderness: *penin.* England **67** 54N 0
Holdrege: U.S.A. **53** 40N 99W
Holguín: Cuba **59** 21N 76W
Holland: U.S.A. **51** 43N 86W
Holland: *see* Netherlands
Hollick-Kenyon Plat.: Antarctica **128** 78S 105W
Hollywood: California, U.S.A. **52** 34N 118W
Hollywood: Florida, U.S.A. **51** 26N 80W
Holstebro: Denmark **70** 56N 9E
Holyhead: Wales **67** 53N 5W
Holy I.: England **67** 56N 2W
Homestead: U.S.A. **51** 25N 80W
Homewood: U.S.A. **57** 42N 88W
Homs: Libya **100** 33N 14E
Homs: Syria **82** 35N 37E
Honan: *Prov.*, *see* Henan
HONDURAS: *cap.* Tegucigalpa **58/9** 15N 87W
Hönefoss: Norway **70** 60N 10E
Honghu: China **89** 30N 113E
Hongjiang: China **89** 27N 110E
HONG KONG: *cap.* Victoria **89** 22N 114E
Honshu: *i.*, Japan **90** 36N 137E
Hood, Mt.: U.S.A. **52** 45N 122W
Hooghly: *r.*, India **84** 22N 88E
Hopeh: *Prov.*, *see* Hebei
Hopewell: U.S.A. **51** 37N 77W
Hopkinsville: U.S.A. **51** 37N 87W
Hoquiam: U.S.A. **52** 47N 124W
Hormuz, Str. of: Iran/Oman **83** 27N 56E
Horn, Cape: Chile **60** 56S 67W
Hornell: U.S.A. **54** 42N 78W
Hoshangabad: India **84** 23N 78E
Hot Springs: Ark., U.S.A. **50** 35N 93W
Hot Springs: S. Dakota, U.S.A. **53** 43N 104W
Houghton Lake: U.S.A. **24** 44N 85W
Houma: China **88** 36N 111E
Houma: U.S.A. **50** 30N 91W
Houston: U.S.A. **50** 30N 95W
Hovd: Mongolia **79** 48N 91E
Howe, Cape: Australia **94** 37S 150E
Howrah: India **84** 23N 88E
Hoy: *i.*, Scotland **67** 59N 3W
Hradec Králové: Czech. **70** 50N 16E
Hsinchu: Taiwan **89** 25N 121E
Hsinhsiang: *see* Xinxiang
Huadian (Chaoyangchen): China **87** 43N 126E
Huaian: China **88** 33N 119E
Huainan (Hwainan): China **88** 33N 117E
Huaiyang: China **88** 34N 115E
Huaiyin: China **88** 34N 119E
Huaiyuan: China **88** 33N 117E
Hualien: Taiwan **89** 24N 121E
Huallaga: *r.*, Peru **60** 8S 76W
Huambo: Angola **102** 13S 16E
Huancayo: Peru **60** 12S 75W
Hubei (Hupeh): *Prov.*, China **89** 31N 112E
Hubli: India **84** 15N 75E
Huang: *r.*, China **88** 37N 118E
Huangchuan: China **88** 32N 115E
Huangshi: China **89** 30N 115E
Huangyan: China **89** 29N 121E
Huddersfield: England **67** 54N 2W
Hudson: *r.*, U.S.A. **55** 42N 74W
Hué: Vietnam **85** 16N 107E
Huelva: Spain **69** 37N 7W
Huesca: Spain **69** 42N 0
Hufhuf: Saudi Arabia **83** 25N 49E
Hughenden: Australia **94** 21S 144E
Huhhot (Kweisui): China **88** 41N 112E
Huiyang: China **89** 23N 114E
Huize: China **85** 26N 103E
Hull: England **67** 54N 0
Hulunchi: *I.*, China **87** 49N 118E
Humber: *r.*, England **67** 54N 0
Humboldt: *r.*, U.S.A. **52** 40N 119W
Humboldt Glacier: Greenland **1** 80N 63W
Hunan: *Prov.*, China **89** 27N 111E
Hunedoara: Romania **71** 46N 23E
HUNGARY:*cap.* Budapest **70/1** 47N 20E
Hunger Steppe: U.S.S.R. **81** 47N 70E
Huntingdon: England **67** 52N 0
Huntingdon: U.S.A. **56** 41N 74W
Huntington: Indiana, U.S.A. **51** 41N 86W
Huntington: W. Va., U.S.A. **51** 38N 82W
Huntly: N.Z. **95** 37S 175E
Huntsville: Alabama, U.S.A. **51** 35N 87W
Huntsville: Texas, U.S.A. **50** 31N 96W
Hunyuan: China **88** 40N 114E
Hupeh: *Prov.*, *see* Hubei
Huron: U.S.A. **53** 44N 98W
Hürth: W. Germany **68** 51N 7E
Hurunui: *r.*, N.Z. **95** 43S 172E
Huskvarna: Sweden **70** 58N 14E
Hutchinson: U.S.A. **53** 38N 98W
Huzhou: China **89** 31N 120E
Hwainan: *see* Huainan
Hwange (*formerly* Wankie): Zimbabwe **102** 18S 26E
Hwang (Yellow): *r.*, *see* Huang
[illegible]
Hyderabad: *& reg.*, India **84** 17N 78E
Hyderabad: Pakistan **84** 25N 68E
Hyères: France **69** 43N 6E
Hyuga: Japan **90** 32N 132E

I

Iaşi: Romania **71** 47N 28E
Ibadan: Nigeria **100** 7N 4E
Ibagué: Colombia **60** 4N 75W
Ibiza: *i.* & *town*, Balearic Is. **69** 39N 2E
Ica: Peru **60** 14S 76W
ICELAND: *cap.* Reykjavík **103** — —
Ichikawa: Japan **90** 36N 140E
Ichinomiya: Japan **90** 35N 137E
Ichinoseki: Japan **90** 39N 141E
Idaho: *State*, U.S.A. **52** 44N 115W
Idaho Falls: *city*, U.S.A. **52** 43N 112W
Igarka: U.S.S.R. **79** 67N 86E
Iglesias: Sardinia **69** 39N 8E
Iguaçu: *r.*, Brazil **61** 25S 54W
Iguala: Mexico **58** 18N 100W
Iida: Japan **90** 36N 138E
Iizuka: Japan **90** 34N 131E
Ijsselmeer (Zuider Zee): Netherlands **68** 53N 5E
Ikaria: *i.*, Greece **71** 38N 26E
Ilebo: Zaïre **102** 4S 21E
Ilfracombe: England **67** 51N 4W
Ilhéus: Brazil **60** 15S 39W
Iligan: Philippines **91** 8N 124E
Illinois: *State*, U.S.A. **50/51** 40N 90W
Il'men', L.: U.S.S.R. **80** 58N 32E
Iloilo: Philippines **91** 11N 122E
Ilorin: Nigeria **100** 9N 5E
Imabari: Japan **90** 34N 133E
Imatra: Finland **70** 61N 29E
Imperia: Italy **69** 44N 8E
Imphal: India **85** 25N 94E
Inari: *I.*, Finland **70** 69N 28E
Inchon: S. Korea **87** 37N 127E
Indaw: Burma **86** 24N 96E
Independence: U.S.A. **53** 37N 96W
INDIA (Bharat): *cap.* New Delhi **84/85** — —
Indiana: *State*, U.S.A. **51** 40N 86W
Indianapolis: U.S.A. **51** 40N 86W
Indigirka: *r.*, U.S.S.R. **79** 68N 146E
INDONESIA: *cap.* Jakarta **91** — —
Indore: India **84** 23N 76E
Indus: *r.*, S.W. Asia **84** 26N 68E
Ingolstadt: W. Germany **70** 49N 11E
Inn: *r.*, W. Germ./Austria **70** 47N 12E
Inner Mongolia: *see* Nei Monggol
Innisfail: Australia **94** 18S 146E
Innsbruck: Austria **71** 47N 11E
Inowrocław: Poland **70** 53N 18E
International Falls: *city*, U.S.A. **53** 48N 93W
Inverary: Scotland **67** 56N 5W
Invercargill: N.Z. **95** 46S 168E
Inverness: Scotland **67** 57N 4W
Ioánnina (Yannina): Greece **71** 40N 21E
Ionian Is.: Greece **71** 38N 20E
Ionian Sea **71** 38N 18E
Ios: *i.*, Greece **71** 37N 25E
Iowa: *State*, U.S.A. **53** 42N 93W
Iowa City: U.S.A. **53** 42N 92W
Ipoh: Malaysia **85** 5N 101E
Ipswich: England **67** 52N 1E
Iquique: Chile **60** 20S 70W
Iquitos: Peru **60** 4S 73W
Iraklion (Candia): Crete **71** 35N 25E
IRAN: *cap.* Tehrān **83** — —
Irapuato: Mexico **58** 21N 101W
IRAQ: *cap.* Baghdād **82/83** 33N 44E
IRELAND, REPUBLIC OF: *cap.* Dublin **67** — —
Irish Sea **67** 53N 5W
Irkutsk: U.S.S.R. **79** 52N 105E
Iron Gates: *gorge*, Yugo./Rom. **71** 45N 23E
Iron Knob: *town*, Australia **94** 33S 137E
Iron Mt.: U.S.A. **52** 43N 117W
Iron Mountain: *city*, U.S.A. **53** 46N 88W
Ironwood: U.S.A. **53** 46N 90W
Irawaddy: *r.*, Burma **85** 24N 96E
Irtysh: *r.*, U.S.S.R. **81** 57N 73E
Irvington: U.S.A. **56** 41N 74W
Ise: Japan **90** 34N 137E
Isère: *r.*, France **69** 45N 5E
Isfahan: Iran **83** 33N 52E
Ishim: *r.*, U.S.S.R. **81** 54N 67E
Ishimbay: U.S.S.R. **80** 53N 56E
Ishinomaki: Japan **90** 38N 141E
Ishpeming: U.S.A. **53** 46N 88W
Isiro: Zaïre **102** 3N 28E
Iskenderun: Turkey **82** 37N 36E
ISLAMABAD: Pakistan **84** 34N 73E
Islay: *i.*, Scotland **67** 55N 6W
Ismailia: Egypt **82** 30N 32E
Isna: Egypt **82** 25N 33E
ISRAEL: *cap.* Jerusalem **82** 32N 35E
Issyk-Kul': *I.*, U.S.S.R. **81** 42N 77E
Istanbul: Turkey **71** 41N 29E
Istra: *penin.*, Yugoslavia **71** 45N 14E
Itabuna: Brazil **60** 15S 39W
Itajai: Brazil **61** 27S 49W
ITALY: *cap.* Rome **69/71** — —
Itapetininga: Brazil **61** 24S 48W
Itasca: U.S.A. **57** 42N 88W
Ithaca: U.S.A. **54** 42N 77W

Ivano-Frankovsk: U.S.S.R. 70 49N 25E
Ivanovo: U.S.S.R. 80 57N 41E
Ivdel': U.S.S.R. 81 61N 60E
Iwaki: Japan 90 37N 141E
Iwakuni: Japan 90 34N 132E
Iwanuma: Japan 90 38N 141E
Izhevsk: U.S.S.R. 80 57N 53E
Izmir: Turkey 71 38N 27E
Izmit: Turkey 82 41N 30E
Izu-Shotō: *is.*, Japan 90 34N 139E

J

Jabal Akhdhar: *mtn.*, Oman 83 24N 57E
Jabalpur: India 84 23N 80E
Jabal Shammar: *plat.*, Saudi Arabia 82 27N 41E
Jabal Tuwaiq: *mtns.*, Saudi Arabia 83 25N 46E
Jablonec: Czechoslovakia 70 51N 15E
Jaca: Spain 69 43N 1W
Jackson: Mich., U.S.A. 51 42N 84W
Jackson: Miss., U.S.A. 50 32N 90W
Jackson: Tenn., U.S.A. 51 36N 89W
Jackson Bay: N.Z. 95 44S 169E
Jacksonville: Fla., U.S.A. 51 30N 82W
Jacksonville: Ill. U.S.A. 50 40N 90W
Jacobabad: Pakistan 84 28N 69E
Jaén: Spain 69 38N 4W
Jaffa: *see* Tel Aviv-Jaffa
Jaffna: Sri Lanka 84 10N 80E
Jaipur: India 84 27N 76E
Jaisalmer: India 84 27N 71E
JAKARTA (Djakarta): Indonesia 91 6S 107E
Jalalabad: Afghanistan 83 34N 71E
Jalapa: Mexico 58 20N 97W
JAMAICA: *cap.* Kingston 59 18N 77W
Jamaica Bay: U.S.A. 56 41N 74W
Jambi: Indonesia 91 2N 104E
Jambol: Bulgaria 71 12N 27E
James: *r.*, S. Dakota, U.S.A. 53 44N 98W
James: *r.*, Va., U.S.A. 51 37N 78W
Jamestown: N.Y., U.S.A. 51 42N 79W
Jamestown: N. Dakota, U.S.A. 53 47N 99W
Jammu: India 84 33N 75E
Jammul & Kashmir: *disputed State*, India 84 35N 77E
Jamnagar: India 84 22N 70E
Jamshedpur: India 84 23N 86E
Janesville: U.S.A. 53 43N 89W
JAPAN: *cap.* Tokyo 90 — —
Japan, Sea of 87 40N 135E
Japan Trench: Pacific Ocean 104 35N 145E
Japen: *i.*, Indonesia 94 2S 136E
Jasło: Poland 70 50N 22E
Jauf: Saudi Arabia 82 30N 40E
Java: *i. & sea*, Indon. 91 7S 110E
Jaxartes: *r.*, *see* Syr Dar'ya
Jayapura: Indonesia 95 3S 141E
Jebba: Nigeria 100 9N 4E
Jebel Aulia Dam: Sudan 82 15N 32E
Jebel el Akhdar: *hills*, Libya 82 32N 21E
Jedburgh: Scotland 67 55N 3W
Jeddah: Saudi Arabia 82 22N 39E
Jefferson City: U.S.A. 50 39N 92W
Jelenia Góra: Poland 51N 16E
Jena: E. Germany 70 51N 12E
Jerez: Spain 69 37N 6W
Jersey: *i.*, Channel Isles 68 49N 1W
Jersey City: U.S.A. 56 41N 74W
JERUSALEM: Israel/Jordan 82 32N 35E
Jessore: Bangladesh 84 23N 89E
Jesup: U.S.A. 51 32N 82W
Jhansi: India 84 25N 79E
Jhelum: *r.*, Pakistan 84 31N 72E
Jiamusi: China 87 47N 130E
Jian: China 89 27N 115E
Jiangmen: China 89 23N 113E
Jiangsu (Kiangsu): *Prov.*, China 88 33N 119E
Jiangxi (Kiangsi): *Prov.*, China 89 27N 115E
Jiangyan: China 88 32N 120E
Jiangyin: China 88 32N 120E
Jianou: China 89 27N 118E
Jianshi: China 89 31N 110E
Jiaoxian: China 88 36N 120E
Jiawang: China 88 34N 117E
Jiaxing: China 89 31N 121E
Jibhalanta: *see* Uliastay
Jieshou: China 88 33N 115E
Jieyang: China 89 24N 116E
Jihlava: Czechoslovakia 70 39N 16E
Jilin (Kirin): China 87 44N 126E
Jiménez: Mexico 58 27N 105W
Jinan (Tsinan): China 88 37N 117E
Jingdezhen: China 89 29N 117E
Jingjiang: China 88 32N 120E
Jinhua: China 89 29N 120E
Jining: China 87 35N 117E
Jinsha Jiang: *r.*, China 85 26N 103E
Jinshi: China 89 30N 112E
Jinxian: China 88 39N 122E
Jinzhou: China 88 41N 121E
Jiujiang: China 89 30N 116E
Jiuquam: China 86 40N 99E
Jixian: China 88 35N 114E
João Pessoa: Brazil 60 7S 35W
Jodhpur: India 84 26N 73E
Jofra Oasis: Libya 100 30N 15E
Jogjakarta: *see* Yogyakarta
Johannesburg: S Afr. 102 26S 28E
Johnson City: U.S.A. 51 36N 82W
Johnstown: U.S.A. 54 40N 79W
Johor Babru: Malaysia 85 1N 104E
Joinvile: Brazil 61 26S 49W
Joliet: U.S.A. 57 42N 88W
Jolo: *i.*, Philippines 91 6N 121E
Jonesboro: U.S.A. 50 36N 91W
Jonglei: Sudan 101 7N 31E
Jonköping: Sweden 70 58N 14E
Joplin: U.S.A. 50 37N 94W
JORDAN: *cap.* Amman 82 31N 37E
Jordan: *r.*, Israel/Jordan 82 32N 36E
Jorhat: India 85 27N 94E
Jos.: & *plateau*, Nigeria 100 10N 9E
Joseph Bonaparte Gulf: Australia 94 14S 128E
Jotunheimen: *mtns.*, Norway 70 61N 9E
Juan Fernández Is.: Pacific Ocean 60 34S 79W
Juba: Sudan 101 5N 32E
Juba: *r.*, Somali Rep 101 2N 42E
Júcar. *r.*, Spain 69 39N 1W
Juiz de Fora: Brazil 61 22S 43W
Jullundur: India 84 31N 76E
Junction City: U.S.A. 53 39N 97W
Juneau: U.S.A. 22 58N 134W
Junin: Argentina 61 35S 61W
Jur: *r.*, Sudan 101 9N 28E
Jura, The: *mtns.*, France/Switz. 69 47N 6E
Jura: *i. & sound*, Scotland 67 56N 6W
Juruá: *r.*, Brazil 60 5S 67W
Juruena: *r.*, Brazil 60 11S 58W
Juticalpa: Honduras 58 15N 86W
Jylland: *Reg.*, Den. 68 36N 9E

K

K2: *mtn.*, China/Kashmir 84 36N 77E
Kabaena. *i.*, Indonesia 91 5S 122E
KABUL: Afghanistan 83 35N 69E
Kabwe: Zambia 102 15S 29E
Kaduna: Nigeria 100 11N 7E
Kafue: Zambia 102 16S 28E
Kagoshima: Japan 90 32N 131E
Kaifeng: China 88 35N 115E
Kai Is.: Indonesia 91 6S 133E
Kaikohe: N.Z. 95 35S 174E
Kaikoura: & *Range*, N.Z. 95 42S 173E
Kailas Range: China 84 32N 81E
Kaimanawa Range: New Zealand 95 39S 176E
Kainji Dam: Nigeria 100 10N 5E
Kaipara Harbour: New Zealand 95 36S 174E
Kaiserslautern: W. Ger. 68 49N 8E
Kaitangata: N.Z. 95 46N 170E
Kakinada: India 84 17N 82E
Kalachinsk: U.S.S.R. 81 55N 75E
Kalahari Desert: Southern Africa 102 24S 23E
Kalamai: Greece 71 37N 22E
Kalamazoo: U.S.A. 51 42N 86W
Kalat: Pakistan 84 29N 67E
Kalemie: Zaïre 102 6S 29E
Kalgan: *see* Zhangjiakou
Kalgoorlie: Australia 94 31S 122E
Kalinin: U.S.S.R. 80 57N 36E
Kaliningrad: U.S.S.R. 70 55N 20E
Kalispell: U.S.A. 52 48N 114W
Kalisz: Poland 70 52N 18E
Kalmar: Sweden 70 57N 16E
Kaluga: U.S.S.R. 80 55N 36E
Kalush: U.S.S.R. 70 49N 25E
Kama: *r.*, U.S.S.R. 80 55N 51E
Kamaishi: Japan 90 39N 142E
Kamaran Is: Yemen P.D.R. 83 15N 42E
Kamchatka: *penin.*, U.S.S.R. 79 55N 160E
Kamchatka Bay: U.S.S.R. 79 55N 163E
Kamenets Podol'skiy: U.S.S.R. 70 49N 26E
Kamenskoye: U.S.S.R. 79 63N 165E
Kamensk-Uralskiy: U.S.S.R. 81 57N 62E
Kamet: *mtn.*, India/China 84 31N 79E
Kamina: Zaïre 102 9S 25E
KAMPALA: Uganda 102 0 33E
Kampot: Kampuchea 85 11N 104E
KAMPUCHEA (*formerly* **CAMBODIA**) *cap.* Phnom Penh 85 — —
Kamyshlov: U.S.S.R. 81 57N 63E
Kananga: Zaïre 102 6S 22E
Kanazawa: Japan 90 37N 137E
Kanchanaburi: Thailand 85 14N 99E
Kanchipuram: India 84 13N 80E
Kandahar: Afghanistan 83 32N 66E
Kandalaksha: U.S.S.R. 70 67N 32E
Kandi: Benin 100 11N 3E
Kandla: India 84 23N 70E
Kandy: Sri Lanka 84 7N 81E
Kangaroo I.: Australia 94 36S 137E
Kangchenjunga; *mtn.*, Nepal/India 84 27N 88E
Kangding: China 87 30N 102E
Kangean Is.: Indonesia 91 7S 116E
Kanin, C.: U.S.S.R. 78 68N 45E
Kankakee: U.S.A. 51 41N 88W
Kankan: Guinea 100 10N 9W
Kannapolis: U.S.A. 51 35N 80W
Kano: Nigeria 100 12N 8E
Kanonji: Japan 90 34N 134E
Kanoya: Japan 90 31N 131E
Kanpur: India 84 26N 80E
Kansas: *State*, U.S.A. 50 39N 98W
Kansas City: Kansas, U.S.A. 50 39N 95W
Kansas City: Mo., U.S.A. 50 39N 95W
Kansk: U.S.S.R. 81 56N 95E
Kansu: *Prov.*, *see* Gansu
Kaohsiung: Taiwan 89 23N 120E
Kaolack: Senegal 100 14N 16W
Kaposvár: Hungary 71 46N 18E
Kapurthala: India 84 31N 75E
Kara: U.S.S.R. 78 69N 65E
Kara-Bogaz-Gol: *bay*, U.S.S.R. 80 42N 54E
Karabuk: Turkey 82 41N 32E
Karachi: Pakistan 84 25N 67E
Karaganda: U.S.S.R. 81 50N 73E
Karakoram Pass: China/India 84 35N 76E
Kara-Kum: *desert*, U.S.S.R. 81 39N 60E
Kara Sea: U.S.S.R. 78 72N 62E
Kara-Tau: *mtns.*, U.S.S.R. 81 44N 68E
Karaul: U.S.S.R. 79 70N 83E
Karbalā: Iraq 83 33N 44E
Kargil: India 84 35N 76E
Kariba Dam: Zimbabwe/Zambia 102 17S 29E
Karl-Marx-Stadt: E. Germany 70 51N 13E
Karlovac: Yugoslavia 71 45N 16E
Karlovy Vary: Czech. 70 50N 13E
Karlskoga: Sweden 70 59N 15E
Karlskrona: Sweden 70 56N 16E
Karlsruhe: W. Germany 68 49N 8E
Karlstad: Sweden 70 59N 13E
Karnataka: *State*, India 84 14N 76E
Kárpathos: *i.*, Greece 71 36N 27E
Kartaly: U.S.S.R. 81 53N 60E
Karviná: Czechoslovakia 70 50N 18E
Karwar: India 84 15N 74E
Kasai: *r.*, Zaïre 102 4S 19E
Kasaoka: Japan 90 34N 133E
Kasese: Uganda 102 0 30E
Kāshān: Iran 83 34N 51E
Kashi (Kashgar): China 81 39N 76E
Kashiwazaki:Japan 90 37N 138E
Kaskaskia: *r.*, U.S.A. 51 39N 89W
Kasli: U.S.S.R. 81 56N 61E
Kásos: *i.*, Greece 71 35N 27E
Kassala: Sudan 101 15N 36E
Kassel: W. Germany 68 51N 9E
Kataba: Zambia 102 16S 25E
Katahdin, Mt.: U.S.A. 51 46N 69W
Katerini: Greece 71 40N 23E
Katherine: Australia 94 14S 133E
Kathiawar: *penin.*, India 84 22N 71E
KATMANDU: Nepal 84 28N 85E
Katoomba: Australia 94 34S 150E
Katowice: Poland 70 50N 19E
Katrineholm: Sweden 70 59N 16E
Kattegat: *str.*, Denmark/Sweden 70 57N 11E
Kauai: *i.*, Hawaiian Is. 104 22N 160W
Kaufbeuren: W. Germany 70 48N 11E
Kaufman: U.S.A. 50 33N 96W
Kaunas: U.S.S.R. 80 55N 24E
Kaura Namoda: Nigeria 100 13N 7E
Kavacha: U.S.S.R. 79 60N 170E
Kavālla: Greece 71 41N 24E
Kavieng: Papua New Guinea 94 3S 151E
Kawagoe: Japan 90 36N 139E
Kawaguchi: Japan 90 36N 140E
Kawasaki: Japan 90 36N 140E
Kawerau: N.Z. 95 38S 177E
Kayes: Mali 100 14N 11W
Kayseri: Turkey 82 39N 36E
Kazach'ye: U.S.S.R. 79 71N 136E
Kazakh S.S.R.: U.S.S.R. 80/81 — —
Kazakh Uplands: U.S.S.R. 81 49N 75E
Kazalinsk: U.S.S.R. 81 46N 62E
Kazan: U.S.S.R. 80 56N 49E
Kazanlák: Bulgaria 71 43N 25E
Kazatin: U.S.S.R. 70 50N 29E
Kéa: *i.*, Greece 71 38N 24E
Kearney: U.S.A. 53 41N 99W
Kebbi: *r.*, Nigeria 100 13N 4E
Kecskemét: Hungary 71 47N 20E
Kediri: Indonesia 91 8S 112E
Keene: U.S.A. 55 43N 72W
Keetmanshoop: Namibia 102 26S 18E
Kelang: Malaysia 85 3N 101E
Kelso: U.S.A. 52 46N 123W
Keluang: Malaysia 85 2N 103E
Kemerovo: U.S.S.R. 81 55N 86E
Kemi: Finland 70 66N 25E
Kendal: England 67 54N 3W
Kenitra: Morocco 100 34N 7W
Kenmare: R. of Irel. 67 52N 10W
Kenmare: *r.*, Rep. of Irel. 67 52N 10W
Kenmore: U.S.A. 53 49N 102W
Kennebec: *r.*, U.S.A. 51 45N 70W
Kennett: U.S.A. 50 36N 90W
Kennewick: U.S.A. 52 46N 119W
Kenosha: U.S.A. 51 43N 88W
Kensington: U.S.A. 57 39N 77W
Kentucky: *State*, U.S.A. 51 37N 85W
Kentucky, L.: U.S.A. 51 36N 88W
KENYA: *cap.* Nairobi 102 0 37E
Kenya, Mt.: Kenya 102 0 37E
Keokuk: U.S.A. 50 40N 92W
Kerala: *State*, India 84 10N 76E
Kerch': U.S.S.R. 81 45N 36E
Kerki: U.S.S.R. 81 38N 65E
Kérkira (Corfu): & *i.*, Greece 71 40N 20E
Kermadec Islands: & *trench*, Pacific Ocean 104 30S 179W
Kermān: Iran 82 30N 57E
Kerulen: *r.*, Mongolia 87 48N 111E
Kesennuma: Japan 90 39N 142E
Keswick: England 67 55N 3W
Ketchikan: U.S.A. 22 55N 132W
Kettering: England 67 52N 1W
Kewanee: U.S.A. 51 41N 90W
Keweenaw Penin.: U.S.A. 53 47N 88W
Key West: U.S.A. 51 25N 82W
Khabarovsk: U.S.S.R. 79 48N 135E
Khairpur: Pakistan 84 28N 69E
Khalkis: Greece 71 38N 24E
Khandwa: India 84 22N 76E
Khaniá: (Canea) Crete 71 35N 24E
Khanka, L.: U.S.S.R. 79 45N 133E
Khan Tengri: *mtn.*, U.S.S.R. 81 42N 80E
Khanty-Mansiysk: U.S.S.R. 81 61N 69E
Khanzi: Botswana 102 22S 22E
Kharagpur: India 84 22N 87E
Kharan Kalat: Pakistan 84 28N 65E
Kharg: *i.*, Iran 83 29N 50E
Khar'kov: U.S.S.R. 80 50N 36E
KHARTOUM: Sudan 101 16N 33E
Khasi Hills: India 84 26N 91E
Khatanga: U.S.S.R. 79 72N 102E
Khayelisha: S. Africa 102 34S.19E
Khemmarat: Thailand 85 16N 105E
Kherson: U.S.S.R. 80 47N 33E
Khimki: U.S.S.R. 72 55N 38E
Khiumaa: *i.*, *see* Hiiumaa
Khiva: U.S.S.R. 81 41N 60E
Khmel'nitsky: U.S.S.R. 70 50N 27E
Khodzheyli: U.S.S.R. 81 42N 60E
Kholmsk: U.S.S.R. 79 47N 142E
Khorog: U.S.S.R. 81 37N 72E
Khorramshahr: Iran 83 30N 48E
Khotin: U.S.S.R. 70 49N 27E
Khrom-Tau: U.S.S.R. 81 50N 58E
Khulna: Bangl. 84 23N 90E
Khurasan: *reg.*, Iran 83 35N 57E
Khuzistan: *reg.*, Iran 83 31N 49E
Khyber Pass: Afghan/Pak. 83 34N 71E
Kiangsi: *Prov.*, *see* Jiangxi
Kiangsu: *Prov.*, *see* Jiangsu
Kidderminster: England 67 52N 2W
Kiel: W. Germany 70 54N 10E
Kielce: Poland 70 51N 21E
Kiev: U.S.S.R. 70 51N 30E
KIGALI: Rwanda 102 2S 30E
Kigoma: Tanzania 102 5S 30E
Kii-suidō: *chan., Japan* 90 34N 135E
Kikinda: Yugoslavia 71 46N 20E
Kikwit: Zaïre 102 5S 19E
Kildare: R. of Ireland 67 53N 7W
Kilimanjaro: *mtn.*, Tanzania 102 3S 37E
Kilkenny: R. of Ireland 67 53N 7W
Killarney: R. of Ireland 67 52N 9W
Kilmarnock: Scotland 67 56N 4W
Kilrush: R. of Ireland 67 53N 9W
Kimberley: S. Africa 102 29S 25E
Kinabalu, Mt.: Mal. 91 6N 116E
Kindu: Zaïre 102 3S 26E
Kineshma: U.S.S.R. 80 57N 42E
King I.: Australia 94 40S 144E
Kingisepp: U.S.S.R. 70 59N 28E
Kingman: Arizona U.S.A. 52 35N 114W
Kingman: Kansas, U.S.A. 53 38N 98W
King's Lynn:England 67 53N 0
King Sound: Austl. 94 17S 123E
Kingsport: U.S.A. 51 37N 84W
Kingston: Australia 94 37S 140E
KINGSTON: Jamaica 59 18N 77W
Kingston: N.Z. 95 45S 169E
Kingston: U.S.A. 55 42N 74W
Kingston upon Hull *see* Hull
Kingsville: U.S.A. 50 28N 98W
KINSHASA: Zaïre 102 4S 15E
Kinston: U.S.A. 51 35N 78W
Kintyre: *penin.*, Scot. 67 55N 6W
Kirgiz S.S.R.: U.S.S.R. 81 42N 75E
KIRIBATI (*formerly* Gilbert Is.), *cap.* Bairiki 104 0 175E
Kirimati (*formerly* Christmas I.): Pacific O. 105 2N 157W
Kirin: *see* Jilin
Kirkcaldy: Scotland 67 56N 3W
Kirkcudbright: Scotland 67 55N 4W
Kirklareli: Turkey 71 42N 27E
Kirksville: U.S.A. 50 40N 93W
Kirkūk: Iraq 83 35N 44E
Kirkwall: Scotland 67 59N 3W
Kirov: U.S.S.R. 80 59N 50E
Kirovabad: U.S.S.R. 80 41N 46E
Kirovograd: U.S.S.R. 80 49N 32E
Kirovsk: U.S.S.R. 81 38N 60E
Kiruna: Sweden 70 68N 20E
Kiryu: Japan 90 36N 139E
Kisangani: Zaïre 102 1N 25E
Kisarazu:Japan 90 35N 140E
Kishinev: U.S.S.R. 80 47N 29E
Kishiwada: Japan 90 34N 135E
Kishm: Afghanistan 81 37N 70E
Kiskunfélegyháza: Hungary 71 47N 20E
Kissimmee: *r.*, U.S.A. 51 27N 81W
Kisumu: Kenya 102 0 35E
Kitaibaraki: Japan 90 37N 141E
Kitakyushu: Japan 90 34N 131E
Kitami: Japan 90 44N 144E
Kíthira: *i.*, Greece 71 36N 23E
Kíthnos: *i.*, Greece 71 37N 24E
Kitwe: Zambia 102 13S 28E
Kivak: U.S.S.R. 79 65N 174W
Kivu, L.: Zaïre 102 2S 29E
Kızılırmak: *r.*, Turkey 82 41N 34E
Kjølen Mtns.: Nor./Sweden 70 65N 15E
Kjustendil: Bulgaria 71 42N 23E
Klagenfurt: Austria 71 47N 14E
Klaipeda: U.S.S.R. 70 56N 21E
Klamath Falls: U.S.A. 52 42N 122W
Klerksdorp: S. Africa 102 27S 26E
Knoxville: U.S.A. 51 36N 84W
Kobe: Japan 90 35N 136E
København: *see* Copenhagen
Koblenz: W. Germany 68 50N 8E
Kōchi: Japan 90 34N 134E
Kodiak I.: U.S.A. 105 57N 154W
Kodok: Sudan 101 10N 32E
Kōfu: Japan 90 36N 139E
Kohat: Pakistan 84 34N 71E
Kohima: India 85 26N 94E
Kokand: U.S.S.R. 81 40N 71E
Kokchetav: U.S.S.R. 81 54N 70E
Kokomo: U.S.A. 51 41N 86W
Kola Penin.: U.S.S.R. 78 67N 38E
Kolhapur: India 84 17N 74E
Köln: *see* Cologne
Kolomna: U.S.S.R. 80 55N 39E
Kolomyya: U.S.S.R. 70 48N 25E
Kolyma Plain: U.S.S.R. 79 68N 155E
Kolyma Range: *see* Gydan Range
Kolyuchin, Gulf of: U.S.S.R. 79 67N 175W
Kolyvan': U.S.S.R. 81 56N 83E
Komatsu: Japan 90 36N 136E
Komárno: Czech. 71 48N 18E
Komba: Zaïre 102 3N 24E
Komotini: Greece 71 41N 25E
Kompong Cham: Kampuchea 85 11N 105E
Kompong Chhnang: Kampuchea 85 12N 105E
Kompong Som (*formerly* Sihanoukville): Kampuchea 85 10N 103E
Komsomol'sk-na-Amur: U.S.S.R. 79 51N 137E
Kongmoon: *see* Jiangmen
Kongola: Zaïre 102 5S 27E
Kongsvinger: Norway 70 60N 12E
Konosha: U.S.S.R. 80 61N 40E
Konotop: U.S.S.R. 80 51N 33E
Konstanz: W. Germany 68 48N 9E
Konya: Turkey 82 38N 32E
Koppeh Dāgh (Koppet Dāgh): *range*, Iran/U.S.S.R. 81 38N 57E
Korçë: Albania 71 41N 21E
Korčula: *i.*, Yugoslavia 71 43N 17E
Kordofan: *Prov.*, Sudan 101 13N 30E
Koriyama: Japan 90 37N 140E
Korosten': U.S.S.R. 70 51N 29E
Kortrijk: Belgium 68 51N 3E
Kos: *i.*, Greece 71 37N 27E
Kosciusko, Mt.: Austl. 94 36N 148E
Kosh-Agach: U.S.S.R. 81 50N 89E
Kosi: *r.*, Nepal/India 84 26N 87E
Košice, Czech. 70 49N 21E
Kosovska Mitrovica: Yugoslavia 71 43N 21E
Kostroma: U.S.S.R. 80 57N 41E
Koszalin: Poland 70 54N 17E
Kota: India 84 25N 76E
Kota Bahru: Malaysia 85 6N 102E

Kota Kinabalu: Malaysia **91** 6N 116E
Kotlas: U.S.S.R. **80** 61N 47E
Kotri: Pakistan **84** 25N 68E
Kounradskiy: U.S.S.R. **81** 47N 75E
Koussou Dam: Côte D'Ivoire **100** 7N 5W
Kovel': U.S.S.R. **70** 51N 25E
Kovrov: U.S.S.R. **80** 56N 41E
Kowloon: Hong Kong **89** 22N 114E
Kozáni: Greece **71** 40N 22E
Kozhikode (Calicut): India **84** 11N 76E
Kpalimé: Togo **100** 7N 1E
Kra, Isthmus of: Thailand **85** 10N 99E
Kragujevac: Yugo. **71** 44N 21E
Krakatau: *volc.*, Indonesia **91** 6S 105E
Kraków: *see* Cracow
Kraljevo: Yugoslavia **71** 44N 21E
Krasnodar: U.S.S.R. **80** 45N 39E
Krasnovodsk: U.S.S.R. **80** 40N 53E
Krasnoyarsk: U.S.S.R. **81** 56N 96E
Krasnyy Kut: U.S.S.R. **80** 51N 47E
Krasnyy Luch: U.S.S.R. **80** 48N 38E
Kratié: Kampuchea **85** 12N 106E
Krefeld: W. Germany **68** 51N 6E
Kremenchug: U.S.S.R. **80** 49N 33E
Kremenets: U.S.S.R. **70** 50N 26E
Krishna: *r.*, India **84** 17N 75E
Krishnanagar: India **84** 23N 88E
Kristiansand: Norway **70** 58N 8E
Kristianstad: Sweden **70** 56N 14E
Kristinehamn: Sweden **70** 59N 14E
Krivoy Rog: U.S.S.R. **80** 48N 33E
Krk: *i.*, Yugoslavia **71** 45N 15E
Kronotskiy Bay: U.S.S.R. **79** 54N 162E
KRUNG THEP: *see* BANGKOK
Kruševac: Yugoslavia **71** 44N 21E
Kruzof I.: U.S.A. **22** 57N 135W
Kuala Dungun: Malaysia **85** 5N 84E
KUALA LUMPUR: Malaysia **85** 3N 102E
Kuala Terengganu: Malaysia **85** 5N 103E
Kuantan: Malaysia **85** 4N 103E
Kuban': *r.*, U.S.S.R. **80** 45N 38E
Kuching: Malaysia **85** 2N 110E
Kudat: Malaysia **91** 7N 117E
Kufra Oases: Libya **101** 25N 22E
Kulunda Steppe: U.S.S.R. **81** 53N 77E
Kulundinskoye, L.: U.S.S.R. **81** 53N 80E
Kumagaya: Japan **90** 36N 139E
Kumamoto: Japan **90** 33N 131E
Kumasi: Ghana **100** 7N 2W
Kumbakonam: India **84** 11N 80E
Kungrad: U.S.S.R. **81** 43N 59E
Kunming: China **85** 25N 103E
Kunshan: China **89** 31N 121E
Kuntsevo: U.S.S.R. **72** 55N 38E
Kupang: Indonesia **91** 10S 124E
Kurashiki: Japan **90** 35N 134E
Kurdistan; *reg.*, Turkey/Iran **82/83** 37N 45E
Kure:Japan **90** 34N 133E
Kurgan: U.S.S.R. **81** 55N 65E
Kuria Muria Is.: Arabian Sea **83** 17N 56E
Kuril: *is.*, *Trench & Ridge*, Pacific O. **104** 45N 150E
Kurnool: India **84** 16N 78E
Kursk: U.S.S.R. **80** 52N 36E
Kurume: Japan **90** 33N 130E
Kushiro: Japan **90** 43N 143E
Kushka: U.S.S.R. **81** 35N 62E
Kushva: U.S.S.R. **81** 58N 60E
Kustanay: U.S.S.R. **81** 53N 64E
Kütahya: Turkey **82** 39N 30E
Kutaisi: U.S.S.R. **80** 42N 42E
Kutch, Gulf of: India **84** 23N 70E
Kutno:Poland **70** 52N 19E
KUWAIT: *cap.* Kuwait (Al-Kuwayt) **83** 29N 48E
Kuybyshev: U.S.S.R. **81** 55N 78E
Kuybyshev: U.S.S.R. **80** 53N 50E
Kuzbass: *reg.*, U.S.S.R. **81** 55N 85E
Kwangsi Chuang: *Prov.*, *see* Guanxi Zhuang
Kwangtung: *Prov.*, *see* Guangdong
Kweichow: *Prov.*, *see* Guizhou
Kweisui: *see* Huhhot
Kwekwe (Que Que): Zimbabwe **102** 19S 30E
Kyle of Lochalsh: Scotland **67** 57N 6W
Kyoga, L.: Uganda **102** 2N 33E
Kyōga-saki: *pt.*, Japan **90** 36N 135E
Kyōto: Japan **90** 35N 136E
Kyūshū: *i.*, Japan **90** 33N 131E
Kyushū-sanchi: *mtns.*, Japan **90** 32N 131E
Kyushu-Palau Ridge: Pacific Ocean **104** 20N 136E
Kyzl: U.S.S.R. **79** 52N 95E
Kyzyl-Kum: *desert*, U.S.S.R. **81** 43N 64E
Kzyl-Orda: U.S.S.R. **81** 45N 65E

L

Labuan: *i.*, Malaysia **91** 5N 15E
Laccadive Is.: *see* Lakshadweep
Laccadive Sea: Indian Ocean **84** 12N 73E
Lachlan: *r.*, Australia **94** 33S 148E
Laconia: U.S.A. **51** 43N 72W
La Coruña (Corunna): Spain **69** 43N 8W
La Crosse: U.S.A. **53** 44N 91W
Ladakh Ra.: India **84** 34N 78E
Ladoga, L.: U.S.S.R. **80** 61N 31E
Ladysmith: S. Africa **102** 28S 30E
Lae: Papua New Guin. **94** 7S 147E
La Fayette: U.S.A. **51** 40N 87W
Lafayette: U.S.A. **50** 30N 92W
Laghouat: Algeria **100** 34N 3E
LAGOS: Nigeria **100** 6N 3E
La Grande: U.S.A. **52** 45N 118W
La Grange: Ga., U.S.A. **51** 33N 85W
La Grange: Ill., U.S.A. **57** 42N 88W
La Guaira: Venez. **59** 11N 67W
Laguna Madre: U.S.A. **50** 26N 97W
LA HABANA: *see* HAVANNA
Lahore: Pakistan **84** 32N 75E
Lahti: Finland **70** 61N 26E
Laiyang: China **88** 37N 121E
Lajes: Brazil **61** 28S 50W
La Junta: U.S.A. **50** 38N 104W
Lake Bluff: U.S.A. **57** 42N 88W
Lake Charles: *city*, U.S.A. **50** 30N 93W
Lake City: U.S.A. **51** 30N 83W
Lake District: *reg.*, Eng. **67** 54N 3W
Lake Forest: U.S.A. **57** 42N 88W
Lakeland: U.S.A. **51** 28N 82W
Lake Zurich: U.S.A. **57** 42N 88W
Lakhimpur: India **84** 28N 81E
Lakshadweep (Laccadive Is.): Indian Ocean **86** 12N 73E
La Línea, Spain **69** 36N 5W
Lame Deer: U.S.A. **52** 46N 107W
Lamesa: U.S.A. **50** 33N 102W
Lamia: Greece **71** 39N 22E
Lampedusa: *i.*, Italy **71** 36N 13E
Lanak Pass: China/Kashmir **84** 34N 80E
Lanark: Scotland **67** 56N 4W
Lancaster: England **67** 54N 3W
Lancaster: Ohio, U.S.A. **51** 40N 83W
Lancaster: Pa., U.S.A. **54** 40N 76W
Lanchow: *see* Lanzhou
Landerneau: France **68** 48N 4W
Land's End: England **67** 50N 6W
Landshut: W. Germany **70** 49N 12E
Langres: France **68** 48N 5E
Langres, Plateau de: France **68** 48N 5E
Langsa: Indonesia **85** 4N 98E
Langshan: *mtns.*, China **88** 42N 109E
Lang Son: Vietnam **85** 22N 107E
Lansing: Ill., U.S.A. **57** 42N 88W
Lansing: Mich., U.S.A. **51** 43N 85W
Lanús: Argentina **61** 35S 58W
Lanxi: China **89** 29N 119E
Lanzarote: *i.*, Canary Islands **100** 29N 13W
Lanzhou (Lanchow): China **87** 36N 104E
Laoag: Philippines **91** 18N 120E
Lao Cai: Vietnam **85** 23N 104E
Laon: France **68** 50N 4E
LAOS: *cap.* Vientiane **85** 18N 104E
LA PAZ: Bolivia **60** 16S 68E
La Plata: Argentina **61** 35S 58W
Laptev Sea: U.S.S.R. **79** 75N 125E
Laptev Strait: U.S.S.R. **79** 73N 142E
L'Aquila: Italy **71** 42N 13E
Larache: Morocco **69** 35N 6W
Laramie: U.S.A. **53** 41N 106W
Laredo: U.S.A. **50** 28N 99W
Lárisa: Greece **71** 40N 22E
Laristan: *reg.*, Iran **83** 28N 54E
Larne: N. Ireland **67** 55N 6W
la Rochelle: France **69** 46N 1W
la Roche-sur-Yon: Fr. **69** 47N 1W
La Romana: Dominican Rep. **59** 19N 69W
Larsen Ice Shelf: Antarctica **128** 68S 64W
Lasa (Lhasa): China **84** 30N 91E
Las Cruces:U.S.A. **52** 32N 107W
La Serena: Chile **60** 30S 71W
Lashio: Burma **85** 23N 98E
Las Palmas: Canary Islands **100** 28N 15W
La Spezia: Italy **71** 44N 10E
Las Piedras: Uruguay **61** 35S 56W
Lassen Peak: U.S.A. **52** 41N 121W
Lastoursville: Gabon **102** 1S 13E
Las Vegas: Nevada, U.S.A. **52** 36N 115W
Las Vegas: N. Mexico, U.S.A. **53** 36N 105W
Latakia: Syria **82** 36N 36E
Latina: Italy **71** 41N 13E
Latvian S.S.R.: U.S.S.R. **80** 57N 35E
Launceston: Australia **94** 41S 147E
Laurel: Miss., U.S.A. **51** 32N 89W
Laurel: Mont., U.S.A. **52** 46N 109W
Lausanne: Switzerland **69** 46N 7E
Laut: *i.*, Indonesia **91** 4S 116E
Laval: France **68** 48N 1W
Laverton: Australia **94** 29S 123E
Lawrence: U.S.A. **55** 43N 71W
Lawton: U.S.A. **50** 35N 98W
Lead: U.S.A. **53** 44N 104W
LEBANON: *cap.* Beirut **82** 34N 36E
Lebanon: U.S.A. **51** 36N 86W
Lecce: Italy **71** 40N 18E
Lechang: China **89** 25N 113E
le Creusot: France **69** 47N 4E
Lee: *r.*, R. of Ireland **67** 52N 9W
Leeds: England **67** 54N 2W
Leeds: U.S.A. **53** 48N 100W
Leeuwarden: Neth. **68** 53N 6E
Leeuwin, C.: Australia **94** 34S 115E
Leeward Is.: W. Indies **59** 17N 63W
Legaspi: Philippines **91** 13N 124E
Leghorn (Livorno): Italy **71** 44N 10E
Legnica: Poland **70** 51N 16E
Leh: India **84** 34N 78E
le Havre: France **68** 50N 0
Leicester: England **67** 53N 1W
Leigh Creek: *town*, Australia **94** 31S 138E
Leipzig: W. Germany **70** 51N 12E
Leizhou Peninsula: China **87** 21N 110E
le Mans: France **68** 48N 0
Lemont: U.S.A. **57** 42N 88W
Lena: *r.*, U.S.S.R. **79** 64N 126E
Leninabad: U.S.S.R. **81** 40N 70E
Leninakan: U.S.S.R. **80** 41N 44E
Leningrad: U.S.S.R. **80** 60N 30E
Leninogorsk: U.S.S.R. **81** 50N 84E
Lenin Pk.: U.S.S.R. **81** 39N 73E
Leninsk-Kuznetskiy: U.S.S.R. **81** 55N 86E
Lens: France **68** 50N 3E
Leoben: Austria **71** 47N 15E
Leominster: U.S.A. **55** 43N 72W
León: Mexico **58** 21N 102W
León: Spain **69** 43N 6W
Leonora: Australia **94** 29S 121E
Leping: China **89** 29N 117E
le Puy: France **69** 45N 4E
Lérida: Spain **69** 42N 1E
Lesbos: *i.*, Greece **71** 39N 26E
Leskovac: Yugoslavia **71** 43N 22E
Les Landes: *reg.*, France **69** 44N 1W
LESOTHO: *cap.* Maseru **102** 29S 27E
les Sables d'Olonne: France **69** 47N 2W
Lesser Antilles: *arch.*, West Indies **59** 15N 62W
Leszno: Poland **70** 52N 17E
Leticia: Colombia **60** 4S 70W
Letpadan: Burma **85** 18N 96E
Leveque, C.: Australia **94** 17S 123E
Leverkusen: W. Ger. **68** 51N 7E
Levittown: U.S.A. **56** 41N 74W
Lewes: England **67** 51N 0
Lewis: *i.*, Scotland **67** 58N 7W
Lewiston: Maine, U.S.A. **51** 44N 70W
Lewiston: Wash., U.S.A. **52** 46N 117W
Lewistown: U.S.A. **52** 47N 109W
Lexington: Ken., U.S.A. **51** 38N 84W
Lexington: Mass., U.S.A. **55** 42N 71W
Leydsdorp: S. Africa **102** 24S 31E
Leyte: *i.*, Philippines **91** 11N 125E
Lhasa: *see* Lasa
Lhokseumawe: Indon. **85** 5N 97E
Lianxian: China **89** 25N 112E
Lianyungang: China **88** 35N 120E
Lianzhou: *see* Hepu
Liaodong Peninsula: China **88** 40N 122E
Liaodongwan: *bay*, China **88** 41N 121E
Liaoning: *Prov.*, China **88** 41N 121E
Liaoyang: China **88** 42N 124E
Libby: U.S.A. **52** 48N 116W
Liberal: U.S.A. **53** 37N 101W
Liberec: Czech. **70** 51N 15E
LIBERIA: *cap.* Monrovia **100** 7N 10W
Libertyville: U.S.A. **57** 42N 88W
LIBREVILLE: Gabon **102** 0 10E
LIBYA: *cap.* Tarābulus (Tripoli) **100/101** — —
Libyan Desert: Libya/Egypt **101** 25N 25E
Libyan Plat: Egypt **101** 30N 27E
Lichinga (Vila Cabral): Mozambique **102** 13S 35E
Licking: *r.*, U.S.A. **51** 38N 84W
Lida: U.S.S.R. **70** 54N 25E
Lidköping: Sweden **70** 58N 13E
LIECHTENSTEIN: *cap.* Vaduz **71** 47N 10E
Liège: Belgium **68** 51N 6E
Lienz: Austria **71** 47N 13E
Liepāja: U.S.S.R. **70** 57N 21E
Liffey: *r.*, R. of Ireland **67** 53N 6W
Likasi: Zaire **102** 11S 27E
Liling: China **89** 28N 113E
Lilla Baelt: *str.*, Den. **68** 55N 10E
Lille: France **68** 51N 3E
Lillestrøm: Norway **70** 60N 11E
LILONGWE: Malawi **102** 14S 34E
LIMA: Peru **60** 12S 77W
Lima: U.S.A. **51** 41N 84W
Limassol: Cyprus **82** 40N 33E
Limerick: R. of Ireland **67** 53N 9W
Límnos: *i.*, Greece **71** 40N 25E
Limoges: France **69** 46N 1E
Limpopo: *r.*, Africa **111** 23S 33E
Linares: Mexico **58** 25N 100W
Linares: Spain **69** 38N 4W
Lincoln: England **67** 53N 1W
Lincoln: U.S.A. **53** 41N 97W
Lincolnwood: U.S.A. **57** 42N 87W
Lindau: W. Germany **70** 48N 10E
Line Is.: Pacific O **104/105** 0 158W
Linfen: China **88** 36N 112E
Lingen: W. Germany **68** 52N 7E
Lingga: *i.*, Indonesia **91** 0 105E
Lingling: China **89** 26N 112E
Linguère: Senegal **100** 15N 15W
Linhai: China **89** 29N 121E
Linköping: Sweden **70** 58N 16E
Linqing: China **88** 37N 116E
Linru: China **88** 34N 113E
Linton: U.S.A. **53** 46N 100W
Linyi: China **88** 35N 118E
Linz: Austria **70** 48N 14E
Lion, Golfe du: France **69** 43N 4E
Lipari Is.: Italy **71** 38N 15E
Lipetsk: U.S.S.R. **80** 53N 40E
LISBON, Portugal **69** 39N 9W
Lisburne, Cape: U.S.A. **79** 69N 166W
Lisburne, C.: U.S.A. **12** 69N 166W
Lishui: China **89** 28N 120E
Lisianski: *i.*, Pacific O. **104** 27N 175W
Lisieux: France **68** 49N 0
Lisle: U.S.A. **57** 42N 88W
Lismore: Australia **94** 29S 153E
Lithgow: Australia **94** 33S 150E
Lithuanian S.S.R.: U.S.S.R. **80** 55N 24E
Little Bitter Lake: Egypt **101** *Inset*
Littlefield: U.S.A. **50** 34N 102W
Little Minch: *chan.*, Scotland **67** 58N 7W
Little Rock: U.S.A. **50** 35N 92W
Liuhe: China **88** 32N 119E
Liuzhou: China **89** 24N 109E
Livermore, Mt.: U.S.A. **50** 30N 105W
Liverpool: England **67** 53N 3W
Livingstone *now* Maramba
Livingstone Falls: Zaire **102** 5S 14E
Livingstonia: Malawi: **102** 10S 34E
Livorno: *see* Leghorn
Liyang: China **89** 32N 120E
Lizard Point: England **67** 50N 5W
Ljubljana: Yugoslavia **71** 46N 14E
Llandrindod Wells: Wales **67** 52N 3W
Llandudno: Wales **67** 53N 4W
Llanelli: Wales **67** 52N 4W
Llano Estacado: *plat.*, U.S.A. **50** 33N 103W
Lleyn: *penin.*, Wales **67** 53N 5W
Lobito: Angola **102** 12S 14E
Lockport: U.S.A. **57** 42N 88W
Lod (Lydda): Israel **82** 32N 35E
Lodwar: Kenya **102** 7S 36E
Łódź: Poland **70** 52N 19E
Lofoten Is.: Norway **70** 69N 15E
Logan: Utah, U.S.A. **52** 42N 112W
Logan W. Va., U.S.A. **51** 38N 82W
Logansport: U.S.A. **51** 41N 85W
Logrono: Spain **69** 42N 2W
Loire: *r.*, France **68** 47N 1W
Loja: Spain **69** 37N 4W
Lolland: *i.*, Denmark **70** 55N 11E
Lomas de Zamora: Arg. **61** 35S 58W
Lombard: U.S.A. **57** 42N 88W
Lomblen: *i.*, Indonesia **91** 8S 123E
Lombok: *i.*, & *str.*, Indonesia **91** 8S 116E
LOME: Togo **100** 6N 1E
Lomond, L.: Scotland **67** 56N 5W
LONDON: England **67** 52N 0
Londonderry: N. Ireland **67** 55N 7W
Londrina: Brazil **61** 23S 51W
Long Bay: U.S.A. **51** 34N 79W
Long Beach: *city*, Calif., U.S.A. **52** 34N 118W
Long Beach: *city*, N.Y., U.S.A. **56** 41N 73W
Longford: R. of Ireland **67** 54N 8W
Long I.: The Bahamas **59** 23N 75W
Long I.: *& Sd.*, U.S.A. **56** 41N 73W
Longmont: U.S.A. **53** 40N 105W
Longreach: Australia **94** 23S 144E
Longview: Oregon, U.S.A. **52** 46N 123W
Longview: Texas, U.S.A. **50** 33N 95W
Longxi *see* Zhangzhou
Long Xuyen: Vietnam **85** 10N 105E
Lookout, C.: U.S.A. **51** 35N 77W
Lorain: U.S.A. **51** 41N 83W
Lorca: Spain **69** 38N 2W
Lord Howe Rise: Pacific Ocean **104** 31S 165E
Lorient: France **68** 48N 3W
Lorne, Firth of: Scot. **67** 56N 6W
Los Alamos: U.S.A. **52** 36N 106W
Los Angeles: U.S.A. **37** 34N 118W
Lossiemouth: Scotland **67** 58N 3W
Lot: *r.*, France **69** 44N 1E
Louislade Archipelago: Coral Sea **94** 11S 153E
Louisiana: *State*, U.S.A. **50** 33N 93W
Louisville: U.S.A. **51** 38N 86W
Loup City: U.S.A. **50** 41N 99W
Lourdes: France **69** 43N 0
Louviers: France **68** 49N 1E
Lowell: U.S.A. **55** 43N 71W
Lower California: *State*, Mexico **58** 27N 113W
Lower Hutt: New Zealand **95** 41N 175E
Lower Tunguska: *r.*, U.S.S.R. **79** 64N 95E
Lowestoft: England **67** 52N 2E
Lowville: U.S.A. **51** 44N 75W
Loyalty Is.: Pac. O. **104** 20S 165E
Lualaba: *r.*, Zaire **102** 6S 26E
Lu'an: China **88** 32N 117E
LUANDA: Angola **102** 9S 13E
Luang Prabang: Laos **85** 20N 102E
Luanshya: Zambia **102** 13S 28E
Lubango (Sá da Bandiera): Angola **102** 15S 14E
Lubbock: U.S.A. **50** 34N 102W
Lübeck: *& bay*, W. Germany **70** 54N 11E
Lublin; Poland **70** 51N 23E
Lubok Sikiping: Indonesia **85** 0 100E
Lubumbashi: Zaire **102** 12S 27E
Lucena: Spain **69** 37N 4W
Luchiang: Taiwan **89** 24N 120E
Lucin: U.S.A. **52** 41N 114W
Lucknow: India **84** 27N 81E
Lüda (Lüta): China **88** 39N 121E
Lüdenscheid: W. Ger. **68** 51N 8E
Luderitz: Namibia **102** 27S 15E
Ludhiana: India **84** 31N 76E
Ludington: U.S.A. **24** 44N 86W
Ludlow: U.S.A. **52** 35N 116W
Ludvika: Sweden **70** 60N 15E
Lufeng: China **89** 23N 116E
Lufkin: U.S.A. **50** 31N 95W
Lugo: Spain **69** 43N 8W
Lugoj: Romania **71** 46N 22E
Luleå: Sweden **70** 66N 22E
Lüleburgaz: Turkey **71** 41N 27E
Lumberton: U.S.A. **51** 34N 79W
Lumsden: N.Z. **95** 46S.168E
Lund: Sweden **70** 56N 13E
Lundy I.: England **67** 51N 5W
Lune: *r.*, England **67** 54N 3W
Lüneburg: Germany **70** 53N 10E
Lüneburger Heide (Lüneburg Heath) **70** 53N 10E
Luo: *r.*, China **88** 36N 109E
Luohe: China **88** 34N 114E
Luoyang: China **88** 35N 112E
Lurgan: N. Ireland **68** 54N 6W
Luristan: *reg.*, Iran **83** 33N 48E
LUSAKA: Zambia **102** 15S 28E
Lusambo: Zaire **102** 5S 23E
Lushai Hills: India **85** 23N 93E
Lushan: China **88** 33N 113E
Lüshun: China **88** 39N 121E
Lüta: *see* Lüda
Luton: England **67** 52N 0
Lutsk: U.S.S.R. **70** 51N 25E
LUXEMBOURG: *cap.* Luxembourg **68** 50N 6E
Luxor: Egypt **82** 26N 33E
Luzern (Lucerne): Switzerland **68** 47N 8E
Luzon: *i.*, Phil. **91** 15N 121E
L'vov: U.S.S.R. **70** 50N 24E
Lyakhov Is.: U.S.S.R. **79** 73N 142E
Lyallpur: *now* Shah Faisalabad
Lydda: *see* Lod
Lydenburg: S. Africa **102** 25S 30E
Lyme Bay: England **67** 51N 3W
Lynchburg: U.S.A. **51** 37N 79W
Lyon: France **69** 46N 5E
Lyons: U.S.A. **57** 42N 88W
Lys'va: U.S.S.R. **81** 58N 58E
Lyttleton: N.Z. **95** 44S 173E
Lyubertsy: U..S.R. **72** 55N 38E
Lyublino: U.S.S.R. **72** 55N 38E

M

Ma'ān: Jordan **82** 30N 36E
Maanshan:China **88** 32N 119E
Maarianhamina: Fin. **70** 60N 20E
Maastricht: Neth. **68** 51N 6E
McAlester: U.S.A. **50** 35N 96W
McAllen: U.S.A. **50** 26N 98W
Macao: *Prov.*, Asia **89** 22N 113E
Macapa: Brazil **60** 0 51W
McComb: U.S.A. **50** 31N 90W
McCook: U.S.A. **50** 40N 101W
Macdonnell Ranges: Australia **94** 24S 132E
Maceió: Brazil **60** 10S 36W
Macerata: Italy **71** 43N 13E
McGehee: U.S.A. **50** 34N 91W
Macgillycuddy's Reeks: *mtns*, R. of Ireland **67** 52N 10W
Machilipatnam (Bandar): India **84** 16N 81E
McIntosh: U.S.A. **53** 46N 101W
Mackay: Australia **94** 21S 149E

Mackay, L.: Australia **94** 23S 128E
Mackenzie: Guyana **60** 6N 58W
Mackinac, Str. of: U.S.A. **24** 45N 85W
McKinney: U.S.A. **50** 33N 97W
McLean: U.S.A. **57** 39N 77W
McMurdo: Antarctica **128** 78S 168E
Macias Nguema Biyogo: *see* Bioko
Mâcon: France **69** 46N 5E
Macon: U.S.A. **51** 33N 84W
Macquarie I.: Pac. O. **104** 55S 159E
McRae: U.S.A. **51** 32N 83W
MADAGASCAR *(formerly* Malagasy Republic) *cap.* Antananarivo **102** *Inset*
Madang: Papua New Guinea **94** 5S 146E
Madeira: *i.*, Atlantic Ocean **100** 33N 17W
Madeira: *r.*, Brazil **60** 5S 61W
Madeira: U.S.A. **52** 37N 120W
Madhya Pradesh: *State*, India **84** 23N 78E
Madison: Florida, U.S.A. **51** 30N 84W
Madison: Ind., U.S.A. **51** 39N 85W
Madison: S. Dakota, U.S.A. **53** 44N 97W
Madison: Wisc., U.S.A. **53** 43N 89W
Madisonville: U.S.A. **51** 37N 88W
Madiun: Indonesia **91** 8S 112E
Madras: India **84** 13N 80E
MADRID: Spain **69** 40N 4W
Madura: *i.*, Indon. **91** 7S 113E
Madurai: India **84** 10N 78E
Maebashi: Japan **90** 36N 139E
Mafikeng: S. Africa **102** 26S 25E
Magadan: U.S.S.R. **79** 60N 150E
Magallenes: *see* Punta Arenas
Magdalena: *r.*, Colombia **60** 7N 74W
Magdeburg: E. Ger. **70** 52N 12E
Magelang: Indonesia **91** 7S 110E
Magellan, Str. of: Chile/Arg. **60** 53S 70W
Maggiore, Lake: Italy/Switzerland **69** 46N 9E
Magnitogorsk:U.S.S.R. **81** 53N 59E
Magnolia: U.S.A. **50** 33N 93W
Magwe: Burma **85** 20N 95E
Mahajanga (Majunga): Madagascar **102** 16S 46E
Mahanadi: *r.*, India **84** 22N 83E
Maharashtra: *State*, India **84** 24N 76E
Maha Sarakham: Thailand **85** 16N 104E
Mahia Penin.: N.Z. **84** 39S 178E
Mahón: Minorca **69** 40N 4E
Maidstone: England **67** 51N 1E
Maiduguri: Nigeria **100** 12N 13E
Maimana: Afghan **83** 36N 65E
Main: *r.*, W. Germany **70** 50N 10E
Mai Ndombe, L.: Zaïre **102** 2S 17E
Maine: *State*, U.S.A. **51** 45N 70W
Mainland: *i.*, Orkney Is. **67** 59N 3W
Mainz: W. Germany **68** 50N 8E
Maiskhal: Bangladesh **84** 21N 92E
Maitland: Australia **94** 33S 152E
Maizuru: Japan **90** 36N 135E
Majorca: *see* Mallorca
Majunga: *see* Mahajanga
Makeni: Sierra Leone **100** 9N 12W
Makarikari Salt Pan: Botswana **102** 21S 26E
Makassar, Str. of: Indonesia **91** 5S 120E
Makeyevka: U.S.S.R. **80** 48N 38E
Makhachkala: U.S.S.R. **80** 43N 48E
Makkah (Mecca): Saudi Arabia **82** 21N 40E
Makó: Hungary **71** 46N 20E
Makran: *reg.*, Iran/Pakistan **83** 26N 62E
Makushino: U.S.S.R. **81** 55N 67E
Malabar Coast: India **84** 12N 75E
MALABO: Equatorial Guinea **100** 2N 10E
Malacca, Str. of: Malaysia/Indon. **85** 2N 102E
Malaga: Spain **69** 37N 4W
MALAGASY REP.: *see* **MADAGASCAR**
Malaita: *i.*, Solomon Is. **94** 9S 161E
Malakal: Sudan **102** 10N 32E
Malang: Indonesia **91** 8S 112E
Malanje: Angola **102** 9S 16E
Malar, L.: Sweden **70** 59N 17E
Malatya: Turkey **82** 38N 38E
MALAWI: *cap.* Lilongwe **102** 13S 34E
Malawi (Nyasa), Lake: Africa **102** 13S 34E
Malaya: *see* Peninsular Malaysia
MALAYSIA: *Fed. cap.* Kuala Lumpur **91** 5N 110E
Malbork: Poland **70** 54N 19E
Malden I.: Pacific O. **105** 5S 155W
Malebo, Pool: *l.*, Zaïre **102** 4S 15E
Malema: Mozambique **102** 15S 37E
Malheur L.: U.S.A. **52** 43N 119W
MALI: *cap.* Bamako **100** 15N 5W
Malin Head: R. of Ireland **67** 55N 7W
Malinmore Head: R. of Ireland **67** 55N 9W
Mallaig: Scotland **67** 57N 6W
Mallorca (Majorca): *i.*, Spain **69** 39N 3E
Mallow: R. of Ireland **67** 52N 9W
Malmesbury: S. Africa **102** 33S 19E
Malmö: Sweden **70** 56N 13E
Malonga: Zaïre **102** 10S 23E
MALTA: *cap.* Valletta **71** 36N 14E
Malta: U.S.A. **52** 48N 108W
Malvan: India **84** 16N 73E
Mamaroneck: U.S.A. **56** 41N 74W
Man, I. of: United Kingdom **67** 54N 5W
Manaar: & *gulf*, Sri Lanka **84** 9N 80E
Manado: Indonesia **91** 2N 125E
MANAGUA: Nic. **58** 12N 86W
MANAMA: Bahrain **83** 26N 51E
Mana Pass: China **84** 31N 79E
Manaus: Brazil **60** 3S 60W
Manchester: England **67** 54N 2W
Manchester: U.S.A. **55** 43N 71W
Mandalay: Burma **85** 22N 96E
Mandan: U.S.A. **53** 47N 101W
Mandasor: India **84** 24N 75E
Mangalore: India **84** 13N 75E
Mangyshlak Penin.: U.S.S.R. **80** 44N 51E
Manhattan, Kansas: U.S.A. **50** 39N 97W
Manhattan: N.Y., U.S.A. **56** 41N 74W
MANILA: Philippines **91** 15N 121E
Manipur: *State*, India **85** 25N 94E
Manisa: Turkey **71** 39N 28E
Manistee: *r.*, U.S.A. **24** 45N 85W
Manistique: U.S.A. **24** 46N 86W
Manizales: Colombia **60** 5N 76W
Manjra: *r.*, India **84** 18N 76E
Mankato: U.S.A. **53** 44N 94W
Mannheim: W. Ger. **68** 49N 8E
Manokwari: Indonesia **91** 1S 134E
Manresa: Spain **69** 42N 2E
Mansfield: U.S.A. **51** 41N 83W
Manta: Ecuador **60** 1S 81W
Mantua (Mantova): Italy **71** 45N 11E
Manus: *i.*, Papua New Guinea **94** 3S 147E
Manzala, L.: Egypt **101** *Inset*
Manzanillo: Cuba **59** 20N 77W
Manzanillo: Mexico **58** 19N 104W
MAPUTO: Mozambique **102** 26S 33E
Maracaibo: & *lake*, Venezuela **59** 11N 72W
Maracay: Venezuela **59** 10N 68W
Maramba *(formerly* Livingstone): Zambia **102** 18S 26E
Marble Bar: Australia **94** 21S 120E
Marburg: W. Germany **68** 51N 9E
Mar Chiquita, Laguna: Argentina **61** 31S 62W
Marcos Paz: Argentina **61** 35S 59W
Marcus I.: Pacific O. **104** 25N 154E
Marcus Necker Rise: Pacific Ocean **104** 20N 170E
Marcy, Mt.: U.S.A. **51** 44N 74W
Mar del Plata: Arg. **60** 38S 58W
Mardin: Turkey **82** 37N 41E
Marfa: U.S.A. **50** 30N 104W
Marganets: U.S.S.R. **81** 48N 67E
Margarita *i.*; Venezuela **59** 11N 64W
Margate: England **67** 51N 1E
Mariana Is.: *& Trench*: Pacific Ocean **104** 18N 145E
Maria van Diemen, C.: New Zealand **95** 34S 173E
Maribor: Yugoslavia **71** 47N 16E
Mariinsk: U.S.S.R. **81** 56N 88E
Marinett: U.S.A. **53** 45N 88W
Maringá: Brazil **61** 23S 52W
Marion: Ind., U.S.A. **51** 41N 86W
Marion: Ohio, U.S.A. **51** 41N 83W
Maritime Alps: France **69** 44N 7E
Markovo: U.S.S.R. **79** 65N 170E
Marmande: France **69** 44N 0
Marmara, Sea of: Turkey **71** 41N 28E
Marne: *r.*, France **68** 49N 4E
Marquesas Is.: Pac. O. **105** 10S 140W
Marquette: U.S.A. **53** 46N 87W
Marrakesh: Mor. **100** 32N 8W
Marra Mts.: Sudan **101** 13N 24E
Marree: Australia **94** 30S 138E
Marsala: Sicily **71** 38N 12E
Marseille: France **69** 43N 5E
Marshall: U.S.A. **50** 33N 94W
Marshall Is.: Pac. O. **104** 10N 166E
Marshalltown: U.S.A. **50** 42N 93W
Marshfield: U.S.A. **53** 45N 90W
Martaban, G of: Burma **91** 16N 97E
Martha's Vineyard: *i.*, U.S.A. **55** 41N 71W
Martin: Czechoslovakia **70** 49N 19E
Martinique: *i.*, West Indies **59** 15N 61W
Martinsville: U.S.A. **51** 37N 80W
Marton: N.Z. **95** 40S 175E
Mary (Merv): U.S.S.R. **81** 38N 62E
Maryborough: Australia **94** 25S 153E
Maryland: *State*, U.S.A. **51** 38N 75W
Maryville: U.S.A. **51** 36N 84W
Mascara: Algeria **69** 35N 0
MASERU: Lesotho **102** 29S 27E
Mashhad: Iran **83** 36N 60E
Masira: *i.*, Oman **83** 20N 59E
Mask, L.: R. of Ireland **67** 54N 9W
Mason City: U.S.A. **53** 43N 93W
Massachusetts:*State*, U.S.A. **55** 42N 73W
Massawa: Ethiopia **101** 16N 39E
Massena: U.S.A. **51** 45N 75W
Massif Central: France **69** 46N 3E
Masterton: N.Z. **95** 41S 176E
Mastung: Pakistan **84** 30N 67E
Masuda: Japan **90** 35N 132E
Matadi: Zaïre **102** 6S 14E
Matagorda I.: U.S.A. **50** 28N 97W
Matamoros: Mexico **50** 26N 97W
Matanzas: Cuba **59** 23N 82W
Matapan, C., Greece **71** 36N 22E
Mateka Falls: Zaïre **102** 5S 15E
Matera: Italy **71** 41N 17E
Mathura: India **84** 27N 78E
Mato Grosso, Plat. of: Brazil **60** 15S 54W
Matrah: Oman **83** 24N 58E
Matrûh: Egypt **82** 32N 27E
Matsudo: Japan **90** 36N 140E
Matsue:Japan **90** 35N 133E
Matsumoto: Japan **90** 36N 138E
Matsuyama: Japan **90** 34N 133E
Matsuzaka: Japan **90** 35N 137E
Mattoon: U.S.A. **51** 39N 88W
Maturin: Venezuela **59** 10N 63W
Maui: *i.*, Hawaiian Is. **105** 20N 155W
Maumee: *r.*, U.S.A. **51** 41N 84W
Maumere: Indonesia **91** 8S 122E
MAURITANIA: *cap.* Nouakchott **100** 20N 10W
Mawlaik: Burma **85** 24N 94E
May, C.: U.S.A. **51** 39N 75W
Mayfield: U.S.A. **51** 36N 89W
Maykop: U.S.S.R. **80** 45N 40E
Maymyo: Burma **85** 22N 96E
Mayoumba: Gabon **102** 4S 11E
Maywood: U.S.A. **57** 42N 88W
Mazar-i-Sharif: Afghanistan **83** 37N 67E
Mazatlán: Mexico **58** 23N 107W
MBABANE: Swaziland **102** 26N 31E
Mbala: Zambia **102** 9S 32E
Mbandaka: Zaïre **102** 0 18E
Mbuji-Mayi: Zaïre **102** 6S 24E
Mead Lake: U.S.A. **52** 36N 114W
Mecca: *see* Makkah
Medan: Indonesia **85** 4N 99E
Médéa: Algeria **69** 36N 3E
Medellin: Colombia **60** 6N 76W
Medgidia: Romania **71** 44N 28E
Mediaş: Romania **71** 46N 25E
Medina: Saudi Arabia **82** 25N 40E
Medinat-ash-Sha'b: Yemen P.D.R. **83** 13N 45E
Mediterranean Sea **100/101** — —
Mednogorsk: U.S.S.R. **81** 51N 58E
Meekatharra: Austl. **94** 27S 119E
Meerut: India **84** 29N 77E
Mega: Ethiopia **101** 4N 38E
Mégara: Greece **71** 38N 23E
Meghalaya: *State*, India **84** 26N 91E
Mahajanga: Madagascar **102** 15S 46E
Meiktila: Burma **85** 21N 96E
Meixian: China **89** 24N 116E
Mekambo: Gabon **102** 1N 14E
Meknès: Morocco **100** 34N 5W
Mekong: *r.*, S.E. Asia **85** 33N 96E
Melaka: Malaysia **85** 2N 102E
Melanesia: *reg.*, Pacific O. **104** — —
Melbourne: Austl. **94** 38S 145E
Melbourne: U.S.A. **51** 28N 81W
Melilla: (Sp.) Africa **69** 35N 3W
Melo: Uruguay **61** 32S 54W
Melrose Park: U.S.A. **57** 42N 88W
Melun: France **68** 49N 3E
Melville I.: Austl. **94** 11S 131E
Memphis: *hist.*, Egypt **82** 30N 31E
Memphis: U.S.A. **51** 35N 90W
Menderes: *r.*, Turkey **82** 37N 27E
Mendoza: Argentina **60** 33S 69W
Mène: Congo **102** 2N 16E
Mengzi: China **85** 23N 103E
Menominee: U.S.A. **53** 45N 88W
Menongue: Angola **102** 15S 18E
Menorca (Minorca): *i.*, Spain **69** 40N 4E
Mentawai Is.: Indon. **91** 3S 100E
Mentekab: Malaysia **85** 3N 102E
Meramec: *r.*, U.S.A. **50** 38N 91W
Merano: Italy **71** 47N 11E
Merauke: Indon. **94** 9S 140E
Mercara: India **84** 12N 76E
Merced: U.S.A. **52** 37N 120W
Mercedes: Buenos Aires, Arg. **61** 35S 60W
Mercedes: San Luis, Arg. **61** 34S 66W
Mercedes: Uruguay **61** 33S 58W
Mergui: Burma **85** 12N 98E
Mergui Archipelago: Burma **85** 10N 97E
Mérida: Mexico **58** 21N 90W
Mérida: Spain **69** 39N 6W
Meridian: U.S.A. **51** 32N 89W
Meridional, Meseta: *plat.*, Spain **69** 39N 5W
Merowe: Sudan **82** 18N 32E
Mersey: *r.*, England **67** 53N 3W
Mersin: Turkey **82** 37N 34E
Merthyr Tydfil: Wales **67** 52N 3W
Merv: *see* Mary
Mesa: U.S.A. **52** 33N 112W
Mesabi Ra.: U.S.A. **53** 48N 93W
Messina: *& str.*, Sicily **71** 38N 16E
Messina: S. Africa **102** 23S 30E
Methuen: U.S.A. **55** 43N 71W
Mettur: India **84** 12N 78E
Metz: France **68** 49N 6E
Mexicali: Mexico **52** 33N 115W
Mexican Plat.: Mex. **58** 24N 103W
MEXICO: *cap.* Mexico City **58** — —
Mexico, Gulf of: **58/59** 25N 90W
MEXICO CITY (Ciudad de Mexico): Mexico **58** 19N 99W
Miami: Ariz., U.S.A. **52** 33N 111W
Miami: Fla., U.S.A. **51** 26N 80W
Miami: Okla., U.S.A. **50** 37N 95W
Miami: *r.*, U.S.A. **51** 39N 85W
Miami Beach: U.S.A. **51** 26N 80W
Mianeh: Iran **83** 37N 47E
Michelson Mt.: U.S.A. **20** 69N 144W
Michigan, Lake: U.S.A./Canada **53** 44N 87W
Michigan City: U.S.A. **51** 42N 86W
Micronesia: *reg.*, Pacific Ocean **104** — —
Mid-Atlantic Ridge: Atlantic Ocean **103** — —
Middleburg: S. Africa **102** 26S 30E
Middle Atlas: *mtns.*, Morocco **100** 33N 5W
Middlesboro: U.S.A. **51** 37N 84W
Middlesbrough: Eng. **67** 55N 1W
Middletown: N.Y., U.S.A. **55** 41N 74W
Middletown: Ohio, U.S.A. **51** 40N 84W
Midland: Mich., U.S.A. **24** 44N 84W
Midland: Texas, U.S.A. **50** 32N 102W
Midnapore: India **84** 22N 87E
Midway I.: Pacific O. **104** 29N 179W
Midwest: U.S.A. **52** 43N 106W
Mielec: Poland **70** 50N 21E
Mieres: Spain **69** 43N 6W
Mihara: Japan **90** 34N 133E
Mijares: *r.*, Spain **69** 40N 0
Milan (Milano): Italy **71** 45N 9E
Milbank: U.S.A. **53** 45N 97W
Mildura: Australia **94** 34S 142E
Miles City: U.S.A. **53** 46N 106W
Milford Haven: Wales **67** 52N 5W
Milford Sound: N.Z. **95** 44S 168E
Milk: *r.*, U.S.A. **52** 48N 109W
Millau: France **69** 44N 3E
Milledgeville: U.S.A. **51** 33N 83W
Mille Lacs: *l.* U.S.A. **53** 46N 94W
Millinocket: U.S.A. **51** 46N 69W
Milos: *i.*, U.S.A. **71** 37N 24E
Milwaukee: U.S.A. **51** 43N 88W
Min: *r.*, China **89** 27N 117E
Minamata: Japan **90** 32N 130E
Minas: Uruguay **61** 34S 55W
Minatitlán: Mexico **58** 17N 95W
Mindanao: *i.*, Phil. **91** 8N 125E
Minden: U.S.A. **50** 33N 93W
Mindoro: *i.*, Phil. **91** 13N 121E
Mine Hd.: R. of Irel. **67** 52N 8W
Mineral Wells: U.S.A. **50** 33N 98W
Minneapolis: U.S.A. **53** 45N 93W
Minnesota: *State*, U.S.A. **53** 47N 95W
Minorca: *see* Menorca
Minot: U.S.A. **53** 48N 101W
Minsk: U.S.S.R. **70** 54N 28E
Minusinsk: U.S.S.R. **81** 54N 92E
Miraflores Locks: Panama Canal **58** *Inset*
Miram Shah: Pak. **84** 33N 70E
Miranda de Ebro: Spain **69** 43N 3W
Mirim, Lagoa: *l.*, Brazil **61** 31S 51W
Mirtoon Sea: Greece **71** 37N 24E
Mirzapur: India **84** 25N 82E
Misawa: Japan **90** 41N 141E
Miskolc: Hungary **70** 48N 21E
Misoöl: *i.*, Indon. **91** 2S 130E
Mississippi: *r.*, U.S.A. **50** 31N 92W
Mississippi: *State*, U.S.A. **50/51** 33N 90W
Missoula: U.S.A. **52** 47N 114W
Missouri: *r.*, U.S.A. **53** 39N 94W
Missouri: *State*: U.S.A. **50** 39N 93W
Misurata: Libya **100** 32N 15E
Mitchell: U.S.A. **53** 44N 98W
Mitchell: *r.*, Queens., Australia **94** 16S 142E
Mitilíni: Greece **71** 39N 26E
Mito: Japan **90** 36N 141E
Mitu: Colombia **60** 1N 70W
Mitumba Mts.: Zaïre **102** 3S 29E
Miyako: Japan **90** 40N 142E
Miyakonojo:Japan **90** 32N 131E
Miyazaki: Japan **90** 32N 131E
Mizoram: *State*, India **85** 23N 93E
Mladá Boleslav: Czech. **70** 50N 15E
Mlawa: Poland **70** 53N 20E
Moascar: Egypt **101** *Inset*
Mobara: Japan **90** 35N 140E
Mobaye: Central Afr. Republic **101** 4N 22E
Moberly: U.S.A. **53** 39N 92W
Mobile: U.S.A. **51** 31N 88W
Mocâmedes: *now* Namibe
Mocuba: Moz. **102** 17S 37E
Modena: Italy **71** 45N 11E
Modesto: U.S.A. **52** 38N 121W
MOGADISCIO: Somali Republic **101** 2N 45E
Mogil'ev Podol'skiy: U.S.S.R. **70** 48N 28E
Mogocha: U.S.S.R. **79** 53N 120E
Mogollon Plateau: U.S.A. **52** 35N 111W
Mogoyto: U.S.S.R. **87** 55N 110E
Mointy: U.S.S.R. **81** 47N 74E
Mojave Desert: U.S.A. **52** 35N 117W
Mold: Wales **67** 53N 3W
Moldavian S.S.R.: U.S.S.R. **70/71** 47N 28E
Mollendo: Peru **60** 17S 72W
Molndal: Sweden **70** 58N 12E
Molopo: *r.*, S. Afr. **102** 26S 23E
Moluccas (Maluku): *is.*, Indon. **91** 0 127E
Molucca Sea: Indon. **91** 0 125E
Mombasa: Kenya **102** 4S 39E
Mombetsu:Japan **90** 44N 143E
MONACO: *cap.* Monaco **69** 44N 7E
Monaghan: R. of Ireland **67** 54N 7W
Monchegorsk: U.S.S.R. **70** 68N 33E
Mönchen-Gladbach: W. Germany **68** 51N 6E
Monclova: Mexico **58** 27N 101W
Mong Cai: Vietnam **85** 22N 108E
MONGOLIA *cap.* Ulan Bator (Ulaanbaatar) **86/87** 47N 105E
Mongu: Zambia **102** 15S 23E
Mongua: Angola **102** 17S 16E
Monmouth: Wales **67** 52N 3W
Monmouth: U.S.A. **53** 41N 91W
Monroe: La., U.S.A **50** 33N 92W
Monroe: Michigan, U.S.A. **51** 42N 83W
Monroeville: U.S.A. **51** 31N 87W
MONROVIA: Liberia **100** 6N 11W
Mons: Belgium **68** 50N 4E
Montana: *State*, U.S.A. **52** 47N 110W
Montargis: France **68** 48N 3E
Montauban: France **69** 44N 1E
Montauk Pt.: U.S.A. **55** 41N 72W
Montclair: U.S.A. **56** 41N 74W
Mont-de-Marsan: Fr. **69** 44N 1W
Monte Bello Is.: Australia **94** 20S 115E
Montego Bay: *town*, Jamaica **59** 18N 78W
Montélimar: France **69** 45N 5E
Monterey: *& Bay*, U.S.A. **52** 37N 122W
Monterrey: Mexico **58** 26N 100W
MONTEVIDEO: Uruguay **61** 35S 56W
Montgomery: U.S.A. **51** 32N 86W
Montgomery: Wales **67** 53N 3W
Montluçon: France **69** 46N 3E
Montpelier: U.S.A. **51** 44N 73W
Montpellier: France **69** 44N 4E
Montreux: Switz. **69** 46N 7E
Montrose: U.S.A. **52** 38N 108W
Montserrat: *i.*, West Indies **59** 17N 62W
Monywa: Burma **85** 22N 95E
Moorhead: U.S.A. **53** 47N 97W
Moosehead, L: U.S.A. **51** 46N 69W
Moradabad: India **84** 29N 79E
Morava: *r.*, Czech. **70** 49N 17E
Moray Firth: Scot. **67** 58N 4W
Moreau: *r.*, U.S.A. **53** 45N 102W
Morelia: Mexico **58** 20N 101W
Morgan City: U.S.A. **50** 30N 91W
Morgantown: U.S.A. **51** 40N 80W
Morioka: Japan **90** 40N 141E
Morlaix: France **68** 49N 4W
MOROCCO: *cap.* Rabat **100** 32N 5W
Morón: Cuba **59** 22N 78W
Morondava: Madagascar **102** 20S 45E
Morotai: *i.*, Indon. **91** 3N 128E
Morpeth: England **67** 55N 2W
Morristown: U.S.A. **56** 41N 75W
Morton Grove: U.S.A. **57** 42N 87W
Moscow: U.S.A. **52** 47N 117W
MOSCOW: U.S.S.R. **80** 56N 37E
Mosel (Moselle): *r.*, Fr./W. Ger. **68** 50N 7E
Moses Lake: *city*, U.S.A. **52** 47N 119W
Moshi: Tanzania **102** 3S 37E
Moss: Norway **70** 59N 11E
Most: Czech. **70** 50N 14E
Mostaganem: Algeria **69** 36N 0
Mostar: Yugoslavia **71** 43N 18E
Mosul: Iraq **83** 36N 43E
Motala: Sweden **70** 59N 15E
Motueka: N.Z. **95** 41S 173E
Moulins: France **69** 47N 3E
Moulmein: Burma **85** 17N 97E
Moultrie: U.S.A. **51** 31N 84W
Moundsville: U.S.A. **51** 40N 81W
Mountain Home: U.S.A. **52** 43N 116W
Mount Eba; *town*, Australia **94** 30S 136E
Mount Gambier: *town*, Australia **94** 38S 141E
Mount Isa: *town*, Australia **94** 21S 140E
Mount Lyell: *town*, Australia **94** 42S 146E
Mount Magnet: *town*, Australia **94** 28S 118E
Mount Morgan: *town*, Australia **94** 24S 150E
Mount Pleasant: *city*, U.S.A. **24** 44N 85W

Mount Prospect: *city*, U.S.A. **57** 42N 88W
Mount Vernon: *city*, Ill., U.S.A. **51** 38N 89W
Mount Vernon: *city*, N.Y., U.S.A. **56** 41N 74W
Mount Vernon: *city*, Wash., U.S.A. **52** 48N 122W
Mourne Mts.: N. Irel. **67** 54N 6W
Moyale: Kenya **102** 4N 39E
MOZAMBIQUE: *cap*. Maputo **102** — —
Mozambique: Moz. **102** 15S 40E
Mozambique Chan. **102** 15S 41E
Mozyr': U.S.S.R. **70** 52N 29E
Mpanda: Tanzania **102** 6S 31E
Mtwara: Tanzania **102** 10S 40E
Muang Khon Kaen: Thailand **85** 16N 103E
Muang Lampang: Thailand **85** 18N 99E
Muang Nan: Thailand **85** 19N 101E
Muang Phrae: Thailand **85** 18N 100E
Muang Phitsanulok: Thailand **85** 17N 100E
Muar: Malaysia **85** 2N 103E
Muchinga Mts.: Zambia **102** 13S 32E
Mudanjiang: China **87** 45N 130E
Mufulira: Zambia **102** 13S 28E
Muğla: Turkey **82** 37N 28E
Muhammad Qol: Sudan **82** 21N 37E
Mukachevo: U.S.S.R. **70** 48N 23E
Mukallā: Yemen P.D.R. **83** 15N 49E
Mukden: *see* Shenyang
Mülheim an der Ruhr: W. Germany **68** 51N 7E
Mulhouse: France **68** 48N 7E
Mull: *i.*, Scotland **67** 56N 6W
Müller Mts.: Indon. **91** 1N 114E
Mull Hd.: Scotland **67** 59N 3W
Mullingar: R. of Irel. **67** 54N 7W
Mull of Oa.: Scotland **67** 56N 6W
Multan: Pak. **84** 30N 71E
Muna: *i.*, Indonesia **91** 5S 122E
Muncie: U.S.A. **51** 40N 85W
Mundelein: U.S.A. **57** 42N 88W
Mungbere: Zaïre **102** 3N 28E
Munich (München): W. Germany **70** 48N 12E
Münster: W. Ger. **68** 52N 8E
Muong Sing: Laos **85** 21N 101E
Murchison: *r.*, Austl. **94** 27S 116E
Murcia: Spain **69** 38N 1W
Mureşul: *r.*, Romania **70** 46N 24E
Murfreesboro:U.S.A. **51** 36N 86W
Murmansk: U.S.S.R. **78** 69N 33E
Murom: U.S.S.R. **80** 56N 42E
Muroran: Japan **90** 42N 141E
Murray: *r.*, Austl. **94** 35S 139E
Murray Bridge: Australia **94** 35S 139E
Murrumbidgee: *r.*, Australia **94** 35S 146E
Murwillumbah: Australia **94** 28S 153E
MUSCAT: Oman **83** 24N 59E
Muscatine: U.S.A. **51** 41N 91W
Muskegon: *r.*, U.S.A. **24** 44N 85W
Muskogee: U.S.A. **50** 36N 95W
Mussourie: India **84** 30N 78E
Mustafakemalpaşa: Turkey **71** 40N 28E
Mustang *I.*: U.S.A. **50** 27N 97W
Muswellbrook: Austl. **94** 32S 151E
Mutare (*formerly* Umtali): Zimbabwe **102** 19S 33E
Muyun-Kum: *desert*, U.S.S.R. **81** 44N 71E
Muzaffarnagar **84** 30N 78E
Muzaffarpur:India **84** 26N 85E
Muzon, C.: U.S.A. **22** 55N 133W
Mwanza: Tanzania **102** 3S 33E
Mweru, L.: Zambia/Zaïre **102** 9S 29E
Myingyan: Burma **85** 21N 95E
Myitkyina: Burma **85** 26N 97E
Mymensingh: Bangl. **84** 25N 90E
Mysore: India **84** 12N 77E
My Tho: Vietnam **85** 10N 106E

N

Naas: R. of Ireland **67** 53N 7W
Nachingwea: Tanzan. **102** 10S 39E
Nacogdoches: U.S.A. **50** 32N 95W
Nadym: U.S.S.R. **78** 65N 73E
Naestved: Denmark **70** 55N 12E
Nafud: *desert*, Saudi Arabia **82** 28N 41E
Nagahama: Japan **90** 35N 136E
Naga Hills: India/Burma **85** 26N 95E
Nagaland: *State*, India **85** 26N 95E
Nagano: Japan **90** 37N 138E
Nagaoka: Japan **90** 37N 139E
Nagapattinam: India **84** 11N 80E
Nagasaki: Japan **90** 33N 130E
Nagercoil: India **84** 8N 77E
Nagoya: Japan **90** 35N 137E
Nagpur: India **84** 21N 79E
Nagykanizsa: Hung. **71** 46N 16E
Naha: Okinawa I. **87** 26N 127E
Naini Tal: India **84** 29N 80E
Nairn: Scotland **67** 58N 4W
NAIROBI: Kenya **102** 2S 37E
Najaf: Iraq **83** 32N 44E
Najd: *reg.*, Saudi Arabia **82/83** 26N 42E
Najran: Saudi Arabi **83** 17N 44E
Nakaminato: Japan **90** 36N 141E
Nakatsu: Japan **90** 34N 131E
Nakhon Phanom: Thailand **85** 17N 105E
Nakhon Ratchasima: Thailand **85** 15N 102E
Nakhon Sawan: Thailand **85** 16N 100E
Nakhon Si Thammarat: Thailand **85** 8N 100E
Nakuru: Kenya **102** 0 36E
Namangan: U.S.S.R. **81** 41N 72E
Nambour: Austl. **94** 27S 153E
Nam Dinh: Vietnam **85** 20N 106E
Namib Desert: Namibia **102** 23S 15E
Namibe (Moçâmedes): Namibia **102** 15S 12E
NAMIBIA: *cap.*, Windhoek **102** — —
Nampa: U.S.A. **52** 44N 117W
Nampula: Moz. **102** 15S 40E
Namsos: Norway **70** 64N 11E
Namur: Belgium **68** 50N 5E
Nanao: Japan **90** 37N 137E
Nanchang: China **89** 28N 116E
Nancy: France **68** 49N 6E
Nanda Devi: *mtn.*, India **84** 30N 80E
Nander: India **84** 17N 77E
Nangchen Japo: *mtn.*, China **86** 33N 94E
Nanjing (Nanking): China **88** 32N 119E
Nanling: *mtns.*, China **89** 25N 112E
Nanning: China **89** 23N 108E
Nanping: China **89** 27N 118E
Nansei Is.: *see* Ryukyu Is.
Nantes: France **68** 47N 2W
Nantong: China **88** 32N 121E
Nanumea: *i.*, Tuvalu **104** 5S 176E
Nanxiong: China **89** 25N 114E
Nanyang: China **88** 33N 112E
Nanyuki: Kenya **102** 0 37E
Nao C. de la: Spain **69** 39N 0
Napa: U.S.A. **52** 38N 122W
Napier: N.Z. **95** 39S 177E
Naples: Italy **71** 41N 14E
Nara: Japan: **90** 35N 136E
Narayanganj: Bangl. **84** 24N 90E
Narbada: *r.*, India **84** 22N 75E
Narbonne: France **69** 43N 3E
Naruto: Japan **90** 34N 135E
Narva: U.S.S.R. **80** 59N 28E
Narvik: Norway **70** 68N 17E
Nar'yan-Mar: U.S.S.R. **78** 67N 53E
Nashua: U.S.A. **55** 43N 72W
Nashville: U.S.A. **51** 36N 87W
Nasik: India **84** 20N 74E
Naşiriyah: Iraq **83** 31N 46E
NASSAU: The Bahamas **59** 25N 77W
Nassau Mts.: Indonesia **94** 4S 136E
Nasser, L.: Egypt **82** 23N 33E
Nässjö: Sweden **70** 58N 15E
Natal: Brazil **60** 6S 35W
Natal: *Prov.*, S. Afr. **102** 28S 31E
Natchez: U.S.A. **50** 32N 91W
Natchitoches: U.S.A. **50** 33N 93W
Natuna Is.: Indon. **85** 4N 108E
Naturaliste: Cape Australia **94** 34S 115E
NAURU: *cap.* Nauru **104** 1S 167E
Navan: R. of Irel. **67** 54N 7W
Navarin, C.: U.S.S.R. **79** 62N 179E
Navasota: *r.*, U.S.A. **50** 31N 96W
Návpaktos: Greece **71** 38N 21E
Návplion: Greece **71** 38N 23E
Náxos: *i.*, Greece **71** 37N 26E
Nayoro: Japan **90** 44N 142E
Nazareth: Israel **82** 33N 35E
Naze, The: *cape*, England **67** 52N 1E
Nazilli: Turkey **71** 38N 28E
N'DJAMENA: Chad **100** 12N 15E
Ndjole: Gabon **102** 0 11E
Ndola: Zambia **102** 13S 29E
Neagh, L.: N. Irel. **67** 55N 6W
Nebit-Dag: U.S.S.R. **80** 40N 55E
Nebraska: *State*, U.S.A. **53** 42N 100W
Nebraska City: U.S.A. **53** 41N 96W
Neches: *r.*, U.S.A. **50** 31N 95W
Negev: *desert*, Israel **82** 30N 35E
Negro: *r.*, Argentina **60** 40S 64W
Negro: *r.*, Brazil **60** 1S 64W
Negros: *i.*, Phil. **91** 10N 123E
Nehbandān: Iran **83** 32N 60E
Nei Monggol (Inner Mongolia) **79** 45N 120E
Neisse (Nysa) *r.*, Pol/E. Ger. **70** 52N 15E
Neiva: Colombia **60** 3N 75W
Nellore: India **84** 14N 80E
Nelson: N.Z. **95** 41S 173E
Néma: Mauritania **100** 17N 7E
Neman: *r.*, U.S.S.R. **70** 53N 25E
Nemuro: Japan **90** 43N 145E
Nenagh: R. of Irel. **67** 53N 8W
Nene: *r.*, England **67** 53N 0
Nenjiang: China **87** 49N 125E
Neosho: *r.*, U.S.A. **50** 38N 96W
NEPAL: *cap.* Katmandu **84** 28N 85E
Nerchinsk: U.S.S.R. **79** 52N 116E
Neryungri: U.S.S.R. **79** 57N 125E
Ness, L: Scotland **67** 57N 4W
NETHERLANDS: *cap.* Amsterdam **68** 52N 5E
Neubrandenburg: E. Germany **70** 53N 13E
Neuchâtel: Switzerland **69** 47N 7E
Neuquén: Argentina **60** 39S 68W
Neuse: *r.*, U.S.A. **51** 35N 78W
Neuss: W. Germany **68** 51N 7E
Nevada: *State*, U.S.A. **52** 39N 117W
Nevada City: U.S.A. **52** 39N 121W
Never: U.S.S.R. **79** 54N 124E
Nevers: France **69** 47N 3E
Nevis: *i.*, St. Christopher-Nevis **59** 17N 63W
New Amsterdam: *i.*, Indian Ocean **104** 38S 78E
Newark: N.J., U.S.A. **56** 41N 74W
Newark: Ohio, U.S.A. **51** 40N 82W
New Bedford: U.S.A. **55** 42N 71W
New Bern: U.S.A. **51** 35N 77W
Newberry: U.S.A. **24** 46N 85W
New Braunfels: U.S.A. **50** 30N 98W
New Britain: *i.*, Papua, New Guineau **94** 6S 150E
New Brunswick: U.S.A. **56** 40N 74W
Newbury: England **67** 51N 1W
New Caledonia: *i.*, Pacific Ocean **94** 21S 165E
Newcastle: Australia **94** 33S 152E
New Castle: Pa., U.S.A. **51** 41N 80W
Newcastle: Wyo., U.S.A. **53** 44N 104W
Newcastle upon Tyne: England **67** 55N 2W
New Delhi: India **84** 28N 77E
New Forest: *reg.*, England **67** 51N 2W
New Guineau: *i.*, S.E. Asia **94** 5S 140E
New Hampshire: *State*, U.S.A. **51** 44N 72W
Newhaven: England **67** 51N 0
New Haven: U.S.A. **55** 41N 73W
New Hebrides: *is., now* **VANUATU**
New Hyde Park: U.S.A. **56** 41N 74W
New Iberia: U.S.A. **50** 30N 92W
New Ireland: *i.*, Papua New Guinea **94** 3S 152E
New Jersey: *State*, U.S.A. **54/55** 40N 75W
Newman: Austl. **94** 23S 120E
New Mexico: *State*, U.S.A. **52/53** 34N 107W
Newnan: U.S.A. **51** 33N 85W
New Orleans: U.S.A. **50** 30N 90W
New Plymouth: N.Z. **95** 39S 174E
Newport: Wales **67** 52N 3W
Newport: Rhode Island, U.S.A. **55** 41N 71W
Newport: Vt., U.S.A. **51** 45N 72W
Newport News: U.S.A. **51** 37N 76W
New Providence: *i.*, The Bahamas **59** 25N 77W
New Rochelle: U.S.A. **56** 41N 74W
Newry: N. Ireland **67** 54N 6W
New Siberian Is. *see* Novosibirskiye Ostrova
New South Wales: *State*, Australia **94** 32S 146E
Newton: Iowa, U.S.A. **50** 42N 93W
Newton: Kansas, U.S.A. **53** 38N 97W
New Ulm: U.S.A. **53** 44N 95W
New York: U.S.A. **56** — —
New York: *State*, U.S.A. **54/55** — —
NEW ZEALAND: *cap.* Wellington **95** — —
Ngami, Lake: Bots **102** 21S 23E
N'Gaounderé: Cameroun **100** 7N 14E
Ngauruhoe: *mtn.*, N.Z. **95** 39S 175E
Ngorongoro Conservation Area: Tanzania **102** 3S 36E
Nguru: Nigeria **100** 13N 10E
Nha Trang: Vietnam **85** 12N 109E
NIAMEY: Niger **100** 14N 2E
Nias *i.*, Indonesia **85** 1N 98E
NICARAGUA: *cap.* Managua **58/59** 13N 85W
Nicaragua, Lake: Nic. **58** 11N 85W
Nice: France **69** 44N 7E
Nicobar Is.: Ind. O. **85** 7N 93E
NICOSIA: Cyprus **82** 35N 33E
Nienburg: W. Ger. **68** 53N 9E
NIGER: *cap.* Niamey **100** 17N 10E
Niger: *r.*, W. Africa **100** 8N 6E
NIGERIA: *cap.* Lagos **100** — —
Nihoa: *i.*, Hawaiian Is. **104** 22N 162W
Niigata: Japan **90** 38N 139E
Niihama: Japan **90** 34N 133E
Niihau: *i.*, Hawaiian Is. **104** 22N 162W
Nijmegen: Neth. **68** 52N 6E
Nikolayev: U.S.S.R. **80** 47N 32E
Nikolayevsk: U.S.S.R. **79** 53N 142E
Nikopol: U.S.S.R. **80** 48N 34E
Nikšić: Yugoslavia **71** 43N 19E
Nikumaroru (*formerly* Gardner I.): Pacific Ocean **104** 5S 175W
Nile: *r.*, N. Africa **101** 21N 31E
Niles: U.S.A. **57** 42N 88W
Nilgin Hills: India **84** 11N 77E
Nîmes: France **69** 44N 4E
Nimule: Sudan **101** 4N 32E
Nineveh: *hist.* Iraq **83** 37N 43E
Ningbo: China **89** 30N 122E
Ningxia (Ninghsia Hui): *Prov.*, China **88** 37N 106E
Niobrara: *r.*, U.S.A. **53** 43N 99W
Niort: France **69** 46N 0
Niš: Yugoslavia **71** 43N 22E
Niterói: Brazil **61** 23S 43W
Nith: *r.*, Scotland **67** 55N 4W
Nitra: Czechoslovakia **70** 48N 18E
Nizamabad: India **84** 17N 78E
Nizhne-Angarsk: U.S.S.R. **87** 56N 110E
Nizhneudinsk: U.S.S.R. **86** 55N 99E
Nizhniy-Tagil: U.S.S.R. **81** 58N 60E
Nobeoka: Japan **90** 33N 132E
Noboribetsu: Japan **90** 42N 141E
Nome: U.S.A. **79** 65N 165W
Nong Khai: Thailand **85** 18N 103E
Nordhausen: E. Ger. **70** 52N 11E
Nordvik: U.S.S.R. **79** 74N 110E
Norfolk: Nebraska, U.S.A. **53** 42N 97W
Norfolk: Va., U.S.A. **51** 37N 76W
Norfolk Broads: *reg.*, England **67** 53N 1E
Norfolk I.: Pac. O. **104** 29S 168E
Norfolk, L.: U.S.A. **50** 36N 92W
Noril'sk: U.S.S.R. **79** 69N 90E
Norman: *r.*, Austl. **94** 19S 142E
Normanton: Austl. **94** 18S 141E
Norrköping: Sweden **70** 59N 16E
Norseman: Austl. **94** 32S 122E
Northallerton: Eng. **67** 54N 1W
Northam: Australia **94** 32S 117E
North American Basin: Atlantic Ocean **103** 32N 55W
Northampton: England **67** 52N 1W
Northampton: U.S.A. **55** 42N 73W
North Bend: U.S.A. **52** 43N 124W
North Bergen: U.S.A. **56** 41N 74W
Northbrook: U.S.A. **57** 42N 88W
North Canadian: *r.*, U.S.A. **50** 37N 103W
North Cape: N.Z. **95** 34S 173E
North Cape: Norway **70** 71N 26E
North Carolina: *State*, U.S.A. **51** 35N 80W
North Channel: Scot./N. Irel. **67** 55N 6W
North Chelmsford: U.S.A. **55** 43N 71W
North Chicago: U.S.A. **57** 42N 88W
North Dakota: *State*, U.S.A. **53** 47N 100W
North Dvina: *r.*, U.S.S.R. **78** 63N 43E
NORTHERN IRELAND: *cap.* Belfast **67** — —
Northern Sporades: *is.*, Greece **71** 39N 24E
Northern Territory: Australia **94** 20S 135E
North Foreland: *cape*, England **67** 51N 1E
North Island: N.Z. **95** — —
NORTH KOREA: *cap.* Pyŏngyang **87** 40N 127E
Northlake: U.S.A. **57** 42N 88W
North Minch: *chan.*, Scotland **67** 58N 6W
North Platte: *& r.*, U.S.A. **53** 41N 100W
North Sea **68** — —
North Uist: *i.*, Scot. **67** 58N 7W
North West Highlands: Scotland **67** 57N 5W
Northwest Pacific Basin: Pacific Ocean **104** 35N 155E
North York Moors: England **67** 54N 1W
Norton Sound: *bay*, U.S.A. **79** 64N 163W
Norwalk: U.S.A. **55** 41N 73W
NORWAY: *cap.* Oslo **70** — —
Norwich: England **67** 53N 1E
Norwood: U.S.A. **55** 42N 71W
Noshiro: Japan **90** 40N 140E
Nossob: *r.*, Africa **102** 26S 21E
Nossi Bé: *i.*, Madagascar **102** 13S 48E
Noto-Hanto: *penin.*, Japan **90** 37N 137E
Nottingham: England **67** 53N 1W
Nouadhibou: Mauritania **100** 21N 17W
NOUAKCHOTT: Mauritania **100** 18N 17W
Nouméa: New Hebrides **94** 22S 167E
Novaya Zemlya: *is.*, U.S.S.R. **78** 75N 60E
Novgorod: U.S.S.R. **80** 58N 31E
Novi Pazar: Yugo **71** 43N 20E
Novi Sad: Yugo. **71** 45N 20E
Novocherkassk: U.S.S.R. **80** 47N 40E
Novograd Volynskiy: U.S.S.R. **70** 51N 28E
Novo Hamburgo: Brazil **61** 30S 51W
Novokuznetsk: U.S.S.R. **81** 54N 87E
Novomoskovsk: U.S.S.R. **80** 54N 38E
Novonazyvayevka: U.S.S.R. **81** 56N 72E
Novorossiysk: U.S.S.R. **80** 45N 38E
Novosibirsk: U.S.S.R. **81** 55N 83E
Novosibirskiye Ostrova (New Siberian Is.): *is.*, U.S.S.R. **79** 76N 140E
Novouzensk: U.S.S.R. **80** 50N 48E
Novyy Port: U.S.S.R. **79** 67N 74E
Nowa Sól: Poland **70** 52N 16E
Nowy Sacz: Poland **70** 50N 21E
Nubian Desert: Sud. **101** 21N 33E
Nueces: *r.*, U.S.A. **50** 28N 98W
Nueva Rosita: Mexico **58** 28N 101W
Nuevitas: Cuba **59** 22N 77W
Nuevo Laredo: Mex. **58** 27N 100W
Nullarbor Plain: Australia **94** 30S 128E
Numazu: Japan **90** 35N 139E
Nunivak I.: U.S.A. **104** 60N 166W
Nürnberg (Nuremberg): W. Germany **70** 49N 11E
Nuseybin: Turkey **82** 37N 41E
Nushki: Pakistan **84** 29N 66E
NUUK (*formerly* Godthaab): Greenland **1** 64N 52W
Nuwara Eliya: Sri Lanka **84** 7N 81E
Nyahururu: Kenya **102** 0 36E
Nyala: Sudan **101** 12N 25E
Nyasa (Malawi), L.: Africa **102** 13S 34E
Nyenchen Tanglha Range: China **84** 30N 90E
Nyíregyháza: Hung. **70** 48N 22E
Nykøbing: Denmark **70** 55N 12E
Nyköping: Sweden **70** 59N 17E
Nyngan: Australia **94** 32S 147E
Nysa: Poland **70** 51N 18E
Nysa (Neisse): *r.*, Pol./E. Ger. **70** 50N 15E

O

Oahu: *i.*, Hawaiian Is. **105** 21N 158W
Oak Brook: U.S.A. **57** 42N 88W
Oakdale: U.S.A. **52** 38N 121W
Oakham: England **67** 53N 1W
Oakland: U.S.A. **52** 38N 122W
Oak Lawn: U.S.A. **57** 42N 88W
Oak Park: Illinois, U.S.A. **57** 42N 88W
Oak Ridge: U.S.A. **51** 36N 84W
Oamaru: N.Z. **95** 45N 171E
Oaxaca: Mexico **58** 17N 97W
Ob': *r.*, U.S.S.R. **78** 63N 65E
Ob': Gulf of: U.S.S.R. **78/9** 67N 76E
Oban: Scotland **67** 56N 5W
Obbia: Somali Rep. **101** 5N 48E
Oberhausen: W. Ger. **68** 51N 7E
Obidos: Brazil **60** 2S 56W
Obihiro: Japan **90** 43N 143E
Obi Is.: Indonesia **91** 2S 128E
Ocala: U.S.A. **51** 29N 82W
Ocean I.: Pacific O. **104** 1S 170E
Odate: Japan **90** 40N 141E
Odawara: Japan **90** 35N 139E
Odemis: Turkey **71** 38N 28E
Odense: Denmark **70** 55N 10E
Oder (Odra): *r.*, E. Ger./Pol. **70** 53N 14E
Odessa: U.S.A. **50** 32N 102W
Odessa: U.S.S.R. **80** 46N 31E
Oeno I.: Pacific O. **105** 24S 130W
Ofunato: Japan **90** 39N 142E
Ogaden: *reg.*, Ethiopia **101** 7N 43E
Ogaki: Japan **90** 35N 137E
Ogbomosho: Nigeria **100** 8N 4E
Ogden: U.S.A. **52** 41N 112W
Ohai: N.Z. **95** 46S 168E
Ohakune: N.Z. **95** 39S 175E
Ohio: *r.* U.S.A. **51** 37N 89W
Ohio: *State*, U.S.A. **51** 40N 83W
Oise: *r.*, France **68** 49N 2E
Oita: Japan **90** 33N 132E
Oka: *r.*, U.S.S.R. **80** 55N 40E
Okanogan: *r.*, U.S.A. **52** 49N 120W
Okaya: Japan **90** 36N 138E
Okayama: Japan **90** 35N 134E
Okazaki: Japan **90** 35N 137E
Okeechobee, L.: U.S.A. **51** 27N 81W
Okhotsk: U.S.S.R. **79** 59N 143E
Okhotsk, Sea of **79** 55N 150E
Oki-gunto: *i.*, Japan **90** 36N 133E
Okinawa: *i.*, Japan **87** 27N 128E
Oklahoma: *State*, U.S.A. **50** 35N 97W
Oklahoma City: U.S.A. **50** 35N 98W
Oklawaha: *r.*, U.S.A. **51** 29N 82W
Okmulgee: U.S.A. **50** 36N 96W
Okovango Basin: Botswana **102** 19S 23E
Okt'abr'sk: U.S.S.R. **81** 49N 57E
Öland: *i.*, Sweden **70** 57N 17E
Oldenburg: W. Ger. **68** 53N 8E
Olduvai Gorge: Tanzania **102** 3S 35E
Olean: U.S.A. **54** 42N 78W
Olekminsk: U.S.S.R. **79** 60N 120E
Olenek: *r.*, U.S.S.R. **79** 71N 120E
Oléron, Ile d': Fr. **69** 46N 1W
Olomouc: Czech. **70** 50N 17E
Olsztyn: Poland **70** 54N 20E
Olympia: U.S.A. **52** 47N 123W
Olympic Nat. Park: U.S.A. **52** 48N 124W
Olympus: *mtn.*, Greece **71** 40N 22E
Omagh: N. Ireland **67** 55N 7W
Omaha: U.S.A. **53** 41N 96W
OMAN: *cap.* Muscat. **83** 20N 57E
Oman, Gulf of: Iran/Oman **83** 25N 57E
Omdurman: Sudan **82** 16N 32E
Ommaney, C.: U.S.A. **22** 56N 135W
Omsk: U.S.S.R. **81** 55N 73E
Omuta: Japan **90** 33N 131E
Omutinskoye: U.S.S.R. **81** 56N 68E
Onega, L.: U.S.S.R. **80** 63N 35E
O'Neill: U.S.A. **53** 42N 99W
Oneonta: U.S.A. **54** 42N 75W
Onslow Bay: U.S.A. **51** 34N 77W

Ontario, Lake: Canada/U.S.A. 51 44N 78W
Oodnadatta: Austl. 94 27S 135E
Ooldea: Australia 94 30S 132E
Ootacamund: India 84 11N 77E
Opava: Czech. 70 50N 18E
Opelika: U.S.A. 51 33N 85W
Opelousas: U.S.A. 50 31N 92W
Opole: Poland 70 51N 18E
Oporto: Portugal 69 41N 9W
Opotiki: N.Z. 95 38S 177E
Opunake: N.Z. 95 39S 174E
Oradea: Romania 71 47N 22E
Oran: Algeria 69 36N 1W
Orange: Australia 94 33S 149E
Orange: France 69 44N 5E
Orange: N.J., U.S.A. 56 41N 74W
Orange: Texas, U.S.A. 50 30N 94W
Orange: r., S. Africa/Namibia 102 28S 18E
Orangeburg: U.S.A. 51 33N 81W
Orange Free State: Prov., S. Africa 102 29S 27E
Orbost: Australia 94 39S 149E
Ord: r., Australia 94 16S 128E
Ordos: plat., China 88 39N 108E
Ordzhonikidze: U.S.S.R. 80 43N 45E
Örebro: Sweden 70 59N 15E
Oregon: State, U.S.A. 52 44N 120W
Oregon City: U.S.A. 52 45N 123W
Orekhovo-Zuyevo: U.S.S.R. 80 55N 39E
Orel': U.S.S.R. 80 53N 36E
Orem: U.S.A. 52 40N 112W
Orenburg: U.S.S.R. 80 52N 55E
Orense: Spain 69 42N 8W
Orihuela: Spain 69 38N 1W
Orinoco: r., Venez. 59 8N 64W
Orissa: State, India 84 20N 84E
Oristano: Sardinia 69 40N 9E
Orizaba: Mexico 58 19N 97W
Orkney Is.: Scotland 67 59N 3W
Orlando: U.S.A. 51 29N 81W
Orléans: France 68 48N 2E
Orosháza: Hungary 71 47N 21E
Orsk: U.S.S.R. 81 51N 59E
Oruro: Bolivia 60 18S 67W
Osage: r., U.S.A. 50 38N 94W
Osaka: Japan 90 35N 135E
Osh: U.S.S.R. 81 41N 73E
Oshkosh: U.S.A. 53 44N 88W
Oshogbo: Nigeria 100 8N 5E
Osijek: Yugoslavia 71 46N 19E
Oskaloosa: U.S.A. 53 41N 93W
Oskarshamn: Sweden 70 57N 16E
OSLO: Norway 70 60N 11E
Oslofjorden: fd., Norway 70 59N 11E
Osmanabad: India 84 18N 76E
Osnabruck: W. Ger. 68 52N 8E
Ostend: Belgium 68 51N 3E
Ostrava: Czech. 70 50N 18E
Ostrovnoye: U.S.S.R. 79 68N 164E
Ostrowiec Swietokrzyski: Pol. 70 51N 21E
Ostrów Wielkopolski: Poland 70 52N 18E
Osumi Is.: Japan 87 31N 131E
Oswego: U.S.A. 51 43N 76W
Otago Penin: N.Z. 95 46S 171E
Otaru: Japan 90 43N 141E
Otranto, Strait of: Italy/Albania 71 40N 18E
Otsu: Japan 90 35N 136E
Ottawa: Ill., U.S.A. 51 41N 89W
Ottawa: Kansas, U.S.A. 53 39N 95W
Ouachita: r., U.S.A. 50 33N 92W
OUAGADOUGOU: Burkina 100 12N 2W
Ouargla: Algeria 100 32N 5E
Oubangui: r., Africa 101 4N 21E
Oudtshoorn: S.Afr. 102 34S 22E
Oujda: Morocco 100 35N 2W
Oulu: & lake, Fin. 70 65N 25E
Ou-sammyaku: mtns., Japan 90 39N 141E
Ouse: r., East Anglia, England 67 53N 0
Outer Hebrides: is., Scotland 67 58N 7W
Oviedo: Spain 69 43N 6W
Owen, Mt.: N.Z. 95 42S 172E
Owen Falls: Uganda 102 0 33E
Owens, L.: U.S.A. 52 36N 118W
Owensboro: U.S.A. 51 38N 87W
Owen Stanley Range: Papua New Guinea 94 9S 147E
Owyhee Res.: & r., U.S.A. 52 43N 118W
Oxford: England 67 52N 1W
Oxnard: U.S.A. 52 34N 119W
Oxus: r. see Amu Dar'ya
Ozark Plateau: U.S.A. 50 37N 93W
Ozarks, L. of the: U.S.A. 50 38N 93W
Ózd: Hungary 70 48N 20E
Ozu: Japan 90 33N 133E

P

Pachuca: Mexico 58 20N 99W
Pacific Grove: U.S.A. 52 37N 122W
Pacific Ocean 104/5 — —
Padang: Indonesia 91 1S 100E
Padangsidimpuan: Indonesia 85 1N 99E
Padre I.: U.S.A. 50 27N 97W
Padua (Padova): Italy 71 45N 12E
Paducah: U.S.A. 51 37N 89W
Paisley: Scotland 67 56N 4W
Pajakumbuh: Indon. 85 0 100E
Pakanbaru: Indonesia 85 1N 102E
PAKISTAN: cap. Islamabad 84 — —
Pak Lay: Laos 85 18N 101E
Pakokku: Burma 85 21N 95E
Pakse: Laos 85 15N 105E
Pakwach: Uganda 102 8S 31E
Palatine: U.S.A. 57 42N 88W
Palatka: U.S.A. 51 30N 82W
Palawan: i., Phil. 91 10N 119E
Palembang: Indonesia 91 3S 105E
Palencia: Spain 69 42N 5W
Palermo: Sicily 71 38N 13E
Palestine: U.S.A. 50 32N 96W
Palghat: India 84 11N 76E
Palisade: U.S.A. 52 41N 116W
Palk Strait: India/Sri Lanka 84 10N 80E
Palliser, C.: N.Z. 95 42S 175E
Palma de Mallorca: Mallorca 69 40N 3E
Palmas, C., Liberia 100 4N 8W
Palmer Land: Antarctica 128 64S 63W
Palmerston North: New Zealand 95 40S 176E
Palmyra I.: Pac. O. 104 6N 162W
Palos, C. de: Spain 69 38N 1W
Pamiers: France 69 43N 2E
Pamirs: mtns., U.S.S.R./Afghanistan 81 37N 73E
Pamlico Sd.: U.S.A. 51 35N 76W
Pampa: reg., Argentina 60 33S 64W
Pampa: U.S.A. 50 35N 101W
Pamplona: Spain 69 43N 2W
PANAMA: cap. Panamá 59 8N 80W
Panama Canal 58 Inset
Panama City: U.S.A. 51 30N 86W
Panay: i., Phil. 91 11N 122E
Pančevo: Yugoslavia 71 45N 21E
Pangong Ra.: China 84 34N 80E
Panjim: India 84 15N 74E
Pantar: i., Indonesia 91 8S 124E
Pantelleria: i., Italy 71 37N 12E
Panyu: China 89 23N 113E
Papua: territ., Papua New Guinea 94 7S 145E
PAPUA NEW GUINEA: cap. Port Moresby 94 5S 145E
Pará: r., Brazil 60 1S 48W
Paraburdoo: Austl. 94 23S 118E
Paracel Is.: S. China Sea 91 16N 112E
PARAGUAY: cap. Asunción 60 23S 58W
Paraguay: r., S. Am. 61 26S 58W
Parakou: Benin 100 9N 3E
PARAMARIBO: Surinam 60 6N 55W
Paramus: U.S.A. 56 41N 74W
Paramushir: i., U.S.S.R. 79 51N 155E
Paraná: Argentina 61 32S 60W
Paraná: r., S.Am. 61 25S 53W
Paranaguá: Brazil 61 26S 48W
Parbati: r., India 84 23N 77E
Parbhani: India 84 19N 77E
Pardubice: Czech. 70 50N 16E
PARIS: France 72 49N 2E
Paris: U.S.A. 50 34N 96W
Parkersburg: U.S.A. 51 39N 82W
Park Range: U.S.A. 52 40N 107W
Park Rapids: town, U.S.A. 53 47N 95W
Park Ridge: U.S.A. 57 42N 88W
Parma: Italy 71 45N 10E
Parma: U.S.A. 51 41N 82W
Parnaíba: Brazil 60 3S 42W
Parnassós: mtn., Greece 71 38N 22E
Páros: i., Greece 71 37N 25E
Parsons: U.S.A. 53 37N 95W
Partizansk: U.S.S.R. 79 43N 133E
Pasadena: U.S.A. 52 34N 118W
Pascagoula: & r., U.S.A. 51 30N 89W
Pasco: U.S.A. 52 46N 119W
Pasir Mas: Malaysia 85 6N 102E
Passaic: U.S.A. 56 41N 74W
Passau: W. Germany 70 49N 13E
Passero, C.: Sicily 71 37N 15E
Passo Fundo: Brazil 61 28S 52W
Pasto: Colombia 60 1N 77W
Patagonia: reg., Arg. 60 45S 70W
Paterson: U.S.A. 56 41N 74W
Pathankot: India 84 32N 76E
Pathfinder Res.: U.S.A. 52 42N 107W
Patiala: India 84 30N 76E
Patna: India 84 26N 85E
Patos, Lagoa dos: Brazil 61 31S 51W
Pátrai (Patras): Greece 71 38N 22E
Pattani: Thailand 85 6N 101E
Pau: France 69 43N 0
Paulistana: Brazil 60 8S 41W
Pavia: Italy 69 45N 9E
Pavlodar: U.S.S.R. 81 52N 77E
Pawtucket: U.S.A. 55 42N 71W
Payette: & r., U.S.A. 52 44N 117W
Paysandú: Uruguay 61 32S 58W
Pearl: r., U.S.A. 50 32N 90W
Pease: r., U.S.A. 50 34N 100W
Peć: Yugoslavia 71 43N 20E
Pechenga: U.S.S.R. 70 70N 31E
Pechora: U.S.S.R. 78 65N 57E
Pechora: r., U.S.S.R. 80 63N 56E
Pecos: & r., U.S.A. 50 31N 104W
Pécs: Hungary 71 46N 18E
Pedro, Pt.: Sri Lanka 84 10N 80E
Pedro Miguel Locks: Panama Canal 58 Inset
Peebles: Scotland 67 56N 3W
Pee Dee: r., U.S.A. 51 34N 79W
Peel: I. of Man 67 54N 5W
Pegasus Bay: N.Z. 95 43S 173E
Pegu: Burma 85 17N 96E
Peipus, L.: U.S.S.R. 80 58N 27E
PEKING (BEIJING): China 88 40N 116E
Pelican Point: Namibia 102 23S 14E
Peloponnese: penin., Greece 71 38N 22E
Pelotas: Brazil 61 32S 52W
Pelusium, Bay of: Egypt 101 Inset
Pematangsiantar: Indonesia 85 2N 99E
Pemba: i., Tanzan. 102 5S 40E
Pembroke: Wales 67 52N 5W
Pendembu: Sierra Leone 100 8N 11W
Pendleton: U.S.A. 52 46N 119W
Pend Oreille, L.: U.S.A. 52 48N 116W
Penganga: r., India 84 20N 77E
P'enghu Liehtao (Pescadores): is., Taiwan 89 24N 120E
Peninsular Malaysia (Malaya): Malaysia 85 4N 102E
Pennar: r., India 84 14N 77E
Pennines: mtns., Eng. 67 54N 2W
Pennsylvania: State, U.S.A. 51 41N 77W
Penobscot: r., U.S.A. 51 45N 68W
Pensacola: U.S.A. 51 30N 87W
Pentland Firth: Scot. 67 59N 3W
Penza: U.S.S.R. 80 53N 45E
Penzance: England 67 50N 6W
Peoria: U.S.A. 51 41N 90W
Perche, Collines du: hills, France 68 49N 1E
Pereira: Colombia 60 5N 76W
Pergamino: Arg. 61 34S 61W
Périgueux: France 69 45N 1E
Perm: U.S.S.R. 80 57N 55E
Pernik: Bulgaria 71 43N 23E
Perpignan: France 69 43N 3E
PERSIA: see IRAN
Persian Gulf: see Gulf, The
Perth: Australia 94 32S 116E
Perth: Scotland 67 56N 3W
Perth Amboy: U.S.A. 56 41N 74W
PERU: cap. Lima 60 10S 75W
Peru Basin: Pacific O. 105 15S 85W
Peru-Chile Trench: Pacific Ocean 105 20S 75W
Perugia: Italy 71 43N 12E
Pesaro: Italy 71 44N 13E
Pescadores: is., see P'enghu Liehtao
Pescara: Italy 71 42N 14E
Peshawar: Pakistan 84 34N 71E
Peterborough: Eng. 67 53N 0
Peterhead: Scotland 67 57N 2W
Petersburg: Alaska, U.S.A. 22 57N 133W
Petersburg: Va., U.S.A. 51 37N 78W
Petoskey: U.S.A. 24 45N 85W
Petrila: Romania 71 45N 23E
Petrolina: Brazil 60 10S 40W
Petropavlovsk: U.S.S.R. 81 55N 69E
Petropavlovsk-Kamchatskiy: U.S.S.R. 79 53N 159E
Petrópolis: Brazil 61 23S 43W
Petroşeni: Romania 71 45N 23E
Petrozavodsk: U.S.S.R. 80 62N 35E
Petukhovo: U.S.S.R. 81 55N 68E
Phanom Dongrak: mtns., Thailand 83 14N 103E
Phan Rang: Vietnam 85 12N 109E
Phan Thiet: Vietnam 85 10N 108E
Phatthalung: Thailand 85 8N 100E
Phenix City: U.S.A. 51 32N 85W
Phet Buri: Thailand 85 13N 99E
Philadelphia: U.S.A. 54 40N 75W
PHILIPPINES, THE: cap. Manila 91 10N 123E
Philippine Sea 104 18N 130E
PHNOM PENH: Kampuchea 85 11N 105E
Phoenix: U.S.A. 52 34N 112W
Phoenix I. now Rawaki
Phoenix Is.: Pac. O. 104 3S 175W
Phong Saly: Laos 85 21N 102E
Phuket: Thailand 85 8N 98E
Piatra-Neamţ: Rom. 71 47N 26E
Picton: N.Z. 95 41S 174E
Piedras Negras: Mex. 58 29N 101W
Pierre: U.S.A. 53 44N 100W
Pietermaritzburg: South Africa 102 30S 30E
Pigeon: r., U.S.A./Canada 53 48N 90W
Pikeville: U.S.A. 51 37N 83W
Piła: Poland 70 53N 17E
Pilsen: see Plzeň
Pinang: i., Malaysia 85 5N 100E
Pinar del Río: Cuba 59 22N 84W
Pindus Mts.: Greece 71 40N 21E
Pine Bluff: U.S.A. 50 34N 92W
Pine Island Sound: U.S.A. 51 27N 82W
Pines, I. of: Cuba 59 22N 83W
Pingdingshan: China 88 34N 113E
Pinghu: China 89 31N 121E
Pingliang: China 88 35N 107E
Pingxiang: China 89 28N 114E
Pingyao: China 88 37N 112E
Pinsk: U.S.S.R. 70 52N 26E
Piombino: Italy 71 43N 10E
Piracicaba: & r., Brazil 61 23S 48W
Piraieus: Greece 71 38N 24E
Pírgos: Greece 71 38N 22E
Pisa: Italy 71 44N 10E
Pistoia: Italy 71 44N 11E
Pit: r., U.S.A. 52 41N 121W
Pitcairn I.: Pac. O. 105 25S 130W
Piteşti: Romania 71 45N 25E
Pittsburg: Kansas, U.S.A. 53 37N 95W
Pittsburg: Texas, U.S.A. 50 33N 95W
Pittsburgh: U.S.A. 51 40N 80W
Piura: Peru 60 5S 81W
Plainfield: U.S.A. 56 41N 74W
Plata, Rio de la: r., S. America 61 35S 57W
Platte: r., U.S.A. 53 41N 100W
Plattsburg: U.S.A. 51 45N 74W
Plauen: E. Germany 70 50N 12E
Plenty, Bay of: N.Z. 95 38S 177E
Plentywood: U.S.A. 53 49N 105W
Pleven: Bulgaria 71 43N 25E
Płock: Poland 70 53N 20E
Ploeşti: Romania 71 45N 26E
Plovdiv: Bulgaria 71 42N 25E
Plunge: U.S.S.R. 70 56N 22E
Plymouth: England 67 50N 4W
Plzeň (Pilsen): Czech. 70 50N 13E
Po: r., Italy 71 45N 10E
Pocatello: U.S.A. 52 43N 112W
Pointe Noire: Congo 102 5S 12E
Poitiers: France 69 47N 0
Pokaran: India 84 27N 72E
POLAND: cap. Warsaw 70 52N 20E
Poltava: U.S.S.R. 80 50N 35E
Poltuvil: Sri Lanka 84 7N 82E
Polunochnoye: U.S.S.R. 81 62N 60E
Pomeranian Bay: E. Ger./Pol. 70 54N 14E
Pompton Lakes: town, U.S.A. 56 41N 74W
Ponape: i., Pacific O. 104 8N 159E
Ponca City: U.S.A. 50 37N 97W
Ponce: Puerto Rico 59 18N 67W
Pondicherry: India 84 12N 80E
Ponta Grossa: Brazil 61 24S 47W
Ponta Porã: Brazil 60 22S 56W
Pontchartrain, L.: U.S.A. 50 30N 90W
Pontevedra: Spain 69 42N 9W
Pontiac: U.S.A. 51 43N 83W
Pontianak: Indonesia 85 0 109E
Pontic Mts.: Turkey 82 42N 35E
Pontivy: France 68 48N 3W
Pontoise: France 72 49N 2E
Poole: England 67 51N 2W
Poona: see Pune
Poopo, L.: Bolivia 60 18S 67W
Popayan: Colombia 60 2N 77W
Poplar Bluff: U.S.A. 50 37N 90W
Popocatepetl: volc., Mexico 58 19N 99W
Porbandar: India 84 22N 70E
Pordenone: Italy 71 46N 13E
Porcupine: r., Canada/U.S.A. 20 67N 142W
Pori: Finland 70 61N 22E
Portalegre: Portugal 69 39N 7W
Port Angeles: U.S.A. 52 48N 123W
Port Antonio: Jam. 59 18N 76W
Port Arthur: U.S.A. 50 30N 94W
Port Augusta: Austl. 94 32S 138E
PORT-AU-PRINCE: Haiti 59 19N 72W
Port Blair: Andaman Is. 85 12N 93E
Port Chalmers: N.Z. 95 46S 171E
Port Chester: U.S.A. 56 41N 74W
Port Dickson: Mal. 85 2N 102E
Port Elizabeth: South Africa 102 34S 26E
Port Fuad: Egypt 101 Inset
Port Harcourt: Nig. 100 5N 7E
Port Hedland: Austl. 94 20S 119E
Port Huron: U.S.A. 51 43N 82W
Portland: Maine, U.S.A. 51 44N 70W
Portland: Oregon, U.S.A. 52 46N 123W
Portland, Bill of: hd., England 67 51N 2W
Portlaoighise: R. of Ireland 67 53N 7W
Port Lincoln: Austl. 94 35S 136E
Port Macquarie: Australia 94 31S 153E
PORT MORESBY: Papua New Guinea 94 9S 147E
Port Nolloth: S. Afr. 102 29S 17E
Pôrto Alegre: Brazil 61 30S 51W
PORT OF SPAIN: Trinidad & Tobago 59 11N 61W
Porto Novo: Benin 100 6N 3E
Pôrto Velho: Brazil 60 9S 64W
Port Pirie: Australia 94 33S 138E
Portree: Scotland 67 57N 6W
Portrush: N. Ireland 67 55N 7W
Port Safaga: Egypt 82 27N 34E
Port St. Joe: U.S.A. 51 30N 85W
Port Said: Egypt 82 31N 32E
Portsmouth: England 67 51N 1W
Portsmouth: N.H., U.S.A. 55 43N 71W
Portsmouth: Ohio, U.S.A. 51 39N 83W
Portsmouth: Va., U.S.A. 51 37N 76W
PORT STANLEY see STANLEY
Port Sudan: Sudan 82 20N 37E
Port Sulphur: U.S.A. 51 29N 90W
Port Talbot: Wales 67 52N 4W
Port Taufiq: Egypt 101 Inset
PORTUGAL: cap. Lisbon 69 — —
Port Washington: U.S.A. 56 41N 74W
Porz: W. Germany 68 51N 7E
Posadas: Argentina 61 27S 56W
Poteet: U.S.A. 50 29N 99W
Potenza: Italy 71 41N 16E
Poti: U.S.S.R. 80 42N 42E
Potomac: U.S.A. 57 39N 77W
Potomac: r., U.S.A. 51 38N 77W
Potosi: Bolivia 60 20S 66W
Potrerillos: Chile 60 26S 69W
Potsdam: E. Germany 70 52N 13E
Potsdam: U.S.A. 51 45N 75W
Pottstown: U.S.A. 54 40N 76W
Poughkeepsie: U.S.A. 55 42N 74W
Poverty Bay: N.Z. 95 39S 178E
Powder: r., U.S.A. 53 45N 106W
Poyang: & l., China 89 29N 116E
Poznań: Poland 70 52N 17E
PRAGUE (Praha): Czechoslovakia 70 50N 14E
Prato: Italy 71 44N 11E
Přerov: Czechoslovakia 70 49N 17E
Prescott: U.S.A. 52 35N 112W
Presidente Prudente: Brazil 60 22S 52W
Prešov: Czech. 70 49N 21E
Presque Isle: city, U.S.A. 51 47N 68W
Preston: England 67 54N 3W
Prestwick: Scotland 67 55N 5W
PRETORIA: Republic of South Africa 102 26S 28E
Préveza: Greece 71 39N 21E
Příbam: Czechoslovakia 70 50N 14E
Prichard: U.S.A. 51 31N 88W
Prilep: Yugoslavia 71 41N 22E
Prince of Wales I.: U.S.A. 22 56N 133W
Princeton, U.S.A. 54 40N 75W
Pripet (Pripyet): r. & marshes, U.S.S.R. 80 52N 29E
Priština: Yugoslavia 71 43N 21E
Prizren: Yugoslavia 71 42N 21E
Progreso: Mexico 58 21N 90W
Prokop'yevsk: U.S.S.R. 81 54N 86E
Prome: Burma 85 19N 95E
Prospect Heights: U.S.A. 57 42N 88W
Prosser: U.S.A. 52 46N 120W
Providence: U.S.A. 55 42N 71W
Providence, C.: N.Z. 95 46S 166E
Provins: France 68 49N 3E
Provo: U.S.A. 52 40N 112W
Pruszków: Poland 70 52N 21E
Prut: r., U.S.S.R./Romania 71 48N 27E
Przemyśl: Poland 70 50N 23E
Pskov: U.S.S.R. 70 58N 28E
Pucheng: China 89 28N 119E
Puebla: Mexico 58 19N 98W
Pueblo: U.S.A. 53 38N 105W
Puerto Aisén: Chile 60 45S 73W
Puerto Ayacucho: Venezuela 60 6N 66W
Puerto Cabello: Venezuela 59 10N 68W
Puerto Deseado: Arg. 60 48S 66W
Puerto Limón: Costa Rica 59 10N 83W
Puerto Montt: Chile 60 41S 71W
Puerto Pañasco: Mex. 52 31N 114W
PUERTO RICO: cap. San Juan 59 18N 66W
Pukekohe: N.Z. 95 37S 175E
Pula: Yugoslavia 71 45N 14E
Pulaski: U.S.A. 51 37N 81W
Pullman: U.S.A. 52 47N 117W
Punakha: Bhutan 84 28N 90E
Pune (Poona): India 84 18N 74E
Punjab: State, India 84 30N 75E
Punta Arenas: Chile 60 53S 71W
Puri: India 84 20N 86E
Purnea: India 84 26N 88E
Purús: r., Brazil 60 5S 64W
Pusan: S. Korea 87 35N 129E
Pushkin: U.S.S.R. 80 59N 30E
Putian: China 89 26N 119E
Putoran Mts.: U.S.S.R. 79 69N 95E

Puttalam: Sri Lanka **84** 8N 80E
Putumayo: *r.*, S. Am. **60** 2S 72W
Puyang: China **88** 36N 115E
Pyatigorsk: U.S.S.R. **80** 44N 43E
Pyinmana: Burma **85** 20N 96E
PYONGYANG: N. Korea **87** 39N 126E
Pyramid Lake: U.S.A. **52** 40N 120W
Pyramids: *hist.*, Egypt **82** 30N 31E
Pyrenees: *mtns.*, France/Spain **69** 43N 0

Q

Qahremanshar: Iran **83** 34N 47E
Qaidam Pendi (Tsaidam Swamps): China **86** 37N 95E
Qasr Farafra: Egypt **101** 27N 28E
QATAR: *cap.* Doha **83** 25N 51E
Qattara Depression: Egypt **82** 29N 28E
Qazvīn: Iran **83** 36N 50E
Qena: Egypt **82** 26N 33E
Qila Saifullah: Pakistan **84** 31N 69E
Qingdao (Tsingtao): China **88** 36N 120E
Qinghai: *lake*, China **86** 37N 100E
Qingjiang: China **89** 28N 116E
Qingyuan: China **89** 24N 113E
Qinhuangdao: China **88** 40N 120E
Qinlingshan: *mtns.*, China **88** 34N 108E
Qiqihar: China **87** 47N 124E
Qomsheh: (*formerly* Shahrezā) **83** 32N 52E
Quanzhou: China **89** 25N 119E
Queen Adelaide Arch.: Chile **60** 52S 75W
Queen Maud Land: Antarctica **128** 75S 10E
Queens: U.S.A. **56** 41N 74W
Queensland: *State*, Australia **94** 23S 145E
Queenstown: N.Z. **95** 45S 169E
Quelimane: Moz. **102** 18S 37E
Quelpart I.: *see* Cheju I.
Quemoy: *see* Chinmen
Que Que: *now* Kwekwe
Querétaro: Mexico **58** 21N 100W
Quetta: Pakistan **84** 30N 67E
Quezon City: Phil. **91** 15N 121E
Quilon: India **84** 9N 76E
Quilpie: Australia **94** 27S 144E
Quimper: France **68** 48N 4W
Quincy: U.S.A. **55** 42N 71W
Qui Nhon: Vietnam **85** 13N 109E
QUITO: Ecuador **60** 0 78W
Qulbala: Angola **102** 6S 15E
Qum: Iran **83** 35N 50E
Qunfidha: Sau. Arab. **82** 19N 41E
Quorn: Australia **94** 32S 138E
Quwaiiya: Sau. Arab. **83** 24N 45E.
Quxian: China **89** 29N 119E

R

RABAT: Morocco **100** 34N 7W
Rabaul: Papua New Guinea **94** 4S 152E
Rach Gia: Vietnam **85** 10N 105E
Racibórz: Poland **70** 50N 18E
Racine: U.S.A. **51** 43N 88W
Radom: Poland **70** 51N 21E
Radomsko: Poland **70** 51N 19E
Radstadt: Austria **71** 47N 13E
Ragusa: Sicily **71** 37N 15E
Raichur: India **84** 16N 77E
Rainier, Mt.: U.S.A. **52** 47N 122W
Raipur: India **84** 21N 82E
Rajahmundry: India **84** 17N 82E
Rajasthan: *State*, India **84** 27N 74E
Rajkot: India **84** 22N 71E
Rajshahi: Bangladesh **84** 24N 88E
Rakaia: *r.*, N.Z. **95** 44S 172E
Raleigh: U.S.A. **51** 36N 79W
Raleigh Bay: U.S.A. **51** 35N 76W
Rambouillet: France **72** 49N 2E
Rampur: India **84** 29N 79E
Ranchi: India **84** 23N 85E
Randers: Denmark **70** 56N 10E
Rangitaiki: *r.*, N.Z. **95** 38S 177E
RANGOON: Burma **85** 17N 96E
Rangpur: Bangladesh **84** 26N 89E
Rann of Kutch: *marsh*, India/Pak. **84** 24N 69E
Rapid City, U.S.A. **53** 44N 103W
Ras al Hadd: *cape*, Oman **83** 23N 60E
Rasht: Iran **83** 37N 50E
Ras Lanuf: Libya **101** 30N 19E
Rathlin I.: N. Irel. **67** 55N 6W
Ratlam: India **84** 23N 75E
Ratnagiri: India **84** 17N 73E
Raton: U.S.A. **53** 37N 105W
Raukumara Ra.: N.Z. **95** 38S 178E
Ravenna: Italy **71** 44N 12E
Ravi: *r.*, Pakistan **84** 31N 72E
Rawaki (*formerly* Phoenix I.): Pacific Ocean **104** 3S 171W
Rawalpindi: Pakistan **84** 34N 73E
Rawson: Argentina **60** 43S 65W
Raymond: U.S.A. **52** 47N 124W
Reading: England **67** 51N 1W
Reading: U.S.A. **54** 40N 76W
Recherche, Arch. of the: Australia **94** 34S 122E
Rechitsa: U.S.S.R. **70** 52N 30E
Recife: Brazil **60** 8S 35W
Recklinghausen: W. Germany **68** 52N 7E
Red: *r.*, Can./U.S.A. **53** 48N 97W
Red: *r.*, U.S.A. **50** 31N 92W
Red Basin of Sichuan: China **89** 30N 105E
Red Bluff: U.S.A. **52** 40N 122W
Red Cedar: *r.*, U.S.A. **53** 45N 92W
Redding: U.S.A. **52** 41N 122W
Redfield: U.S.A. **53** 45N 99W
Red L.: U.S.A. **53** 48N 95W
Red Sea **82** — —
Red Sea Hills: Egypt **82** 27N 33E
Red Wing: U.S.A. **53** 45N 93W
Regensburg: W. Ger. **70** 49N 12E
Reggio di Calabria: Italy **71** 38N 16E
Reggio nell'Emilia: Italy **71** 45N 11E
Reidsville: U.S.A. **51** 36N 80W
Reims: France **68** 49N 4E
Remscheid: W. Germany **68** 51N 7E
Rendsburg: W. Germany **70** 54N 10E
Rengat: Indonesia **85** 0 102E
Rennes: France **68** 48N 2W
Reno: U.S.A. **52** 39N 120W
Republican: *r.*, U.S.A. **53** 40N 97W
REPUBLIC OF SOUTH AFRICA *cap.*, Pretoria **102** — —
Resistencia: Arg. **61** 27S 59W
Reşiţa: Romania **71** 45N 22E
Réthimnon: Crete **71** 35N 25E
Reus: Spain **69** 41N 1E
Reutlingen: W. Ger. **68** 48N 9E
Revilla Gigedo Is.: Pacific Ocean **105** 19N 112W
Rewari: India **84** 28N 76E
Rexburg: U.S.A. **52** 44N 112W
Reykjanes Ridge: Atlantic Ocean **100** 60N 31W
Reynosa: Mexico **50** 26N 98W
Rezā īyeh: *see* Orumiyeh
Rheinhausen: W. Germany **68** 51N 7E
Rhine: *r.*, Europe **68** 52N 6E
Rhode Island: *State*, U.S.A. **55** 42N 72W
Rhodes (Ródhos): *i. & town*, Greece **71** 36N 28E
RHODESIA: *now* **ZIMBABWE**
Rhodope Mts.: Bulg. **71** 42N 24E
Rhône: *r.*, Europe **69** 45N 5E
Rhum: *i.*, Scotland **67** 57N 6W
Rhyl: Wales **67** 53N 4W
Riau Arch.: Indon. **91** 0 105E
Ribble: *r.*, England **67** 53N 2W
Ribeirão Prêto: Brazil **60** 21S 48W
Riberalta: Bolivia **60** 11S 66W
Riccarton: N.Z. **95** 44S 173E
Richard's Bay: S. Afr. **102** 29S 32E
Richfield: U.S.A. **52** 39N 112W
Richland: U.S.A. **52** 46N 119W
Richmond: Indiana, U.S.A. **51** 40N 85W
Richmond: Ky., U.S.A. **51** 38N 84W
Richmond: N.J., U.S.A. **56** 41N 74W
Richmond: Virginia, U.S.A. **51** 38N 77W
Richwood: U.S.A. **51** 38N 81W
Ridgewood: Ill., U.S.A. **57** 42N 88W
Ridgewood: N.Y., U.S.A. **56** 41N 74W
Riesa: E. Germany **70** 51N 13E
Riga: *& gulf*, U.S.S.R. **80** 57N 24E
Rijeka: Yugoslavia **71** 45N 15E
Rimini: Italy **71** 44N 13E
Rio Branco: Brazil **60** 10S 68W
Río Cuarto: Arg. **61** 33S 64W
Rio de Janeiro: Brazil **61** 23S 43W
Río Gallegos: Arg. **60** 52S 69W
Rio Grande: Brazil **61** 32S 52W
Rio Grande: *r.*, U.S.A./Mexico **58** 29N 102W
Rio Grande do Sul: *State*, Brazil **61** 30S 53W
Ritter, Mt.: U.S.A. **52** 38N 120W
Rivera: Uruguay **61** 31S 56W
Riverside: Calif., U.S.A. **52** 34N 117W
River Forest: *town*, U.S.A. **57** 42N 88W
Riverside: Ill., U.S.A. **57** 42N 88W
RIYADH: Saudi Arabia **83** 25N 47E
Roanoke: U.S.A. **51** 37N 80W
Roanoke Rapids: *city*, U.S.A. **51** 37N 78W
Robstown: U.S.A. **50** 28N 97W
Rochefort: France **69** 46N 1W
Rochester: Minn., U.S.A. **53** 44N 92W
Rochester: N.H., U.S.A. **55** 43N 71W
Rochester: N.Y., U.S.A. **54** 43N 78W
Rock: *r.*, U.S.A. **51** 42N 89W
Rockall Plateau: Atlantic Ocean **103** 58N 14W
Rockford: U.S.A. **51** 42N 89W
Rockhampton: Australia **94** 23S 151E
Rock Hill: *city*, U.S.A. **51** 35N 81W
Rock Island: *city*, U.S.A. **50** 41N 91W
Rock Springs: *city*, U.S.A. **52** 42N 109W
Rockville Centre: U.S.A. **56** 41N 74W
Rockwood: U.S.A. **51** 46N 70W
Rocky Ford: *city*, U.S.A. **50** 38N 104W
Rocky Mount: *city*, U.S.A. **51** 36N 78W
Rocky Mts.: Canada/U.S.A. **52** 55N 117W
Rodez: France **69** 44N 3E
Ródhos (Rhodes): *i. & town*, Greece **71** 36N 28E
Rogers City: U.S.A. **24** 45N 85W
Rogers, Mt.:U.S.A. **51** 37N 82W
Rolla: U.S.A. **50** 38N 92W
Roman: Romania **71** 47N 26E
ROMANIA: *cap.* Bucharest **70/1** — —
Romanovka: U.S.S.R. **87** 53N 113E
ROME: Italy **71** 42N 12E
Rome: U.S.A. **51** 34N 85W
Romorantin: France **68** 47N 2E
Roosevelt I.: Antarc. **128** 80S 161W
Rosario: Argentina **61** 33S 61W
Roseburg: U.S.A. **52** 43N 123W
Roseires: Sudan **101** 12N 34E
Roselle: U.S.A. **57** 42N 88W
Rosenheim: W. Ger. **70** 48N 12E
Rosetta: Egypt **82** 32N 30E
Ross Ice Shelf: Antarctica **128** 80S 180
Rosslare: R. of Ireland **67** 52N 6W
Ross Sea: Antarctica **128** 76S 175W
Rostock: E. Germany **70** 54N 12E
Rostov: U.S.S.R. **80** 47N 40E
Roswell: U.S.A. **53** 33N 105W
Rothesay: Scotland **67** 56N 5W
Roti: *i.*, Indonesia **91** 10S 124E
Rotorua: N.Z. **95** 38S 176E
Rotterdam: Neth. **68** 52N 4E
Roubaix: France **68** 51N 3E
Rouen: France **68** 49N 1E
Roundup: U.S.A. **52** 46N 109W
Rourkela: India **84** 22N 85E
Rovno: U.S.S.R. **70** 51N 26E
Roxburgh: N.Z. **95** 46S 169E
Royale, Isle: U.S.A. **53** 48N 89W
Royan: France **69** 46N 1W
Ruahine Range: N.Z. **95** 40S 176E
Ruapehu: *mtn.*, N.Z. **95** 39S 176E
Rub al Khali: *desert*, Saudi Arabia **83** 20N 50E
Rubtsovsk: U.S.S.R. **81** 52N 81E
Rudnichnyy: U.S.S.R. **80** 60N 52E
Rugao: China **88** 33N 121E
Rugby: England **67** 52N 1W
Rügen: *i.*, E. Germany **70** 54N 13E
Ruhr, The: *district*, W. Ger. **68** *Inset*
Rukwa, L.: Tanzania **102** 8S 32E
Rum Jungle: Austl. **94** 13S 131E
Rumoi: Japan **90** 44N 142E
Ruse: Bulgaria **71** 44N 26E
Russian Soviet Fed. Socialist Rep.: U.S.S.R. **78/9** — —
Rutland: U.S.A. **51** 44N 73W
Rutog: China **84** 34N 80E
Ruvuma: *r.*, Africa **102** 11S 37E
Ruwenzori, Mt.: Uganda **102** 1N 30E
RWANDA: *cap.* Kigali **102** 2S 30E
Ryazan': U.S.S.R. **80** 55N 40E
Rybach'ye: U.S.S.R. **81** 43N 76E
Rybinsk: *now* Andropov-Rybinsk
Rybnik: Poland **70** 50N 19E
Ryukyu Is. (Nansei Is.): Japan **87** 27N 127E
Ryukyu Trench: Pacific Ocean **104** 27N 130E
Rzeszów: Poland **70** 50N 22E
Rzhev: U.S.S.R. **80** 56N 35E

S

Saalfeld: E. Germany **70** 51N 11E
Saarbrücken: W. Ger. **68** 49N 7E
Saaremaa: *i.*, U.S.S.R. **70** 58N 23E
Šabac: Yugoslavia **71** 45N 20E
Sabadell: Spain **69** 42N 2E
Sabah: *State*, Malaysia **91** 5N 118E
Sabinas: Mexico **58** 28N 101W
Sable, Cape: U.S.A. **51** 25N 81W
Saco: U.S.A. **51** 43N 70W
Sacramento: *& r.*, U.S.A. **52** 39N 121W
Sacramento Mts.: U.S.A. **50** 34N 105W
Sa da Bandeira: *see* Lubango
Sado: *i.*, Japan **90** 38N 138E
Safford: U.S.A. **52** 32N 110W
Safi: Morocco **100** 32N 9W
Saga: Japan **90** 33N 130E
Sagaing: Burma **85** 21N 96E
Saginaw: U.S.A. **24** 44N 84W
Saginaw Bay: U.S.A. **24** 44N 84W
Sagua la Grande: Cuba **59** 23N 80W
Sahara Desert: North Africa **100/1** — —
Saharan Atlas: *mtns.*, Algeria **100** 33N 3E
Saharanpur: India **84** 30N 78E
Sai: *r.* India **84** 26N 82E
Saigon: *now* Ho Chi Minh City
St. Albans: England **67** 52N 0
St. Andrews: Scot. **67** 56N 3W
St. Augustine: U.S.A. **51** 30N 81W
St. Bees Head: Eng. **67** 55N 4W
St. Bride's Bay: Wales **67** 52N 5W
St. Brieuc: France **68** 49N 3W
ST. CHRISTOPHER - NEVIS (ST. KITTS-NEVIS), *cap.* Basse Terre **59** 17N 63W
St. Cloud: U.S.A. **53** 46N 94W
St. David's Head: Wales **67** 52N 5W
St. Denis: France **72** 49N 2E
St. Dizier: France **68** 49N 5E
Saintes: France **69** 46N 1W
St. Étienne: France **69** 45N 4E
St. Francis: *r.*, U.S.A. **50** 35N 90W
St. Gallen: Switz. **68** 47N 9E
St. George: U.S.A. **52** 37N 114W
St. George, C.: U.S.A. **51** 30N 85W
St. George's Chan.: Wales/R. of Irel. **67** 52N 6W
St. Germain-en-Laye: France **72** 49N 2E
St. Helena: *i.*, Atl. O. **103** 16S 8W
St. Helena Bay: South Africa **102** 32S 18E
St. Helens: England **62** 53N 3W
St. John: *r.*, U.S.A./Can. **51** 47N 69W
St. Johns: *r.*, U.S.A. **51** 30N 82W
St. Joseph: Mo., U.S.A. **50** 40N 95W
St. Joseph: *& r.*, Mich., U.S.A. **51** 42N 87W
St. Kitts: *see* **ST. CHRISTOPHER-NEVIS**
St. Lawrence: *I.*, Bering Sea **104** 63N 170W
St. Lô: France **68** 49N 1W
St. Louis: U.S.A. **50** 39N 90W
St. Louis: Senegal **100** 16N 16W
ST. LUCIA: *cap.* Castries **59** 14N 61W
St. Malo: France **68** 49N 2W
St. Martin: *i.*, West Indies **59** 18N 63W
St. Mary's: Australia **94** 42S 148E
St. Marys: U.S.A. **54** 41N 79W
St. Nazaire: France **68** 47N 2W
St. Paul: U.S.A. **53** 45N 93W
St. Paul, C.: Ghana **100** 6N 1E
St. Paul Rocks: Atlantic Ocean **103** 0 30W
St. Petersburg: U.S.A. **51** 28N 83W
St. Pierre and Miquelon: *is.*, Atlantic Ocean **41** 47N 56W
St. Pölten: Austria **70** 48N 16E
St. Quentin: France **68** 50N 3E
St. Thomas: *i.*, West Indies **59** 18N 65W
St. Tropez: France **69** 43N 7E
ST. VINCENT AND THE GRENADINES: *cap.*, Kingstown **59** 13N 61W
Saipan: *i.*, Pac. O. **104** 15N 145E
Saiwūn: Yemen P.D.R. **83** 16N 49E
Sakaka: Sau. Arab. **82** 30N 40E
Sakakawea, L.: *see* Garrison Dam Res.
Sakata: Japan **90** 39N 140E
Sakhalin: *i.*, U.S.S.R. **79** 50N 143E
Sakhalin Bay: U.S.S.R. **79** 54N 141E
Sakishima Group: *is.*, Japan **87** 24N 124E
Salado: *r.*, Argentina **61** 30S 61W
Salala: Oman **83** 17N 54E
Salamanca: Spain **69** 41N 6W
Salaqi: China **88** 41N 111E
Sala y Gómez: *i.*, Pacific Ocean **105** 26S 105W
Salekhard: U.S.S.R. **78** 66N 66E
Salem: India **84** 12N 78E
Salem: Mass, U.S.A. **55** 42N 71W
Salem: Oregon, U.S.A. **52** 45N 123W
Salem: Va., U.S.A. **51** 37N 80W
Salerno: Italy **71** 41N 15E
Salgótarján: Hungary **70** 48N 20E
Salida: U.S.A. **53** 38N 106W
Salima: Malawi **102** 14S 35E
Salina: U.S.A. **53** 39N 98W
Salinas: U.S.A. **52** 37N 122W
Saline: *r.*, U.S.A. **50** 34N 92W
Salisbury: *& Plain.*, England **67** 51N 2W
SALISBURY *now* HARARE
Salmon: *r.*, U.S.A. **52** 45N 116W
Salmon River Mts.: U.S.A. **52** 45N 115W
Salonica: *see* Thessalonica
Sal'sk: U.S.S.R. **80** 47N 42E
Salt: *r.*, U.S.A. **50** 40N 92W
Salta: Argentina **61** 25S 65W
Saltillo: Mexico **58** 25N 101W
Salt Lake City: U.S.A. **52** 41N 112W
Salt Range: Pakistan **84** 33N 73E
Salto: Uruguay **61** 31S 58W
Salueen (Salween): *r.*, Burma **86** 20N 98E
Salvador (Bahia): Brazil **60** 13S 38W
Salzburg: Austria **70** 48N 13E
Salzgitter: W. Ger. **70** 52N 10E
Sama de Langreo: Spain **69** 43N 6W
Samah: *see* Ya Xian
Samar: *i.*, Phil. **91** 12N 125E
Samarinda: Indon. **91** 0 117E
Samarkand: U.S.S.R. **81** 40N 67E
Samarra: Iraq **83** 34N 44E
Sambalpur: India **84** 22N 84E
Sambor: U.S.S.R. **70** 50N 23E
Sam Neua: Laos **85** 20N 104E
Sámos: *i.*, Greece **71** 38N 27E
Samothrace: *i.*, Greece **71** 40N 26E
Samsun: Turkey **82** 41N 36E
SAN'A: Yemen **83** 15N 44E
Sanandaj: Iran **83** 35N 47E
San Angelo: U.S.A. **50** 31N 100W
San Antonio: U.S.A. **50** 29N 99W
San Antonio: *r.*, U.S.A. **50** 29N 97W
San Benito Is.: Mex. **58** 28N 115W
San Bernardino: U.S.A. **52** 34N 117W
San Blas, C.: U.S.A. **51** 30N 85W
San Carlos de Bariloche: Arg. **60** 41S 71W
San Clemente: *i.*, U.S.A. **52** 33N 118W
San Cristóbal: Venez. **60** 8N 72W
Sancti Spíritus: Cuba **59** 22N 79W
Sandakan: Malaysia **91** 6N 118E
San Diego: U.S.A. **52** 33N 117W
Sandpoint: U.S.A. **52** 48N 117W
Sandusky: U.S.A. **51** 41N 83W
San Felix I.: Pac. O. **60** 26S 80W
San Fernando: Mexico **58** 25N 98W
San Fernando: Phil. **91** 17N 120E
Sanford: Fla., U.S.A. **51** 29N 80W
Sanford: Maine, U.S.A. **51** 43N 71W
Sanford: N.C., U.S.A. **51** 35N 79W
San Francisco: Argentina **61** 31S 62W
San Francisco: *r.*, U.S.A. **52** 33N 109W
San Francisco: U.S.A. **52** 38N 122W
Sangar: U.S.S.R. **79** 64N 127E
Sangli: India **84** 17N 74E
Sangre de Cristo Range: U.S.A. **53** 37N 105W
Sanhe: China **88** 40N 117E
Sanjo: Japan **90** 38N 139E
San Joaquin: *r.*, U.S.A. **52** 37N 120W
SAN JOSÉ: Costa Rica **59** 10N 84W
San José: U.S.A. **52** 37N 122W
San José: *r.*, U.S.A. **52** 35N 108W
San José de Mayo: Uruguay **61** 34S 57W
San Juan: Argentina **60** 32S 69W
SAN JUAN: Puerto Rico **59** 18N 66W
San Juan Mts.: U.S.A. **52** 37N 107W
San Justo: Argentina **61** 31S 61W
San Lorenzo: Ecuador **60** 1N 79W
San Luis: Argentina **61** 33S 66W
San Luis Obispo: U.S.A. **52** 35N 121W
San Luis Potosí: Mex. **58** 22N 101W
San Marcos: U.S.A. **50** 30N 98W
SAN MARINO: *cap.*, San Marino **71** 44N 12E
San Miguel de Tucumán: Arg. **61** 27S 65W
San Nicholas: Argentina **61** 33S 60W
San Pedro: *r.*, U.S.A. **52** 33N 111W
San Rafael: Arg. **60** 35S 68W
San Remo: Italy **69** 44N 8E
SAN SALVADOR: El Salvador **58** 14N 89W
San Salvador de Jujuy: Argentina **61** 24S 65W
San Sebastián: Spain **69** 43N 2W
San Severo: Italy **71** 42N 15E
Santa Ana: U.S.A. **52** 34N 118W
Santa Barbara: *& chan.*, U.S.A. **52** 34N 120W
Santa Barbara Is.: U.S.A. **52** 34N 120W
Santa Catalina: *i. & gulf*, U.S.A. **52** 33N 118W
Santa Clara: Cuba **59** 22N 80W
Santa Clara: U.S.A. **52** 37N 122W
Santa Cruz: Bolivia **60** 18S 63W
Santa Cruz: U.S.A. **52** 37N 122W
Santa Cruz: *i.*, U.S.A. **52** 34N 120W
Santa Cruz de Tenerife: Canary Islands **100** 28N 16W
Santa Fe: Argentina **61** 32S 61W
Santa Fe: U.S.A. **53** 36N 106W
Santa Maria: Brazil **61** 30S 54W
Santa Maria: U.S.A. **52** 35N 120W
Santa Marta: Col. **59** 11N 74W
Santana do Livramento: Brazil **61** 31S 55W
Santander: Spain **69** 43N 4W
Santa Paula: U.S.A. **52** 34N 119W
Santarém: Brazil **60** 2S 55W
Santarém: Portugal **69** 39N 9W
Santa Rosa: Arg. **60** 37S 64W
Santa Rosa: Calif., U.S.A. **52** 38N 123W
Santa Rosa: N. Mex., U.S.A. **53** 35N 105W
Santa Rosa: *i.*, U.S.A. **52** 34N 120W
SANTIAGO: Chile **60** 33S 71W
Santiago: Dom. Rep. **59** 20N 71W
Santiago: *r.*, Mexico **58** 21N 104W
Santiago de Compostelo: Spain **69** 43N 9W
Santiago de Cuba: Cuba **59** 20N 76W
Santiago del Estero: Argentina **61** 28S 64W
Santo André: Brazil **61** 24S 47W
Santo Angelo: Brazil **61** 28S 54W
SANTO DOMINGO: Dom. Repub. **59** 19N 70W
Santos: Brazil **61** 24S 46W
Sanyuan: China **79** 35N 109E
São Bernardo do Campo: Brazil **61** 24S 47W
São Francisco: *r.*, Brazil **60** 12S 43W
São João da Boa Vista: Brazil **61** 22S 47W
São José dos Campos: Brazil **61** 23S 46W
São Leopoldo: Brazil **61** 30S 51W
São Luís: Brazil **60** 3S 44W
Saone: *r.*, France **68** 46N 5E

São Paulo: Brazil **61** 24S 46W
São Roque, C. de: Brazil **60** 5S 35W
São Vicente: Brazil **61** 24S 46W
São Vicente, Cabo de (C. St. Vincent): Portugal **69** 37N 9W
Sapporo: Japan **90** 43N 141E
Saragossa: *see* Zaragoza
Sarajevo: Yugo. **71** 44N 18E
Saranac Lake: *city*, U.S.A. **51** 44N 74W
Saransk: U.S.S.R. **80** 54N 45E
Sarasota: U.S.A. **51** 27N 83W
Saratov: U.S.S.R. **80** 52N 46E
Saravane: Laos **85** 15N 106E
Sarawak: *State*, Malaysia **91** 3N 113E
Sardinia: *i.*, Medit. Sea **69** 40N 9E
Sargasso Sea **103** 30N 60W
Sarh: Chad **101** 9N 18E
Sark: *i.*, Chan. Is. **68** 50N 2W
Sarny: U.S.S.R. **70** 51N 27E
Sarpsborg: Norway **70** 59N 11E
Sarrebourg: France **68** 49N 7E
Sarthe: *r.*, France **68** 48N 0
Sasebo: Japan **90** 33N 130E
Sassari: Sardinia **69** 41N 9E
Satara: India **84** 17N 74E
Satpura Range: India **84** 22N 77E
Satu-Mare: Romania **70** 48N 23E
SAUDI ARABIA: *cap.* Riyadh **82/83** — —
Saugor: India **84** 24N 79E
Sauk Center: U.S.A. **53** 46N 95W
Sault Ste. Marie: U.S.A. **24** 46N 84W
Sava: *r.*, Yugoslavia **71** 45N 17E
Savannah: *& r.*, Ga., U.S.A. **51** 32N 81W
Savannah: Tenn., U.S.A. **51** 35N 88W
Savannakhet: Laos **85** 17N 105E
Savona: Italy **69** 44N 8E
Sawu: *i. & sea*, Indon. **91** 10S 122E
Sayaboury: Laos **85** 19N 102E
Sayn Shanda: Mong. **79** 45N 110E
Scapa Flow: *inlet*, Scotland **67** 59N 3W
Scarborough: Eng. **67** 54N 0
Schaumburg: U.S.A. **57** 42N 88W
Schenectady: U.S.A. **55** 43N 74W
Schleswig: W. Ger. **70** 54N 10E
Schweinfurt: W. Ger. **70** 50N 10E
Schwerin: E. Ger. **70** 54N 11E
Scilly, Is. of: Eng. **67** 50N 6W
Scoresbysund: Greenland **1** 71N 23W
Scotia Sea: S. Atlantic Ocean **103** 57S 50W
SCOTLAND: *cap.*, Edinburgh **67** — —
Scottsbluff: U.S.A. **53** 42N 104W
Scranton: U.S.A. **54** 41N 76W
Scunthorpe: England **67** 54N 1W
Seattle: U.S.A. **52** 48N 122W
Sebha Oasis: Libya **100** 27N 15E
Sedalia: U.S.A. **50** 39N 93W
Sedan: France **68** 50N 5E
Segamat: Malaysia **85** 2N 103E
Segovia: Spain **69** 42N 4W
Segovia: *r.*, Hond./Nicaragua **59** 15N 84W
Ségre: *r.*, Spain **69** 42N 1E
Segura: *r.*, Spain **69** 38N 2W
Seine: *r.*, France **68** 49N 1E
Seine, Baie de la: Fr. **68** 49N 1W
Sekondi-Takoradi: Ghana **100** 5N 2W
Selby: England **67** 54N 1W
Selenga: *r.*, Mongolia **87** 49N 101E
Selety-Tengiz, L.: U.S.S.R. **81** 53N 73E
Selkirk: Scotland **67** 56N 3W
Selma: U.S.A. **51** 32N 87W
Selvas: *geog. reg.*, Brazil **60** 6S 65W
Semarang: Indonesia **91** 7S 110E
Seminoe Res.: U.S.A. **52** 42N 107W
Semiozernoye: U.S.S.R. **81** 52N 64E
Semipalatinsk: U.S.S.R. **81** 50N 80E
Semnān: Iran **83** 35N 53E
Sendai: Honshu, Japan **90** 38N 141E
Sendai: Kyushu, Japan **90** 32N 130E
Seneca L.: U.S.A. **54** 43N 77W
SENEGAL: *& r., cap.* Dakar **100** 15N 15W
Sennar: *& dam.*, Sudan **82** 13N 34E
Sens: France **68** 48N 3E
SEOUL (KYONGSONG): S. Korea **87** 38N 127E
Septentrional, Meseta: *plat.*, Spain **69** 42N 5W
Serang: Indonesia **91** 6S 106E
Seremban: Malaysia **85** 3N 102E
Serengeti Nat. Park: Tanzania **102** 3S 35E
Sergino: U.S.S.R. **81** 66N 65E
Seria: Brunei **91** 4N 114E
Serian: Malaysia **85** 1N 111E
Serra da Mantigueira: *mtns.*, Brazil **61** 22S 45W
Serov: U.S.S.R. **81** 60N 60E
Serowe: Botswana **102** 23S 27E
Serra do Mar.: *mtns.*, Brazil **61** 27S 49W
Serra dos Parecis: *mtns.*, Brazil **60** 12S 60W
Serra Geral: *mtns.*, Brazil **61** 25S 51W
Sérrai: Greece **71** 41N 23E
Sète: France **69** 43N 4E
Sétif: Algeria **69** 36N 5E
Setúbal: Portugal **69** 38N 9W
Sevan, L.: U.S.S.R. **80** 41N 46E
Sevastopol': U.S.S.R. **80** 45N 34E
Severn: *r.*, England **67** 52N 2W
Severnaya Zemlya: *is.*, U.S.S.R. **79** 79N 95E
Severodvinsk: U.S.S.R. **78** 65N 40E
Severoural'sk: U.S.S.R. **81** 60N 60E
Seville: Spain **69** 37N 6W
Sèvres: France **72** 49N 2E
Seward Peninsula: U.S.A. **79** 66N 165W
Seymour: U.S.A. **50** 33N 99W
Sfax: Tunisia **100** 35N 11E
'S.-Gravenhage: *see* Hague, The
Shabwah: Yemen P.D.R. **83** 16N 47E
Shache (Yarkand): China **81** 38N 77E
Shackleton Range: Antarctica **116** 82S 25W
Shah Faisalabad (formerly Lyallpur): Pakistan **84** 31N 73E
Shahjahanpur: India **84** 28N 80E
Shahrezā: *now* Qomsheh
Shahrūd: *now* Emamrud
Shakhty: U.S.S.R. **80** 48N 40E
Shalym: U.S.S.R. **81** 53N 88E
Shamrock: U.S.A. **50** 35N 100W
Shandong (Shantung): *Prov.*, China **88** 36N 117E
Shandong Peninsula: China **88** 37N 120E
Shanghai: China **89** 31N 121E
Shangqiu: China **88** 34N 116E
Shangrao: China **89** 28N 118E
Shangshui: China **88** 33N 115E
Shangzhi (Chuho): China **79** 45N 128E
Shannon: *r.*, R. of Ireland **67** 53N 9W
Shansi: *Prov.*, *see* Shānxi
Shan States: Burma **85** 22N 98E
Shantou (Swatow): China **89** 23N 117E
Shantung: Prov., *see* Shandong
Shānxi (Shansi): *Prov.*, China **88** 37N 112E
Shănxi (Shensi): *Prov.*, China **88** 35N 109E
Shaoguan: China **89** 25N 113E
Shaoxing: China **89** 30N 121E
Shaoyang: China **89** 27N 111E
Sharjah: U.A.E. **83** 25N 55E
Sharon: U.S.A. **51** 41N 81W
Shasta, Lake: U.S.A. **52** 41N 122W
Shasta, Mt.: U.S.A. **52** 41N 122W
Shawnee: U.S.A. **50** 35N 97W
Sheboygan: U.S.A. **53** 44N 88W
Sheffield: England **67** 53N 1W
Sheffield: U.S.A. **51** 35N 88W
Shelby: U.S.A. **52** 48N 112W
Shelbyville: U.S.A. **51** 35N 86W
Shelekhov Bay: U.S.S.R. **79** 60N 157E
Shenandoah: *r.*, U.S.A. **51** 38N 79W
Shensi: *Prov.*, *see* Shănxi
Shenyang (Mukden): China **88** 42N 123E
Shepparton: Austl. **94** 36S 145E
Shepetovka: U.S.S.R. **70** 50N 27E
Sheridan: U.S.A. **52** 45N 107W
Sherlovaya Gora: U.S.S.R. **79** 51N 116E
Sherman: U.S.A. **50** 34N 97W
Shetland Is.: Scot. **67** 60N 2W
Sheyenne: *r.*, U.S.A. **53** 48N 99W
Shibeli: *r.*, Ethiopia/Somali Republic **101** 6N 43E
Shigatse: *see* Xigaze
Shijiazhuang: China **88** 38N 115E
Shikoku: *i.*, Japan **90** 34N 134E
Shilong: China **89** 23N 114E
Shillong: India **84** 26N 92E
Shimoga: India **84** 14N 76E
Shimonoseki: Japan **90** 34N 131E
Shimizu: Japan **90** 35N 138E
Shingu: Japan **90** 34N 136E
Shiogama: Japan **90** 38N 141E
Shipki Pass: India/China **84** 32N 79E
Shirakawa: Japan **90** 37N 140E
Shiranuka: Japan **90** 39N 144E
Shirāz: Iran **83** 30N 53E
Shisanzhan: China **79** 51N 126E
Shizuoka: Japan **90** 35N 139E
Shkodër: Albania **71** 42N 19E
Sholapur: India **84** 18N 76E
Shortland Is.: Solomon Is. **94** 7S 156E
Shreveport: U.S.A. **50** 32N 94W
Shrewsbury: England **67** 53N 3W
Shuangliao: China **87** 44N 123E
Shunde: China **89** 23N 113E
Shwebo: Burma **85** 23N 96E
Sialkot: Pakistan **84** 32N 75E
SIAM: *see* **THAILAND**
Siam, Gulf of **85** 10N 102E
Sian: *see* Xi'an
Siauliai: U.S.S.R. **80** 56N 23E
Sibenik: Yugoslavia **71** 44N 16E
Sibi: Pakistan **84** 30N 68E
Sibiu: Romania **71** 46N 25E
Sibolga: Indonesia **85** 2N 99E
Sibu: Malaysia **85** 2N 112E
Sichuan(Szechwan): *Prov.*, China **89** 30N 105E
Sicilian Channel: Medit. Sea **71** 37N 12E
Sicily: *i. & Reg.*, Italy **71** — —
Sidi-bel-Abbès: Alg. **69** 35N 1W
Sidney: U.S.A. **53** 48N 104W
Sidra: Libya **101** 31N 18E
Sidra, Gulf of: Libya **101** 32N 17E
Siegburg: W. Germany **68** 51N 7E
Siegen: W. Germany **68** 51N 8E
Siem Reap: Kampuchea **85** 13N 103E
Siena: Italy **71** 43N 11E
SIERRA LEONE: *cap.*, Freetown **100** 8N 12W
Sierra Madre, Eastern: *mtns.*, Mexico **58** 25N 100W
Sierra Madre, Southern: *mtns.*, Mexico **58** 17N 100W
Sierra Madre, Western: *mtns.*, Mexico **58** 25N 105W
Sierra Morena: *mtns.*, Spain **69** 38N 5W
Sierra Névada: *mtns.*, Spain **69** 37N 3W
Sierra Nevada: *mtns.*, U.S.A. **52** 38N 120W
Sighet Marmatier: Romania **70** 48N 24E
Sihanoukville: *now* Kompong Som
Siirt: Turkey **82** 38N 42E
Sikeston: U.S.A. **51** 37N 89W
Sikhote Alin' Range: U.S.S.R. **79** 47N 137E
Sikkim: *State*, India **84** 27N 88E
Silchar: India **85** 25N 93E
Silistra: Bulgaria **71** 44N 27E
Silver Spring: U.S.A. **57** 39N 77W
Silverton: Colorado, U.S.A. **52** 38N 108W
Silverton: Oregon, U.S.A. **52** 45N 123W
Simanggang: Malaysia **85** 1N 111E
Simeulue: *i.*, Indon. **85** 3N 96E
Simferopol': U.S.S.R. **80** 45N 34E
Simla: India **84** 31N 77E
Simpson Desert: Australia **94** 25S 137E
Sinabang: Indonesia **85** 2N 96E
Sinai: *penin. & mtn.*, Egypt **82** 28N 34E
Sind: *Prov.*, Pakistan **84** 26N 69E
SINGAPORE: *cap. Singapore* **85** 1N 104E
Singaradja: Indon. **91** 8S 115E
Singkawang: Indon. **85** 1N 109W
Singkep: *i.*, Indon. **91** 1S 104E
Sinkiang Uighur A.R.: *see* Xinjiang Weiwuer Zizhiqu
Sintang: Indonesia **85** 0 111E
Sinuiju: N. Korea **87** 40N 124E
Sioux City: U.S.A. **53** 42N 96W
Sioux Falls: *city*, U.S.A. **53** 44N 97W
Siretul: *r.*, Romania **71** 47N 26E
Sirte: Libya **100** 31N 17E
Sisak: Yugoslavia **71** 45N 16E
Sisseton: U.S.A. **53** 46N 97W
Sistān: *geog. reg.*, Iran/Afghan. **83** 31N 61E
Sitapur: India **84** 27N 81E
Sittang: *r.*, Burma **85** 18N 97E
Sivas: Turkey **82** 40N 37E
Siwa: Egypt **101** 29N 25E
Skagerrak: *str.*, Denmark/Nor. **68** 57N 8E
Skagway: U.S.A. **22** 59N 135W
Skegness: England **67** 53N 0
Skien: Norway **68** 59N 10E
Skikda: Algeria **69** 37N 7E
Skiros: *i.*, Greece **71** 39N 25E
Skive: Denmark **70** 57N 9E
Skokie: U.S.A. **57** 42N 88W
Skopje: Yugoslavia **71** 42N 21E
Skövde: Sweden **70** 58N 14E
Skovorodino **87** 54N 124E
Skye: *i.*, Scotland **67** 57N 6W
Slavonski Brod.: Yugoslavia **71** 45N 18E
Slieve Donard: *mtn.*, N. Ireland **67** 54N 6W
Sligo: R. of Ireland **67** 54N 8W
Sliven: Bulgaria **71** 43N 26E
Slonim: U.S.S.R. **70** 53N 25E
Słupsk: Poland **70** 54N 17E
Slutsk: U.S.S.R. **70** 53N 28E
Smederovo: Yugoslavia **71** 45N 21E
Smoky Hill: *r.*, U.S.A. **53** 39N 100W
Smolensk: U.S.S.R. **80** 55N 32E
Snaefell: *mtn.*, I. of Man. **67** 54N 4W
Snake: *r.*, U.S.A. **52** 46N 118W
Snowdon: *mtn.*, Wales **67** 53N 4W
Snyder: U.S.A. **50** 33N 101W
Sochi: U.S.S.R. **80** 44N 40E
Society Is.: Pac. O. **105** 17S 150W
Socotra: *i.*, Arab. Sea **83** 13N 54E
Soda Mts.: Libya **100** 29N 15E
Södertälje: Sweden **70** 59N 18E
Sofala (Beira): Moz. **102** 20S 35E
SOFIYA: Bulgaria **71** 43N 23E
Söke: Turkey **71** 38N 27E
Sokoto: Nigeria **100** 13N 5E
Soligorsk: U.S.S.R. **70** 53N 28E
Solingen: W. Germany **68** 51N 7E
SOLOMON ISLANDS: *cap.* Honiara **94** 10S 155E
Solothurn: Switz. **68** 47N 8E
Solway Firth: Eng./Scotland **67** 55N 4W
SOMALI REPUBLIC: *cap.*, Mogadiscio **101** — —
Sombor: Yugoslavia **71** 46N 19E
Sombrero: *i.*, West Indies **59** 18N 63W
Somerset: U.S.A. **51** 37N 85W
Somerville: N.J., U.S.A. **54** 41N 75W
Somme: *r.*, France **68** 50N 2E
Son: *r.*, India **84** 24N 81E
Søndre Strømfjord: Greenland **1** 67N 52W
Songea: Tanzania **102** 11S 36E
Songhuahu (Sungari Res.): China **87** 43N 127E
Songjiang: China **89** 31N 121E
Songkhla: Thailand **85** 7N 101E
Son La: Vietnam **85** 21N 104E
Sonoyta: Mexico **52** 32N 113W
Sopot: Poland **70** 54N 19E
Sopron: Hungary **71** 48N 16E
Soria: Spain **69** 42N 2W
Sorocaba: Brazil **61** 23S 48W
Soroki: U.S.S.R. **70** 48N 28E
Souk Ahras: Algeria **69** 36N 8E
Souris: *r.*, U.S.A./Canada **53** 49N 101W
Sousse: Tunisia **100** 36N 11E
Southampton: Eng. **67** 51N 1W
South Australia: *State*, Australia **94** 30S 135E
South Bend: U.S.A. **51** 42N 86W
South Carolina: *State*, U.S.A. **51** 34N 81W
South China Sea **91** 15N 115E
South Dakota: *State*, U.S.A. **53** 45N 100W
South Downs: Eng. **67** 51N 0
Southeast Pacific Basin: Pacific Ocean **105** 45S 100W
Southend-on-Sea: England **67** 52N 1E
Southern Alps: N.Z. **95** 43S 170E
Southern Cross: Australia **94** 31S 119E
Southern Ocean **104/105** — —
Southern Uplands: Scotland **67** 55N 4W
South Georgia: *i.*, Atlantic Ocean **60** 54S 37W
South Island: N.Z. **95** — —
SOUTH KOREA: *cap.* Seoul **87** 37N 127E
South Orkney Is.: Southern Ocean **128** 61S 45W
Southport: England **67** 54N 3W
South Sandwich Trench: Southern O. **103** 57S 25W
South Shetland Is.: Antarctica **128** 62S 60W
South Sioux City: U.S.A. **53** 42N 96W
South Urst: *i.*, Scot. **67** 57N 7W
SOUTH WEST AFRICA *see* **NAMIBIA**
Southwest Pacific Basin: Pacific Ocean **105** 35S 150W
Southwest Cape: New Zealand **95** 47S 168E
Sovetsk: U.S.S.R. **70** 55N 22E
Sovetskaya Gavan (Soviet Harbour): U.S.S.R. **79** 49N 140E
Soweto: South Africa **102** 26S 28E
SPAIN: *cap.*, Madrid **69** — —
Spanish Town: Jam. **59** 18N 77W
Sparks: U.S.A. **52** 40N 120W
Spartanburg: U.S.A. **51** 35N 82W
Spárti: Greece **71** 37N 22E
Spasskoye: U.S.S.R. **81** 52N 69E
Speedwell, C.: U.S.S.R. **78** 75N 55E
Spencer, C.: U.S.A. **22** 58N 136W
Spencer Gulf: Austl. **94** 34S 137E
Spenser Mts.: N.Z. **95** 42S 173E
Spey: *r.*, Scotland **67** 57N 3W
Spitsbergen (Svalbard): *i.*, Arctic Ocean **78** 78N 20E
Split: Yugoslavia **71** 44N 16E
Spokane: U.S.A. **52** 48N 117W
Spoleto: Italy **71** 43N 13E
Springbok: S. Africa **102** 30S 18E
Springdale: U.S.A. **50** 36N 94W
Springfield: Colo., U.S.A. **53** 37N 103W
Springfield: Illinois, U.S.A. **51** 40N 90W
Springfield: Mass., U.S.A. **55** 42N 73W
Springfield: Mo., U.S.A. **50** 37N 93W
Springfield: Ohio, U.S.A. **51** 40N 84W
Springfield: Oregon, U.S.A. **52** 44N 123W
Springfield: Va., U.S.A. **57** 39N 77W
Spurn Hd.: England **67** 54N 0
Sretensk: U.S.S.R. **79** 52N 118E
SRI LANKA: *cap.* Colombo **84** 7N 81E
Srinagar: India **84** 34N 75E
Stafford: England **67** 53N 2W
Stamford: U.S.A. **55** 41N 74W
Stanke Dimitrov: Bulgaria **71** 42N 23E
STANLEY: Falkland Is. **60** 52S 58W
Starachowice: Pol. **70** 51N 21E
Stara Zagora: Bulg. **71** 42N 26E
Stargard Szczeciński: Poland **70** 53N 15E
Starogard Gdański: Poland **70** 54N 19E
Start Pt.: England **67** 50N 4W
State College: *city*, U.S.A. **54** 41N 78W
Staten I.: U.S.A. **56** 41N 74W
Statesville: U.S.A. **51** 36N 81W
Staunton: U.S.A. **51** 38N 79W
Stavanger: Norway **68** 59N 6E
Stavropol': U.S.S.R. **80** 45N 42E
Stendal: E. Germany **70** 53N 12E
Steppes: *geog. reg.*, U.S.S.R. **78** 50N 70E
Sterling: Colorado, U.S.A. **53** 41N 103W
Sterling: Ill., U.S.A. **51** 42N 90W
Sterlitamak: U.S.S.R. **80** 54N 56E
Steubenville: U.S.A. **51** 40N 81W
Stevens Point: *city*, U.S.A. **53** 45N 89W
Stewart I.: N.Z. **95** 47S 168E
Steyr: Austria **70** 48N 14E
Stickney: U.S.A. **57** 42N 88W
Stillwater: U.S.A. **50** 36N 97W
Štip: Yugoslavia **71** 42N 22E
Stirling: Scotland **67** 56N 4W
STOCKHOLM: Sweden **70** 59N 18E
Stockport: England **67** 53N 2W
Stockton: U.S.A. **52** 38N 121W
Stockton-on-Tees: England **67** 55N 1W
Stockton Plateau: U.S.A. **50** 30N 102W
Stoke-on-Trent: Eng. **67** 53N 2W
Stonehaven: Scot. **67** 57N 2W
Stonington I.: Antarctica **128** 67S 67W
Store Bælt: *str.*, Den. **68** 55N 11E
Stornoway: Scot. **67** 58N 6W
Stour: *r.*, Dorset, England **67** 51N 2W
Stoyba: U.S.S.R. **87** 53N 132E
Stralsund: E. Germany **70** 54N 13E
Strangford L.: N. Ireland **67** 54N 6W
Stranraer: Scotland **67** 55N 5W
Strasbourg: France **68** 49N 8E
Stratford on Avon: England **67** 52N 2W
Stratford: N.Z. **95** 39S 174E
Straubing: W. Ger. **70** 49N 12E
Strawberry Mt.: U.S.A. **52** 44N 119W
Stromboli: *volc.*, Italy **71** 39N 15E
Stryy: U.S.S.R. **70** 49N 24E
Stuart Highway: Australia **94** 20S 134E
Stuttgart: W. Germany **68** 49N 9E
Stuttgart: U.S.A. **50** 35N 91W
Suakin: Sudan **101** 19N 37E
Subotica: Yugoslavia **71** 46N 20E
Suchow (Tungshan): *see* Xuzhou
Suchow: *see* Suzhou
Suck: *r.*, R. of Irel. **67** 53N 8W
Sucre: Bolivia **60** 19S 65W
SUDAN: *cap* Khartoum **101** — —
Sudeten Mts.: Czech./Poland **70** 51N 16E
Sue Peaks: *mtn.*, U.S.A. **50** 30N 103W
Suez: *& gulf*, Egypt **82** 30N 32E
Suez Canal: Egypt **101** *inset*
Suffolk: U.S.A. **51** 37N 77W
Sui: Pakistan **84** 29N 69E
Suir: *r.*, R. of Ireland **67** 52N 7W
Suitland: U.S.A. **57** 39N 77W
Suizhong: China **88** 40N 120E
Sukagawa: Japan **90** 37N 140E
Sukhona: *r.*, U.S.S.R. **80** 60N 42E
Sukhumi: U.S.S.R. **80** 43N 41E
Sukkur: Pakistan **84** 28N 69E
Sula Is.: Indonesia **91** 2S 125E
Sulaiman Range: Pakistan **84** 30N 70E
Sulawesi: *see* Celebes
Sulphur Springs: U.S.A. **50** 33N 96W
Sulu Sea: Phil. **91** 8N 120E
Sumatra: *i.*, Indon. **91** 0 100E
Sumba: *i.*, Indonesia **91** 10S 120E
Sumbawa: *i.*, Indon. **91** 8S 117E
Sumen: Bulgaria **71** 43N 27E
Sumgait: U.S.S.R. **80** 40N 50E
Summan Dahna: *desert*, Saudi Arabia **83** 26N 47E
Summit: Ill., U.S.A. **57** 42N 88W
Summit: N.J., U.S.A. **56** 41N 74W
Sumoto: Japan **90** 34N 135E
Sumter: U.S.A. **51** 34N 80W
Sumy: U.S.S.R. **80** 51N 35E
Sunbury: U.S.A. **54** 41N 77W
Sundarbans: *district*, India/Bangladesh **84** 22N 90E
Sunda Str.: Indon. **91** 6S 106E
Sunderland: England **67** 55N 1W
Sundsvall: Sweden **70** 62N 17E
Sungai Petani: Mal. **85** 6N 100E
Sungari Res.: *see* Songhuahu
Suo-nada: *gulf*, Japan **90** 34N 132E
Superior: U.S.A. **53** 47N 92W
Superior, L.: U.S.A./Canada **53** 47N 90W
Suphan Buri: Thailand **85** 14N 100E
Suqian: China **88** 34N 118E
Sur (Tyre): Lebanon **82** 33N 35E
Surabaja: Indonesia **91** 7S 113E
Surakarta: Indonesia **91** 7S 111E
Surat: India **84** 21N 73E
Surat Thani: Thai. **85** 9N 99E
Surgut: U.S.S.R. **81** 61N 73E
SURINAM: *cap.* Paramaribo **60** 4N 56W
Susquehanna: *r.*, U.S.A. **54** 40N 76W
Susuman: U.S.S.R. **79** 63N 148E
Sutlej: *r.*, Pakistan/India **84** 30N 73E
Suwa: Japan **90** 36N 138E
Suwannee: *r.*, U.S.A. **51** 30N 83W

Suxian: China **88** 34N 117E
Suzhou (Suchow): China **89** 32N 121E
Suzuka: Japan **90** 35N 137E
Svalbard: *see* Spitsbergen
Svendborg: Den. **70** 55N 11E
Sverdlovsk: U.S.S.R. **81** 57N 61E
Svetozarevo: Yugo. **71** 44N 21E
Svir': *r.*, U.S.S.R. **80** 61N 34E
Svobodnyy: U.S.S.R. **87** 51N 128E
Swale: *r.*, England **67** 54N 2W
Swan Hill: *town*, Australia **94** 35S 144E
Swansea: Wales **67** 52N 4W
Swatow: *see* Shantou
SWAZILAND: *cap.* Mbabane **102** 27S 32E
SWEDEN: *cap.* Stockholm **70** — —
[illegible]
Sweetwater Canal: Egypt **101** *Inset*
Swellendam: S. Afr. **102** 34S 20E
Swilly, L.: R. of Irel. **67** 55N 8W
Swindon: England **67** 52N 2W
Swinoujście: Poland **70** 54N 14E
SWITZERLAND: *cap.* Bern **68/69** 47N 8E
Sydney: Australia **94** 34S 151E
Syktyvkar: U.S.S.R. **80** 62N 51E
Sylacauga: U.S.A. **51** 33N 86W
Sylhet: Bangladesh **84** 25N 92E
Syracuse: Sicily **71** 37N 15E
Syracuse: U.S.A. **54** 43N 76W
Syr Dar'ya (Jaxartes): *r.*, U.S.S.R. **81** 43N 67E
SYRIA: *cap.* Damascus **82** — —
Syrian Desert: Middle East **82** 32N 40E
Syzran': U.S.S.R. **80** 53N 48E
Szczecin: Poland **70** 53N 15E
Szczecinek: Poland **70** 54N 17E
Szechwan: *Prov.*, *see* Sichuan
Szeged: Hungary **71** 46N 20E
Székesfehérvár: Hung. **71** 47N 18E
Szolnok: Hungary **71** 47N 20E
Szombathely: Hung. **71** 47N 17E

T

Tabaueran (*formerly* Fanning I.): Pac. O. **104** 4N 159W
Tabora: Tanzania **102** 5S 33E
Tabriz: Iran **83** 38N 46E
Tacheng (Chuguchak): China **81** 47N 83E
Tacloban: Philippines **91** 11N 125E
Tacna: Peru **60** 18S 70W
Tacoma: U.S.A. **52** 47N 122W
Taconite Harbour: U.S.A. **24** 46N 91W
Tacuarembó: Uruguay **61** 32S 56W
Tadzhik S.S.R.: U.S.S.R. **81** 38N 72E
Taegu: S. Korea **87** 36N 128E
Taejon: S. Korea **87** 37N 127E
Taff: *r.*, Wales **67** 52N 3W
Tafilalet Oasis: Mor. **100** 31N 4W
Taganrog: U.S.S.R. **80** 47N 39E
Tagus (Tajo): *r.*, Port./Sp. **69** 40N 8W
Tahiti: *i.*, Pacific O. **105** 18S 150W
Tahoe, Lake: U.S.A. **52** 39N 120W
Tai, Lake: China **89** 31N 121E
Taian: China **88** 36N 117E
T'aichung: Taiwan **89** 24N 121E
Taihape: N.Z. **95** 40S 176E
T'ainan: Taiwan **89** 23N 120E
T'AIPEI: Taiwan **89** 25N 122E
T'aipeihsien: Taiwan **89** 25N 121E
Taipeh Shan: *ra.*, *see* Dabieshan
Taiping: Malaysia **85** 5N 101E
Taishan: China **89** 22N 113E
T'aitung: Taiwan **89** 23N 121E
TAIWAN: *cap.* T'aipei **89** 24N 121E
Taixing: China **88** 32N 120E
Taiyuan: China **88** 38N 112E
Ta'iz: Yemen **83** 14N 44E
Taizhou: China **88** 32N 120E
Tak: Thailand **85** 17N 99E
Takada: Japan **90** 37N 138E
Takamatsu: Japan **90** 34N 134E
Takaoka: Japan **90** 37N 137E
Talara: Peru **60** 5S 81W
Talaud Is.: Indon. **91** 4N 127E
Talavera de la Reina: Spain **69** 40N 5W
Talbot, C.: Austl. **94** 14S 127E
Talca: Chile **60** 35S 72W
Talladega: U.S.A. **51** 33N 86W
Tallahassee: U.S.A. **51** 30N 84W
Tallinn: U.S.S.R. **80** 59N 25E
Tamale: Ghana **100** 9N 1W
Tamar: *r.*, England **67** 51N 4W
Tamatave: *see* Toamasina
Tambov: U.S.S.R. **80** 53N 41E
Tamil Nadu: *State*, India **84** 10N 78E
Tampa: *& bay*, U.S.A. **51** 28N 82W
Tampere: Finland **70** 61N 24E
Tampico: Mexico **58** 23N 98W
Tamsag Bulag: Mongolia **79** 47N 117E
Tamworth: Australia **94** 31S 151E
Tana, L.: Ethiopia **101** 12N 37E
Tanabe: Japan **90** 34N 135E
TANANARIVE: *see* ANTANANARIVO
Tandil: Argentina **60** 37S 59W
Tanezrouft: *geog. reg.*, Algeria **100** 23N 0
Tanga: Tanzania **102** 5S 39E
Tanganyika, L.: Afr. **102** 8S 30E
Tanggu: China **88** 39N 118E
Tangier: Morocco **69** 36N 6W
Tangshan: China **88** 40N 118E
Tanimbar Is.: Indon. **91** 7S 131E
Tanjongbalai: Indon. **85** 3N 100E
Tanta: Egypt **82** 31N 31E
TANZANIA: *cap.* Dodoma **102** — —
Tapajos: *r.*, Brazil **60** 6S 57W
Tapa Shan: *mts.*, *see* Dabashan
Tapti: *r.*, India **84** 21N 75E
Tara: U.S.S.R. **81** 57N 75E
TARABULUS (TRIPOLI): Libya **100** 33N 13E
Tarakan: Indonesia **91** 3N 118E
Taranto: *& gulf*, Italy **71** 40N 17E
Tararua Ra.: N.Z. **95** 41S 175E
Tarawa: *i.*, Kiribati **104** 1N 173E
Tarbes: France **69** 43N 0
Tarcoola: Australia **94** 31S 135E
Taree: Australia **94** 32S 152E
Tarim He: *r.*, China **86** 41N 83E
Tarko-Sale: U.S.S.R. **79** 65N 78E
Tarlac: Philippines **91** 15N 121E
Târnovo: Bulgaria **71** 43N 26E
Tarnow: Poland **70** 50N 21E
Tarragona: Spain **69** 41N 1E
Tarsus: Turkey **82** 37N 35E
Tartary, Gulf of: U.S.S.R. **79** 50N 140E
Tartu: U.S.S.R. **80** 58N 27E
Tarutung: Indonesia **85** 2N 99E
Tashkent: U.S.S.R. **81** 41N 69E
Tasman, Mt.: N.Z. **95** 44S 170E
Tasman Bay: New Zealand **95** 41S 173E
Tasmania: *i. & State*, Australia **94** 42S 146E
[illegible]
Tassili n'Ajjer: *plat.*, Algeria **100** [illegible]
Tatabánya: Hung. **71** 48N 18E
Tatarsk: U.S.S.R. **81** 55N 76E
Tateyama: Japan **90** 35N 140E
Tatry: *mtns.*, Czech. **70** 49N 20E
Taubaté: Brazil **61** 23S 46W
Taumarunui: N.Z. **95** 39S 175E
Taungdwingy: Burma **85** 20N 96E
Taunggyi: Burma **85** 21N 97E
Taunton: England **67** 51N 3W
Taunton: U.S.A. **55** 42N 71W
Taupo: *& lake*, N.Z. **95** 39S 176E
Tauranga: N.Z. **95** 38S 176E
Taurus Mts.: Turkey **82** 37N 35E
Tavda: *& r.*, U.S.S.R. **81** 58N 65E
Tavistock: England **67** 51N 4W
Tavoy: Burma **85** 14N 98E
Tawitawi: *i.*, Phil. **91** 5N 120E
Tay: *r.*, Scotland **67** 56N 3W
Tay, L.: Scotland **67** 56N 4W
Taymyr, L.: U.S.S.R. **79** 75N 102E
Taymyr Peninsula: U.S.S.R. **79** 75N 105E
Tay Ninh: Vietnam **85** 12N 106E
Tayshet: U.S.S.R. **81** 56N 97E
Tbilisi: U.S.S.R. **80** 42N 45E
Tczew: Poland **70** 54N 19E
Teague: U.S.A. **50** 32N 96W
Te Anau, L.: N.Z. **95** 45S 168E
Te Awamatu: N.Z. **95** 38S 175E
Tecuci: Romania **71** 46N 27E
Tees: *r.*, England **67** 55N 1W
Teesside: *reg.*, England **67** 55N 1W
Tegal: Indonesia **91** 7S 109E
TEGUCIGALPA: Honduras **58** 14N 87W
TEHRĀN: Iran **83** 35N 51E
Tehuacán: Mexico **58** 18N 97W
Tehuantepec: *gulf & isthmus*, Mexico **58** 17N 94W
Teifi: *r.*, Wales **67** 52N 4W
Tekely: U.S.S.R. **81** 45N 79E
Tekirdağ: Turkey **71** 41N 27E
Tel-Aviv-Jaffa: Israel **82** 32N 35E
Tell Atlas: *mtns.*, Algeria **69** 37N 7E
Tell el Kebir: Egypt **101** *inset*
Telok Anson: Malaysia **85** 4N 101E
Telukbetung: Indon. **91** 5S 105E
Temir-Tau: U.S.S.R. **81** 50N 73E
Temple: U.S.A. **50** 31N 97W
Temuco: Chile **60** 39S 73W
Tenali: India **84** 16N 81E
Tenerife: *i.*, Canary Is. **100** 28N 16W
Tengchong: China **85** 25N 98E
Tengiz, L.: U.S.S.R. **81** 50N 69E
Tenkiller Ferry Res.: U.S.A. **50** 36N 95W
Tennant Creek: *town*, Australia **94** 20S 134E
Tennessee: *r. & State*, U.S.A. **51** 36N 88W
Ten Thousand Is.: U.S.A. **51** 26N 82W
Tepic: Mexico **58** 21N 105W
Teramo: Italy **71** 43N 14E
Teresina: Brazil **60** 5S 43W
Termez: U.S.S.R. **81** 37N 67E
Ternate: *i.*, Indon. **91** 1N 127E
Terni: Italy **71** 43N 13E
Ternopol': U.S.S.R. **70** 50N 26E
Terracina: Italy **71** 41N 13E
Terre Haute: U.S.A. **51** 39N 87W
Teruel: Spain **69** 40N 1W
Tessenei: Ethiopia **101** 15N 37E
Test: *r.*, England **67** 51N 1W
Tete: Mozambique **102** 16S 34E
Tetuan: Morocco **69** 36N 5W
Texarkana: U.S.A. **50** 33N 94W
Texas: *State*, U.S.A. **50** 32N 100W
Texas City: U.S.A. **50** 29N 95W
Texel: *i.*, Neth. **68** 53N 5E
Texoma, L.: U.S.A. **50** 34N 97W
Tezpur: India **84** 27N 93E
THAILAND: *cap.* Bangkok (Krung Thep) **85** 15N 102E
Thakhek: Laos **85** 17N 105E
Thal: *desert*, Pakistan **84** 32N 72E
Thames: N.Z. **95** 37S 176E
Thames: *r.*, England **67** 52N 0
Thanh Hoa: Vietnam **85** 19N 105E
Thanjavur: India **84** 11N 79E
Thar Desert: India/Pakistan **84** 27N 72E
Thásos: *i.*, Greece **71** 41N 25E
Thaton: Burma **85** 16N 97E
Thayetmyo: Burma **85** 19N 95E
Thebes: *hist.*, Egypt **82** 26N 33E
The Dalles: U.S.A. **52** 46N 121W
The Hague: *see* Hague
Thermopolis: U.S.A. **52** 44N 108W
Thessalonica (Salonica): Greece **71** 41N 23E
Thief River Falls: *city*, U.S.A. **53** 48N 96W
Thionville: France **68** 49N 6E
Thira: *i.*, Greece **71** 36N 25E
Thomasville: Ala., U.S.A. **51** 32N 88W
Thomasville: Ga., U.S.A. **51** 31N 84W
Three Kings Is.: N.Z. **95** 34S 172E
Three Points, C.: Ghana **100** 5N 2W
Thu Dau Mot: Vietnam **85** 11N 107E
Thule: Greenland **1** 76N 68W
Thun: Switz. **69** 47N 8E
Thursday I.: Austl. **94** 11S 142E
Thurso: Scotland **67** 59N 3W
Tianjin (Tientsin): China **88** 39N 117E
Tianmen: China **89** 31N 113E
Tiaret: Algeria **69** 35N 1E
Tiber: *r.*, Italy **71** 43N 12E
Tibesti: *highlands*, Chad **100/101** — —
Tibet Aut. Reg. (Xizang Zizhiqu): China **86** 33N 85E
Tien Shan: *range*, China/U.S.S.R. **81** 42N 80E
Tientsin: *see* Tianjin
Tierra del Fuego: *i.*, Argentina/Chile **60** 54S 67W
Tiffin: U.S.A. **51** 41N 83W
Tigris: *r.*, Turkey/Iraq **83** 35N 44E
Tihama: *plain*, Sau. Arab. **82** 20N 41E
Tijuana: Mexico **52** 32N 117W
Tiksi: U.S.S.R. **79** 72N 129E
Tilburg: Neth. **68** 52N 5E
Tilbury: England **67** 51N 0
[illegible]
Timaru: N.Z. **95** 44S 171E
Timbuktu: *see* Tombouctou
Timişoara: Romania **71** 46N 21E
Timor: *i. & sea*, Indonesia **91** 10S 125E
Timsah, L.: Egypt **101** *Inset*
Tipperary: R. of Ireland **67** 52N 8W
TIRANË: Albania **71** 41N 20E
Tiraspol': U.S.S.R. **71** 47N 30E
Tire: Turkey **71** 38N 28E
Tiree: *i.*, Scotland **67** 56N 7W
Tîrgovişte: Romania **71** 45N 25E
Tîrgu-Jiu: Romania **71** 45N 23E
Tîrgu Mureş: Romania **71** 46N 25E
Tiruchirappalli: India **84** 11N 79E
Tirunelveli: India **84** 9N 78E
Tissamaharama: Sri Lanka **84** 6N 81E
Tista: *r.*, Bangl./India **84** 27N 89E
Titicaca, Lake: Peru/Bolivia **60** 16S 69W
Titograd: Yugoslavia **71** 42N 19E
Titovo Užice: Yugo. **71** 44N 20E
Titov Veles: Yugo. **71** 42N 22E
Tivoli: Italy **71** 42N 13E
Tlemcen: Algeria **69** 35N 1W
Toamasina (Tamatave): Madagascar **102** 18S 49E
Toba, Lake: Indon. **85** 3N 99E
Tobago: *i.*, Trinidad & Tobago **59** 11N 61W
Tobol': *r.*, U.S.S.R. **81** 56N 66E
Tobol'sk: U.S.S.R. **81** 58N 68E
Tobruk: Libya **82** 32N 24E
Tocantins: *r.*, Brazil **60** 4S 50W
Toccoa: U.S.A. **51** 35N 84W
TOGO: *cap.* Lomé **100** 8N 1E
Tokelau: *is.*, Pac. O. **104** 9S 171W
Tokushima: Japan **90** 34N 134E
Tokuyama: Japan **90** 34N 132E
TOKYO: Japan **90** 36N 140E
Tolbuhin: Bulgaria **71** 44N 28E
Toledo: *& mtns.*, Spain **69** 40N 4W
Toledo: Ohio, U.S.A. **51** 42N 84W
Toledo: Oregon, U.S.A. **52** 45N 124W
Toliara (Tulear): Madagascar **102** 23S 44E
Tolo, G. of: Indon. **91** 2S 122E
Tolstoy, C.: U.S.S.R. **79** 59N 155E
Toluca: Mexico **58** 19N 100W
Tomakomai: Japan **90** 43N 142E
Tomaszów Mazowiecki: Poland **70** 52N 20E
Tomatlán: Mexico **58** 20N 105W
Tombigbee: *r.*, U.S.A. **51** 32N 88W
Tombouctou (Timbuktu): Mali **100** 17N 3W
Tomini, Gulf of: Indonesia **91** 0 121E
Tom Price: Australia **94** 23S 118E
Tomsk: U.S.S.R. **81** 56N 85E
TONGA: *cap.* Nuku'alofa **104** 20S 175W
Tongchuan: China **88** 35N 109E
Tongguan: China **88** 35N 110E
Tonghua: China **87** 42N 126E
Tongling: China **89** 31N 118E
Tongxian: China **88** 40N 117E
Tonkin, Gulf of: *see* Bei bu Wan
Tonle, Sap: *L.*, Kampuchea **85** 13N 104E
Tønsberg: Norway **70** 59N 11E
Tooele: U.S.A. **52** 41N 112W
Toowoomba: Austl. **94** 28S 152E
Topeka: U.S.A. **50** 39N 96W
Torbay: England **67** 51N 3W
Torne: *r.*, Sweden/Finland **70** 68N 19E
Tororo: Uganda **102** 1N 34E
Torrens, L.: Austl. **94** 31S 137E
Torreón: Mexico **58** 26N 103W
Torres Strait: Austl. **94** 10S 142E
Torridge: *r.*, England **67** 51N 4W
Tortosa: Spain **69** 41N 1E
Toruń: Poland **70** 53N 19E
Tosa-wan: *bay*, Japan **90** 33N 134E
Tottori: Japan **90** 36N 134E
Touba: Senegal **100** 15N 16W
Touggourt: Algeria **100** 33N 6E
Toul: France **68** 49N 6E
Toulon: France **69** 43N 6E
Toulouse: France: **69** 44N 1E
Toungoo: Burma **85** 19N 96E
Tournai: Belgium **68** 51N 3E
Tours: France **68** 47N 1E
Townsville: Austl. **94** 19S 147E
Toyama: Japan **90** 37N 137E
Toyohashi: Japan **90** 35N 137E
Toyota: Japan **90** 35N 137E
Trabzon: Turkey **82** 41N 40E
Tralee: R. of Ireland **67** 52N 10W
Tranås: Sweden **70** 58N 15E
Trang: Thailand **85** 8N 100E
Transkei: *self-governing State*, South Africa **102** 31S 29E
Transvaal: *Prov.*, Rep. of South Africa **102** 25S 29E
Transylvanian Alps: Romania **71** 45N 24E
Trapani: Sicily **71** 38N 12E
Traverse City: U.S.A. **24** 45N 85W
Trenčín: Czechoslovakia **70** 49N 18E
Trent: *r.*, England **67** 53N 1W
Trento: Italy **71** 46N 11E
Trenton: Missouri, U.S.A. **50** 40N 94W
Trenton: N.J., U.S.A. **54** 40N 75W
Treviso: Italy **71** 46N 12E
Trier: W. Germany **68** 50N 7E
Trieste: Italy **71** 46N 14E
Trikkala: Greece **71** 40N 22E
Trincomalee: Sri Lanka **84** 8N 81E
Trinidad: U.S.A. **53** 37N 105W
TRINIDAD & TOBAGO: *cap.* Port of Spain **59** 10N 61W
Trinity: *r.*, U.S.A. **50** 31N 96W
Tripoli: Lebanon **82** 34N 36E
TRIPOLI: Libya *see* TARABULUS
Tripolis: Greece **71** 38N 22E
Tripura: *State*, India **84** 24N 92E
Tristan da Cunha: *i.*, Atlantic Ocean **103** 38S 12W
Trivandrum: India **84** 8N 77E
Trnava: Czechoslovakia **70** 48N 18E
Troitsk: U.S.S.R. **81** 54N 62E
Trollhättan: Sweden **70** 58N 12E
Tromsø: Norway **70** 70N 19E
[illegible]
[illegible]
Troy: Ala., U.S.A. **51** 32N 86W
Troy: N.Y., U.S.A. **55** 43N 74W
Troy: *hist.*, Turkey **82** 40N 26E
Troyes: France **68** 48N 4E
Trujillo: Honduras **58** 16N 86W
Trujillo: Peru **60** 8S 79W
Truro: England **67** 50N 5W
Truth or Consequences: U.S.A. **52** 33N 107W
Tsaidam Swamps: *see* Qaidam Pendi
Tsangpo: *r.* China **88** 29N 86E
Tselinograd: U.S.S.R. **81** 51N 71E
Tsimlyansk Res.: U.S.S.R. **80** 48N 43E
Tsinan: *see* Jinan
Tsingtao: *see* Qingdao
Tsinkiang: *see* Quanzhou
Tsinling Shan: *see* Qinlingshan
Tsu: Japan **90** 35N 137E
Tsuchiura: Japan **90** 36N 140E
Tsugaru-kaikyo: *str.*, Japan **90** 41N 140E
Tsukumi: Japan **90** 33N 132E
Tsumeb: Namibia **102** 19S 18E
Tsuruga: Japan **90** 36N 136E
Tsuruoka: Japan **90** 39N 140E
Tsushima: *is.*, Japan **90** 34N 129E
Tsuyama: Japan **90** 35N 134E
Tuam: R. of Ireland **67** 54N 9W
Tuamotu Arch.: Pacific Ocean **105** 15S 140W
Tuapse: U.S.S.R. **80** 44N 39E
Tubai Is.: Pac. O. **105** 25S 150W
Tubarão: Brazil **61** 28S 49W
Tübingen: W. Ger. **68** 49N 9E
Tucson: U.S.A. **52** 32N 111W
Tucumcari: U.S.A. **53** 35N 104W
Tucupita: Venez. **59** 9N 62W
Tudela: Spain **69** 42N 2W
Tufts Abyssal Plain: Pacific Ocean **105** 45N 140W
Tugssâq: Greenland **1** 73N 55W
Tula: U.S.S.R. **80** 54N 37E
Tulare: U.S.A. **52** 36N 119W
Tulcea: Romania **71** 45N 29E
Tulear: *see* Toliara
Tulia: U.S.A. **50** 35N 102W
Tullahoma: U.S.A. **51** 35N 86W
Tullamore: R. of Ireland **67** 53N 7W
Tulsa: U.S.A. **50** 36N 96W
Tumaco: Colombia **60** 2N 79W
Tumkur: India **84** 13N 77E
Tumpat: Malaysia **85** 6N 102E
Tunbridge Wells: England **67** 51N 0
Tungabhadra: *r.*, India **84** 16N 76E
Tungting, L.: *see* Dongting, L.
Tunis: Tunisia **100** 37N 10E
TUNISIA: *cap.* Tunis **100** 35N 10E
Tunja: Colombia **60** 6N 73W
Tunxi: China **89** 30N 118E
Tupelo: U.S.A. **51** 34N 89W
Turanian Plain: U.S.S.R. **81** 43N 60E
Turbo: Colombia **59** 8N 77W
Turda: Romania **71** 47N 24E
Turfan Depression: *see* Turpan Depression
Turgay: *& r.*, U.S.S.R. **81** 50N 64E
Turgutlu: Turkey **71** 39N 28E
Turin: Italy **69** 45N 8E
Turkana (Rudolf), L.: Kenya **102** 4N 36E
Turkestan: U.S.S.R. **81** 43N 68E
TURKEY: *cap.* Ankara **82** — —
Turkmen S.S.R.: U.S.S.R. **80/81** 39N 57E
Turks Is.: W. Indies **59** 22N 71W
Turku: Finland **70** 60N 22E
Turlock: U.S.A. **52** 37N 121W
Turnagain, C.: N.Z. **95** 40S 177E
Turnu Măgurele: Romania **71** 44N 25E
Turnu Severin: Romania **71** 45N 23E
Turpan: China **86** 43N 89E
Turpan Depression: China **79** 43N 89E
Tuscaloosa: U.S.A. **51** 33N 88W
Tushino: U.S.S.R. **72** 55N 38E
Tuticorin: India **84** 9N 78E
TUVALU: *(formerly* Ellice Is.), *cap.*, Funafuti **104** 8S 180
Tuxpan de Rodriguez Cano: Mexico **58** 21N 97W
Tuxtla Gutiérrez: Mexico **58** 17N 93W
Tuy Hoa: Vietnam **85** 13N 109E
Tuz, L.: Turkey **82** 38N 33E
Tuzla: Yugoslavia **71** 45N 19E
Tweed: *r.*, England/Scotland **67** 56N 2W
Twin Bridges: U.S.A. **52** 45N 112W
Twin Falls: *city*, U.S.A. **52** 43N 115W
Tygda: U.S.S.R. **79** 53N 126E
Tyler: U.S.A. **50** 32N 95W
Tyne: *r.*, England **67** 32N 2W
Tynemouth: England **67** 55N 1W
Tyre: *see* Sur
Tyrrhenian Sea **71** 40N 12E
Tywi: *r.*, Wales **67** 52N 4W
Tyumen': U.S.S.R. **81** 57N 65E
Tzepo: *see* Zibo

U

Ube: Japan **90** 34N 131E
Uberaba: Brazil **60** 20S 48W
Uberlândia: Brazil **60** 19S 48W
Ubon Ratchathani: Thailand **85** 15N 105E
Ubsa Nor.: *l.*, Mong. **86** 50N 93E

Ubundi: Zaïre **102** 0 25E
Ucayali: *r.*, Peru **60** 7S 74W
Udaipur: India **84** 25N 74E
Uddevalla: Sweden **70** 58N 12E
Udine: Italy **71** 46N 13E
Udon Thani: Thailand **85** 17N 103E
Ueda: Japan **90** 36N 138E
Uelzen: W. Germany **68** 53N 10E
Ufa: *& reg.*, U.S.S.R. **80** 55N 56E
UGANDA: *cap.*, Kampala **102** 1N 32E
Uinta Mts.: U.S.A. **52** 41N 111W
Ujjain: India **84** 23N 76E
Ujung Pandang: Indonesia **91** 5S 119E
Ukhta: U.S.S.R. **80** 63N 54E
Ukiah: U.S.A. **52** 39N 123W
Ukrainian S.S.R.: U.S.S.R. **80** 50N 30E
ULAN BATOR (ULAANBAATAR): Mongolia **87** 47N 107E
Ulan Gom: Mongolia **79** 50N 92E
Ulangur Hu: *l.*, China **86** 47N 87E
Ulan-Ude: U.S.S.R. **79** 52N 107E
Uldza: Mongolia **87** 49N 112E
Uliastay (Jibhalanta): Mongolia **79** 47N 97E
Ullapool: Scotland **67** 58N 5W
Ulm: W. Germany **70** 48N 10E
Ulu-Tau: *range*, U.S.S.R. **81** 49N 67E
Ul'yanovsk: U.S.S.R. **80** 54N 48E
Uman': U.S.S.R. **70** 49N 30E
Umarkot: Pakistan **84** 25N 70E
Umeå: Sweden **70** 64N 20E
Umm Samim: *salt flats*, Oman **83** 22N 56E
Umtali: *now* Mutare
Unayzah (Anaiza): Saudi Arabia **83** 26N 44E
Union: U.S.A. **56** 41N 74W
UNION OF SOVIET SOCIALIST REPUBLICS: *cap.*, Moscow **78/79** — —
Uniontown: U.S.A. **51** 40N 80W
UNITED ARAB EMIRATES: *cap.*, Abu Dhabi **83** 24N 55E
UNITED KINGDOM OF GREAT BRITAIN & N. IRELAND: *cap.*, London **67** — —
UNITED STATES OF AMERICA: *cap.*, Washington, D.C. **50/53** — —
Uozu: Japan **90** 37N 137E
Upper Hutt: New Zealand **95** 41S 175E
UPPER VOLTA: *now* **BURKINA**
Uppsala: Sweden **70** 60N 18E
Ur: *hist.*, Iraq **83** 31N 46E
Urakawa: Japan **90** 42N 143E
Ural: *r.*, U.S.S.R. **80** 52N 53E
Ural Mts.: U.S.S.R. **81** 55N 59E
Ural'sk: U.S.S.R. **80** 51N 51E
Urawa: Japan **90** 36N 140E
Ure: *r.*, England **67** 54N 2W
Urfa: Turkey **82** 37N 39E
Uruapan: Mexico **58** 19N 102W
Uruguaiana: Brazil **61** 30S 57W
URUGUAY: *cap.* Montevideo **61** 32S 56W
Uruguay: *r.*, S. Am. **61** 29S 56W
Urumqi (Wulumuchi): China **86** 44N 87E
Usa: Japan **90** 34N 131E
Üsküdar: Turkey **82** 41N 29E
Usol'ye: U.S.S.R. **79** 53N 103E
Uspallata Pass: Chile/Arg. **60** 33S 70W
Uspenskiy: U.S.S.R. **81** 49N 73E
Ussuriysk: U.S.S.R. **79** 44N 132E
Usti: Czechoslovakia **70** 51N 14E
Ust'-Kamenogorsk: U.S.S.R. **81** 50N 83E
Ust'-Kut: U.S.S.R. **79** 57N 105E
Ust-Urt Plateau: U.S.S.R. **80/81** 44N 57E
Ust' Uyskoye: U.S.S.R. **81** 54N 65E
Usuki: Japan **90** 33N 132E
Utah: *State*, U.S.A. **52** 39N 112W
Utah Lake: U.S.A. **52** 40N 112W
Utica: U.S.A. **54** 43N 75W
Utrecht: Neth. **68** 52N 5E
Utsunomiya: Japan **90** 37N 140E
Uttaradit: Thailand **85** 17N 100E
Uttar Pradesh: *State*, India **84** 27N 80E
Uvalde: U.S.A. **50** 29N 100W
Uwajima: Japan **90** 33N 133E
Uyuni: Bolivia **60** 20S 67W
Uzbek S.S.R.: U.S.S.R. **81** 41N 62E
Uzhgorod: U.S.S.R. **70** 49N 22E

V

Vaal: *r.*, S. Africa **102** 27S 28E
Vaasa: Finland **70** 63N 22E
Vác: Hungary **71** 48N 19E
Valdai Hills: U.S.S.R. **80** 57N 34E
Valdepeñas: Spain **69** 39N 3W
Valdés Penin.: Arg. **60** 43S 64W
Valdivia: Chile **60** 40S 74W
Valdosta: U.S.A. **51** 31N 83W
Valence: France **69** 45N 5E
Valencia: *& gulf*, Spain **69** 39N 0
Valencia: Venez. **59** 10N 68W
Valenciennes: France **68** 50N 4E
Valentia: *i.*, R. of Irel. **61** 52N 10W
Valjevo: Yugoslavia **71** 44N 20E
Valladolid: Spain **69** 42N 5W
Vallejo: U.S.A. **52** 38N 122W
VALLETTA: Malta **71** 36N 14E
Valley Stream: *town*, U.S.A. **56** 41N 74W
Valparaiso: Chile **60** 33S 72W
Vals, Cape: Indon. **94** 8S 137E
Van: *& lake*, Turkey **83** 39N 43E
Vancouver: U.S.A. **52** 46N 123W
Väner, L.: Sweden **70** 59N 13E
Vänersborg: Sweden **70** 58N 12E
Vannes: France **68** 48N 3W
Vanua Levu: *i.*, Fiji **104** 16S 179E
VANUATU (*formerly* New Hebrides): *cap.* Vila **94** 17S 167E
Var: *r.*, France **69** 44N 7E
Varanasi: India **84** 25N 83E
Varanger Penin.: Norway **70** 71N 29E
Varaždin: Yugoslavia **71** 46N 16E
Vardar: *r.*, Yugo./Greece **71** 41N 22E
Varna: Bulgaria **71** 43N 28E
Värnamo: Sweden **70** 57N 14E
Västerås: Sweden **70** 60N 17E
Västervik: Sweden **70** 58N 17E
Vätter, L.: Sweden **70** 58N 14E
Vaupés: *r.*, Col. **60** 1N 71W
Växjö: Sweden **70** 57N 15E
Vaygach I.: U.S.S.R. **78** 70N 59E
Velikiye Luki: U.S.S.R. **80** 56N 31E
Vellore: India **84** 13N 79E
Venado Tuerto: Argentina **61** 34S 62W
Vendee, Collines de: *hills*: France **69** 47N 1W
Vendôme: France **68** 48N 1E
VENEZUELA: *cap.*, Caracas **60** 7N 65W
Venezuela, Gulf of: Venezuela **59** 11N 71W
Venice: *& gulf*, Italy **71** 45N 12E
Ventspils: U.S.S.R. **70** 57N 22E
Veracruz: Mexico **58** 19N 96W
Verde: *r.*, U.S.A. **52** 34N 112W
Verdigris: *r.*, U.S.A. **50** 38N 96W
Verdon: *r.*, France **69** 44N 6E
Verdun: France **68** 49N 5E
Vereeniging: S. Afr. **102** 26S 28E
Verkhoyansk: U.S.S.R. **79** 68N 134E
Verkhoyansk Range: U.S.S.R. **79** 65N 130E
Vermilion L.: U.S.A. **53** 48N 93W
Vermilion: *r.*, U.S.A. **53** 44N 97W
Vermont: *State*, U.S.A. **51** 44N 73W
Vernal: U.S.A. **52** 40N 110W
Vernon: U.S.A. **50** 34N 99W
Véroia: Greece **71** 41N 22E
Verona: Italy **71** 45N 11E
Versailles: France **72** 49N 2E
Verviers: Belgium **68** 51N 6E
Vesuvius: *volc.*, Italy **71** 41N 15E
Viborg: Denmark **70** 56N 9E
Vicente López: Arg. **61** 35S 57W
Vicenza: Italy **71** 46N 11E
Vichy: France **69** 46N 3E
Vicksburg: U.S.A. **50** 32N 91W
VICTORIA: Hong Kong **89** 22N 114E
Victoria: *r.*, Austl. **94** 16S 130E
Victoria: *State*, Austl. **94** 37S 145E
Victoria: U.S.A. **50** 29N 97W
Victoria Falls: Zimbabwe **102** 18S 26E
Victoria Land: Antarctica **128** 75S 160E
Victoria, L.: Africa **102** 1S 33E
Victoria West: South Africa **102** 31S 23E
Vidin: Bulgaria **71** 44N 23E
VIENNA: Austria **70** 48N 16E
Vienna: U.S.A. **57** 39N 77W
Vienne: France **69** 46N 5E
VIENTIANE: Laos **85** 18N 103E
VIETNAM: *cap.*, Hanoi **85** 15N 105E
Vigo: Spain **69** 42N 9W
Vijayawada: India **84** 16N 81E
VILA: Vanuatu **94** 18S 168E
Vila Cabral: *now* Lichinga
Vila de João Bala: *now* Xai-Xai
Vila Velha: Brazil **60** 3N 51W
Villach: Austria **71** 47N 14E
Villahermosa: Mexico **58** 18N 93W
Villa Maria: Argentina **61** 32S 63W
Villeneuve-sur-Lot: France **69** 44N 1E
Villeurbanne: France **69** 46N 5E
Vilnius: U.S.S.R. **80** 55N 25E
Viña del Mar: Chile **60** 33S 72W
Vincennes: U.S.A. **51** 39N 88W
Vindhya Ra.: India **84** 23N 77E
Vineland: U.S.A. **54** 39N 75W
Vinh: Vietnam **85** 19N 106E
Vinh Loi: Vietnam **85** 9N 105E
Vinkovci: Yugoslavia **71** 45N 19E
Vinnitsa: U.S.S.R. **70** 49N 28E
Virgin: *r.*, U.S.A. **52** 37N 114W
Virginia: *State*, U.S.A. **51** 37N 78W
Virginia: U.S.A. **53** 48N 93W
Virgin Is.: W. Indies **59** 18N 65W
Vishakhapatnam: India **84** 18N 83E
Visalia: U.S.A. **52** 36N 119W
Visby: Sweden **70** 58N 18E
Viseu: Portugal **69** 41N 8W
Vistula: *r.*, Poland **70** 53N 19E
Vitebsk: U.S.S.R. **80** 55N 30E
Viti Levu: *i.*, Fiji **104** 18S 178E
Vitim: *& r.*, U.S.S.R. **79** 60N 113E
Vitória: Brazil **60** 20S 40W
Vitoria: Spain **69** 43N 3W
Vitória da Conquista: Brazil **60** 15S 41W
Vizianagaram: India **84** 18N 83E
Vladimir: U.S.S.R. **80** 56N 40E
Vladimir Volynskiy: U.S.S.R. **70** 51N 25E
Vladivostok: U.S.S.R. **79** 43N 132E
Vlissingen (Flushing): Netherlands **68** 51N 4E
Vlorë: Albania **71** 40N 20E
Volga: *r.*, U.S.S.R. **80** 50N 45E
Volga Hills: U.S.S.R. **80** 51N 45E
Volgograd: U.S.S.R. **80** 49N 45E
Vologda: U.S.S.R. **80** 59N 40E
Vólos: Greece **71** 39N 23E
Vol'sk: U.S.S.R. **80** 52N 47E
Volta Lake: *& dam*. Ghana **100** 7N 0
Volta Redonda: Braz. **61** 23S 44W
Vorkuta: U.S.S.R. **78** 67N 64E
Voronezh: U.S.S.R. **80** 52N 39E
Voroshilovgrad: U.S.S.R. **80** 48N 40E
Vosges: *mtns.*, Fr. **68** 48N 7E
Vraca: Bulgaria **71** 43N 24E
Vršac: Yugoslavia **71** 45N 21E
Vryburg: S. Africa **102** 27S 25E
Vukovar: Yugoslavia **71** 45N 19E
Vyaz'ma: U.S.S.R. **80** 55N 34E
Vyborg: U.S.S.R. **80** 61N 29E
Vyshniy-Volochek: U.S.S.R. **80** 58N 35E

W

Wabash: *r.*, U.S.A. **51** 38N 88W
Waccasassa Bay: U.S.A. **51** 29N 83W
Waco: U.S.A. **50** 32N 97W
Waddenzee: Neth. **68** 53N 5E
Wadena: U.S.A. **53** 46N 95W
Wadi Halfa: Sudan **82** 22N 31E
Wad Medani: Sudan **82** 14N 34E
Wagga Wagga: Austl. **94** 35S 147E
Wahpeton: U.S.A. **53** 46N 97W
Waiau: *& r.*, N.Z. **95** 43S 173E
Waigeo: *i.*, Indonesia **91** 0 131E
Waikaremoana, L.: N.Z. **95** 39S 177E
Waikato: *r.*, N.Z. **95** 38S 176E
Waingapu: Indon. **91** 10S 120E
Waipara: N.Z. **95** 43S 173E
Waipawa: N.Z. **95** 40S 177E
Wairau: *r.*, N.Z. **95** 41S 174E
Wairoa: N.Z. **95** 39S 177E
Waitaki: *r.*, N.Z. **95** 45S 171E
Waitangi: N.Z. **95** 35S 174E
Waitara: N.Z. **95** 39S 174E
Wakatipu, L.: N.Z. **95** 45S 168E
Wakayama: Japan **90** 34N 135E
WaKeeney: U.S.A. **53** 39N 100W
Wakefield: England **67** 54N 1W
Wake I.: Pac. O. **104** 20N 167E
Wakkanai: Japan **90** 45N 142E
Wałbrzych: Poland **70** 51N 16E
WALES: *cap.*, Cardiff **67** — —
Wallachia: *Old Reg.*: Romania **71** 44N 25E
Walla Walla: U.S.A. **52** 46N 118W
Walsall: England **67** 53N 2W
Walsenburg: U.S.A. **53** 38N 105W
Walvis Bay: *town*, S. Afr. **102** 23S 15E
Wanaka, L.: N.Z. **95** 44S 169E
Wanganui: *& reg.*, New Zealand **95** 40S 175E
Wankie: *now* Hwange
Wanne-Eickel: W. Ger. **68** 52N 7E
Wantagh: U.S.A. **56** 41N 73W
Wanxian, Hebei: China **88** 39N 115E
Wanxian, Sichuan: China **89** 31N 108E
Warangal: India **84** 18N 80E
Warren: Idaho, U.S.A. **52** 45N 116W
Warren: Minn., U.S.A. **53** 48N 97W
Warren: Ohio, U.S.A. **51** 41N 81W
Warren: Pa., U.S.A. **51** 42N 79W
Warrnambool: Australia **94** 38S 143E
Warroad: U.S.A. **53** 49N 95W
WARSAW: Poland **70** 52N 21E
Warwick: England **67** 52N 2W
Warwick: U.S.A. **55** 42N 71W
Wash, The: *bay*, England **67** 53N 0
WASHINGTON, D.C.: U.S.A. **57** 39N 77W
Washington: Ind., U.S.A. **51** 39N 87W
Washington: N.C., U.S.A. **51** 36N 77W
Washington: *State*, U.S.A. **52** 47N 120W
Washington, Mt.: U.S.A. **51** 44N 71W
Waterbury: U.S.A. **55** 42N 73W
Waterford: R. of Irel. **67** 52N 7W
Waterloo: U.S.A. **53** 42N 92W
Watertown: N.Y., U.S.A. **51** 44N 76W
Watertown: S. Dak., U.S.A. **53** 45N 97W
Waterville: U.S.A. **51** 45N 70W
Watsonville: U.S.A. **52** 37N 122W
Wattenscheid: W. Ger. **68** 51N 7E
Wau: Sudan **101** 7N 27E
Waukegan: U.S.A. **57** 42N 87W
Wausau: U.S.A. **53** 45N 90W
Waxahachie: U.S.A. **50** 32N 97W
Waycross: U.S.A. **51** 31N 83W
Wayne: U.S.A. **56** 41N 74W
Waynesboro: U.S.A. **51** 38N 79W
Weald, The: *geog. reg.*, England **67** 51N 0
Wear: *r.*, England **67** 55N 2W
Weaverville: U.S.A. **52** 41N 123W
Webster: U.S.A. **55** 42N 72W
Weddell Sea: Antarctica **128** 72S 40W
Weed: U.S.A. **52** 41N 122W
Wei: *r.*, China **88** 37N 116E
Weiden: W. Germany **70** 50N 12E
Weifang: China **88** 37N 118E
Weihai: China **88** 38N 122E
Weimar: E. Germany **70** 51N 11E
Weinan: China **88** 34N 109E
Weirton: U.S.A. **51** 41N 81W
Weiser: U.S.A. **52** 44N 117W
Weissenfels: E. Ger. **70** 51N 12E
Wejherowo: Poland **70** 55N 18E
Wellesley Is.: Austl. **94** 17S 139E
WELLINGTON: N.Z. **95** 41S 175E
Wells: U.S.A. **52** 41N 115W
Wels: Austria **70** 48N 14E
Welshpool: Wales **67** 53N 3W
Wenatchee: U.S.A. **52** 47N 121W
Wendover: U.S.A. **52** 41N 114W
Wenshan: China **85** 23N 104E
Wenzhou: China **89** 28N 121E
West Australian Basin: Indian Ocean **104** 20S 100E
West Bengal: *State*, India **84** 23N 87E
Westbury: U.S.A. **56** 41N 74W
Westchester: U.S.A. **57** 42N 88W
West Dvina (Daugava): *r.*, U.S.S.R. **80** 56N 28E
Western Australia: *State*, Australia **94** 25S 120E
Western Ghats: *range*, India **84** 15N 75E
WESTERN SAHARA: *cap.*, El Aaiún **100** 25N 14W
WESTERN SAMOA: *cap.*, Apia **104** 12S 172W
Western Sayan Mts.: U.S.S.R. **81** 52N 91E
Western Sierra Madre: *see* Sierra Madre, Western
Western Springs: U.S.A. **57** 42N 88W
West Indies **59** — —
West Irian: *State*, Indonesia **94** 5S 137E
Weston: Malaysia **91** 5N 116E
Weston-super-Mare: England **67** 51N 3W
Westphalia: *Land*, W. Germany **68** 52N 7E
Westport: N.Z. **95** 42S 172E
Westport: R. of Ireland **67** 54N 10W
Westport: U.S.A. **55** 41N 73W
West Siberian Plain: U.S.S.R. **78/79** 60N 73E
West Virginia: *State*, U.S.A. **51** 38N 80W
Westwood: U.S.A. **52** 40N 121W
Wetar: *i.*, Indonesia **91** 7S 126E
Wexford: R. of Irel. **67** 52N 6W
Wey: *r.*, England **67** 51N 1W
Weymouth: England **67** 51N 2W
Weymouth: U.S.A. **55** 42N 71W
Whakatane: N.Z. **95** 38S 177E
Whangarei: N.Z. **95** 36S 174E
Wharton Basin: Indian Ocean **104** 16S 107E
Wheaton: Ill., U.S.A. **57** 42N 88W
Wheaton: Md., U.S.A. **57** 39N 77W
Wheeler L.: U.S.A. **51** 35N 87W
Wheeling: U.S.A. **51** 40N 81W
White: *r.*, Arkansas, U.S.A. **50** 35N 91W
White: *r.*, Indiana, U.S.A. **51** 39N 87W
White: *r.*, S. Dak., U.S.A. **53** 44N 100W
Whitefish: U.S.A. **52** 48N 115W
White Nile (Bahr el Jebel): *r.*, Sudan **101** 7N 31E
White Plains: U.S.A. **55** 41N 74W
White Sea: U.S.S.R. **78** 65N 37E
White Volta: *r.*, West Africa **100** 12N 2W
Whiting: U.S.A. **57** 42N 87W
Whitney, Mt.: U.S.A. **52** 37N 118W
Whyalla: Australia **94** 33S 138E
Wichita: U.S.A. **50** 38N 97W
Wichita: *r.*, U.S.A. **50** 34N 100W
Wichita Falls: *city*, U.S.A. **50** 34N 98W
Wick: Scotland **67** 58N 3W
Wicklow: R. of Irel. **67** 53N 6W
Wicklow Mts.: R. of Ireland **67** 53N 6W
Wiener-Neustadt: Austria **70** 48N 16E
Wiesbaden: W. Ger. **68** 50N 8E
Wigan: England **67** 53N 3W
Wight, I. of: Eng. **67** 51N 1W
Wigtown: Scotland **67** 55N 4W
Wilhelmshaven: W. Germany **68** 54N 8E
Wilkes-Barre: U.S.A. **54** 41N 76W
Wilkes Land: Antarctica **128** 70S 115E
Willamette: *r.*, U.S.A. **52** 45N 123W
Williamson: U.S.A. **51** 37N 82W
Williamsport: U.S.A. **54** 41N 77W
Williston: U.S.A. **53** 48N 104W
Willmar: U.S.A. **53** 45N 95W
Wilmette: U.S.A. **57** 42N 88W
Wilmington: Del., U.S.A. **54** 40N 76W
Wilmington: N.C., U.S.A. **51** 34N 78W
Wilson: U.S.A. **51** 36N 78W
Wiluna: Australia **94** 27S 120E
Winchester: England **67** 51N 1W
Winchester: Ky., U.S.A. **51** 38N 84W
Winchester: Va., U.S.A. **54** 39N 78W
Windermere: *l.*, England **67** 54N 3W
WINDHOEK: Namibia **102** 22S 17E
Wind River Range: U.S.A. **52** 43N 110W
Windsor: England **67** 51N 1W
Windward Is.: W. Indies **59** 13N 62W
Windward Passage: Cuba/Haiti **59** 20N 73W
Winfield: U.S.A. **50** 37N 97W
Winnemucca: *& l.*, U.S.A. **52** 41N 118W
Winner: U.S.A. **53** 43N 100W
Winnetka: U.S.A. **57** 42N 88W
Winnibago, L.: U.S.A. **53** 44N 88W
Winona: U.S.A. **51** 33N 90W
Winslow: U.S.A. **52** 35N 111W
Winston-Salem: U.S.A. **51** 36N 80W
Winter Haven: U.S.A. **51** 28N 82W
Winterthur: Switz. **68** 48N 9E
Winton: Australia **94** 22S 143E
Wisconsin: *State*, U.S.A. **53** 45N 90W
Wisconsin Rapids: U.S.A. **53** 44N 90W
Wismar: E. Germany **70** 54N 11E
Witten: W. Germany **68** 51N 7E
Wittenberge: E. Ger. **70** 53N 12E
Włocławek: Poland **70** 53N 19E
Wolf: *r.*, U.S.A. **53** 45N 89W
Wolf Point: *town*, U.S.A. **53** 48N 105W
Wollongong: Austl. **94** 34S 151E
Wolverhampton: England **67** 53N 2W
Wonsan: N. Korea **87** 39N 127E
Woodland: U.S.A. **52** 39N 122W
Woodville: N.Z. **95** 40S 176E
Woodville: U.S.A. **50** 31N 94W
Woodward: U.S.A. **50** 36N 99W
Woomera: Australia **94** 31S 137E
Woonsocket: U.S.A. **55** 42N 72W
Worcester: England **67** 52N 2W
Worcester: S. Africa **102** 34S 20E
Worcester: U.S.A. **55** 42N 72W
Workington: Eng. **67** 55N 3W
Worth: U.S.A. **57** 42N 88W
Wrangell: U.S.A. **22** 57N 132W
Wrath, C.: Scotland **67** 59N 5W
Wrexham: Wales **67** 53N 3W
Wrocław: Poland **70** 51N 17E
Wuchang: China **89** 30N 114E
Wugang: China **89** 27N 111E
Wuhan: China **89** 30N 114E
Wuhsi: *see* Wuxi
Wuhu: China **89** 31N 118E
Wuishan: *mtns.*, China **89** 27N 117E
Wulanhaote: China **87** 46N 122E
Wulumuchi: *see* Urumqi
Wuppertal: W. Ger. **68** 51N 7E
Würzburg: W. Ger. **70** 50N 10E
Wusong: China **89** 31N 121E
Wuwei: China **89** 31N 118E
Wuxi (Wuhsi): China **88** 32N 120E
Wuzhou: China **89** 24N 111E
Wye: *r.*, England **67** 52N 3W
Wyndham: Austl. **94** 15S 128E
Wyoming: *State*, U.S.A. **52/53** 43N 107W

X

Xai-Xai: Mozambique **102** 25S 34E
Xánthi: Greece **71** 41N 25E
Xi: *r.*, China **89** 23N 111E
Xiamen (Amoy): China **89** 24N 117E
Xi'an (Sian): China **88** 34N 109E
Xiang: *r.*, China **89** 28N 113E
Xiangcheng: China **88** 34N 113E
Xiangfan: China **88** 32N 112E
Xiangtan: China **89** 28N 113E
Xiaogan: China **89** 31N 114E
Xiashi: *see* Haining
Xieng Khouang: Laos **85** 19N 103E
Xigaze (Shigatse): China **86** 29N 89E
Xinghua: China **88** 33N 120E
Xingtai: China **88** 37N 114E
Xingu: *r.*, Brazil **60** 7S 53W
Xinhui: China **89** 23N 113E
Xining: China **87** 37N 102E
Xinjiang Weiwuer Zizhiqu (Sinkiang Uighur Aut. Reg.): **86** 40N 85E
Xinxiang: China **88** 35N 114E
Xinyang: China **88** 32N 114E

Xizang Zizhiqu (Tibet Aut. Reg.) **86** 33N 85E
Xuancheng: China **89** 31N 119E
Xuanhua: China **88** 41N 115E
Xuchang: China **88** 34N 114E
Xuzhou (Suchow, Tungshan): China **88** 34N 117E

Y

Yaan: China **87** 30N 103E
Yakima: *& r.*, U.S.A. **52** 47N 120W
Yakutat: U.S.A. **22** 60N 139W
Yakutsk: U.S.S.R. **79** 62N 130E
[illegible]
[illegible]
Yamal Peninsula: U.S.S.R. **78** 70N 70E
Yamatu: China **81** 46N 84E
Yamethin: Burma **85** 20N 96E
Yamoussoukro: Côte D'Ivoire **100** 7N 5W
Yampa: *r.*, U.S.A. **52** 40N 108W
Yamuna: *r.*, India **84** 25N 81E
Yanbu: Saudi Arabia **82** 24N 38E
Yancheng: China **88** 33N 120E
Yangjiang: China **89** 22N 112E
Yangliuqing: China **88** 39N 117E
Yangquan: China **88** 38N 113E
Yangtze: *r.*, China **89** 31N 118E
Yangzhou: China **88** 32N 120E
Yantai (Chefoo): China **88** 37N 121E
Yanzhou: China **88** 36N 117E
YAOUNDÉ: Cameroun **100** 4N 11E
Yaraka: Australia **94** 25S 144E
Yarkand: *see* Shache
Yaroslavl': U.S.S.R. **80** 58N 40E
Yatsushiro: Japan **90** 33N 131E
Yawatahama: Japan **90** 33N 132E
Ya Xian: China **85** 18N 110E
Yazd: Iran **83** 32N 54E
Yazoo: *r.*, U.S.A. **50** 33N 90W
Yazoo City: U.S.A. **50** 33N 90W
Ye: Thailand **85** 15N 98E
Yellow Sea: China/Korea **87** 35N 122E
Yellowstone: *L. & Nat. Park*, U.S.A. **52** 45N 111W
Yellowstone: *r.*, U.S.A. **52** 46N 108W
YEMEN: *cap.*, San'a **83** 15N 44E
YEMEN P.D.R.: *cap.* Aden **83** 15N 50E
Yenakiyevo: U.S.S.R. **80** 48N 38E
Yenangyaung: Burma **86** 20N 95E
Yenisey: *r.*, U.S.S.R. **79** 58N 88E
Yenisey, Gulf of: U.S.S.R. **79** 72N 83E
Yeniseysk: U.S.S.R. **81** 58N 92E
Yeovil: England **67** 51N 3W
Yerevan: U.S.S.R. **80** 40N 44E
Yeysk: U.S.S.R. **80** 46N 38E
Yibin: China **87** 29N 105E
[illegible]
Yinchuan: China **88** 38N 106E
Yingkou: China **88** 40N 122E
Yinshanmai: *desert*, China **88** 42N 108E
Yiyang: China **89** 29N 112E
Yogyakarta (Jogjakarta) **91** 8S 110E
Yokkaichi: Japan **90** 35N 137E
Yokohama: Japan **90** 35N 140E
Yokosuka: Japan **90** 35N 140E
Yokote: Japan **90** 39N 140E
Yonago: Japan **90** 35N 133E
Yonkers: U.S.A. **56** 41N 74W
Yonne: *r.*, France **68** 48N 3E
York: England **67** 54N 1W
York, Cape: Austl. **94** 11S 143E
York: Nebr., U.S.A. **53** 41N 98W
York: Pa., U.S.A. **54** 40N 77W
Yoshkar-Ola: U.S.S.R. **80** 57N 48E
Youghal: R. of Irel. **67** 52N 8W
Youngstown: U.S.A. **51** 41N 81W
Yreka: U.S.A. **52** 42N 123W
Yuan: *r.*, China **89** 29N 110E
Yuanling: China **89** 28N 110E
Yuba City: U.S.A. **52** 39N 122W
Yubari: Japan **90** 43N 142E
Yucatan Channel: Mexico/Cuba **58** 22N 86W
Yucatán Penin.: Mexico **58** 20N 88W
Yuci: China **88** 38N 113E
Yueyang: China **89** 29N 113E
YUGOSLAVIA: *cap.* Belgrade **71** — —
Yukagir Plateau: U.S.S.R. **79** 66N 157E
Yulin: China **88** 38N 109E
Yuma: U.S.A. **52** 33N 115W
Yuncheng: China **88** 35N 111E
Yunnan: *Prov.*, China **85** 25N 103E
Yunxian (Yunyang): China **88** 33N 111E
Yushu: China **86** 33N 97E
Yuxian: China **88** 34N 113E
Yuyao: China **89** 30N 121E
Yuzhno Sakhalinsk: U.S.S.R. **79** 47N 143E

Z

Zabul: Iran **83** 31N 62E
Zacatecas: Mexico **58** 23N 103W
Zadar: Yugoslavia **71** 44N 15E
Zagreb: Yugoslavia **71** 46N 16E
Zagros Mts.: Iran **83** 32N 50E
Zāhēdān: Iran **83** 29N 61E
ZAÏRE: *cap.*, Kinshasa **102** — —
Zaïre: *r.*, Zaïre **102** 2N 21E
Zakopane: Poland **70** 49N 20E
Zalaegerszeg: Hungary **71** 47N 17E
Zambezi: *r.*, Africa **102** 16S 34E
ZAMBIA: *cap.* Lusaka **102** — —
Zamboanga: Phil. **91** 7N 122E
Zamora: Spain **69** 41N 6W
Zamość: Poland **70** 51N 23E
Zanesville: U.S.A. **51** 40N 82W
Zanthus: Australia **94** 31S 123E
Zanzibar: *i. & town*, Tanzania **102** 6S 39E
Zapala: Argentina **60** 39S 70W
Zaporozh'ye: U.S.S.R. **80** 48N 35E
Zaragoza (Saragossa): Spain **69** 42N 1W
Zárate: Argentina **61** 34S 59W
Zaria: Nigeria **100** 11N 8E
Żary: Poland **70** 52N 15E
Zaysan, L.: U.S.S.R. **81** 48N 84E
Zeila: Somali Rep. **101** 11N 43E
Zenica: Yugoslavia **71** 44N 18E
Zeya: U.S.S.R. **79** 54N 127E
Zgierz: Poland **70** 52N 19E
Zhangjiakou (Changkiakow, Kalgan): China **88** 41N 115E
Zhangjiang: China **87** 22N 110E
Zhangzhou (Longxi): China **89** 24N 118E
Zhaoan: China **89** 24N 117E
Zhaoqing (Gaoyao): China **89** 23N 112E
Zhaotong: China **85** 27N 103E
Zhdanov: U.S.S.R. **80** 47N 37E
Zhejiang (Chekiang): *Prov.*, China **89** 29N 120E
Zhengding: China **88** 38N 114E
Zhengzhou (Chengchow): China **88** 35N 113E
Zhenjiang: China **88** 32N 120E
[illegible]
[illegible]
Zhlobin: U.S.S.R. **70** 53N 30E
Zhmerinka: U.S.S.R. **70** 49N 28E
Zhongshan: China **89** 22N 113E
Zhoushan: China **89** 30N 122E
Zhuoxian: China **88** 40N 116E
Zhuzhou: China **89** 28N 113E
Zibo (Tzepo): China **88** 37N 118E
Zielona Góra: Pol. **70** 52N 16E
Žilina: Czech. **70** 49N 19E
ZIMBABWE (*formerly* Rhodesia): *cap.* Harare **102** — —
Zinder: Niger **100** 14N 9E
Zlatoust: U.S.S.R. **81** 55N 60E
Znojmo: Czech. **70** 49N 16E
Zolochev: U.S.S.R. **70** 50N 25E
Zomba: Malawi **102** 15S 35E
Zongo: Zaïre **102** 4N 18E
Zonguldak: Turkey **82** 41N 32E
Zouar: Chad **100** 20N 17E
Zrenjanin: Yugo. **71** 45N 20E
Zuara: Libya **100** 33N 13E
Zuider Zee: *see* Ijsselmeer
Zuni: *r.*, U.S.A. **52** 35N 109W
Zunyi: China **89** 28N 107E
Zurich: Switzerland **68** 47N 8E
Zwickau: E. Germany **70** 51N 12E
Zwolle: Neth. **68** 53N 6E
Zyrardów: Poland **70** 52N 20E

Canadian Statistics

1. Land Area, Population 1961-1986 and Population Density, 1986

Province or territory	AREA Land area km²	Total km²*	POPULATION 1961	1971	1981	1986	POPULATION DENSITY 1986** km²
Newfoundland	371 635	405 720	458	522	568	568	1.5
Prince Edward Island	5 660	5 660	105	112	123	127	22.4
Nova Scotia	52 841	55 490	737	789	847	873	16.5
New Brunswick	71 569	73 440	598	635	696	710	9.9
Québec	1 357 655	1 540 680	5 259	6 028	6 438	6 540	4.8
Ontario	916 734	1 068 580	6 236	7 703	8 625	9 114	9.9
Manitoba	547 704	649 950	922	988	1 026	1 071	2.0
Saskatchewan	570 113	652 330	925	926	968	1 010	1.8
Alberta	638 233	661 190	1 332	1 628	2 238	2 375	3.7
British Columbia	892 677	947 800	1 629	2 185	2 744	2 889	3.2
Yukon Territory	531 844	483 450	15	18	23	24	0.04
Northwest Territories	3 246 389	3 426 320	23	35	46	52	0.01
Canada	9 203 054	9 970 610	18 238	21 568	24 343	25 354	2.8

*Includes both land and fresh water
**Based on land area not total area
Canada Year Book 1988.

2. Comparison Between Built-on and Total Land Areas and Percentage Distribution of Built-on Land Area, 1981

Province/ Territory	Total Land Area[1] 000 000 ha	1981 Built-on Area 000 ha	Built-on as % of Total	Percentage Increase 1951-1981	% DISTRIBUTION OF BUILT-ON AREA: Urban & Rural Settlement	Rural Transportation	Farmstead
Newfoundland	37.0	128.0	0.3	75.8	61.5	38	0.5
Prince Edward Island	0.6	33.9	6.0	18.5	13	79	8
Nova Scotia	5.3	174.9	3.3	41.3	42.5	55	2.5
New Brunswick	7.2	350.6	4.9	68.0	73	25	2
Québec	135.6	795.4	0.6	91.9	52	42	6
Ontario	89.1	1 183.3	1.3	55.3	45	45	10
Manitoba	54.8	397.8	0.7	63.4	29	57	14
Saskatchewan	57.0	744.4	1.3	13.0	10	73	17
Alberta	64.4	1 418.4	2.2	145.2	52	41	7
British Columbia	93.0	521.4	0.6	94.5	53	42	5
Territories	377.8	29.8	0.01	161.4	25	74	1
Total	922.0	5 777.9	0.6	71.4	44	47	9

[1] Excludes inland water.

J.A.G. Hansen, "Built-on Lands: Definition and Canadian Area Estimates", *Plan Canada* 23/4 (1984): 122-133.

State of the Environment Report for Canada, 1986.

3. Selected Demographic Rates[1] and Indexes, Canada, the Provinces and Territories, 1981-82[2] and 1982-83[2]

	Year	Nfld.	P.E.I.	N.S.	N.B.	Qué.	Ont.	Man.	Sask.	Alta.	B.C.	Yukon	N.W.T.	Canada
Birth rate	1981-82	18.2	16.2	14.8	15.4	14.6	14.1	15.9	12.7	18.3	14.9	23.9	25.9	15.1
	1982-83	17.5	15.9	13.8	14.9	14.8	14.0	16.2	17.2	17.5	14.6	23.8	23.9	14.8
Total fertility rate[3]	1981-82	1 976	1 868	1 633	1 698	1 623	1 615	1 822	2 122	1 928	1 659	2 142	2 979	1 704
Death rate	1981-82	5.8	8.2	7.7	7.5	6.7	7.2	8.4	7.7	5.4	7.1	5.8	4.6	7.0
	1982-83	5.4	8.0	8.1	7.6	6.8	7.2	8.2	7.7	5.3	7.2	5.5	4.1	7.0
Life expectancy at birth	Male	72.0	72.8	71.1	70.9	71.0	72.3	72.1	72.6	72.0	72.6		—	71.9
(1981)[4,5]	Female	78.5	80.5	78.2	78.7	78.7	79.0	78.7	79.9	78.9	79.4		—	78.9
Rate of natural increase	1981-82	12.4	8.1	6.6	7.9	7.9	6.9	7.5	9.9	12.9	7.8	18.0	21.4	8.1
	1982-83	12.1	7.8	5.6	7.3	7.5	6.8	8.0	9.5	12.2	7.4	18.4	19.8	7.9
Net migration rate	1981-82	-9.7	-6.1	-0.9	-4.0	-1.1	3.6	1.2	1.6	22.1	8.8	7.0	9.6	3.8
	1982-83	3.0	2.4	2.6	3.5	-1.5	4.6	3.5	4.0	1.9	4.7	-82.9	5.4	2.4
Rate of total increase	1981-82	2.7	2.0	5.7	3.9	6.8	10.5	8.7	11.5	35.0	16.6	25.0	31.0	11.9
	1982-83	15.1	10.2	8.2	10.8	6.0	11.4	11.5	13.5	14.1	12.1	-64.5	25.2	10.3
Percentage of women 15-40 in total population on December 1	1981	22.0	20.7	21.5	21.7	22.7	21.7	20.8	20.1	23.4	21.7	25.7	23.0	22.0
	1982	22.2	20.7	21.6	21.8	22.7	21.7	20.9	20.2	23.5	21.7	25.3	23.3	22.1
Percentage of population 65 and over on December 1	1981	7.8	12.3	11.0	10.2	8.9	10.2	12.0	12.1	7.3	11.0	3.2	2.9	9.8
	1982	8.0	12.4	11.2	10.4	9.2	10.3	12.1	12.2	7.3	11.2	3.3	2.8	9.9

[1] Per 1 000.
[2] Census year: from June 1, 1981 to May 31, 1982.
[3] The total fertility rate represents the number of children born to 1 000 women during their childbearing years.
[4] Life expectancy at birth is accurate to one decimal place (tenths of years).
[5] Preliminary data.

Statistics Canada, 1981 Census of Canada and unpublished data, Health Division and Demography Division.

Current Demographic Analysis: Report on the Demographic Situation in Canada 1983.

4. Life Expectancy at Birth, Selected Countries

Country	Year	Males (M) years	Females (F) years
Japan	1984	74.54	80.18
Sweden	1983	73.62	79.61
Switzerland	1981-82	72.70	79.60
Netherlands	1982-83	72.75	79.48
Denmark	1982-83	71.50	77.50
France	1981	70.41	78.47
Canada	1983-85	72.92	79.83
Spain	1975	70.41	76.21
Australia	1983	72.09	78.72
Israel	1983	72.52	75.92
United States	1983	71.00	78.30
England and Wales	1981-83	71.34	77.35
Cuba	1977-78	71.45	74.91
Italy	1974-77	69.69	75.91
Poland	1983	67.04	75.16
Portugal	1975	65.09	72.86

Note: Some countries report only combined male and female life expectancy. For example (1980-1985 average): Nigeria 48.5, Brazil 63.4, India 52.5, China 67.4, and Saudi Arabia 56.0.

Canada Year Book 1988.

5. Families by Family Structure, 1976, 1981, and 1986

	PERCENTAGE		
Family structure	1976	1981	1986
Husband-wife families	90.2	88.7	87.3
Lone-parent families	9.8	11.3	12.7
Male parent	1.7	2.0	2.3
Female parent	8.1	9.3	10.4
Total families	100.0	100.0	100.0

Canada Year Book 1988

6. Age Groups and Sex Ratio of Canada's Population, Census Years, 1901 to 1986[1]

	PER CENT OF TOTAL POPULATION									
Age Group	1901	1911	1921	1931	1941	1951	1961	1971	1981	1986
0-4	12.0	12.3	12.0	10.4	9.1	12.3	12.4	8.4	7.3	7.2
5-9	11.5	10.9	12.0	10.9	9.1	10.0	11.4	10.5	7.3	7.1
10-14	10.8	9.7	10.4	10.4	9.6	8.1	10.2	10.7	7.9	7.1
15-19	10.4	9.5	9.2	10.0	9.7	7.6	7.9	9.8	9.5	7.6
20-24	9.6	9.9	8.1	8.8	9.0	7.8	6.5	8.8	9.6	8.9
25-34	14.9	17.0	15.3	14.4	15.7	15.5	13.6	13.4	17.3	17.9
35-44	11.7	12.0	13.2	12.9	12.5	13.3	13.1	11.7	12.2	14.4
45-54	8.3	8.6	9.1	10.4	10.7	10.0	10.3	10.6	10.3	10.1
55-64	5.7	5.5	5.9	6.4	7.9	7.7	7.1	8.0	8.8	9.2
65-69	2.0	1.8	2.0	2.2	2.7	3.1	2.7	2.9	3.5	3.6
70+	3.1	2.8	2.8	3.3	4.0	4.7	5.0	5.2	6.2	7.0
Total	100.0	100.0	100.0	100.0	100.0	100.0	100.0	100.0	100.0	100.0
Sex ratio[2]	105.0	112.9	106.4	107.4	105.3	102.4	102.2	100.2	98.3	97.4

[1] Excluding Newfoundland in censuses prior to 1951.
[2] Males per 100 females.

Canadian Urban Trends, National Perspective, Vol. I. Printed with the permission of the Ministry of State for Urban Affairs and Copp Clark Publishing. *Canada Year Book 1988.*

7. Population of Census Metropolitan Areas, Census Years

Census Metropolitan Area	1961	1971	1976	1981[1,2]	1986
Calgary	279 062	403 319	469 917	625 966	671 326[3]
Chicoutimi-Jonquière	127 616	133 703	128 643	158 229	158 468
Edmonton	359 821	495 702	554 228	740 882	785 465[3]
Halifax	193 353	222 637	267 991	277 727	295 990
Hamilton	401 071	498 523	529 371	542 095	557 029
Kitchener	154 864	226 846	272 158	287 801	311 195
London	226 669	286 011	270 383	326 817	342 302
Montréal	2 215 627	2 743 208	2 802 485	2 862 286	2 921 357[3]
Oshawa	—	120 318[1]	135 196	186 446	203 543
Ottawa-Hull	457 038	602 510	693 288	743 821	819 263
Québec	379 067	480 502	542 158	583 820	603 267
Regina	113 749	140 734	151 191	173 226	186 521
Saint John, NB	98 083	106 744	112 974	121 012	121 265
St. Catharines-Niagara	257 796	303 429	301 921	342 645	343 258
St. John's, Nfld.	106 666	131 814	143 390	154 835	161 901
Saskatoon	95 564	126 449	133 750	175 058	200 665
Sherbrooke	—	—	—	125 183	129 960
Sudbury	127 446	155 424	157 030	156 121	148 877
Thunder Bay	102 085	112 093	119 253	121 948	122 217
Toronto	1 919 409	2 628 043	2 803 101	3 130 392	3 427 168
Trois-Rivières	—	—	—	125 343	128 888
Vancouver	826 798	1 082 352	1 166 348	1 268 183	1 380 729
Victoria	155 763	195 800	218 250	241 450	255 547[3]
Windsor	217 215	258 643	247 582	250 885	253 988
Winnipeg	476 543	540 262	578 217	592 061	625 304

[1] Adjusted due to boundary changes
[2] Based on 1986 Census Metropolitan area.
[3] Excludes population of one or more incompletely enumerated Native reserves or Native settlements.

Canada Year Book 1988.

8. Immigration to Canada by Country or Region of Last Permanent Residence, 1946 to 1950, 1963 to 1967, 1975, and 1985

Country	Annual Average 1946-50	Annual Average 1963-67	1975	1985
Asia	1 001	11 150	47 382	38 597[1]
British Isles	32 081	42 946	36 076	4 454
United States	8 777	15 199	21 055	6 669
West Indies	446	3 993	17 800	5 691
Portugal	22	6 495	8 547	1 342
Italy	4 010	24 360	5 978	650
Greece	568	6 523	4 062	551
France	956	6 266	3 891	1 401
Germany (West)	1 996	8 541	3 469	1 578
Netherlands	5 193	2 905	1 448	466
Others	31 537	26 363	29 646	22 903
Total	86 078	154 027	187 881	84 302

Immigration and Population Statistics, Manpower and Immigration; *Canadian Statistical Review*, July 1976, Statistics Canada. *Canada Yearbook 1988.*

[1] Vietnam (10 404), Hong Kong (7 380), and India (4 028) were the main originating countries.

9. Intended Destination of Immigrants, 1985

Province or Territory	Male	Female	Total
Newfoundland	161	164	325
Prince Edward Island	57	56	113
Nova Scotia	476	498	974
New Brunswick	318	291	609
Québec	7 449	7 435	14 884
Ontario	19 218	21 512	40 730
Manitoba	1 754	1 661	3 415
Saskatchewan	945	960	1 905
Alberta	4 243	4 758	9 001
British Columbia	5 590	6 649	12 239
Yukon and Northwest Territories	55	52	107
Canada	40 266	44 036	84 302

Canada Year Book 1988.

10. Population by Mother Tongue, 1981 and 1986

Language	1981[1]		1986	
	No.	%	No.	%
English	14 684 365	60.3	15 334 085	60.6
French	6 127 530	25.2	6 159 740	24.3
Non-official languages				
Aboriginal	150 235	0.6	138 060	0.5
Italian	499 920	2.1	455 820	1.8
Portuguese	159 295	0.7	153 985	0.6
Spanish	64 575	0.3	83 130	0.3
German[2]	485 375	2.0	438 680	1.7
Yiddish	27 945	0.1	22 665	0.1
Dutch	136 500	0.6	123 670	0.5
Ukrainian	258 575	1.1	208 415	0.8
Russian	28 525	0.1	24 860	0.1
Polish	116 095	0.5	123 120	0.5
Finnish	31 130	0.1	25 770	0.1
Hungarian	77 630	0.3	69 000	0.3
Greek	116 835	0.5	110 350	0.4
Arabic[3]	44 425	0.2	40 665	0.2
Punjabi	49 670	0.2	63 640	0.3
Chinese	212 785	0.9	266 560	1.1
Vietnamese	28 325	0.1	41 560	0.2
Tagalog (Filipino)	36 195	0.1	42 420	0.2
Other languages	409 270	1.7	428 205	1.7
Sub-total, single response	23 745 200	97.5	24 354 390	96.2
Multiple response	597 980	2.5	954 940	3.8
Canada[4]	24 343 180	100.0	25 309 330	100.0

[1] Since multiple responses are shown in this table, the 1981 data do not correspond to those previously released.
[2] Includes Alsacians in 1986.
[3] Includes Maltese in 1981.
[4] The figures for 1986 exclude the population on 136 incompletely enumerated Native reserves and settlements. The total population on these reserves was estimated to be about 45 000 in 1986.

Canada Year Book 1988.

11. Employed, Unemployed, and Average Income by Province, 1981 and 1985

Province**	Employed* (%)		Unemployed (%)		Average Family Income Constant 1985 $	
	1981	1985	1981	1985	1981	1985
Newfoundland	52.6	53.0	13.9	21.3	32 390	29 629
Prince Edward Island	58.7	61.9	11.2	13.2	29 463	30 943
Nova Scotia	57.3	58.8	10.2	13.8	31 370	34 349
New Brunswick	56.2	56.8	11.5	15.2	30 916	31 473
Québec	61.5	62.2	10.3	11.8	35 774	35 068
Ontario	67.6	68.0	6.6	8.0	40 920	41 775
Manitoba	64.8	65.8	5.9	8.1	35 856	34 829
Saskatchewan	63.5	66.4	4.7	8.1	36 561	34 866
Alberta	72.3	71.9	3.8	10.1	43 943	40 736
British Columbia	65.1	64.3	6.7	14.2	41 766	37 968

* Population employed as a % of the total population over 15 years of age.
** Statistics not available for the Territories.

Canada Year Book 1988.

12. Lumber Production and Shipments and Value of All Shipments of the Sawmill and Planing Industry, 1968 and 1984

PROVINCE OR TERRITORY	PRODUCTION		QUANTITY SHIPPED		VALUE OF SHIPMENTS	
	1968	1984	1968	1984	1968	1984
	m^3	m^3	m^3	m^3	$000	$000
Newfoundland	17 310	89 212	25 213	n.a.	931	n.a.
Prince Edward Island	6 563	37 756	2 305	n.a.	73	n.a.
Nova Scotia	511 294	460 314	439 751	280 464	15 572	39 986
New Brunswick	627 963	1 066 323	663 549	997 548	24 886	99 198
Québec	3 801 653	8 852 128	3 631 322	8 413 907	135 075	827 781
Ontario	1 985 433	4 558 587	1 736 936	3 941 761	76 824	432 529
Manitoba	79 890	137 592	68 055	134 722	1 849	14 918
Saskatchewan	199 185	519 921	251 602	480 943	8 767	41 641
Alberta	805 896	2 405 457	909 442	2 683 004	29 950	220 966
British Columbia	17 317 436	30 861 348	18 171 589	29 858 746	707 896	3 056 786
Yukon & Northwest Territories	17 296	—	18 646	—	584	—
Canada	25 369 913	48 988 638	25 918 404	46 801 846	1 002 407	4 735 555

Canada Year Book 1970 – 71 and *1988; Canada Forestry Statistics,* Statistics Canada, 1973.

13. Pulp Production, 1964, 1973, and 1984

	1964	1973	1984
	10^3 t	10^3 t	10^3 t
Québec	4 720	5 590	6 371
British Columbia	2 564	5 336	5 370
Ontario	3 009	3 668	4 366
Other Provinces	2 170	3 965	4 356
Total Production	12 464	18 559	20 464

Canada Year Book 1972 and *1988; Canadian Forestry Statistics*, Statistics Canada, 1973.

14. Volume of Wood Cut, by Province (000 m^3)

Province or Territory	1980	1984
Newfoundland	2 795	2 889
Prince Edward Island	278	413
Nova Scotia	4 544	3 559
New Brunswick	8 387	8 378
Québec	31 687	36 519
Ontario	21 322	28 130
Manitoba	2 335	1 698
Saskatchewan	3 330	2 726
Alberta	5 933	8 457
British Columbia	74 654	74 556
Yukon and Northwest Territories	115	177
Canada	155 380	167 502

Canada Year Book 1988.

15. Exports of Pulp and Newsprint to Britain, United States and All Countries, 1980 and 1985

COMMODITY AND YEAR	BRITAIN		UNITED STATES		ALL COUNTRIES	
	Quantity t	Value $000	Quantity t	Value $000	Quantity t	Value $000
Pulp						
1980	377 944	205 773	3 515 798	1 911 688	7 244 311	3 866 989
1985	337 365	161 875	3 550 645	1 827 634	7 024 185	3 393 793
Newsprint						
1980	433 593	250 930	6 209 403	2 924 483	7 706 840	3 676 468
1985	272 954	158 724	6 948 988	4 688 940	8 274 702	5 407 368

Canada Year Book 1988.

16. Canada's Forest Inventory, 1981

PROVINCE OR TERRITORY	INVENTORIED FOREST LAND (000 km^2)					VOLUME[3] (000 000 m^3)		
	Inventoried forest land[1]	Productive forest land[2]				Softwoods	Hardwoods	Total
		Crown provincial	Crown federal	Private and others	Total			
Newfoundland	142	79	1	4	85	429	34	463
Prince Edward Island	3	—	—	3	3	22	11	33
Nova Scotia	41	6	—	22	29	137	65	202
New Brunswick	65	29	2	31	62	338	178	516
Québec	624	469	2	63	533	3 089	1 044	4 133
Ontario	432	331	6	39	377	2 075	1 123	3 198
Manitoba	240	132	3	4	140	439	196	635
Saskatchewan	123	84	5	—	89	293	191	484
Alberta	331	199	17	—	216	781	657	1 438
British Columbia	566	437	5	16	458	7 438	404	7 842
Yukon	242	—	67	—	67	214	40	254
Northwest Territories	615	—	143	—	143	315	131	446
Total	3 425	1 767	252	183	2 202	15 570	4 074	19 644

[1] Land primarily intended for growing, or currently supporting, forest.
[2] Productive forest land available for growing and harvesting forest crops. Excludes reserved forest land by law not available, as in national parks, some provincial parks, game refuges, water conservation areas, nature preserves and military areas.
[3] Merchantable volume on production forest land.

Canada Year Book 1988.

17. Quantity and Value of Sea and Inland Fish Landed, 1962, 1972, and 1984

PROVINCE OR TERRITORY	QUANTITY			LANDED VALUE		
	1962	1972	1984	1962	1972	1984
	t	t	t	$000	$000	$000
Newfoundland	249 127	295 135	450 584	17 222	35 723	162 244
Prince Edward Island	17 065	25 780	38 521	4 361	9 540	38 301
Nova Scotia	197 682	286 856	394 504	30 928	66 375	265 280
New Brunswick	92 746	162 144	100 012	9 182	19 923	75 567
Québec	60 512	83 210	84 240	5 534	11 138	57 711
Ontario	28 924	19 589	22 667	5 341	8 119	35 105
Manitoba	16 374	11 101	13 040	4 229	4 523	18 106
Saskatchewan	6 822	4 864	3 508	1 478	1 634	3 998
Alberta	4 093	2 202	1 420	714	727	1 248
British Columbia	311 517	153 060	169 168	49 067	75 128	242 935
Yukon & Northwest Territories	2 968	1 625	1 163	859	866	1 459
Totals	987 813	1 045 566	1 278 827	128 915	233 696	901 954

Canada Year Book 1969, 1975 and *1988.*

18. Number of Fishermen and Fish Processing Establishments, by Province, 1984

Province	Number of Fishermen	Fish Processing Establishments	Fish Processing Employees
Nfld.	27 617	99	8 637
P.E.I.	3 399	19	712
N.S.	13 235	100	5 793
N.B.	6 665	74	3 829
Québec	8 500	39	1 859
Ontario[1]	1 588	15	n.a.
B.C.	17 299	49	2 972
Other[1]	5 600	2	n.a.

[1] Mainly freshwater fisheries.

Canada Year Book 1988.

19. Market Value of Major Fishery Products, 1984

$000

Atlantic Coast		Pacific Coast	
1. Cod	419 761	1. Herring	98 955
2. Lobster	174 218	2. Sockeye salmon	85 665
3. Crab	125 945	3. Coho salmon	59 636
4. Herring	120 739	4. Spring salmon	46 582
5. Flounder and Sole	79 854	5. Other salmon	84 359
6. Scallops	76 864		
Total Atlantic Coast	1 392 868	Total Pacific Coast	466 887
Total Inland Fishery	119 685		

Canada Year Book 1988.

20. Net Income and Cash Receipts from Farming Operations, by Province, 1982 and 1986 ($000 000)

Province	NET INCOME 1982	NET INCOME 1986	CASH RECEIPTS 1982	CASH RECEIPTS 1986
Newfoundland	7.7	9.9	35.5	45.2
Prince Edward Island	30.0	50.6	164.2	189.9
Nova Scotia	48.7	79.8	232.5	267.6
New Brunswick	44.6	61.2	198.7	226.4
Québec	642.2	1 066.4	2 799.4	3 226.8
Ontario	714.9	1 421.6	4 858.9	5 457.9
Manitoba	220.2	503.1	1 703.7	2 073.6
Saskatchewan	986.7	738.8	4 027.6	4 130.3
Alberta	629.6	720.1	3 825.4	3 758.9
British Columbia	152.9	214.6	943.8	1 003.1
Canada	3 477.7	4 866.1	18 789.7	20 379.6

Canada Year Book 1988.

21. Area and Production of Major Field Crops by Province[1], Various Years

FIELD CROP AND PROVINCE	AREA (000 ha)				TOTAL PRODUCTION (000 t)			
	Average 1945-49	Average 1963-67	1974	1986	Average 1945-49	Average 1963-67	1974	1986
Wheat	**9 823**	**11 630**	**9 391**	**14 217**	**9 873**	**18 473**	**14 220**	**31 850**
Québec	5	9	24	60	6	16	42	185
Ontario								
Winter	248	159	168	253	493	433	519	925
Spring	16	8	4	28	22	14	8	79
Manitoba	968	1 324	1 200	1 983	1 306	2 145	1 715	4 501
Saskatchewan	5 775	7 575	6 160	8 782	5 035	11 523	8 872	18 643
Alberta	2 766	2 509	1 800	3 035	2 939	4 262	2 994	7 348
British Columbia	42	44	28	63	71	74	52	128
Oats	**4 605**	**3 284**	**2 442**	**1 555**	**5 034**	**5 773**	**3 929**	**3 906**
Prince Edward Island	44	35	20	12	63	67	43	31
New Brunswick	71	32	20	15	95	53	35	31
Québec	550	430	250	125	508	654	367	260
Ontario	601	547	198	117	876	1 118	361	273
Manitoba	584	633	480	243	756	1 046	663	601
Saskatchewan	1 634	718	760	405	1 481	1 258	1 157	941
Alberta	1 058	849	680	607	1 157	1 505	1 234	1 696
British Columbia	37	28	26	24	70	51	54	57
Barley	**2 628**	**2 670**	**4 600**	**4 952**	**3 074**	**5 042**	**8 585**	**15 026**
Prince Edward Island	2	5	8	26	4	12	23	85
Nova Scotia	2	1	2	6	3	3	6	16
New Brunswick	4	2	4	10	7	4	10	28
Québec	34	6	21	195	41	13	36	580
Ontario	94	79	136	235	163	195	337	762
Manitoba	706	282	720	627	914	501	1 154	1 872
Saskatchewan	942	775	1 600	1 457	936	1 463	2 787	4 006
Alberta	835	1 462	2 040	2 307	980	2 761	4 093	7 446
British Columbia	8	57	68	89	16	91	139	231
Soybeans	**29**	**103**	**178**	**405**	**41**	**202**	**300**	**988**
Ontario	29	103	178	405	41	202	300	988

21. Area and Production of Major Field Crops by Province[1], Various Years (continued)

FIELD CROP AND PROVINCE	AREA (000 ha)				TOTAL PRODUCTION (000 t)			
	Average 1945-49	Average 1963-67	1974	1986	Average 1945-49	Average 1963-67	1974	1986
Mixed Grains	**490**	**646**	**724**	**471**	**999**	**1 726**	**1 831**	**1 306**
Prince Edward Island	19	19	30	30	43	56	99	90
Québec	76	40	50	45	112	90	106	120
Ontario	366	320	328	223	804	998	993	631
Manitoba	7	61	80	45	11	129	136	112
Saskatchewan	5	49	80	53	6	103	145	123
Alberta	13	148	148	65	17	328	331	204
Flaxseed	**466**	**713**	**600**	**805**	**241**	**518**	**363**	**1 067**
Manitoba	180	397	300	445	108	263	180	584
Saskatchewan	210	177	220	324	85	136	119	432
Alberta	58	122	80	36	35	102	64	51
Rapeseed	**16**	**468**	**1 304**	**2 776**	**673**	**430**	**1 200**	**3 887**
Ontario	—	—	—	34	—	—	—	67
Manitoba	—	47	200	425	—	41	193	590
Saskatchewan	16	192	600	1 052	673	195	544	1 497
Alberta	—	229	480	1 194	—	194	442	1 656
British Columbia	—	—	—	71	—	—	—	77
Shelled Corn	**98**	**291**	**584**	**1 087**	**280**	**1 468**	**2 589**	**6 514**
Québec	—	—	66	260	—	—	293	1 270
Ontario	92	286	516	801	273	1 450	2 291	5 131
Manitoba	5	2	2	20	8	4	5	86
Potatoes	**167**	**118**	**112**	**114**	**1 801**	**2 183**	**2 427**	**2 850**
Prince Edward Island	18	18	18	28	272	403	467	810
New Brunswick	24	23	23	21	396	551	608	507
Québec	47	29	21	20	406	389	382	420
Ontario	37	20	17	13	363	427	368	334
Manitoba	8	9	14	17	64	119	222	353
Tame Hay	**4 214**	**5 121**	**5 355**	**5 501**	**15 176**	**21 368**	**23 604**	**30 663**
Prince Edward Island	88	72	51	51	302	296	204	242
Nova Scotia	161	90	60	73	634	429	288	394
New Brunswick	214	100	64	70	678	430	251	323
Québec	1 584	1 345	1 070	990	5 013	5 495	4 518	6 100
Ontario	1 348	1 354	1 080	1 072	5 559	6 701	5 733	8 165
Manitoba	130	407	500	587	504	1 571	2 177	3 084
Saskatchewan	192	467	800	728	617	1 579	2 903	2 722
Alberta	376	1 114	1 480	1 619	1 243	3 949	6 078	7 893
British Columbia	121	174	250	308	624	917	1 451	1 724
Fodder Corn	**162**	**212**	**419**	**324**	**3 183**	**5 594**	**10 043**	**9 525**
Québec	28	26	64	80	549	705	1 855	2 300
Ontario	123	166	336	202	2 531	4 579	7 697	5 806
Manitoba	6	15	11	16	53	213	190	327
Alberta	—	—	—	10	—	—	—	454
British Columbia	2	2	7	10	38	77	299	499

[1] Only provinces with over 10 000 ha in a particular crop are listed.

Canada Year Book 1961, 1970-71, 1975, and *1988.*

22. Canadian Wheat Statistics, 1983, 1984, and 1985

	1983	1984	1985
Carryover from previous crop year (000 t)	9 983.3	9 189.7	7 598.0
Production (000 t)	26 505.1	21 199.4	24 252.3
Total supply (000 t)	36 488.4	30 389.1	31 850.3
Exports (000 t)	21 764.8	17 541.9	17 683.0
Domestic use (000 t)	5 533.9	5 250.1	5 598.3
Carryover at end of crop year (000 t)	9 189.7	7 598.0	8 569.0
Cash receipts ($000 000)	4 253.7	4 198.8	3 071.4

Canada Year Book 1988.

23. Exports of All Canadian Wheat and Wheat Flour, by Country of Final Destination, Crop Years 1983-84 to 1985-86 (000 t)

Region	1983-84	1984-85	1985-86
Western Europe Total	**2 238.3**	**1 302.0**	**1 536.2**
United Kingdom	955.1	633.1	701.7
Italy	742.3	221.0	367.0
Eastern Europe Total	**6 890.9**	**6 284.6**	**5 506.0**
Poland	52.0	90.9	23.0
USSR	6 760.9	6 019.1	5 219.5
Middle East Total	**2 262.8**	**1 990.8**	**1 393.6**
Africa Total	**1 050.3**	**716.3**	**809.1**
Algeria	813.3	507.8	491.9
Asia Total	**6 317.9**	**4 740.5**	**5 535.6**
People's Republic of China	3 513.9	2 844.4	2 614.5
South America Total	**1 501.2**	**1 485.1**	**1 420.7**
Brazil	1 363.0	1 152.1	986.2
Central America and Antilles Total	**1 432.7**	**853.0**	**1 200.1**
Cuba	1 052.8	779.4	1 136.6
North America Total	**70.0**	**169.5**	**281.3**
Total	**21 764.3**	**17 541.8**	**17 682.7**

Canada Year Book 1988.

24. Major World Wheat Producers, 1966, 1976, and 1986

	1966		1976		1986	
	Production 000 t	% of World Total	Production 000 t	% of World Total	Production 000 t	% of World Total
USSR	100 499	32.6	96 900	23.2	92 300	17.2
China	25 700[1]	8.3	43 003[1]	10.3	89 002[1]	16.6
USA	35 699	11.6	58 444	14.0	56 972	10.6
India	10 424	3.4	28 336	6.8	46 885	8.7
Canada	22 516	7.3	23 523	5.6	31 850	5.9
France	11 297	3.7	16 089	3.9	26 587	5.0
Turkey	9 715	3.2	16 500	4.0	19 000	3.5
Australia	12 570	4.1	12 000	2.9	17 356	3.2
Pakistan	3 933	1.3	8 636	2.1	13 923	2.6
UK	3 475	1.1	4 773	1.1	13 874	2.6
Total	308 259	100.0	417 478	100.0	535 842	100.0

[1] FAO estimate

FAO Production Yearbook 1967, 1976, and *1986.*

25. Value of Mineral Production[1]

Year	Total value $000	Value per capita $	Year	Total value $000	Value per capita $	Year	Total value $000	Value per capita $
1886	10 221	2.23	1930	279 874	27.42	1975	13 346 994	588.05
1890	16 763	3.51	1935	312 344	28.84	1980	31 841 758	1 331.49
1895	20 506	4.09	1940	529 825	46.55	1981	32 410 481	1 328.62
1900	64 421	12.15	1945	498 755	41.31	1982	33 831 494	1 373.59
1905	69 079	11.51	1950[2]	1 045 450	76.24	1983	38 539 005	1 548.62
1910	106 824	15.29	1955	1 795 311	114.37	1984	43 789 031	1 742.91
1915	137 109	17.18	1960	2 492 510	139.48	1985	44 733 540	1 762.55
1920	227 860	26.63	1965	3 714 861	189.11	1986[p]	33 854 397	1 321.51
1925	226 583	24.38	1970	5 722 059	268.68			

[1] Includes fuels.
[2] Value of Newfoundland production included from 1950.
[p] Preliminary

Canada Year Book 1988.

26. Value of Production of Principal Minerals, 1976, 1982, and 1986 ($000)

	1976	1982	1986
Metals			
Antimony	n.a.	2 455	23 910
Cobalt	11 769	38 741	56 242
Copper	1 126 156	1 195 083	1 567 988
Gold	207 796	968 012	1 715 392
Iron Ore	1 241 263	1 201 256	1 254 758
Lead	129 388	197 335	204 427
Molybdenum	91 873	159 142	113 942
Nickel	1 232 143	600 936	1 075 467
Silver	175 128	415 204	310 102
Uranium (U_3O_8)	n.a.	837 468	923 838
Zinc	862 296	1 036 096	1 304 107
Total — All Metals	5 241 151	6 874 197	8 944 159
Non-metals			
Asbestos	445 523	364 795	300 586
Gypsum	22 906	46 608	80 613
Peat	22 500	49 738	74 502
Potash (K_2O)	361 442	630 562	579 022
Quartz	13 895	31 864	42 834
Salt	75 691	156 620	241 611
Sodium Sulphate	24 878	47 462	33 413
Sulphur, in smelter gas	15 454	42 027	66 983
Sulphur, elemental	63 339	569 928	927 083
Total — All non-metals	1 142 516	1 973 801	2 668 790
Structural materials			
Clay products	92 110	95 993	180 353
Cement	339 159	673 653	790 846
Lime	54 099	142 081	206 400
Sand and gravel	320 800	554 608	596 603
Stone	209 600	263 249	426 306
Total — All structural materials	1 015 768	1 729 584	2 200 508

Canada's Mineral Production, Preliminary Estimate, Statistics Canada, 1976.

Canada Year Book 1988.

27. Crude Oil and Equivalent Production and Value, 1983 to 1986

ITEM AND PROVINCE OR TERRITORY	PRODUCTION[1] (000 m³)				VALUE ($000 000)			
	1983	1984	1985	1986	1983	1984	1985	1986
Crude oil								
Ontario	84	90	112	136	17	20	25	15
Manitoba	738	793	821	825	153	170	181	95
Saskatchewan	9 536	10 813	11 588	11 622	1 783	2 180	2 370	1 270
Alberta	55 415	60 020	57 147	53 185	11 090	12 602	12 401	6 334
British Columbia	2 097	2 108	1 970	2 029	407	436	411	258
Northwest Territories	169	175	1 118	1 410	19	20	195	108
Sub-total, crude oil	68 039	73 999	72 756	69 207	13 469	15 428	15 583	8 080
Pentanes[2]								
Saskatchewan	20	30	26	28	4	6	5	4
Alberta	5 161	5 333	5 645	5 655	1 021	1 123	1 225	500
British Columbia	114	131	125	139	22	27	28	15
Northwest Territories	—	—	32	49	—	—	6	4
Sub-total, pentanes[2]	5 295	5 494	5 828	5 871	1 047	1 156	1 264	523
Synthetic crude oil[3]								
Alberta	10 713	9 681	12 775	16 007	2 625	2 386	2 807	1 636
Total	84 047	89 174	91 359	91 085	17 141	18 970	19 654	10 239

[1] Marketable production.
[2] A product of gas plants.
[3] Includes experimental crude oil.

Canada Year Book 1988.

28. Oil Refining, by Province, 1985

Province or territory	No.	Capacity 000 m³/yr	% of total
Newfoundland	—	—	—
Nova Scotia	2	5 906	5.0
New Brunswick	1	13 505	11.6
Québec	4	22 276	19.0
Ontario	7	39 175	33.5
Manitoba	—	—	—
Saskatchewan	2	2 121	2.7
Alberta	6	23 143	19.8
British Columbia	6	9 683	8.3
Northwest Territories	1	168	0.1
Total	29	115 977	100.0

Canada Year Book 1988

29. Canada's Crude Oil Imports, by Major Country, 1983 and 1986 ($000 000)

Country	1983	1986
United Kingdom	200	1 328
Nigeria	192	367
Venezuela	826	311
U.S.A.	423	220
Iran	524	193
Saudi Arabia	93	184
Mexico	645	157
Total Imports	3 319	2 885

Canada Year Book 1988.

30. Natural Gas Production and Value, 1983 to 1986

PROVINCE	PRODUCTION (000 000 m³)				VALUE ($000 000)			
	1983	1984	1985	1986	1983	1984	1985	1986
New Brunswick	2	1	1	1	—	—	—	—
Ontario	461	486	521	504	46	61	65	66
Saskatchewan	909	1 225	1 614	1 814	35	62	93	118
Alberta	57 336	62 476	67 482	62 558	5 958	6 688	6 681	6 106
British Columbia	6 262	6 619	7 282	6 819	347	398	475	431
Yukon and Northwest Territories	163	179	229	201	17	18	20	22
Total	65 133	70 986	77 129	71 897	6 403	7 227	7 334	6 743

Canada Year Book 1988.

31. Coal Production and Value, by Type and Province, 1983 to 1986

TYPE AND PROVINCE	PRODUCTION (000 t)				VALUE ($000 000)			
	1983	1984	1985	1986	1983	1984	1985	1986
Bituminous								
Nova Scotia	2 986	3 093	2 800	2 695	145	162	169	165
New Brunswick	565	564	560	490	30	30	30	26
Alberta	7 315	7 630	7 841	6 994	349	321	307	275
British Columbia	11 687	20 775	23 110	20 362	574	1 017	1 102	940
Sub-total, bituminous	22 553	32 062	34 311	30 541	1 098	1 530	1 608	1 406
Sub-bituminous								
Alberta	14 564	15 422	16 871	18 225	122	137	151	160
Lignite								
Saskatchewan	7 760	9 917	9 672	8 281	84	127	125	100
Total	44 877	57 401	60 854	57 047	1 304	1 794	1 884	1 666

Canada Year Book 1988.

32. Electricity Generated and Consumed, by Province, 1983 to 1986 (000 MW h)

PROVINCE OR TERRITORY	GENERATION				DOMESTIC DEMAND			
	1983	1984	1985	1986	1983	1984	1985	1986
Newfoundland	40 155	45 648	41 494	40 600	7 829	8 532	8 633	8 800
Prince Edward Island	12	2	2	12	473	494	522	570
Nova Scotia	6 165	7 236	7 457	7 400	6 209	6 867	6 904	7 200
New Brunswick	11 657	12 396	11 401	12 200	8 185	9 361	9 385	10 600
Québec	110 498	122 179	137 028	148 600	114 160	123 709	132 794	140 100
Ontario	117 889	120 606	121 783	125 700	102 309	110 357	112 713	117 300
Manitoba	22 090	21 489	22 777	24 100	12 039	12 806	13 514	13 900
Saskatchewan	10 389	11 543	11 838	11 900	9 529	10 919	10 223	10 100
Alberta	29 127	31 160	33 432	34 900	27 100	28 968	30 929	32 200
British Columbia	47 174	52 379	59 124	50 800	41 271	42 154	44 750	45 200
Yukon and Northwest Territories	695	778	846	950	612	702	774	880
Total	395 851	425 416	447 182	457 162	329 716	354 869	371 141	386 850

Canada Year Book 1988

33. Trade in Energy, 1983 to 1985 ($000 000)

Item	1983	1984	1985
Crude oil and equivalent			
Exports	3 457	4 404	5 917
Imports	3 319	3 376	3 700
Balance	138	1 028	2 217
Petroleum products[1]			
Exports	1 344	1 676	1 956
Imports	756	1 411	1 421
Balance	588	265	535
Natural gas			
Exports	3 847	3 923	3 912
Imports	—	—	—
Balance	3 847	3 923	3 912
Liquefied petroleum products[2]			
Exports	1 051	1 106	991
Imports	195	136	122
Balance	856	970	869
Coal			
Exports	1 232	1 820	1 996
Imports	838	1 091	886
Balance	394	729	1 110
Coal products			
Exports	15	30	34
Imports	104	112	137
Balance	-89	-82	-103
Electric energy			
Exports	1 228	1 378	1 408
Imports	2	13	8
Balance	1 226	1 365	1 400
Radioactive ores			
Exports	63	334	232
Imports	112	100	76
Balance	49	234	156
Elements and isotopes			
Exports	368	541	590
Imports	15	15	28
Balance	353	526	562
Total			
Exports	12 605	15 212	17 036
Imports	5 341	6 254	6 378
Balance	7 264	8 958	10 658

[1] Contains values of selected petroleum products including products destined for non-energy consumption such as asphalt and lubricating oils and grease.
[2] Includes petroleum refinery and natural gas processing plant propane and butane.

Canada Year Book 1988.

34. Cargoes Loaded and Unloaded at Principal Canadian Ports, by Province, 1985 (000 t)

PROVINCE AND PORT	INTERNATIONAL		COASTWISE		TOTAL
	Loaded	Unloaded	Loaded	Unloaded	1985
NEWFOUNDLAND	1 295.6	1 104.6	243.3	2 351.4	4 995.0
PRINCE EDWARD ISLAND	66.6	9.6	—	598.0	674.3
NOVA SCOTIA	8 386.1	5 679.4	4 239.9	2 065.5	20 370.9
Halifax	4 105.9	5 393.5	2 871.2	1 327.1	13 697.8
Port Hawkesbury	1 441.7	151.7	100.6	144.9	1 838.8
NEW BRUNSWICK	3 422.5	4 879.1	1 082.4	902.5	10 286.5
Saint John	2 580.2	3 962.2	1 074.7	561.5	8 178.7
QUÉBEC	52 142.0	18 988.1	12 780.4	19 228.5	103 139.0
Sept-Îles-Pointe-Noire	17 599.0	714.7	3 474.3	544.1	22 332.1
Port-Cartier	17 345.1	1 203.5	1 073.6	2 175.4	21 797.7
Montréal[1]	5 910.1	5 957.2	2 592.3	4 727.3	19 186.9
Québec City[2]	4 037.1	1 788.7	829.1	3 703.8	10 358.7
Baie Comeau	3 028.4	1 096.1	244.3	2 243.6	6 612.5
Sorel	1 622.3	335.5	56.3	2 870.3	4 884.4
Lévis	281.0	3 501.8	529.8	33.9	4 346.6
Port-Alfred	225.3	2 749.5	—	97.5	3 072.4
Havre Saint-Pierre	323.2	—	2 506.2	10.9	2 840.4
Trois-Rivières	975.4	361.9	23.5	700.8	2 061.7
ONTARIO	9 828.4	24 199.1	22 164.5	15 293.6	71 485.5
Thunder Bay	2 833.2	135.7	13 958.4	429.1	17 356.4
Hamilton	381.8	5 308.9	167.9	4 447.3	10 305.9
Nanticoke	261.3	5 976.4	236.6	2 238.2	8 712.5
Sarnia-Courtright	1 445.4	2 976.1	1 395.7	330.3	6 147.5
Sault Ste Marie	165.5	4 569.4	136.0	389.7	5 260.6
Windsor-Walkerville	1 250.9	813.2	929.4	427.0	3 420.5
Clarkson	347.8	171.1	89.4	2 609.1	3 217.5
Toronto	64.5	825.7	56.4	769.8	1 716.5
Goderich	690.7	—	657.4	222.1	1 570.2
MANITOBA	359.0	—	21.4	—	380.5
Churchill	359.0	—	21.4	—	380.5
BRITISH COLUMBIA	67 920.5	5 807.8	21 152.5	21 121.4	116 002.2
Vancouver	48 849.5	3 029.7	2 237.0	2 111.9	56 228.2
Prince Rupert	9 275.4	16.6	364.9	308.2	9 965.1
New Westminster	1 155.5	1 346.4	1 353.0	1 656.2	5 511.1
Howe Sound	9.0	—	1 431.6	2 855.6	4 296.2
North Arm Fraser River	5.4	76.1	1 819.8	1 964.0	3 865.1
Nanaimo	1 187.4	62.0	143.0	1 227.7	2 620.2
Crofton	807.1	57.4	178.8	1 451.9	2 495.2
Duncan Bay-Campbell River	662.6	56.9	493.3	1 274.3	2 487.2
Kitimat	1 463.4	662.2	119.7	159.5	2 404.8
NORTHWEST TERRITORIES	—	0.9	32.3	155.9	189.2
Total	143 420.7	60 668.8	61 716.9	61 716.9	327 523.3

[1] Data for the port of Montréal exclude shipping activities at Contrecoeur.
[2] Data for the port of Quebéc exclude shipping activities at Lévis.

Canada Year Book 1988.

35. Principal Commodities in Water-borne Cargo Loaded and Unloaded at Ports Handling Large Tonnage, 1985 (000 t)

PORT AND COMMODITY		INTERNATIONAL		COASTWISE		TOTAL
		Loaded	Unloaded	Loaded	Unloaded	
Vancouver[1]	Coal	18 150.4	—	53.6	1.4	18 205.4
	Wheat	6 377.4	—	—	—	6 377.4
	Sulphur	5 362.3	—	—	—	5 362.3
	Potassium chloride (muriate of potash)	2 839.2	—	—	—	2 839.2
	Other chemicals and related products	2 260.0	52.5	140.8	—	2 453.5
	Lumber and timber	2 006.0	15.3	77.7	113.8	2 212.8
	Fuel oil	636.7	69.0	1 154.5	—	1 860.2
	Wood pulp	1 416.7	12.7	62.1	—	1 491.5
	Rapeseed	1 473.0	—	—	—	1 473.0
	Barley	1 358.5	—	—	—	1 358.5
	Gasoline	697.0	7.1	538.5	—	1 242.6
	Pulp	809.8	—	1.0	345.4	1 156.2
	Coke of petroleum and coal	1 105.0	12.1	17.7	—	1 134.8
	Other commodities	4 357.3	2 861.0	191.1	1 651.3	9 060.7
Total, Vancouver[1]		48 849.5	3 029.7	2 237.0	2 111.9	56 228.1
Sept-Îles-Pointe-Noire	Iron ore, concentrates and scrap	17 182.9	—	3 454.1	—	20 637.0
	Coal	334.4	349.9	11.8	—	696.1
	Other commodities	81.8	364.8	8.4	544.1	999.1
Total, Sept-Îles-Pointe-Noire		17 599.1	714.7	3 474.3	544.1	22 332.2
Port-Cartier	Iron ore, concentrates and scrap	14 401.3	2.0	1 040.1	—	15 443.4
	Wheat	1 786.8	206.9	5.8	1 608.2	3 607.7
	Corn	796.9	545.2	—	196.6	1 538.7
	Other commodities	360.1	449.4	27.7	370.6	1 207.8
Total, Port-Cartier		17 345.1	1 203.5	1 073.6	2 175.4	21 797.6
Montréal[2]	Wheat	1 896.3	—	—	2 358.4	4 254.7
	Fuel oil	373.4	481.5	1 091.7	553.9	2 500.5
	Crude petroleum	442.1	289.3	888.2	13.2	1 632.8
	Other chemicals and related products	530.4	772.0	1.0	9.3	1 312.7
	Gasoline	19.5	577.6	360.3	241.1	1 198.5
	Other commodities	2 648.4	3 836.8	251.1	1 551.4	8 287.7
Total, Montréal[2]		5 910.1	5 957.2	2 592.3	4 727.3	19 186.9
Thunder Bay	Wheat	561.5	8.3	9 995.3	—	10 565.1
	Coal	—	113.7	1 988.6	—	2 102.3
	Potassium chloride (muriate of potash)	1 465.4	—	238.0	—	1 703.4
	Barley	—	—	726.2	—	726.2
	Iron ore, concentrates and scrap	—	—	483.3	—	483.3
	Flaxseed	248.5	—	10.8	—	259.3
	Other commodities	557.9	13.7	516.2	429.1	1 516.9
Total, Thunder Bay		2 833.3	135.7	13 958.4	429.1	17 356.5
Halifax	Crude petroleum	—	3 704.0	—	753.9	4 457.9
	Gypsum	2 474.5	—	505.1	—	2 979.6
	Fuel oil	185.2	370.9	1 464.3	202.8	2 223.2
	Gasoline	41.4	84.4	719.5	131.7	977.0
	Other commodities	1 404.8	1 234.2	182.3	238.7	3 060.0
Total, Halifax		4 105.9	5 393.5	2 871.2	1 327.1	13 697.7
Québec City[3]	Wheat	2 296.7	27.0	5.7	2 189.2	4 518.6
	Iron ore, concentrates and scrap	1 042.4	743.5	—	—	1 785.9
	Fuel oil	27.4	100.6	533.9	165.8	827.7
	Other commodities	670.7	917.6	289.5	1 348.8	3 226.6
Total, Québec City[3]		4 037.2	1 788.7	829.1	3 703.8	10 358.8
Hamilton	Iron ore, concentrates and scrap	147.3	1 109.2	93.6	4 016.7	5 366.8
	Coal	—	3 568.9	—	52.0	3 620.9
	Other commodities	234.5	630.8	74.3	378.6	1 318.2
Total, Hamilton		381.8	5 308.9	167.9	4 447.3	10 305.9

[1] Includes Roberts Bank.
[2] Data for the port of Montréal exclude shipping activities at Contrecoeur.
[3] Data for the port of Québec exclude shipping activities at Lévis.

Canada Year Book 1988.

36. Motor Vehicles Registered for Road Use, by Province and Territory, 1981 and 1985

Province or territory	1981	1985
Newfoundland	209 482	257 693
Prince Edward Island	68 396	76 126
Nova Scotia	515 689	529 267
New Brunswick	365 951	416 805
Québec	2 878 827	2 974 099
Ontario	5 057 801	5 179 918
Manitoba	662 407	739 488
Saskatchewan	692 023	697 160
Alberta	1 748 918	1 729 287
British Columbia	1 616 614	2 175 032
Yukon	18 119	20 479
Northwest Territories	17 255	23 271
Canada	13 851 482	14 818 625

Canada Year Book 1988.

37. Length of Mainline Track Operated, by Area, 1984[1] (kilometres)

Newfoundland	240
Prince Edward Island	—
Nova Scotia	712
New Brunswick	1 101
Québec	4 696
Ontario	15 044
Manitoba	2 824
Saskatchewan	4 019
Alberta	3 730
British Columbia	6 300
Northwest Territories	—
United States	575
Total	39 242

[1] Includes all mainline track operated under ownership, joint-ownership, lease, contract or trackage rights.

Canada Year Book 1988.

38. Summary of Canadian Commercial Aviation, Operational Statistics, 1955-85

Year	Passengers 000	Passenger kilometres 000 000	Cargo kilograms 000	Mail kilograms 000	Hours flown 000
1955	2 763	1 983	105 163	11 008	623
1960	4 830	4 507	95 401	15 709	879
1965	6 832	8 729	128 618	22 879	1 128
1970	12 031	18 605	256 420	30 068	1 669
1975	20 493	31 539	362 711	45 032	2 466
1980	28 554	46 996	399 418	59 978	3 091
1985 (estimated)	29 030	48 812	498 199	82 458	2 434

Canada Year Book 1988.

39. Measures of Bilateral Trade Between Canada and the United States, 1981-85 ($000 000 000 Canadian)

YEAR	SOUTHWARD TRADE			NORTHWARD TRADE			TRADE BALANCE		
	Canadian exports[1]	US imports[2]	Reconciled data	Canadian imports[3]	US exports[4]	Reconciled data	Canada	US	Reconciled data
1981	55.8	55.6	56.7	54.1	47.5	53.6	1.4	8.2	3.4
1982	57.8	57.3	59.0	48.0	41.6	47.1	9.8	15.7	12.1
1983	66.5	64.3	67.6	54.3	47.2	53.1	12.2	17.1	14.4
1984	85.2	86.1	86.9	69.1	60.2	66.9	16.1	25.9	20.0
1985	93.2	94.2	95.0	74.6	64.5	73.5	18.6	29.7	21.5

[1] Canadian exports to the US as recorded by Canada.
[2] Canadian exports to the US as recorded by the US.
[3] US exports to Canada as recorded by Canada.
[4] US exports to Canada as recorded by the US.

Canada Year Book 1988.

40. Total Imports, Exports and Trade Balance on a Balance-of-payments Basis, 1972-86

YEAR	IMPORTS		EXPORTS[1]			
	Value $000 000	Percentage change from previous year	Value $000 000	Percentage change from previous year	Trade balance $000 000	Ratio of exports to imports %
1972	18 272	19.3	20 222	13.7	1 950	110.7
1974	30 003	36.0	32 738	27.0	1 035	105.9
1976	36 608	7.8	38 166	13.5	1 558	104.3
1978	49 048	18.1	53 361	19.9	4 313	108.8
1980	67 903	11.0	76 681	16.9	8 778	112.9
1982	66 739	-13.5	84 560	0.2	17 821	126.7
1984	91 493	25.2	112 219	23.7	20 726	122.7
1986	110 498	7.5	120 631	0.3	10 133	109.2

[1] Includes domestic exports and re-exports.

Canada Year Book 1988.

41. Major Export Commodities, 1986

	$000 000
1. Passenger automobiles and chassis	17 936.4
2. Motor vehicle parts, except engines	9 563.6
3. Newsprint paper	5 667.3
4. Trucks, truck tractors and chassis	5 212.2
5. Lumber, softwood	4 863.1
6. Wood pulp and similar pulp	4 072.5
7. Crude petroleum	3 774.0
8. Precious metals, including alloys	3 131.5
9. Wheat	2 835.8
10. Natural gas	2 482.9
11. Aluminum, including alloys	2 345.1
12. Petroleum and coal products	2 108.5
13. Coal and other crude bituminous substances	1 851.0
14. Motor vehicle engines and parts	1 849.1
15. Aircraft parts, except engines	1 446.4
Total exports	120 520.9

Canada Year Book 1988.

42. Major Import Commodities, 1986

	$000 000
1. Motor vehicle parts, except engines	14 729.0
2. Passenger automobiles and chassis	12 061.7
3. Electronic computers	4 193.1
4. Trucks, truck tractors and chassis	2 947.2
5. Crude petroleum	2 884.6
6. Motor vehicle engines	2 486.7
7. Precious metals, including alloys	1 869.8
8. Outerwear, all kinds	1 751.4
9. Organic chemicals	1 615.6
10. Aluminum and other metal ores	1 596.1
11. Electronic tubes and semi conductors	1 351.4
12. Aircraft parts, except engines	1 196.1
13. Aircraft with engines	1 126.5
14. Plastic materials not shaped	976.1
15. Paper and paperboard	924.1
Total imports	112 678.0

Canada Year Book 1988.

43. Exports: Principal Nations, 1986

	$000 000
1. United States	93 182.3
2. Japan	5 940.5
3. United Kingdom	2 718.3
4. West Germany	1 317.3
5. U.S.S.R.	1 221.6
6. China	1 112.5
7. France	1 010.6
8. Netherlands	1 001.7
9. South Korea	972.9
10. Belgium and Luxembourg	844.2
All countries	120 520.9

Canada Year Book 1988.

44. Imports: Principal Nations, 1986

	$000 000
1. United States	77 337.0
2. Japan	7 626.3
3. United Kingdom	3 721.2
4. West Germany	3 453.2
5. South Korea	1 749.4
6. Taiwan	1 744.7
7. Italy	1 671.4
8. France	1 585.3
9. Mexico	1 179.6
10. Hong Kong	1 041.0
All countries	112 678.0

Canada Year Book 1988.

45. Foreign Investment in Canada, 1970 and 1984 ($000 000 Canadian)

Item	1970	1984
Foreign direct investment in Canada	26 423	81 776
Manufacturing	10 767	32 301
Oil and gas	6 574	20 947
Mining and smelting	3 231	4 946
Utilities	442	710
Merchandising	1 699	6 388
Financial	2 910	13 225
Other	800	3 259
Total, foreign portfolio and other investment in Canada	25 576	190 946
Total, foreign investment in Canada	51 999	272 722

Canada Year Book 1988.

46. Canada's Investment Abroad, 1970 and 1984 ($000 000 Canadian)

Item	1970	1984
Canada's direct investment abroad	6 188	41 725
Manufacturing	3 207	19 247
Merchandising	278	1 845
Mining and smelting	378	3 058
Oil and gas	492	7 387
Utilities	1 225	1 557
Financial	421	7 053
Other	187	1 578
Total, Canada's portfolio and other investment abroad	15 805	78 170
Total, Canada's investment abroad	21 993	119 895

Canada Year Book 1988.

47. Value of Shipments of Goods of Own Manufacture, by Province ($000 000)

Province or territory	1969	1979	1981	1983	1984
Newfoundland	242.4	1 028.0	1 241.3	1 174.8	1 170.3
Prince Edward Island	56.9	212.5	247.0	285.2	289.0
Nova Scotia	731.5	3 212.5	3 822.6	3 891.5	4 595.4
New Brunswick	708.9	2 970.5	3 844.2	3 504.8	4 092.3
Québec	12 810.2	39 117.3	50 139.1	52 098.4	56 990.5
Ontario	23 847.8	76 220.2	93 989.5	103 885.0	121 726.4
Manitoba	1 230.0	3 914.7	4 977.0	4 957.0	5 036.1
Saskatchewan	530.4	1 863.3	2 503.6	2 619.5	2 851.6
Alberta	1 849.3	8 940.0	13 437.1	13 850.3	15 287.8
British Columbia	3 917.8	14 627.8	16 793.4	16 998.2	17 979.3
Yukon and Northwest Territories	5.2	26.3	34.9	49.0	51.3
Canada	45 930.4	152 133.1	191 029.7	203 313.7	230 070.1

Canada Year Book 1988

48. Summary Statistics, Annual Census of Manufacturers, 1965-84[1]

Year	Establishments No.[1]	PRODUCTION AND RELATED WORKERS			Cost of fuel and electricity $000	Cost of materials and supplies used $000	Value of shipments of goods of own manufacture $000	Value added $000
		Number	Man-hours paid 000	Wages $000				
1965	33 310	1 115 892	2 384 002	5 012 345	675 641	18 622 213	33 889 425	14 927 764
1970	31 928	1 167 063	2 450 058	7 232 256	903 264	25 699 999	46 380 935	20 047 801
1975	30 100	1 271 786	2 613 062	12 699 228	1 805 398	51 177 942	88 427 031	36 105 457
1980	35 495	1 346 187	2 780 203	22 162 309	4 448 859	99 897 576	168 058 662	65 851 774
1984	36 464	1 240 816	2 583 486	28 294 553	7 306 383	136 133 629	230 070 091	88 667 660

[1] The increase in the number of establishments between 1975 and 1980 was largely a result of the addition of 4 962 small establishments by improved coverage.

Canada Year Book 1976-77, 1988.

49. Selected Principal Statistics on Manufacturing Activity of the Leading Industries Ranked by Value of Shipments of Goods of Own Manufacture, 1984

	Establishments	Value of shipments $000 000	Value added $000 000
Canada			
1 Petroleum products[1]	33	22 958	2 527
2 Motor vehicles	21	20 750	4 100
3 Meat and meat products[2]	536	8 277	1 451
4 Primary steel industries	28	7 095	2 746
5 Sawmill and planing mill products	1 328	6 265	2 410
6 Newsprint	43	6 191	2 925
7 Non-ferrous smelting and refining	30	4 383	2 231
8 Industrial organic chemicals	50	4 296	835
9 Pulp	37	3 740	1 593
10 Motor vehicle engines and parts	33	3 602	1 494
Newfoundland			
1 Fish products	99	401	192
2 Sawmill and planing mill products	62	9	5
Prince Edward Island			
1 Fish products	19	52	18
2 Mixed fertilizer	6	18	4
Nova Scotia			
1 Fish products	100	389	128
2 Newspapers, magazines, and periodicals	23	67	53
3 Feed (livestock)	11	66	7
4 Sawmill and planing mill products	101	60	28
5 Soft drinks	7	52	20
6 Canned and preserved fruit and vegetables	10	44	15
7 Meat and meat products[2]	10	39	5
8 Ready-mix concrete	14	33	11
9 Bread and other bakery products	16	31	16
10 Other commercial printing	58	24	14
New Brunswick			
1 Pulp	6	508	146
2 Fish products	74	200	63
3 Sawmill and planing mill products	79	185	63
4 Fluid milk	5	65	21
5 Bread and other bakery products	9	46	27
6 Soft drinks	6	45	14
7 Feed (livestock)	8	41	5
8 Newspapers, magazines, and periodicals	15	37	26
9 Fabricated structural metal	5	32	15
10 Wooden doors and windows	16	29	12
Québec			
1 Petroleum products[1]	4	5 055	724
2 Newsprint	22	2 797	1 321
3 Non-ferrous smelting and refining	12	2 726	1 353
4 Meat and meat products[2]	133	2 117	304
5 Dairy products (excluding fluid milk)	72	1 937	432
6 Sawmill and planing mill products	415	1 329	573
7 Aircraft and aircraft parts	54	1 172	762
8 Commercial printing	739	978	512
9 Spun yarn and woven cloth	46	942	327
10 Stamped and pressed metal products	121	934	173
Ontario			
1 Motor vehicles	11	18 179	3 320
2 Petroleum products[1]	[illegible]	[illegible]	[illegible]
3 Primary steel industries	14	5 828	2 297
4 Motor vehicle engines and parts	24	3 594	1 489
5 Other motor vehicle accessories and parts	142	2 870	1 462
6 Industrial organic chemicals	26	2 756	411
7 Meat and meat products[2]	195	2 662	590
8 Commercial printing	1 221	1 802	1 008
9 Other food products	126	1 787	688
10 Motor vehicle stamping	71	1 610	738
Manitoba			
1 Meat and meat products[2]	38	547	87
2 Agricultural implements	34	331	138
3 Aircraft and aircraft parts	10	156	105
4 Feed (livestock)	39	143	28
5 Other commercial printing	106	124	63
6 Fluid milk	7	104	30
7 Newspapers, magazines, and periodicals	38	103	76
8 Other dairy products	20	95	21
9 Other food products	13	82	22
10 Soft drinks	8	78	36
Saskatchewan			
1 Meat and meat products[2]	35	346	70
2 Agricultural implements	39	123	67
3 Newspapers, magazines, and periodicals	54	87	65
4 Feed (livestock)	22	85	21
5 Soft drinks	10	54	32
6 Ready-mix concrete	48	52	21
7 Sawmill and planing mill products	8	52	20
8 Other commercial printing	60	41	24
9 Machine shop industries	45	27	18
10 Bread and other bakery products	17	27	16
Alberta			
1 Petroleum products[1]	7	4 277	339
2 Meat and meat products[2]	71	1 939	221
3 Industrial organic chemicals	9	990	352
4 Chemical fertilizers	6	544	130
5 Construction and mining machinery	97	425	217
6 Feed (livestock)	69	301	53
7 Steel pipe and tube	5	284	98
8 Other dairy products	30	272	71
9 Sawmill and planing mill products	47	269	115
10 Newspapers, magazines, and periodicals	61	232	179
British Columbia			
1 Sawmill and planing mill products	354	3 666	1 359
2 Petroleum products[1]	7	2 245	253
3 Pulp	16	1 536	675
4 Newsprint	4	1 025	517
5 Meat and meat products[2]	40	491	144
6 Fluid milk	20	434	102
7 Fish products	49	390	144
8 Other commercial printing	278	207	118
9 Newspapers, magazines, and periodicals	63	195	147
10 Shipbuilding and repair	15	193	126

Manufacturing Industries of Canada: National and Provincial Areas, 1984, Statistics Canada Catalogue 31-203.

[1] Excluding lubricating oil and grease.
[2] Excluding poultry.

50. Retail Trade, by Kind of Business and by Province, 1982-85

Kind of business and province	1982 $000 000	1983 $000 000	1984 $000 000	1985 $000 000
Kind of business				
Combination stores (groceries and meat)	19 906.2	21 027.4	22 341.4	23 776.7
Grocery, confectionery and sundries stores	4 938.4	5 209.7	5 703.1	6 154.8
All other food stores	1 945.9	2 048.8	2 144.6	2 325.6
Department stores	10 208.1	10 930.5	11 384.9	12 038.6
General merchandise stores	2 080.1	2 312.0	2 395.1	2 698.9
General stores	1 898.4	1 909.8	1 890.9	1 982.7
Variety stores	1 071.3	1 129.9	1 207.0	1 266.9
Motor vehicle dealers	14 413.0	17 198.0	20 846.5	26 026.6
Used car dealers	461.5	501.1	559.0	654.9
Service stations	8 728.5	8 949.5	9 732.5	11 100.7
Garages	1 376.2	1 345.8	1 580.9	1 484.2
Automotive parts and accessories stores	2 175.0	2 492.9	2 606.2	2 801.8
Men's clothing stores	1 113.7	1 249.8	1 323.5	1 324.1
Women's clothing stores	1 913.0	2 137.0	2 396.4	2 777.2
Family clothing stores	1 275.1	1 487.1	1 575.4	1 867.4
Specialty shoe stores	135.2	147.4	162.8	212.0
Family shoe stores	882.4	967.8	1 008.3	1 075.8
Hardware stores	887.6	984.0	1 046.5	1 157.6
Household furniture stores	1 209.5	1 551.0	1 698.7	1 542.2
Household appliance stores	381.9	487.4	453.0	527.4
Furniture, TV, radio and appliance stores	510.0	669.8	831.5	1 144.9
Pharmacies, patent medicine and cosmetics stores	3 913.7	4 294.0	4 727.2	5 356.6
Book and stationery stores	465.9	513.8	565.3	715.4
Florists	380.6	400.7	452.8	471.5
Jewellery stores	822.5	837.9	867.1	932.0
Sporting goods and accessories stores	1 289.9	1 401.1	1 640.5	1 868.3
Personal accessories stores	1 378.5	1 416.6	1 559.3	1 719.4
All other stores	11 876.6	12 642.2	13 379.8	14 442.3
Total	97 638.5	106 243.0	116 079.9	129 446.3
Province or territory				
Newfoundland	1 761.2	1 970.5	2 071.1	2 254.1
Prince Edward Island	412.4	471.7	520.7	547.5
Nova Scotia	3 097.8	3 533.8	4 048.0	4 579.6
New Brunswick	2 448.6	2 719.3	2 927.4	3 171.5
Québec	23 496.8	25 783.8	29 005.9	31 782.3
Ontario	35 543.3	39 446.1	43 465.7	49 003.6
Manitoba	3 830.0	4 099.9	4 513.7	5 200.8
Saskatchewan	4 042.1	4 357.1	4 354.4	4 704.0
Alberta	10 941.3	11 303.5	11 833.4	13 523.5
British Columbia	11 766.2	12 256.9	13 004.6	14 303.6
Yukon and Northwest Territories	298.8	300.3	334.8	375.8

Canada Year Book 1988.

51. Highlights from Nation-wide Emissions Inventory of Air Contaminants, 1980

Contaminant[1]	Total Emissions (000 000 t)	Major Contributors by Category: Category	%	Major Contributors by Source: Source	% of Category
Particulate Matter	1.9	Industrial Processes	64.0	Mining and rock quarrying	16.6
				Iron ore mining	12.9
				Sulphate pulping	8.7
				Coal industry	8.4
				Iron and steel production	6.3
				Grain handling	5.1
				Sawmills	4.4
				Primary copper & nickel processing	4.1
				Primary aluminum	3.3
		Miscellaneous	12.9	Slash burning	82.3
		Fuel combustion/stationary sources	16.2	Power utilities	47.6
				Fuelwood combustion	28.3
Sulphur Oxides (as SO_2)	4.6	Industrial Processes	67.1	Primary copper & nickel processing	61.0
				Natural gas processing	12.3
				Iron ore mining	5.2
				Tar sands operations	4.8
				Primary lead & zinc products	3.8
		Fuel combustion/stationary sources	29.9	Power utilities	55.6
				Industrial fuel combustion	33.2
				Commercial fuel combustion	6.1
				Residential fuel combustion	4.8
Hydrocarbons	2.0	Industrial Processes	28.9	Petrochemical industry	36.9
				Coal industry	26.9
				Petroleum refining	23.4
		Transportation	40.3	Gasoline motor vehicles	77.3
		Miscellaneous	25.8	Gasoline/diesel marketing	46.1
				Application of surface coatings	27.7
				General solvent use	15.0
Nitrogen Oxides (as NO_2)	1.7	Transportation	62.1	Gasoline motor vehicles	42.1
				Diesel engines	38.7
				Railroads	10.0
		Fuel combustion/stationary sources	33.8	Industrial fuel combustion	45.8
				Power utilities	39.4

[1] Open sources such as agricultural tilling, unpaved roads, etc. contribute significantly to emissions of particulate matter; similarly, forest fires are important contributors to emissions of hydrocarbons and particulate matter. These sources have been excluded here because the focus is on man-made sources that could be important to urban pollution.

Personal Communication, F. Vena, Environmental Protection Service, Environment Canada,1985.

State of the Environment Report for Canada, 1986.

52. Provincial/Territorial and Local Government Environmental Expenditures[1] (current dollars)

	ENVIRONMENTAL EXPENDITURES AND PERCENTAGE CHANGE					
Jurisdiction	$000 1972-73	$000 1977-78	Percentage change 1972-73/ 1977-78	$000 1981-82	Percentage change 1977-78/ 1981-82	Environmental as percentage of total expenditures 1981-82
Newfoundland	11 794	29 079	146.6	51 488	77.1	3.8
Prince Edward Island	2 682	7 937	195.9	10 458	31.8	3.0
Nova Scotia	8 219	23 399	184.7	46 200	97.4	2.2
New Brunswick	12 096	35 291	191.8	52 225	48.0	2.9
Québec	83 873	253 320	202.0	404 485	59.7	2.0
Ontario	218 020	424 629	94.8	619 802	46.0	3.2
Manitoba	25 187	53 228	111.3	69 374	30.3	2.9
Saskatchewan	5 914	13 192	123.1	29 091	120.5	1.2
Alberta	36 250	119 147	228.7	562 684	372.3	8.1
British Columbia	70 672	188 389	166.6	384 500	104.1	5.6
Northwest Territories	1 243	16 665	1 241.0	20 725	24.4	5.3
Yukon	280	3 245	1 059.0	3 568	10.0	2.6
Local Governments	762 717	1 848 283	142.3	2 533 807	37.1	n.a.
Federal Government	361 988	783 431	116.4	1 510 472	92.8	2.2

[1] Because institutional structures differ from one jurisdiction to another, direct comparisons are unrealistic.

State of the Environment Report for Canada, 1986.

53. Sources of SO_2 and NO_x Emissions, Canada and the United States, 1980

	SO_2 000 000 t/a		NO_x[2] 000 000 t/a	
	U.S.A.	Canada	U.S.A.	Canada
Electrical Utilities	15.8	0.77	5.6	0.26
Residential/Commercial/ Industrial Fuel Combustion	3.2	0.61	4.2	0.34
Non-ferrous Smelters	1.4	2.09[1]		
Transportation	0.8	0.14	8.5	1.08
Other Industrial Processes & Miscellaneous	2.9	1.03	1.0	0.08
Total	24.1	4.64	19.3	1.75

[1] Copper, nickel, lead and zinc smelters only.
[2] NO_x reported as NO_2

United States-Canada Memorandum of Intent on Transboundary Air Pollution, Executive Summaries of Work Group Reports, February 1983; Environment Canada, Environmental Protection Service, Personal Communication, 1985.

State of the Environment Report for Canada, 1986.

54. High and Low Temperatures and Precipitation Data for Typical Stations in Various Districts

DISTRICT AND STATION	TEMPERATURES (CELSIUS)						PRECIPITATION		
	Mean. Jan.	Mean July	Highest on record	Lowest on record	Av. dates of freezing temperatures (0°C or lower)		Total (all forms) mm	Snowfall cm	Av. number of days (all forms)
					Last in spring	First in autumn			
Newfoundland									
Island									
Belle Isle	-9.6	9.3	22.8	-35.0	June 21	Sept. 29	898.8	255.5	161
Labrador									
Cartwright	-13.2	12.7	36.1	-37.8	June 19	Sept. 13	953.7	440.0	183
Maritime Provinces									
Prince Edward Island									
Charlottetown A	-7.1	18.3	34.4	-28.1	May 16	Oct. 14	1 169.4	330.6	174
Nova Scotia									
Annapolis Royal	-4.0	18.1	32.8	-27.2	May 23	Sept. 29	1 279.9	254.3	152
Sydney A	-4.7	17.7	35.0	-25.6	May 23	Oct. 14	1 399.9	317.9	186
New Brunswick									
Grand Falls	-12.2	18.2	36.7	-43.3	June 22	Aug. 28	1 012.4	306.7	105
Québec									
Northern									
Fort Chimo A	-23.3	11.4	32.2	-46.7	June 17	Sept. 3	504.2	245.2	163
Southern									
Montréal McGill	-8.7	21.8	36.1	-33.9	May 12	Sept. 30	1 020.1	242.8	163
Sherbrooke	-9.8	20.0	36.7	-41.1	June 7	Sept. 16	949.9	253.2	169
Ontario									
Northern									
Thunder Bay A	-15.4	17.6	37.2	-41.1	May 17	Sept. 28	711.8	213.0	138
Southern									
Parry Sound	-9.9	19.1	37.8	-41.1	May 24	Sept. 17	1 093.5	330.6	162
Toronto	-4.6	22.0	40.6	-32.8	May 23	Sept. 22	800.5	139.2	134
Prairie Provinces									
Manitoba									
The Pas A	-22.7	17.7	36.7	-49.4	May 24	Sept. 11	453.7	170.0	131
Winnipeg A	-19.3	19.6	40.6	-45.0	May 21	Sept. 16	525.5	125.5	120
Saskatchewan									
Saskatoon A	-19.3	18.5	40.0	-47.8	May 15	Sept. 22	348.8	113.1	108
Alberta									
Edmonton A	-15.0	17.4	34.4	-48.3	May 14	Sept. 8	466.1	135.7	124
British Columbia									
Pacific Coast and Coastal Valleys									
Victoria	4.1	15.4	35.0	-15.6	Apr. 8	Oct. 29	647.2	32.0	138
Southern Interior									
Princeton A	-7.9	17.8	41.7	-42.8	June 1	Sept. 14	344.5	167.5	115
Central Interior									
Barkerville	-10.7	12.1	35.6	-46.7	June 28	Aug. 16	1 043.9	538.4	177
Northern Interior									
Fort Nelson A	-23.8	16.6	36.7	-51.7	May 25	Sept. 9	451.8	186.5	134
Yukon									
Dawson	-30.7	15.6	35.0	-58.3	May 28	Aug. 28	306.1	137.1	114
Whitehorse A	-20.7	14.1	34.4	-52.2	June 8	Aug. 30	261.2	136.6	120
Northwest Territories									
Mackenzie Basin									
Fort Good Hope	-31.3	16.3	34.4	-55.6	June 2	Aug. 21	281.9	131.6	97
Hay River A	-25.8	15.8	35.6	-48.3	June 2	Sept. 1	339.9	165.0	117
Barrens									
Baker Lake	-33.0	11.0	30.6	-50.6	June 23	Aug. 30	234.6	100.0	106
Coppermine	-30.1	9.7	32.2	-50.0	June 24	Aug. 23	202.3	100.7	109
Arctic Archipelago									
Eureka	-36.4	5.4	19.4	-55.3	July 27	Aug. 3	64.0	44.1	55
Frobisher Bay A	-25.6	7.6	24.4	-45.6	June 28	Aug. 27	432.6	255.5	146
Resolute A	-32.1	4.1	18.3	-52.2	July 10	July 20	131.4	83.8	96

A = Airport.

Canada Year Book 1988.